MONOPOLIES AND MERGERS COMMISSION

# Films

A report on the supply of films for exhibition in cinemas in the UK

Presented to Parliament by the Secretary of State for Trade and Industry by Command of Her Majesty
October 1994

LONDON: HMSO

Cm 2673

£28.40 net

# Members of the Monopolies and Mergers Commission as at 28 July 1994

Mr G D W Odgers  *(Chairman)*
Mr P H Dean CBE[1]  *(Deputy Chairman)*
Mr D G Goyder  *(Deputy Chairman)*
Mr H H Liesner CB  *(Deputy Chairman)*
Mr A G Armstrong
Mr I S Barter
Professor M E Beesley CBE
Mrs C M Blight
Mr P Brenan[1]
Mr J S Bridgeman
Mr R O Davies
Professor S Eilon
Mr J Evans
Mr N H Finney OBE
Sir Archibald Forster
Sir Ronald Halstead CBE
Ms P A Hodgson
Mr M R Hoffman
Mr D J Jenkins MBE
Mr A L Kingshott
Mr N F Matthews
Professor J S Metcalfe CBE[1]
Professor A P L Minford
Mr J D Montgomery
Dr D J Morris
Professor J F Pickering
Mr L Priestley
Mr M R Prosser
Dr A Robinson
Mr J K Roe[1]
Dr L M Rouse
Mrs E C Tritton QC[1]
Professor G Whittington

    Mr A J Nieduszynski  *(Secretary)*

---

[1] These members formed the group which was responsible for this report under the chairmanship of Mr P H Dean.

## Note by the Department of Trade and Industry

In accordance with section 83(3) and (3A) of the Fair Trading Act 1973, the Secretary of State has excluded from the copies of the report, as laid before Parliament and as published, certain matters, publication of which appears to the Secretary of State to be against the public interest, or which he considers would not be in the public interest to disclose and which, in his opinion, would seriously and prejudicially affect certain interests. The omissions are indicated by a note in the text.

# Contents

## Part I—Summary and Conclusions

*Page*

*Chapter* 1 Summary .................................................................... 3
2 Conclusions ................................................................ 6

## Part II—Background and evidence

*Chapter* 3 Background to the inquiry ............................................. 63
4 The market for films in the UK ...................................... 70
5 Financial results .......................................................... 117
6 Views of third parties ................................................... 134
7 Views of the leading exhibitors ..................................... 157
8 Views of the leading distributors .................................. 192
9 Views of the other distributors in the complex monopoly group ..... 246

*Appendices* (The numbering of the appendices indicates the chapters to which they relate.)

1.1 The reference and conduct of the inquiry ..................... 259
2.1 Schedule of practices engaged in by the members of the complex monopoly group ............................................. 261
2.2 Original list of persons in whose favour the complex monopoly situation was provisionally considered to exist ............. 262
3.1 Summary of the Monopolies Commission's 1966 report on *Films* .... 263
3.2 Summary of the MMC's 1983 report on *Films* ............... 266
3.3 The Films (Exclusivity Agreements) Order 1989 .............. 271
4.1 Distributors and exhibitors in the UK ............................ 273
4.2 Taxation: a summary of the main issues affecting film production in the UK .................................................................. 280
4.3 SFD *Standard Conditions for licensing the commercial exhibition of a film or films* .............................................................. 282
4.4 Survey of operators of independent cinemas in the UK ..... 295
4.5 Cinema nuts: comparisons between different distributors ..... 304
4.6 The market in the USA ................................................. 307
4.7 Shares of rental payments and box office receipts ........... 309
4.8 Locations affected directly by alignment ....................... 313
4.9 Effects of alignment on MGM Cinemas' and Odeon's smaller cinemas ....................................................................... 314
4.10 Case studies .............................................................. 318
4.11 Pattern of release for UIP's film *Ghost* ....................... 320
4.12 Booking of films by distributors ................................... 321
5.1 Financial performance and licensing arrangements of the distributors .. 324
5.2 Financial performance of the five leading exhibitors ....... 335
6.1 Independent exhibitors and distributors who gave evidence ..... 346
Glossary ........................................................................... 348
Index ................................................................................ 353

# Part I

# Summary and Conclusions

# 1 Summary

**Introduction**

1.1. We have been asked to investigate the supply of films for exhibition in cinemas in the UK. When making this reference to us the Director General of Fair Trading indicated that his own enquiries into the industry had been prompted by complaints from independent cinemas about difficulties in obtaining popular films from distributors. He added that most of the major companies were vertically integrated and followed practices which could lead to the exclusion of independent producers, distributors and exhibitors from the market; and that although there had been changes in the market since the previous MMC report in 1983, he considered competition remained restricted to such an extent that a full investigation was appropriate. Our terms of reference are set out in Appendix 1.1. The EC Commission is also currently considering applications for clearance under EC competition law of certain joint ventures in the industry.

**Background**

1.2. The theatrical distribution market was worth £103 million in 1993. The five leading distributors, Buena Vista, Columbia, Fox, UIP and Warner Distributors, all of which are affiliated to Hollywood studios, accounted for about three-quarters of receipts from film rentals in the period 1990 to 1993. Each distributor's shares fluctuate quite widely from year to year, reflecting the success of individual films. Several independent distributors, of which the largest are Entertainment, First Independent, Guild and Rank Film Distributors, make up the balance of this market. The leading distributors are mainly in business to distribute the films of their respective Hollywood studios, though most also distribute independently-produced films to a limited extent. The independent distributors compete to obtain independently-produced films.

1.3. In the exhibition market there are likewise five leading players: two owners of long-standing circuits, MGM Cinemas and Odeon, and three recent US-owned entrants specializing in the operation of multiplex cinemas, Natl Amusements, UCI and Warner Theatres. These five exhibitors account for almost four-fifths of the £289 million box office receipts in 1993, numerous independent exhibitors making up the balance. All the leading exhibitors except Odeon have some ownership link, direct or indirect, with a Hollywood studio, but these links are not as close as those between the Hollywood studios and their respective distribution affiliates.

1.4. The relationship between the distributors and the exhibitors is complex and symbiotic. Neither side currently dominates the other, though independent exhibitors are at a bargaining disadvantage *vis-à-vis* the leading distributors, as are independent distributors *vis-à-vis* the leading exhibitors.

1.5. The industry has been transformed since our 1983 report and is still undergoing change. By July 1994 71 new multiplex cinemas had been built and others are under construction or planned. Exhibitors have also invested heavily in refurbishing older cinemas and converting them to multi-screen use. There has been a substantial increase in the number of cinemas which show popular films on first release. Advertising and publicity budgets have risen strongly. Audiences have doubled after many years of continual decline. Cinema admission prices are not excessive. In contrast to the resurgence which has occurred in cinema-going, however, British film production during the last ten years has languished.

1.6. A large and growing proportion of the revenues from the exploitation of films comes from the rental and sale of video cassettes and from various forms of television broadcasting. But while the cinema now represents perhaps only a quarter of total revenues, it remains highly important because the success of a film in the cinema is seen as the key to its success in these other markets too.

## The monopoly situations

1.7. We find that one scale monopoly situation and one complex monopoly situation exist within the meaning of the Fair Trading Act 1973. The scale monopoly situation involves MGM Cinemas, which over the period 1990 to 1993 made just over a quarter of exhibitors' total rental payments for the licensing of films for exhibition in UK cinemas.

1.8. The complex monopoly situation involves the five leading distributors, the four independent distributors named in paragraph 1.2 and the five leading exhibitors, and is based on our finding of the existence of a number of uncompetitive practices in the industry. The more significant of these are discussed below.

## Public interest issues

1.9. The scale monopoly situation does not in itself raise concerns for the public interest. The market share of MGM Cinemas is only just over 25 per cent, and there are other strong players in the exhibition market whose market shares are not far below.

1.10. We find two of the practices inherent in the complex monopoly situation to be against the public interest. The first is alignment: the practice whereby, in the first instance, a distributor normally offers its films to, and discusses the timing and release strategy for those films with, its aligned circuit, ie either MGM Cinemas or Odeon. In locations where both circuits operate directly competing cinemas, aligned distributors normally supply films to their aligned circuit but not the other. This practice, by reducing competition for screens among aligned distributors and reducing pressure on the two circuits to compete for films on merit, makes the market less responsive to consumer preferences. We condemned it in our 1983 report, but stopped short of making a recommendation because of the then parlous plight of the industry. The industry is now stronger and we make recommendations intended to bring this practice to an end.

1.11. The second practice which we find to be against the public interest concerns minimum exhibition periods. Distributors sometimes insist on lengthy minimum exhibition periods—perhaps four weeks or longer—as a condition of supplying exhibitors with prints of popular films. This practice creates problems particularly for single-screen cinemas or those with few screens, reducing their freedom to respond to consumer demand, and adds to the difficulties faced by independent distributors in getting their films shown. We recommend that minimum exhibition periods should be restricted to a maximum of two weeks on first release and one week subsequently.

1.12. Relevant to the exhibitors' complaints which led up to this inquiry is the issue of refusal to supply. The established arrangements for calculating rentals, which command industry-wide support from both distributors and exhibitors, have the effect of reducing distributors' receipts if a given audience is divided between two cinemas. Distributors therefore refuse supply in circumstances where to supply another cinema would split the potential audience and reduce their profits. Given the extent of competition in both the distribution and exhibition markets, we consider it reasonable for distributors to determine supply with a view to maximizing profits on individual films. We propose, however, the establishment of some independent machinery to consider exhibitors' complaints.

1.13. Another issue is vertical integration, to which critics of the film industry frequently point as distorting the market and creating barriers to entry, particularly for British films. All the Hollywood studios rely upon their respective affiliates to distribute their films in the UK. Given the state of competition among the studios and in the distribution market generally, we do not object to this practice, which is common world-wide. Four of the seven Hollywood studios also have ownership links with UK exhibitors. We have examined whether these links result in dealings between distributors and exhibitors being other than at arm's length. Our analysis shows a slight degree of preference between vertically linked parties at the margin, but the evidence does not warrant an adverse public interest finding. We suggest nevertheless that certain indicators should be monitored by the Office of Fair Trading so that the matter is kept under review.

## Overview

1.14. Film production is an expensive and very risky business. Profitability depends on the success of a small number of films. The Hollywood studios account for a high proportion of box office receipts in the UK, but there is vigorous competition between them and no one studio dominates.

1.15. We regret that the proportion of culturally British films to be seen in UK cinemas is low, but we do not attribute this to any conspiracy or other improper behaviour on the part of the Hollywood studios or their UK affiliates. The Hollywood studios are skilled in producing and promoting films that the UK public wants to see. They have the advantage of operating in the much bigger US market, which enables them to make films with high production costs and hence to attract the most popular stars. In deciding which films to release in the UK and how to promote them, the studios benefit from the experience of prior distribution in the USA. Exhibitors are eager to show films which have proved popular in the USA and which are heavily promoted, and the shared language makes the UK market particularly receptive to US films.

1.16. We do not therefore under-estimate the problems which British film-makers face in competing against Hollywood. But UK exhibitors are interested in showing any films which they think will have popular appeal, irrespective of origin, and recent examples demonstrate that it is possible for British films to compete successfully for screen space. In so far as British film-makers produce popular films our recommendations, if implemented, may incidentally facilitate the showing of these in UK cinemas. But the main difficulties faced by the British film industry are beyond the scope of this inquiry.

1.17. The transformation of the industry over the last decade has worked well for consumers. Further changes may be expected. Today, apart from the practices we have criticized, competition in the markets under investigation is effective.

# 2 Conclusions

## Contents

| | Paragraph |
|---|---|
| Background | 2.1 |
|   EC aspects | 2.4 |
| The monopoly situations | 2.5 |
|   Findings on scale monopoly situation | 2.7 |
|   Findings on complex monopoly situation | 2.11 |
|   Persons in whose favour the monopoly situations exist | 2.36 |
| The relevant markets | |
|   Market definition | 2.42 |
|   Production | 2.49 |
|   Distribution | |
|     Factual position | 2.59 |
|     Analysis of market dynamics | 2.68 |
|   Exhibition | |
|     Factual position | 2.76 |
|     Analysis of market dynamics | 2.82 |
|   Determination of rental payments | 2.89 |
|   Risk and risk management | 2.92 |
|   Aggregated financial results | 2.98 |
|   Changes since the last MMC report | 2.100 |
| Public interest issues | 2.105 |
|   Complaints and concerns | 2.106 |
|   Issues arising from scale monopoly situation | 2.111 |
|   Issues arising from complex monopoly situation | 2.112 |
|     Alignment by distributors and exhibitors | 2.113 |
|     Exclusivity | 2.130 |
|     Refusal to supply | 2.142 |
|     Minimum exhibition periods | 2.155 |
|     Restrictions on screen use | 2.165 |
|     Distributors' influence over exhibitors' admission prices | 2.174 |
|     Observance of the SFD *Standard Conditions* | 2.181 |
|     Co-ordination of release dates | 2.188 |
|     Conditional booking | 2.192 |
|     Vertical integration | 2.197 |
|     Difficulties faced by British film-makers | 2.218 |
| Summary of conclusions on monopoly situations and adverse findings | 2.227 |
| Recommendations | 2.230 |
| Overview | 2.250 |

# Background

2.1. The matter of the supply of films for exhibition in cinemas in the UK (the reference goods) has been referred to us under the monopoly provisions of the Fair Trading Act 1973 (the Act) by the Director General of Fair Trading (DGFT). In making the reference the DGFT said that his own enquiries had been prompted initially by complaints from independent cinemas about difficulties in obtaining popular films from distributors. He added that most of the major companies were vertically integrated and followed practices which could lead to the exclusion of independent producers, distributors and exhibitors from the market. Although there had been changes in the market since the previous MMC report in 1983, the DGFT considered that competition remained restricted to such an extent that it was appropriate for the MMC to undertake a fresh investigation.

2.2. There have been two previous MMC reports into the supply of films, in 1966[1] and 1983.[2] The conclusions of these reports are summarized in paragraphs 3.3 to 3.7 and in Appendices 3.1 and 3.2. It is sufficient to note here that the 1983 report found that the practices of alignment and barring operated against the public interest, and that the two leading cinema circuits were able to exercise market power to delay the release of popular films to other exhibitors. The MMC considered the possibility, as a remedy for the adverse effects of alignment, of requiring the two circuits to divest some of their cinemas but concluded that, in view of the industry's continuing decline, such action was not practicable. The Commission did, however, recommend that the barring system should be prohibited, and that popular films should not be exhibited for more than four weeks unless they were made available to all other competing cinemas which sought to show them.

2.3. Following that report the Office of Fair Trading (OFT) set up an experimental scheme for a year in Glasgow and Manchester in which the distributors agreed to negotiate exclusivity arrangements with exhibitors case by case, rather than in accordance with standard barring arrangements, and to provide prints of films to subsequent-run cinemas four weeks after they opened at first-run cinemas. The OFT encountered difficulties both in mounting the experiment and in evaluating the results, in view of other changes which were happening in the market. Nevertheless it recommended that action should be taken to implement the MMC's recommendations on both these points. In subsequent consultations, however, the Department of Trade and Industry (DTI) found that there was strong opposition to the imposition of a four-week limit on the length of time which first-run cinemas could exhibit a popular film without its being made available to competing cinemas, and the proposal was dropped. On the other hand the Secretary of State proceeded with the introduction of an Order[3] under the Act to prohibit the practice of barring, and this came into effect in April 1989.

## EC aspects

2.4. In carrying out our inquiry we have to take account of relevant provisions of the laws of the EC as well as domestic UK law. Article 85.1 of the Treaty of Rome prohibits agreements between companies which may affect trade between member states and which prevent, restrict or distort competition. In July 1989 the EC Commission granted an exemption from those provisions under Article 85.3 to United International Pictures BV

---

[1]*Films: a report on the supply of films for exhibition in cinemas*, HC 206, October 1966.

[2]*Films: a report on the supply of films for exhibition in cinemas*, Cmnd 8874, May 1983.

[3]The Films (Exclusivity Agreements) Order 1989: see Appendix 3.3.

(UIP BV), a distribution joint venture between three of the Hollywood studios. UIP BV's UK subsidiary is one of the leading distributors here. The exemption expired in July 1993 and the EC Commission is considering UIP BV's request for a renewal. In January 1993 the EC Commission received an application for negative clearance or exemption under Article 85.3 for United Cinemas International Multiplex BV (UCI BV), a joint venture in exhibition between two of the three partners in UIP BV. UCI BV's UK subsidiary is one of the leading exhibitors here. The EC Commission is not expected to reach decisions on either of these two applications before 1995. We visited the EC Commission at the half-way stage in our inquiry for a general discussion about these cases and their relationship to our inquiry.

# The monopoly situations

2.5. Our terms of reference (Appendix 1.1) require us to investigate and report on whether a monopoly situation exists in relation to the supply of films for exhibition in cinemas in the UK, and if so by virtue of which provisions of sections 6 to 8 of the Act the monopoly situation is taken to exist, and in whose favour the situation exists.

2.6. Section 6 of the Act deals with monopoly situations in the supply of goods, and section 7 in the supply of services. Distributors supply prints of films to exhibitors on rental terms, together with a licence permitting the exhibitor to show the film to the public. It seems to us reasonable to regard this as a supply of goods, and that section 6 is therefore the relevant section for the purposes of this inquiry. It envisages different kinds of monopoly situation, usually referred to as 'scale' and 'complex'.

## Findings on scale monopoly situation

2.7. A scale monopoly situation under section 6(1)*(a)* or *(b)* is taken to exist when at least one-quarter of all goods of a particular description which are supplied in the UK are supplied by or to the same person, or by or to members of the same group of interconnected bodies corporate. We consider that the supply of films for exhibition in cinemas should be measured by value—as represented by distributors' rental receipts from cinema exhibitors—averaged over a four-year period. Distributors' receipts in any one year may be heavily influenced by the success or failure of a small number of films, whereas receipts over a four-year period give a better indication of a distributor's underlying performance. This was the approach followed by our predecessors in the 1983 report and, having considered the matter afresh, we believe it continues to be the appropriate one.

2.8. At one stage in our inquiry our calculations indicated that over the four years 1990 to 1993 inclusive United International Pictures (UK) (UIP) received over 25 per cent of distributors' total rentals from the licensing of films for exhibition in cinemas in the UK. Our final calculations (Table 4.2) show that UIP's share was 24.9 per cent, just below the threshold referred to in paragraph 2.7. We therefore make no finding of a scale monopoly situation in respect of UIP.

2.9. Table 4.2 also shows that over the same period Warner Bros Distributors Limited (Warner Distributors) received 27.7 per cent of distributors' total rentals. Warner Distributors used to have an agreement with The Walt Disney Company (Walt Disney) to distribute the latter's films in the UK. Walt Disney established its own UK distribution company, Buena Vista International (UK) Limited (Buena Vista), to take over that function with effect from November 1992. We therefore consider that it is both realistic and fair to measure Warner Distributors' share of supply by reference to its receipts for films other than Walt Disney's. Table 4.2 shows that, on this basis, Warner Distributors' share of total rental receipts in 1990 to 1993 was only 17.0 per cent.

2.10. As to the category of persons to whom supplies are made, which in this inquiry means cinema exhibitors, we consider that market share can again be appropriately measured over the same four-year period even though year-to-year fluctuations are less marked than in distribution. Table 4.8 shows that over this period Metro-Goldwyn-Mayer Cinemas Ltd (MGM Cinemas) made 26.7 per cent of exhibitors' total rental payments for the exhibition of films in UK cinemas. We conclude that a monopoly situation exists by virtue of section 6(1)(a) of the Act (a scale monopoly) in that at least one-quarter of the films which are supplied for exhibition in cinemas in the UK are supplied to MGM Cinemas.

## Findings on complex monopoly situation

2.11. A complex monopoly situation under section 6(1)(c) and (2) of the Act is taken to exist when at least one-quarter of all goods of a particular description which are supplied in the UK are supplied by or to members of the same group consisting of two or more persons (not being a group of interconnected bodies corporate), who, whether voluntarily or not and whether by agreement or not, so conduct their respective affairs as in any way to prevent, restrict or distort competition in connection with the production or supply of goods of that description.

2.12. In our issues letter of 14 February 1994 we informed the following distributors and exhibitors of our provisional finding that a complex monopoly situation existed in respect of the supply of films for exhibition in cinemas in the UK in that they conducted their affairs in one or more of the ways (the practices) described in paragraph 2.13:

*Distributors*

Buena Vista
Columbia Pictures Corporation Limited (Columbia)
Entertainment Film Distributors Limited (Entertainment)
First Independent Films Limited (First Independent)
Guild Film Distribution Limited (Guild)
Rank Film Distributors Limited (RFD)
Twentieth Century Fox Film Company Limited (Fox)
UIP
Warner Distributors

*Exhibitors*

MGM Cinemas
Natl Amusements (UK) Ltd (Natl Amusements)
Odeon Cinemas Limited (Odeon)
United Cinemas International (UK) Limited (UCI)
Warner Bros Theatres Limited  ⎫
Warner Bros Theatres (UK) Limited  ⎭ (together Warner Theatres)

In our view there are no other distributors or exhibitors whose involvement in the markets is sufficiently great for their conduct to have the effect of preventing, restricting or distorting competition.

2.13. The practices referred to in paragraph 2.12 are:

*(a)* distributors systematically offering their films to the cinemas of either MGM Cinemas or Odeon in places where they are in competition one with the other, but not to both (alignment by distributors);

*(b)* MGM Cinemas and Odeon accepting films from distributors in accordance with the practice of alignment (alignment by exhibitors);

*(c)* distributors supplying, and exhibitors accepting, individual films on the basis that a particular cinema will have the exclusive right to show a film within a specified area and for a specified period (exclusivity);

*(d)* distributors refusing to supply individual films to exhibitors who request them, either at all or at the time requested, for reasons other than creditworthiness and the need to cover the costs of supply (refusal to supply);

*(e)* distributors requiring exhibitors to show a film at particular cinemas for a minimum period exceeding seven days (minimum exhibition periods);

*(f)* distributors requiring exhibitors to show a film at all times during the licence period at which films are normally shown at the cinema in question (except for children's matinées and late night shows) (restrictions on screen use);

*(g)* distributors supplying, and exhibitors accepting, films on terms which require exhibitors to charge such admission prices during licence periods as shall be agreed by the distributors (distributor influence over admission prices);

*(h)* distributors and exhibitors observing the *Standard Conditions for Licensing the Commercial Exhibition of a Film or Films* (the *Standard Conditions*) issued by the Society of Film Distributors Limited (SFD) (observance of SFD *Standard Conditions*); and

*(i)* distributors and exhibitors with related companies based overseas reserving important decision-making functions (for example, as regards which films should be released or shown in the UK and as regards release strategies) to such companies (overseas-based decision-taking).

We invited the parties concerned to comment on our provisional finding and on the issues which appeared to us to arise from it.

2.14. The parties all commented in writing and several of them attended hearings. Four parties—Buena Vista, First Independent, MGM Cinemas and Natl Amusements—made no comment on our provisional finding. Guild said that it did not agree that a complex monopoly existed but presented no arguments in support of this view. Entertainment disputed its inclusion in the complex monopoly group but gave no reason other than that it was the only true independent in the list and did not own or control cinemas. UIP said that it did not believe the practices listed were complex monopoly practices which were restrictive and/or affected the public interest but its submissions essentially addressed the practices' effects on the public interest, not whether they prevented, restricted or distorted competition. UCI's submissions were also of this nature and it did not challenge the complex monopoly finding as such or UCI's inclusion in it. Columbia questioned the inclusion of certain of the practices.

2.15. Warner Distributors and Warner Theatres raised more detailed arguments, while The Rank Organisation Plc (Rank), on behalf of its subsidiaries RFD and Odeon, and Fox made submissions in considerable detail on various aspects of the provisional monopoly situation and the practices. These arguments and submissions are set out in paragraphs 7.12 to 7.14 and 8.22 to 8.24 of this report, a number of specific points being referred to below.

2.16. We have carefully considered the representations described or referred to in paragraphs 2.14 and 2.15, as well as all the other evidence bearing on our provisional finding of a complex monopoly situation. It is important to recognize that, in considering whether such a situation exists, we are concerned with whether the practices which we have identified prevent, restrict or distort competition and not with the question, entirely separate under the Act, of whether they constitute facts which operate or may be expected to operate against the public interest.

2.17. Before we examine the practices themselves, there is a preliminary matter which we have to consider, namely which of the parties participates in which of the practices (bearing in mind that we have provisionally identified 15 companies which may be included in a complex monopoly group and nine practices). We have therefore set out in Appendix 2.1 a schedule of the practices in which we have concluded that each of the companies engages.

2.18. In some instances a company contended that it did not engage in a particular practice, or a number of the practices, while we have been unable to take this view. Warner Distributors said that it did not engage in many of the practices which had given rise to complaints and allegations of anti-competitive behaviour, and believed that its policy relating to the provision of prints was considerably more liberal than that of many of its competitors. But the company's arguments were concerned with the effect of the practices, particularly in so far as Warner Distributors was involved in them, on the public interest. Its submissions made clear that it engaged in all the distributor practices except for exclusivity.

2.19. Fox said that the conduct identified by the MMC as giving rise to a complex monopoly was not conduct in which it engaged. It argued, first, that it did not engage in alignment in any consequential sense. Fox explained that it normally approached Odeon to discuss the release strategy for its films and would either offer Odeon booking priority or explain why it was not doing so. There was no obligation or understanding that it would give precedence to Odeon. We do not find these arguments convincing. Fox provided a list of the films, totalling 57, which it had released since January 1991 or was due to release in the latter part of 1994. Of these, Fox regarded 39 as having been first offered to Odeon, 4 to MGM and 14 to some other exhibitor. Fox also provided a list of Odeon cinemas where key releases were normally shown in preference to competing MGM Cinemas sites. We are satisfied that Fox's practice in relation to the offering of its films to Odeon constitutes an example of alignment as we have defined it.

2.20. Fox further argued that it did not engage in the practices concerning minimum exhibition periods and restrictions on screen use to any significant degree. When it did so, it was in order to maximize its profits and recover its costs, including its advertising and promotional expenses. Fox said that it pressed for minimum periods longer than seven days in special circumstances, where for example it had committed itself to make a large investment in advertising a film. We noted that its preferred playing time for *Mrs Doubtfire*, which it released in January 1994 with 350 prints, was three weeks minimum plus holdover although it agreed bookings of two weeks in a small minority of cases. Fox told us that conflicts arose in that sometimes an exhibitor wanted to cut short the agreed run of a film whereas Fox would insist on the full contracted playing time if it considered the film sufficiently successful to warrant it. As to restrictions on screen use, Fox incorporates in its licensing agreements the *Standard Conditions*, including the provision that, in the absence of specific agreement to the contrary, the exhibitor 'shall exhibit the film at all times during the licence period at which films would normally be exhibited at the cinemas at the time of the signing of the Agreement (excluding children's matinees and late night shows)' (see text at Appendix 4.3). We consider that this evidence shows that Fox does engage in these two practices.

2.21. Fox also said that it did not in practice exercise control over exhibitors' prices: it had not prohibited exhibitors from lowering their prices when they had wished to do so. The practice referred to in paragraph 2.13*(g)* is based on another of the provisions in the *Standard Conditions* which, as we noted in paragraph 2.20, Fox incorporates in its licensing agreements. We consider that the inclusion of the provision can in itself be expected to influence exhibitors' behaviour and is sufficient ground for believing that Fox engages in this practice too.

2.22. Entertainment said that it did not consider that it was aligned to either of the two main circuits. It agreed, however, that for films to which it planned to give a wide release it sought exhibition dates in the first instance from Odeon. We believe that its relationship with Odeon constitutes alignment even though it applies to a smaller proportion of Entertainment's films than is the case with the leading distributors.

2.23. We now address the question whether the practices themselves prevent, restrict or distort competition in the supply of the reference goods.

## *Alignment by distributors and exhibitors*

2.24. Distributors aligned to either MGM Cinemas or Odeon (the two main circuit exhibitors) normally offer their films in the first instance to their aligned exhibitor and plan their release strategies in consultation with it. These arrangements are long-standing. In 20 locations where both these exhibitors have cinemas, the films of UIP and Warner Distributors are normally offered to, and hence shown by, MGM Cinemas but not Odeon, while the films of the other leading distributors and certain independent distributors are normally offered to and shown by Odeon but not MGM Cinemas. The competition for these screens does not take place equally among all distributors, but is largely restricted to the distributors which are aligned with the exhibitor in question. Correspondingly, in these locations MGM Cinemas does not normally seek to book the films of distributors which are aligned to Odeon, nor does Odeon seek to book the films of UIP and Warner Distributors. We are satisfied that the practice of alignment represents a form of market sharing and restricts competition.

## *Exclusivity*

2.25. Where a distributor gives an exhibitor the exclusive right to show a film, for a specified period and within a specified area, it follows that no other cinema in that area can show the film in competition until the period of exclusivity has ended. Although two of the leading distributors told us that they never, or hardly ever, granted exclusivity to an exhibitor, and four of the five leading exhibitors told us that they never sought contractual exclusivity, Odeon negotiates exclusivity for many of the films it shows. We are satisfied that the practice exists to a significant extent (it is engaged in by three of the leading distributors and the four independent distributors in the complex monopoly group, as well as one of the two main circuit exhibitors (ie Odeon)) and that it restricts competition. The fact that, as Fox and Rank argued (among other points), the practice involves the exercise of intellectual property rights does not, in our view, affect the position.

## *Refusal to supply*

2.26. It is similarly our view that, where a distributor refuses to supply a print of a film to an exhibitor who requests one, the exhibitor is prevented from showing the film in competition with other cinemas which receive prints of the film. Evidence which we have received from distributors, of how they decided on their distribution strategies for films, satisfied us that all distributors refuse to supply prints to exhibitors, where to do so would not fit in with the distributors' strategies. We consider that this practice too restricts competition.

## *Minimum exhibition periods*

2.27. All the distributors told us that their licensing agreements with exhibitors required the film to be shown for a specified minimum period of at least seven days. For the more popular films the period was two weeks or more. Although the distributors told us that they agreed to shorten the period if a film's box office receipts were disappointing, we received evidence from the Cinema Exhibitors' Association (CEA) and from individual exhibitors that exhibitors were often refused permission to take a film off early (see paragraphs 6.5 and 6.6 and paragraph 18 (Statement 2) of Appendix 4.4). Indeed some distributors told us that they would refuse permission if they considered their film was achieving reasonable takings but an exhibitor wanted to replace it with another film which it thought would do better. Having considered this varied evidence, we conclude on balance that this practice restricts competition by preventing exhibitors from showing another film which they would prefer to show, and thus restricting the ability of other distributors to make bookings for their films.

## *Restrictions on screen use*

2.28. The distributors all incorporate the *Standard Conditions* in their licensing agreements, including the provision quoted in paragraph 2.20. They argued that sharing of screens with other films could be negotiated case by case. But the CEA told us that permission to do so was not given sufficiently often. Most distributors, according to the CEA, demanded that only their film should be shown during the normal exhibition day. Some gave permission for other films to be shown on the same screen but imposed unsuitable limitations as to the timing of such showings (see paragraphs 6.8 to 6.11). A significant proportion of the respondents to our survey of independent exhibitors said that distributors always or usually refused them permission to show other films if asked (see paragraph 18 (Statement 5) of Appendix 4.4). The distributors' evidence made clear that, while they sometimes gave permission for other films to be shown on a screen which they had booked for one of their films, there were also times when they would not do so, for example if the film were aimed primarily at children but the distributor wanted to see if it appealed to adult audiences as well. Balancing the different strands of this evidence, we take the view that the practice does restrict competition in that exhibitors are restricted in their ability to compete for audiences by showing other films at certain times, and other distributors are less able to get their films shown.

## Distributor influence over admission prices

2.29. The *Standard Conditions* provide that 'the Exhibitor shall charge such admission prices at the cinema during the licence period as shall be agreed by the Distributor'. The distributors told us that they did not in practice exercise influence or control over admission prices but that since a reduction in admission prices could affect the distributor's rentals it was only reasonable that it should be consulted about proposed changes. We received evidence from the CEA that distributors sometimes refused permission for reductions in admission prices (see paragraph 6.13), and the minutes of SFD meetings showed that distributors had taken action against unauthorized price promotions undertaken by exhibitors (see paragraph 4.132). The leading exhibitors told us that they regarded this provision of the *Standard Conditions* as reasonable given that distributors' rentals depended on exhibitors' admission prices; they freely entered into licensing agreements with distributors which included it. We consider that this is a practice engaged in jointly by the distributors and exhibitors in the complex monopoly group. Use of the *Standard Conditions* is widespread in the industry and the inclusion of this provision has the effect of restricting exhibitors' ability to compete by cutting prices.

## Observance of SFD Standard Conditions

2.30. As to the *Standard Conditions* themselves, the leading exhibitors could, if they so decided, propose the use of their own conditions: their acceptance of the *Standard Conditions* is a matter of choice. We therefore consider that this practice too is one jointly engaged in by distributors and exhibitors. The evidence shows that the use of the *Standard Conditions* is almost universal and we consider that this situation restricts individual parties' ability to compete by offering different terms.

## Overseas-based decision-taking

2.31. Finally, as regards overseas-based decision-taking, we included this suggested practice in our provisional finding because of submissions that the Hollywood studios sometimes insisted on films being released in the UK which their distribution subsidiaries did not think would succeed here with, it was argued, some consequent distortion of competition. Having considered this matter further and taken into account the representations of the parties, we have concluded that there is insufficient evidence to justify reliance on such a practice in support of the complex monopoly situation which is in question here. Consequently, there is no reference to it in the schedule in Appendix 2.1.

## Other points

2.32. Before stating our conclusion, we advert to two points of a more general nature. First, Warner Distributors argued that it was inappropriate for the MMC to include, in the complex monopoly finding, such a varied range of practices which, it said, had very different effects on competition (see paragraph 8.23). We do not agree. We believe it now to be settled law that similarity in the practices of members of a complex monopoly group is not necessary.[1] In the present circumstances, we consider that, having regard to the

---

[1] *R v MMC and another ex parte Ecando Systems Limited*: unreported judgments of Simon Brown J on 30 September 1991 and of the Court of Appeal on 12 November 1992.

interaction between the practices and their combined effect on the market, we are fully justified in identifying the group as we have done.

2.33. Secondly, we provisionally identified a group comprising both distributors and exhibitors. Although no question of substance appears to us to be involved we have considered whether, if only as a technical matter, it might be preferable instead to identify two groups, comprising each of those categories respectively. We have concluded that, in the circumstances, this would be neither necessary nor sensible, having regard to what we believe to be the commercial reality of the market and industry concerned and bearing in mind that a similar approach was adopted in our previous report (paragraphs 8.4 and 8.5 of that report).

2.34. We have given the distributors and exhibitors listed in paragraph 2.12 the opportunity to comment on this point. No objection has been made to the identification of one group only, other than on behalf of Fox, whose solicitors submitted that, having regard to the wording of section 6 of the Act, it would be more appropriate for the MMC to conclude (if the conditions described in that section were fulfilled) that separate complex monopoly situations prevailed in favour of distributors and in favour of exhibitors. We are not persuaded by this view.

*Conclusion on complex monopoly situation*

2.35. Having had regard to the views which we have set out in paragraphs 2.16 to 2.34 and the evidence in Chapters 4, 6, 7, 8 and 9, we have concluded that a monopoly situation exists by virtue of section 6(1)*(c)* and (2) of the Act (a complex monopoly situation) in that the parties listed in paragraph 2.12 (being members of one and the same group for the purpose of these provisions) so conduct their respective affairs as to restrict competition in connection with the supply of the reference goods by engaging in the practices listed in paragraph 2.13 (excluding subparagraph *(i)*), and supply at least one-quarter of the reference goods. As has already been mentioned, a schedule of the practices in which we have concluded that each of the parties engages appears in Appendix 2.1, while Tables 4.2 and 4.8 show that the supply requirement (see paragraph 2.11) is satisfied.

## Persons in whose favour the monopoly situations exist

2.36. Our terms of reference require us to report in favour of what person or persons the monopoly situations which we have identified exist. In our issues letter we informed the parties of our relevant provisional findings, that is to say that:

*(a)* the scale monopoly situation relating to MGM Cinemas existed in favour of MGM Cinemas and Crédit Lyonnais SA (Crédit Lyonnais); and

*(b)* the complex monopoly situation existed in favour of the companies provisionally identified as members of the complex monopoly group (whose names appear in paragraph 2.12) and the persons listed in Appendix 2.2.

Consequently, the persons in whose favour these monopoly situations were provisionally found to exist were:

*(c)* MGM Cinemas;

(d) the other members of the complex monopoly group; and

(e) the persons listed in Appendix 2.2.

The persons referred to in *(e)* were ultimate holding companies (in one case an ultimate controlling shareholder) and some intermediate holding companies of members of the complex monopoly group.

2.37. Several parties, in particular Columbia and UIP, argued that their ultimate holding companies had no involvement in their business and no other interest beyond that of controlling shareholders and should therefore not be regarded as persons in whose favour the complex monopoly situation existed. We do not accept that, as a general matter, ultimate or intermediate holding companies, or controlling shareholders, may not, where appropriate, be identified as such persons—nor that involvement in the business concerned is a necessary condition for the identification of such a person. We have not overlooked the fact that previous reports of the MMC have identified shareholders as persons in whose favour the relevant monopoly situation existed.[1] More particularly, however, we regard it as correct, and consistent with the practice of the MMC, to give primary consideration to the circumstances of the instant case; as was stated in the report on *Contact lens solutions*[2] (paragraph 8.40):

> We do not consider that it would be consistent with our statutory duties to attempt to define all the circumstances in which persons, not themselves suppliers of the goods or services concerned, would be persons in whose favour a monopoly situation existed. The facts of a particular case are necessarily of particular relevance ...

2.38. The present circumstances suggest to us that, in considering this question, the most reasonable approach is not in relation to a shareholding as such, but to that factor combined with the ownership or operation, by the shareholding company concerned, of a film studio, together with the close participation of the studio in the control and operations of the UK distributor concerned. The evidence recorded in Chapters 4, 5 and 8 indicates that UK cinema release is part of the studios' global distribution strategies and that their distribution subsidiaries are being effectively run as branches of the studio parent, their costs being largely met by and the net revenues largely remitted to the parent. With this background in mind and having considered the arguments of the parties, we have reviewed our provisional findings as regards persons in whose favour the monopoly situations exist in the light of the approach described at the outset of this paragraph. Our conclusions on the matter are set out in paragraph 2.40.

2.39. To the extent that reviewing our provisional findings required the identification of certain additional companies in relation to the monopoly situations—namely MCA Inc, Metro-Goldwyn-Mayer Inc (MGM Inc) and Paramount Pictures Corporation (Paramount)—they were informed of the position.

2.40. We have therefore concluded that the monopoly situations which we have identified exist in favour of the following persons:

(a) as regards the scale monopoly situation relating to MGM Cinemas (paragraph 2.10), MGM Cinemas; and

---

[1] eg *Carbonated drinks*, Cm 1625, August 1991, paragraphs 10.8 to 10.12, 10.18 to 10.22; *Contact lens solutions*, Cm 2242, May 1993, paragraphs 8.32 to 8.46, 8.51, 8.67, 8.85 and 8.95.

[2] See previous footnote.

*(b)* as regards the complex monopoly situation (paragraphs 2.11 to 2.35), the members of the complex monopoly group (see paragraph 2.12) and the following:

Fox Inc;
MCA Inc;
MGM Inc;
Paramount;
Sony Pictures Entertainment Inc;
Time Warner Inc; and
Walt Disney.

2.41. Having reached these conclusions on the existence of a monopoly situation and on the questions in subparagraphs *(a)* and *(b)* in our terms of reference (see Appendix 1.1), we have to consider the remaining questions, *viz*:

*(c)* whether any steps (by way of uncompetitive practices or otherwise) are being taken by that person or persons for the purpose of exploiting or maintaining the monopoly situation and if so by what uncompetitive practices or in what other way;

*(d)* whether any action or omission on the part of that person or persons is attributable to the existence of that monopoly situation and if so what action or omission and in what way it is so attributable; and

*(e)* whether any facts found by the Commission in pursuance of their investigations under the preceding provisions of this paragraph operate or may be expected to operate against the public interest.

Before doing so, we describe and analyse the main facts about the relevant markets.

# The relevant markets

## Market definition

2.42. The first question to arise is whether the viewing of films in the cinema is part of a wider market which includes the viewing of films on television screens, whether from video cassettes, free television or pay television.

2.43. A distributor normally releases a film in successive periods to these different outlets, starting with the cinema release and proceeding through video rental, pay television, video sale and free television. Thus consumers wanting to see the latest releases have no alternative but to visit the cinema. Consumers who are prepared to wait may see video rental or television broadcasts as lower-cost alternatives to the cinema. But there is also evidence that the growth in film-watching on the small screen has stimulated interest in the cinema, and that a successful cinema release increases demand for a film when it is released to video and television outlets. It is not clear how these various factors interact.

2.44. Cinema-going is in any event a different kind of experience compared with watching films on television screens at home. It involves an outing, seeing the film on a big screen with appropriate sound equipment, and being in company with other members of the public. We therefore consider that the supply of cinema services is a separate market (we refer to this as the exhibition market) and that the supply of films for exhibition in cinemas (the distribution market) is also separate from the supply of films for other kinds of viewing (see paragraphs 4.17 to 4.22).

2.45. A second question is whether these markets should be viewed as a whole or broken down, for example on a geographical basis or as between different types of film. Many cinemas are geographically isolated from other cinemas and do not face much competition from other exhibitors. The bulk of box office receipts, however, is derived from the main centres of population where, in most cases, cinemas are in direct competition with each other. The competitive position of an exhibitor also depends to some extent on the number and quality of all the cinemas which it owns: this is particularly true of the two main circuit exhibitors.

2.46. Moreover in considering whether to supply particular cinemas, and on what terms, distributors have to consider not only the competitive position of each cinema in its local market but also the competition from other distributors. When determining their release strategies for individual films, distributors begin by assessing the likely level of demand in the UK as a whole; while exhibitors, in reaching their booking decisions, assess which of the films available to them will generate the greatest box office takings. Both these decisions depend crucially on the supply of, and potential demand for, other films to be released around the same time. Distributors plan their promotional campaigns for the UK as a whole and much of their advertising, notably on television, is placed on a national basis.

2.47. For these reasons we consider that, while there are elements of competition which are local, or are particular to individual films, it is sensible to view both the distribution and exhibition markets as national in scope for the purposes of economic analysis.

2.48. Cinemas compete with other forms of leisure activity such as pubs, bowling alleys, concerts and television. They have to provide an entertainment experience which customers perceive as giving value for money compared with those other activities. While the existence of these alternatives represents a long-term competitive constraint on cinemas—they undoubtedly contributed to the prolonged decline in cinema attendances from 1950 until the mid-1980s—we consider that they are not such close substitutes as to be regarded as part of the same market (see paragraphs 4.23 to 4.26).

## Production

2.49. The making of a feature film is a complex commercial operation which requires the co-ordination of several component activities. It can be very expensive: the average cost of films made by the US Hollywood studios in 1993 was around £20 million. It is also a very risky activity, the general pattern being that most films lose money for their producers, a few break even and a few make big profits.

2.50. The making of big-budget films for international distribution has long been dominated by the Hollywood studios: Columbia Picture Industries Inc and TriStar Pictures Inc (Columbia/TriStar), MCA Inc which owns the Universal studio (MCA/Universal), MGM Inc, Paramount, Twentieth Century Fox Film Corporation (20th Century Fox), Walt Disney and Warner Bros. Four of these are now owned by non-US parents: Columbia/TriStar which is owned by Sony Corporation, MGM Inc which was acquired by Crédit Lyonnais (the French state-owned bank) as a result of loan default, MCA/Universal whose parent is Matsushita Electric Industrial Co Limited and 20th Century Fox which is a subsidiary of The News Corporation Limited.

2.51. The production of a film cannot begin until the necessary financial backing has been secured. In most cases this requires an assurance that arrangements to distribute the finished product are in place. The Hollywood studios have their own distribution organizations and are able to finance production from their own resources or—increasingly as production budgets in the USA have risen—via co-production arrangements with independent companies.

2.52. There are no large, integrated UK companies involved in making their own films on a substantial scale. Typically therefore a UK production company has to pre-sell the distribution rights to a separate distribution company, which contributes towards the production budget either by making an advance against the expected distribution profits or by giving guarantees against which the production company can raise bank finance.

2.53. Many British films are made by companies formed specially for the purpose of making a single film, raising money from investors willing to put money into high-risk ventures (and encouraged to do so by tax concessions). While such individuals may recycle any profits from one venture into another, there is a general absence of companies which can spread the risks over a slate of films, reinvesting the profits from the few successes into new production on a planned, long-term basis. The budgets for British films are small in comparison with US films and the producers are not in a position to compete for the well-known directors and stars whose involvement is generally—though not invariably—necessary for a film to be a big hit at the box office.

2.54. Television companies have been an important source of finance for British films in the last ten years or so. It is acknowledged in the industry that investment in film production by television companies, particularly the BBC and Channel Four, has enabled films to be made which would otherwise not have been, and some of these have achieved a degree of success at the cinema box office. But Mr David Puttnam suggested to us that their involvement may have caused producers and directors to place less emphasis on making films likely to appeal to cinema audiences (see paragraphs 6.78 and 6.79). Another probable effect of their involvement is to reduce the prospective revenues from distribution to other outlets, partly because distributors generally prefer to acquire all forms of distribution rights, including for television, as a package so that they can control their exploitation to the best overall advantage, and partly because the early showing of a film on free television is likely to reduce demand from other outlets.

2.55. Because of the international nature of the film industry there are problems of definition in classifying films by nationality. In this report we define a British film as one for which the UK was the prime source of the ideas or cultural values portrayed; and a British-made film as one whose producer was British or which was produced in the UK by an overseas producer. These definitions are not watertight. According to the British Film Institute (BFI) total investment in British-made films declined from £426 million in 1984 to £185 million in 1992, and the average production budget roughly halved from £8 million to £4 million (all figures at 1992 prices). The BFI and the Producers Alliance for Cinema and Television (PACT) gave evidence to us about the reasons, in their view, for this decline (see Chapter 6).

2.56. The number of films released annually for cinema exhibition in the UK in the last ten years has fluctuated in the range 215 to 256 (see Table 4.3). This is somewhat lower than the number of releases in other large European countries. In recent years about 60 per cent of releases have been US films, between 10 and 20 per cent British and between 20 and 30 per cent from other countries.

2.57. The share of the UK box office going to US-made films in 1992, 86 per cent, was higher than for most other European countries. But whereas the US share of the UK box office has been consistently over 80 per cent for years, other European countries experienced a strong increase in the US share during the 1980s from much lower levels: see Table 4.1.

2.58. The industry distinguishes two broad categories of film: mainstream (sometimes referred to as 'commercial') and arthouse. While there is no precise definition of these terms, mainstream films are those aimed at a wide audience while arthouse films are of more specialized interest. The term arthouse is, for example, used to refer to most foreign-language films released in the UK. Some films start out as arthouse but attract a wider audience than expected: these are referred to as cross-overs. Some cinemas, particularly in London, specialize in showing arthouse films. In our inquiry we have been mainly, but not exclusively, concerned with mainstream films, which generate the great bulk of box office receipts and rentals.

## Distribution

### *Factual position*

2.59. The distribution companies operating in the UK theatrical market fall into two groups. The five leading distributors—Buena Vista, Columbia, Fox, UIP and Warner Distributors—are each owned by one or more of the Hollywood studios. Their main role is to distribute the films made or acquired by their parent companies. They do not have to bid or pay in advance for the UK distribution rights to those films but act as sales and marketing arms of their respective groups. Their role is to advise on which films should be released for UK cinema exhibition, to draw up and implement release and marketing strategies and to sell exhibition rights to cinema operators (ie to book films into individual screens). In most cases their release costs—covering advertising, promotion and the manufacture of prints—are for the account of their parents. In return the distributors remit their rental receipts to their parents, as payment for the distribution rights, after retaining a proportion of income acceptable to the Inland Revenue as representing a fair reflection of the profits of the UK-based activity. These arrangements are described in more detail in Chapter 5.

2.60. The remaining distributors, whom we refer to as the independent distributors, do not have access to an assured supply of films from within their respective corporate groups. These companies trade on their own account, bidding for distribution rights to films made by independent producers (ie production companies other than the Hollywood studios) and making financial commitments on an arm's length basis. Although we identified 24 such independent distributors, most of them operate on a small scale and specialize in handling arthouse films. Only four, all of which are involved in the mainstream as well as the arthouse part of the market, took more than 1 per cent of rental receipts from cinema exhibitors in the period 1990 to 1993:

*(a)* Entertainment, a private company;

*(b)* First Independent, a subsidiary of HTV Group Plc, holder of the ITV franchise for Wales;

*(c)* Guild, which is now (since 1992) owned by the French conglomerate Chargeurs SA, a shareholder in the satellite broadcaster British Sky Broadcasting Ltd (BSkyB); and

(d) RFD, which is owned by Rank and is therefore a sister company of Odeon, one of the two main circuit exhibitors. Although RFD invests in film production on a significant scale (mainly in co-productions led by US independents), it has to acquire rights to most of the films which it distributes in the open market.

2.61. In 1993 total rentals accruing to distributors from the exhibition of films in UK cinemas were about £103 million. The leading distributors accounted for 83 per cent of the total, UIP being the biggest with 31 per cent followed by Warner Distributors with 22 per cent, Columbia 15 per cent, Buena Vista 11 per cent and Fox 4 per cent. Among the independents Guild and Entertainment had 5 per cent each, RFD 2 per cent and First Independent 1 per cent (see Table 4.2).

2.62. Distributors determine their marketing plans and release patterns on a film-by-film basis taking into account the type of film; the estimated size and composition of its potential audience; other films likely to be released around the same time; the number of cinemas available and willing to take the film; and the budget available to support the release. Some of these factors interact: for example, the distributor's judgment of the potential audience size helps to determine how much it can justify spending on promotion.

2.63. For films expected to be popular, the leading distributors start discussions with whichever of the two main circuit exhibitors (MGM Cinemas and Odeon) they are aligned with up to 12 months before the film is expected to be ready for UK theatrical release. They aim to agree a release date, taking account of both their own and the exhibitor's knowledge of other films expected to be released around the same time, and to reserve screens on a provisional basis (a process often referred to as 'pencilling in'). The distributors may also have early discussions with some of the other leading exhibitors. When the film becomes available for viewing by exhibitors, the distributor seeks to make firm bookings of screens, starting with both the main circuit exhibitors, and moving on to the specialist multiplex operators (see paragraph 2.76(b)) and finally the independent exhibitors. Their degree of success in making bookings enables the distributors to finalize their plans for advertising and other promotional activity, although much of the expenditure may have to be committed in advance.

2.64. Independent distributors are not often in a position to plan so far ahead because they are not involved with the films they handle from the outset, as the integrated distributors are. Moreover it appears to be more difficult for independent distributors to persuade exhibitors to 'pencil in' their films before they become available for viewing, and they may consequently experience some difficulty in obtaining the bookings they want. In other respects, the release process is similar to that of the leading distributors.

2.65. Advertising and promotion are very important aspects of film distribution. It is now not unusual for a distributor to spend more than £1 million on the promotion of a major release. The revival of cinema audiences has enabled distributors to justify increased promotional expenditure, which in turn has contributed to the further growth in audiences. Television advertising is usually the biggest component of film advertising budgets, followed by national newspapers, posters, cinema trailers and radio. But editorial comment in the media, often stimulated by the availability of stars or directors for interviews, is also a crucial element. A variety of other promotional techniques is used, for example the simultaneous release of music from the film on CD and cassette, merchandising agreements with clothing companies or fast food chains.

2.66. All the leading distributors and the main independents are members of the SFD, the trade association which represents distributors of films for UK theatrical exhibition. As noted in paragraph 2.13, the SFD has issued *Standard Conditions* for the licensing of the commercial exhibition of films. All its members use these conditions in their agreements with exhibitors although they are not obliged to do so. The SFD has committees, made up of representatives from member companies, dealing with sales, advertising and promotion, and (exhibitor) irregularities.

2.67. With the growth in rentals and sales of video cassettes and more recently in pay television, revenues from cinema exhibition have been falling as a proportion of total revenues from the exploitation of films and now stand at around a quarter of the total. None of the leading distributors of films in the UK theatrical market deals with sales to the video and television markets, these being the responsibility of related companies in the UK or the USA.

## *Analysis of market dynamics*

2.68. The distribution subsidiaries of the Hollywood studios have a strong position, taking 77 per cent of total rentals in the period 1990 to 1993 as a whole. In only one year in the last six has their collective share dipped below this level. The fortunes of individual companies have varied rather more, however: UIP's share in any one year has ranged between 18 and 39 per cent in this period, and Fox's between 4 and 14 per cent. Warner Distributors has been the most consistently successful in that its share did not fall below 25 per cent in any year between 1988 and 1992. In 1993, however, after it lost the business of distributing Disney films, its share fell to 22 per cent and on the past record of Warner Bros' own films can be expected to fall further (see paragraph 2.9). Concentration within the group of majors has fallen: whereas in 1988 to 1990 UIP and Warner Distributors had a combined share in the range 62 to 72 per cent, the range in the three subsequent years has been 44 to 53 per cent.

2.69. The shares taken by independent distributors have also been variable. The two most successful in recent years have been RFD and Guild, the latter a new entrant since 1983. RFD took 11 per cent of rentals in 1991 but its share fell sharply to around 2 per cent in the two latest years. Guild's share rose from below 1 per cent in 1988 and 1989 to 14 and 10 per cent in 1991 and 1992 respectively but fell back to 5 per cent in 1993.

2.70. Some of the leading distributors argued that market share was not a useful indicator of a company's strength in this market since everything depended on the individual film. A studio's track record of producing and distributing successful films was no guarantee of success in future and conferred no market power. There is something in this, as witness the fluctuating fortunes of the leading distributors individually and the ability of Guild to achieve a substantial share very quickly on the back of an agreement with an independent US production company, Carolco Pictures Inc (Carolco), which produced a series of highly successful films. But the Hollywood studios have dominated the industry for many years and we were satisfied that the expectation that they would produce a continuing flow of attractive films gave their distribution subsidiaries influence with exhibitors.

2.71. In principle distributors compete with each other in the following ways:

— in acquiring distribution rights;

— in securing release dates, making bookings with exhibitors and maximizing the screening time of their films; and

— in advertising and promotion.

In practice the leading distributors largely have distribution rights handed to them on a plate by their US parents, whose films are not available for other distributors to bid for. To a small extent the leading distributors compete to pick up rights to independent films but such pick-ups by the Hollywood studios are usually made on an international scale by their US-based distribution companies which then license the UK subsidiaries to distribute them in the UK alongside the studios' own films.

2.72. Independent distributors compete to establish relationships, such as output deals, with independent production companies—both Guild and RFD obtain most of their films as a result of such arrangements with US independent producers—and in bidding for rights to other independent films on a one-off basis. They find themselves in competition with the Hollywood studios in doing so. Since they are not in a position to match the studios' spending power, they rely on their ability to spot producers and films whose potential is not immediately apparent. Independent distributors told us that the strength of competition often required them to make bids at pre-production stage. In this respect their operations are much riskier than those of the leading distributors.

2.73. Competition for release dates for films which are expected to be popular is mainly a matter of securing dates from MGM Cinemas and Odeon, the two main circuit exhibitors. This is because the specialist multiplex operators, the only other exhibitors with a sizeable market share, are generally able to accommodate all films offered to them which have commercial potential, whereas MGM Cinemas and Odeon still have a large number of sites with fewer than four screens. There is keen competition for the most desirable dates, notably at Christmas and other holiday periods.

2.74. Competition for screen-time concerns the number of sites in which a film is booked, which screens the film will be shown on, for how many weeks the film will be shown and on how many showings per week. The general view seems to be that the UK as a whole is 'under-screened'. International comparisons of numbers of screens in relation to admissions, and the low level of rentals in the UK by international standards, appear to support this view (see paragraphs 4.94 and 4.135). We were told that the position varied in different parts of the country and at different times of year. Some multiplex operators with 12- or 14-screen sites find that there is a shortage of commercial films at times. The more common situation, however, is that screens are in short supply in relation to the number of films on release. UCI, all of whose cinemas have large numbers of screens, said that there were nonetheless times when it had to take films off that were doing reasonably well in order to make way for new releases. This aspect of competition is heavily influenced by the quality of the films and exhibitors' judgments of them. Price competition is confined to a small proportion of cases where distributors—and sometimes exhibitors—seek special terms.

2.75. Financial results may be expected to give some indication of the state of competition and the relative strength of the companies. For the leading distributors taken as a group, operating profit before payment for distribution rights expressed as a percentage of turnover fell from 46 per cent in 1989 to 14 per cent in 1991 before recovering to 39 per cent in 1993 (see Table 5.5). This dip may have been partly a function of the recession but was also due to the fact that both Guild and RFD had a successful year in 1991 and took audiences away from the leading distributors. Profitability of individual companies on the same measure is highly volatile, UIP's ranging from [ * ] per cent, for example, and Columbia's from [ * ] per cent (see Appendix 5.1, Table 8). Measured over the period 1989 to 1993 as a whole, profitability of the individual companies varied broadly with size, UIP averaging [*] per cent, Warner Distributors [*] per cent, Columbia [*] per cent, Fox [*] per cent and Guild [*] per cent. Various factors influence these results, in particular the number of blockbusters released.

---

*Figures omitted. See note on page iv.

## Exhibition

### *Factual position*

2.76. UK cinema operators fall into four groups:

*(a)* the two main circuit exhibitors, MGM Cinemas and Odeon. Both have a national chain of cinemas, MGM Cinemas having a total of 119 sites at July 1994 and Odeon 73;

*(b)* three US-owned companies—UCI, Natl Amusements and Warner Theatres—which have entered the market in the last ten years by building multiplex cinemas. By July 1994 UCI had 26 sites, Natl Amusements had 10 sites and Warner Theatres 9;[1]

*(c)* several small chains of cinemas, most of which are confined to one part of the country; and

*(d)* a large number of exhibitors which operate one or two cinemas.

We refer to those in groups *(a)* and *(b)* as the leading exhibitors and to the rest as the independent exhibitors.

2.77. In 1993 UK box office receipts totalled some £289 million (see Table 4.7). MGM Cinemas was the market leader with 26 per cent of this total and UCI was second with 21 per cent, followed closely by Odeon with 20 per cent. Natl Amusements and Warner Theatres had 8 per cent and 5 per cent respectively. No other exhibitor had more than 1 per cent.

2.78. The most striking development in the exhibition market since the last MMC report in 1983 has been the growth in multiplexes, purpose-built cinemas with at least five and usually eight or more screens. By July 1994 there were 71 multiplexes, less than 10 per cent of the total number of cinemas (around 750) but with one-third of the number of screens and generating about 40 per cent of total admissions.

2.79. The leading exhibitors seek to plan their future programmes well in advance so far as the booking of new releases is concerned. Because there is uncertainty as to how popular films will prove to be, however, the exhibitors have to preserve a considerable degree of flexibility to respond to audience demand. They prefer to commit themselves to show a particular film for no more than one or two weeks, although they sometimes yield to distributors' requests to make firm bookings for three, four or even five weeks for films expected to be particularly popular (blockbusters). If a film does well, the exhibitor will keep it for longer than the contracted period; but if a film performs below expectations, distributors frequently agree to shorten the run. Exhibitors usually change their programmes on Fridays, and those with multi-screen cinemas do not make final decisions about the films to be shown until the preceding Monday, when negotiations take place with the distributors, in the light of the weekend's takings, about which films will be kept on and which taken off to make way for new releases.

---

[1]Warner Theatres can reasonably be regarded as a new entrant although it has for many years operated what is now the Warner West End cinema in Leicester Square. Similarly UCI operates two long-standing West End cinemas owned by an associated company, Cinema International Corporation UK (CIC), as well as its chain of modern multiplexes. These older cinemas are included in the figures quoted above.

2.80. Most of the leading exhibitors' admission prices vary considerably from one cinema to another. They do not vary according to the film being shown, however: the exhibitors told us that to charge higher prices for selected films would alienate customers and imply that other films were not worth seeing. Prices are noticeably lower in places where two of the leading exhibitors have cinemas close to each other (except for the West End of London where prices are generally much higher than elsewhere). Although prices vary widely from place to place, however, the average adult evening admission charges in 1993 for the five leading exhibitors were in a relatively narrow range, from £3.41 for Warner Theatres to £3.82 for Odeon. Most exhibitors make considerable use of concessionary prices for particular categories of people (such as children, pensioners and students) and for the less popular days of the week or times of day. In 1993 these had the effect of reducing the average realized seat price by about a quarter (35 per cent for Warner Theatres) below the average full adult prices quoted above (see Table 4.11). Our survey of independent exhibitors (see paragraph 2.106 and Appendix 4.4) showed that in early 1994 most of them charged a full adult price of less than £3.50.

2.81. The CEA is the only trade association representing exhibitors in the UK. It told us that its membership accounted for approximately 90 per cent of cinema operators in the UK, including all the leading exhibitors. The CEA's evidence to us is summarized in Chapter 6.

## *Analysis of market dynamics*

2.82. In 1980 the two main circuits held some 60 per cent of the exhibition market (measured by rentals paid), two minor circuits held 14 per cent and the rest 26 per cent. By 1993 the three specialist multiplex operators (see paragraph 2.76(*b*)) had captured 34 per cent of the market (measured by box office receipts), compared with 45 per cent for the two main circuits and 21 per cent for independent exhibitors. UCI in particular has become a strong third force, overtaking Odeon's share in the last two years. In addition while Natl Amusements and Warner Theatres have shares of only around 8 per cent and 5 per cent respectively, they are able to obtain most films on first release and thus present direct competition to the big three in places where they have cinemas in the same catchment area.

2.83. Exhibitors compete through:

— location;
— facilities offered;
— films exhibited; and
— pricing of tickets.

2.84. As regards competition for sites, the position is different for MGM Cinemas and Odeon on the one hand, which have long-standing sites and have decisions to make on which to retain as well as whether to build new cinemas, and the three recent multiplex entrants on the other. Odeon has chosen to compete mainly by upgrading and multi-screening its existing sites while MGM has built enough new multiplexes to make it the second-largest multiplex operator behind UCI. There is keen competition for sites in areas of high population density.

2.85. The facilities offered—standard of projection and sound equipment, seating, spaciousness and layout, car parking and above all a wide choice of films—are the principal means by which multiplex cinemas have been able to compete successfully against traditional cinemas and have attracted new audiences. Their growth has obliged other exhibitors to invest in upgrading their sites or, in many cases, face the alternative of closing down. Some independent exhibitors who have invested in new or existing sites appear to be doing well but many continue as low-priced outlets offering second-run films while others have withdrawn.

2.86. Exhibitors compete for films by investing in their cinemas, so that they can give the distributor the prospect of attracting good audiences, and by the terms they offer. The most important aspect of the terms, namely the basis of calculating rentals, is normally settled on an annual basis so that negotiation about individual films takes place only where special terms are involved. The period of exhibition, the question of sharing screens and the choice of screens are factors more likely to be at issue when bookings are discussed with distributors.

2.87. We have seen (paragraph 2.80) that exhibitors' admission prices vary from place to place and that concessionary prices for children, students and pensioners are an important feature. These facts suggest that exhibitors have to have regard to customers' ability and willingness to pay the prices charged. While the average realized prices of three of the leading exhibitors (MGM Cinemas, UCI and Natl Amusements) rose in real terms between 1988 and 1993, they remained below Odeon's average price which rose in line with inflation. International comparisons suggest that UK prices are a little below the EC average (see paragraph 4.121). The absolute level of admission prices (see paragraph 2.80) does not seem to us to be excessive. Exhibitors augment their income by selling refreshments at relatively high margins.

2.88. As to profitability, Odeon is the only one of the leading exhibitors to have achieved a historic cost return on capital employed (ROCE) of more than [*] per cent in any of the last five years (see Appendix 5.2, Table 9). An important influence on ROCE has been the heavy capital investments which all the leading exhibitors have incurred in building and upgrading cinemas. Odeon has been by far the most profitable exhibitor on this measure thanks to its many old cinemas whose costs have largely been written off. Its ROCE fell from nearly [*] per cent in 1989 to [*] per cent in 1993, however, as a result of its investment programme to upgrade existing, and in a few cases build new, cinemas which caused its capital employed figure to rise sharply.

## Determination of rental payments

2.89. On average over the period 1989 to 1993, and in 1993 itself, the leading exhibitors paid to the distributors about 36 per cent of their box office receipts as rental for the films licensed (see Appendix 5.2, Table 9). There are three main methods of calculating rentals:

(a) the nut method, whereby a monetary figure (the nut) is agreed for each screen. In principle the nut is meant to reflect the screen's weekly operating costs plus an element for profit but in practice the agreed figure is the result of a negotiation between the exhibitor and the distributor. The rental is the higher of 25 per cent of the total box office takings and 90 per cent of takings above the nut;

(b) the sliding scale method, under which the percentage of weekly box office takings paid as rental rises, usually from a minimum of 25 per cent to a maximum of 50 per cent in steps of five percentage points, as the takings rise above pre-set break figures; and

(c) the datum scale method, whereby the rental is 25 per cent of the takings up to a break figure and 75 per cent thereafter subject to an overall maximum of 50 per cent.

Other methods, such as a flat percentage, are used by a small minority of exhibitors.

*Figures omitted. See note on page iv.

2.90. The exhibitor chooses which method of calculation to use but the nut and break figures are agreed with distributors. For the most part the exhibitor agrees figures with one of the leading distributors and, if satisfied with them, then seeks to persuade other distributors to work to the same figures. We did find cases where exhibitors used different figures for different distributors, however (see paragraphs 2.205 to 2.207). MGM Cinemas, the three specialist multiplex operators and some independent exhibitors use the nut method, Odeon and other independents use the sliding scale method and yet other independents use the datum scale method.

2.91. Most distributors told us that they sometimes sought special terms for blockbusters, particularly from exhibitors using the sliding and datum scale methods. These terms usually entailed increasing the maximum rate of payment above 50 per cent if takings exceeded the normal 50 per cent break figure by more than a specified level. Less frequently distributors sought to negotiate a minimum rental above the normal 25 per cent from exhibitors using the nut method. (Since the nut method yields 90 per cent of incremental receipts above a certain level to the distributor, with no overall maximum rate, there is less cause for distributors to want to depart from the normal terms in dealing with exhibitors using that method.) Nut and break figures are reassessed at intervals, typically once a year, at the exhibitor's instigation but there is no presumption that the distributor will agree to an increase.

## Risk and risk management

2.92. Throughout our inquiry the high-risk nature of film-making has been emphasized to us. Every film is different. When a new film is being planned the following of well-tried formulae and the involvement of a well-known director and stars can improve the prospects of success, but a high degree of uncertainty remains. Films with big budgets tend to attract bigger audiences than those with small budgets but the potential losses are correspondingly greater. Even for the Hollywood studios, with all their experience, financial backing and distribution networks, most films lose money. The studios do, however, make a relatively large number of films and are therefore able to spread their risk and rely on the high profits made on a small number of films to offset the losses on the majority and generate a positive return overall.

2.93. Similarly at the level of distribution to cinemas, a substantial budget for prints and advertising is a necessary but not a sufficient condition for a film to become a box office hit. Information which the distributors gave us about individual films showed that many did not recover their distribution costs from the theatrical release, while a small proportion yielded very high returns. The rental figure of 36 per cent referred to in paragraph 2.89 is the average of a wide range, with many films yielding the normal minimum of 25 per cent but a few popular films generating rentals of 45 to 50 per cent (see paragraphs 5.8 to 5.10).

2.94. We noted in paragraph 2.67, however, that a large and growing proportion of the revenues from the exploitation of films comes from the rental and sale of video cassettes and from various forms of television broadcasting. But while cinema now represents a minority of the total market for films it remains highly important, because the success of a film in the cinema usually has a big influence on its success in the video markets and on the amounts which broadcasters are prepared to pay for the television rights. Some of the distributors said that expenditure on the theatrical release of a film was seen as an investment which generated returns from video and television as well as the cinema. They were therefore prepared to accept a degree of loss on theatrical distribution in the expectation that the overall return to their parent companies from all forms of distribution would be favourable. Others argued that the amounts at stake in theatrical distribution, which as we have seen may be £1 million or more for a potentially popular film, were too great for such an approach to be justified; they would not give a film a wide release if they did not think there was a chance of recouping the costs in the theatrical market. The leading distributors told us that the terms of their affiliated companies' agreements to supply films to BSkyB were not generally linked to the budgets for the films' UK theatrical release.

2.95. The exhibitor takes the risk of committing screens, usually for at least seven days, to show films which may or may not attract audiences and hence generate the revenue needed to cover the high fixed costs of owning and operating cinemas. The exhibitor will want to know about the film's success if it has previously been released in other countries (usually the USA) and about the distributor's marketing plans. Until a film opens in the UK market, however, there remains significant uncertainty as to how well it will perform here. Some exhibitors may prefer to wait until after a film's release before committing themselves to it, but they take the risk that the potential audience will have seen the film elsewhere and that the interest generated by the publicity surrounding its release will have subsided.

2.96. Many of the arrangements and practices in the industry were explained to us as being part of the industry's efforts to manage these undoubted risks. This was true in particular of the systems for determining rentals. These systems, which appear to exist in one form or another in most parts of the world, are all based on the sharing of box office takings according to certain agreed formulae rather than the fixing of a price in advance (see paragraph 2.89).

2.97. The relationship between distributors and exhibitors is therefore symbiotic, but also involves elements of conflict. At the overall level distributors and exhibitors have common interests. Distributors depend on exhibitors to show their films and benefit directly, via rentals, from the exhibitors' success in attracting audiences to their cinemas. Exhibitors depend on a supply of popular films to attract audiences and benefit from distributors' success in promoting them. At the level of the individual cinema, however, the interests of exhibitor and distributor do not always coincide. A profit-maximizing strategy for the release of a particular film will lead a distributor to limit the number of cinemas that receive a first-run print and individual exhibitors' preferences may not therefore be met. The potential for conflict also arises in the share-out of the box office receipts. Distributors told us that average percentage rentals paid by exhibitors in the UK were very low by international standards. Some of them argued that the shortage of screens in the UK put exhibitors in a strong position and enabled them to resist pressure for higher rentals. MGM Cinemas, on the other hand, argued that the fall in percentage rentals in recent years was due to the growth of multiplex cinemas. These were able to keep films on for longer periods as audiences declined, so that while percentage rentals fell, the absolute amounts grew. MGM Cinemas emphasized that the majors operated on a global scale and that the UK was but a small part of the world market. Their UK distribution subsidiaries could therefore afford to take a tough line on any issue which they perceived as threatening their wider interests. We noted, however, that the distributors did not always get their way: even when UIP, the biggest of them, was negotiating special terms for *Jurassic Park*, the most successful film ever released, it was not able to dictate terms to the leading exhibitors but had to compromise (see paragraph 7.6).

## Aggregated financial results

2.98. The results of our analysis of the accounts of the leading distributors and exhibitors are set out in Chapter 5. Over the period 1989 to 1993 the turnover (revenues) of the five leading distributors totalled some £353 million, nearly all of it in the form of rental payments from exhibitors. They spent £156 million, equivalent to 44 per cent of turnover, on advertising and publicity and £43 million (12 per cent of turnover) on prints. After indirect costs their operating profits before payment for distribution rights totalled £124 million, representing 35 per cent of turnover. We regard this figure (return on turnover, or ROT) as the best measure of the performance of the vertically integrated distributors (though it is not a measure of overall profit since it takes no account of production costs). After payment, mostly to their parent companies, for distribution rights, the distributors were left with a profit of only 1.3 per cent of turnover.

2.99. Exhibition, unlike distribution, is capital-intensive because of the magnitude of the investment in cinemas. ROCE is therefore the best measure of the exhibitors' profitability. We found that average ROCE for the five leading exhibitors together, on a restated historic cost basis, rose from only 8.5 per cent in 1989 to 15.3 per cent in 1993. According to their accounts, without the revenue from the sale of refreshments (known in the industry as concession income) the five exhibitors taken together would have achieved little more than a break-even result: see Table 5.9.

## Changes since the last MMC report

2.100. It is no exaggeration to say that the distribution and exhibition markets in the UK have been transformed compared with the parlous plight described in the previous MMC report in 1983. That inquiry found an exhibition industry in a state of long-term decline, with total admissions having fallen from 327 million in 1965 to 84 million in 1981. The number of cinemas had fallen by more than half over that period and the number of seats by more than two-thirds. The report noted that the industry had not attracted people into its cinemas in competition with other forms of entertainment, and that its ability to compete was further threatened by the rapid growth in sales of video recorders (1983 report, paragraph 8.6). The exhibition market had for many years been dominated by the two main circuits, then owned by EMI Cinemas Ltd and Rank Leisure Ltd, and there seemed little prospect of new entry presenting a challenge to their position.

2.101. Since then the three specialist multiplex operators have entered the exhibition market (see paragraph 2.76*(b)*). The first purpose-built multiplex was opened in 1985 by American Multiplex Cinemas Inc (AMC)—whose burgeoning chain of cinemas was subsequently acquired by UCI in 1988—and by July 1994 the three entrants had 42 multiplexes between them. Some incumbent exhibitors have responded by investing both in the construction of new multiplexes and in upgrading, and putting more screens in, some of their existing cinemas. The 71 multiplexes built in the UK as a whole by July 1994 have a total of 638 screens. This accounts, broadly, for the whole of the growth in the total number of screens in the UK since 1985. The CEA told us that over £600 million had been invested by exhibitors since 1984/85. We were told of a further 13 multiplexes that were under construction or planned.

2.102. We can now see that total admissions bottomed out at 54 million in 1984, the year after the previous MMC report was published, and have since grown every year, more than doubling to reach about 114 million by 1993. The investment in cinemas has clearly been a major contributor to this recovery, although increases in the number of attractive films and in distributors' expenditure in promoting them have also contributed. These elements are interrelated.

2.103. Another significant change since the last report has been a substantial increase in the number of cinemas showing popular films on first release. The reasons for this lie in developments in both exhibition and distribution. As regards the former, there has been the major growth of multiplexes referred to in paragraph 2.101. These have come to occupy a strong market position, justifying a place in the first run. On the distributor side, greater use has been made of television advertising, usually bought nationally, which together with other forms of advertising and promotion require a wide release of prints if distributors are to capitalize fully on the impact. Distributors now need, moreover, to tap the theatrical market more quickly as films have also to be released into the video channel and this may occur as early as six months after theatrical release. They therefore supply more cinemas on first run—not only multiplexes—and there has been a sharp decline in the extent to which the two main circuit exhibitors enjoy exclusivity over others. This is also partly due to the 1989 Order which implemented a recommendation of the previous MMC report that the practice of barring should be prohibited (see paragraphs 2.3 and 2.133). To cater for a wider first run, distributors have had to increase the number of prints, but the increased cost has been justified by the growth in box office receipts and hence rentals.

2.104. At the time of the previous MMC report the films of the seven large Hollywood studios (see paragraph 2.50) were distributed by three joint-venture companies in the UK. Of these only UIP, which distributes the films of MGM Inc, Paramount and MCA/Universal, remains: each of the other four studios now has its own separate distribution subsidiary in the UK.

# Public interest issues

2.105. We turn now to the remaining questions in our terms of reference (see paragraph 2.41). We summarize the main areas of concern and complaint which have been put to us, including the cultural argument for intervention in the market. We then consider in turn the various practices underlying our complex monopoly finding and the issues which we raised with the members of the complex monopoly group (see paragraph 2.12).

## Complaints and concerns

2.106. The complaints and concerns which were put to us fell into two broad categories. First, a number of independent exhibitors have complained about various aspects of distributors' behaviour, notably difficulties in obtaining films on first release, minimum playing times and restrictions on screen use. These complaints are set out in Chapter 6. We carried out a survey of independent exhibitors in general, partly in order to test the extent of dissatisfaction on these matters. The results are given in Appendix 4.4. The CEA also reported to us the results of a major consultation exercise which it carried out among its members: see paragraph 6.2. Since these complaints concern some of the practices which underlie our finding of a complex monopoly situation, we deal with them in the following sections of this chapter.

2.107. Secondly, we received representations that British producers experienced difficulties in securing an adequate showing for their films. This was said to be due to a bias in favour of the distribution and exhibition of US films in the UK. US films were preferred by exhibitors because they had already been market tested, enjoyed substantial advertising support and consequently represented a much reduced risk compared with British (or indeed other non-US) films. The problem was exacerbated by the shortage of screens in the UK and by restraints exercised by the leading distributors over exhibitors. A high level of concentration in both distribution and exhibition, and the close vertical links between the two sectors, discouraged new entrants, reduced competition and enabled the Hollywood studios to control the market to the detriment of other producers. Difficulties in securing adequate distribution in turn militated against new investment in UK independent film production. PACT was the principal spokesman of these views (see paragraphs 6.52 to 6.70) but was supported by the BFI (paragraphs 6.92 to 6.108) and Mr Michael Henry (paragraphs 6.118 to 6.145).

2.108. The BFI emphasized that there was a cultural element to these concerns. Despite the growth in cinema audiences and in the video and television markets, the public had not enjoyed a greater variety of films. The exhibition of British films was being marginalized. They tended to be shown at smaller, independent cinemas and the BFI-supported regional film theatres, while the new multiplex cinemas showed almost exclusively US films. The decline in British film production was not due to a deficiency of UK talent, as was witnessed by the success of British films, directors, actors and others in winning US Academy Awards. The BFI argued that film was the most significant medium for expressing the cultural identity of a nation. It was unacceptable for this cultural form to be dominated by overseas interests to such an extent that less than 10 per cent of the audience share went to indigenous films, barriers to entry for independent producers were practically insurmountable, new talent therefore had to go abroad to work and audiences could not express their preferences because their choice was restricted.

2.109. We recognize that films have a cultural as well as an economic dimension. This is a complicated field, however. The cultural origin of a film may be different from the place of production, and different again from the national origin of the production or distribution company. For example, some films celebrating UK themes and values are made by Hollywood studios and/or distributed by the major US-owned distributors (recent instances include *The Remains of the Day*, *Shadowlands* and two versions of the *Robin Hood* story); while some films celebrating US themes and values are made by British production companies (eg *Posse* which was produced by Working Title, a subsidiary of PolyGram, which also produced *Four Weddings and a Funeral*).

2.110. For the purposes of this inquiry we have not attempted to make cultural judgments. We have, however, considered whether practices in the UK distribution and exhibition markets cause difficulties for British film-makers and we return to this theme below (see paragraphs 2.218 to 2.226).

## Issues arising from scale monopoly situation

2.111. As shown in paragraph 2.10, the market share of MGM Cinemas only narrowly exceeds the 25 per cent level which is the definition of a scale monopoly situation under the Act. There are other strong players in the exhibition market whose market shares are not far below that of MGM Cinemas, which does not come close to enjoying a position of dominance. It conducts its business in ways which have much in common with its competitors and engages in some of the practices which underlie our finding of a complex monopoly situation. We consider that its status as a scale monopolist does not raise any issues which are different from those which we examine in the context of the complex monopoly situation. We therefore conclude that, in relation to the scale monopoly situation, there are no steps, actions or omissions, such as are referred to in paragraphs *(c)* and *(d)* of our terms of reference, nor any facts which operate or may be expected to operate against the public interest.

## Issues arising from complex monopoly situation

2.112. We now consider the issues which arise from our finding of a complex monopoly situation. We begin with the effects on the public interest of the eight practices which we have found to restrict competition (see paragraphs 2.13 and 2.35) and we then deal with four other matters. We raised all these matters with the members of the complex monopoly group in our issues letter to them dated 14 February 1994.

### *Alignment by distributors and exhibitors*

2.113. For the purpose of the complex monopoly situation, the practices of alignment by distributors and by exhibitors were described in paragraph 2.13*(a)* and *(b)* and discussed in paragraph 2.24. In considering these in the context of the public interest, it appears to us more convenient to treat them as one practice which, consistently with our expression of it in paragraphs 2.13 and 2.24, we would describe (as in paragraph 4.159) as an arrangement whereby, in the first instance, a distributor normally offers its films to, and discusses the timing and release strategy for those films with, its aligned circuit, ie either MGM Cinemas or Odeon; so that in locations where MGM Cinemas and Odeon operate directly competing cinemas (other than multiplexes), aligned distributors normally supply prints of their films to the cinemas of their aligned circuit but not to those of the other circuit. UIP and Warner Distributors are aligned with MGM Cinemas; and the other leading distributors, together with some independent distributors, are aligned with Odeon. We invited the members of the complex monopoly group to comment on whether alignment made the market less responsive to consumer preferences.

2.114. The leading distributors submitted that the effect of alignment was much reduced since the time of the MMC's 1983 report (which reached the conclusion that alignment operated against the public interest: see paragraph 2.2). As a result of cinema closures over the years they said that there were now only around 20 locations where MGM Cinemas and Odeon both operated cinemas other than multiplexes and where alignment determined to which of them a particular distributor's films were supplied. (We refer to these as 'the aligned locations'.) Elsewhere a distributor would supply cinemas of both circuits according to their individual merits and whether they fitted the release strategy for individual films. Distributors also reached decisions to supply multiplexes and independent cinemas without any regard to alignment. The growth of multiplexes, in particular, had greatly diluted the importance of alignment in influencing release patterns.

2.115. Most of the leading distributors also argued that alignment was a sensible way of conducting business, reducing the uncertainty and costs which would be entailed in having to negotiate each release with the two main circuit exhibitors from scratch. Alignment was thus one of the industry's techniques for reducing risk. The benefits were enjoyed by independent distributors as well as the leading distributors.

2.116. Entertainment said that the close relationships between leading distributors and the two circuits, particularly MGM Cinemas, put other parties at a disadvantage. Alignment enabled the leading distributors to reserve screens many months in advance, even if the film they eventually released was different from the title for which space had been reserved. Independent distributors were unable to do this and found difficulty in booking screens because of this pre-emption by the leading distributors.

2.117. One independent distributor claimed that the circuits gave preferential rental terms to those among the leading distributors which were aligned to them.

2.118. MGM Cinemas and Odeon submitted that the impact of alignment was much reduced. MGM Cinemas agreed that it had, to a degree, a preferential relationship with UIP and Warner Distributors which extended to its whole circuit. Odeon denied that this was true of its relationship with its aligned distributors. Both accepted that alignment gave them a say in the setting of release dates but denied that this gave them an unfair advantage over other exhibitors. On Entertainment's complaint about booking practices, MGM Cinemas said that it reserved dates on the same basis for independent releases as for those of the majors: the difference was that few independent releases had the clear commercial potential that would lead it to reserve dates without seeing the film. Odeon said that it had early discussions with many distributors about forthcoming films. Although it sometimes 'penciled in' dates for exhibition as a result of such discussions, these were all subject to its being able to view the film. Its practice in this respect was identical for independent distributors and for those owned by the Hollywood studios. Both MGM Cinemas and Odeon denied that they reserved dates for distributors, as opposed to specific films.

2.119. Alignment is a form of market sharing, restricting competition between the two circuits and among aligned distributors. It exists because the two circuits still have substantial numbers of cinemas which have few screens and are therefore unable to accommodate all the films which are given a wide release. Distributors align themselves with one circuit or the other in order to reduce the risk that their films will not receive an adequate release. They have early discussions with their aligned circuit with a view to arranging the basic framework of a release pattern. (Subsequently they often talk to the other circuit, the three specialist multiplex operators, and sometimes the larger independent exhibitors with a view to completing the release plan.) Part of the arrangement is that in the aligned locations the film will be supplied to the cinema of the aligned circuit and normally not to the cinema of the other circuit.

2.120. From the evidence given to us by various parties who practise alignment we believe that there are currently 20 aligned locations, namely:

Aberdeen;
Blackpool;
Bournemouth;
Brighton;
Bristol;
Cardiff;
Edinburgh;
Glasgow;
Leeds;
Leicester;
Liverpool;
London:
  Fulham Road (MGM Cinemas)—High Street, Kensington (Odeon);
  Hampstead (MGM Cinemas)—Swiss Cottage (Odeon);
  Streatham (both);
Norwich;
Nottingham;
Plymouth;
Portsmouth;
Reading; and
Southend.

The list is subject to change as cinemas close or (conceivably) open. Multiplex cinemas are not affected, however, even if built in an aligned location by one of the two circuits, because of the convention now established in the industry that multiplexes are supplied with prints of all films given a wide release. The number of locations affected has fallen over the years as a result of closures by one or the other circuit, although RFD told us that the number of Odeon cinemas currently affected had not changed since 1990.

2.121. The restriction on competition that is inherent in the practice of alignment has the following adverse consequences:

*(a)* it reduces competition for screens among aligned distributors, making it probable that some films achieve a wider showing than they would on merit and others a narrower;

*(b)* it reduces the pressure on MGM Cinemas and Odeon to ensure that their cinemas can compete for prints of first-release films on merit; and

*(c)* to the extent that some films would otherwise be shown in both an MGM Cinemas and an Odeon cinema in a given location, it reduces consumers' choice of cinema in which to see a given film.

We take each of these points in turn.

2.122. Concerning *(a)*, distributors argued that alignment did not enable them to book screens for non-commercial films. But the purpose of alignment for distributors is to reduce the risk of not securing an adequate release for their films. The relationship means that at the margin the exhibitor is more likely to take a film of uncertain appeal, or to book it into more screens, than it otherwise would. In 1992 the cinemas in the 20 aligned locations, where alignment bites directly, accounted for 32 per cent of total box office takings in the case of Odeon and 17 per cent in the case of MGM Cinemas. The combined total represented 11 per cent of total box office receipts in the UK market in that year. Moreover, this effect is not confined to the aligned locations: aligned distributors generally take a bigger share of the box office in the two circuits' smaller cinemas outside the aligned locations than their (the respective distributors') success in the market as a whole would indicate (see paragraphs 4.166 and 4.167).

2.123. As regards *(b)*, the two circuit exhibitors argued that they had to be competitive in order to retain the business of their aligned distributors. We note, however, that it is many years since there was any change in aligned relationships. Although Odeon claimed that it was particularly keen to be competitive with MGM Cinemas in the aligned locations, we received no evidence that distributors put any pressure on the two circuits to improve their cinemas in these locations. The comments of MGM Cinemas on our proposed remedy (see paragraphs 7.20 to 7.22) made clear that it regarded alignment as providing a degree of protection for some of its cinemas in the aligned locations.

2.124. The two circuit exhibitors further argued that they faced competition from other cinemas, particularly multiplexes, in several of the aligned locations. There are in fact other cinemas than the aligned MGM Cinemas and Odeon sites in 10 of the 17 aligned locations outside London (disregarding arthouse and part-time cinemas) and we were told of plans to build new multiplexes in five of the 17 locations. The leading distributors told us that they took decisions on which other cinemas to supply without regard to alignment or to Odeon's policy on exclusivity (see paragraph 2.138). They can therefore be expected to supply these other cinemas as well as the MGM Cinemas or Odeon sites if they consider that to do so would increase their net rentals. Nevertheless these other cinemas are unlikely in most cases to present such direct competition to the aligned cinemas of the two circuits as the circuits do to each other.

2.125. As regards *(c)*, we accept that it is more important for cinema-goers to have a choice of film in a given area than a choice of cinemas in which to see a given film. It is in any case unsafe to assume that, absent alignment, the distributors would supply prints to both the MGM Cinemas and Odeon cinemas in the areas affected. Commercial considerations would restrict the number of films for which that was done. Other and more detrimental effects for the consumer are indicated in paragraph 2.129.

2.126. As regards Entertainment's claim that aligned distributors were able to reserve screens well in advance of release dates (paragraph 2.116), we were satisfied by the explanations which the two circuits gave about their booking practices, accounts which accorded with what we were told by the leading distributors.

2.127. In investigating the claim that aligned distributors enjoyed favourable rental terms (paragraph 2.117) we found that there had been differentials in some of MGM Cinemas' sites and that the pattern was broadly as had been claimed. But the differentials were generally modest and MGM Cinemas told us that they had disappeared when its nut figures were revised in 1994. The differentials which previously existed are likely to have resulted from the relative bargaining strength of particular distributors rather than from alignment (see paragraph 2.207). Odeon told us that it used the same break figures and percentage steps for all distributors except that it used somewhat higher break figures for films which it considered of above average commercial risk. In practice these films did not attract big audiences and the rental was always at the minimum 25 per cent rate, so the higher break figures made no difference. Odeon also agreed to higher maximum rentals on films expected to be particularly popular. In practice these were nearly always films which were released by the leading distributors. Odeon stressed, however, that the decision to depart from normal terms for these two categories of film was always based on its judgment of the film itself, regardless of the identity of the distributor.

2.128. It is difficult to disentangle the effects of alignment from other factors, such as Odeon's negotiation of exclusivity (see paragraphs 2.138 to 2.139) and the power which the two circuits enjoy simply by virtue of their size. Nevertheless we are satisfied that we have done so and we believe that alignment by distributors and exhibitors restricts competition, for the reasons given in paragraph 2.121*(a)* and *(b)*. We also believe that the disadvantages of alignment outweigh the benefits which the parties claimed for it (paragraph 2.115). We conclude that alignment is a step, by way of uncompetitive practice (the uncompetitive practices concerned having been identified in paragraph 2.121*(a)* and *(b)*) taken, for the purpose of exploiting or maintaining the monopoly situation, by MGM Cinemas, Odeon and the distributors shown in the schedule in Appendix 2.1 as engaging in this practice.

2.129. We further conclude that alignment represents a fact which operates, and may be expected to operate, against the public interest. In paragraph 2.121*(a)* and *(b)* we have noted two adverse consequences of the practice, in making it probable that some films achieve a wider or narrower showing than their merits justify and in reducing competition for prints of first-release films. We therefore conclude that the particular effect, adverse to the public interest, which alignment has is that it makes the market for the supply of films for exhibition in cinemas in the UK less responsive to consumer preference.

## *Exclusivity*

2.130. We define exclusivity to mean the practice of distributors supplying, and exhibitors accepting, individual films on the basis that a particular cinema will have the exclusive right to show a film within a specified area for a specified period. It results from an agreement between distributor and exhibitor and is normally, though not always, referred to in the licensing contract. The practice is therefore to be distinguished from cases where the distributor of its own volition confers *de facto* exclusivity on a cinema simply by deciding not to supply prints concurrently to competing cinemas.

2.131. At the time of the 1983 report (and for many years before that) exclusivity took the form of barring. This was the system whereby many cinemas were barred as a matter of course from receiving prints of newly-released films until a certain number of weeks after they had first been shown by cinemas of the two leading circuits. The 1983 report found that this practice operated against the public interest because it failed to allow sufficient competition during the full period in which films were released (1983 report, paragraph 8.31), and it was eventually outlawed by the 1989 Order which in essence prohibited exclusivity agreements covering more than one film (see paragraph 2.3). Since the Order came into force, therefore, exclusivity has had to be negotiated on a film-by-film basis.

2.132. An even more important development in relation to exclusivity has been the success of multiplexes in obtaining prints on first release regardless of whether they are near to, and compete with, cinemas of the two leading circuits. Warner Distributors said that this success stemmed from an episode in 1987 when for the first time a multiplex had been opened within the catchment area of cinemas belonging to the two main circuits. Warner Distributors wanted to supply a print to the new multiplex on first release but told us that Cannon (the predecessor of MGM Cinemas) threatened to cancel all its bookings for the film if Warner Distributors did not observe the normal bars. When despite this Warner Distributors decided to stick to its intentions, not only Cannon but also Odeon cancelled all their bookings for the film. The film therefore opened at a much reduced number of sites. It nevertheless proved an immediate success and the two circuits soon requested prints.

2.133. Mr Sumner Redstone, who with members of his family is the owner of Natl Amusements, also told us of difficulties which had been experienced in obtaining films in the early stages when there were very few multiplexes. The two circuit exhibitors had said to the distributors that if they gave prints to new multiplexes they (the circuits) would not play the films in other parts of the country where there were no multiplexes. Natl Amusements had made strong representations to the distributors about these problems, stressing that it was in their interests to encourage the development of multiplexes in order to reinvigorate the market and hence generate greater revenues. UCI told us that it experienced some difficulties in obtaining prints in the late 1980s but that those had now been overcome, partly thanks to the 1989 Order. Odeon said that it continued to seek exclusivity over multiplexes on a film-by-film basis (as permitted by the Order) but rarely succeeded. We understand the current position is that all multiplexes receive prints of all films given a wide release as a matter of routine.

2.134. Although exclusivity is, as a result of those developments, much less significant than it used to be, we nevertheless considered whether it unduly restricted consumers' choice of cinemas in which to see particular films on first release; whether it harmed independent exhibitors; and whether it deterred new entry and investment in exhibition.

2.135. Distributors other than RFD told us that, outside the West End of London, only Odeon of the leading exhibitors requested exclusivity. UIP and Warner Distributors said that they never acceded to Odeon's requests. The other leading distributors said that they met Odeon's requests if to do so fitted in with their own commercial objectives, ie if they would in any case not have supplied prints to the cinemas against which Odeon sought exclusivity. No distributor said that it was coerced by Odeon into granting exclusivity to the detriment of its own commercial interests.

2.136. Distributors argued that the substantial new entry in exhibition since 1983, particularly via the construction of multiplex cinemas, as well as new investment in existing cinemas, demonstrated that exclusivity had not deterred entry and investment. Nor was it likely to result in undue restrictions on consumer choice.

2.137. The four major exhibitors other than Odeon said that they did not seek contractual exclusivity. The three specialist multiplex operators nevertheless all submitted that the practice should not be prohibited: the market should decide. MGM Cinemas said that it considered the negotiation of exclusivity arrangements to be against the spirit of the 1989 Order on barring and would prefer the practice outlawed. It explained that it considered the negotiation of exclusivity by an exhibitor to be anti-competitive, a means by which a large exhibitor could misuse its power to damage smaller competitors. It wanted decisions on which cinemas received prints to be in the hands of distributors. MGM Cinemas suffered from Odeon's demands for exclusivity only in London, however.

2.138. Odeon said that all distributors granted contractual exclusivity in some circumstances; it was not aware of any differences between them in their attitudes to exclusivity. For its own part, Odeon said that it sought exclusivity for many of the films it exhibited and usually succeeded in negotiating some exclusivity against neighbouring cinemas, although rarely against multiplexes. It listed 30, out of its (then) total of 72 cinemas, where it sought exclusivity and named the competing cinemas against which it did so. Twenty of these Odeon cinemas are in locations subject to alignment, and in most of these locations there are other competing cinemas as well as one of MGM Cinemas'. In these locations, therefore, Odeon uses exclusivity, as well as alignment, to protect its cinemas against local competition on many of the films which it shows. Nevertheless only one of the independent exhibitors listed by Odeon in the 30 locations complained to us about difficulties in obtaining prints, and these difficulties did not appear to result from Odeon's policy.

2.139. Since the distributors say that they only grant contractual exclusivity to Odeon where it suits their own interests, the question arises whether the practice makes any difference to what would happen anyway. Odeon agreed that its negotiation of exclusivity was to some extent a matter of 'belt and braces' but said that the practice also provided greater certainty particularly in border-line cases where the distributor, left to itself, might choose to book a film into a competing cinema concurrently.

2.140. We accept that it may be necessary for an exhibitor to have the assurance of exclusive supply if it is to take the risk of devoting a screen to the showing of a film of limited appeal. This may be particularly true of the arthouse part of the exhibition market, for which the potential audiences outside London appear to be relatively small. But we also attach importance to the danger which MGM Cinemas emphasized, namely that a big exhibitor may use the power of its circuit to pressurize distributors into refusing supply to smaller competitors, as Cannon and Odeon attempted to do in 1987.

2.141. We have considered whether exclusivity represents an action attributable to the monopoly situation but have concluded that, in the present circumstances, this is not the case. Moreover in taking account of the evidence outlined above, it appears to us that the practical impact of exclusivity is currently small and we conclude that it does not represent a fact which operates or may be expected to operate against the public interest.

## *Refusal to supply*

2.142. We are concerned under this heading with distributors' refusal to supply individual films to exhibitors who request them, either at all or at the time requested, for reasons other than the exhibitor's creditworthiness and the need to cover the costs of supply. These consist primarily of the cost of making an additional print (if none is already available). We were told that most prints cost around £700 to £1,000 to make, the main variable being the length of the film.

2.143. Distributors said that selection of exhibitors to receive prints was done with the aim of maximizing profits. Decisions about which cinemas to supply had to take account of the dilution effect, whereby splitting a given size of audience between two cinemas would reduce rental receipts. More generally it was essential for distributors to retain control of supply decisions so that release strategies could be planned and carried out in the way best calculated to maximize the return on each individual film. Cinemas not supplied on first release were usually supplied on second run if they so wished: cases of an absolute refusal to supply were rare and were made solely on commercial grounds (eg a poor payment record).

2.144. The major exhibitors supported the distributors' right to determine the optimal number of prints for each release and their allocations to cinemas. This fostered competition among exhibitors to attract audiences by the quality of their cinemas and hence persuade distributors to supply first-run prints. The CEA told us that the availability of first-run prints had improved since the last MMC inquiry. This was, it said, acknowledged by all exhibitors although some felt that their own access to first-run product had decreased as a result of the opening of new competing screens.

2.145. Complaints about non-availability of prints were one of the principal reasons for this inquiry being mounted. Chapter 6 summarizes the representations we received from 15 exhibitors (14 small independents and one small circuit operator). Most of these complaints were about the late supply of prints, not absolute refusals to supply, some blaming the distributors' preference for allocating films to multiplexes.

2.146. In our survey of independent exhibitors (Appendix 4.4), between 42 and 55 per cent of respondents said that each of the major distributors provided prints of popular films only after they had been on release for more than a certain number of weeks. Between 40 and 52 per cent said that this was also true of each of the four independent distributors listed.

2.147. The distributors told us that they did not keep records of cases where they refused exhibitors' requests for prints. We therefore asked them to keep such a record for the period from November 1993 to February 1994. The results, which are summarized in Appendix 4.12, showed that refusals to supply were few in relation to the number of bookings made in the period. Some of the films with the highest incidence of refusals were those which the distributor had decided to release gradually, in order to build up interest via favourable reviews and 'word of mouth' reactions. In most other cases the distributors explained that they had refused supply because of a judgment that they would maximize profits by supplying just one exhibitor in the area and not splitting the audience.

2.148. Distributors argued that for them to be obliged to supply exhibitors on request would deprive them of the ability to exploit the distribution rights which they had acquired, as a result of their own or their parent companies' investments, according to their own commercial judgment. This would be contrary to the fundamental principles of the protection of intellectual property rights which were enshrined in UK and EC law and in international conventions.

2.149. The distributors' main reason for refusing to supply creditworthy exhibitors with prints on first release stems from the arrangements by which film rentals are determined (see paragraph 2.89). The use of break and nut figures ensures that distributors' share of the revenue from showing a film exceeds the normal minimum of 25 per cent only if the box office takings exceed certain thresholds. If a given audience is divided between two cinemas, the distributor's share of the total takings is therefore likely to be lower than if the audience is concentrated in one cinema. If, on the other hand, the rental were expressed as a flat 36 per cent (the present average level of rental in the UK market) the distributor's receipts would be the same in both cases, although the extra costs of supplying a second cinema would still have to be weighed in the balance. In practice the calculation which a profit-maximizing distributor has to make is whether the supply of a print to a second cinema would increase the combined rentals from the two cinemas, as a result of attracting incremental admissions, more than it would increase supply costs.

2.150. The general view of the exhibitors who gave evidence was that the existing methods of calculating rentals were necessary to reduce exhibitors' risks in the event that a film did not attract large audiences. The idea of switching to a flat percentage rental, a method which is used in a small minority of cases, did not commend itself to them. The CEA argued that the normal rental arrangements, which served exhibitors well, might be jeopardized if distributors were obliged to supply more prints than they judged optimal, since they would look to restore their position in other ways, such as imposing higher minimum rentals. We were told that arrangements requiring exhibitors to bid for films, including the offer of guaranteed minimum rental amounts, which were sometimes used in the USA had proved very damaging for smaller exhibitors when films failed to live up to expectations (see paragraph 7.44).

2.151. We conclude that refusal to supply represents an action, attributable to the monopoly situation, on the part of the distributors in whose favour it exists, which are able to impose the practice on exhibitors. We have noted, from the schedule in Appendix 2.1, that the practice is common to all such distributors.

2.152. As things stand, distributors are able to determine supply in a wholly discretionary way and according to criteria which may vary from film to film. A distributor might, for example, threaten to refuse supply of a popular film unless an exhibitor agreed to take another, less popular film which it would not otherwise choose; or might withhold supply from cinemas whose admission prices it considered too low in an attempt to force up prices and hence rentals. We received very little evidence that distributors behaved in this way.

2.153. As regards refusal to supply with a view to maximizing profits on individual films, we consider this to be unobjectionable provided there is effective competition in both the distribution and exhibition sectors. Given the riskiness of the film business and the established rental arrangements, which command general support, it is necessary for distributors to retain control over their release strategies if the full potential of each film is to be realized at lowest cost. As there are some 750 cinemas in the UK and the most popular films have, at most, 350 to 400 prints, it follows that even for the biggest films only about half of all cinemas receive prints on first release. The number of complainants may therefore be seen as relatively small. The situation is, indeed, a great deal healthier than it was at the time of the last inquiry. There has been a substantial increase in the average number of prints supplied of popular films, to the benefit not only of the new multiplexes but also independent exhibitors, more of whom receive prints on first release. Nor is there clear evidence that cinemas are refused prints on second run without good cause. It is in distributors' interests to supply prints to other exhibitors when first-run cinemas finish with them, since at that stage the marginal costs of supply are very low and even modest rental payments improve the distributors' financial position.

2.154. Our findings are generally reassuring as to the way in which the distributors have exercised their undoubted power *vis-à-vis* independent exhibitors, in the sense that we have not found evidence which would support a conclusion that distributors have exercised their right to refuse supply in an unreasonable manner. We conclude that the practice is a fact which does not, and may be expected not to, operate against the public interest. It is understandable, however, that small exhibitors should be concerned about supply, particularly if their cinemas face competition from multiplexes. Failure to obtain first-run prints can greatly reduce their income and hence their ability to invest in their cinemas in order to counter multiplex competition (although some of the leading distributors and exhibitors argued that it is because such exhibitors have not invested before that they do not now receive first-run prints). We believe it is desirable that there should be some independent machinery to consider exhibitors' complaints with a view to reassuring both existing exhibitors and potential entrants that future refusal to supply will not be unfairly discriminatory. We return to this subject in paragraph 2.245.

## *Minimum exhibition periods*

2.155. In our issues letter we referred to this practice as 'distributors requiring exhibitors to show a film at particular cinemas for a minimum period exceeding seven days'. We asked the parties to comment on the possibility that the practice harmed smaller distributors by restricting their access to screens; harmed exhibitors by reducing their revenue; and unduly restricted consumer choice.

2.156. The leading distributors argued that the question of minimum exhibition periods was one of the key elements in their negotiations with exhibitors concerning the supply of prints and could not be seen in isolation from the other elements, in particular the decision whether to supply a print on first run and the rental terms. It was necessary for distributors to have some assurance as to how long a film would be shown so that they could plan their distribution strategies and decide on release costs. Distributors spent heavily on publicity and advertising for films expected to be popular, and needed the freedom to negotiate minimum exhibition periods in order to have a reasonable opportunity to generate an adequate return. Most said that it was not their standard practice to look for minimum periods longer than seven days. For those films where they did so, they did not insist that an exhibitor should continue to show a film whose box office performance was below expectations. But they would hold the exhibitor to the contractual period in cases where the distributor considered that its film was doing reasonable business but the exhibitor wished to replace it with another which the exhibitor thought would do better.

2.157. Entertainment said that the leading distributors were able to obtain longer minimum periods than it could. Their ability to impose unreasonable periods on the exhibition circuits exacerbated the difficulties faced by other distributors in securing bookings and hence restricted consumer choice. But Rank said that independent distributors acquired exceptional films only occasionally and at a high price: it was particularly important that they should be able to exploit these films to the full in order to recoup their release costs. Rank said that it was the strength of the film which determined a distributor's ability to negotiate an extended period. RFD, Guild and First Independent did not feel that they were denied access to screens as a result of minimum periods negotiated by the major distributors.

2.158. The specialist multiplex exhibitors said that they regarded the negotiation of minimum periods as part of a normal commercial relationship. They found the distributors were flexible in exercising their contractual rights—though Natl Amusements implied that there was room for improvement—and they had enough screens to be able to show films from independent distributors which had commercial potential. UCI and Warner Theatres argued that distributors would be likely to insist on some *quid pro quo* in the form of tougher rental terms if their freedom to negotiate minimum periods were curtailed.

2.159. Odeon said that it normally booked films for seven days plus holdover and rarely had difficulties with those films for which distributors sought longer periods. But MGM Cinemas said that two weeks rather than one was the norm. It argued that a distributor made a commercial judgment regarding the amount of money to be spent on promoting a film and should be happy to let the market decide whether its judgment was correct. The policy of seeking extended playing times could be interpreted as an attempt by distributors to prevent the release of competing films. MGM Cinemas acknowledged, however, that most distributors allowed exhibitors to take a film off early when box office receipts fell significantly below expectations.

2.160. The CEA told us that it had found, as a result of its consultation exercise, that minimum periods were the major difficulty for the majority of operators. Their length had increased and was now rarely less than two weeks, often more. Long minimum runs created problems especially where cinemas had fewer than four screens. A growing trend among distributors was to demand long minimum runs when a film had been on release for some time. The CEA added that distributors did not distinguish between cinemas according to the number of screens: the periods they specified were reasonable in some circumstances but totally unreasonable in others. Hence the practice discriminated against cinemas with fewer screens. Problems arose when two attractive films competed for space. It was difficult to get distributors' agreement to terminate runs early. If a distributor had available a print of another current film, it might agree to the run for the first film being cut short as long as it was replaced by the other.

2.161. In reply to our survey of independent exhibitors (see Appendix 4.4), several respondents said that a minimum run of three to four weeks did not make commercial sense, particularly for one-screen cinemas in small towns or country areas. About 47 per cent of respondents said that the distributor always or usually refused permission for a film to be taken off early, while 36 per cent said that such permission was given.

2.162. Information we received from the leading distributors showed that for the most part they did not seek to license films to exhibitors for periods of more than two weeks. In the period from January 1993 to March 1994, for example, Columbia released 17 films; it set a playing time of one week for eight of these, two weeks for seven, three weeks for one and four weeks for one. In the period November 1993 to February 1994 UIP sought a minimum period of two weeks for six out of eight main films and four weeks for the other two. The flexibility with which distributors implemented this aspect of their release strategies varied: some were prepared to agree to shorter periods for cinemas with few screens, others were not, at least in relation to their most popular films. Warner Distributors said that its normal practice was to negotiate extended minimum periods *only* from cinemas with fewer than four screens, on the grounds that it was only in such cinemas that there was a real risk of its films being taken off prematurely.

2.163. The evidence shows that this is an area of difficulty, with very different perceptions on the part of most of the leading distributors and exhibitors on the one hand and MGM Cinemas, Entertainment and many independent exhibitors on the other. The problem arises not with multiplex cinemas, which generally have enough screens to accommodate all commercial films and can (subject to the distributor's agreement) switch them between screens according to demand, but with cinemas with fewer than four screens. These account for the great majority of independent exhibitors and the bulk of MGM Cinemas' sites. In dealing with these cinemas, distributors use minimum periods to bolster their share of screen-time and to reduce risk. This in turn enables them to justify spending increased sums on advertising and promotion. But in reducing their own risks, distributors reduce exhibitors' freedom to respond to consumer demand. We also do not discount Entertainment's argument that extended minimum periods exacerbate the difficulties which independent distributors experience in obtaining bookings even though Guild, First Independent and RFD said that this was not their experience.

2.164. We have had regard to the evidence on the length of the minimum periods sought by distributors, and the fact that they show some flexibility both in negotiating periods in the first place and in subsequently agreeing to curtail showings of films which perform disappointingly. We have also taken note of the distributors' arguments that minimum periods reduce risks and enable films to be more effectively promoted. Nevertheless we conclude that the negotiation of minimum exhibition periods is a step taken by way of uncompetitive practice—in that exhibitors are prevented from showing other films which they would prefer to show—by the distributors shown in the schedule in Appendix 2.1 as engaging in this practice, for the purpose of exploiting and maintaining the monopoly situation. We further conclude that this practice is a fact which operates and may be expected to operate against the public interest, by reason of the particular effect that consumer choice is restricted.

## *Restrictions on screen use*

2.165. This practice, whereby distributors require exhibitors to show a film at all times during the licence period at which films are normally shown at the cinema in question (except for children's matinées and late night shows), has some affinity with the previous one, and has potentially similar effects (see paragraph 2.155).

2.166. The leading distributors argued that in booking films it was essential for them to know the extent of the exhibitor's commitment since that helped to determine the booking's potential benefits for the distributor. The restriction on screen use was part of the mechanism by which rental payments were assessed, since the house nut or break figures were set on the assumption that all performances were of the same film. It was essential that the distributor was able to renegotiate the rental when the film shared a screen. The question of sharing screens arose particularly with films aimed mainly at children. The distributor might want to see if such films attracted an adult audience as well, as *Aladdin* had done. If they did not, distributors were flexible, for example in agreeing that the film could be shown in a smaller screen in the evening, or have a reduced number of showings (subject to an amendment to the rental terms).

2.167. Rank said that given the cost of prints and the limitations on their availability, the distributor needed to ensure that each print was used as effectively as possible. If an exhibitor was not willing to show a film at all performances, the distributor would prefer to place the film with another who was. Guild considered that it was not denied access to screens by restrictions on screen use imposed by other distributors.

2.168. Two of the leading exhibitors said that most distributors—but not Buena Vista (see paragraph 2.171)—were prepared to negotiate variations in screen usage. Rank, whose evidence covered both RFD and Odeon, maintained that any reduction in the number of times a film was shown per week would be likely to reduce distributors' income and hence increase risks, and would reduce the efficiency with which prints were used. MGM Cinemas, however, told us that films appealing principally to children often performed very badly on the main evening show. Only rarely did distributors permit the film to be moved to a smaller screen or the screen to be shared with another film, despite the fact that this was demonstrably more efficient to both the distributor and exhibitor. MGM Cinemas considered that distributors showed greater flexibility than they used to, but more was needed.

2.169. According to the CEA, its members found that distributor permission for screen-sharing was given sparingly, although more often than in the past. This caused particular problems for cinemas with fewer than four screens and those situated in small towns or suburbs. Some distributors which allowed screen-sharing ignored the local licensing provisions and market situation, or might impose arbitrary screening times which were unsuitable.

2.170. In our survey of independent exhibitors (Appendix 4.4), about one-half of respondents said that the major distributors specified no screen-sharing (55 per cent for Buena Vista); between 34 and 44 per cent said that this was also true of the four independent distributors listed. Several respondents said that providing programmes for all sections of the community demanded a variety of films and timings through the week. 22 per cent of respondents said that distributors always or usually refused them permission to show other films if asked, while 65 per cent said that permission was not refused.

2.171. There was more criticism of Buena Vista on this topic than of other distributors, by some of the leading exhibitors as well as in our survey of independent cinemas. Buena Vista submitted that this was because it distributed more family films than all the other leading distributors together. As a result it received many more requests for other films to be played in the evenings during periods when it had booked the screen. Buena Vista believed that many of its family films were suitable for all audiences although some exhibitors did not; nevertheless, for four of the five classic Disney animated films which it had released in its first 18 months, Buena Vista had agreed from the outset that a different film could be shown in the evening.

2.172. Clearly these restrictions do inhibit exhibitors' ability to use their screens to the best advantage, as they judge it, in meeting consumer demand. Because of the shortage of screens in the UK it is important that exhibitors should not be unreasonably hindered in this way. But there is also force in the distributors' argument that they need to know where they stand in entering into a licensing agreement and that the number of showings of a film needs to be agreed between the two parties and not simply left to the exhibitors' discretion. The *Standard Conditions* specify that the distributor's agreement to a variation in shows may be sought after a licence agreement has been signed 'and shall not be unreasonably withheld'. We have noted that, in contrast with the variation of minimum exhibition periods, the majority of independent exhibitors responding to our survey said that distributors were willing to agree to their requests to show other films; and that both MGM Cinemas and the CEA consider that matters have improved in this respect (whereas the CEA considered that the length of minimum periods had increased over the years and become more of a problem).

2.173. For these reasons we believe, on balance, that the imposition by distributors of restrictions on screen use does not represent a step taken to exploit or maintain the monopoly situation. Nor do we consider that it produces facts which operate or may be expected to operate against the public interest. This is another aspect of the relationship between distributors and exhibitors which is likely to give rise to continued difficulty, however, and we believe it could usefully be brought within the ambit of the complaints machinery which we propose for dealing with cases of refusal to supply (see paragraphs 2.154, 2.245 and 2.246).

## *Distributors' influence over exhibitors' admission prices*

2.174. In this section we deal with the fact that the use of the *Standard Conditions* leads distributors to supply, and exhibitors to accept, films on terms which require exhibitors to charge such admission prices during licence periods as shall be agreed by the distributors.

2.175. Distributors said that the need for this provision sprang from the fact that rentals were calculated as a share of box office takings. It was unacceptable for exhibitors to have a unilateral right to cut admission prices and hence to cut distributors' rentals below the level assumed when the licence agreement had been reached. It might suit exhibitors, for example, to reduce admission prices in order to attract bigger audiences and hence boost concession (ie refreshment) sales, the profits from which accrued only to exhibitors.

Generally, however, distributors told us that in practice they did not exercise control or influence over admission prices. Columbia, for example, said that it usually consented to exhibitors' price promotions when consulted in advance even though, in many cases, any resulting increase in admissions would be unlikely to compensate it for the price reductions.

2.176. The leading exhibitors assured us that it was they who set admission charges: regular increases were not discussed with the distributors. They accepted that the arrangements for determining rentals gave distributors a legitimate right to approve price promotions. (MGM Cinemas did not accept the idea, however, that exhibitors might cut admission prices in order to boost concession income since the bigger the audience the less was taken in concession sales per head.) The leading exhibitors maintained that distributors' right to approve price changes did not cause price levels to be higher than they would otherwise be, although MGM Cinemas said that greater flexibility in price variation procedures was desirable.

2.177. Minutes of meetings of SFD committees showed that distributors became concerned during the first half of 1993 about the growth in price promotions by exhibitors, such as 'two seats for the price of one', which had not been cleared with distributors in advance. The SFD President reported to the Sales Managers Committee in June 1993 that the Society's intervention had led to the curtailment of such promotions.

2.178. It might be regarded as undesirable in principle that distributors should have the ability to influence exhibitors' admission prices in this way. In other sectors of the UK economy distributors are prohibited by the Resale Prices Act 1976 from seeking to maintain the resale prices at which their goods are sold by retailers. (It is our understanding that the Resale Prices Act does not apply to the supply of films because exhibitors do not sell on to consumers the goods—ie the prints of films—which distributors supply them with.) Price promotions in other consumer markets are therefore generally a matter for retailers to decide unilaterally. But in those markets retailers are not usually able to pass on to their suppliers, without prior agreement, the reductions in revenue which result from price cuts. It is the automatic linkage of rentals to admission prices in the film industry which creates a need for distributors to be consulted about price changes which would affect their income under licence agreements already entered into. As indicated in paragraph 2.150, we found no enthusiasm among exhibitors for departing from the revenue-sharing approach to the calculation of rentals.

2.179. We therefore accept that, in these circumstances, the contractual right which distributors have to approve exhibitors' admission prices is reasonable. We have, however, been alert to any indications that the right was being exercised so as to push up prices (and hence rentals) or to restrict price competition among exhibitors. As noted in paragraph 2.87, we do not believe that the general level of admission prices in the UK is excessive. The SFD activity described in paragraph 2.177 shows that distributors were concerned at what they saw as a proliferation of unauthorized price promotions, but in doing so they were seeking to protect their contractual rights. We received evidence that exhibitors do cut prices at cinemas with a view to boosting audience size (see paragraph 7.87), while UCI told us that in its experience distributors usually responded favourably to proposals for price cuts if it could show that they were part of a well-thought-out commercial strategy.

2.180. Taking account of the full range of evidence bearing on this question we do not consider that distributors' ability to influence exhibitors' admission prices is a step taken to exploit or maintain the monopoly situation. Nor do we consider that it is a fact which operates, or may be expected to operate, against the public interest.

## *Observance of the SFD* Standard Conditions

2.181. The last of the practices underlying the complex monopoly situation is the observance by distributors and exhibitors of the *Standard Conditions* for the licensing of the exhibition of films.

2.182. The leading distributors acknowledged that the *Standard Conditions* were in widespread use but argued that they had no anti-competitive effect. They had been negotiated between the SFD and the CEA, not imposed by distributors, and were a convenient and efficient way of dealing with the routine aspects of licensing agreements. The important provisions, such as rental arrangements and minimum periods, were subject to separate negotiation. The SFD had made clear that it was willing to consider proposals for amending the *Standard Conditions* that the CEA might want to put forward. The leading distributors tended to favour the continued use of the *Standard Conditions* but some said that they would not object to negotiating individual conditions with exhibitors.

2.183. Columbia said that if the *Standard Conditions* were prohibited, the larger distributors and exhibitors would be likely to produce their own standard contracts, the larger companies imposing their desired terms on the smaller. The *Standard Conditions* had been negotiated by parties of equal bargaining power and tended to redress the imbalance of power between individual contracting parties. Entertainment considered that it would suffer if the *Standard Conditions* were scrapped since the leading distributors would have the power to negotiate better terms than it could.

2.184. Most of the leading exhibitors favoured the retention of the *Standard Conditions* while submitting that the present text was biased in favour of distributors. UCI, however, felt that the widespread use of the *Standard Conditions* might discourage the kind of bilateral negotiation and contracts which were characteristic of many industries. It would prefer the 'background terms' to be negotiated on an individual basis and was considering whether to seek to adopt its own version.

2.185. The CEA submitted that the *Standard Conditions* did not reflect current trading conditions and were burdensome to small exhibitors. The CEA believed the exhibitors should not have to abide by conditions which required them to obtain distributors' permission before making changes to the operation of their businesses. The CEA had agreed with the SFD that the *Standard Conditions* should be reviewed but after an initial exercise to bring the document into a usable state the SFD had not proceeded to the second, more substantive stage, saying only that it would consider further amendments which the CEA put to it in writing. The CEA considered that this was not in the spirit of what had been agreed and would on past experience be an exercise in futility. It favoured the use of standard terms and conditions that were evenly balanced, so as to protect the weaker players from unreasonable demands, and believed the best course was for it and the SFD to meet regularly to keep the *Standard Conditions* under review. At our request the CEA identified specific elements of the present text which it thought were in need of revision, but it asked that we should not put these to the SFD for comment at that juncture because there were other matters to which it wanted to give priority.

2.186. We have addressed separately two of the most important elements of the *Standard Conditions*, namely the treatment of restrictions on screen use and distributors' right to approve exhibitors' admission prices. For the rest, we can see the theoretical advantages in having standard contractual conditions to govern the 'nuts and bolts' of licensing agreements in this industry, where the interests of the two parties are so closely intertwined, provided they are well balanced. We can understand the CEA's view that the present document is more detailed and intrusive than should be necessary for the generality of exhibitors. But it must be a matter for the two associations to resume the review of the *Standard Conditions* in a constructive spirit with a view to agreeing a revised version which will command the support of both sides, which is manifestly not the case at present.

2.187. We for our part do not find that the use of the *Standard Conditions* in itself is a matter for concern as regards the public interest.

## *Co-ordination of release dates*

2.188. We asked the leading parties to comment on the view that by co-ordinating the release dates of their films, distributors reduced consumers' choice of first-release films at any given time and crowded out other distributors.

2.189. The leading distributors acknowledged that information about likely release dates was widely available but denied that there was collaboration between distributors. Release dates were normally set in consultation with the two main circuit exhibitors as part of the alignment relationship (see paragraph 2.113). A decision by a distributor to shift a release date to avoid a clash with a similar type of film benefited consumers by bringing about a more even flow of releases. Smaller distributors remained free to set their own release dates.

2.190. Leading exhibitors shared these views. Natl Amusements argued that to the extent that distributors scheduled release dates to ensure minimum overlap, this was a logical business practice which allowed revenues to be maximized and brought associated benefits to consumers. UCI, however, told us that distributors competed for access to screens at particularly popular times of the year, such as Christmas and the other school holidays. It believed that a more even pattern of releases might be desirable in order to avoid films crowding each other out at peak periods. Nevertheless the availability of information about distributors' release plans enabled all distributors to take their own decisions according to their assessment of what was best for the particular film.

2.191. We have noted that the setting of release dates is an important aspect of competition among distributors (see paragraph 2.73). Since screens are a limited resource, particularly if needed in large numbers simultaneously for the release of a potentially popular film, it is understandable that distributors want to plan ahead as best they can and avoid clashes with similar films. The setting of release dates in consultation with MGM Cinemas and Odeon, which is unavoidable for many films as long as those exhibitors have significant numbers of cinemas with only a few screens, means that a degree of co-ordination is bound to occur. Independent distributors did not complain that they were disadvantaged by this process and having reviewed the evidence we do not believe that it raises concerns for the public interest.

## *Conditional booking*

2.192. In our survey of independent exhibitors (see Appendix 4.4) we asked whether distributors required exhibitors to take a film they might not otherwise have chosen in return for being supplied with a film they did want. Very few respondents said that this was the case. More significant numbers said that there were informal understandings to this effect in their dealings with the five leading distributors and Guild. The proportions of respondents who said that this was true of Columbia and, to a lesser extent, Warner Distributors were noticeably higher than for other distributors.

2.193. All the leading distributors said that they did not engage in conditional booking. Columbia firmly denied that it engaged in the practice, either in the sense of imposing a requirement or expressing an expectation that exhibitors would book one film as a condition of receiving another. This had been Columbia's policy for many years. Columbia explained that its small team of salesmen had to conduct sales discussions by telephone with large numbers of exhibitors in a very short space of time. Inevitably the conversations would cover the availability of prints for more than one film. Columbia inferred from our survey results that a minority of exhibitors had taken discussions of this kind as suggesting subtle or implied pressure on the exhibitor to agree to conditional bookings. But Columbia's salesmen were under instruction not to book conditionally, and no such pressure was in fact exerted. Columbia did not know why more exhibitors had identified Columbia as engaging in informal conditional booking than had identified other distributors but thought it might be due to the fact that the survey had been conducted at a time when it had two films on release—*The Remains of the Day* and *The Age of Innocence*—which were of great interest but which Columbia had decided for marketing reasons to issue in limited print numbers.

2.194. We contacted most of the exhibitors who had identified Columbia in this connection and asked for further particulars. Some told us that they had not intended to identify Columbia, while others said that Columbia was no worse in this respect than other distributors, but several maintained that Columbia was worse than all or most of the others. Most were unwilling for their identity to be revealed to Columbia, which was therefore unable to comment on the cases concerned; it commented in detail on the cases which were identified. Columbia also listed 18 cinemas which had refused one of its films, all of which had been offered prints of another, popular film, in the early stages of its release, a few months later.

2.195. Warner Distributors also denied that it engaged in conditional booking. The ability to persuade an exhibitor of the commercial value of the film was an important part of the distributor's function. Exhibitors and distributors needed to maintain good working relationships since they had to negotiate and deal on a daily basis and from year to year. As part of maintaining this relationship exhibitors might be prepared to accept films even where they had doubts about their commercial potential, rather than simply 'cherry-picking' the safest, most popular films. This was a feature of any industry where suppliers and buyers had to conduct business together and was not related in any way to the alleged existence of the complex monopoly. Such a relationship also operated in the public interest in encouraging exhibitors to show films of uncertain appeal. But Warner Distributors' sales force were under instruction not to engage in conditional booking. They were paid a basic salary plus an annual bonus but the latter was not based on any quantifiable measure of their performance in booking films. There were many instances of independent exhibitors refusing to screen films offered to them by Warner Distributors, which nevertheless continued to offer them films on first release.

2.196. The allegations of conditional booking have been difficult for us to investigate because of exhibitors' understandable unwillingness, in most cases, to be identified as complainants, leaving the distributors in the position of having to respond to the complaints only in general terms. The issue arises because of the imbalance of power between the leading distributors and some independent exhibitors (others who operate as the only cinema in a given area may be in a strong position because they have few screens to fill and can choose from among the films of all the distributors). We note that there were very few charges of explicit conditional booking, and that the CEA did not raise this with us as an area of difficulty. The proportion of respondents to our survey who said that they had been subject to informal conditional booking was significant, but our further enquiries in following up those comments (see paragraph 2.194) showed that the results could be taken as giving only a broad indication of the position. On the balance of the evidence we do not believe they provide a sufficient basis for distinguishing between the behaviour of different distributors. Given the way that business is conducted and the importance of relationships between individuals, as explained by Columbia and Warner Distributors, it is not surprising that a minority of exhibitors should at times feel that they were being put under a degree of pressure to take films which they were not seeking. But we accept and welcome the categorical statements by all the distributors that they do not engage in conditional booking. These statements should give some reassurance to independent exhibitors. We for our part reach no adverse finding on this subject. Given the scope for misunderstandings, however, we suggest that distributors should re-emphasize the instructions to their salesmen. We also believe this issue could usefully be brought within the framework of the machinery we propose for dealing with complaints (see paragraphs 2.245 and 2.246).

## Vertical integration

2.197. Critics of the film industry frequently point to the vertical links between companies involved in production, distribution and exhibition as having potentially distorting effects on the market and creating barriers to entry. It is suggested in particular that the Hollywood studios use their interests in distribution and exhibition in the UK to control the market and secure favourable treatment for their own films at the expense of others.

2.198. It is important to understand the facts about the extent of such vertical integration. The ownership links affecting the main players are as follows:

- (a) All the big seven Hollywood studios have UK distribution interests, four (Columbia/TriStar, 20th Century Fox, Walt Disney and Warner Bros) having their own separate subsidiaries while the other three (MGM Inc, Paramount and MCA/Universal) each have a one-third share in UIP.

- (b) Warner Bros also has a wholly-owned exhibition subsidiary, Warner Theatres, the fifth largest exhibitor.

- (c) Two of the three partners in UIP (MCA/Universal and Paramount) jointly own UCI, which is effectively the joint-second largest exhibitor along with Odeon.

- (d) Crédit Lyonnais wholly owns both MGM Inc, the studio, and MGM Cinemas, the largest exhibitor. But MGM Cinemas told us that it now reported, via its immediate parent, straight to Crédit Lyonnais in Paris. Beyond the common ownership, it had no remaining connection with MGM Inc. (MGM Inc has in any event produced few films in recent years.)

- (e) Natl Amusements, the fourth largest exhibitor, is owned by Mr Sumner Redstone, a US citizen, and members of his family. Mr Redstone and his family are also indirectly the majority shareholders in Viacom Inc, which acquired the Paramount studio during our inquiry.

- (f) Rank wholly owns both RFD and Odeon.

- (g) Three Hollywood studios—Columbia/TriStar, 20th Century Fox and Walt Disney—have no exhibition interests in the UK.

2.199. The distribution subsidiaries of the Hollywood studios told us that their primary function was to distribute the films made or acquired by their parent companies. Some of them also acquire the UK distribution rights to independent films but on a small scale. Those with vertical links to exhibitors said that their relationship was at arm's length, as with unrelated exhibitors, except for flagship cinemas in the West End of London. They neither gave nor received preferential treatment. The leading exhibitors all told us that they booked films on their merits, regardless of identity of the distributor.

2.200. In the following paragraphs we look at four aspects of conduct which shed light on this issue—patterns of trading between vertically linked distributors and exhibitors, differential rental terms, exhibitors' decisions on which films to take off and keep on, and the question of distortions in the decisions of vertically linked exhibitors to invest in multiplexes—before reaching an overall judgment on the significance of vertical integration in this market.

*Patterns of trading between vertically linked distributors and exhibitors*

2.201. Information on the individual distributors' shares of the box office takings and rental payments of each exhibitor (see Appendix 4.7) showed that UIP had a somewhat greater share of UCI's business than of the exhibition market as a whole, particularly in 1991 and 1992 (though not 1993).

2.202. UCI emphasized that its policy was to show all commercially viable product in its multiplexes irrespective of the identity of either producer or distributor. It assessed the commercial prospects of each film and chose whether to exhibit any film on the basis of the revenues that UCI expected the film to generate. When deciding which films to keep on at the end of each week, UCI reviewed new films available against films already playing and allocated films across its screens with a view to generating the highest possible attendances and revenues. Its success in selecting films to meet customer demand was demonstrated by the fact that it achieved the highest levels of attendance per screen and per seat of all the leading exhibitors. UCI submitted information based on box office takings which, it said, showed that UCI had no bias in favour of any particular distributor (see Appendix 4.7).

2.203. UIP stressed that its policy and practice were to seek to show each of its films in those cinemas, regardless of ownership, which it believed would maximize its return from that film (subject to the alignments, which did not affect the supply of films to multiplexes). Given the quality of multiplexes, UIP sought to book the majority of its films into all multiplexes. It treated UCI no differently from any other multiplex operator and its experience was that it received substantially identical treatment, both on bookings and holdovers, from all multiplex operators. UIP was unable to comment on the MMC's rental comparisons because it did not have access to all relevant information but on the figures which were available to it, based on admissions and box office receipts, it could find no evidence of any systematic preference in its trading with UCI (see Appendix 4.7). It pointed out that neither UIP nor UCI was much involved in the specialist or arthouse part of the market, which UIP estimated accounted for around 3 per cent of total box office receipts. The MMC's comparisons therefore overstated the difference between the percentage of UIP's box office receipts, and the percentage of total UK box office receipts, generated by UCI.

2.204. Our figures suggest that UCI displayed a modest degree of preference for UIP films in 1991 and 1992, but not 1993. The pattern is neither consistent nor very marked and we do not believe that much weight can be placed on this finding.

*Differential rental terms*

2.205. We analysed the extent to which the leading exhibitors used different nut figures as the basis for calculating rental payments to different distributors. There have been differences of this kind with three of the exhibitors, generally on a small scale.

2.206. MGM Cinemas' nut figures in 1993 were lowest for UIP and Warner Distributors, its two aligned distributors. For Columbia and Fox the nuts were on average between 1 and 2 per cent higher, and for Entertainment about 5 per cent higher, than those for UIP and Warner Distributors. UCI's nut figures were the same for all distributors at most of its sites but at seven (out of 23) there were differences during 1993, with the nuts for Fox and UIP being 4 to 6 per cent lower than for Warner and Columbia at six sites but 13 per cent higher at one site. Three of Warner Theatres' multiplexes had differential nuts and five did not. While differences on individual screens were significant, the overall average difference was less than 1 per cent, with UIP and Warner Distributors having slightly more favourable terms than Columbia and Fox. Natl Amusements used the same nut figures, and Odeon the same break figures, for all the distributors in our analysis, although Odeon required special terms for films which it regarded as being of above average commercial risk. A fuller account of this analysis is set out in Appendix 4.5.

2.207. The figures do not show a pattern of systematic preferences between vertically linked parties, but UIP enjoyed the most favourable treatment, jointly with Warner Distributors, from MGM Cinemas; and jointly with Fox from UCI. Warner Distributors enjoyed the most favourable treatment from Warner Theatres jointly with UIP. The likely explanation for these differentials is that UIP and Warner Distributors enjoy the best treatment because they are the biggest distributors.

*Exhibitors' decisions on which films to take off and keep on*

2.208. We also carried out a sample study of the circumstances in which films were taken off by exhibitors to make way for new releases. In the case of MGM Cinemas and UCI the data showed that films were quite often kept on although they had generated lower box office receipts than other films which were taken off. Most of these were films that were being shown for a small number of matinée performances, however. Leaving these cases on one side, the extent to which films were kept on or taken off in circumstances which did not reflect box office takings was not significant (see paragraphs 4.156 to 4.158).

*Investments in multiplex cinemas by vertically linked exhibitors*

2.209. Two exhibitors suggested that UCI's and Warner Theatres' investments were not made on a wholly commercial basis, viewed as stand-alone investments in exhibition, but were justified partly by the increased rentals which they generated for their parent studios' films.

2.210. UCI and Warner Theatres agreed that their investments had been designed to help revitalize the UK exhibition sector with a view to benefiting their parent studios' films, among others. Both companies rejected the charge that these investments were not commercial, however, saying that they did not proceed with any project to build a new multiplex unless it was expected to yield an internal rate of return of at least 20 per cent before tax. Most of their cinemas which were now operational were on target to achieve this return. Both companies supplied information in support of these claims.

2.211. Our analysis of the companies' accounts shows that UCI's ROCE (excluding the two West End cinemas owned by CIC) reached [ * ] per cent in 1991 and has broadly maintained that level in the two subsequent years. Warner Theatres' profitability on this measure (excluding the Warner West End) has been rising strongly and reached [ * ] per cent in 1993. Although these levels of ROCE are well below the [*] per cent hurdle rate of return which both companies use in appraising individual projects, it is not unreasonable that they should expect their profitability to rise if the market continues to grow. It is too early to judge what their profitability will be in the long term. At present it is not markedly out of line with that of MGM Cinemas or Natl Amusements. Odeon's profitability is higher because of its many older cinemas, the cost of which has been mainly written off. There is no firm basis for thinking that UCI's or Warner Theatres' investments are motivated by different criteria from those of other leading exhibitors.

*Conclusions on vertical integration*

2.212. As regards ownership links between production and distribution, the prime purpose of the leading distributors is to distribute the films of their parent companies. To the extent that they acquire independent films for distribution, the distributors' skills and resources may enable those films to reach a wider public than they otherwise would. Another effect may be to leave less room for independent distributors, but that is part of the competitive process and we received no evidence—and no complaints from independent distributors—that the leading distributors abused their position in this respect. As to the terms on which they agree to distribute independent films, we see no reason why, as Mr Michael Henry argued (see paragraph 6.120), the leading distributors should offer the same terms as for their parent companies' films. Since none of them is in a dominant position it would be unreasonable to expect them to deal with independent parties on the same footing as their connected companies. There is keen competition both among the leading distributors and with independent distributors to acquire the rights to independent films with clear commercial potential, so there is no question of the producers having to accept oppressive terms.

2.213. So far as the UIP joint venture is concerned, we noted in paragraph 2.4 that the EC Commission is currently considering an application for the renewal of UIP BV's exemption under Article 85.3 of the Treaty of Rome and is therefore considering this matter on an EC-wide basis.

2.214. As regards ownership links extending from production and distribution through to exhibition, we have carefully investigated the parties' claims that dealings between related distributors and exhibitors take place on an arm's length basis. There is some evidence of preference between vertically linked parties at the margin. UCI generated higher box office receipts and rentals for UIP in 1991 and 1992 than the latter's share of the overall market, or of the business of Natl Amusements, the other exhibitor whose operation most closely resembles UCI. But this apparent preference was not evident to the same degree in 1990 and disappeared in 1993. The evidence of differential nut figures does not demonstrate clearly that UIP or Warner Distributors received favourable treatment because of their ownership links to the exhibitors concerned.

2.215. The investments of UCI and Warner Theatres (and Natl Amusements) have played a major part in the transformation of the exhibition market over the last ten years. Coming after a long period of decline and low investment by incumbent exhibitors, who failed or were slow to embrace the multiplex concept, this initiative took boldness and vision. The effect on both the distribution and exhibition markets has been overwhelmingly beneficial. We are not impressed with, and the facts do not support, the argument that these investments have had the effect of distorting the exhibition market.

---

*Figures omitted. See note on page iv.

2.216. As regards the acquisition of Paramount by Viacom Inc (see paragraph 2.198(e)), UCI told us that it had received no direction from its partners that it should change its stance towards Natl Amusements, which it regarded as a competitor. MCA Inc pointed out that while it had a half share in UCI it had no financial relationship with Viacom; it would therefore be very concerned to ensure that the relationship between UCI and Natl Amusements did not change. Mr Redstone told us that he did not expect the relationships between UIP, Natl Amusements and UCI to be changed by the merger. We received no evidence which cast any doubt on these statements.

2.217. Apart from the use of flagship cinemas in the West End of London, preference between vertically linked distributors and exhibitors appears to be largely absent. All exhibitors have to look to unrelated distributors for the majority of the films they show. From a commercial standpoint it makes most sense for the corporate groups to treat exhibition as a separate profit centre, so that they can effectively motivate staff and retain the confidence of all unrelated distributors that they will received fair treatment. The Hollywood studios have been successful in making films with popular appeal and do not need to require their exhibition subsidiaries to discriminate in favour of their own product. In view of the concerns which have been expressed to us, however, and bearing in mind the indications of slight preference to which we have referred, we suggest that certain indicators should be monitored by the OFT so that the matter is kept under review (see paragraph 2.247).

## *Difficulties faced by British film-makers*

2.218. We referred in paragraphs 2.107 and 2.108 to the concern in some quarters, notably among British film producers, about the unhealthy state of British film production, in contrast to the much improved condition of the exhibition sector. Numerous possible explanations for this state of affairs have been put forward, including the dominance of the Hollywood studios, the attitude of distributors and exhibitors to British films, the structure and financing of the film production industry in this country, the UK tax regime, the relative lack of government incentives and the kind of films which British producers and directors make.

2.219. Most of these are outside our terms of reference. We observe that, while the fortunes of the British film industry have fluctuated over the years, the dominance of Hollywood has been an issue for decades. The Hollywood studios have the advantage of operating in the much bigger US market, enabling them to make films with high production costs and hence to attract the most popular stars. In deciding which films to release in the UK and how to promote them, the studios benefit from the experience of prior distribution in the USA which we were told is usually, though not invariably, a good guide to a film's prospects in the UK. Correspondingly UK exhibitors are eager to show films which have proved popular with US audiences, particularly if their distributors are able to spend heavily on advertising and promoting them. It is of course open to British film-makers to release their films first in the USA, as was done with *Four Weddings and a Funeral*, but this may not be appropriate for all films.

2.220. Because of the shared language, the UK is particularly open to the import of films from the USA. It is therefore not surprising that the US share of box office takings in the UK is higher than in most other European countries. But we noted that the US share of the market in continental Europe has risen strongly in the last ten years (see Table 4.1) despite the fact that some of the countries, notably France, have elaborate and well-funded systems of financial support for domestic producers. This suggests that the US industry has become even more competitive in recent years, releasing a large number of films which have proved attractive to international audiences. By contrast the difficulties which European producers have in gaining audiences outside their home market are the subject of anxious debate, as witness the EC Commission's recent Green Paper on options for strengthening the EC audio-visual sector (see paragraph 3.37).

2.221. No single distributor dominates the market and there is effective competition both among the leading distributors and between them and independent distributors. Contrary to the implication of the arguments advanced by the BFI and Mr Michael Henry, we do not believe that the Hollywood studios or their UK affiliates have any public duty positively to facilitate the making or distribution of British films. They told us that they were always interested in opportunities to invest in promising film projects or to distribute independent films with commercial potential, and there are notable examples of their doing so. We consider it healthy that such decisions should be taken according to commercial criteria.

2.222. We have, however, considered whether any of the practices and structural factors dealt with earlier in this chapter are inimical to the effective distribution and exhibition of British, and indeed other independent, films.

2.223. We have found that alignment makes the market less responsive to consumer preferences than it should be. If the remedies we recommend prove effective (see paragraph 2.238), the market should work that much better. We believe this will help to improve the prospects for attractive films from any source to achieve their potential in the exhibition market.

2.224. Our finding against the negotiation of extended minimum exhibition periods is based on the view that it restricts consumer choice by reducing exhibitors' freedom to show the films they consider will best meet their customers' preferences. To the extent that British films come into that category, our recommendation for constraining this practice (see paragraph 2.244), if implemented, will incidentally benefit them.

2.225. We have not found that the other practices which we have examined operate against the public interest. In particular, we have concluded that the vertical links which exist between distributors and exhibitors are not in themselves putting independent films at a disadvantage. Exhibitors are interested in showing any films which they think will have popular appeal, irrespective of origin, and judge them on their merits.

2.226. Our general view therefore is that the problems facing the British film industry lie for the most part beyond the scope of this inquiry. We regret that the proportion of culturally British films to be seen in UK cinemas is low. The recent success of *Howard's End, Much Ado About Nothing, The Remains of the Day, Shadowlands* and *Four Weddings and a Funeral* demonstrates, however, that it is possible for such films to achieve effective releases in the UK and to do well both here and abroad. Our common language with the USA, while making the UK market more receptive to US films, also represents an opportunity for British film-makers which their continental counterparts do not share. We do not underestimate the difficulties of competing against Hollywood, but those difficulties stem from the advantages which Hollywood enjoys, and the studios' undoubted achievements in capitalizing on them, not from any conspiracy or other improper behaviour on the part of them or their UK affiliates.

# Summary of conclusions on monopoly situations and adverse findings

2.227. We have concluded that a scale monopoly situation exists in relation to the reference goods by virtue of section 6(1)*(a)* of the Act (see paragraph 2.10). We have concluded that this monopoly situation exists in favour of MGM Cinemas (see paragraph 2.40).

2.228. We have also concluded that a complex monopoly situation exists by virtue of section 6(1)*(c)* and (2) in that the distributors and exhibitors listed in paragraph 2.12 so conduct their respective affairs as to restrict competition in the supply of the reference goods by engaging in the practices listed in paragraph 2.13 (except subparagraph *(i)*), and supply at least one-quarter of the reference goods (see paragraph 2.35). We have further concluded that this situation exists in favour of such distributors and exhibitors and the persons listed in paragraph 2.40(*b*).

2.229. Having carefully considered the facts found in the course of our inquiry, including those which flow from and relate to the complex monopoly situation which we have identified, we have concluded that the following are facts which operate, and may be expected to operate, against the public interest:

— alignment by distributors and exhibitors, with the particular effect, adverse to the public interest, specified in paragraph 2.129; and

— minimum exhibition periods, with the particular effect, adverse to the public interest, specified in paragraph 2.164.

# Recommendations

2.230. We are required by section 54(3) of the Act to consider what action (if any) should be taken for the purpose of remedying or preventing the adverse effects we have identified, and we may if we think fit make recommendations as to such action.

## Alignment

2.231. We condemned alignment in our 1983 report, but stopped short of making a recommendation because of the then parlous plight of the industry. The industry is now stronger and we believe the practice should be brought to an end. We invited the parties' views on two alternative possibilities: first, that distributors and exhibitors might be prohibited from entering into any agreement or arrangement with each other relating to the showing of a film at a cinema, other than an agreement or arrangement which covered one cinema only, was made solely on the merits of that cinema, and contained no condition as to the showing of that or any other film in any other cinema; and secondly, that the practice of alignment might simply be prohibited outright. We proposed also that distributors should be required to submit information to the OFT every six months showing, for each film distributed, the cinemas of MGM Cinemas and Odeon to which prints had been supplied *(a)* on first release and *(b)* subsequently.

2.232. The two circuit exhibitors which engage in alignment, the majority of distributors who responded, and the CEA saw objections to the first possible remedy. They argued that it would undermine efficiency by preventing distributors from dealing with exhibitors on a whole-circuit basis. Moreover there would always be room for argument over whether a cinema was selected on its merits. It would be difficult to demonstrate compliance. The remedy also went wider than was necessary to deal with alignment, not least because it would prohibit the negotiation of exclusivity which was quite a different matter. The same parties were also opposed to the second possibility, mainly on the grounds that it would create uncertainty as to what it was that distributors would not be permitted to do. Two of the leading distributors, however, did not object to either proposal. The majority of distributors who responded said that the proposed regular reporting to the OFT would be unnecessarily burdensome. Two of them did not object. These views are more fully recorded in Chapters 6, 7 and 8.

2.233. Alignments are informal, with no contractual obligation on either side. The devising of a remedy which would be effective without having other undesirable consequences is therefore not straightforward. We do not seek to prevent early discussions between distributors and exhibitors about film releases but we consider that these, and the subsequent booking of individual cinemas, should take place on a more competitive basis. It seems to us that there is no good reason why distributors should not discuss their forthcoming releases with both the circuits at around the same time. As regards the great majority of the circuits' cinemas, which do not compete with each other in the same local markets, the circuits now largely complement each other from the distributors' point of view and there is no need for a preferential relationship with one of them even if that were thought acceptable from the standpoint of the public interest. As for the 20 aligned locations, we see no reason why distributors should not in each case choose between the two cinemas on their merits—except for blockbusters where they might wish to supply both—in the same way as they choose between competing cinemas of other exhibitors.

2.234. The first possible remedy focuses on this last point. It would not prevent a distributor having preferential early discussions with one circuit, but it would change the framework of the discussions in that the circuit would not be able to count on getting the film for its cinemas in all the 20 aligned locations. We do not believe the remedy would prevent distributors from booking screens with exhibitors' central booking staff as long as the choice of screens was made for each one individually on its merits. Since distributors generally have a good knowledge of the exhibitors' individual cinemas, and make most of their bookings on this basis already, we see no serious practical difficulties about this. We acknowledge, however, that it might be difficult to demonstrate that the bookings had been made in this way, given the range of considerations which may reasonably enter into a distributor's judgment of the merits; and correspondingly difficult for a complainant to demonstrate that a booking had *not* been made in this way.

2.235. Adverting to a point made by the parties about the scope of this possible remedy (see paragraph 2.232), we agree that the remedy should be concerned only with agreements or arrangements to show films in cinemas owned by MGM Cinemas and Odeon in a specified list of aligned locations. (As noted in paragraph 2.120, however, the list of aligned locations is subject to change and would have to be updated if the need arose.) We proposed (paragraph 2.231) that the formulation of this remedy would contain 'no condition as to the showing of that or any other film in any other cinema'. We would now envisage that the allusion should be to 'any other cinema *operated by the same exhibitor*'.

2.236. The second possible remedy would outlaw both aspects of alignment, *viz* the holding of early discussions about film releases with one circuit in preference to the other and the systematic booking of films into all the cinemas of either circuit in preference to the other in the 20 aligned locations (here again, the list of locations in paragraph 2.120 would have to be updated as necessary). Being expressed as a negative requirement, this alternative would arguably be less intrusive than the other and is limited in terms to dealing with the practice which we have found to operate against the public interest.

2.237. We are quite clear that either of these remedies would need to be accompanied by some form of regular reporting to the OFT which should be continued until such time as the DGFT was satisfied that the pattern of supply of films was no longer determined by the practice objected to. The principal requirement would be information about the supply of prints to the cinemas of the two circuits, but the OFT might also want to seek other information, concerning for example the timing of early discussions about forthcoming releases, and the criteria by which particular supply decisions had been taken. We do not believe the particular proposal we made (see the last sentence of paragraph 2.231) would be unduly burdensome and we are fortified in this view by the fact that two of the leading distributors agreed.

2.238. On balance we prefer the second alternative. We therefore recommend that the practice of alignment, as described in paragraph 2.113, should be prohibited. We also recommend that the parties involved in alignment (as shown in the schedule in Appendix 2.1) should be required to supply such information to the DGFT as he may request to enable him to monitor compliance with the substantive remedy. We envisage that this would include, though would not necessarily be limited to—this would be a matter for the DGFT—the supply by distributors at regular intervals of the information referred to in the last sentence of paragraph 2.231.

## Minimum exhibition periods

2.239. We invited the parties to comment on the possibility that minimum exhibition periods might be abolished or restricted to a maximum of two weeks on first release and one week subsequently.

2.240. Leading distributors said that minimum periods were not imposed by distributors but decided jointly: the remedy would represent interference with a successful system based on free negotiation in the light of market conditions. If the possibility of negotiating extended minimum periods were denied they would have to look for other ways of reducing their risks, for example by securing better rental terms. Two distributors said that the remedy would create particular difficulties for children's films, the exploitation of which was concentrated in the holiday periods. RFD said that it was especially important for independent distributors to be able to exploit to the full the exceptional films which they acquired rarely and at high prices.

2.241. Two of the leading exhibitors expressed concern that distributors would require a higher rental in the first two weeks, and perhaps minimum rental guarantees, if they were unable to secure extended minimum exhibition periods. UCI said that it would prefer to negotiate freely and not be circumscribed by regulation. Natl Amusements suggested that, rather than restrictions being imposed, the SFD establish a procedure for exhibitor and distributor to negotiate an agreement based on the performance of the film in question. The CEA was undecided whether the length of run which could be demanded by a distributor should be dealt with by an Order or an agreed code of practice.

2.242. We have considered these views carefully. Most of the leading parties did not accept that the practice of minimum exhibition periods was harmful and their views on the possible remedy are coloured by that position. It is mainly independent exhibitors—and, to a degree, independent producers and distributors—who are disadvantaged by the practice. Having reached the conclusion that the practice operates and may be expected to operate against the public interest, we believe the choice lies essentially between a remedy on the lines of that which we put to the parties and a code of practice with accompanying machinery.

2.243. The number of films for which distributors seek minimum periods of more than two weeks is quite small. That is not to deny the significance of the practice, because the films affected are the potentially most popular ones, taking a disproportionate share of box office receipts; while from the point of view of an exhibitor with a single-screen cinema, even three or four films a year with minimum periods of four weeks can take up a sizeable proportion of screen-time. But the point is that the number of films affected, if minimum periods were restricted to two weeks, would be small and those which proved popular would in any case be kept on for longer periods if so agreed between exhibitor and distributor during the period of exhibition. We do not think a code of practice is necessary to deal with this issue. A period of two weeks is long enough, in our view, for an exhibitor to be required to keep a film on. Anything less than two weeks on first release would represent a much greater disruption of present practice and this could not be justified by the extent of the detriment we have found. On the other hand once a film has been shown for a time, the potential audience for a cinema showing it on second or subsequent run is reduced and at that stage a one-week maximum is appropriate.

2.244. We therefore recommend that minimum exhibition periods to be included in licensing agreements should be restricted, in respect of any cinema, to a maximum of two weeks on first release and one week subsequently.

## Other matters

2.245. As stated in paragraph 2.154, we believe there should be some independent machinery to consider exhibitors' complaints about refusals by distributors to supply films. Similarly in paragraphs 2.173 and 2.196 we noted that restrictions on screen use and the question of conditional booking were also likely to be a cause of continued difficulty between distributors and exhibitors and could usefully be brought within the ambit of the same machinery.

2.246. What we have in mind, in general terms, is that the CEA and the SFD would each appoint one representative to a panel. These would sit with two independent members, one of whom would act as chairman, as a committee for the purpose of considering complaints on any of these subjects and to make recommendations. The CEA and the SFD would draw up guidelines, taking account of the evidence and arguments in our report, which the committee would refer to in reaching its decisions. The OFT might be able to help with the drawing up of the guidelines.

2.247. On the question of vertical integration between production and distribution interests on the one hand and exhibitors on the other, we have suggested in paragraph 2.217 that certain indicators be monitored by the OFT. We propose that the five leading exhibitors should supply the OFT annually with figures showing the proportions of their box office receipts and rental payments which are attributable to films licensed by each of the five leading distributors. They would also inform the OFT of the extent to which (if at all) their standard rental terms—ie the nut or break figures for each cinema—vary from one distributor to another.

2.248. These proposals do not flow from the adverse effects which we have identified and do not therefore have the status of statutory recommendations. We hope nevertheless that the parties will agree to adopt them, recognizing their potential for contributing to harmonious relationships in the industry and public confidence in its trading practices.

2.249. The 1989 Order which prohibited the practice of barring seems to have played a useful part in helping to open up the exhibition market (see paragraphs 2.3, 2.103 and 2.133). It should be kept in operation.

# Overview

2.250. The film industry comprises three interrelated markets each of which—to the extent that they fall within the scope of our inquiry—we have found to be competitive. In production, the Hollywood studios appear to compete vigorously with each other and with independent US production companies. The UK production sector is fragmented and there are no substantial, integrated players.

2.251. In distribution the affiliates of the Hollywood studios compete with each other and with independent distributors in the distribution of completed films, albeit the competition here is qualified by a number of practices which we have identified and on which, where appropriate, we have made recommendations.

2.252. Exhibition is much more competitive than at the time of the previous MMC report in 1983 thanks mainly to the entry of three US-owned companies and the rapid development of multiplex cinemas. The 1989 Order prohibiting barring seems to have helped to open up the market. Exhibitors face pressure from other leisure activities as well as from each other. Admission prices are not excessive.

2.253. The relationship between distributors and exhibitors is complex. The leading distributors and leading exhibitors have some links in common back to Hollywood, but the Hollywood connection is not the governing element of their relationship, which is symbiotic. Neither side currently dominates the other, though independent exhibitors are at a bargaining disadvantage *vis-à-vis* the leading distributors, as are independent distributors *vis-à-vis* the leading exhibitors. As more screens are built, and the concentration among exhibitors lessens, some shift of power may be occurring in favour of the distributors.

2.254. Film-making is a high-risk business. Every film is different and the costs, which are very large for most popular films, have to be incurred up front without any assurance that the film will succeed at the box office, or in the video and television markets which bring an increasing proportion of the revenues. Profitability depends on the success of a small number of films. The industry organizes itself to manage this risk, notably by the arrangements for determining rentals which share box office takings between distributors and exhibitors.

2.255. The position of independent distributors seems precarious although the evidence does not suggest they are about to become extinct. The main reason for the precariousness is that the Hollywood film industry is skilled at turning out and promoting films that the UK public wants to see, and is prepared to commit huge financial resources to that end. Independent distributors have to compete in the open market for the rights to distribute independent films. With notable exceptions, these do not generally turn out to be blockbusters.

2.256. We have found that the alignments which still exist, if in an attenuated form, between distributors and the two main circuit exhibitors make the market less responsive to consumer preference than it otherwise would be, and we have recommended that they be brought to an end.

2.257. Most of the complaints and concerns expressed to us can be divided into two categories. First, there are complaints on the part of a relatively small number of independent exhibitors about the difficulty of obtaining popular—ie mainly US—films on first release. There is also a wider concern among exhibitors about minimum playing times and about restrictions on screen use. Secondly, we received representations about the difficulties in securing exhibition for British films and about an alleged bias against independently-produced British and other European films.

2.258. As regards the first category of complaint, we find no evidence that distributors have acted improperly in refusing to supply films. We consider it reasonable for distributors to determine supply with a view to maximizing profits on individual films, provided there is effective competition in both the distribution and exhibition markets. This is now generally the case, apart from the particular uncompetitive practices which we have criticized. Indeed we believe that most of the complaints on this matter have arisen as a result of increased competition brought about directly or indirectly by the building of multiplexes, the overall impact of which has been much to the benefit of cinema-goers. We propose, however, the establishment of some independent machinery to consider exhibitors' complaints on this and certain other matters.

2.259. We share exhibitors' concerns about minimum playing times, which restrict consumer choice, and we have made a recommendation to deal with the problem. On balance we have concluded that restrictions on screen use are not harmful, however.

2.260. As regards the second category of complaint, our analysis of relevant markets does not lend much support to the view that the difficulties of British film-makers are attributable to practices in, or the structure of, the distribution and exhibition sectors in the UK. These difficulties lie mainly beyond the scope of our inquiry. Nevertheless, in so far as British film-makers produce popular films our recommendations, if implemented, may incidentally facilitate the showing of these on UK cinema screens.

2.261. The transformation of the industry over the last decade has worked well for UK consumers: many popular films have been released, exhibitors have invested heavily in new and existing cinemas and audiences have doubled after many years of continual decline. Further changes may be expected. Today, apart from the practices we have criticized, competition in the markets under investigation is effective.

2.262. Background information on the industry, and the evidence on which our conclusions are based, can be found in Chapters 3 to 9 which form Part II of our report.

P H DEAN *(Chairman)*

P BRENAN

J S METCALFE

J K ROE

E C TRITTON

A J NIEDUSZYNSKI *(Secretary)*

28 July 1994

# Part II

# Background and evidence

# 3 Background to the inquiry

## Contents

| | Paragraph |
|---|---|
| Reasons for the reference | 3.1 |
| Previous reports | 3.2 |
| The OFT's experimental scheme | 3.9 |
| The Films (Exclusivity Agreements) Order 1989 | 3.14 |
| Trade Disputes Committee and Appeals Tribunal | 3.16 |
| The 1984 Government White Paper on *Film Policy* | 3.17 |
| The Downing Street seminar | 3.20 |
| British Film Commission | 3.22 |
| Department of National Heritage | 3.23 |
| Pan-European audio-visual support schemes | 3.26 |
| GATT Uruguay Round: audio-visual services | 3.30 |
| Article 85 exemption applications | 3.33 |
| The 1994 EC Green Paper | 3.37 |
| Consultations with EC Commission and Centre National de la Cinématographie | 3.38 |

## Reasons for the reference

3.1. On 29 September 1993 the DGFT referred to the MMC the matter of the existence or possible existence of a monopoly situation in relation to the supply of films for exhibition in cinemas in the UK. He explained in a press release that his enquiries into the industry had initially been prompted by complaints from independent cinemas about their difficulties in obtaining popular films from the major distributors, despite changes put into place following an earlier MMC investigation. The DGFT said that most major companies were vertically integrated and followed practices which could lead to the exclusion of independent producers, distributors and exhibitors from the market. He was aware of the changes that had taken place since the 1983 MMC report, such as the emergence of multiplex cinemas, but considered that competition remained restricted to such an extent that it was appropriate for the MMC to undertake a fresh investigation and decide whether any aspects of the industry continued to operate against the public interest. A reference was accordingly made to the MMC on 29 September 1993; the terms of reference are set out in Appendix 1.1.

## Previous reports

3.2. The supply of films has been investigated on two previous occasions. In September 1964 the supply in Great Britain of films to exhibitors for exhibition in cinemas was referred to the Monopolies Commission (the Commission) under the provisions of the Monopolies and Restrictive Practices (Inquiry and Control) Act 1948. The Commission's report *Films: A Report on the Supply of Films for Exhibition in Cinemas* (the 1966 report) was published in October 1966. In December 1980 the supply of films to exhibitors for exhibition in cinemas in Great Britain was referred to the MMC under the provisions of the Act. The MMC's report *Films: A Report on the Supply of Films for Exhibition in Cinemas* (the 1983 report) was published in May 1983.

*The 1966 report*

3.3. The 1966 report found that the introduction of a larger measure of competition into film exhibition would be advantageous both to the industry and the public. Competition was found to be deficient partly because of the various practices that were customary in the industry, but mainly because of the structure of the industry which resulted from the dominant position of the two main exhibition circuits. The Commission concluded that to give the industry a new and competitive structure would mean breaking up the circuits, but that would be a drastic step the results of which would be uncertain. Instead the Commission recommended a series of less drastic remedies which were intended to eliminate practices which restricted competition. Although each remedy individually could not be expected to have far-reaching consequences, the Commission believed that, provided they were all carried out, their combined effect should be to permit the development of greater and more effective competition. A summary of the conclusions and recommendations of the 1966 report, and the action taken in response to them, is at Appendix 3.1.

*The 1983 report*

3.4. The 1983 report found that scale monopoly situations existed in favour of two distributors and the two major exhibition circuits. The systems of alignments and barring were found to give rise to complex monopoly situations which operated and might be expected to operate against the public interest. Divestment was considered in the case of alignments. But taking into account the then market circumstances (the decline in cinema audiences, the continuing need to close cinemas and the fact that some cinemas were making losses) the MMC concluded that such a remedy was not practicable and could not be recommended. The MMC recommended that the barring system cease to operate and be replaced by arrangements under which exclusivity would be negotiated for each film hire agreement on a case-by-case basis.

3.5. Delays in the release of popular films to exhibitors other than the two major exhibition circuits were found to be a consequence of the market power which the circuits possessed as scale monopolists. This was reinforced by the system of alignments. It was recommended that popular films should not be exhibited for more than four weeks unless they had been made available to all other competing cinemas which sought to show them.

3.6. The MMC recommended changes to the procedures and membership of the Trade Disputes Committee (TDC) and the Appeals Tribunal, both of which had been established after the 1966 report. It was recommended that the TDC be empowered to deal with disputes relating to the extent of competition between individual cinemas and with disputes or complaints in connection with film hire agreements in certain circumstances. The arrangements for awarding allocations of product to independent exhibitors should continue and the TDC should give reasons for its decisions.

3.7. The MMC recommended that the undertakings which the major exhibition circuits gave, as a result of the 1966 report, to extend further the practice of giving trial runs to certain films whose appeal to the public was in doubt, and giving limited or partial circuit bookings to films of limited or minority appeal, should be allowed to lapse. Concern was expressed at the possibility of further concentration in the industry in Great Britain.

3.8. A summary of the conclusions and recommendations of the 1983 report is at Appendix 3.2.

## The OFT's experimental scheme

3.9. In December 1983 the DTI announced that undertakings on barring and on the release of popular films, on the lines recommended by the MMC (see paragraphs 3.4 and 3.5), would be sought in respect of two or more major cities only, initially for a trial period of six months, to assess their effectiveness in practice. In February 1984 the DGFT was invited to consult with the relevant parties with a view to obtaining such undertakings. Glasgow and Manchester were chosen as the trial cities (where new distribution policies were implemented), with Liverpool and Birmingham acting as the control cities (where existing distribution arrangements continued).

3.10. The OFT sought undertakings from distributors that, in the two experimental cities, they would only negotiate exclusivity arrangements with exhibitors on a case-by-case basis; that all subsequent-run cinemas would be able to exhibit any film four weeks after its opening at a first-run cinema; and that quarterly questionnaires covering both the trial and control areas would be returned to the OFT.

3.11. The experiment ran between May 1985 and May 1986 and included all cinemas within a 14-mile radius of each of the four city centres. In reporting on the experiment, the OFT noted that the MMC's recommendations were highly controversial within the industry, and that the experiment had been difficult to mount because of both this and the need for undertakings from the large number of participants concerned. A large amount of information had to be collected and analysed by the OFT in order to identify any changes of behaviour as a result of the experiment. As had been anticipated from the difficulty of the negotiations prior to the experiment, the less than full-hearted co-operation from some of the larger distributors and exhibitors resulted in information which was in some ways no more than adequate. Information from smaller distributors and exhibitors was patchy, delayed and incomplete and, at the outset, many of them had been ignorant of the preceding negotiations.

3.12. In addition, the experiment took place against a background of coincidental factors, notably the unexpected upturn in cinema audiences generally and the increasing use of widespread release of particular films backed by television promotions, which complicated assessment of its results. The OFT felt it necessary to supplement its examination of the detailed information received with case studies of particular films, as well as seeking general comments from the participants.

3.13. The OFT acknowledged that its conclusions from the experiment were not decisive but recommended that action should be taken against the practice of barring and to ensure the earlier release of popular films by means of an Order under the Act.

## The Films (Exclusivity Agreements) Order 1989

3.14. In late 1987 the DTI initiated a consultation period on a draft Order which would *(a)* effectively prohibit the practice of barring, and *(b)* impose a limit of four weeks on the length of time for which first-run cinemas could exhibit a popular film without it being made available to competing cinemas on normal commercial terms. The consultation revealed widespread support for *(a)* but strong opposition to *(b)*, which was not proceeded with.

3.15. Following a further period of consultation with the industry, an order prohibiting the practice of barring came into effect in April 1989 (Appendix 3.3). The 1989 Order made it unlawful for an exhibitor or a distributor to make or carry out an agreement relating to the supply of any film for exhibition at a cinema in Great Britain if the agreement contained or provided for terms about exclusivity relating to more than one film (but excluding agreements relating to not more than three films in respect of their exhibition at the cinema in question as a single programme). Effectively, therefore, distributors and exhibitors were required to negotiate exclusivity on a film-by-film basis.

## Trade Disputes Committee and Appeals Tribunal

3.16. Developments in the industry between 1983 and 1989 led the DTI and the OFT to agree that the remit envisaged for the TDC (see paragraph 3.6) had disappeared. The recommendations relating to the TDC were considered to be no longer relevant, particularly as the question of allocation of product was addressed by the 1989 Order. We understand that, while the TDC has not formally been wound up and the CEA elects members to sit if required, it has not been active in recent years.

## The 1984 Government White Paper on *Film Policy*

3.17. The White Paper entitled *Film Policy* issued in July 1984 spoke of considerable optimism in the British film production sector, noting strong indications of a rekindling of interest in making commercial British films, and growing market opportunities abroad. A very different picture was painted in respect of the exhibition sector, which was characterized by declines in admissions, box office takings and the number of cinema screens. While other countries had shown a long-term decline in admissions, nowhere had it been so steep or so apparently continuous and irreversible as in the UK.

3.18. The White Paper described as outmoded aspects of the existing regulatory framework. Considerable attention was focused on the Eady Levy, which was raised on the price of cinema admissions. The principal reason for the introduction of the levy in 1957 was to divert money from film exhibition to support domestic film production. The White Paper stated the Government's belief that statutory recycling mechanisms, such as the levy, were not an efficient means of encouraging an economic activity that should essentially be oriented towards the market. It noted that the levy was no longer fulfilling its original purpose with much of the payout going to distributors rather than to producers. Moreover, the levy was an unreasonable burden on the exhibition sector.

3.19. The White Paper stated the Government's intention to remove the levy as part of a shift in its approach to the film industry away from statutory intervention and towards the creation of a business environment that would encourage innovation and reward success. The Eady Levy was terminated in 1985.

## The Downing Street seminar

3.20. In June 1990 British film producers were invited to discuss the industry's problems and opportunities at a seminar hosted by the then Prime Minister. It was agreed at the seminar that, *inter alia*: the Government would provide £5 million over the next three years to help British producers seeking to enter European co-productions; a working party, chaired by the DTI, would be set up to examine the structure of the industry and how to attract greater private sector finance to UK film production; the industry should explore whether changes were needed to the tax regime for film production and report to Treasury Ministers; the Government would continue discussions in Europe on how best to support the film production industry, notably through the MEDIA programme; and the Government would study proposals from the industry, including the idea of a Film Commission, to improve the promotion of British films in the UK and overseas.

3.21. The working party examining the structure and financing of the industry was unable to agree its report and is now defunct. The industry working group's proposals on changes to the tax regime were submitted to Treasury Ministers in 1991 and partially implemented in the Finance Act 1992.

## British Film Commission

3.22. The British Film Commission (BFC) was launched in May 1991, following the Downing Street Seminar, and became fully operational in 1992. Its purposes are: to promote the UK as a location for the production of, *inter alia*, feature films; provide a comprehensive information service to producers; and to facilitate filming in the UK.

## Department of National Heritage

3.23. In 1992 the Department of National Heritage (DNH) took over the film industry responsibilities of the DTI. Its stated objectives in relation to film are: to help reverse the decline in British film production since 1985; to promote the UK as a location for producing feature films; to expand the opportunities for access to high-quality films from Britain and elsewhere; and to foster international co-operation in production, distribution and exhibition of films.

3.24. The DNH provides funding of approximately £17 million a year to the BFI, the national body charged with responsibility for encouraging the understanding and development of moving-image culture in all its forms. The BFI's concerns range across all aspects of film, television and video including production, distribution, archiving, education and publishing. The DNH also provides a £2 million annual grant to British Screen Finance Limited (British Screen), a private sector company whose current shareholders are Rank, MGM Cinemas, Channel Four Television Corporation (Channel 4) and Granada Television Limited. British Screen operates three film support schemes under which funding is provided, respectively, to low to medium budget feature films, short films and script development. Its remit requires it to support projects which it believes might not otherwise proceed to production, including a high proportion of projects which explore British themes, cultural values or current concerns and which involve new talent. British Screen typically provides about 20 per cent of a film's production budget. As a general rule the loan is available as an equity investment which is recouped by British Screen from world-wide receipts at least *pari passu* with other co-financiers. Between 1986 and November 1992 it committed funds of £31.7 million, including support of £29.5 million for 75 feature films.

3.25. The European Co-Production Fund (ECPF) was set up in 1991, following the Downing Street Seminar, with Government funding of £5 million over three years (see paragraph 3.20). The fund, which is administered by British Screen, exists to promote collaboration between producers in the UK and other EC member states, by providing funds to enable them to invest in feature films and film development work.

## Pan-European audio-visual support schemes

3.26. The UK is a member of, and contributes financially to, three major pan-European audio-visual support schemes: MEDIA, Audio-Visual EUREKA and Eurimages.

### *MEDIA*

3.27. MEDIA is an EC programme, the purpose of which is to stimulate the economic development of the European audio-visual industry sector and to help create the right environment for small and medium-sized businesses to collaborate and develop. Its aims are to: stimulate and increase the European audio-visual sector; increase European production and distribution companies' share of world markets; encourage a business-like approach to the industry; and develop the use of new technologies. MEDIA was provided with a 200 million ECU (approximately £140 million) fund for its first five years of operation, of which the UK provides approximately £28 million.

### *Audio-Visual EUREKA*

3.28. Audio-Visual EUREKA, an initiative involving 33 European countries, the EC Commission and the Council of Europe, is aimed at strengthening the European audio-visual industry by encouraging: the emergence of a more transparent and dynamic audio-visual market on a European scale; a favourable framework for financing the production and co-production of original European works; the launching of actions and concrete co-operation projects; the widest possible distribution of European programmes; the development and widest possible diffusion of production from countries having a limited geographical or linguistic coverage; all aspects of audio-visual production; and the promotion of European technologies. Audio-Visual EUREKA does not support projects by means of financial backing.

### *Eurimages*

3.29. Eurimages is a Council of Europe fund which supports programmes in three categories: co-production of feature length fiction films; co-production of creative documentaries; and support for distribution or broadcasting of works, including dubbing, subtitling and manufacturing of release prints. In 1993 its budget amounted to approximately 122 million French francs (£14.6 million at an exchange rate of 8.34 French francs to £1). The UK's contribution is approximately £5.5 million over three years.

## GATT Uruguay Round: audio-visual services

3.30. In December 1993, as part of the broader conclusion of the GATT Uruguay Round, agreement was reached on the General Agreement on Trade in Services (GATS). GATS provides a framework of general rules covering trade in all services, requiring, for example, that regulations and agreements affecting trade in services should be transparent. GATS also lays down rules for the scheduling of commitments by signatories on market access and on national treatment—the equal treatment of domestic and foreign companies—made during the Round. Sectors not covered in a signatory's schedule of commitments remain subject to the general provisions of GATS. Article XIX requires members to enter into successive rounds of negotiations, beginning not later than five years from the date of entry into force of GATS and periodically thereafter, with a view to achieving a progressively higher level of liberalization.

3.31. During the negotiation process, the EC sought to achieve some form of individual treatment of the audio-visual services sector by, for example, including an annex in the GATS package which, in effect, would have removed the audio-visual sector from the liberalizing elements of the agreement. The USA for its part sought to conclude a package with the EC that would have gone beyond the services element of the negotiations. In particular, it wished any deal with the EC to address the question of access for US film producers to copyright levies raised in some EC member states on the sale of blank audio and video tapes.

3.32. In the event neither of these aims was achieved. The EC has committed itself to no particular liberalization measures, its GATS obligations being solely to secure transparency and share information with other parties to the agreement on any new measures taken by the EC or its member states. Through exemptions from the most favoured nation clause, eg for Eurimages, most aspects of the existing audio-visual policy have been secured.

## Article 85 exemption applications

3.33. In 1982 the EC Commission received from UIP BV, on behalf of MCA Inc, Metro Goldwyn Mayer Film Co and Paramount, an application for negative clearance or alternatively an exemption from the provisions of Article 85(1) of the Treaty of Rome in respect of joint-venture agreements and related agreements concerning the distribution of feature films.

3.34. The agreements as notified contained several provisions which prevented the granting of an exemption. Following discussions with the EC Commission, the notifying parties presented a number of amendments to the agreements in order to meet its objections. In July 1989 the EC Commission granted an exemption, declaring the provisions of Article 85(1) of the Treaty of Rome inapplicable for the period 27 July 1988 to 26 July 1993 to the basic agreement and to the accompanying agreements between the parent companies or subsidiaries of them and the joint venture company, subject to certain obligations.

3.35. In October 1993 the EC Commission invited third parties to submit observations they might have on UIP BV's request, submitted in June 1993, for renewal of the exemption. A decision on the request is not expected before 1995.

3.36. In January 1993 the EC Commission received from Paramount Communications BV (Paramount BV), MCA International BV (MCA BV) and UCI BV an application for negative clearance or alternatively an exemption from the provisions of Article 85(1) of the Treaty of Rome in respect of a joint-venture agreement concerning the acquisition, development, operation and management of a chain of cinemas in various countries through UCI BV and its direct or indirect subsidiaries. No decision on the application is expected before 1995.

## The 1994 EC Green Paper

3.37. In April 1994 the EC Commission issued a Green Paper which examined options for strengthening the EC's audio-visual sector. The paper, entitled *Strategy Options to Strengthen the European Programme Industry in the Context of the Audiovisual Policy of the European Union*, emphasized the cultural importance of films and the need to develop a strong, forward-looking industry able to compete in world markets, to help European culture to flourish and to create jobs. The paper posed a number of questions about how these objectives were to be achieved. The EC Commission has embarked on a series of consultations on the options advanced in the Green Paper, with a view to presenting proposals for action by the EC authorities.

## Consultations with EC Commission and Centre National de la Cinématographie

3.38. During the course of the inquiry, MMC members and staff met with officials of the EC Commission in Brussels and the French Centre National de la Cinématographie (CNC) in Paris. Discussions with the EC Commission focused on the Article 85 exemption applications (see paragraphs 3.33 to 3.36), state aids in the film industry, European audio-visual support schemes and the cultural importance of the film industry. Discussions with the CNC focused on the experience of the French film industry in competing against US films, financial support to the industry and European support schemes.

# 4 The market for films in the UK

## Contents

*Paragraph*

| | |
|---|---|
| Introduction and background | 4.1 |
|     Certification and release of films in the UK | 4.3 |
|     Ancillary markets | 4.8 |
|     Returns and risks of film-making | 4.12 |
|     Defining the market | 4.14 |
|     Distributors and exhibitors of films in the UK | 4.27 |
|         Film distributors | 4.30 |
|         Film exhibitors | 4.32 |
| Film production | 4.35 |
|     Financing of films | 4.38 |
|     Production of films in the UK | 4.40 |
|     Difficulties facing film production in the UK | 4.43 |
|     Access to distribution | 4.51 |
| Film distribution | |
|     Main changes in film distribution since 1983 | 4.52 |
|     Size of market and growth trends | 4.56 |
|     Distributors' market shares | 4.59 |
|     Activities of film distributors in the UK | |
|         Functions of the distributors | 4.62 |
|         Aspects of competition between distributors | 4.64 |
|         Decisions on which films to distribute in the UK | 4.70 |
|         Distributors' trade associations | 4.74 |
|     Prospects for new entry | 4.77 |
| Film exhibition | |
|     Main changes in film exhibition since 1983 | 4.82 |
|     Independent exhibitors | 4.84 |
|     Size of the market | 4.87 |
|     Exhibitors' market shares | 4.96 |
|     Multiplex cinemas | 4.101 |
|     Activities of film exhibitors in the UK | |
|         The booking of films | 4.108 |
|             Advertising and promotion | 4.113 |
|             Cinema Exhibitors' Association | 4.114 |
|     Ticket prices | 4.115 |
|     New investment | 4.122 |
|     Prospects for new entry | 4.126 |
|     Appeals procedure | 4.130 |
| Relationships between distributors and exhibitors | |
|     The SFD's *Standard Conditions* | 4.131 |
|     Rental payments | 4.135 |
|     Vertical integration and links between companies | 4.143 |
|     Alignment | 4.159 |
|     Barring | 4.168 |
|     Exclusivity | 4.169 |
|     Refusal to supply a film | 4.173 |
|     Conditional booking | 4.180 |
|     Minimum exhibition periods | 4.183 |
|     Restrictions on screen use | 4.188 |
|     Competition and the balance of power between distributors and exhibitors | 4.192 |

# Introduction and background

4.1. In this chapter we principally describe the distribution and exhibition of films in the UK. The chapter begins with background information on the supply of films, a consideration of the main characteristics of the market for films and a brief introduction to the leading companies competing in this market. We then take a brief look at film production before turning in more detail to distribution and exhibition.

4.2. As mentioned in paragraph 3.23, the government department with responsibilities for the film industry in the UK is the DNH. The BFI (see paragraph 3.24) is the national body with responsibility for promoting the development and understanding of the moving image (film, video and television) as an integral element in the cultural life of the country. It does this in conjunction with the Welsh Arts Council, the Scottish Film Council and the Northern Ireland Film Council. About half of the BFI's funding comes from the DNH, the remainder being raised from the BFI's various revenue-earning activities, membership subscriptions, sponsors and donations. As well as undertaking a wide range of activities concerning film, television and video (including production, distribution, exhibition, archives, education and publishing), the BFI is responsible for the National Film and Television Archive, the three-screen National Film Theatre and the Museum of the Moving Image (these last two being situated at the South Bank complex in London), and it provides support for 46 regional film theatres (RFTs) in the UK. The BFI produces both feature films and short films, as well as supporting regional film and video projects (further information about, and from, the BFI is given in paragraphs 6.92 to 6.108).

## Certification and release of films in the UK

4.3. The number of feature films *classified* by the British Board of Film Classification (BBFC) in 1993 for exhibition in cinemas in the UK was 350. This compares with around 500 feature films a year in the early 1970s, a subsequent low of 278 in 1981, and a recent peak of 396 in 1990. The average number of feature films classified by the BBFC over the last ten years has been around 350 a year. The BBFC also classifies shorter films such as short features, trailers and advertisements (in 1993 it classified 32 short features, 331 trailers and 137 advertisements).

4.4. In 1993 the BBFC also classified a little over 3,700 videos, including 699 trailers and 62 advertisements. Over the period 1985 to 1992 it classified about nine times as many video versions of feature films as it did feature films for exhibition in cinemas. Many of these were, however, from back catalogues of older films which were being released on video for the first time or had previously been released on video without needing to be classified (the Video Recordings Act 1984 requires that most videos should be classified before release, including films and television programmes which have not been exhibited in cinemas).

4.5. The number of feature films *released* by distributors to cinemas in any year is lower than the number classified in that year by the BBFC. The BFI found that 241 titles were released in 1992;[1] this compares with 319 that were classified that year. Some films submitted for classification are not subsequently released, and some are foreign language films not destined for general release.

4.6. Over the four years 1989 to 1992, 1,046 new feature films were released to cinemas in the UK (an average of some 260 a year), compared with 1,276 in Germany, 1,555 in France, 1,718 in Italy and 1,850 (including 158 re-releases) in the USA. Of the 241 feature films released in the UK in 1992, the BFI identified 136 (56 per cent) as US-made. US-made films accounted for about 86 per cent of UK box office revenue that year, while the 25 British-made films accounted for about 4 per cent of the box office (see paragraph 4.40 for an explanation of these terms).

4.7. In terms of box office revenue, US-made films have held between 80 and 90 per cent of both the UK and the Irish Republic markets for more than ten years. In other EC countries the share of US-made films, while generally less than in the UK, has increased considerably since the early 1980s

---

[1] See the BFI's *Film and Television Handbook 1994*, Table 15, page 42.

(see Table 4.1). In Germany it increased from 55 per cent in 1982 to 83 per cent in 1992, in Spain from 46 to 77 per cent, in Italy from 32 to 69 per cent and in France from 30 to 58 per cent.

TABLE 4.1  Share of US-made films in the film exhibition markets in various EC countries

*per cent*

| | US-made films: share of box office | | |
|---|---|---|---|
| | 1982 | 1987 | 1992 |
| France | 30 | 44 | 58 |
| Italy | 32 | 48 | 69 |
| Belgium | 43 | 62 | 73 |
| Spain | 46 | 58 | 77 |
| Denmark | 50 | 55 | 78 |
| Netherlands | 51 | 64 | 79 |
| Germany | 55 | 58 | 83 |
| Luxembourg | 62 | 65 | N/A |
| Portugal | 44 | 67 | 85 |
| **UK** | **82** | **89** | **86** |
| Irish Republic | 86 | 80 | 88 |
| Greece | 51 | 81 | 93 |

Sources: 1982 & 1987: Council of Europe document number MM-CM (93) 1, Appendix IV, February 1993.
1992: *White Book of the European Exhibition Industry* (Synthesis Vol, p19), Media Salles, March 1994.

## Ancillary markets

4.8. Since the MMC's 1983 report there has been a marked increase in the importance of ancillary markets, first from the hire or sale of video cassettes and, more recently, from pay television. The video market for films only emerged during the early 1980s, but then grew very quickly, led by the video rental market from about 1983, and followed by the video sell-through market from about 1988. The arrival of cable and satellite broadcasting has greatly increased the number of television channels, some exclusively showing feature films. Pay television, either broadcast from satellites or received via cable, has developed in the UK since 1990. A distinction, therefore, should be drawn between free television (ie television financed largely by either an annual fee or by the revenue from advertisements, and normally, but not exclusively, received directly from ground-based transmitters), and pay television (received from satellites or cables, and paid for by subscription related to the number and types of channel received).

4.9. The audio-visual sector continues to benefit from advances in technology. It is expected that UK television viewers will eventually be readily able to watch broadcast films on a pay-per-view basis or via cables as video on demand. Experiments are already taking place in California with the direct transmission of films to cinemas via cable. This would give audiences high-quality pictures and sound without incurring the cost of making individual prints for each cinema, although there are huge investment costs involved.

4.10. The rapid growth, since the early 1980s, of ancillary markets (also known as the secondary markets) has meant that the theatrical release of films now probably accounts for around one-quarter of the total revenue generated by feature films over their full life cycle. Because of the time lags between the different forms of exhibition (see paragraph 4.19), and because distribution to the video and television markets is often undertaken by different companies, it is difficult to establish the share of revenues between these different markets. The information provided to us by four of the leading distributors in the UK showed cinema takings in the UK varying between 23 and 35 per cent of total revenues. These figures are consistent with estimates recently published in *Screen Digest*[1] which show that of the US studios' world-wide total revenues from feature films of $14.5 billion in 1993, 48 per cent came from video markets (compared with 12 per cent in 1983) and 27 per cent from theatrical exhibition markets (57 per cent in 1983). The remaining categories were free television (11 per cent),

---

[1] *Screen Digest*, Vol 7(8), 4 May 1994, page 10.

pay television (8 per cent) and other markets, including video discs and pay-per-view (6 per cent). In the US domestic market alone (estimated to be worth $8.6 billion in 1993), the video market accounted for 51 per cent of revenues, and the theatrical market for 25 per cent.

4.11. The growth of video and television as means of watching films is also shown by consumer expenditure figures. The BFI noted, for example, that in 1992 consumer expenditure on video rental, video sell-through and film subscription channels was almost four times as much as expenditure on cinema visits.[1]

## Returns and risks of film-making

4.12. Investment in films is very risky. Every film is different, combining the different artistic and creative talents of numerous individuals from the initial ideas, through script development, design, acting, photography, background music and editing, to marketing the final product, including advertising and promotion. Until the finished film is finally released for exhibition in cinemas, it is difficult to tell whether it will be a success. What is certain, however, is that the film's investors will not see any return for their money at all until the film has been exhibited to paying customers. While the unpredictability of the returns from films can to a limited extent be managed (eg by the regular production of formulaic films containing what past experience has shown to be the important ingredients of successful films), it is the case, and the industry continues to expect, that only about one-fifth of new films will make a healthy profit from their theatrical release, a further one-fifth will break even, and the rest will lose money for those financing them (though some films will recoup these losses from the ancillary markets).

4.13. Exhibitors have the first call on the bulk of the box office takings generated by films. In the UK they retain on average about 64 per cent of box office revenue (to cover their own costs and to provide a contribution to their profits, though they may in fact make losses on some films), and pay about 36 per cent to distributors as film rentals. The distributors in turn retain about two-thirds of their rental receipts to cover their own costs, mostly in promoting and marketing the film. It is important to recognize that these are averages, and that for many films the receipts accruing to the distributor are not sufficient to cover the release costs (see paragraph 5.10). On average, about 12 per cent is left of box office revenue after the exhibitors have taken their share and the distributors have recovered their costs. This is then available to recover the film production and financing costs, and finally to make a contribution to the producers' profits (which may or may not be reinvested in the production of subsequent films). Paragraphs 5.4 to 5.7 have a more detailed analysis of 'shares of the cake' in terms of both box office takings and total cinema revenue.

## Defining the market

4.14. Our terms of reference relate to 'the supply of films for exhibition in cinemas in the UK' and define 'films' as 'any record, however made, capable of being used as a means of showing a sequence of visual images as a moving picture'. While under this definition films are goods (usually 35mm colour prints[2]), cinema-goers are aware only of the 'moving picture' element, ie the sequence of 'visual images' presented to them on cinema screens. The goods are not purchased by, or otherwise physically passed on to, cinema-goers; instead the exhibitor provides facilities for consumers to view the film as a moving picture.

---

[1] See the BFI's *Film and Television Handbook 1994*, Table 4, page 26.

[2] Video cassettes have so far hardly been used at all for the showing of films in cinemas (though they may in the future). This inquiry is therefore about the supply of films as prints. Common usage does not distinguish between 'film' and 'print' when referring to the supply of films to cinemas.

4.15. The term 'films' includes feature films, short features, trailers and advertisements as shown in cinemas.[1] However, we have confined our inquiry to feature films, which we have defined as films over 72 minutes in length and made for theatrical release. This was the area of concern to the DGFT when making this reference to us, and feature films comprise by far the preponderant part of films made for theatrical exhibition.

4.16. Two main questions of market definition arise: first, whether films shown in cinemas are part of the same market as films shown on television (whether broadcast or replayed from video cassettes); and second, whether the market for films shown in cinemas should be broken down, for the purposes of the economic analysis, either by geographic region or by different types of film.

4.17. Cinema, video and television are different means of viewing feature films. Producers and distributors have taken advantage of these different ways to release films through each medium in succession to maximize their returns. People wanting to see the latest feature film have to see it in a cinema. Those who are prepared to wait (or who want to see it again in their own homes) may wait for the video version. Others wait rather longer to see it on television.

4.18. There are conflicting views about how the growing availability of films on television and video has affected cinema attendances. On the one hand, it is suggested that they are lower cost alternatives to seeing a film in the cinema, that they compete directly with cinemas, and have had an adverse impact on the number of cinema admissions. On the other hand, it is also suggested that the growth in film-watching on the small screen has created a much greater public awareness of new films when they are first shown in cinemas, and that this partly accounts for the revival in cinema-going in the last decade (see paragraph 4.87).

4.19. Because of the growing importance of video and television outlets for feature films, the time available for a film to earn revenue during its theatrical release has decreased considerably. Distributors operate a system of standard time delays, or holdback periods, after films are first released for exhibition in cinemas before they are made available through the other media. While in some countries these delays are laid down by government regulation, in the UK they are matters of convention within the industry, but appear nonetheless to be widely observed. The periods after the delays, when films become available in a particular medium, are referred to as 'windows'. In the UK the release window for the video versions of films normally opens six months after cinema release (but can be up to 12 months or more, particularly for sell-through versions). For pay television the window normally opens 12 months after cinema release (but can be up to 18 months). For free television the window normally opens three years after cinema release in respect of US films; for other films the timing is flexible but the window rarely opens within a year of cinema release.[2]

4.20. The general view in the industry appears to be that a film's successful cinema release is good for its video sales, and that people who regularly view films on video are also regular cinema-goers (this is one of the findings of the CAVIAR surveys—see paragraph 4.68). The video version of a feature film may be seen by many more people than saw it at the cinema. Even so, the video viewing of feature films supplements, rather than substitutes for, cinema viewing. The relationship is not so clear when it comes to the watching of films broadcast on television: regular viewers of feature films on both pay television and free television tend not to be regular cinema-goers.

---

[1]The MMC reported four years ago on aspects of the supply of cinema screen advertising services. This was published as *The Supply of Cinema Advertising Services: a report on the supply in the United Kingdom of cinema advertising services*, Cm 1080, HMSO, May 1990.

[2]Under an agreement reached under the auspices of the British Screen Advisory Council in September 1988, a minimum production cost of £4 million was set for the purpose of determining whether an English language film should be subject to holdback as regards release to free television. This figure was to be increased each subsequent year by the increase in the retail price index (RPI) plus 3.5 per cent (subject to a maximum increase in any one year of £300,000), but in practice this is not a calculation that has been strictly undertaken each year. The understanding in the industry at present is that the current figure should be taken to be £5.5 million to £6 million.

4.21. Feature films supplied for exhibition in cinemas are normally:

— in a distinctive form (ie 35mm or 70mm prints rather than video tapes);
— shown in distinctive buildings, most of which were designed for this purpose;
— projected on to wide screens with appropriate sound equipment; and
— intended to be seen collectively by large groups of people.

The collective experience is part of the enjoyment of viewing films in cinemas, in contrast to seeing them on video cassette or via television, both of which are meant for private showings.

4.22. The characteristics of the supply of films which we have described in paragraphs 4.17 to 4.21 lead us to the view that, despite the very considerable changes in both the means and opportunities for viewing feature films since 1983, it remains sensible to regard the supply of films for exhibition in cinemas in the UK as a separate and distinct market (we refer to this as 'the distribution market').

4.23. The second issue of market definition is whether the market should be analysed as a single entity or whether it should be subdivided in some way (see paragraph 4.16). This needs to be looked at in the context of the related market for the supply of cinema services ('the exhibition market'). To show films, cinemas need prints from distributors: there is no alternative. There are two main constraints on the charges and other conditions of supply that film distributors may seek from exhibitors:

*(a)* the competitive position of each cinema in its own local market; and

*(b)* the extent and nature of competition between film distributors.

These constraints vary over time according to the number of different film titles currently available on release, the numbers of prints made for each title, and the number of suitable screens at which they can be shown.

4.24. We have considered whether the exhibition market is a national or a local one. We noted, for example, that in its analysis of the UK exhibition market Fox currently identifies 498 different local exhibition markets. (While its main criteria include travel time and each cinema's local reputation, Fox recognizes that such a classification inevitably involves an element of judgment.) Of these, 387 are, in Fox's view, monopoly markets (ie cinemas, including several city centre arthouse cinemas, which do not face strong local competition) and the other 111 are competitive markets (including all the principal provincial cities). We discuss later various elements of the exhibition market, including, for example, the existence of national chains of cinemas, exhibitors' policies on admission charges and the booking of films, and the bargaining relationship between exhibitors and distributors. These elements, among others, lead us to the view that competition in the exhibition market is driven primarily by factors which have a clearly national dimension, and justify looking at it on a national basis, while not ignoring aspects of local competition.

4.25. The process by which the supply of feature films is related to the likely demand is not the setting of cinema admission charges, since these do not vary from one film to another, but the allocation of cinema screens. If a film is expected to be in great demand, prints are made available for a larger number of screens and the cinemas may also extend the period for which they are shown. This is in turn the outcome of two separate decisions: first, the distributor's assessment as to the likely level of demand for a film and decision about the number of prints to be made; and secondly, the exhibitors' decisions about which of the films currently available will generate the greatest revenue and should be shown on their screens. Both of these decisions will depend on the supply of and demand for concurrently available films and the number of screens at any one site, ie on competition from other films. This means, too, that although a key feature of this market is that all films are unique, it would be inappropriate to subdivide the distribution market (eg into different categories of films) in order to analyse competition.

4.26. Cinemas as a group also compete against other calls on their potential customers' leisure time and income, eg television viewing, pubs, discos, theatres, concerts, bowling alleys and leisure centres. While these are not close substitutes for cinema-going, the existence of other leisure activities is a longer-term competitive constraint on cinemas, helping to explain, for example, the marked decline in cinema attendances during the 1950s and 1960s (a period when television was building up a huge audience). For continued commercial success, cinemas have to provide audiences with an entertainment experience which they perceive as being good value for money, in terms of both the quality of the films shown and the quality of other exhibition services provided (eg sound systems, comfortable seating, cleanliness, etc) compared with other leisure activities. While the availability of other leisure activities may bring competitive pressures on cinemas over the longer term, however, they do not have such an immediate impact on film exhibitors as to be regarded as being in the same market.

## Distributors and exhibitors of films in the UK

4.27. In their 1983 report the MMC noted that, while in 1965 (the time of their first report on the supply of films) all the ten major distributors had operated independently of each other, by 1981 three joint distribution companies had been formed. The film distribution sector had become highly concentrated with six distributors accounting for 90 per cent or more of film rental payments (the 1983 report, paragraph 8.13). The report concluded, among other things, that:

> within a single system of decision-making operated by EMI and its aligned distributors on the one hand, and by Rank and its aligned distributors on the other, there is effective control of some 60 per cent of the film exhibition market and a still greater share of the film distribution market in Great Britain [the 1983 report, paragraph 8.17].

4.28. The industry has evolved further since 1983. While a small number of film distributors continue to be the main suppliers of films, their identity has changed with the dissolution of certain joint ventures and the creation of separate distribution companies (see paragraph 4.53). The effects of these changes, together with the impact of new entrants, is reflected in the somewhat lower concentration figures found during this inquiry. The five leading distributors now account for about 77 per cent of rental payments from cinemas (see paragraph 4.60). On the exhibition side, the rapid growth of operators of multiplex cinemas in the mid- to late 1980s has been a strikingly important development (see paragraphs 4.101 to 4.107).

4.29. We now identify the main companies currently operating in the UK market, first the distributors and then the exhibitors. Later in this chapter we deal with vertical integration and the links between companies in the industry (see paragraphs 4.143 to 4.158).

### *Film distributors*

4.30. There are two broad types of distributor supplying films to cinemas in the UK. First, there are the five distributors who are vertically linked to Hollywood-based studios. These distributors, Buena Vista, Columbia, Fox, UIP and Warner Distributors, are each primarily sales and marketing entities responsible for the theatrical distribution in the UK of films that have been made or acquired by their parent companies. A brief outline of the ownership, history and main recent films of these five distributors is given in Appendix 4.1. We refer to these five distributors, for convenience, as the 'leading distributors'. We refer to all the other distributors in the UK as the 'independent distributors' or the 'independents'.

4.31. There are currently about 24 independent distributors active in the UK. They trade on their own account. While some of the independents aim to acquire the UK distribution rights for mainstream films (and may find themselves in direct competition with the leading distributors for some of these titles), many specialize in acquiring the rights to arthouse films. One independent distributor, Guild, alone accounted for half of the receipts of all the independent distributors in the UK in 1992. There were seven independents who distributed ten or more new titles in that year: Guild, RFD, Entertainment, Mayfair Entertainment UK Ltd (Mayfair), Electric Pictures, Artificial Eye Film Co (Artificial Eye) and Metro Tartan Ltd. We regard RFD as an independent distributor, although its parent company, Rank, owns Pinewood Studios Limited (Pinewood) and has a half share in Universal Studios in Florida, as well as owning Odeon. Neither Pinewood nor Universal Studios produces films, both being providers of studio facilities to production companies. All the independents named in this paragraph, except Guild and Entertainment, have interests in cinema exhibition in the UK.

*Film exhibitors*

4.32. There are now five main exhibitors in the UK (compared with the four identified by the MMC in 1983). They are: MGM Cinemas, Odeon, UCI, Natl Amusements and the two affiliated companies Warner Bros Theatres Limited (operating the Warner West End cinema) and Warner Bros Theatres (UK) Limited (operating a chain of multiplex cinemas). We refer to these last two companies jointly as Warner Theatres, unless there is a specific need to distinguish them. UCI[1] and Natl Amusements, together with Warner Theatres' multiplex cinemas, have entered the UK market since the MMC last reported. We refer to these five exhibitors as the 'leading exhibitors' (where appropriate, MGM Cinemas and Odeon are also referred to as the two 'main circuit exhibitors'). We refer to all other exhibitors as 'independent exhibitors'. A brief outline of the ownership and recent history of each the leading exhibitors is set out in Appendix 4.1, and a description of the links between some of these leading exhibitors and some of the leading distributors is given in paragraphs 4.147 to 4.158.

4.33. Some of the independent exhibitors operate several cinemas each within a region of the UK, but do not have national coverage. The largest of these exhibitors is Hutchinson Leisure Group of Companies Ltd, a subsidiary of Apollo Leisure (UK) Limited (Apollo), which operates mostly in North-West England, North Wales, the Midlands and Yorkshire. Others include Robins Cinemas Ltd (Robins) which operates a number of cinemas in various parts of Great Britain, CAC Leisure Limited (whose cinemas are known as Caledonian Cinemas) operating in Scotland, the Ward Anderson group of cinemas operating in Northern Ireland (and is a leading exhibitor in the Irish Republic), Charles Scott Cinemas operating in the West of England, Cinema Ltd (which also owns Artificial Eye) operating in London, Bloom Theatres Limited (trading as Mainline Pictures) operating in London and the South-East, and Oasis Cinemas Ltd operating in London and Edinburgh. Most of the other independent exhibitors operate one or two single- or twin-screen cinemas.

4.34. There are around 750 commercial cinemas in the UK, some of which are only part-time. Of the 750 cinemas, almost half are single-screen cinemas and a further third are two- or three-screen cinemas. The rest (about one-fifth) are cinemas with more than three screens (see also paragraphs 4.90 and 4.91).

# Film production

4.35. Feature films, in both their financing and production, fall broadly into one of two categories, international or local. International films are intended to have strong commercial potential, can be made in any of several countries, generally have an internationally acceptable theme or style, and are made with a view to distribution in many countries. Local films tend to reflect national themes, customs and preoccupations. They are usually made in the local language and in the country where they are to be exhibited. As a generalization, most international films are made in English, while the second category includes mostly films made in other languages. English language films produced specifically for the UK market will be at a significant disadvantage (eg in the amount that can be spent on their production) compared with those produced with a world-wide audience in mind.

4.36. A feature film is the product of three basic specialist activities: the producer's talents in making a film from an outline or an idea; the financier's talents in identifying promising film proposals and supporting the film-maker; and the film distributor's talents in developing a marketing and distribution plan aimed at maximizing the film's revenues. While the production of a feature film

---

[1]UCI also manages two cinemas in the West End of London which are owned by CIC. Unless otherwise indicated, we have included data (eg on box office and film rental payments) relating to these two CIC-owned cinemas as part of UCI's data.

requires a script, budget, casting, production crew, and plans or arrangements for the distribution and marketing of the film when it has been finished, none of this can be put in place without the film producer having first secured the necessary financial backing.

4.37. As was noted in paragraph 4.12, investment in film production is very risky, and the return unpredictable. The production of films can be very expensive: the average cost of films made by the US Hollywood studios reached almost $30 million (or about £20 million) in 1993, about two and a half times (in nominal terms) the cost ten years earlier (see also paragraph 4.42). The production budgets for some US films have recently exceeded $60 million. *Screen Digest* recently published (see paragraph 4.10) estimates showing that of the US studios' total world-wide revenues from feature films in 1993, 59 per cent came from the US domestic market and 41 per cent came from sales outside the USA (the figures for theatrical rental only were 55 per cent from the US market and 45 per cent from the rest of the world). The average expenditure per film on promotion and advertising is now a further $14 million in the USA alone (approaching three times the level of ten years ago). While there is no guarantee that the more spent on making and marketing a film the more successful that film will be at the box office, low-budget films do not normally include the best-known film stars, expensive special effects, sets or costumes, and such films rarely achieve the biggest successes at the box office.

## Financing of films

4.38. Most films made by the Hollywood studios are internally funded. Profits from the distribution of their successful films, after meeting the losses on unsuccessful ones, are used to finance new productions. Even the major studios, however, often need outside financial backing for their particularly expensive productions, as do other film production companies for most of their films. The main sources of non-studio finance are: pre-production advances from theatrical and video film distributors; financial guarantees from sales agents against the value of overseas sales; television broadcasters, including the growing number of pay-television companies; banks, financial markets and other arm's length investors; and grants from governments and other public bodies.

4.39. More than one source is normally needed to finance an independently-produced film, ie a film made by a producer outside the Hollywood studios. Part of the challenge facing such independent producers is the cultivation of, and drawing upon, the various sources of finance, and determining the right combination needed in a particular case.

## Production of films in the UK

4.40. As so many different contributions (finance, script development, production, direction, casting, locations, etc) go into the production of each feature film, it is often difficult to classify them into countries of origin. For the purposes of this inquiry we considered it sufficient to use two broad definitions: one concerned with the production of the film (eg 'British-made', by which we mean any feature film which was produced or co-produced by a UK production company or which was made in the UK by an overseas producer), and the other indicating the country which was the prime source of the ideas or cultural values portrayed in the film (eg 'British film'). Neither definition is watertight.

4.41. The number of British-made films produced annually (whether intended for the cinema or for television) has fluctuated since 1980, being as low as 24 in 1981, and as high as 60 in 1990 and 67 in 1993 (of which 35 were co-productions and eight were US films). In relation to other EC countries, the rate of production of British-made films has been about the same as in Spain, and a little lower than in Germany. France (155 films in 1992) and Italy (127 films in 1992) are the major film-producing countries in the EC. Research published recently in *European FilmFile*[1] showed that, at the end of 1993, 2,745 feature film projects were in progress in 34 different European countries, of which 553 (20 per cent) were in the UK. However, of the 2,745 films only 646 (24 per cent) were

---

[1]*European FilmFile*, Volume 3, Winter 1993-4.

already in production or at a later stage: the others (including 493 in the UK) were planned, in development or on hold.

4.42. The BFI estimates that the average budget for British-made films has declined substantially in real terms since 1983. In 1992 it was £3.9 million compared with £8.2 million (at 1992 prices) in 1983. We were told by Channel 4 that both it and British Screen routinely looked at film proposals which had average budgets of £1.25 to £1.5 million. The average budget for French films in 1992 was £3.25 million and in Italy it was £1.85 million. Commenting on these figures, the BFI's *Film and Television Handbook 1994* notes (page 20) that 'unlike the UK, neither France nor Italy is fishing in the same talent pool as Hollywood'.

## Difficulties facing film production in the UK

4.43. We received a number of submissions drawing our attention to the apparent paradox that the film industry in the UK is at the same time both successful and, at least in the view of some, in decline. In particular, it was noted that while over the last eight or so years annual cinema audiences have been growing quickly and British films have continued to win more than their share of international awards, investment in film production in the UK has declined sharply; according to BFI estimates, in 1984 investment in British-made films (as defined in paragraph 4.40) amounted to about £426 million (at 1992 prices), but by 1992 the figure had dropped to about £185 million.

4.44. Many of the requirements for film production are present in the UK. These include ideas for plots, script writers, actors, directors, producers, various types of production talent (eg set design, photographers, special effects experts, etc), studio facilities and expertise in finding outdoor locations. Skills in the British film industry are widely acclaimed around the world.

4.45. We noted, too, that film studios in the UK are fully occupied at present, with a lot of interest being shown for 1995. Pinewood told us that the general level of film production there was higher now than it had been for some time. Pinewood noted particularly that a number of high-budget US films were using its studios in 1994. It hoped that this indicated an increasing willingness of US film producers to use UK facilities. Similarly, Shepperton Studios told us that there had been a tremendous upsurge in film production in the UK in late 1993 and early 1994, resulting in a shortage of stage facilities, and that it expected this momentum to continue into 1995.

4.46. One of the main problems facing the producers of British films is the spreading of risk. This means not just the spreading of risks across many different films, only a minority of which will be financially successful, but also the spreading of the risk between the production, distribution and exhibition sectors (bearing in mind, too, the prospects of revenues from the video and television markets). Film production in the UK has been very fragmented, with many British films being made by companies formed specially for the purpose of making a single film even if those financing it may be associated with other films. It has therefore generally not been possible for individual production companies to offset the failures of some films by the successes of others. The BFI told us that in the ten years to 1989, 464 feature films were made by 352 production companies, and that 250 of these companies existed to produce only one film (see also paragraph 6.97).

4.47. Television broadcasters, particularly the BBC and Channel 4, have been an important source of finance for British film production in the last ten years or so. A few films financed partly from this source have achieved international success in the cinema, for example *Four Weddings and a Funeral*, *Much Ado about Nothing*, *Peter's Friends*, *The Crying Game*, *Howard's End*, *Letter to Brezhnev* and *A Room with a View*. But some in the industry take the view that reliance on this source of finance may distance the film producer from the cinema audience (eg see the evidence of Mr Puttnam in paragraphs 6.78, 6.79 and 6.82). Television broadcasters may also impose restrictions, in return for their financial support, which adversely affect the film's opportunities for theatrical exhibition in the UK. On the other hand, when acting solely as purchasers of completed films, television companies are important sources of additional revenue. Both RFD and Entertainment drew our attention to the advantage which, they considered, was enjoyed by the Hollywood studios as a result of their output deals with BSkyB. BSkyB has recently entered into output deals with British Screen, PolyGram and Guild and is discussing similar deals with other British distributors. BSkyB told us that its deals with

British film-makers brought them benefits that were unique in Europe, guaranteeing as they did nearly 9 per cent of production budgets, and involving no content requirements, no credits, and no distortion of release patterns.

4.48. The amounts available from UK government sources are relatively low compared with a number of other countries (eg France, Germany and Australia). See also the account given in Chapter 3 of the main sources of UK and EC support for film production in the EC. Banks and private financiers seem unwilling to commit significant sums to the high-risk business of film production in the UK. Reasons that have been put forward for this attitude include the experience of past losses made by UK production companies (notably EMI Films Ltd and Rank).

4.49. Other important factors affecting the financing of film production in the UK are exchange rates and taxation. Relative changes in exchange rates over time will affect the costs of film production in the UK compared with other countries: changes in the sterling/dollar exchange rate are, for example, thought to have contributed to the increase in the number of films currently being produced in the UK. Two aspects of the tax regime in the UK have been alleged to cause difficulties for film production. The first concerns tax relief for expenditure on film production and for new investment in film production facilities, and the second concerns the treatment of income tax (and in particular, bilateral and other taxation agreements between different countries). Taxation issues are summarized in Appendix 4.2.

4.50. We received extensive submissions about the difficulties faced by UK film producers from the BFI, PACT and others. These are summarized in Chapter 6.

## Access to distribution

4.51. Unless a production company decides to set up its own distribution operation (a subject which is dealt with in the next section), it must look to either the leading distributors or to independent distributors to handle the film's distribution and marketing in the UK. The leading distributors told us that their primary purpose was to distribute the films of their parent studios. However, some said that they did acquire independently-made films, usually made by independent producers in the USA, but sometimes made by those in other countries, including the UK. The business of independent distributors depends largely on the acquisition of the distribution rights for films made by independent production companies.

# Film distribution

## Main changes in film distribution since 1983

4.52. While there have been a number of new entrants into this industry over the years, as well as distributors leaving it, the general picture, at least since the early 1960s, is one of the continuing importance of a limited number of distributors, albeit in a variety of combinations. In their 1983 report, the MMC noted that the leading six distributors were Columbia-EMI-Warner Distributors Ltd, UIP, UK Film Distributors Ltd, RFD, ITC Film Distributors Ltd, and Brent Walker Distributors Ltd. The first four of these were direct descendants of the ten companies which the MMC found in 1966 to supply practically all first feature films, and the first three are still the main distributors now, although their corporate identities have undergone further change.

4.53. Two of the joint ventures functioning in 1983, Columbia-EMI-Warner and UK Film Distributors, have broken up and each individual member is now responsible for the distribution of its own product or that of its parent company. Columbia-EMI-Warner (which became Columbia-Cannon-Warner following Cannon's acquisition of the EMI film business in 1986) split in November 1987 into two new distribution companies, Columbia and Warner Distributors. Cannon, by then owned by Pathé Communications Corporation, acquired MGM Inc in 1990. UK Film Distributors, which was jointly formed by 20th Century Fox and Walt Disney to distribute the films of both companies in the

UK, ceased to trade in December 1987. 20th Century Fox then established its own distribution company. Between 1988 and 1992 Walt Disney films were distributed in the UK by Warner Distributors, but the distribution agreements were terminated and Buena Vista began to distribute Walt Disney films in the UK from November 1992.

4.54. Several of the smaller film distributors that were in business at the time of the last MMC report have now ceased trading (eg New Realm, Golden Era, Miracle Films and Sunn Classic). Some of the independent distributors who began distributing films to cinemas after 1983 did not continue in business for very long (eg Palace Pictures, Virgin Vision, Anglo American and Castle Target).

4.55. Two companies which were primarily concerned with video have expanded their interest in the distribution of films for theatrical release: Guild and Entertainment have both emerged since the late 1980s to become significant competitors in the market for theatrical film distribution. Some of today's larger independent distributors have expanded through acquisition. Mayfair acquired both Curzon and Hobo, and in May 1994 announced the merger of its distribution interests with those of Artificial Eye. HTV Group plc acquired Miracle Films and Vestron Film and Video Distribution Ltd and formed them into First Independent in 1990.

## Size of market and growth trends

4.56. We measured the size of the distribution market by reference to receipts by distributors of film rentals over the four-year period 1990 to 1993. This information is shown in Table 4.2, together with figures for 1988 and 1989. The distributors are listed there in the order of their market shares in 1993. The distributors in Table 4.2 are split into three groups: the five leading distributors; the four largest independent distributors; and the remaining independents.

4.57. The film distribution market in 1993 was worth a little over £103 million (see Table 4.2). In nominal terms, this is almost double the figure for 1988. Growth in the market has been irregular because of the varying fortunes of individual films from year to year and the effects of recession on the economy more generally. The most important factor in bringing about the growth in the size of the market has been the growth of cinema attendances during this period: attendances increased by about one-third from 1988 to 1993.

4.58. This increase in the size of the market was not reflected in the number of films released for exhibition. Table 4.3 shows the number of new feature films on general release each year in the UK. This fell from 360 in 1970 to 219 in 1980, and (except for one year) varied from 215 to 256 a year subsequently. While the number of releases increased between 1986 and 1989 from 215 to 241, it dropped back in 1991 to 216 before rising again to 242 in 1993.

TABLE 4.2 Distributors' rental receipts (excluding VAT) from the licensing of films for exhibition in cinemas in the UK in each of the calendar years 1988 to 1993

| Distributor | 1988 £m | 1988 % | 1989 £m | 1989 % | 1990 £m | 1990 % | 1991 £m | 1991 % | 1992 £m | 1992 % | 1993 £m | 1993 % | 1990 to 1993 £m | 1990 to 1993 % |
|---|---|---|---|---|---|---|---|---|---|---|---|---|---|---|
| *Leading distributors* | | | | | | | | | | | | | | |
| UIP | 22.8 | 39.2 | 29.5 | 36.7 | 25.5 | 30.9 | 15.2 | 17.9 | 16.2 | 18.9 | 32.0 | 30.9 | 88.9 | 24.9 |
| Warner Distributors | 17.6 | 30.2 | 28.4 | 35.3 | 25.9 | 31.4 | 21.9 | 25.7 | 27.9 | 32.5 | 23.2 | 22.4 | 98.9 | 27.7 |
| of which*: Warner Bros films | 6.6 | 11.3 | 15.0 | 18.7 | 11.7 | 14.2 | 10.1 | 11.9 | 16.2 | 18.9 | 22.7 | 22.0 | 60.7 | 17.0 |
| Walt Disney films | 11.0 | 18.9 | 13.4 | 16.7 | 14.2 | 17.2 | 11.8 | 13.9 | 11.7 | 13.6 | 0.5 | 0.5 | 38.2 | 10.7 |
| Columbia | 3.9 | 6.7 | 7.0 | 8.7 | 6.6 | 8.0 | 6.7 | 7.9 | 14.4 | 16.8 | 15.0 | 14.5 | 42.8 | 12.0 |
| Buena Vista | - | - | - | - | - | - | - | - | 1.9 | 2.2 | 11.8 | 11.4 | 13.7 | 3.8 |
| Fox | 3.2 | 5.5 | 3.1 | 3.9 | 5.7 | 6.9 | 11.7 | 13.7 | 7.9 | 9.2 | 4.0 | 3.9 | 29.3 | 8.2 |
| **Sub-total: leading distributors** | **47.5** | **81.6** | **68.0** | **84.6** | **63.7** | **77.1** | **55.5** | **65.2** | **68.3** | **79.5** | **86.0** | **83.2** | **273.6** | **76.6** |
| *Main independent distributors* | | | | | | | | | | | | | | |
| Guild | 0.3 | 0.5 | 0.6 | 0.7 | 3.9 | 4.7 | 12.2 | 14.3 | 8.6 | 10.0 | 5.1 | 4.9 | 29.8 | 8.3 |
| Entertainment | 0.7 | 1.2 | 0.3 | 0.4 | 0.9 | 1.1 | 1.6 | 1.9 | 1.5 | 1.7 | 4.9 | 4.7 | 8.9 | 2.5 |
| RFD | 2.4 | 4.1 | 3.1 | 3.9 | 3.3 | 4.0 | 9.1 | 10.7 | 2.1 | 2.4 | 2.2 | 2.1 | 16.7 | 4.7 |
| Vestron | 0.9 | 1.5 | 0.8 | 1.0 | - | - | - | - | - | - | - | - | - | - |
| First Independent | - | - | - | - | 0.1 | 0.1 | 2.1 | 2.5 | 1.5 | 1.7 | 0.8 | 0.8 | 4.5 | 1.3 |
| **Sub-total: main independents** | **4.3** | **7.4** | **4.8** | **6.0** | **8.2** | **9.9** | **25.0** | **29.4** | **13.7** | **15.9** | **13.0** | **12.6** | **59.9** | **16.8** |
| Total: above listed distributors | 51.8 | 89.0 | 72.8 | 90.5 | 71.9 | 87.0 | 80.5 | 94.6 | 82.0 | 95.5 | 99.0 | 95.7 | 333.5 | 93.4 |
| *Other independent distributors* | | | | | | | | | | | | | | |
| **Sub-total: other independents†** | **6.4** | **11.0** | **7.6** | **9.5** | **10.7** | **13.0** | **4.6** | **5.4** | **3.9** | **4.5** | **4.4** | **4.3** | **23.6** | **6.6** |
| Total: all independents† | 10.7 | 18.4 | 12.4 | 15.4 | 18.9 | 22.9 | 29.6 | 34.8 | 17.6 | 20.5 | 17.4 | 16.8 | 83.5 | 23.4 |
| **Total: all distributors†** | **58.2** | **100.0** | **80.4** | **100.0** | **82.6** | **100.0** | **85.1** | **100.0** | **85.9** | **100.0** | **103.4** | **100.0** | **357.1** | **100.0** |

*Source:* MMC, based on data from the companies, the SFD and Entertainment Data International Ltd.

*Approximate breakdown of Warner Distributors' rental income according to its two main sources of supply during the period up to November 1992.
†Estimated.

TABLE 4.3  **Number of new feature films released for general exhibition in cinemas in the UK**

| Year | Number of films | Proportion of films released which were: | | |
|---|---|---|---|---|
| | | US films % | British films % | Other films % |
| 1955 | 350 | 57 | 23 | 19 |
| 1960 | 333 | 43 | 24 | 34 |
| 1965 | 302 | 36 | 23 | 41 |
| 1970 | 360 | 34 | 24 | 42 |
| 1975 | 282 | 46 | 25 | 29 |
| 1980 | 219 | 56 | 19 | 26 |
| 1981 | 225 | 60 | 14 | 26 |
| 1982 | 293 | 48 | 18 | 35 |
| 1983 | 226 | 48 | 15 | 38 |
| 1984 | 245 | 60 | 11 | 29 |
| 1985 | 256 | 52 | 15 | 33 |
| 1986 | 215 | 57 | 14 | 29 |
| 1987 | 216 | 57 | 20 | 23 |
| 1988 | 237 | 60 | 12 | 28 |
| 1989 | 241 | 55 | 21 | 24 |
| 1990 | 240 | 66 | 10 | 23 |
| 1991 | 216 | 72 | 11 | 17 |
| 1992 | 222 | 56 | 14 | 29 |
| 1993* | 242 | 61 | 10 | 29 |

*Sources:* 1955/81: MMC's 1983 report on the supply of films (Table 2.1).
1982/93: BFI.

*Provisional figures.
*Note:* The BFI told us that the number of films shown for each year in Table 4.3 refers to films of 40 or more minutes in length distributed for the first time. The figures exclude re-releases, films which had only a short run at one cinema (eg some films shown at the National Film Theatre and the Institute of Contemporary Arts in London and at RFTs), and all films made on 16mm film. The BFI regards this definition of films, a narrower one than that used to compile the BFI data mentioned in paragraphs 4.5 and 4.6, as presenting a truer picture of theatrical films distribution in the UK for the purposes of the MMC's inquiry.

## Distributors' market shares

4.59. Distributors' rental income in any one year may be heavily influenced by the success or failure of a small number of films. We have therefore assessed their market shares on the basis of rental receipts over four years, selecting the period 1990 to 1993. Table 4.2 shows that over this period UIP received 24.9 per cent of distributors' total rentals from the licensing of films for exhibition in cinemas in the UK. Over the same period Warner Distributors received 27.7 per cent of distributors' total rentals, but within this figure 10.7 per cent was generated by Walt Disney films, which Warner Distributors no longer handles.

4.60. The next largest distributors during this period were Columbia (12.0 per cent) and Fox (8.2 per cent). The five leading distributors accounted for about 77 per cent of rental revenues, and the seven largest distributors (the leading distributors together with Guild and RFD) a little under 90 per cent. The share held by the leading distributors declined from about 85 per cent in 1989 to 65 per cent by 1991, but has since risen to 83 per cent. The decline in 1990 and 1991 was due largely to the growth in the rental income achieved by Guild and RFD. These two companies have had less success in subsequent years, but Entertainment's share grew in 1993.

4.61. In 1993 the five leading distributors accounted for only about 35 per cent of the new titles released in the UK (see Table 4.4). In contrast, while the independent distributors accounted for about 65 per cent of the new titles released in 1993, they only earned about 17 per cent of the rentals in that year. This pattern is not unusual: as the BFI has pointed out,[1] a few blockbuster films account for most of the box office and rental figures each year.

---

[1] See the BFI's *Film and Television Handbook 1994*, pages 37 and 42.

TABLE 4.4 **Distributors' shares of films released in the UK and measured by number of titles, box office revenues and rental receipts, 1993**

| Distributor | Number of titles in 1993 | Percentage of all titles | Percentage of box office revenues | Percentage of rental receipts |
|---|---|---|---|---|
| *Leading distributors* | | | | |
| UIP | 26 | 10.7 | 25.6 | 30.9 |
| Warner Distributors | 20 | 8.3 | 23.3 | 22.4 |
| Columbia | 13 | 5.4 | 16.7 | 14.5 |
| Buena Vista | 18 | 7.4 | 12.2 | 11.4 |
| Fox | 8 | 3.3 | 4.5 | 3.9 |
| Sub-total: leading distributors | 85 | 35.1 | 82.3 | 83.2 |
| *Other distributors* | | | | |
| Sub-total: other distributors | 157 | 64.9 | 17.7 | 16.8 |
| Total | 242 | 100.0 | 100.0 | 100.0 |

*Source:* MMC and the BFI.

# Activities of film distributors in the UK

## Functions of the distributors

4.62. The leading distributors' main role is to organize the successful theatrical distribution of their parent companies' films in the UK. All the leading distributors told us that they also distributed (to varying degrees) independently-produced films (though Columbia and Fox have distributed very few in recent years). The leading distributors' arrangements for acquiring the UK distribution rights are described in Appendix 5.1. All the leading distributors distribute films in the UK only for theatrical exhibition: the video and television rights for these films in the UK are handled by other, associated, companies.

4.63. Independent distributors have to acquire distribution rights on an arm's length basis in competition with other distributors. They largely acquire distribution rights for films made by independent production companies, and normally seek these rights for all the UK film markets, including video and television (they may have to compete to acquire all a film's rights outside the USA, and sometimes for the US rights as well). They are also likely to be involved in a variety of co-financing and other deals with independent production companies. Some independent distributors (notably Guild, RFD, Entertainment and First Independent) aim to acquire the distribution rights for mainstream commercial films, and may have to compete with the leading distributors in so doing. Other independent distributors in the UK concentrate on arthouse films and largely compete amongst themselves, although we were told that the leading distributors were taking an increasing interest in acquiring rights to the more commercial arthouse films, ie the potential 'cross-overs'. As is shown in Appendix 4.1, a number of successful British films have been distributed by independent distributors in recent years.

## Aspects of competition between distributors

4.64. There is significant competition between individual films for access to screens and for audiences. Information about likely release dates is known widely in the industry many months in advance. This enables distributors to try to plan their own release dates so as to avoid direct clashes with competing films of the same type. The marketing plan and release patterns for new feature films are determined on a film-by-film basis by their distributors. The following considerations are taken into account: the type of film and its potential audience; other films likely to be released around the same time by the same or other distributors; the number of cinemas available and willing to take the film; the budget available to support the release; and the success of the same film in other countries, particularly the USA.

4.65. The basic release patterns widely used in the industry are:

— *mass release*: 250 to 400 prints released simultaneously to take advantage of a concentrated national media campaign;

— *wide release*: for films with popular appeal, based on 150 to 250 prints directed to certain geographic areas;

— *limited release*: using 75 to 150 prints for cinemas in densely-populated areas; and

— *selected release*: usually three to five prints for specially selected venues known to have audiences interested in less popular or specialized films.

Other forms of release may also be chosen but are less common. For example: a *staggered release*, which is based on word of mouth response in large conurbations helping to establish a film thought to have a difficult message to convey but with good commercial potential nevertheless; and a *platform release*, whereby a film is released at one or a very limited number of cinemas in London's West End before it is given a wider release elsewhere in the country.

4.66. Advertising and promotional activities are a major feature of competition between distributors, and appear now to be more important in determining the commercial success of a new release than at the time of the MMC's 1983 report (see also paragraph 5.24). Advertising and promoting films encompasses a wide range of activities including in-cinema marketing (especially 'trailers', and point-of-sale promotions), advertisements on television and radio, poster advertising and also interviews with actors, directors and producers. Music from films is sometimes released simultaneously on CDs and cassettes. Merchandising agreements may also be made, eg with clothing companies or fast-food retailers.

4.67. Distributors told us that the revival in cinema-going in the late 1980s resulted partly from their increased advertising and promotional activities. The revival, together with the potential benefits from the exploitation of ancillary rights, made it possible in turn to spend more heavily on advertising and promotional activities than when theatrical attendances had been declining. In contrast to the phased releases which were quite common at the time of the last MMC report, distributors increasingly favour releasing a film simultaneously across the UK in order to maximize the impact of national marketing campaigns. These now often incorporate advertisements on television, which, we were told, were usually placed country-wide.

4.68. Films themselves are potent marketing tools, in that virtually all the creative material used in any promotional campaign will be derived from them. The results of the latest CAVIAR survey (CAVIAR 11, February 1994[1]) show that, while people hear or read about films from several sources, the most frequently mentioned sources are television (33 per cent television advertisements, and 30 per cent television editorial comment, eg in various film review programmes), and word of mouth (29 per cent of visits). Other sources frequently quoted are national newspapers (24 per cent), posters and cinema trailers (17 per cent and 16 per cent), and the radio (10 per cent for both radio advertising and editorial). As these figures indicate, many of the respondents quoted more than one source.

4.69. Price competition between distributors does not appear to be significant because the methods used by the great majority of exhibitors to calculate rental payments for films have the effect of automatically increasing the rentals for films that perform well at the box office. In particular, distributors do not normally offer exhibitors (though occasionally exhibitors may seek) more favourable rental terms for showing particular films which have low or uncertain expectations. They may, however, seek to obtain special terms for films with particularly strong commercial potential.

---

[1]The Cinema and Video Industry Audience Research (CAVIAR) survey of cinema audiences is undertaken late each autumn on behalf of the Cinema Advertising Association Ltd (CAA). CAVIAR 11 reported the results of the survey undertaken by BMRB International between 19 October and 22 November 1993.

*Decisions on which films to distribute in the UK*

4.70. All the leading distributors told us that, in deciding which films to distribute, they relied on their assessment of the commercial prospects for each film. As already mentioned, the leading distributors largely concentrate on distributing films produced or acquired by their parent companies (see paragraph 4.62). Independent distributors search intensely for the distribution rights to independently-produced films.

4.71. UIP said that its policy was to seek a broad range of films, and that it would consider and, on occasions, seek to obtain films which it considered had limited or specialist appeal. It emphasized that it applied the same tests to its partners' films as it did to those of third parties when assessing their commercial viability, and that it might, after viewing a partner's new film, advise the partner that it did not consider theatrical distribution advisable in the UK. UIP told us that its partners frequently picked up independent films, 162 of them over the last six years. Between 1988 and 1992 UIP had distributed six films in the UK which had been produced in the UK by third parties, and a seventh, *Shadowlands*, was distributed early in 1994. These third party films generated, on average, 1 per cent of UIP's annual rental receipts.

4.72. Warner Distributors said that between 1988 and 1993 it handled 14 independent films, the rights to which had been acquired by Warner Bros International. Warner Distributors explained to us that Warner Bros International had the final say as to which Warner Bros films it released in the UK, and that occasionally Warner Bros International had decided (for its own reasons) to release a film in the UK which Warner Distributors did not consider to be commercially viable.

4.73. Columbia told us that, while it was not a primary part of its business to distribute films produced by third parties, it was not subject to any legal or internal constraints preventing it from distributing such films. In recent years it had not received many commercially attractive proposals to distribute the films of independent producers. In Columbia's view, this was because of the existence of strong independent distributors such as Guild, First Independent and Entertainment, whose principal source of supply was independent producers. Fox listed 35 independent films which it distributed between 1988 and 1993, but only one of these was acquired after 1989.

*Distributors' trade associations*

4.74. The SFD is the main trade association representing film distributors in the UK. There are currently 11 members, including all the leading distributors and the larger independents (see paragraph 6.39). Most of the smaller film distributors are not members of the SFD, but it told us that there were no restrictions which prevented them joining should they wish to. We also heard from the Independent Film Distributors' Association, formed in the early 1970s, which now loosely represents a few independent distributors (eg Artificial Eye, Contemporary Films, Electric Pictures and Mainline Pictures).

4.75. The SFD told us that its prime purposes were to provide a forum and focus for the discussion of matters of common interest to those engaged in film distribution in the UK and, where appropriate, to act as a voice in relation to the common interests of its members. The SFD did not, it said, play any role in the day-to-day business of its members (other than to the extent that they used its published *Standard Conditions*—see next paragraph), nor did it speak for any of its members on policy matters, eg decisions on the release of films or the revenue-sharing terms negotiated between distributors and exhibitors. The SFD's governing body is its Council, which comprises the managing directors of its member companies and is chaired by the SFD's President. The SFD's two main committees are its Publicity Directors' Committee and its Sales Managers' Committee. It also has an Irregularities Committee which comprises the managing directors of its member companies. This meets as required to consider reports of malpractice at cinemas revealed through checks made on the SFD's behalf by an outside agency. During the course of this inquiry we examined the minutes of all the SFD's committee meetings which took place during 1993.

4.76. The SFD has issued *Standard Conditions* which contain terms and conditions for the licensing and exhibition of films in cinemas in the UK. The *Standard Conditions* are reproduced in full in

Appendix 4.3. We were told by the SFD that its members were free to vary the *Standard Conditions* or not to use them at all. In practice, however, all the members use the *Standard Conditions* as the basis for licence agreements with exhibitors (see also paragraphs 4.131 to 4.134).

## Prospects for new entry

4.77. The two main factors affecting access to film distribution rights in the UK are the extent to which such rights are freely traded (ie are available to whichever distributor offers the most attractive deal to the original copyright holder), and the size and timing of the financial commitment required of the distributor, notably the expenditure on prints and trailers, on advertising and promotion, and the amount and terms offered for the UK distribution rights.

4.78. With few exceptions, new entrants are not able to obtain the UK distribution rights for films produced by the Hollywood studios, because most of these mainstream films are distributed by companies which have vertical links with those studios. Some independent distributors have, however, achieved significant success in the UK, usually by distributing independently-produced US films (eg Guild, which has a relationship with Carolco whereby all its theatrical productions are released in the UK by Guild).

4.79. The acquisition of film rights from independent production companies can entail quite complicated financial deals which bring together several different interested parties. RFD explained the various means by which it had invested in US film production in return for distribution rights outside North America. The types of deals RFD has entered into include co-financing deals with US producers and distributors for the joint financing of a series of films, purchase deals by which RFD acquires the rights to a single film in a specific territory, output deals whereby RFD agrees to distribute all films made or acquired by the licensor either for a specific period or for a specific number of films, and first-look deals by which RFD has first refusal of the chance to invest in and acquire distribution rights for films proposed by particular production companies (these are more fully described in Appendix 5.1, paragraphs 20 to 31). Apart from the amounts which may have to be paid in advance for the distribution rights, distributors must find increasingly large sums for advertising and promoting a film. Experience shows that for most films these costs will not be recovered from theatrical exhibition alone, if at all, so the distributor needs to have sufficient financial resources to spread its risks over a substantial portfolio of films.

4.80. Once a distributor has acquired the rights to a new film, there is still the need to find screen space for it. We were frequently told that there was a shortage of suitable screens, both in number and quality, in certain parts of the UK and at certain times of the year, on which to show newly-released films. This raises the question of ease of entry into exhibition (which is dealt with in paragraphs 4.126 to 4.129). We have also looked at the effects of some of the practices of the leading distributors and exhibitors to see whether they create unnecessary difficulties, eg the negotiation of extended minimum exhibition periods. These practices are discussed in the last section of this chapter. Difficulties in obtaining a suitable theatrical release in the UK may also affect the returns available for the film from the video and television markets.

4.81. The experience of the last ten years suggests that while theatrical distributors can enter and survive in the UK market, consolidation and growth are more difficult. Few independent distributors have shown long-term significant success, and their market shares have fluctuated widely (as indeed have those of the leading distributors—see Table 4.2). There is no strong evidence that over the last ten years the leading distributors serving the UK market have been seriously threatened by new entrants other than in the short term.

# Film exhibition

## Main changes in film exhibition since 1983

4.82. Over the last ten years the exhibition sector has undergone a remarkable revival after many years of decline. Since 1984 admissions, the number of screens, and box office revenues have all increased substantially. During this period the exhibition market has been transformed. The main changes include a number of acquisitions and amalgamations involving existing exhibitors, the closure of many cinemas, the building of new ones and above all the entry into the market by three operators of multiplex cinemas. As a result of these changes the market for film exhibition is less concentrated than it was ten years ago, and the nature of competition is now significantly different.

4.83. In 1993 the two main circuit exhibitors, MGM Cinemas and Odeon, accounted for almost 46 per cent of box office revenues (excluding VAT) from the showing of films in UK cinemas, compared with 60 per cent for EMI and Odeon in 1983. MGM Cinemas has undergone several changes of ownership and has made a number of acquisitions during this period (see Appendix 4.1). The development of multiplex cinemas, which has been such a striking feature of the exhibition sector in the last decade, is discussed in paragraphs 4.101 to 4.107.

## Independent exhibitors

4.84. In July 1994 the five leading exhibitors operated 1,156 screens, some 60 per cent of the total number in the UK. There are a few other exhibitors who individually operate more than ten screens (they are mentioned in paragraph 4.33).

4.85. We sent a short postal questionnaire in early December 1993 to all the other independent exhibitors we could identify in order to obtain some quantitative data and their views on a number of matters relevant to the present inquiry. We received 178 replies, representing an effective response rate of 50 per cent. The responses to this questionnaire are summarized in Appendix 4.4. The questionnaire responses confirmed that most of the independents were operators of one cinema with a single screen. Some of the independent cinemas in rural areas and at university sites receive financial and programming assistance from the BFI (see paragraph 4.2). The survey suggested that total box office receipts of all independent cinemas in 1993 were about £60 million excluding VAT, compared with about £229 million for the leading exhibitors in the same year (see Table 4.7).

4.86. Film programming at the National Film Theatre in London and at the 46 RFTs is carried out by, or with the advice of, the BFI. The BFI also supports some of the RFTs with grants and provides film booking and publicity services to most of them.

## Size of the market

4.87. From a low point of 54 million in 1984, cinema admissions rose to 114.4 million in 1993 (see Figure 4.1). This doubling in the number of admissions in less than ten years reversed a decline which had been a feature of the market since about 1950. The recovery in cinema attendances, up to levels last seen in the mid-1970s, has contrasted with the continuing trend of falling audiences and numbers of screens in much of the rest of Europe, although a number of countries, including France and Germany, saw a significant increase in admissions in 1993.

4.88. Factors which may have led to the increase in cinema admissions in the UK include:

— increased advertising of films, particularly on television and in national newspapers and magazines;

— greater public awareness of films as a result of, for example, the arrival of video cassettes and film channels on pay television;

FIGURE 4.1

**Cinema admissions in the UK, 1980 to 1993**

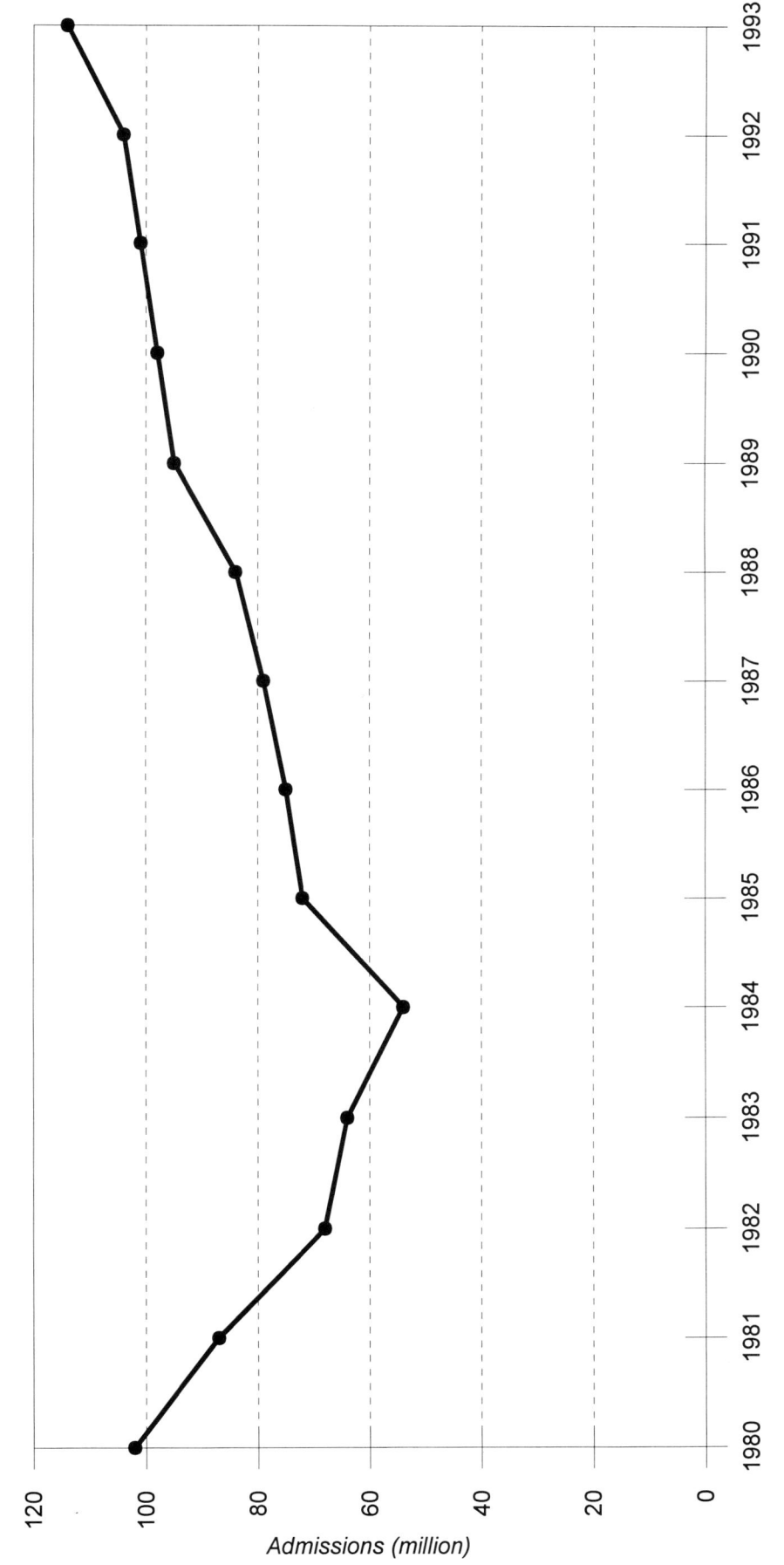

*Source:* MMC based on company data.

— a flow of new films with wide popular appeal, many with large production budgets (encouraged by the better revenue prospects arising from the growth of the ancillary markets) enabling some spectacular visual and sound effects which encourage the public to see the films on the big screen (eg films such as *Crocodile Dundee*, the *Indiana Jones* trilogy and *Jurassic Park*);

— the development of multiplex cinemas, and the refurbishment of many other cinemas; and

— growth in car ownership and the motorway network, which has increased the accessibility of the new out-of-town cinemas.

4.89. Expenditure on cinema admissions in 1992, at 0.07 per cent of household expenditure, has varied only a little in proportionate terms since 1985 (see Table 4.5). Expenditure on television licences and video rentals amounted to about 1.2 per cent of household spending in 1985, but declined to 0.9 per cent by 1992. Expenditure on theatres, sporting events and other forms of entertainment has accounted for a growing proportion of consumer spending over the years, reaching 1.2 per cent by 1992.

TABLE 4.5  **Household expenditure on entertainment in the UK**

*per cent*

|  | 1980 | 1985 | 1990 | 1992 |
|---|---|---|---|---|
| Cinema admissions | 0.11 | 0.06 | 0.07 | 0.07 |
| Television and video rental; television licences | N/A* | 1.18 | 0.85 | 0.88 |
| Theatres, sporting events, and other entertainment | 0.84 | 0.86 | 0.99 | 1.17 |

*Source:* MMC, based on figures published by the Central Statistical Office in *Family Spending*, HMSO, 1993.

*This category was a much wider one in 1980 (including, for example, the purchase and repair of televisions and radios), so the figures are not comparable with those of the later years shown in the table.

4.90. In 1945 there were 4,723 cinema screens in Great Britain in 4,723 cinemas. By July 1994 there were 1,929 screens in 753 cinemas (see Table 4.6). The number of screens reached a low point in 1984 (when there were 1,246 screens at 660 cinemas), and the number of cinemas reached a low point of 648 (but with 1,299 screens) in 1987. About half of all cinemas in the UK have only one screen, and about 85 per cent of cinemas have three or fewer screens.

TABLE 4.6 **Numbers of cinemas and screens in the UK, July 1994**

| Exhibitor | Cinemas | Per cent of total | Screens | Per cent of total | Average number of screens per cinema |
|---|---|---|---|---|---|
| *Leading exhibitors* | | | | | |
| MGM Cinemas (MGM and Cannon cinemas) | 119 | 15.8 | 394 | 20.4 | 3.3 |
| Odeon | 73 | 9.7 | 319 | 16.5 | 4.4 |
| UCI* | 26 | 3.5 | 232 | 12.0 | 8.9 |
| Natl Amusements (Showcase cinemas) | 10 | 1.3 | 127 | 6.6 | 12.7 |
| Warner Theatres | 9 | 1.2 | 84 | 4.4 | 9.3 |
| Sub-total | 237 | 31.5 | 1,156 | 59.9 | 4.9 |
| *Main independent exhibitors* | | | | | |
| Apollo | 19 | 2.5 | 54 | 2.8 | 2.8 |
| Robins | 15 | 2.0 | 30 | 1.5 | 2.0 |
| Ward Anderson group | 12 | 1.6 | 39 | 2.0 | 3.2 |
| CAC Leisure (Caledonian cinemas) | 6 | 0.8 | 13 | 0.7 | 2.1 |
| Charles Scott Cinemas | 6 | 0.8 | 8 | 0.4 | 1.3 |
| Panton Film Distributors (Coronet cinemas) | 5 | 0.7 | 11 | 0.6 | 2.2 |
| Mainline Pictures (Screen cinemas) | 5 | 0.7 | 8 | 0.4 | 1.6 |
| Cinema Ltd | 4 | 0.5 | 5 | 0.3 | 1.2 |
| Graves (Cumberland) Ltd | 4 | 0.5 | 5 | 0.3 | 1.2 |
| Sub-total | 76 | 10.1 | 173 | 9.0 | 2.3 |
| *Small independent exhibitors* | | | | | |
| Sub-total† | 440 | 58.4 | 600 | 31.1 | 1.4 |
| **Total** | **753** | **100.0** | **1,929** | **100.0** | **2.6** |

*Source:* MMC, based on CAA data and questionnaire returns.

*Including the Empire and Plaza Cinemas in London's West End which are managed by UCI.
†Estimate. The figures include an estimated 60 cinemas which do not take on-screen advertising (and thus are not included in CAA data), RFTs and some part-time cinemas.

4.91. The increasing number of cinemas and of cinema screens since the mid-1980s is shown in Figure 4.2. Since 1984 the number of cinema screens in the UK has increased by about 50 per cent. During this same period 638 multiplex screens were opened, and the net change in the number of screens in cinemas other than multiplexes was quite small. In fact, there appears to have been very little change in the number of single-screen cinemas for a number of years, and changes in the number of non-multiplex screens are largely the net result of increases brought about by the splitting of some two- and three-screen cinemas into four- or more screen cinemas, partly offset by the complete closure of others.

4.92. In their 1983 report the MMC showed that there had been a significant fall in the seating capacity of cinemas in Great Britain: between 1970 and 1981 the numbers of seats fell from 1.5 to 0.6 million. Since then seating capacity has fallen a little further, to about 0.5 million by 1993. But as a result of the increase in admissions over this same period capacity utilization, as measured by admissions per seat per week, has increased one and a half times (from about 2.6 in 1981 to about 4.0 by 1993).

4.93. In 1992 the UK had the highest cinema seat capacity utilization rate, at 3.8 admissions per seat per week, of any country in the EC. The next highest figures were for the Irish Republic, Denmark and Belgium (each over 3 admissions per seat per week), and the lowest figures were for Italy, Greece and Spain (each about 1.8 per week), with France at 2.3 per week and Germany 2.8 per week. The EC average was 2.4.

4.94. In relation to its size of population, the UK has one of the lowest numbers of cinema screens in Europe. There are now about 4,400 screens in France, 3,600 in Germany, and 3,000 in Italy, compared with the figure of about 1,929 in the UK. In 1992 the UK had one screen for every 33,000 people, compared with one for every 22,000 in Germany, 19,000 in Italy and 13,000 in France. In terms of numbers of admissions per screen per week, the UK's figure of about 1,134 (for 1992) was higher than any other EC country, including Portugal (978), Spain (887), Belgium (736), Germany (561), Italy (532) and France (506). The EC average was about 650.

FIGURE 4.2

**Numbers of cinemas and cinema screens in the UK,* 1980 to 1993**

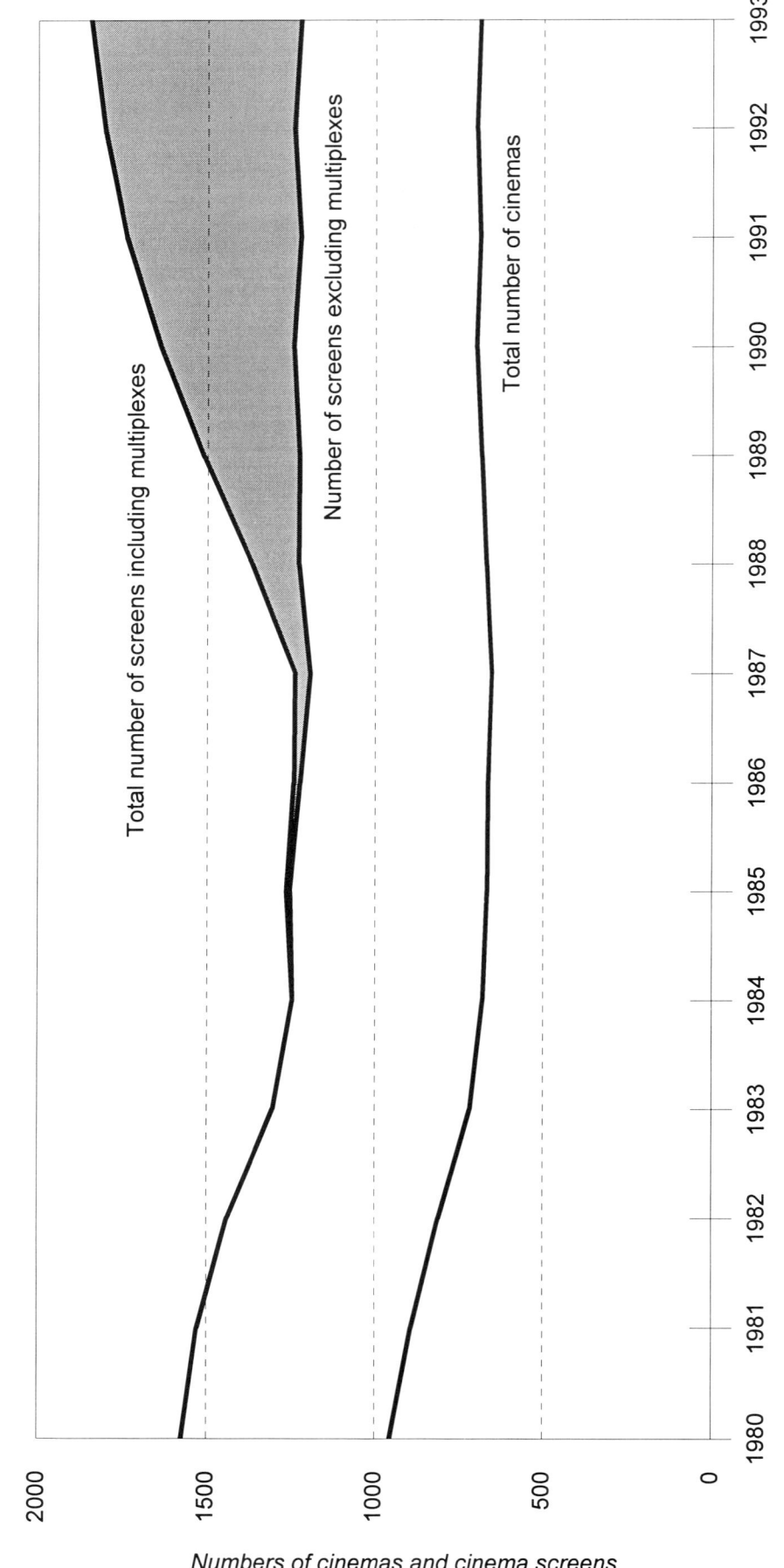

*Source:* CAA.

*Data up to 1984 exclude Northern Ireland.

4.95. There are now about 7 million regular cinema-goers, ie people who claim to visit the cinema at least once a month, in the UK. CAVIAR 11 (see paragraph 4.68) found that cinema-going is at its greatest among young people, particularly those aged 18 and 19 years, of whom about 38 per cent are regular visitors. Of the other younger age groups, about one-third of 12- to 17-year-olds and about 35 per cent of 20- to 24-year-olds are also regular cinema-goers. The level of cinema-going falls rapidly with increasing age: about 11 per cent of those aged 35 to 44 are regular visitors, and of those over 44 years of age only about 3 per cent are regular visitors. There is a seasonal pattern to cinema attendances, influenced mainly by school holidays and by the weather. For example, poor summer weather enhances the appeal of cinema-going compared with outdoor entertainment.

## Exhibitors' market shares

4.96. We measured the size of the exhibition market, using both exhibitors' box office receipts and their film rental payments, over the four-year period 1990 to 1993 although we also looked at figures for 1988 and 1989. The box office figures are given in Table 4.7 and the film rental figures are in Table 4.8 (in both tables the leading exhibitors are listed in order of their market shares in the latest year, 1993). Also included in Tables 4.7 and 4.8 are figures for the independent exhibitors, which we have estimated mostly on the basis of data supplied to us by the leading distributors.

4.97. The exhibition market measured in terms of box office, excluding VAT, was worth about £289 million in 1993 (see Table 4.7). This is almost double, in nominal terms, the figure for 1988. Box office takings, including VAT, in the UK have risen from £136 million in 1984 (including levy) to about £340 million by 1993, with most of this increase being due to inflation and the recovery in admissions (though there has also been some real increase in ticket prices, particularly at multiplex cinemas (see paragraph 4.118)).

4.98. Measured by film rental payments, MGM Cinemas is the largest exhibitor, with an average market share of just under 27 per cent over the four-year period 1990 to 1993 (see Table 4.8). (Although year-to-year fluctuations in exhibition are less than in distribution, for consistency we chose to measure market shares on the same basis for the distribution and the exhibition markets.) The next two largest exhibitors are Odeon (a little under 21 per cent) and UCI (20 per cent). UCI's market share, including the two CIC-owned cinemas in the West End, has grown from almost 12 per cent in 1988 to about 22 per cent by 1993. Between them, the five leading exhibitors accounted for about 78 per cent of film rental payments to distributors over the four-year period. Their share of rentals has been increasing over the years, from just under 70 per cent in 1988 to almost 80 per cent in 1993, thanks to the rapid growth of the three specialist multiplex operators.

4.99. Market shares measured in terms of box office receipts are not in general significantly different from those measured by rental payments. A comparison of the data in Tables 4.7 and 4.8 shows that for most of the years 1988 to 1993 (but not for 1991 and 1993), the five leading exhibitors accounted for a smaller share of rental payments than of box office. In other words, on average they tended to pay a slightly smaller share of their box office receipts as rentals to the distributors than did the independent exhibitors. In 1991 the opposite appears to have been the case, ie the five leading exhibitors accounted for a higher share of rental payments than of box office, and in 1993 their share was about the same under both measures.

4.100. While we have measured the size of the exhibition market in terms of film rental payments and box office receipts, it should be remembered that exhibitors also generate revenue from concession income (the sale of drinks, popcorn, confectionery and so on) as well as from screen advertising. While this revenue arises from the exhibitors' function as an exhibitor of films, distributors are not entitled to receive a share of it. For the five leading exhibitors these activities contributed about 22 per cent of total revenue during the five-year period 1989 to 1993 (see paragraph 5.34).

TABLE 4.7 Exhibitors' box office receipts, excluding VAT, from the showing of films in cinemas in the UK, 1988 to 1993

| Exhibitor | 1988 £m | 1988 % | 1989 £m | 1989 % | 1990 £m | 1990 % | 1991 £m | 1991 % | 1992 £m | 1992 % | 1993 £m | 1993 % | 1990 to 1993 £m | 1990 to 1993 % |
|---|---|---|---|---|---|---|---|---|---|---|---|---|---|---|
| *Leading exhibitors* | | | | | | | | | | | | | | |
| MGM Cinemas | 53.1 | 35.5 | 60.5 | 31.5 | 58.0 | 26.9 | 64.5 | 26.0 | 70.0 | 27.8 | 73.8 | 25.5 | 266.4 | 26.5 |
| UCI (including CIC) | 15.8 | 10.6 | 28.5 | 14.9 | 40.0 | 18.4 | 47.2 | 19.0 | 51.4 | 20.4 | 59.5 | 20.6 | 198.1 | 19.7 |
| Odeon | 35.9 | 24.0 | 43.0 | 22.4 | 48.3 | 22.4 | 55.3 | 22.3 | 51.0 | 20.3 | 56.5 | 19.6 | 211.1 | 21.0 |
| Natl Amusements | 1.0 | 0.7 | 5.7 | 3.0 | 14.0 | 6.5 | 15.9 | 6.4 | 17.8 | 7.1 | 23.5 | 8.1 | 71.2 | 7.1 |
| Warner Theatres | 3.7 | 2.5 | 4.1 | 2.1 | 7.6 | 3.5 | 10.4 | 4.2 | 11.2 | 4.5 | 15.7 | 5.4 | 44.8 | 4.4 |
| **Sub-total** | **109.5** | **73.2** | **141.8** | **73.9** | **167.9** | **77.1** | **193.3** | **77.8** | **201.4** | **80.1** | **229.0** | **79.2** | **791.6** | **78.6** |
| *Independent exhibitors* | | | | | | | | | | | | | | |
| **Sub-total\*** | **40.0** | **26.8** | **50.0** | **26.1** | **50.0** | **22.9** | **55.0** | **22.2** | **50.0** | **19.9** | **60.0** | **20.8** | **215.0** | **21.4** |
| **Total\*** | **149.5** | **100.0** | **191.8** | **100.0** | **217.9** | **100.0** | **248.3** | **100.0** | **251.4** | **100.0** | **289.0** | **100.0** | **1006.6** | **100.0** |

Source: MMC, based on data from the companies.

\*Estimated by the MMC.

TABLE 4.8 Exhibitors' rental payments for the showing of films in cinemas in the UK, 1988 to 1993

| Exhibitor | 1988 £m | 1988 % | 1989 £m | 1989 % | 1990 £m | 1990 % | 1991 £m | 1991 % | 1992 £m | 1992 % | 1993 £m | 1993 % | 1990 to 1993 £m | 1990 to 1993 % |
|---|---|---|---|---|---|---|---|---|---|---|---|---|---|---|
| *Leading exhibitors* | | | | | | | | | | | | | | |
| MGM Cinemas | 21.1 | 36.3 | 24.2 | 30.1 | 20.8 | 25.2 | 22.0 | 25.9 | 25.9 | 30.2 | 26.8 | 25.9 | 95.5 | 26.7 |
| UCI (including CIC) | 6.8 | 11.6 | 12.2 | 15.2 | 14.5 | 17.6 | 16.5 | 19.4 | 17.9 | 20.8 | 22.6 | 21.9 | 71.5 | 20.0 |
| Odeon | 14.0 | 24.1 | 17.0 | 21.1 | 17.5 | 21.2 | 20.0 | 23.5 | 17.4 | 20.3 | 18.4 | 17.8 | 73.3 | 20.5 |
| Natl Amusements | 0.4 | 0.7 | 2.0 | 2.5 | 4.8 | 5.8 | 5.4 | 6.3 | 5.9 | 6.9 | 7.9 | 7.6 | 24.0 | 6.7 |
| Warner Theatres | 1.4 | 2.4 | 2.0 | 2.5 | 2.6 | 3.1 | 3.4 | 4.0 | 3.4 | 4.0 | 5.4 | 5.2 | 14.8 | 4.1 |
| Statistical adjustment* | -3.1 | -5.3 | -2.4 | -3.0 | +0.9 | +1.1 | -0.7 | -0.8 | -3.0 | -3.5 | +0.9 | +0.9 | -1.9 | -0.5 |
| **Sub-total** | **40.6** | **69.8** | **55.0** | **68.4** | **61.1** | **74.0** | **66.6** | **78.3** | **67.5** | **78.6** | **82.0** | **79.3** | **277.2** | **77.6** |
| *Independent exhibitors* | | | | | | | | | | | | | | |
| Sub-total† | 17.6 | 30.2 | 25.4 | 31.6 | 21.5 | 26.0 | 18.5 | 21.7 | 18.4 | 21.4 | 21.4 | 20.7 | 79.9 | 22.4 |
| **Total†** | **58.2** | **100.0** | **80.4** | **100.0** | **82.6** | **100.0** | **85.1** | **100.0** | **85.9** | **100.0** | **103.4** | **100.0** | **357.1** | **100.0** |

Source: MMC, based on data from the companies.

*Because of different accounting periods and other relatively minor differences, the data provided to us by the leading exhibitors about their rental payments to the leading distributors did not match exactly the equivalent data provided to us by the leading distributors about their rental receipts from the leading exhibitors. In the event, it did not prove possible to eliminate entirely the resulting differences. We therefore used the figures supplied by the leading distributors in compiling the data for Table 4.8, and adjusted the exhibitors' data as necessary in order to bring them into line with the distributors' figures.
†Estimated by the MMC.

## Multiplex cinemas

4.101. Multiplex cinemas are purpose-built cinemas (as opposed to conversions) with multiple screens (at least 5 and usually between 8 and 12), located mainly on green-field sites (often as part of a larger shopping or leisure complex). They incorporate modern audio and visual equipment, a large foyer with a wide selection of refreshments, and free car parking. Multiplex operators claim to offer an 'entertainment experience' for the consumer in secure and very comfortable surroundings. These new cinemas have stimulated further investment in older cinemas, many of which have been modified and upgraded (eg by converting single-screen cinemas into multi-screen cinemas, and by installing new equipment).

4.102. The rapid development of multiplexes in the late 1980s is apparent from Table 4.9. By July 1994 there were 71 multiplex cinemas in the UK (with two more due to open in August 1994), accounting for about one-tenth of all cinema sites, about one-third of all screens, and about one-quarter of all cinema seats. By the end of 1993, about 40 per cent of all visits to UK cinemas were to multiplex cinemas. The locations of all 71 multiplex cinemas are shown in Figure 4.3, together with the 13 locations where multiplex cinemas are expected to open in the next few years. Table 4.9 indicates that the pace of openings of multiplexes slowed down between 1991 and 1993. Warner Theatres told us that it planned to open a further seven multiplexes by 1995, while other leading exhibitors are also planning to add a few to their chains of multiplexes. Some operators are considering the desirability of opening new so-called miniplex cinemas (ie newly-built cinemas with fewer than five screens) in locations where a larger cinema could not be financially justified.

TABLE 4.9  **Multiplex cinemas in the UK**

| Year | Multiplex sites | Multiplex screens | As % of all screens* |
|---|---|---|---|
| 1985 | 1 | 10 | 1 |
| 1986 | 2 | 18 | 1 |
| 1987 | 5 | 44 | 3 |
| 1988 | 14 | 139 | 10 |
| 1989 | 29 | 285 | 19 |
| 1990 | 41 | 387 | 24 |
| 1991 | 58 | 516 | 29 |
| 1992 | 64 | 562 | 32 |
| 1993 | 70 | 625 | 32 |
| 1994 | 71 | 638 | 33 |

*Source:* MMC, based on data from the companies, CAA and Dodona Research.

*That is, as a percentage of those screens which accepted advertising (not all cinema operators accept advertisements for showing on their screens).

4.103. The first multiplex cinema, The Point in Milton Keynes, was opened in late 1985 by AMC, a US exhibition company unconnected to production and distribution interests. In 1988 AMC sold its chain of 19 multiplex cinemas, either built or under development, to UCI, a joint venture between CIC NV and United Artists Communications Inc (UA) which continued to develop the chain. CIC NV then transferred its multiplex interests to UCI which, since 1990, has been owned by Paramount and MCA Inc following UA's decision to withdraw from the joint venture. UCI continues to be the largest operator of multiplexes in the UK, where it now has 225 screens at 24 sites (see Table 4.10).

TABLE 4.10  **Operators of multiplex cinemas in the UK, as at July 1994**

|  | Multiplex sites | As % of sites | Multiplex screens | As % of screens | Multiplex seats | As % of seats |
|---|---|---|---|---|---|---|
| UCI | 24 | 33.8 | 225 | 35.3 | 50,687 | 32.9 |
| MGM Cinemas | 17 | 23.9 | 125 | 19.6 | 30,765 | 20.0 |
| Natl Amusements | 10 | 14.1 | 127 | 19.9 | 32,718 | 21.2 |
| Warner Theatres* | 9 | 12.7 | 84 | 13.1 | 23,176 | 15.0 |
| Odeon | 8 | 11.3 | 56 | 8.8 | 13,256 | 8.6 |
| Independent cinemas† | 3 | 4.2 | 21 | 3.3 | 3,567 | 2.3 |
| Total | 71 | 100.0 | 638 | 100.0 | 154,169 | 100.0 |

*Source:* MMC, based on data from the companies and as published in *Screen Digest*, February 1994.

*Including the nine-screen Warner West End, which is a city centre multi-screen conversion rather than a purpose-built cinema.
†All in Northern Ireland, ie The Movie House cinemas in Glengormley (six screens, which opened in 1990) and in Belfast (eight screens, which opened in late 1992), and the Strand Omniplex in Londonderry (seven screens, which opened in October 1993).

4.104. The next largest operator of multiplex cinemas is MGM Cinemas which has 17. Natl Amusements, now the fourth largest exhibitor in the UK (after MGM Cinemas, Odeon and UCI), is owned through intermediate holding companies by Mr Sumner Redstone (a US citizen) and members of his family. It opened its first Showcase multiplex in Nottingham in 1988, and by the end of 1993 it was operating ten, all of them with 12 or 14 screens (its 11th cinema is due to open in Bristol in August 1994). Warner Theatres opened its first multiplex in Bury in 1989 and has since opened a further seven, with 75 screens in total (excluding the recently reopened nine-screen Warner West End in London). Odeon currently operates eight multiplex cinemas, and is due to open its ninth in Taunton in August 1994. There are three independent multiplex cinemas in Northern Ireland.

4.105. Unlike many other cinemas, multiplex cinemas expect to receive on first release most of the films they want to show. However, when multiplex cinemas first appeared in the UK this was not the case (see paragraph 8.103 and also paragraphs 7.51 and 7.59).

4.106. UCI told us that until 1989 certain aligned distributors refused to supply films for some of its cinemas until up to four weeks after first release. This practice effectively ended in 1989 when the Order prohibiting barring came into effect (see paragraphs 3.14, 3.15 and 4.168). All distributors of mainstream (as opposed to arthouse) films now appear to regard the supply of first-release films to all multiplexes (as well as the two main circuits) as their highest priority in planning the release of popular films and determining the number of prints to be made.

4.107. With their large numbers of screens, multiplex operators have more scope to keep on films that are performing well, and also to switch films with lesser appeal from larger auditoriums to smaller ones. From the point of view of the cinema-goer, the presence of so many screens in one cinema makes for a wide choice of films. Some of the multiplex operators, however, told us that they had found it difficult to attract audiences for arthouse films, and that they now showed such films only to a small extent, eg on one screen for one day a week.

## Activities of film exhibitors in the UK

### The booking of films

4.108. In the UK, release dates for new films are set for Fridays so that new releases can attract the best potential audiences over the coming weekend. Every Monday discussions take place between exhibitors and distributors, in the light of the previous weekend's box office figures, about which films are to be kept on at cinemas for the show-week beginning the following Friday and which are to be taken off to make way for new films. Sometimes difficult negotiations can take place, particularly when the distributor thinks that the film should be kept on and the exhibitor wants to take it off, but the negotiations have to be completed quickly so that exhibitors can meet their copy deadlines for advertising their programmes in local newspapers.

4.109. The leading exhibitors seek to plan their future programmes, and make their film bookings for new releases, well in advance. This is very important for organizing marketing and pre-release publicity. Because of the uncertainty about how well films will perform, exhibitors maintain considerable flexibility to determine their programmes in detail week by week to respond to consumer demand. Decisions on which films to book are made centrally, with relatively little discretion given to local managers. Local managers may be involved in the decisions about which screens, in a multiple-screen cinema, films should be shown on, and whether or not there may be scope (given the interests of the local area) for special presentations (eg late night shows, the showing of films of local interest one weekday evening a week, or even supporting or establishing a local film club). Independent cinemas do not plan as far ahead as the leading exhibitors, and beyond the month ahead they may have no firm knowledge of what particular films they will be showing. One of the more frequent complaints of independent exhibitors was about their difficulties in obtaining popular films from the leading distributors.

4.110. Leading exhibitors told us that they selected those films which they judged would maximize cinema attendances, subject to providing a broad range of films for the public. They recognized the need to encourage demand for films which had limited audience appeal; when exhibited in selected cinemas and at certain times these could attract reasonable audiences. When films have been first released in the USA, their performance there provides a useful, but not infallible, indicator to their likely appeal to UK audiences.

4.111. MGM Cinemas told us that it reserved dates well in advance for major releases, but these reservations were only provisional until its bookings department had viewed the films. If MGM Cinemas was unsure of a film's commercial potential, it insisted on seeing it before reserving dates. Few films from independent distributors had the clear commercial potential to justify advance reservations of dates, and it was at times difficult for independent distributors to find dates if their films became available for viewing at short notice. Odeon said that, following discussions with any distributor, it might 'pencil in' dates for exhibition, but all such provisional bookings were subject to viewing by its booking staff.

4.112. The general practice in the industry is that a film distributor seeking a broad release for a film normally speaks first to whichever of the two main circuits, MGM Cinemas or Odeon, it is aligned (see paragraph 4.159). Subsequently, the three multiplex operators are informed of the agreed release dates, and offered the same films for the same dates.

*Advertising and promotion*

4.113. The advertising and promotion of films are mainly carried out by the distributors (see paragraph 4.66), though the leading exhibitors may participate in national advertising and promotional activities in support of particular films, and all exhibitors normally place advertisements in local newspapers giving details of films and the times of performances at their cinemas. In addition, some cinema-based promotional and advertising activity does take place (eg posters outside the cinema or in the entrance foyer or, where space allows, more extensive displays in the foyer), and this can, we were told, have a favourable impact on the success of films of less obvious commercial potential.

*Cinema Exhibitors' Association*

4.114. The CEA is the only trade association representing cinema exhibitors. It said that its membership accounted for approximately 90 per cent of cinema operators in the UK, including the five leading exhibitors as well as most independent exhibitors. The CEA's views are summarized in paragraphs 6.2 to 6.18.

## Ticket prices

4.115. It is the common practice among exhibitors to set prices on the basis of the particular cinema or screen and not on the basis of an individual film. Exhibitors generally believe that to charge more for the most attractive films would alienate customers and would suggest that the films for which ticket prices were lower were not worth seeing. However, prices do vary by locality, with none of the major exhibitors having a uniform national admission price. The quality of the cinema may also be reflected in the price: the more modern and better-equipped multiplexes tend to charge higher prices than the older cinemas.

4.116. Within a given cinema, prices vary according to category of customer (lower prices being generally offered to children, pensioners and students), and according to the day of the week and time of the day. Concessions to those categories of customers mentioned have a substantial effect on box office takings.

4.117. There is not much difference in average prices charged among the leading exhibitors. Table 4.11 sets out, for each of them, the average adult evening admission charge and the average realized seat price (both for 1993). Our survey of independent cinemas (see paragraph 4.85 and Appendix 4.4) found that, on the whole, admission charges to independent cinemas were slightly lower than for cinemas operated by the leading exhibitors.

TABLE 4.11 **Average price levels of the leading exhibitors**

| | (a)<br>Average adult<br>evening admission<br>charge in 1993<br>£ | (b)<br>Average realized<br>seat price<br>in 1993<br>£ | (c)<br>(a) − (b)<br>as % of<br>(a)<br>% |
|---|---|---|---|
| MGM Cinemas (124 cinemas) | 3.55 | 2.69 | 24 |
| Odeon (64 cinemas*) | 3.82 | 2.93 | 23 |
| UCI (23 cinemas) | 3.71 | 2.68 | 28 |
| Natl Amusements (10 cinemas) | 3.79 | 2.73 | 28 |
| Warner Theatres (8 cinemas) | 3.41 | 2.21 | 35 |

*Source:* MMC, from information supplied by the leading exhibitors.

*That is, those 64 of its cinemas where prices are uniform throughout the week for all screens. At Odeon's eight other cinemas prices vary by screen and/or day.

4.118. Table 4.12 sets out the changes in average realized seat prices between 1988 and 1993. The table shows that MGM Cinemas, UCI and Natl Amusements have increased their prices significantly faster than inflation (as measured by the increase in the RPI), whereas the increase in Odeon's prices over the period was virtually the same as that of the index (despite the fact that during this period, mainly during 1990 and 1991, it introduced premium-priced seats in its cinemas). The figures may reflect in part improvements in the average quality of the cinemas in a given chain. For example, MGM Cinemas said that increases in its average prices was partly the consequence of the closure of some of its cheaper cinemas. While Odeon still had the highest average realized prices at the end of the period, it said that this to some extent reflected the fact that it had a relatively high proportion of its cinema seats in the more expensive London area. In contrast, the fall in Warner Theatres' average price is largely due to the opening of new multiplex cinemas outside London with lower admission charges than those at its Warner West End cinema in London, which was its only cinema until mid-1989.

TABLE 4.12 **Average realized seat prices, 1988 to 1993 (nominal prices, unadjusted for inflation)**

|  | 1988 £ | 1989 £ | 1990 £ | 1991 £ | 1992 £ | 1993 £ | % change 1988 to 1993 |
|---|---|---|---|---|---|---|---|
| MGM Cinemas: multiplexes | 1.89 | 2.04 | 2.38 | 2.67 | 2.84 | 2.83 | +50 |
| other cinemas | 1.87 | 1.94 | 2.19 | 2.51 | 2.58 | 2.62 | +40 |
| Odeon | 2.20 | 2.34 | 2.49 | 2.78 | 2.93 | 2.93 | +33 |
| UCI | 1.74 | 2.03 | 2.35 | 2.44 | 2.60 | 2.68 | +54 |
| Natl Amusements | 1.88 | 2.19 | 2.49 | 2.59 | 2.62 | 2.73 | +45 |
| Warner Theatres | 3.31 | 3.18 | 2.92 | 2.78 | 2.41 | 2.38 | −28 |
| Retail price index |  |  |  |  |  |  | +32 |

*Source:* MMC.

4.119. There are a number of factors that constrain prices in the wider context of the leisure sector. The availability of films on video cassette (either through rental or purchase) is likely to have some influence on exhibitors' prices. Some account in setting prices has to be taken of alternatives to a visit to the cinema, for example attending a theatre or concert, or a visit to a pub or restaurant. The prices charged by other cinemas in the locality provides a more immediate constraint. This is less effective in areas of lower population density, where the nearest competing cinema may be many miles away, but prices are noticeably lower in some places where two of the leading exhibitors have cinemas close to each other. (This does not apply to the West End of London, where prices are markedly higher than in the rest of the UK.)

4.120. We have also been given evidence of competitive price responses. In some cases this took the form of lower admission charges as an inducement to increased admissions, in part at the expense of nearby cinemas. In other cases there have been price promotions, such as 'two seats for the price of one', that have been introduced by the major chains as well as by independent exhibitors.

4.121. We also considered whether cinema admission charges in the UK tended to be higher or lower than those in other European countries. We have seen two international comparisons of cinema prices, namely the *European Cinema Yearbook 1993 (ECY)* and *Screen Digest* September 1993, both of which suggested that average admission charges in the UK have in recent times been slightly lower than the average in other EC countries.

## New investment

4.122. Cinema exhibitors have invested heavily during the past decade in the building of new cinemas and screens, the installation of new projection and audio equipment, the provision of comfortable seating in tiered auditoriums in order to improve line of sight and the provision of car-parking facilities. The CEA told us that, based on a survey it had conducted, £601 million had been invested in new screens, refurbishment and car-parking facilities since 1984/85. Capital expenditure by the five leading exhibitors during the six-year period from 1988 to 1993 amounted to almost £390 million (see paragraph 5.44). Whilst much of this new investment has been in the building of multiplexes, considerable investment in the upgrading of existing cinemas in town centres has also occurred (eg Odeon has invested heavily in recent years in the modernization of its existing cinemas and their conversion to multi-screen operation).

4.123. Of the two main circuit exhibitors, MGM Cinemas now has 17 multiplexes and Odeon eight. MGM Cinemas told us that it would have built more in the UK in the period 1986 to 1990 had it not been required to transmit funds to its overseas parent company. There is keen competition between the leading exhibitors for sites suitable for the construction of new multiplex cinemas (see also paragraph 4.127). We were told of several instances where, in public tenders, one or more of the exhibitors withdrew its interest because it appeared that the price had become too high given the likely construction and operating costs.

4.124. Two exhibitors separately expressed their concerns to us that UCI's and Warner Theatres' investment in new multiplex cinemas was not based on strictly commercial grounds viewed as stand-alone investment in exhibition, but rather was justified partly by the increased rentals which UCI and Warner Theatres then generated for their parent studios' films (see also paragraphs 7.181 and 7.182). They suggested to us that if this was in fact the case, competition in the exhibition market in the UK was being distorted by such new investment.

4.125. The MMC's questionnaire survey of independent cinemas (see paragraph 4.85) showed that about 80 per cent of respondents had invested in their cinemas in the three-year period 1991 to 1993. In some cases the sums involved were substantial, up to £0.5 million at one site.

### Prospects for new entry

4.126. The prospects for new entry into the exhibition market are decided largely by three factors: the availability of sites with prospects for successful planning applications (either for new building or for conversion or renovation); the capital costs of entry and access to the necessary finance; and the readiness of distributors to provide prints.

4.127. We were told that it was becoming increasingly difficult to identify new sites for multiplex cinemas. This was a particular problem in the Greater London area. Many of the best sites had already been taken, and competition from other uses, as well as planning restrictions, meant that the opening of new multiplex cinemas was likely to be less frequent than it had been. UCI said that there was fierce competition between itself and other exhibitors for the limited number of suitable sites. So far as smaller cinemas are concerned, we were told that opportunities existed to invest in existing sites, or to build new cinemas in areas not already served by multiplexes.

4.128. Natl Amusements told us that the capital costs of its cinemas varied between £6 million (for its Derby Showcase) to over £10 million (for its Leeds and Teesside cinemas). At the other end of the scale, we understand that the Richmond Filmhouse (a single-screen cinema, but fitted out, we were told, to a high standard) cost about £0.5 million.

4.129. It is now the case, but it was not in their early days, that multiplex cinemas have few difficulties in obtaining prints. Smaller cinemas may face difficulties, particularly in obtaining prints on first release; their success in doing so will depend on whether distributors believe rental payments will cover the cost of the additional prints.

### Appeals procedure

4.130. Differences between distributors and exhibitors are now resolved through negotiation between the parties concerned, rather than by recourse to any procedure involving, for example, representatives of the SFD and the CEA. A formal appeals procedure, involving a TDC and an Appeals Tribunal, was established following the MMC's 1966 report. These arrangements are effectively in abeyance (see paragraph 3.16). The principal purpose of the TDC was to resolve disputes over the application of the old system of barring (see paragraph 4.168). Once barring had been made unlawful by the 1989 Order (see paragraph 3.15), which implemented one of the recommendations of the MMC's 1983 report, this function disappeared, and the machinery has not been used to deal with other complaints.

## Relationships between distributors and exhibitors

### The SFD's *Standard Conditions*

4.131. The *Standard Conditions* (the full text of which is at Appendix 4.3) contain a number of clauses which affect commercial relationships between distributors and exhibitors. For example, they specify that: 'The Exhibitor shall charge such admission prices at the cinema during the licence period as shall be agreed by the Distributor' (Clause 2(g)). This means that the exhibitor has to notify distributors in advance of any proposed price changes. A reduction in admission prices may affect a distributor's willingness to book films into a particular cinema, since the effect is likely to be a reduction in the distributor's rental receipts per admission.

4.132. During the first half of 1993, the SFD became concerned about the growth in the number of price promotions being introduced by exhibitors, such as 'two seats for the price of one'. Some of these promotions, introduced by the major chains as well as independent exhibitors, had not been approved by distributors in advance and were thus unauthorized. The minutes of the meeting of the Sales Managers Committee of the SFD, held on 30 June 1993, recorded a statement by the SFD President that 'the intervention of the Society had led to the curtailment of such promotions'.

4.133. The *Standard Conditions* also limit an exhibitor's freedom to show any other film it may wish to during the licence period for any one film. Thus, according to Clause 5(a), unless the distributor agrees otherwise, an exhibitor must show the licensed film each day of the licence period. Furthermore, Clause 5(b) requires that a film be shown at all times during the day when films would normally be shown (excluding children's matinées and late night shows) unless otherwise agreed by the film's distributor. Exhibitors may not switch a film from one screen to another (Clause 5(d)), nor show another feature film in the same programme (Clause (6)), without the distributor's agreement.

4.134. The SFD explained to us the background to its *Standard Conditions*, and the reasons for introducing some of the provisions (see paragraphs 6.39 and 6.42 to 6.47). The CEA made a number of comments to us about the *Standard Conditions* (see paragraphs 6.12 to 6.15).

## Rental payments

4.135. Data from the leading exhibitors show that the average rental they paid for feature films during the period 1989 to 1993 was about 36 per cent of the box office (excluding VAT) (see Table 5.8). The *ECY* gives a figure of 40 per cent as the average film rental in the UK for each of the years 1989 to 1991. Although the data we received indicate that this estimate was too high, it is lower than equivalent figures (as reported in the *ECY*) in France (48 per cent), Germany (44 per cent), and Italy (41 per cent). Some of the leading distributors told us that the average level of rentals in the UK, expressed in percentage terms, was very low by international standards.

4.136. There are three main methods of calculating rental payments: the nut; the sliding scale; and the datum scale.

(a) The *nut* is a negotiated figure which notionally represents the cinema's costs (including a contribution to overhead costs) for a given screen plus a profit margin (see also Appendix 4.5). The rental for that screen is then the greater of: (i) 25 per cent of the weekly box office; and (ii) 90 per cent of what is left of the weekly box office after deducting the nut (though this percentage may vary between 75 and 90).

*Example:* Assume that the negotiated nut figures for a three-screen cinema are:

|  | £ |
|---|---|
| Screen 1 | 5,231 |
| Screen 2 | 2,846 |
| Screen 3 | 1,923 |
| Total | 10,000 |

In this case, if Screen 1's box office receipts for a film in week 1 were £7,000, the cinema's rental payment to the distributor that week would be the higher of:

(£7,000 − £5,231) × 0.9 = £1,592 and
£7,000 × 0.25 = £1,750

ie £1,750, being 25 per cent of the box office.

If, in the second week, the film was transferred to Screen 2 and the box office receipts fell to £5,000, the rental payment would be the higher of:

(£5,000 − £2,846) × 0.9 = £1,939 and
£5,000 × 0.25 = £1,250

ie £1,939, being 38.9 per cent of the box office.

(b) Under the *sliding scale* method, the percentage of weekly box office takings for each screen paid to the distributor rises (usually from 25 per cent in steps of 5 per cent) as those box office takings rise over the pre-set break figures for the screen. It is usual under this arrangement for the maximum payment to be 50 per cent of the box office, except when special terms (see paragraph 4.140) are agreed on individual films which take the scale above 50 per cent. In some cases, the exhibitor may agree a guaranteed minimum payment to the distributor which is higher than the normal 25 per cent.

*Example:* Effect of the sliding scale method for a two-screen cinema where Screen 1 has a lowest break figure of £6,624 and Screen 2 a lowest break figure of £3,566:

| Film hire rate % | Box office takings (£) Screen 1 £ | Screen 2 £ |
|---|---|---|
| 25 | <6,624 | <3,566 |
| 30 | ≥6,624 | ≥3,566 |
| 35 | 7,609 | 4,097 |
| 40 | 8,593 | 4,627 |
| 45 | 9,583 | 5,160 |
| 50 | 10,568 | 5,690 |

In this case, if Screen 1's box office receipts in week 1 were £10,000, the cinema would pay a rental to the film's distributor that week of £4,500 (ie 0.45 × £10,000). If the box office receipts fell (by 30 per cent) to £7,000 in week 2, the payment to the distributor would fall (by 53 per cent) to £2,100 (ie 0.30 × £7,000). If the film transferred to Screen 2 in week 3, and took only £5,500, the payment to the distributor would rise to £2,475 (ie 0.45 × £5,500).

(c) The *datum scale* is a variation of the sliding scale method.

*Example:* 25% to £2,000 with 75% over and a 50% maximum.

Thus: Net take = £2,200
Rental = (£2,000 × 0.25) + (£200 × 0.75)
= £500 + £150

ie £650, being 29.5 per cent of the box office.

4.137. Another method sometimes used is the *straight percentage*, which is agreed on a film-by-film basis. For example, some distributors supply first-run films to RFTs at a flat rate of 35 per cent. In the case of second-run cinemas, ie those in which the film plays after it has been shown in other cinemas in the same locality, some distributors normally charge a flat fee of 25 per cent, with a minimum guaranteed to cover dispatch costs.

4.138. The different methods of calculating rental payments have been adopted by the various exhibitors as follows:

— *Nut*: MGM Cinemas, UCI, Natl Amusements, Warner Theatres and some independent cinemas.

— *Sliding scale*: Odeon and some independent cinemas.

— *Datum scale*: Some independent cinemas.

— *Straight percentage*: Some independent cinemas, including several RFTs.

4.139. All these methods, to varying degrees, reflect the general desire throughout the industry to manage and share the risk involved in the production, distribution and exhibition of feature films.

Apart from the straight percentage method, their effect is to place most of the risk of a film performing poorly on to the distributor, whose share of the takings rises as the level of receipts rises. If an audience of a given size is spread over two cinemas, the distributor's share of the box office is lower than if the same audience is concentrated in one of the two cinemas. This dilution is more pronounced, particularly for very successful films, in the case of the house nut system than the sliding scale. The desire to avoid audience splitting, with the consequent reduction in rental payments, is one of the most important factors in leading distributors to restrict the number of prints for any film.

4.140. Most distributors said that they sometimes negotiated special terms. For films expected to be very popular, distributors may seek from exhibitors using the house nut method a minimum rental higher than the normal 25 per cent. But special terms apply more often to cinemas not using the house nut method. In such cases distributors may seek to negotiate 'overage' for such films, ie the exhibitor agrees to pay a rental of more than 50 per cent if the film's box office takings exceed the 50 per cent break figure by more than a specified amount. If the particular films are successful, overage terms enable the distributor to take a larger percentage of the box office. Overage terms vary from film to film and from cinema to cinema.

4.141. Several, but not all, distributors said that they consulted other distributors about a particular cinema's break figures or nuts if the exhibitor referred in negotiation to what other distributors had agreed. One distributor said that it checked with other distributors from time to time that they were using the same figures, so that it could take advantage of better figures which another distributor might have been able to negotiate.

4.142. In general, the method of calculating the rental payments is decided by the exhibitor, but the actual nut or break figures have to be agreed with distributors on a cinema-by-cinema basis. Nut and break figures are renegotiated from time to time, usually once a year, at the initiative of exhibitors. One distributor said that the terms negotiated between distributors and exhibitors were affected by alignment: it told us that MGM Cinemas had operated three sets of standard terms, with the most favourable given to its two aligned distributors (UIP and Warner Distributors), slightly less favourable terms to its non-aligned leading distributors (Buena Vista, Columbia and Fox), and the least favourable terms to all the independent distributors. This distributor acknowledged that MGM Cinemas had recently, as an outcome of negotiations during early 1994, placed the major independents on an equal footing with the leading distributors in this respect. Nevertheless, we looked carefully at the nut and break figures for each of the leading exhibitors, as at the end of 1993, to establish whether or not they showed such differentials (see Appendix 4.5).

## Vertical integration and links between companies

4.143. One of the factors that has in the past given rise to concern about competition in the film industry is the number and complexity of links between the companies. The DGFT mentioned vertical links as one of the reasons for the reference to the MMC (see paragraph 3.1).

4.144. The main links are those that involve the seven Hollywood studios. They may be horizontal (mainly in the form of joint ventures) or vertical (ie connecting businesses operating at the three levels of the industry, namely production, distribution and exhibition). Links between companies of different kinds can vary greatly in their commercial significance. Some are formal, for example ownership links, while others may be more a matter of commercial practice.

4.145. Links between the production and distribution of films have traditionally been strong. All the main seven Hollywood studios have adopted the same strategy and either own or have a large share in a distribution company, and the general practice has been to use that company as the studio's sole distributor in the main territories. Four of the seven (Columbia/TriStar, 20th Century Fox, Walt Disney and Warner Bros) have their own respective UK distribution subsidiaries. The other three studios (MGM Inc, Paramount and MCA/Universal) operate a joint-venture distribution company (UIP), each holding a one-third share. A brief outline of the market in the USA is given in Appendix 4.6.

4.146. While independent distributors are also involved, to varying extents, in the financing of films in order to obtain distribution rights, they do not participate in the development of ideas for films, nor do they initiate or have much influence over film production. Rank, in addition to investing in film production through RFD (see paragraph 4.79), also owns Pinewood which, unlike the Hollywood studios, provides studio facilities for film production without itself being involved in film-making.

4.147. Some, but not all, of the Hollywood studios have ownership links with exhibitors. In three cases (Columbia/TriStar, 20th Century Fox and Walt Disney) the studio has no interests in exhibition in the UK. By contrast Paramount and MCA/Universal have formed a joint venture (as they have also done at the distribution level in partnership with MGM Inc) and this company (UCI) is a leading exhibitor in the UK. Natl Amusements has also recently become linked to Paramount, which was acquired by its affiliated company Viacom Inc. Warner Bros is the only studio which has a wholly-owned UK exhibition operation (Warner Theatres). As well as its distribution interests, Rank owns the Odeon exhibition circuit. In the case of MGM Inc, there is also a link between production and exhibition, but an indirect one: the studio and the UK exhibitor (now MGM Cinemas) were both acquired by Mr G Parretti, before his interests came under the control of the French bank Crédit Lyonnais as a result of foreclosure. MGM Cinemas told us that it had no remaining connection with MGM Inc, and that it now reported, via its immediate parent, straight to Crédit Lyonnais. A number of the smaller independent distributors also have modest interests in exhibition.

4.148. Informal links involving distributors and exhibitors are described in paragraph 4.159. The system of 'alignment' connects the Odeon circuit with a number of distributors, and MGM Cinemas' circuit with the two largest distributors.

4.149. We asked each of the leading exhibitors how they decided which films to exhibit in the UK, whether or not any ownership links between them and any film distribution or production company constrained their ability to act independently in choosing films for exhibition in their cinemas, and how readily independent producers obtained access to screens in the UK for their films.

4.150. The general response was that each of the leading exhibitors chose which films to show by reference to their box office potential, although some said that they also aimed to show a varied range of films. The main factors they took into account when deciding which films to show in which cinemas were the cinema's locality and catchment area in relation to the film's potential audience profile. The multiplex operators emphasized the potential size of the box office for the film, with a preference for showing films which were likely to generate the largest audiences. Some multiplex cinemas give limited showings for films which were expected to appeal to a limited audience.

4.151. MGM Cinemas (owned by Crédit Lyonnais) said that it had no links with any film production or distribution companies. UCI said that its ownership links did not constrain its ability to act independently in choosing which films to exhibit, nor did they cause it to treat Paramount, MCA/Universal or UIP differently from other production or distribution companies. Odeon told us that it dealt with RFD on an arm's length and normal commercial basis. Natl Amusements said that its links with Paramount through Viacom Inc did not constrain its ability to act independently in the selection of films for exhibition in its cinemas. Warner Theatres told us that its links with other companies imposed no constraints on the decisions as to which films it exhibited, and that it was treated by Time Warner Entertainment Group as a separate profit centre. It said that all its dealings with Warner Distributors, for example with regard to the setting of play dates, choice of screen, length of run and level of rental, were conducted at arm's length. (See also paragraph 4.161.)

4.152. We looked at the rental receipts for the five leading distributors as well as those for Guild and RFD, and compared for each distributor the shares of its rental receipts accounted for by each of the leading exhibitors in relation to the distributor's share of the distribution market as a whole. The figures are given in seven tables in Appendix 4.7. The figures show that UIP had a somewhat greater share of UCI's business than of the exhibition market as a whole in 1991 and 1992 (though not 1993). It can also be seen that Warner Distributors had a somewhat greater share of Warner Theatres' business, excluding the Warner West End, in 1993.

4.153. Commenting on these figures, UCI emphasized that its policy was to show commercially viable films in its multiplexes irrespective of the identity of either the producer or the distributor. It assessed the commercial prospects of each film and chose whether to exhibit any film on the basis of the revenues that UCI expected the film to generate. When deciding which films to keep on at the end of each week, UCI reviewed new films available against films already playing and allocated films across its screens with a view to generating the highest possible attendances and revenues. Its success in selecting films to meet customer demand was demonstrated by the fact that it achieved the highest levels of attendance per screen and per seat of all the leading exhibitors. UCI submitted information based on box office takings which, it said, showed that UCI had no bias in favour of any particular distributor.

4.154. UIP stressed that its policy and practice were to try to have each of its films exhibited in those cinemas, regardless of ownership, which it believed would maximize its return from that film (subject to the alignments, which did not affect the supply of films to multiplexes anyway). Given the quality of multiplexes, UIP sought to book the majority of its films into all multiplexes. It treated UCI no differently from any other multiplex operator and its experience was that it received substantially identical treatment, both on bookings and holdovers, from all multiplex operators. UIP was unable to comment on the MMC's rental comparisons because it did not have access to all relevant information but on the figures which were available to it, based on admissions and box office receipts, it could find no evidence of any systematic preference in its trading with UCI. It pointed out that neither UIP nor UCI was much involved in the specialist or arthouse part of the market, which UIP estimated accounted for around 3 per cent of total box office receipts. The MMC's comparisons, therefore, overstated the difference between the percentage of UIP's box office receipts, and the percentage of total UK box office receipts, generated by UCI.

4.155. Warner Theatres said that, leaving aside the Warner West End, Warner Distributors' share of its box office receipts, at 26.9 per cent in 1993, was in line with Warner Distributors' overall share which, on the information available to Warner Theatres, was 24.1 per cent in that year.

4.156. In order to test whether exhibitors gave preferential treatment to particular distributors, eg with which they had some ownership or alignment links, we obtained information on the films booked by each of the five leading exhibitors in three of their multiplex cinemas for two six-week periods at the beginning of 1993 and 1994. We examined the gross takings of those films which were kept on from one week to another and also of those films which were taken off, noting in each case the relevant distributor of the film. We chose multiplex cinemas as the basis of this study since, with ten screens or more (eight in the case of Odeon), there was, in principle, some scope for preferential trading compared with those situations (in, say, three-screen cinemas) where pressure on screens is more acute.

4.157. The results showed few occasions where Natl Amusements, Odeon or Warner Theatres retained films with low box office takings at the expense of other films with higher box office takings. UCI appeared to do so to a much greater extent, but it told us that of 50 occasions, in the two periods taken together, where films with low takings were kept on, this was explained in all but three cases by the fact that the films had received relatively few showings, mainly at matinées. Where films were shown in matinées this did not affect the availability of screens for the exhibition of other films in the evening. In UCI's view, the data produced confirmed its statement that it decided which films to keep on and which to take off by reference to their performance at the box office.

4.158. As to the two aligned exhibitors (see next paragraph), we found more occasions in the six-week period in 1994 where films with low takings had been kept on, when other films with higher takings had been taken off, in the case of MGM Cinemas (19 occasions) than Odeon (six occasions). Of those 19 occasions, MGM Cinemas told us that this was explained in 18 cases by their retention for restricted showings, mainly matinées. In the remaining case, MGM told us that it had been asked by the distributor to give up a print to make it available for another exhibitor. Although based on a small sample, this evidence gave no support for the view that MGM Cinemas and Odeon engaged in discrimination in deciding which films to take off and which to keep.

## Alignment

4.159. Alignment is an arrangement whereby, in the first instance, a distributor normally offers its films to, and discusses the timing and release strategy for those films with, its aligned circuit, ie either MGM Cinemas or Odeon. In the 20 locations where MGM Cinemas and Odeon operate directly competing cinemas (other than multiplexes), aligned distributors normally supply prints of their films to the cinemas of their aligned circuit but not to those of the other circuit. Aligned to MGM Cinemas are UIP (in respect of Paramount, MCA/Universal and MGM Inc films) and Warner Distributors. Two leading distributors, Buena Vista and Columbia, together with Entertainment, Guild and RFD are aligned to the Odeon circuit, as is UIP in respect of United Artists' films. Fox explained that it normally approached Odeon to discuss the release strategy for its films and would either offer Odeon booking priority or explain why it was not doing so. There was no obligation or understanding that it would give precedence to Odeon. Fox provided a list of the 57 films which it had released since January 1991 or was due to release in the latter part of 1994. Of these, Fox regarded 39 (68 per cent) as having been first offered to Odeon, 4 to MGM Cinemas and 14 to some other exhibitor. Fox also provided a list of Odeon cinemas where its key releases were normally shown in preference to competing sites operated by MGM Cinemas.

4.160. The different parties to alignment claimed that its impact had been much reduced during the past decade partly as a result of closures of cinemas belonging to the two main circuit exhibitors (RFD told us that the number of Odeon cinemas directly affected by alignment had not changed since 1990), but mostly because of the growth of multiplex cinemas, which were not aligned. We received different lists of the locations where alignment currently determines the allocation of films as between the two circuits: that is, those situations where both Odeon and MGM Cinemas have cinemas in town centres, often a few hundred yards apart, and the films of the aligned distributors will not usually be exhibited concurrently in both cinemas (ie the aligned locations). Of the 20 aligned locations, three are in London (but not in the West End) and 17 are elsewhere (see Appendix 4.8). We refer to MGM Cinemas' and Odeon's cinemas in these locations, together with Odeon's cinemas in the West End of London (see next paragraph), as 'the aligned cinemas'. MGM Cinemas told us that it did not regard any of its West End cinemas as being aligned, but some distributors treated them as such.

4.161. In central London there is a kind of alignment relating to the supply of films by distributors to the few prestigious West End cinemas. Warner Distributors' films for which a platform release is selected are invariably shown in the Warner West End cinema in Leicester Square. In the West End of London, UIP's films are generally shown at either the Empire cinema in Leicester Square or the Plaza cinema in Lower Regent Street (or both), owned by CIC but managed by UCI. Distributors other than Warner Distributors and UIP requiring a West End showcase usually favour either the Odeon West End or the Odeon Leicester Square.

4.162. The direct effects of alignment may be gauged by measuring what proportion of rental payments made by MGM Cinemas and Odeon to their aligned distributors is derived from the cinemas affected (see Table 4.13). The higher figures shown in Table 4.13 for Columbia and Fox reflect the fact that the aligned cinemas represent a higher proportion of Odeon's circuit (currently 73 sites) than of MGM Cinemas' circuit (119 sites), and the importance of Odeon's West End cinemas. The low figures for RFD are due to the fact that relatively few of RFD's films are shown in the prestigious West End cinemas which bring in high rentals. Looked at from the two exhibitors' point of view, the cinemas in the 20 aligned locations accounted for 32 per cent of the total box office takings in 1992 in the case of Odeon and 17 per cent in the case of MGM Cinemas. The addition of cinemas in central London, where a form of alignment exists, would increase these proportions to 45 per cent for Odeon and 21 per cent for MGM Cinemas. The box office takings of the aligned cinemas in the 20 locations represented 11 per cent of total box office receipts in the UK market in 1992, a figure which rises to 14.5 per cent if the central London cinemas are added.

TABLE 4.13 **Alignment and rental payments**

| Distributor | Aligned circuit | Percentage of the aligned circuit's total annual rental payments which arise from its cinemas in the aligned locations | | |
|---|---|---|---|---|
| | | 1991 | 1992 | 1993 |
| UIP | MGM Cinemas | 21.0 | 21.6 | 20.9 |
| Warner Distributors* | MGM Cinemas | 17.7 | 20.0 | 27.8 |
| Columbia | Odeon | 55.6 | 48.2 | 55.6 |
| Fox | Odeon | N/A | N/A | 42.4 |
| RFD | Odeon | 19.6 | 19.6 | 13.6 |

Source: MMC.

*Excluding Walt Disney films.

4.163. Certain distributors argued that alignment helped to minimize uncertainty in this high-risk industry, thus reducing costs. Outside the aligned locations they supplied films to both the main circuits. They also said that since the practice did not affect the supply of films to multiplexes or to independent cinemas, the significance of alignment had been substantially reduced since the MMC's 1983 report (which reached an adverse public interest finding on the issue). The leading distributors and Odeon maintained that the benefits of alignment extended to independent distributors, but this view was not shared by one of the latter, Entertainment (see paragraph 9.11).

4.164. MGM Cinemas told us that it considered alignment was being wrongly applied to two of its cinemas, both in London (see paragraph 7.19). Warner Theatres told us that it was disappointed to find distributors unwilling to use its refurbished Warner West End as a prestigious cinema for the platform release of any of their main films. This reflected their traditional preferences for certain other West End cinemas.

4.165. Although alignment directly affects only 20 locations, plus those in the West End, its indirect influence may be more widespread, for two reasons:

*(a)* there are many MGM Cinemas sites which have fewer than four screens (99 of its 127 cinemas are of this size, compared with 24 out of 72 in the case of Odeon) so reducing choice of screens for distributors other than those aligned to MGM Cinemas; and

*(b)* distributors place their product in the aligned circuit first and only later in the non-aligned circuit.

4.166. In order to measure the extent to which alignment has an impact outside the 20 localities, we made a comparison between each distributor's shares of box office in the smaller cinemas (defined as cinemas with one, two or three screens) of the two circuit exhibitors and its shares in the UK exhibition market as a whole (the total market) in 1992 and 1993 (see Appendix 4.9). In the case of MGM Cinemas, we found that UIP and Warner Distributors took a higher share of both box office and rentals in its 86 smaller cinemas outside the aligned locations than they did in the total market in both 1992 and 1993. The shares of UIP and Warner Distributors of box office and rentals were also higher in these smaller cinemas than in MGM Cinemas' 22 cinemas, outside the aligned locations, with four or more screens. Those distributors not aligned to MGM Cinemas, except Buena Vista, had a lower share of box office and rentals in MGM Cinemas' smaller cinemas than its larger ones, and lower than in the total market. In the case of Buena Vista the reverse was the case, but only marginally so. These findings indicated that even outside the 20 localities, alignment had effects during 1992 and 1993 in MGM Cinemas' smaller cinemas where screen space is at a premium. MGM Cinemas argued that distributors' shares in its small cinemas varied from year to year depending on the relative popularity of films from both its aligned and non-aligned distributors, since only the most popular films would be shown in its smaller cinemas. For example, in the first half of 1994 the relevant box office shares of three non-aligned distributors, Buena Vista, Fox and RFD, had risen sharply in these cinemas due to the popularity of certain individual films, whereas Warner Distributors' share had fallen considerably.

4.167. We also found that both Fox and Columbia took a higher share of box office in Odeon's 13 smaller cinemas than they did in the total market in both 1992 and 1993, and the same was true for Buena Vista in its first full year, 1993. Fox and Columbia also had a higher share of rentals from the Odeon circuit as a whole compared with the total market. UIP and Warner Distributors, which are aligned to MGM Cinemas, both had notably lower shares of box office in Odeon's 13 smaller cinemas than in the total market. They also had lower shares of the Odeon circuit's total box office receipts and rental payments than their shares of the total market. These findings are apparently in line with those relating to MGM Cinemas, indicating that there is an effect of alignment even outside the 20 localities where alignment is acknowledged to bite. However, in Odeon's view the limited sample size and the lack of any clear pattern meant that these findings were inconclusive.

## Barring

4.168. The 1989 Order, which came into force (in respect of Great Britain only) on 4 April 1989, made it unlawful for distributors or exhibitors to make or carry out an agreement for the exhibition of a film at a cinema if that agreement contained exclusivity terms relating to more than one film (except if they were shown as a single programme). This put an end to the system of barring, a long-standing arrangement which determined the order in which competing cinemas systematically received films (see the MMC's 1983 report, paragraphs 2.36 to 2.39, where barring is described more fully). We have been told that the barring of named cinemas no longer occurs, even in Northern Ireland where the Order does not apply, though as noted below contractual exclusivity is sometimes negotiated on a film-by-film basis.

## Exclusivity

4.169. Exclusivity exists, in the sense in which we use the term, where a particular cinema has the exclusive right, conferred by contract, to show a film within a specified area and for a specified period (it is one of the matters covered by the *Standard Conditions*—see Clause 13). This is different, though the practical effects may be similar, from cases where the distributor confers *de facto* exclusivity on a particular cinema by not supplying prints concurrently to competing cinemas.

4.170. We were told by most distributors that, outside the West End, the only leading exhibitor which now requested contractual exclusivity was Odeon. RFD, however, claimed that other exhibitors, including MGM Cinemas, also requested contractual exclusivity (see paragraph 7.56). While some distributors (UIP, Warner Distributors and First Independent) said that they never granted contractual exclusivity outside the West End, others said that they did so if it fitted in with their own commercial objectives (ie if they would in any case have chosen not to supply the competing cinemas against which an exhibitor sought exclusivity). No distributor told us that it had been coerced by Odeon into granting contractual exclusivity to the detriment of its own commercial interests.

4.171. The four leading exhibitors other than Odeon said that they did not seek contractual exclusivity. MGM Cinemas further said that it considered the negotiation of exclusivity arrangements to be against the spirit of the 1989 Order on barring (see paragraph 7.50). Odeon believed that all distributors granted contractual exclusivity in some circumstances, and it was not aware of any differences between them in their attitudes to exclusivity. Odeon also said that it sought exclusivity for many of the films it exhibited, and that it usually succeeded in negotiating some exclusivity against neighbouring cinemas, although not against multiplexes. It listed 30, out of its (then) total of 72 cinemas, where it regularly sought exclusivity and named the competing cinemas against which it did so. Twenty of these cinemas are in locations subject to alignment, and in most of these locations there are other competing cinemas as well as an MGM Cinemas site. See also the comments of some of the distributors, eg in paragraphs 8.93, 8.100, 9.18, 9.19, 9.21 and 9.22.

4.172. Distributors argued that the substantial new entry into and investment in the exhibition market since 1983 demonstrated that exclusivity (and refusal to supply—see below) had neither deterred entry and investment, nor resulted in undue restrictions on consumer choice.

## Refusal to supply a film

4.173. Complaints about non-availability of prints were one of the principal reasons for this inquiry being mounted. We received complaints from 15 independent exhibitors and these are summarized in Chapter 6.

4.174. We have taken refusal to supply to mean a decision taken by a supplier, without reference to the views of any other exhibitor, that it will not supply a film on a particular date to a cinema which requested it. (Decisions to refuse to supply which arise from agreements or understandings with other exhibitors, eg alignment or exclusivity deals with individual exhibitors, are considered elsewhere in this chapter under their respective headings.) It is at the local level that competition between cinemas takes place. Where first-run films are available to one cinema in an area but not to others, this will affect competition in that local market. It was alleged that there were examples of where otherwise viable cinemas had closed because they could no longer obtain first-run films as they had previously.

4.175. Distributors were asked about their policies on refusal to supply. It was clear, from the answers we received, that while both the distributors and the exhibitors had a common interest in maximizing admissions, there are circumstances when exhibitors are refused a print of a particular film at a particular time. Although the distributors' policies on this point were variously described, their main arguments for refusing to supply films to particular cinemas were:

*(a)* that prints were not available; or

*(b)* that it was not commercially viable to supply.

One reason why prints were not made available was that, for whatever reason, the distributor had decided not to make more prints available than had already been issued. This might be because the cost of additional prints was considered to be too high in relation to the rental income it was expected to generate. We were told that new prints normally cost between £700 and £1,000, but it could be up to £2,000 for very long films or films requiring subtitles. But in any case, distributors told us that to supply all cinemas which could be expected even to cover the cost of a print and associated costs was not the way to maximize distributors' profits, since it meant that the larger number of prints would simply spread the audience over a larger number of cinemas (the dilution effect—see paragraph 4.139).

4.176. Refusal to supply (apart from to cinemas which are considered to be credit risks) is thus related to patterns of release and the distributor's decision as to how many prints to make. For example, we noted in the case study material that we asked the leading distributors together with Guild and RFD to provide (see Appendix 4.10) that the leading distributors seemed to make a large number of prints in relation to the number of screens in which their films were shown, resulting in each print being shown in only one or two screens. In contrast, both RFD's and Guild's figures show that individual prints of their films were usually shown at two or more screens (eg each print of RFD's *Silence of the Lambs* was shown at, on average, 4.6 screens, while each print of Guild's *Basic Instinct* was shown at, on average, 2.5 screens). See Appendix 4.11 for one example of a release pattern for a major new film.

4.177. One leading distributor listed some 170 cinemas which it did not usually supply with a print until after initial release. Another referred to what it termed 'second-run theatres', which it said were cinemas which showed a particular film after it had been shown in other cinemas in the area. In general, while distributors denied that there were certain cinemas which they only supplied by way of delayed releases, it is apparent that distributors have a view of the order of priority in which they would allocate prints depending on the film, the cinemas' previous record for attracting audiences and the number of prints the distributor has decided should be made available.

4.178. The leading exhibitors supported the distributors' right to determine the optimal number of prints for each release and their allocations to cinemas. In our survey of independent exhibitors (see paragraph 4.85) between 42 and 55 per cent of respondents said that each of the leading distributors provided prints of popular films only after they had been on release for more than a certain number of weeks. Between 40 and 52 per cent also said that this was true of each of the four independent distributors listed. Films have a short 'shelf-life' in cinemas. They are not mass-produced, and sales generally peak within the first few weeks, and thereafter decline. Refusals to supply films on first-run release therefore affect particular cinemas very much more than would an equivalent refusal (which is in any event rare) in respect of films that have already been on release for some weeks. We asked the leading distributors to keep records, over the period November 1993 to February 1994, of all requests from exhibitors for particular films on particular dates which were refused. We analysed the resulting information, as reported in Appendix 4.12, and found no examples where distributors had been clearly unreasonable when dealing with exhibitors' requests for films.

4.179. In their 1970 general report on refusal to supply,[1] the Monopolies Commission said that the practice of refusing to supply was not *per se* against the public interest, and that its effects on the public interest depended on the circumstances of particular cases. First-run releases are now generally wider (ie involve a greater number of prints) than they were at the time of the MMC's 1983 report. A mass release in the early 1980s, for example, usually involved around 200 prints, whereas ten years later a mass release would normally require 250 to 400 prints: UIP's *Jurassic Park* had 412 prints. Nevertheless there are still a large number of cinemas which usually do not receive first-run films.

## Conditional booking

4.180. All the distributors responding to the MMC's main questionnaire to distributors denied that they ever required an exhibitor to take one film as a condition of being given another. None of the leading exhibitors said that they had experienced such a practice, but some independent exhibitors said that they had, although usually in an informal way.

4.181. Our survey of independent cinemas (see paragraph 4.85) showed that only a very few (about 2 or 3 per cent in relation to any particular distributor) believed that when booking a film they were obliged to accept other, specified films. But about one-quarter said that, in the case of one leading distributor, they believed they were expected to take other films it released, and between 13 and 18 per cent believed this to be the case with other distributors (the proportion depending on the distributor concerned). The proportion of respondents saying that they were expected to take other films was above average in the case of Columbia and, to a lesser extent, Warner Distributors. We put these results from the survey to these two distributors for their comments, and their comments are reported in paragraphs 8.235 and 8.241.

4.182. We contacted most of the exhibitors who had identified Columbia in this connection and asked for further particulars. Some told us that they had not intended to identify Columbia, while others said that Columbia was no worse in this respect than other distributors, but several maintained that Columbia was worse than all or most of the others. Most were unwilling for their identity to be revealed to Columbia, which was therefore unable to comment on the cases concerned; it commented in detail on the cases which were identified. Columbia also listed 18 cinemas which had refused one of its films, all of which had been offered prints of another, popular film, in the early stages of its release, a few months later.

## Minimum exhibition periods

4.183. Distributors generally license films for at least seven days, and often require longer minimum exhibition periods. For example:

(a) Warner Distributors said that it formally requested minimum playing time commitments from cinemas with fewer than four screens, and the period did not exceed four weeks, but there had been exceptions for major films.

---

[1]*Refusal to Supply: a report on the general effect on the public interest of the practices of refusing to supply goods required for business purposes and of entering into certain exclusive supply agreements*, Cmnd 4372, July 1970, HMSO.

*(b)* UIP said that it usually sought two-week minimum periods on first release, and up to four weeks for films considered likely to be particularly successful. Over the period 29 November 1993 to 28 February 1994, UIP sought two-week minimums for six of the eight main films released in or near to the period and four weeks for the other two. For one of the former, *In the Name of the Father*, UIP sought four-week minimums in Northern Ireland but two weeks in Great Britain. For most of its films there was a fair amount of variation around the main pattern of booking periods on first release. Thus for *Schindler's List*, for example, seven of the eleven first-release bookings were for four-week minimums plus holdover, one for four weeks, one for three weeks and two for two weeks. Bookings for dates after first release were usually for shorter periods (for example, in the case of *Schindler's List* 18 of 21 such bookings were for two weeks plus holdover or two weeks only).

*(c)* Columbia listed the running times which it required for all films released since the beginning of 1993. Of 17 films, Columbia set a playing time of one week for eight films, two weeks for seven, three weeks for one and four weeks for one.

*(d)* Fox said that it decided on a film-by-film basis whether to negotiate for a minimum run of more than one week, and that it did press for longer minimum periods in special circumstances (eg for films on which it had committed itself to a large advertising and promotional campaign). Its preferred playing time for *Mrs Doubtfire* (a 350-print release in January 1994), for example, was for a minimum of three weeks plus holdover, though it had agreed to bookings of two weeks in 22 cases.

*(e)* Buena Vista said that it was particularly likely that it would seek a minimum exhibition period on releases with a large number of prints that it had supported with a substantial advertising campaign. For children's or family films it would want to see the film held over school holiday periods. It required a minimum of four weeks (though some leading exhibitors told us that the minimum period had been five weeks) for *Aladdin*, covering the period before and after Christmas 1993.

4.184. The leading distributors argued that the question of minimum exhibition periods was one of the key elements in their negotiations with exhibitors concerning the supply of prints. It should not be seen in isolation from the other elements, in particular from the decisions on whether to supply a print on first run and the rental terms. Distributors all claimed that they were prepared to shorten the minimum exhibition period after the first week if box office returns were poor (bearing in mind, it was argued, that the purpose was not to force exhibitors to keep on relatively unsuccessful films, but to ensure that relatively successful films were not taken off prematurely).

4.185. The specialist multiplex exhibitors said that they regarded the negotiation of minimum exhibition periods as part of a normal commercial relationship. They found that distributors were flexible in exercising their contractual rights (though Natl Amusements implied that there was room for improvement), and they had enough screens to be able to show those films from independent distributors which had commercial potential. Odeon said that while it normally booked films for seven days plus holdover, it rarely had difficulties when distributors sought longer periods. On the occasions when distributors had sought minimum exhibition periods of four or five weeks these had generally been for popular films which Odeon had no difficulty in keeping on anyway. MGM Cinemas on the other hand said that two weeks was the norm; it considered that distributors made commercial judgments regarding the amount of money to be spent on promoting a film and should be happy to let the market decide whether their judgment was correct and, therefore, how long their films should continue to play.

4.186. While the leading exhibitors said that distributors were prepared to shorten the exhibition period if a film performed below expectations, some smaller exhibitors complained that distributors were inflexible in this respect. The CEA told us that minimum exhibition periods were the principal difficulty for the majority of operators. The length had increased and was now rarely less than two weeks, often more. Long minimum exhibition periods carried problems, especially for cinemas with fewer than four screens, as distributors did not distinguish between cinemas according to the number of screens.

4.187. In reply to our survey of independent exhibitors, several respondents said that minimum exhibition periods of three to four weeks did not make commercial sense, particularly for one-screen cinemas in small towns or country areas. About 47 per cent of respondents said that the distributor always or usually refused permission for a film to be taken off early, while 36 per cent said that such permission was given (see Appendix 4.4, paragraph 18, Statement 2).

## Restrictions on screen use

4.188. Distributors normally require exhibitors, during the licence period, to show a particular film at all the times at which films are normally shown at the cinema in question (except for children's matinées and late night shows). The relevant provisions of the *Standard Conditions* are Clauses 5(b) and 6 (see Appendix 4.3).

4.189. The leading distributors told us that these restrictions on screen use were part of the mechanism by which rental payments were assessed, since the house nut or break figures were set on the assumption that all performances at a particular screen during the week were of the same film. In practice, the question of sharing screens rose particularly in connection with children's films. Distributors told us that they might want to see if such films could attract an adult audience as well (eg as *Aladdin* had done), and if not, distributors were flexible, for example in agreeing that the film could be shown in a smaller screen in the evening, or have a reduced number of showings (subject to an amendment to the rental terms).

4.190. Two of the leading exhibitors said that most distributors (but not Buena Vista) were prepared to negotiate variations in screen usage. MGM Cinemas said, however, that while films appealing principally to children often did not perform well as the main evening show, distributors only rarely permitted the film to be moved to a smaller screen or the screen to be shared with another film, despite the fact that this was demonstrably more efficient to both the distributor and exhibitor. Buena Vista said that it was prepared to be flexible with regard to the showing of other films on the same screen at different times (see paragraph 8.119). It said that it distributed more films classified 'U' and 'PG'[1] than all the other leading distributors put together. It was therefore not surprising that Buena Vista was the subject of more complaints than other distributors on this topic (see paragraph 8.120).

4.191. The CEA said that distributor permission for screen sharing was given sparingly, though more often than it was in the past. This caused particular problems for cinemas with fewer than four screens, and for those situated in small towns or suburbs. In our survey of independent exhibitors, about one-half of respondents said that the leading distributors specified no screen-sharing (55 per cent for Buena Vista); between 34 and 44 per cent said that this was also true of the four independent distributors listed. Several respondents said that providing programmes for all sections of the community demanded a variety of films and timings through the week. About 22 per cent said that distributors always or usually refused them permission to show other films if asked, while 65 per cent said that permission was not refused.

## Competition and the balance of power between distributors and exhibitors

4.192. The market in this inquiry is that of the supply of films for exhibition in cinemas in the UK, and the basic unit of supply is the feature film. Competition takes place at three different levels:

*(a)* at the production level for scripts, finance, actors, etc;

*(b)* at the distribution level for screens; and

*(c)* at the exhibition level for films. At all three levels, there is competition for audiences.

---

[1] A 'U' film is for 'Universal' viewing, ie films suitable for all cinema-goers. A 'PG' ('Parental Guidance') film is also considered suitable for general viewing, but some scenes may be unsuitable for young children.

As distribution is the channel through which all films must pass from producer to exhibitor, its organization strongly influences the availability of films for exhibition.

4.193. While distributors compete with each other in various ways (eg in securing release dates, in acquiring screen-time, in attempting to maximize the periods for which their films are screened in cinemas, and in advertising and promotion), the leading distributors largely acquire distribution rights automatically from their US parents, whose films are not available for other distributors to bid for. To a small extent, the leading distributors compete to pick up rights to independent films. Independent distributors compete to establish relationships, such as output deals, with independent production companies, and in bidding for rights to other independent films on a one-off basis. Their principal activities are therefore much riskier than those of the leading distributors, which for the most part, as indicated, do not have to bid for film rights and whose distribution costs are wholly or mainly met by their parent companies.

4.194. Exhibitors compete largely through the location of their cinemas, the facilities offered, the films exhibited and the admission prices. As regards sites, both MGM Cinemas and Odeon have long-standing sites and have to decide which of these they should retain as well as whether to build new cinemas, whereas the three recent multiplex entrants only have to decide which cinemas to build. The facilities offered (eg the standard of projection and sound equipment, seating, spaciousness and layout, car parking and, perhaps above all, choice of films) are the principal means by which cinemas have been able to compete successfully against each other, and attract new audiences. Exhibitors also compete for films, eg by investing in their cinemas and by the terms they offer distributors.

4.195. The high-risk nature of the film business has been emphasized to us many times during the inquiry. At the production level much uncertainty exists as to when, even whether, the production company will receive a return on its investment. At the distribution level, substantial budgets for prints and advertising may be necessary, but are not sufficient conditions for a film to become a box office hit. The exhibitor then takes the risk of committing its screens, usually for at least seven days, to show the films which may or may not attract audiences and hence generate the revenue needed to cover the high costs of owning and operating cinemas.

4.196. Many of the arrangements and practices we looked at during the course of this inquiry were explained to us as being part of the industry's efforts to manage these risks. This was true in particular of the systems for deciding how much exhibitors pay to distributors for the rights to show films. These systems, which appear to exist in one form or another in most parts of the world, are all based on the sharing of box office takings according to certain agreed formulae rather than the fixing of a price in advance. Distributors depend on exhibitors to show their films and benefit directly, via rentals, from the exhibitors' success in attracting audiences to their cinemas, and exhibitors depend on a supply of popular films to attract audiences and benefit from distributors' success in promoting them.

4.197. Distributors told us that average percentage rentals paid by exhibitors in the UK were very low by international standards (they argued, for example, that a shortage of cinema screens in the UK put exhibitors in a strong bargaining position and enabled them to resist pressure for higher rentals). Leading exhibitors, on the other hand, emphasized that the Hollywood studios operated widely throughout the world and that the UK was but a small part of the global market. Their UK distribution subsidiaries could therefore afford to take a tough line on any issue which they perceived as threatening their wider interests. Exhibitors told us, however, that when UIP was negotiating special terms for *Jurassic Park*, the most successful film ever released, it was not able to dictate terms to the leading exhibitors but had to compromise.

4.198. The two previous inquiries into the supply of films observed the strong market position of the two main circuit exhibitors, ie the predecessors of MGM Cinemas and Odeon. Since the late 1980s their position has been radically changed by the successful entry of new exhibitors on a national scale, which not only offer significant competition in the market for exhibiting films, but have also contributed directly to a growth in the number of screens on which the films can be shown. These developments may well have weakened the bargaining power of the exhibitors as opposed to the distributors, but it is unclear how far this shift in bargaining power will go.

# 5 Financial results

## Contents

|  | Paragraph |
|---|---|
| Introduction | 5.1 |
| 'Shares of the cake' | 5.4 |
| Results of individual films | 5.8 |
| Financial results: distributors | 5.11 |
|    Distribution rights | 5.12 |
|    The five leading distributors | 5.14 |
|    Guild | 5.17 |
|    RFD | 5.18 |
|    Commentary on financial results | 5.19 |
| Financial results: exhibitors | 5.26 |
|    Aggregated results | 5.31 |
|    Profitability of the exhibitors | 5.37 |
|       Operating profit per admission | 5.38 |
|       Admissions | 5.43 |
|       Capital employed | 5.44 |
|       Return on capital employed | 5.46 |

## Introduction

5.1. In this chapter we first set out our estimates of the 'shares of the cake', ie the division of *(a)* box office takings and *(b)* total revenues from the exhibition of films in UK cinemas between exhibitors' costs and profits, distributors' costs and profits, and payments for distribution rights. We then look at the results of a selection of individual films to see how the rentals received by the distributors and the contribution after direct costs vary with box office takings.

5.2. We then consider the financial performance of the main distributors. We aggregate financial information from the five leading distributors, Buena Vista, Columbia, Fox, UIP and Warner Distributors, which are all vertically linked to one or more Hollywood studios, to show their overall results from UK film distribution. Table 4.2 shows that these five distributors accounted for some 76.6 per cent of rental receipts from UK film distribution in the calendar years 1990 to 1993 inclusive. We also consider separately the results of the two largest independent distributors, Guild and RFD, which accounted for a further 8.3 per cent and 4.7 per cent of rental receipts respectively in that period.

5.3. Finally, we consider the financial performance of the five leading exhibitors: MGM Cinemas, Natl Amusements, Odeon, UCI and Warner Theatres. Tables 4.7 and 4.8 show that these accounted for 78.6 per cent of cinema box office takings and 77.6 per cent of rental payments to distributors in the calendar years 1990 to 1993 inclusive. In the case of Natl Amusements and UCI we have taken into account relevant parts of the results of their overseas affiliated companies which own some of the UK cinema sites for which Natl Amusements and UCI are the operators. We aggregate the results of these five exhibitors to give their overall profitability from film exhibition in UK cinemas.

## 'Shares of the cake'

5.4. We have examined the 'shares of the cake' in two ways. First, we have looked at the division of box office takings alone, treating other income, such as sales of refreshments (known in the trade as 'concession income') and screen advertising revenue as deductions from exhibitors' costs. Table 5.1 sets out, in percentage terms, our estimates of how box office takings of films distributed by the five leading distributors in their accounting periods 1989 to 1993 were divided between exhibitors' costs and profits, distributors' costs and profits and distributors' payments for distribution rights. Secondly, we have looked at the division of total revenues, not only box office takings, but also concession income, screen advertising and other income. Table 5.2 therefore sets out, as an alternative, the division of these total revenues. For this exercise we have only used information from the five leading distributors and the five leading exhibitors but, as already pointed out, they accounted for 76.6 per cent of rentals received from exhibitors and 78.6 per cent of box office takings respectively.

5.5. Table 5.1 shows that over the period, 45.0 per cent of box office takings went in meeting exhibitors' costs (after deducting concession and other income), 18.8 per cent represented exhibitors' profits before interest and taxation and 23.3 per cent went in meeting distributors' costs. 12.4 per cent was payable, mainly overseas, for the cost of distribution rights. Taken overall, the distributors were left with only a small profit from theatrical exhibition after making these payments, although this takes no account of the streams of income and profit from other forms of exhibition which may be affected by success in the cinema.

TABLE 5.1 **Percentage division of box office takings**

per cent

| | Periods* | | | | | 1989 to |
|---|---|---|---|---|---|---|
| | 1989 | 1990 | 1991 | 1992 | 1993 | 1993 |
| Exhibitors' costs excluding rental payments less concession and other income | 46.3 | 46.5 | 44.7 | 47.4 | 40.6 | 45.0 |
| Exhibitors' profits before interest and tax | 12.8 | 16.7 | 20.8 | 18.7 | 23.4 | 18.8 |
| Distributors' costs less sundry income | 21.6 | 21.3 | 29.7 | 23.8 | 21.6 | 23.3 |
| Cost of distribution rights | 18.6 | 15.2 | 4.5 | 10.1 | 13.4 | 12.4 |
| Distributors' profits after cost of distribution rights | 0.7 | 0.3 | 0.3 | (0.0) | 1.0 | 0.5 |
| Box office takings | 100.0 | 100.0 | 100.0 | 100.0 | 100.0 | 100.0 |

*Source:* MMC using data from the five leading distributors and the five leading exhibitors.

*Company accounting periods ending in the year shown or early in the following year.

5.6. Table 5.2 shows that over the period total revenues were made up of about 72.6 per cent box office takings, 21.5 per cent concession income and 5.9 per cent other income (mainly screen advertising). The table reveals the significance of concession income to the exhibitors. Of these total revenues, some 60.0 per cent went in meeting exhibitors' costs (including the purchase of goods for resale as refreshments etc), 13.7 per cent represented exhibitors' profits before interest and taxation, 16.9 per cent went in meeting distributors' costs and 9.0 per cent was payable, mainly overseas, in payment for distribution rights. The distributors' profit after the cost of distribution rights, but before interest and tax, was 0.4 per cent.

TABLE 5.2 **Percentage division of box office takings and other income**

*per cent*

|  | Periods* | | | | | 1989 to 1993 |
|---|---|---|---|---|---|---|
|  | 1989 | 1990 | 1991 | 1992 | 1993 |  |
| Box office takings | 74.3 | 72.7 | 72.1 | 72.0 | 72.3 | 72.6 |
| Concession income | 19.1 | 21.1 | 21.9 | 22.2 | 22.6 | 21.5 |
| Other income | 6.6 | 6.2 | 6.0 | 5.8 | 5.1 | 5.9 |
| Total revenue | 100.0 | 100.0 | 100.0 | 100.0 | 100.0 | 100.0 |
| Exhibitors' costs excluding rental payments | 60.1 | 61.1 | 60.1 | 62.2 | 57.1 | 60.0 |
| Exhibitors' profits before interest and tax | 9.5 | 12.1 | 15.0 | 13.4 | 16.9 | 13.7 |
| Distributors' costs less sundry income | 16.1 | 15.5 | 21.4 | 17.1 | 15.6 | 16.9 |
| Cost of distribution rights | 13.7 | 11.1 | 3.3 | 7.3 | 9.7 | 9.0 |
| Distributors' profits after cost of distribution rights | 0.6 | 0.2 | 0.2 | (0.0) | 0.7 | 0.4 |
| Total revenue | 100.0 | 100.0 | 100.0 | 100.0 | 100.0 | 100.0 |

*Source:* MMC using data from the five leading distributors and the five leading exhibitors.

*Company accounting periods ending in the year shown or early in the following year.

5.7. Tables 5.1 and 5.2 show that exhibitors' profits (before interest and taxation) have risen as a percentage of both box office receipts and total revenues during the five-year period. Distributors' profits before the cost of distribution rights fell sharply from 1989 to 1991, but they recovered in the two most recent years as both distributors' and exhibitors' costs fell in relation to total revenues. The distributors took some of the strain of the recession by incurring costs in 1991 and 1992 that were higher in relation to rentals than in 1989, 1990 and 1993, and as a result the producers suffered a sharp fall in amounts receivable for distribution rights, not only in terms of percentages of box office takings and total cinema revenues, but also in absolute terms (Table 5.4 shows the fall in the cost of distribution rights in 1991 and 1992). The share of box office takings is shown in Figure 5.1, in which the small profit or loss of the distributors has been combined with payments for distribution rights to give the total share accruing to the Hollywood parent companies.

## Results of individual films

5.8. It is possible to calculate from Tables 5.1 and 5.2 that the rentals paid to distributors amounted to 36.2 per cent of box office takings and 26.3 per cent of exhibitors' turnover for the five years 1989 to 1993; the amount payable to the distributors' parent studios for distribution rights was 12.4 per cent of box office takings and 9.0 per cent of exhibitors' turnover. These percentages were averages for the leading exhibitors and distributors, but were not necessarily representative of individual films.

5.9. We received information from some of the distributors concerning the profitability of the films selected by them for the case studies discussed in Appendix 4.10. This is not a representative sample of films, being taken from the top five, bottom five and a typical five for each distributor. Also the results of individual films may be spread over more than one financial year, so that they cannot be agreed to audited accounts. However, we believe the results of these films give a broad indication of how profitability varies with success at the box office. In Table 5.3 we set out the results of 38 films grouped according to box office takings. For each group, the table gives the average box office takings, rentals, distributor's direct costs and contribution. These same amounts are also shown as a percentage of box office takings.

FIGURE 5.1

**Shares of the cake, based on box office takings**

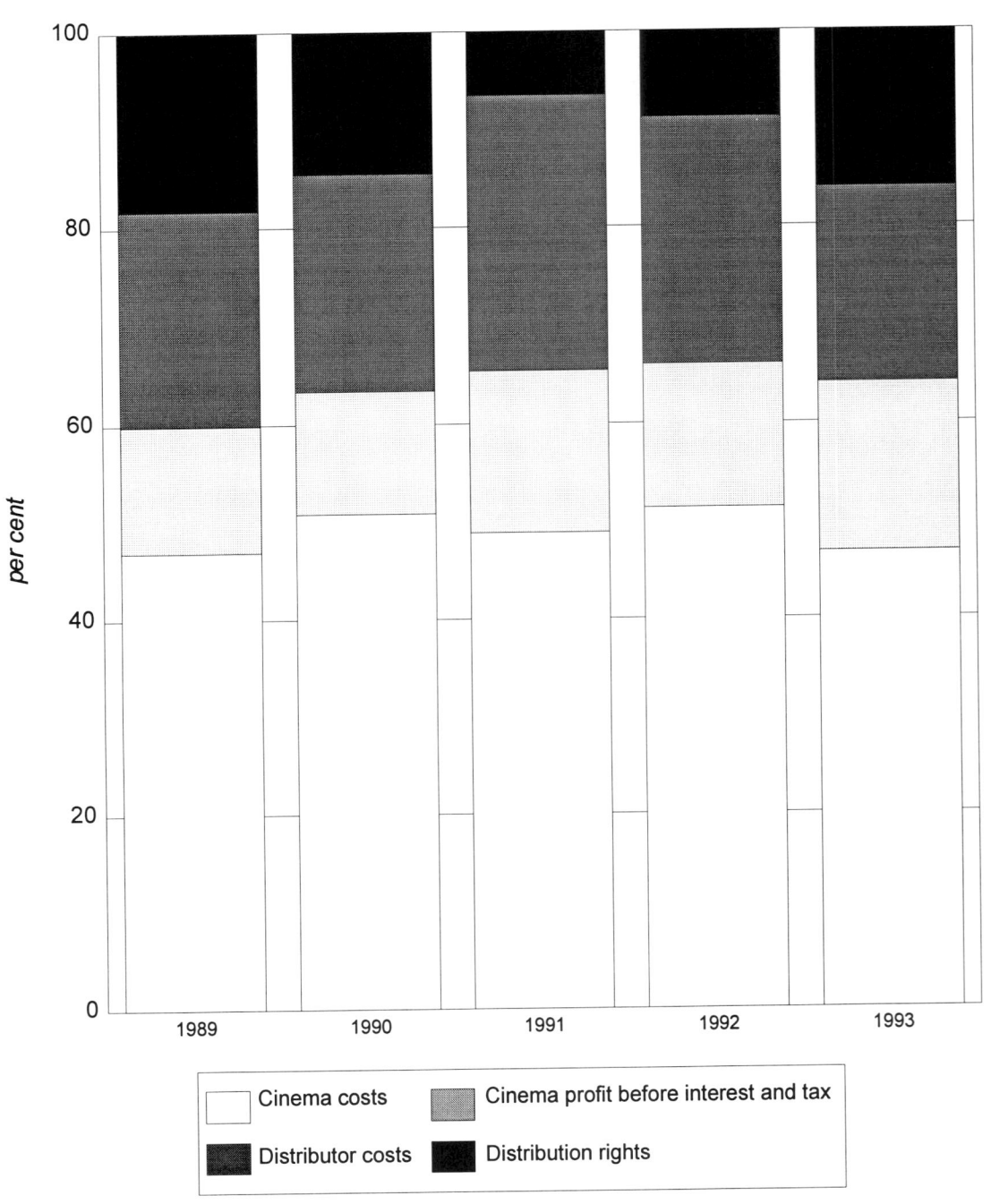

*Source:* MMC using data from the five leading distributors and the five leading exhibitors.

TABLE 5.3 **Average box office takings, rentals, direct costs and contribution of selected films**

£'000

| Range of box office takings | Number of films | Box office takings | Rental receipts | Prints and trailers | Advertising and publicity | Other costs | Contribution* |
|---|---|---|---|---|---|---|---|
| 0 – 1,000 | 6 | 641 | 177 | 92 | 342 | 2 | (259) |
| 1,000 – 2,500 | 11 | 1,713 | 508 | 149 | 433 | 10 | (84) |
| 2,500 – 5,000 | 7 | 3,484 | 1,158 | 185 | 549 | 14 | 410 |
| 5,000 – 10,000 | 4 | 6,491 | 2,473 | 166 | 799 | 67 | 1,441 |
| 10,000 – 20,000 | 10 | 13,157 | 5,803 | 298 | 1,034 | 12 | 4,459 |
| | | *Percentages of box office takings* | | | | | |
| 0 – 1,000 | 6 | 100.0 | 27.6 | 14.3 | 53.3 | 0.4 | (40.4) |
| 1,000 – 2,500 | 11 | 100.0 | 29.7 | 8.7 | 25.3 | 0.6 | (4.9) |
| 2,500 – 5,000 | 7 | 100.0 | 33.2 | 5.3 | 15.7 | 0.4 | 11.8 |
| 5,000 – 10,000 | 4 | 100.0 | 38.1 | 2.6 | 12.3 | 1.0 | 22.2 |
| 10,000 – 20,000 | 10 | 100.0 | 44.1 | 2.3 | 7.8 | 0.1 | 33.9 |

*Source:* MMC using distributors' data.

*Contribution before distributors' indirect costs.

5.10. Table 5.3 shows the effects on the profitability of individual films of the system of nuts and sliding scales (described in paragraphs 4.136 to 4.139) and the relatively small variation in the distributor's direct costs between successful and unsuccessful films. Films with box office takings below £2.5 million received little more than the minimum rental of 25 per cent. Such films made up the majority; we have been told that in both 1992 and 1993 only 39 films had box office takings above £2.5 million. This relatively small number of films would have been generally profitable, increasingly so as box office takings increased. The much greater number of films with box office takings below £2.5 million would, in most cases, have failed to cover the distributor's costs so that there would be no return to the producer from them. *Jurassic Park*, the most successful film during the five years, is not included in the above table. Its rental receipts and contribution as percentages of box office takings were above the highest levels in the table. The presence or absence of succesful films in any year is the principal determinant of a distributor's profitability.

## Financial results: distributors

5.11. We received financial information from the five leading distributors and from the two largest independents, Guild and RFD, and the tables in Appendix 5.1 are based on the statements submitted by them. Although there may be minor inconsistencies in the way in which these seven distributors have classified some items of income, cost and capital employed, we believe these are unlikely to have had a material effect on the results shown. Costs and capital employed that are not wholly attributable to UK film distribution have generally been apportioned by the distributors on a turnover basis. Where a distributor's accounting period does not coincide with the calendar year, figures for the period ending during the year or, in the case of Columbia, early in the following year have been used. All the information on the distributors in this chapter is based on their financial years, sometimes causing small differences from the information in other chapters where a calendar year basis has been used.

### *Distribution rights*

5.12. The five leading distributors are all owned by one or more Hollywood studios which are also their principal suppliers. They generally operate under some form of licensing or franchising agreement, whereby substantially all or most of their rentals, after deduction of operating expenses, are payable to their Hollywood suppliers in consideration of the distribution rights acquired. These arrangements are more fully described in Appendix 5.1. They sometimes acquire distribution rights to films from independent producers on an arm's length basis, but for most of their films they are performing a sales and marketing function for their parent studios. Their business does not require much working capital or fixed assets.

5.13. Guild, RFD and the smaller independent distributors, on the other hand, are usually not connected with the companies from which they obtain distribution rights. They negotiate the acquisition of these rights on an arm's length basis. This frequently involves some participation in the financing of the production of the films in question and assuming some of the associated risks.

## *The five leading distributors*

5.14. Table 5.4 sets out the five leading distributors' aggregated financial results from UK film distribution for their last five accounting periods. Appendix 5.1 contains similar information for each of the five leading distributors.

TABLE 5.4  **The five leading distributors: aggregated results from UK film distribution**

£'000

| | 1989 | 1990 | 1991 | 1992 | 1993 | Total |
|---|---|---|---|---|---|---|
| *Turnover* | | | | | | |
| Gross rentals | 61,569 | 76,747 | 53,780 | 69,325 | 85,204 | 346,625 |
| Other revenue | 876 | 1,560 | 924 | 747 | 2,089 | 6,196 |
| Total | 62,445 | 78,307 | 54,704 | 70,072 | 87,293 | 352,821 |
| *Direct costs* | | | | | | |
| Prints, trailers etc | 6,428 | 8,573 | 8,884 | 8,702 | 10,283 | 42,870 |
| Advertising and publicity | 21,527 | 30,640 | 32,760 | 35,207 | 36,065 | 156,199 |
| Other direct costs | 445 | 515 | 511 | 535 | 824 | 2,830 |
| Total | 28,400 | 39,728 | 42,155 | 44,444 | 47,172 | 201,899 |
| Contribution | 34,045 | 38,579 | 12,549 | 25,628 | 40,121 | 150,922 |
| *Indirect costs* | | | | | | |
| Staff costs | 2,439 | 3,052 | 2,588 | 2,559 | 3,012 | 13,650 |
| Accommodation | 618 | 1,130 | 792 | 941 | 781 | 4,262 |
| General administration | 2,089 | 2,208 | 1,790 | 1,531 | 2,241 | 9,859 |
| Other | (121) | (85) | (182) | (82) | 0 | (470) |
| Total | 5,025 | 6,305 | 4,988 | 4,949 | 6,034 | 27,301 |
| Operating profit before cost of distribution rights | 29,020 | 32,274 | 7,561 | 20,679 | 34,087 | 123,621 |
| Cost of distribution rights | 27,817 | 31,712 | 7,081 | 20,691 | 31,634 | 118,935 |
| Operating profit after payment for distribution rights | 1,203 | 562 | 480 | (12) | 2,453 | 4,686 |
| *Tangible capital employed at period end* | | | | | | |
| Tangible fixed assets | 3,396 | 3,651 | 3,102 | 3,150 | 2,859 | |
| Fixed asset investments | 11 | 11 | 11 | 11 | 11 | |
| Net current assets (excluding net borrowings) | 6,026 | 2,546 | 9,172 | 7,081 | 11,641 | |
| Capital employed | 9,433 | 6,208 | 12,285 | 10,242 | 14,511 | |

*Source:* MMC using the five leading distributors' data.

*Accounting periods ending in the year shown or early in the following year. Columbia's 1992 accounting period covered 13 months and UIP's 1990 accounting period covered 18 months.

5.15. Table 5.5 gives a number of cost and profitability ratios for these distributors, based on the results set out in Table 5.4. We have calculated ROT both before and after the cost of distribution rights. The latter is of little use in measuring financial performance because, as noted in paragraph 5.12, payments to affiliated studios for distribution rights leave only a small profit or loss in the UK. Although in many past monopoly inquiries we have found ROCE to be a useful profitability indicator, we do not find it to be of much assistance in measuring the performance of the leading distributors. They are not engaged in manufacturing and their activities are generally not capital-intensive. With their very small capital employed, ROCE calculated before the cost of distribution rights would usually exceed 100 per cent, while ROCE after these costs would often be small or negative. We believe that for our purposes the best measure of the overall performance of the vertically integrated distributors is ROT before the cost of distribution rights. This is not a measure of overall profit, since it takes no account of the costs incurred by affiliated companies, notably on film production.

TABLE 5.5 **The five leading distributors: aggregated operating ratios from UK film distribution**

| | | | Periods* | | | per cent |
|---|---|---|---|---|---|---|
| | 1989 | 1990 | 1991 | 1992 | 1993 | Total |
| Percentages of turnover | | | | | | |
| Gross rentals | 98.6 | 98.0 | 98.3 | 98.9 | 97.6 | 98.2 |
| Other revenue | 1.4 | 2.0 | 1.7 | 1.1 | 2.4 | 1.8 |
| Prints, trailers etc | 10.3 | 10.9 | 16.2 | 12.4 | 11.8 | 12.1 |
| Advertising and publicity | 34.5 | 39.1 | 59.9 | 50.2 | 41.3 | 44.3 |
| Other direct costs | 0.7 | 0.7 | 1.0 | 0.8 | 0.9 | 0.8 |
| Direct costs | 45.5 | 50.7 | 77.1 | 63.4 | 54.0 | 57.2 |
| Contribution | 54.5 | 49.3 | 22.9 | 36.6 | 46.0 | 42.8 |
| Indirect costs | 8.0 | 8.1 | 9.1 | 7.1 | 6.9 | 7.8 |
| Operating profit (ROT) before distribution rights | 46.5 | 41.2 | 13.8 | 29.5 | 39.1 | 35.0 |
| Cost of distribution rights | 44.6 | 40.5 | 12.9 | 29.5 | 36.3 | 33.7 |
| Operating profit (ROT) after distribution rights | 1.9 | 0.7 | 0.9 | (0.0) | 2.8 | 1.3 |

*Source:* MMC using the five leading distributors' data.

*Accounting periods ending in the year shown or early in the following year. Columbia's 1992 accounting period covered 13 months and UIP's 1990 accounting period covered 18 months.

5.16. Table 7 in Appendix 5.1 gives the rentals, other income and total turnover from UK film distribution for each of the five leading distributors in their last five accounting periods. Table 8 shows for each of these distributors a number of cost and profitability items expressed as percentages of turnover.

## *Guild*

5.17. Although Guild was acquired by Chargeurs SA in 1992, its new parent company has not so far been an important source of films and Guild has retained the character of an independent distributor. Guild provided us with the same information as the leading distributors, but because of its different situation as an independent we have not aggregated its results with theirs in Tables 5.4 and 5.5. However, we have drawn on its information at certain points for purposes of comparison. The results of Guild are set out in Table 9 of Appendix 5.1. [
*Details omitted. See note on page iv.*
]

## *RFD*

5.18. RFD is substantially engaged in a number of activities other than film distribution in the UK. It distributes films in the UK for exhibition on television and for supply as video cassettes. It also distributes films overseas. It told us that it usually bought distribution rights as a single package and could not identify how much of its payments for distribution rights related to theatrical distribution in the UK and how much to its other activities. RFD was therefore unable to provide us with financial information in the form that we had requested. It provided us instead with analyses of its trading profits for the last five years, together with allocations of its indirect costs to UK theatrical distribution. We have used this information in Table 10 of Appendix 5.1.

## Commentary on financial results

5.19. The aggregated annual film rentals of the five leading distributors increased during the period from £61.6 million to £85.2 million (Table 5.4). The erratic trend between 1989 and 1991 was partly accounted for by a change in UIP's accounting date, as a result of which its 1990 accounting period covered 18 months. In Table 5.6 we have restated the aggregated rentals of the leading distributors (both including and excluding Guild and RFD) to adjust for the effects of UIP's 18-month accounting period in 1990 and Columbia's 13-month accounting period in 1992. We have also recalculated these rentals at 1993 prices to exclude the effects of inflation.

TABLE 5.6 **Restatement of aggregate gross rentals to show trends on a yearly basis**

£'000

|  | Periods | | | | |
| --- | --- | --- | --- | --- | --- |
|  | 1989 | 1990 | 1991 | 1992 | 1993 |
| The five leading distributors, Guild and RFD | | | | | |
| At nominal prices | 65,859 | 70,863 | 76,518 | 79,180 | 93,117 |
| At calendar year 1993 prices | 80,297 | 80,204 | 80,996 | 80,605 | 93,231 |
| The five leading distributors only | | | | | |
| At nominal prices | 62,457 | 62,811 | 53,780 | 67,731 | 85,204 |
| At calendar year 1993 prices | 76,101 | 71,158 | 56,966 | 68,967 | 85,314 |
| Annual increase based on 1993 calendar year prices | | | | | per cent |
| The leading distributors, Guild and RFD | | (0.1) | 1.0 | (0.5) | 15.7 |
| The five leading distributors only | | (6.5) | (19.9) | 21.1 | 23.7 |

*Source:* MMC using data from the five leading distributors, Guild and RFD.

5.20. Table 5.6 shows that the 1993 rentals of the five leading distributors were 36.4 per cent higher than their 1989 rentals, but only 12.1 per cent higher when adjusted for inflation. When the rentals of Guild and RFD are included rental growth over these four years was 41.4 per cent, but only 16.1 per cent when adjusted for inflation. Virtually all the growth took place in 1993, helped by the extraordinary success of UIP's *Jurassic Park*. The different year-on-year growth rates when Guild and RFD are included is mostly caused by their exceptional performance in 1991, when the most successful films included *Terminator II* (Guild), *Silence of the Lambs* (RFD) and *Dances with Wolves* (Guild).

5.21. Table 7 of Appendix 5.1 shows that UIP was the largest distributor in terms of film rentals received, with a total of £131.3 million in five and a half years, an average of £23.9 million a year. Its rentals were unusually high in 1993, due to its UK release of *Jurassic Park*. Warner Distributors was next, with rentals of £117.8 million over five years, an average of £23.6 million a year. The loss of the distribution of Disney films to Buena Vista in 1993 was largely offset by the success of films from the Time Warner group in that year. Columbia was third largest, with an average of £10.9 million a year, followed by Fox whose average was £6.5 million a year (the same as Guild).

5.22. Table 5.5 shows that before distribution rights, average ROT for the five leading distributors reached 46.5 per cent in 1989, the highest level in the last five years. The lowest level was 13.8 per cent in 1991 when none of the five distributors had especially successful films. Table 8 of Appendix 5.1 shows that ROT before the cost of distribution rights tended to reflect size. UIP with [ * ] per cent was highest over the period. Warner Distributors was next with [ * ] per cent, followed by Columbia and Fox with [ * ] and [ * ] per cent respectively. Guild averaged [ * ] per cent but varied between [ * ] per cent in 1991 and a negative [ * ] per cent in 1993 (disregarding the heavy percentage loss in 1989 when its film distribution activities were negligible). This may have reflected its lack of an ownership link with a Hollywood studio and the consequent difficulties it faces in having to compete for successful films for distribution. Buena Vista made [ * ] per cent in 1993, its first year of operation.

---

*Figures omitted. See note on page iv.

5.23. The effect of the arrangements made by the leading distributors to acquire distribution rights from their affiliated studios can be seen in Table 5.5. While the aggregate ROT over the period was 35.0 per cent before the cost of distribution rights, it was reduced to a negligible 1.3 per cent after the cost of distribution rights had been deducted.

5.24. Table 5.4 shows that expenditure by the five leading distributors on direct costs increased throughout the period from £28.4 million in 1989 to £47.2 million in 1993. In Table 5.5 it can be seen that these direct costs absorbed 57.2 per cent of turnover over the period and a disproportionately large share (77.1 per cent) in 1991 when rental income was relatively low. Advertising and publicity, the largest element of direct costs, increased from 34.5 per cent of turnover in 1989 to 59.9 per cent in 1991 before falling back to 41.3 per cent in 1993, giving an average of 44.3 per cent over the period. As regards individual distributors, Table 8 of Appendix 5.1 shows that UIP spent least on average at [ * ] per cent of turnover over the five years, partly because of its high revenue from *Jurassic Park*. Columbia, Fox and Warner Distributors all averaged [ * ] to [ * ] per cent. Guild tended to spend most heavily on advertising and publicity in relation to rental receipts, with an overall average of [ * ] per cent of turnover, possibly reflecting its position as an independent. The five leading distributors spent an average of around 12.1 per cent of turnover on prints, trailers etc, varying from [ * ] per cent (UIP) to [ * ] per cent (Columbia), except for Buena Vista, which spent [ * ] per cent in 1993, its first year of operation.

5.25. RFD's results are not directly comparable with those of the other distributors because of the different form in which they are presented. However, its average UK theatrical commission income (Table 10 of Appendix 5.1) was [ * ] per cent of its turnover from UK theatrical distribution, after the cost of acquiring distribution rights. This was, however, before indirect costs of [ * ] per cent and its operating profit of [ * ] per cent after the cost of distribution rights is close to the [ * ] per cent of the five leading distributors. RFD's overall operating profit averaged [ * ] per cent of turnover over the five-year period, but this is not comparable with the results of the other distributors because of the inclusion of RFD's other activities.

## Financial results: exhibitors

5.26. Film exhibition is a capital-intensive activity and the balance sheets of the exhibitors are dominated by the cost of their investment in cinemas. ROCE is therefore a better measure of the profitability of the exhibitors than ROT. In line with their statutory and management accounts, some exhibitors included their cinemas at valuation rather than historical cost in the information provided to us, which has the effect in most instances of substantially reducing ROCE. We therefore asked them to restate their assets at historical cost and to recalculate depreciation on the basis of this cost so that ROCE would reflect the actual return on the amounts invested by them in their exhibition business. We also asked the exhibitors to exclude from capital employed any assets which did not make a contribution to trading profits such as construction in progress. We asked one of the exhibitors, who entered into a sale and leaseback transaction for some of its cinemas but reacquired them three years later, to restate its results to reflect the fact that it continued to enjoy the economic benefits of these assets.

5.27. The statements submitted to us by the five leading exhibitors have been summarized in Tables 1 to 7 of Appendix 5.2. Costs and capital employed that are not wholly attributable to the exhibition of films in UK cinemas have normally been apportioned by the companies on a turnover basis.

5.28. The financial information for MGM Cinemas includes its operations in the Republic of Ireland, which account for 1.9 per cent of turnover. Because of its immateriality, we did not ask MGM Cinemas to undertake a special exercise to eliminate its Irish operation from the results submitted to us. The figures for UCI consolidate 100 per cent of the cinema operations of Milton Keynes Entertainment Company Limited (MKEC) for the five years 1989 to 1993, although MKEC only became a wholly-owned subsidiary in 1993. UCI's results also include those of the two West End

---

*Figures omitted. See note on page iv.

cinemas, the Empire and the Plaza, which it operates on behalf of its affiliate, CIC. In Appendix 5.2 the financial results of UCI are set out in Table 4 and those of CIC in Table 5, but in the rest of the appendix and in this chapter their combined results have been included as those of UCI. Natl Amusements and UCI operate cinemas which are owned by overseas affiliated companies, and we have taken into account the relevant parts of the results of these affiliated companies. In Appendix 5.2 the results of Warner Bros Theatres Limited, which operates the Warner West End cinema, are set out in Table 6 and those of Warner Bros Theatres (UK) Limited, which operates a chain of multiplexes, in Table 7. Thereafter in Appendix 5.2 and in this chapter the combined results of these companies have been included under Warner Theatres.

5.29. Odeon's financial year ends on 31 October and that of Warner Theatres on 30 November, while the financial years of the other three leading exhibitors coincide with the calendar year. All the information on the leading exhibitors in this chapter is based on their financial years, sometimes causing small differences from the information in other chapters where a calendar year basis has been used.

5.30. In paragraph 5.26 we have explained that the results of the exhibitors have been restated when necessary in order to eliminate revaluations of fixed assets. With the results of all the exhibitors on a historical cost basis, those which operate old cinemas with low historical costs and a high level of accumulated depreciation have very high returns. Tables 5 and 6 of Appendix 5.2 show the unusually high ROCE of CIC and Warner Bros Theatres Limited (included in the results of UCI and Warner Theatres respectively). This restatement is also significant in the case of Odeon, which has owned most of its cinemas since the 1930s.

## *Aggregated results*

5.31. Table 5.7 has been compiled from the information on individual exhibitors set out in Tables 1 to 7 of Appendix 5.2. It gives the five leading exhibitors' aggregated financial results from the exhibition of films in UK cinemas for the five years to 1993. Although there may be minor inconsistencies in the way in which the exhibitors have classified some items of income, cost and capital employed, we believe that these are unlikely to have had a material effect on the aggregated results in Table 5.7.

TABLE 5.7  **The five leading exhibitors: aggregated results on exhibition in UK cinemas**

£'000

*Financial years ending in*

|  | 1988 | 1989 | 1990 | 1991 | 1992 | 1993 | Total |
|---|---|---|---|---|---|---|---|
| *Turnover excl VAT* | | | | | | | |
| Box office takings | - | 143,750 | 169,539 | 194,492 | 203,336 | 234,636 | 945,753 |
| Screen advertising | - | 8,222 | 10,983 | 11,950 | 12,221 | 12,242 | 55,618 |
| Concessions | - | 37,003 | 49,172 | 58,951 | 62,603 | 73,323 | 281,052 |
| Other revenue | - | 4,400 | 3,435 | 4,305 | 4,346 | 4,500 | 20,986 |
| Total | - | 193,375 | 233,129 | 269,698 | 282,506 | 324,701 | 1,303,409 |
| *Costs* | | | | | | | |
| Film rental payments | - | 58,766 | 62,333 | 67,146 | 68,989 | 84,381 | 341,615 |
| Concession cost of sales | - | 17,135 | 19,898 | 21,682 | 22,069 | 23,986 | 104,770 |
| Advertising and publicity | - | 5,479 | 7,143 | 8,319 | 9,550 | 9,835 | 40,326 |
| Staff costs | - | 41,007 | 50,200 | 56,727 | 61,677 | 65,448 | 275,059 |
| Depreciation | - | 10,957 | 19,320 | 22,154 | 23,884 | 25,049 | 101,364 |
| Other operating costs | - | 41,694 | 45,942 | 53,232 | 58,379 | 61,162 | 260,409 |
| Total | - | 175,038 | 204,836 | 229,260 | 244,548 | 269,861 | 1,123,543 |
| Operating profit | - | 18,337 | 28,293 | 40,438 | 37,958 | 54,840 | 179,866 |
| *Tangible capital employed at year end* | | | | | | | |
| Tangible fixed assets | 179,689 | 290,452 | 321,230 | 360,670 | 371,915 | 414,746 | |
| Fixed asset investments | 4,160 | 5,781 | 3,857 | 4,276 | 3,716 | 61 | |
| Net current assets (excluding net borrowings) | (21,295) | (26,861) | (33,646) | (33,168) | (31,555) | (31,419) | |
| Capital employed | 162,554 | 269,372 | 291,441 | 331,778 | 344,076 | 383,388 | |
| Average capital employed* | | 215,965 | 280,408 | 311,686 | 337,725 | 358,678 | 295,057 |

*Source:* MMC using the five leading exhibitors' data.

*The calculation of average capital employed of Warner Theatres has been adjusted for the closure of the company's West End cinema between 12 September 1991 and 24 September 1993 for conversion into a nine-screen cinema.

5.32. Table 5.7 shows that in the aggregate the five leading exhibitors' box office takings grew from £143.8 million in 1989 to £234.6 million in 1993, in part reflecting their investment in new cinemas and screens. Table 8 of Appendix 5.2 sets out the components of turnover of the five leading exhibitors in their last five accounting years. It can be seen that MGM Cinemas was the largest exhibitor, with total box office takings of £341.9 million over the five-year period, an average of £68.4 million a year. Odeon was next largest, with £251.6 million over the five years and an annual average of £50.3 million. It was followed by UCI, with £226.6 million over the five years and an annual average of £45.3 million. UCI, however, was growing fast and if the box office takings of its affiliate, CIC, are included it had overtaken Odeon in 1992. Natl Amusements, at £77.0 million, and Warner Theatres, at £48.7 million, were considerably smaller than the other three leading exhibitors but had the highest growth rates in box office takings in 1993.

5.33. Table 5.8 gives a number of significant cost and profitability ratios, including ROT and ROCE, for these five exhibitors, calculated from the information in Table 5.7.

TABLE 5.8 **The five leading exhibitors: aggregated results on exhibition in UK cinemas**

*per cent*

*Financial years ending in*

|  | 1989 | 1990 | 1991 | 1992 | 1993 | Total |
|---|---|---|---|---|---|---|
| *Percentages of turnover* | | | | | | |
| Box office takings | 74.3 | 72.7 | 72.1 | 72.0 | 72.3 | 72.6 |
| Screen advertising revenue | 4.3 | 4.7 | 4.4 | 4.3 | 3.8 | 4.3 |
| Concession income | 19.1 | 21.1 | 21.9 | 22.2 | 22.6 | 21.6 |
| Other revenue | 2.3 | 1.5 | 1.6 | 1.5 | 1.3 | 1.5 |
| | | | | | | |
| Costs | 90.5 | 87.9 | 85.0 | 86.6 | 83.1 | 86.2 |
| Operating profit (ROT) | 9.5 | 12.1 | 15.0 | 13.4 | 16.9 | 13.8 |
| | | | | | | |
| *Other ratios* | | | | | | |
| Film rental payments: box office takings | 40.9 | 36.8 | 34.5 | 33.9 | 36.0 | 36.1 |
| Operating profit: average capital employed (ROCE) | 8.5 | 10.1 | 13.0 | 11.2 | 15.3 | 12.2 |

*Source:* MMC using the five leading exhibitors' data.

5.34. Table 5.8 shows that concession income as a percentage of turnover averaged 21.6 per cent over the five-year period, and rose from 19.1 per cent in 1989 to 22.6 per cent in 1993. Table 8 of Appendix 5.2 indicates that this is partly because of the increasing market share of the multiplex chains which derive a higher proportion of their turnover from concession income than the two main circuits; but the importance of concession income for Odeon and MGM Cinemas also grew over the period. To demonstrate the importance of concessions to the exhibitors, Table 5.9 shows the gross profit from this source and compares this profit with the exhibitors' total operating profit. For the five years 1989 to 1993 the gross profit from concessions of £176.3 million was close to the total operating profit of £179.9 million. If no allowance were made for the share of indirect costs attributable to concessions, film exhibition and the other ancillary activities would have only recorded a very small profit.

TABLE 5.9 **The five leading exhibitors: contribution of concessions**

*£'000*

*Financial years ending in*

|  | 1989 | 1990 | 1991 | 1992 | 1993 | Total |
|---|---|---|---|---|---|---|
| Concession income | 37,003 | 49,172 | 58,951 | 62,603 | 73,323 | 281,052 |
| Concession cost of sales | 17,135 | 19,898 | 21,682 | 22,069 | 23,986 | 104,770 |
| Concession gross profit | 19,868 | 29,274 | 37,269 | 40,534 | 49,337 | 176,282 |
| | | | | | | |
| Total operating profit | 18,337 | 28,293 | 40,438 | 37,958 | 58,840 | 179,866 |

*per cent*

|  | | | | | | |
|---|---|---|---|---|---|---|
| Concession gross profit: | | | | | | |
| total operating profit | 108.3 | 103.5 | 92.2 | 106.8 | 90.0 | 98.0 |
| concession income | 53.7 | 59.5 | 63.2 | 64.7 | 67.3 | 62.7 |

*Source:* MMC using the five leading exhibitors' data.

5.35. According to Table 5.8, the aggregate profitability of the five leading exhibitors, in terms of both ROT and ROCE, improved year on year from 1989 to 1993, except for a slight reversal in 1992. Table 9 of Appendix 5.2 shows that each exhibitor increased its ROCE over these five years except for Odeon—its ROT hardly varied, but its ROCE was more than halved. Odeon told us that if its fixed assets were stated at current market value, instead of historical cost, its ROCE would have shown little movement since 1990.

5.36. Rental payments as a percentage of box office takings are seen in Table 5.8 to have fallen from their highest level for the five-year period of 40.9 per cent in 1989 to a low point of 33.9 per cent in 1992, before recovering to 36.0 per cent in 1993. However, if the box office takings and rental payments of *Jurassic Park* were eliminated from the 1993 results, rental payments would have continued to decline as a percentage of box office takings.

## *Profitability of the exhibitors*

5.37. Three ratios, operating profit per admission, admissions per seat and capital employed per seat, can be combined to give ROCE.[1] In the section following we look at each of these ratios and their components for the leading exhibitors and use them to explain differences in financial performance.

### *Operating profit per admission*

5.38. Table 10 of Appendix 5.2 sets out box office receipts, concession gross profit and the principal variable costs per admission for each of the leading exhibitors. This table is summarized in Table 5.10.

TABLE 5.10 **The five leading exhibitors: average revenues and costs per admission, 1989 to 1993**

£

*Financial years ending*

|  | 1989 | 1990 | 1991 | 1992 | 1993 |
| --- | --- | --- | --- | --- | --- |
| Box office receipts | 2.16 | 2.39 | 2.62 | 2.70 | 2.74 |
| Concession gross profit | 0.30 | 0.41 | 0.50 | 0.54 | 0.58 |
| Film rental | (0.88) | (0.88) | (0.90) | (0.92) | (0.98) |
| Other costs less other revenues | (1.30) | (1.52) | (1.68) | (1.82) | (1.70) |
| Operating profit | 0.28 | 0.40 | 0.54 | 0.50 | 0.64 |
|  |  |  |  |  | '000 |
| Admissions | 66,413 | 70,820 | 74,215 | 75,252 | 85,666 |

*Source:* MMC using the five leading exhibitors' data.

5.39. The leading exhibitors benefited not only from an increase in admissions of 29.0 per cent from 1989 to 1993, but also an increase of more than 125 per cent in profit per admission before interest and tax. Table 10 of Appendix 5.2 gives the performance of the individual exhibitors. In 1989 Warner Theatres only had a single West End cinema, with higher costs and box office receipts per admission than the other exhibitors (although with its growing chain of multiplex cinemas its results have come to resemble more closely those of its competitors). Apart from Warner Theatres, Odeon had the highest box office prices and until 1993 it generated the highest rentals per admission. Natl Amusements, with low operating costs, has emerged as the most profitable exhibitor in terms of operating profit per admission.

5.40. Fixed costs are more usefully considered in terms of cost per seat rather than cost per admission. Table 11 of Appendix 5.2, which sets out the principal fixed costs of each of the leading exhibitors analysed in this way, is summarized in Table 5.11.

---

[1] $\text{ROCE} = \dfrac{\text{Operating profit}}{\text{Admissions}} \times \dfrac{\text{Admissions}}{\text{Ave number of seats}} \times \dfrac{\text{Ave number of seats}}{\text{Ave capital employed}}$

TABLE 5.11 **The five leading exhibitors: average fixed costs per seat, 1989 to 1993**

£

*Financial years ending in*

|  | 1989 | 1990 | 1991 | 1992 | 1993 |
|---|---|---|---|---|---|
| Staff costs | 159.20 | 172.47 | 185.16 | 192.26 | 199.05 |
| Advertising and publicity | 21.27 | 24.54 | 27.15 | 29.77 | 29.91 |
| Depreciation | 42.54 | 66.38 | 72.31 | 74.45 | 76.18 |
| Other operating costs | 161.87 | 157.83 | 173.76 | 181.97 | 186.03 |
|  | 384.88 | 421.22 | 458.38 | 478.45 | 491.17 |

*Units*

| Average number of seats | 257,576 | 291,070 | 306,364 | 320,806 | 328,797 |
|---|---|---|---|---|---|

*Source:* MMC using the five leading exhibitors' data.

5.41. Fixed costs per seat increased by 27.6 per cent from 1989 to 1993. By far the largest increase was the 79.1 per cent for depreciation. This reflected the high capital costs of the new multiplexes and the modernization by MGM Cinemas and Odeon of some of their older cinemas. Advertising and publicity costs increased by more than 40 per cent. Table 11 of Appendix 5.2 shows that from 1989 the new multiplex operators spent far more on these items than MGM Cinemas and Odeon, which responded with increased expenditure, although not on the scale of their new competitors. Staff costs increased by more than 25 per cent and other operating costs per seat by almost 15 per cent. [

*Details omitted. See note on page iv.*

] Natl Amusements benefits from not having to bear the costs of a head office; it is managed from the office of National Amusements Inc in Dedham, Massachussetts.

5.42. We asked the leading exhibitors to give us details of their average number of employees. There are many part-time employees, and the companies have not dealt with them on a consistent basis. It is therefore only possible to make broad comparisons between the exhibitors. Nevertheless, on various measures of productivity (admissions and seats per employee, employees per screen) the new multiplex operators appear to perform better than the traditional circuits which have fewer modern cinemas.

*Admissions*

5.43. All the leading exhibitors except MGM Cinemas have increased the number of seats over the five years, and all have increased the number of screens. When considering profit per seat, one must look not only at profit per admission but also the number of admissions per seat. The number of admissions and the average (not year-end) number of seats for the five leading exhibitors is set out in Table 5.12 and for each of the exhibitors in Table 13 of Appendix 5.2. Over the five years admissions increased by 29.0 per cent and the number of seats by 27.7 per cent, so that admissions per seat in 1993, after a decline from 1990 to 1992, were little changed from 1989.

TABLE 5.12 **The five leading exhibitors: average admissions per seat, 1989 to 1993**

'000

|  | 1989 | 1990 | 1991 | 1992 | 1993 |
|---|---|---|---|---|---|
| Admissions | 66,413 | 70,820 | 74,215 | 75,252 | 85,666 |

*Units*

|  | 1989 | 1990 | 1991 | 1992 | 1993 |
|---|---|---|---|---|---|
| Average number of seats | 257,576 | 291,070 | 306,364 | 320,806 | 328,797 |
| Admissions per seat | 258 | 243 | 242 | 235 | 261 |

*Source:* MMC using the leading exhibitors' data.

*Capital employed*

5.44. Table 5.13 gives the numbers of cinemas and screens of the five leading exhibitors at the end of each of their accounting periods completed in the five years to 1993 and their total capital expenditure (the capital expenditure of the individual exhibitors is given in Table 13 of Appendix 5.2). Capital expenditure reached a peak in 1989 but, despite a subsequent decline in expenditure and the closure of a number of older cinemas by MGM Cinemas and Odeon, the leading exhibitors except MGM Cinemas are still increasing their facilities. MGM Cinemas' expenditure of £26 million on acquisitions in 1989 and 1990, which added five cinemas and ten development sites to its circuit, has not been included in the capital expenditure in Table 5.13. The five leading exhibitors incurred capital expenditure of £388.2 million during the six years 1988 to 1993.

TABLE 5.13 **The leading exhibitors: facilities and capital expenditure, 1988 to 1993**

|  | \multicolumn{6}{c}{*Numbers at period end*} |  |  |  |  |
|---|---|---|---|---|---|---|
|  | 1988 | 1989 | 1990 | 1991 | 1992 | 1993 |
| *Cinemas* |  |  |  |  |  |  |
| MGM Cinemas | 143 | 146 | 138 | 138 | 133 | 127 |
| Natl Amusements | 3 | 7 | 7 | 8 | 9 | 10 |
| Odeon | 72 | 74 | 75 | 74 | 72 | 72 |
| UCI | 11 | 17 | 21 | 23 | 25 | 25 |
| Warner Theatres | 1 | 3 | 5 | 6 | 7 | 9 |
|  | 230 | 247 | 246 | 249 | 246 | 243 |
| *Screens* |  |  |  |  |  |  |
| MGM Cinemas | 386 | 396 | 400 | 443 | 429 | 416 |
| Natl Amusements | 37 | 89 | 89 | 101 | 113 | 127 |
| Odeon | 205 | 233 | 262 | 289 | 310 | 321 |
| UCI | 91 | 146 | 186 | 205 | 217 | 217 |
| Warner Theatres | 5 | 26 | 48 | 57 | 64 | 84 |
|  | 724 | 890 | 985 | 1,095 | 1,133 | 1,165 |
|  |  |  |  |  |  | £'000 |
| Capital expenditure | 69,556 | 104,360 | 67,315 | 61,679 | 47,812 | 37,502 |

*Source:* The five leading exhibitors.

5.45. Table 14 of Appendix 5.2 gives the average capital employed for each of the five leading exhibitors, and the capital employed per seat. MGM Cinemas and Odeon still have a number of older, traditional cinemas (many of which are listed buildings) with low historical costs, which are heavily depreciated, and this is reflected in their lower capital employed per seat than the new multiplex operators. Their expenditure on new and refurbished cinemas has reduced the differences between them and the new multiplex operators.

*Return on capital employed*

5.46. Table 5.14 sets out average operating profit per admission, admissions per seat and average capital employed per seat for each of the leading exhibitors for the five years from 1989 to 1993, together with their return on average capital employed.[1]

---

[1] Table 5.14 shows the components of ROCE listed in paragraph 5.37 (with one of the ratios, capital employed per seat, inverted). For example, for the five leading exhibitors in aggregate, ROCE in 1993 was 0.64 × 261 ÷ 1,091 = 0.153 or 15.3 per cent.

TABLE 5.14 **The five leading exhibitors: components of profitability, 1989 to 1993**

£

*Financial years ending in*

|  | 1989 | 1990 | 1991 | 1992 | 1993 |
|---|---|---|---|---|---|
| *Operating profit per admission* | | | | | |
| MGM Cinemas | [ | | | | |
| Natl Amusements | | *Figures omitted.* | | | |
| Odeon | | *See note on* | | | |
| UCI | | *page iv.* | | | |
| Warner Theatres | | | | | ] |
| *Average* | 0.28 | 0.40 | 0.54 | 0.50 | 0.64 |

Units

|  | 1989 | 1990 | 1991 | 1992 | 1993 |
|---|---|---|---|---|---|
| *Admissions per seat* | | | | | |
| MGM Cinemas | [ | | | | |
| Natl Amusements | | *Figures omitted.* | | | |
| Odeon | | *See note on* | | | |
| UCI | | *page iv.* | | | |
| Warner Theatres | | | | | ] |
| *Average* | 258 | 243 | 242 | 235 | 261 |

£

|  | 1989 | 1990 | 1991 | 1992 | 1993 |
|---|---|---|---|---|---|
| *Capital employed per seat* | | | | | |
| MGM Cinemas | [ | | | | |
| Natl Amusements | | *Figures omitted.* | | | |
| Odeon | | *See note on* | | | |
| UCI | | *page iv.* | | | |
| Warner Theatres | | | | | ] |
| *Average* | 838 | 963 | 1,017 | 1,053 | 1,091 |

per cent

|  | 1989 | 1990 | 1991 | 1992 | 1993 |
|---|---|---|---|---|---|
| *ROCE* | | | | | |
| MGM Cinemas | [ | | | | |
| Natl Amusements | | *Figures omitted.* | | | |
| Odeon | | *See note on* | | | |
| UCI | | *page iv.* | | | |
| Warner Theatres | | | | | ] |
| *Average* | 8.5 | 10.1 | 13.0 | 11.2 | 15.3 |

*Source:* MMC using the leading exhibitors' data.

5.47. For the exhibitors taken together, operating profit per admission improved from 28p to 64p, an increase of more than 125 per cent. This was partly offset by an increase of 40 per cent in capital employed per seat from £838 to £1,091. Admissions per seat, after declining from 1990 to 1992, recovered to their 1989 levels; over the five years the growth in admissions was closely matched by the increased number of seats. Overall, ROCE improved from 8.5 to 15.3 per cent.

5.48. Table 5.14 reveals how the financial performance of the new multiplex operators—Natl Amusements, UCI and Warner Theatres—differs from that of the traditional operators. Even so there are differences between the multiplex operators. UCI is outstanding for the number of admissions per seat; in 1993 it was more than 20 per cent ahead of its nearest competitor. This intensive use of its capacity partly compensates it for having the highest capital cost per seat of all the exhibitors. However, its increasing staff costs and other overheads have led to a fall in profitability in 1992 and 1993. Natl Amusements has benefited from its high profits on concessions and low operating costs, particularly staff costs. Warner Theatres has changed during the five years from the operator of a loss-making West End cinema, used mostly for its parent studio's films, into an increasingly profitable multiplex operator.

5.49. Overall, the ROCE of the multiplex operators has not yet reached their target rates of return and their operating profits have in some years been insufficient to cover their interest costs.

5.50. MGM Cinemas and Odeon, the traditional exhibitors, generally had a lower profit per admission than their newer competitors. They had lower overheads per seat, but this advantage was offset by having fewer admissions per seat than their new competitors, who also had higher concession profits per admission. Their principal advantage is a lower capital employed per seat, a reflection of their large numbers of old cinemas with low historical costs, now largely depreciated, but this advantage has been reduced as they have responded to the construction programmes of their new multiplex competitors with building projects of their own. Odeon's ROCE has fallen from almost [*] per cent in 1989 to around [*] per cent, still comfortably the highest of the major exhibitors.

---

*Figures omitted. See note on page iv.

# 6 Views of third parties

## Contents

*Paragraph*

Exhibition interests
    Cinema Exhibitors' Association .................................... 6.2
    Independent exhibitors ............................................ 6.19
    Mr Geoffrey Henshaw ............................................. 6.35
Distribution interests
    Society of Film Distributors Limited ............................... 6.39
    Small distributors ................................................. 6.48
Production interests
    Producers Alliance for Cinema and Television ....................... 6.52
    Production companies ............................................. 6.71
    Mr David Puttnam ............................................... 6.72
Others
    British Film Institute .............................................. 6.92
    Channel 4 ........................................................ 6.109
    Mr Michael Henry ................................................ 6.118
    Department of National Heritage .................................. 6.146

6.1. In this chapter we summarize the views of the interested parties who gave evidence to us, other than the leading exhibitors (see Chapter 7) and the distributors in the complex monopoly group (see Chapters 8 and 9). We did not receive any representations from individual consumers or from the National Consumers Council or the Consumers' Association.

## Exhibition interests

### Cinema Exhibitors' Association

6.2. The CEA represents approximately 90 per cent of UK cinema operators, including all the leading exhibitors. It gave written evidence and attended a hearing. Its written submission was the result of a major consultation exercise among its members. The CEA told us that whilst all its members agreed with the views expressed, its comments did not represent all the views of all members.[1]

### *Print availability*

6.3. The CEA stated that the availability of first-run prints had improved since the last MMC inquiry. This was acknowledged by all exhibitors. Although some felt that, as new screens opened, their access to first-run prints had decreased, others, who in the past had been only occasionally offered first-run prints, were now nearly always offered them.

---

[1]Odeon, however, told us that its views were not necessarily the same as the CEA's.

6.4. From time to time all exhibitors found that they were unable to book the film that they wanted at the time they wanted it. Most independent exhibitors and the smaller circuits were generally able to book the films that they wanted. Sometimes, however, they did not obtain the number of prints that they wished. The smaller circuits also were not permitted to move the prints around their circuits as they wished at all times.

## *Minimum exhibition periods*

6.5. The major difficulty for most exhibitors was the minimum exhibition periods demanded by distributors. These had increased over the years and were now rarely less than two weeks; they were often more if an exhibitor wished to show a film in the opening weeks. Recent examples of films with minimum playing times exceeding two weeks included *Jurassic Park*, *The Fugitive* and *Aladdin*. The CEA said that a long minimum exhibition period caused problems, especially where a cinema had fewer than four screens. The problems were exacerbated as the number of screens on a site decreased. A minimum exhibition requirement on one film might preclude a smaller cinema from showing another, more popular film during that period. If a film performed below expectations, it was often difficult for the exhibitor to secure the distributor's agreement to it being taken off early.

6.6. There was also a growing trend among distributors to demand a long minimum exhibition period for films which had been on release for some time. This caused particular difficulties for exhibitors in smaller towns and suburbs where a film might already have been exhibited in a nearby cinema. The problem could be more acute where a cinema had a single screen with a large seating capacity.

6.7. The CEA was undecided whether the length of run which could be demanded by a distributor should be dealt with by an Order or an agreed code of practice.

## *Restrictions on screen use*

6.8. The *Standard Conditions* (see Appendix 4.3) laid down that, with the permission of the distributor, another film might be shown 'over and/or under' the main feature. Permission to do so was, according to the CEA, not given sufficiently often, though more frequently than in the past. Most distributors demanded that only their film be shown during the normal exhibition day. This caused particular problems for cinemas with fewer than four screens and those which were situated in small towns or suburbs. Often these cinemas were open only in the evenings, except during school holidays. The insistence that no other film be shown over or under the main booking often deprived a neighbourhood of family entertainment during school holidays. It could also prevent an exhibitor from showing films of wider appeal in the evening.

6.9. Some distributors gave permission for another film to be shown over or under their own film, but imposed arbitrary screening times which were totally unsuitable for the local situation, thereby making the offer unacceptable. For example, a distributor might allow another film to be shown after 8.30 pm. While this might be suitable in urban areas, it was not appropriate in rural areas. The CEA thought the conditions should be more flexible.

6.10. Distributors sometimes gave permission for a film which had played in a cinema for an exclusive run to continue to play in an over or under situation or on a limited number of days. At the same time, they would not make this concession available to nearby second-run cinemas (ie cinemas which did not get films on release date) which had not yet shown the film. This increased the problems for those cinemas.

6.11. The CEA argued that the demand for exclusive use of a screen for one film was abused by distributors. It prevented exhibitors from utilizing screen time to the benefit of the public and could put the viability of cinemas in jeopardy.

*SFD Standard Conditions*

6.12. The CEA stated that the *Standard Conditions* did not take account of the last report of the MMC, did not reflect current trading conditions and used archaic language. The *Standard Conditions* were, in their present form, particularly burdensome to smaller exhibitors.

6.13. It was wrong that exhibitors had to abide by *Standard Conditions* which were biased totally in favour of the distributors, in that exhibitors required the distributors' permission before making changes to the operation of their businesses. It was, for example, unreasonable that exhibitors could not change their ticket prices without first receiving the permission of the distributors. Distributors had refused permission for some exhibitors to reduce their admission prices on Monday evenings when attendances were low. This applied particularly where two cinemas were in competition: the distributor would refuse permission for one to reduce prices in order to undercut the other. The *Standard Conditions* also gave distributors unreasonable rights to intervene in the exhibitors' box office operations.

6.14. The SFD had agreed with the CEA that the *Standard Conditions* should be reviewed and the first part of this exercise, to bring the document to a usable state, had been completed in June 1992. Rather than proceeding to the second, substantive stage of the review, however, the SFD had stated that it would consider further amendments that the CEA put to it in writing. The CEA considered that this was not in the spirit of what had been agreed and would, on past experience, be an exercise in futility.

6.15. The CEA favoured some form of evenly-balanced standard terms and conditions in order to protect, in particular, smaller exhibitors and distributors who did not have the commercial strength to refuse unreasonable demands. The CEA believed the best way to achieve this was by regular meetings with the SFD to review the *Standard Conditions* in the light of changing circumstances and any new legislation. It identified specific elements of the *Standard Conditions* which it thought were particularly in need of revision.

*Exchanges of information*

6.16. The CEA also believed that members of the SFD often shared commercially sensitive information, for example on break figures or house nuts and on creditworthiness, about the membership of the CEA. It observed that since the announcement of the MMC inquiry, different break figures were being agreed by different distributors for the same cinema, but commented that this had happened only rarely in the past.

*Alignment: possible remedy*

6.17. Commenting on our first possible remedy on alignment (see paragraph 7.16), the CEA questioned how the first part of the remedy would operate and how it would be policed. If the offer of a film were to be based only on a cinema's merits, the difficulties independent exhibitors already experienced in obtaining prints on a specific date were likely to be exacerbated. A distributor would simply be able to say that a cinema did not merit the film at that date. If cinemas under the same company's control were to be ignored when negotiating a play date, which was always linked with the amount of film rental, it was likely that rentals would increase. The CEA said that in the case of *Jurassic Park*, where the rental terms originally demanded had been high, major exhibitors had been able to exert pressure on the distributor because of the potential number of screens they offered. This had benefited all exhibitors. If the suggested remedy had been operative when the negotiations had taken place the rental terms would have been higher.

6.18. On the second part of the remedy, the CEA said that distributors were always trying to increase the rental paid by exhibitors and, as making returns to the OFT would increase their costs, they would use this as an excuse to seek higher rental. Asking for information only from MGM Cinemas and Odeon appeared to be discriminatory. Alignment of product, especially when films moved over from arthouse to mainstream cinemas, probably had a greater effect within the arthouse market on the potential income of a film than it did within the mainstream cinemas.

## Independent exhibitors

6.19. Evidence received from the 22 independent exhibitors listed in Appendix 6.1 is summarized below. Six of these exhibitors (Apollo Leisure UK Ltd (Apollo), Cosmo Leisure Group, Full Circle Film and Theatre Company, Hippodrome (Wrexham) Ltd (Hippodrome), North West Leisure (Manchester) Ltd (North West Leisure) and Richmond Filmhouse) attended hearings as well as providing written submissions. We also carried out a survey of independent exhibitors, the results of which are summarized in Appendix 4.4.

### *Availability of prints*

6.20. Fifteen exhibitors complained about non-availability of prints. Most said that they were unable to obtain films on release or within a reasonable period after release. Some blamed the distributors' preference for allocating films to multiplex cinemas.

6.21. North West Leisure said that a two-screen cinema it had owned at the time of the previous MMC inquiry had been forced to close as a result of a multiplex cinema opening nearby. Certain distributors had stopped supplying the cinema with films on release and those that had been shown after a run at the multiplex had collapsed at the box office.

6.22. Hippodrome told us that it had also experienced difficulty in obtaining new releases after two multiplex cinemas opened in a town more than ten miles away. This prevented Hippodrome from competing fairly. If it were squeezed out of business, there would be no local cinema.

6.23. Richmond Filmhouse said that it had had difficulty in obtaining films after a second Odeon cinema had opened in the same town. It was unable to obtain prints on release and in some cases, eg *Much Ado About Nothing*, had been unable to obtain the film at all. It believed that Odeon had persuaded Entertainment, the distributor of the film, to play it at the Odeon, despite a prior agreement that the film would be played at the Richmond Filmhouse. It believed this was because Odeon would be showing the film in many other cinemas throughout the country and Entertainment did not wish to upset their relationship. Richmond Filmhouse said that difficulties in accessing films were a deterrent to independent operators building new multi-screen cinemas. Potential backers would be concerned that, if a new independent cinema was successful, one of the large exhibitors would build a cinema in the same area and block the independent's access to films.

6.24. One exhibitor said that, as a result of the unfair treatment of independent exhibitors by distributors, no capital was available to enable small exhibitors to add more screens to their cinemas. No independent exhibitor or group of independent exhibitors would be willing to invest in building a multiplex cinema when there was every possibility that it would be denied the product to operate.

6.25. Another exhibitor, which had cinemas in the Midlands, North Wales and the North of England, said that, in cases where films were limited to 120 to 150 prints, it was often unable to obtain a sufficient number to cover its circuit. It might typically be offered between one and four prints. The number varied for each film and was often reduced between initial negotiations and play date.

6.26. Another exhibitor believed that some distributors identified particular key towns and refused to supply cinemas in other towns in the same area with first releases. The exhibitor subsequently wrote to say that, since giving its initial evidence to the MMC, its relationship with distributors had improved.

6.27. Queens Film Theatre in Belfast said that distributors were happy to give films to the leading exhibitors under any circumstances, but adopted a different approach when supplying independent cinemas. The circuit exhibitors, particularly MGM Cinemas, had a stranglehold on some of the small distributors, to the detriment of independent cinemas.

## *Conditional booking*

6.28. Two exhibitors complained about conditional booking (see also paragraphs 4.180 to 4.182). Hippodrome told us of two instances where it considered that conditional booking had been practised. In one case, after the exhibitor had refused to take a particular film, the distributor had refused to supply it with three other films. Another distributor had agreed to supply the exhibitor with the two films it wanted on condition that it took two less successful films. Empire Cinema said that, in order to obtain films it wanted, it had to take less popular films.

## *Minimum exhibition periods*

6.29. Nine exhibitors complained of the distributors' tendency to stipulate minimum exhibition periods for films, which meant that they must either wait for some time to show a popular film or play it for a long period with poor attendance. One exhibitor felt that interest in most films waned after two weeks and the public and exhibitors would be better served if a film was moved to another cinema after that period rather than making an exhibitor show it for longer. If this were the case, the second cinema would show the film only two weeks after release. When multiplex cinemas had to take a film for a long period they were able to move it from a large to a smaller screen. However, in these circumstances the print would be earning progressively less and would still be withheld from another venue where it would be the main (or only) feature. The exhibitor thought that distributors might be imposing minimum exhibition periods in order to block the showing of competing films.

## *Restrictions on screen use*

6.30. Five exhibitors complained about distributors' inflexibility over the use of screens to show films under or over the main film. One exhibitor said that, during a school holiday, a distributor had refused to allow it to show a 'U' certificate film in the same auditorium as a '15' certificate film (which was not due to start until 5.00 pm), unless the former finished by 2.00 pm. This meant that the screen was closed for three hours in the afternoon at a time when a potential audience was looking for entertainment.

6.31. Another exhibitor said that a distributor had allowed it to show an adult film as the last performance each day when its children's film was playing in the afternoon. However, the distributor had stipulated that the showing of the adult film could not start before 8.30 pm. This did not allow the exhibitor to adapt to local habits or transport times. Neither would it cater for local licensing conditions which, in some towns, restricted the hours a cinema could show films. The exhibitor said that, in other cases, distributors of adult films would not let it put on a children's film in the afternoon when the main film was newly released.

## *Calculation of rental payments*

6.32. Seven exhibitors complained about the high rental charges for prints. Most of these also complained about the increasing tendency on the part of distributors to impose special terms for popular films. Some said that distributors had refused to increase the break figures applying to their cinemas for several years despite increases in admission charges. One exhibitor said that, to be effective and fair to exhibitors, rental terms should be updated in line with factors such as inflation and increases in admission charges.

6.33. Another exhibitor said that, increasingly over recent years, the 50 per cent ceiling on the rental payable to distributors for a film had been withdrawn, and terms of 75 per cent (or, in a few instances, 90 per cent) of net take in excess of the break figure had been applied, with no maximum.

Initially distributors justified this on the basis of increased promotional activity on major films. In practice most major films, and consequently a high proportion of the business, bore premium terms. It had been the practice that the break figures specific to individual screens were increased in line with inflation. In recent years the increases had been less than the rate of inflation.

## *Availability of British films*

6.34. Richmond Filmhouse said that the choice of films in the cinema was not as wide as it could be. It attributed this to the fact that the large exhibitors were also distributors of US product. Independent multi-screen exhibitors would be more likely to exhibit a wider range of films than the multiplex owners, most of which had their own distribution set-up or other vested interests. The development of networks of independent cinemas would, therefore, encourage distributors to take more risks, and invest more money, in distributing British films. In the view of Mainline Pictures all British films sufficiently commercial enough to play around the UK had done so. The new wave of British films, eg *Raining Stones* and *Naked*, would also be played around the UK, but for how long and in how many screens depended on market forces.

## Mr Geoffrey Henshaw

6.35. Mr Henshaw, North West Leisure (and Chairman of the Independent Exhibitors' Committee of the CEA), gave written evidence as an individual exhibitor and attended a hearing. Giving his views on the general situation, Mr Henshaw told us that distributors always ensured that multiplex cinemas and the major circuits were the first to obtain copies of new releases. Multiplex cinemas were often given two prints of a new film, presumably so that it could be shown at different times on different screens. Remaining copies were then given to independent exhibitors. The allocation of prints to the independent exhibitors appeared to be done on a random basis; no priority was given to cinemas in areas where there was no multiplex or circuit cinema. Some were allowed films only when other cinemas had finished with them. By the time this happened, the films had lost their initial appeal and would not attract large audiences. As multiplex operators and the major circuits extended their exhibition periods, prints for independent exhibitors were put back even further.

6.36. Distributors benefited from extended exhibition periods at multiplex cinemas and this led them to demand similar arrangements from independent exhibitors. Independents, particularly those with single screens, often found that this was not viable, especially when the film had already played extensively in other cinemas. Certain distributors had little sympathy if a film failed to attract customers and usually insisted on the film completing its contract. In the case of the more popular films, in addition to insisting on an extended run, certain distributors imposed special terms which could result in an exhibitor paying the distributor up to 75 per cent of box office takings. If an exhibitor refused the terms it would not get the film.

6.37. Mr Henshaw believed that the consideration given by distributors to the multiplex operators resulted from vertical integration. Distributors gave priority to their own in-house interests without any concern for the traditional British-owned cinemas which had supported them for many years. Mr Henshaw proposed that legislation be introduced which would force distributors to offer films at the same time to all cinemas which were in competition with each other, thus enabling them to compete on a fair and equitable basis.

6.38. We invited Mr Henshaw to comment on our first possible remedy on alignment (see paragraph 7.16). After consulting with six exhibitors, whom he said represented a small cross-section of interested parties in North-West England, he told us that they had no firm views as to the merits or otherwise of the alignment system. The present system did not appear to have any influence on the availability of prints for independent exhibitors. Mr Henshaw supported the idea that distributors should submit information to the OFT on prints supplied to MGM Cinemas and Odeon and proposed that this information be extended to include the supply of prints to independent cinemas.

# Distribution interests

## Society of Film Distributors Limited

6.39. The SFD has the following members: Buena Vista, Columbia, Entertainment, First Independent, Fox, Gala Film Distributors Limited, Guild, Mayfair, RFD, UIP and Warner Distributors. In written evidence, the SFD told us that it aimed to provide a forum for its members' discussions and to represent them on matters of common interest. One of the services it offered was to negotiate with the CEA the *Standard Conditions* (see Appendix 4.3). The SFD thought that the use of these conditions suited both distributors and exhibitors as it meant that little time or effort generally needed to be spent in establishing the formalities of the legal relationships between them. The use of the *Standard Conditions* was entirely a question of convenience and a matter for the free choice of SFD members, who could vary the conditions as they wished, or decline to use them at all. The SFD had not issued any further guidance to its members on any of these conditions. Other than to the extent that they used the *Standard Conditions*, the SFD did not play any part in its members' operations and thus was not involved in decisions on the release of films or negotiations between distributors and exhibitors. With regard to the old SFD Recommendations to its members referred to in the MMC's 1983 report (paragraphs 5.5 to 5.8 of that report), the SFD told us that these had all been rescinded or allowed to lapse. None of them had been acted on by the SFD since the publication of that report.

6.40. The SFD said that the film industry was unlike any other and that it was more competitive than ever before. Each film was unique; its production costs and most of its marketing costs were committed long before it was offered to the public and, accordingly, before the producer or distributor knew how successful it might be. Many films did not attract sufficient consumer interest to enable the marketing costs to be recovered; others recovered sufficient to enable distributors to recoup the marketing costs but not the producer's investment. Although the success of a film did not depend on its cost, most successful films involved substantial investment.

6.41. Similarly, investment in cinemas played a crucial role in attracting audiences. The SFD drew our attention to the high level of investment in exhibition which had been made in the last eight years, not only by the larger companies. More new cinemas had been built in the UK than in any other EC country. This had contributed to the doubling of cinema audiences over this period. In response to increasing consumer demand, distributors had increased the number of prints which were available to exhibitors.

### *Refusal to supply*

6.42. Commenting on our possible remedy on refusal to supply (see paragraph 7.46), the SFD said that it would be undesirable to introduce any form of legislation intended to fetter the judgment of a distributor as to how best to exploit a film. A distributor must reasonably be allowed to determine how many prints to purchase and how to employ them within the strategy determined for the film—whether that were a gradual release with an initially low number of prints or a blanket release using a large number of prints—in order to take maximum advantage of the publicity expenditure. The SFD questioned whether it would be practicable to seek to impose a positive obligation on a distributor to provide prints to any exhibitor which demanded them. To do so would impose extra costs on a distributor and require it to market its product through more outlets than it would otherwise choose, and in a way it did not approve, without giving any compensating advantages in terms of receipts. Indeed, the spread of an audience between two competing cinemas would, in the absence of new or special financial arrangements, almost certainly operate to reduce a distributor's total receipts. The more commercially appealing films would occupy more screens but produce less net revenue. The less commercially attractive films would be squeezed out and lose much-needed revenue; such films would become less and less attractive to distributors considering acquiring rights to distribute in the UK. The public would ultimately have less choice.

*Restrictions on screen use*

6.43. Commenting on our possible remedy on restrictions on screen use (see paragraph 7.69), the SFD said that, because rentals were directly related to box office takings, distributors needed to know in advance the extent to which a film would be exhibited in a cinema during the licence period. There was no reason to believe that most cinema exhibitors considered the restrictions unreasonable.

6.44. If the restrictions were thought to have adverse effects, those effects could be overcome only by imposing restrictions on the distributors which would give the exhibitors complete or limited discretion to show other films during the licence period. Such restrictions would mean that a distributor would, at best, have no more than a limited assurance as to the number of performances its film would receive. This would result in prints being less efficiently used. It would also be likely to result in a reduction in box office receipts for the film in question and, in most cases, to a disproportionate reduction in the distributor's share. If a distributor felt that the overall net return would not justify tying up a print, it might decide not to grant the licence and the exhibitor and consumers would suffer.

*Rental terms*

6.45. Commenting on the possibility that contracts based on box office receipts might be prohibited (see paragraph 7.146), the SFD said that the sharing of box office receipts was the industry norm throughout the developed world. Both the break figures and the nut formulae (see paragraph 4.136) recognized the need of the exhibitor to meet its overheads week by week. This helped some exhibitors to make a sufficient return to stay in business and so contributed to their survival. The alternatives of fixed or guaranteed fees would necessitate weekly negotiation of the fee for each film for each cinema. Exhibitors would face increased uncertainty and greater risk. The SFD did not think this alternative would increase the number of screens or the number of films, or lower admission costs. In its view, it would be more likely to lead to cinema closures, exhibitors' reluctance to risk certain films or certain levels of fees, and increased pressure on the less obviously commercial films competing for screen-time. In the SFD's view, any of these consequences would be contrary to the public interest.

*SFD's response to the CEA's comments on the Standard Conditions*

6.46. Commenting on the CEA's criticism of the *Standard Conditions* (see paragraphs 6.12 to 6.15), the SFD rejected the suggestion that the current *Standard Conditions* did not take account of the last MMC report. Specific changes had been made and agreed with the CEA. The criticism that the conditions did not reflect current trading conditions was felt to be too vague to comment on. The reference to archaic language did not address any substantive issue. The SFD's view was that, since the *Standard Conditions* were intended to be incorporated in whole or in part in legally enforceable contracts, they had to be skilfully drafted. The CEA's suggestion that the conditions were particularly burdensome to smaller exhibitors was not understood, but the SFD would be pleased to consider any specific criticisms on this aspect. The CEA's comment that it was unreasonable that exhibitors could not change their ticket prices without first receiving the permission of the distributor was unrealistic. Such a requirement was fundamental to the overall arrangements between distributors and exhibitors.

6.47. The SFD had asked the CEA to put its proposals in writing but the CEA had failed to do so. The SFD said that it was, and had always been, open to well-considered suggestions to improve its *Standard Conditions*.

## Small distributors

6.48. We received written evidence from five small distributors, two of which (Artificial Eye and Mayfair) announced the merger of their distribution interests during the course of our inquiry. Artificial Eye also attended a hearing. The names of those who gave comments are shown in Appendix 6.1.

*Lack of exhibition outlets*

6.49. Three distributors, Colstar International Limited (Colstar), Artificial Eye and Metro Tartan Ltd (Metro Tartan), said that they had experienced difficulties in finding exhibitors in the commercial market to show independently-produced films. Colstar said that investors were unlikely to support an independent film if its exhibition outlets were not guaranteed. It also said that another result of the way in which major exhibitors dominated the market was the disappearance of the short film. This reduced opportunities for new film-makers and meant that financial backing for such films was not available. Metro Tartan said that, although multiplex cinemas had increased audience levels, they had not improved audience choice as the same distributors were supplying mostly US product. Artificial Eye said that, although some of the multiplex cinemas devoted one night a week to arthouse films, these showings happened long after a film had been released, and because they were only for one night, had no chance to build an audience. The films which it had distributed fairly widely to multiplex cinemas, eg *Cyrano de Bergerac* and *Short Cuts*, had not been as successful in those cinemas as they had been in city-centre arthouse cinemas. The audiences in the two venues were quite different.

*British films*

6.50. Artificial Eye said that the claim by British producers that their films' potential was not realized because of lack of available screens was wishful thinking. There was not really a substantial market for many of these films.

*Video market*

6.51. Oasis Film Distribution Ltd and Artificial Eye commented on the growth of the video market. They said that many films were being released into cinemas in a small way simply as a public relations exercise for the video release.

# Production interests

## Producers Alliance for Cinema and Television

6.52. PACT represents primarily independent television and film producers in the UK. It operates a range of business services, which include running industrial relations agreements with the trade unions involved in feature film production. PACT gave written evidence and attended a hearing.

*Bias against independently-produced UK and European films*

6.53. PACT said that there was a bias in favour of the distribution and exhibition of US films in the UK. Consequently, it was more difficult for independently-produced UK and European films to gain access to British cinema screens. US-produced independent films, having been distributed by the major US studios in North America, would have already achieved substantial market exposure. This put them on an equal footing with films handled by the vertically integrated US studios distributing into the UK market. UK and European independent films lacked this market exposure and usually received a narrow release, ie a small number of prints, and, therefore, restricted marketing and advertising budgets.

6.54. Films from the Hollywood studios, or from US independent production companies but with backing from the studios, were preferred by exhibitors because they had already been extensively market tested in the USA, enjoyed greater advertising support and consequently represented a much reduced risk. UK exhibitors sustained a self-fulfilling prophecy that a non-US film, not handled by a vertically integrated company, would be less attractive to audiences. They were, therefore, less willing to book such films. Denied an effective theatrical release, such films had reduced potential in the increasingly crucial video and television markets. In the case of UK independent films, the near certainty of reduced revenues in their home market made it increasingly difficult to obtain a return on investment. This in turn militated against new investment in UK independent film production. Many UK film-makers now worked for the major US studios because that was the only way they could be sure to get sufficient playing time for their films.

6.55. PACT stated that, unlike in the USA, distributors contributed very little finance to the making of films in the UK. Although the Hollywood studios had distribution organizations in the UK, it was not possible to obtain finance directly from these organizations for the financing of production: instead it was necessary to approach their parent companies in North America.

## *Reduction in choice*

6.56. The bias in favour of US films resulted in a reduction in the choice of films available for viewing. In 1991 there were 267 films released to British cinemas. This was a little over two-thirds of the number released in France and other major European countries and a little over half the number released in the USA. Released with fewer prints, independently-produced films were often unavailable outside London. Despite the publicly supported RFT network, non-metropolitan audiences were often denied access to many of these films. A narrow release also meant that there was frequently a considerable delay between the time a film was first released, when it attracted most media attention, and when it became available to regional cinemas. The delay reduced a film's revenue potential, which typically declined rapidly between three and four weeks after release date.

6.57. PACT acknowledged that the growth of multiplex cinemas had increased the choice of films but said that they were largely filled with US films. Most of them had been built by American companies, and the majority were now controlled by subsidiaries of the Hollywood studios, in order to improve access to the market for their own films and to extend the life of successful films. The benefit for British films was much more marginal.

## *Concentration of film exhibition in the UK*

6.58. PACT said that there were fewer cinema screens per capita in the UK than in any other major market. The UK was under-screened and there were significant barriers to entry which effectively prevented the natural level of growth in the number of screens. These resulted particularly from uncertainty as to whether films would be supplied by the few distributors who controlled most of the available product.

6.59. UK exhibitors charged relatively high prices for cinema tickets, yet retained an unusually large proportion of the box office. In most countries an exhibitor's share of the total ticket price did not exceed 60 per cent. In the UK it was almost 70 per cent. For vertically integrated companies involved in both distribution and exhibition, a high exhibitor share was simply a matter of internal transfer pricing. For independent companies, however, it meant a much smaller return. This ultimately reduced investors' ability to recoup their investment in independently-produced films.

6.60. PACT stated that the restraints exercised by distributors over exhibitors, coupled with a lack of screens, served to reduce further UK and European independent producers' access to the market and the choice of films available to the public. The level of concentration in exhibition, coupled with a comparable level of concentration at the distribution level, and the close links between distribution and exhibition, discouraged new entrants into exhibition. Competition between films and, therefore, producers was reduced. This particularly affected opportunities for UK and independent producers.

## *PACT report on the supply of independent British films in the UK*

6.61. In June 1994 PACT gave us a report on factors influencing the production, distribution and exhibition of independent British films in the UK market. This report was based on an independent study, carried out by consultants on PACT's behalf, to discover whether there was any evidence that independent exhibitors, producers and distributors in the UK faced unfair restraints as a result of the dominant market position of the US majors. In particular, the consultants were asked to collect evidence that either supported or contradicted the following hypotheses:

*(a)* that restraint exercised by the US majors was preventing access by local product to distribution in the UK;

*(b)* that the integration of major distributors/exhibitors resulted in local or independent films being restricted in respect of access to screens, duration of theatrical runs and availability of 'slow-burn' release patterns;

*(c)* that independent exhibitors were being denied access to prints of mainstream films; and

*(d)* that successful independent, and especially British, films had been taken off screens to make way for less successful product of the integrated distributors/exhibitors.

6.62. Questionnaires were sent to independent producers, distributors and exhibitors and respondents were interviewed. The consultants then analysed the budgets, marketing expenditures, release patterns and performance of the top British, European and independent US films released in the UK and USA over the last three years. Other factors that might influence the production, distribution and exhibition of British films were also considered.

6.63. PACT said that the study tested three theories which had been advanced to account for the comparative failure of British films:

*(a)* the lack of competitiveness of the films;

*(b)* the restriction of the market due to the dominance of a small number of large (and mostly US) operators; and

*(c)* a capacity problem in the UK retail sector, especially in cinema exhibition and pay television, which created special difficulties for the low-budget, specialist and cross-over films which were the main element of British film output.

## Conclusions of the report

6.64. PACT concluded that all three explanations were correct, to different degrees. It was also likely that all three factors interacted: US domination undermined the competitiveness of British films, while inadequate capacity prevented differentiation between the two at retail level.

6.65. All three explanations drew attention to the strong but unequal partnership between the British film industry and Hollywood. Most British producers chose to collaborate with Hollywood and saw the location of production and the source of financing of films as matters of little general importance. Hollywood-financed productions had a large equity component, ensuring that most of the risks as well as the benefits of exploitation were taken by the production entity, ie the Hollywood studio. While individual British films thus produced might be outstandingly successful, they could contribute little beyond short-term employment opportunities to the British production sector.

6.66. A few British producers chose to compete with Hollywood. They saw the production location and source of finance as matters of major importance. This was the option favoured by the EC Commission's recent Green Paper on programme production (see paragraph 3.37). European-financed, big-budget productions tended to be funded by a mixture of equity and distribution pre-sales, with an added element of public subsidies and incentives. Much of the risk was thus removed from the production entity, which nevertheless was able to keep a significant share of profits. All else being equal, this approach was most likely to contribute to the success of the European production sector. From the British point of view, however, it offered limited possibilities because of the absence of significant UK corporations engaged in film production and distribution, and of a regulatory environment supportive of British films.

6.67. Some British producers valued creative integrity above commercial considerations and had low budgets and small audiences. Their productions, in the UK as elsewhere in Europe, were usually funded by local broadcasters supplemented by co-production agreements and distribution pre-sales, with little or no equity being retained by the producer. Risk was thus minimized, but so was the producer's share of profits. It was hard, on the basis of these characteristics, for this approach to lift British film production above the level of a cottage industry.

## *Economic characteristics of film production and distribution*

6.68. PACT said that film production and distribution had a high risk profile. They required substantial capital in the long term, and production was best entered into as a function of distribution. A degree of imposed order, via alignments, fixed bookings and trading agreements at retail level, was necessary for the market to work at all. Dismantling that structure or introducing politically-inspired regulatory requirements, such as product quotas, would not necessarily serve the interests of either the industry or the consumer.

## *Public policy*

6.69. There were three, interrelated options for public policy: to concentrate on improving the competitiveness of British films; to limit the barriers to entry erected, wittingly or otherwise, by the major operators; and to encourage greater opportunity in the retail market, especially in cinema exhibition and pay television.

6.70. Striking the correct balance between the three lines of policy was important for two additional reasons: there was significant interdependence between Hollywood and the UK film community; and the economics of multiplex investment, which was crucial to the development of the market as a whole, was finely balanced. However, PACT did not believe this fine balance would be upset by some degree of intervention, providing that legislation took care not to interfere with market forces beyond what was required to establish a level playing field. According to PACT this did not currently exist. The correct public policy was the one which encouraged the greatest success of British films while fostering continued growth and diversity in the market as a whole.

## Production companies

6.71. Although we invited comments from 14 production companies, only one, Adventure Pictures, gave evidence. It said that a film it had produced, *Orlando*, had done exceptionally well in London, where there was an established network of independently-owned cinemas and screens owned by the major chains which specialized in this type of film, but elsewhere it had been dependent on arthouse cinemas. Outside London there were hardly any screens with a reputation for showing quality independent/British films and which had the ability to allow an extended run for a box office success. Adventure Pictures said that quite often Orlando had played to full houses for a week or two at provincial arthouse cinemas and then been taken off in order to make way for the next pre-booked film.

## Mr David Puttnam

6.72. Mr Puttnam, a film producer since 1968, was invited, with Lord Attenborough, to a hearing. Lord Attenborough was unable to attend. Mr Puttnam supplemented the discussion at the hearing with written evidence.

6.73. Mr Puttnam told us that he had initially produced low-budget British films, largely with the help of the then British Film Fund, financed through the Eady Levy. These films, made for the UK market, were financially successful but not particularly ambitious. In 1977 Mr Puttnam had produced *Midnight Express* for Columbia Pictures and this had launched his career as a producer on a larger scale. The films he had made since then had been aimed at world-wide audiences and were financed and distributed accordingly.

## *The audio-visual industry*

6.74. Mr Puttnam said that the December 1993 EC White Paper on growth, employment and competitiveness had identified the audio-visual sector as one of the three areas in which Europe could hope to create significant additional employment before the end of the century. It was, therefore, important that the UK was involved in this industry. Whereas the other two areas which had been identified, bio-technology and energy, had comparatively high levels of government support, the audio-visual sector had a very low level.

6.75. The feature film industry had an importance disproportionate to its actual level of economic activity within the world-wide audio-visual industry. Feature films acted as the principal sales vehicles for other types of programming, eg television.

## *The UK film industry*

6.76. The UK produced culturally distinguished films, most of which were seen on television. These tended to be produced at a modest cost with, consequently, fairly low levels of expectation. Despite their high cultural quality, British films of this type could not consistently compete in the world-wide market and were unlikely to be sustained without some permanent form of support.

6.77. Although, in theory, it might be possible for British films to penetrate the world-wide market, this could not be achieved with only a few films a year. A permanent product flow was necessary to establish British films and their stars and to increase the acceptability of the films in other markets. Mr Puttnam said that it was economically possible to have a national industry which was independent of, and complementary to, the national culture. For example, the UK had been a prolific and successful maker of large-scale action adventure films like the *Indiana Jones*, *Star Wars* and *Superman* productions. While such films did not reflect any aspect of British life, they created significant employment, developed technical and craft skills and attracted additional investment capital into the country.

6.78. Mr Puttnam believed that every year one or two British films, which could have been commercially successful in the UK, failed because of poor distribution resulting from lack of confidence in the films themselves. *The Crying Game* and *Hear My Song* were prime examples. The ease and popularity of television viewing had hampered the competitive presentation of films to their natural audience. The return on investment received by feature film producers had little or no connection with the size of television audiences and this had adversely influenced the development of the film industry in the UK. British film-makers had developed little or no direct relationship with their audience. Their principal concerns tended to be centred on the response of reviewers and those who commissioned programmes.

6.79. The abolition of the Eady Levy had had a catastrophic effect on UK film production. Funding had, to a very great extent, been taken over by Channel 4 and, to a lesser degree, the BBC and was thus coming from product-driven rather than market-driven sources. There was an important role for television in the funding of feature films, but in the UK the influence and the decision-making process were being operated by a medium which had traditionally worked in a unique and extremely rarified market-place. Mr Puttnam said that there was, in reality, very little real competition between the BBC and Channel 4 in pursuing film drama product.

6.80. Although multiplex cinemas had been built to give audiences a wider choice of films, recent history had indicated that the new audiences did not specifically want different types of films, merely more convenience in seeing them. Another cause of decline in production was the UK tax regime. Although the problem was more apparent than real, agents advised US stars that if they worked in the UK their tax liability could be doubled. This created an unnecessary barrier and, as US directors and stars generated a great number of jobs whilst filming, the UK economy was being deprived of both employment and income.

6.81. In the UK as elsewhere in Europe, films were produced regardless of the size of the potential audience. In the USA producers sought the largest audience possible for their work and accordingly undertook sophisticated research. The Hollywood studios identified their audience and invested in marketing based on this research. If the UK distributor of *The Crying Game* had spent more and been more confident with respect to the potential audience, the film could have been far more successful. Research was an invaluable tool and no other highly-capitalized industry addressing a large consumer base would act without maximizing its use.

## *BSkyB*

6.82. Mr Puttnam thought that BSkyB, if properly encouraged, had the opportunity to become another important pillar in the rebuilding of the British film and television industry. It was an organization which was entirely reliant on developing and maintaining its subscriber base and so would nurture a knowledgeable ongoing relationship with its subscription audience.

## *Revenues*

6.83. Mr Puttnam said that when he first entered the industry, the vast majority of revenue from a film came from the cinema box office. As television and then videos had been developed the figures had changed. Cinema box office returns now accounted for only 35 per cent of the average revenue achieved by the average film. He estimated that by the year 2010 the figure could be as low as 5 per cent, with the ancillary markets accounting for the remaining 95 per cent.

## *The French film industry*

6.84. In France the cultural issue was regarded as very important and cultural industries, particularly film, were a political, even an 'electoral' issue. Although the French support system was well developed and open to change, it had not achieved all of its aims. Over the last ten years, the level of French audiences achieved by films produced in other countries had barely changed. Conversely, the level of audiences achieved by French language films had steadily dropped from 90 million to 20 million (half of which in 1993 resulted from only three films). The European industry in general was over-fragmented: too many films were probably being produced and there were too many distributors.

## *The future*

6.85. In order to maintain a healthy film production industry in the UK it was necessary to have some form of permanent support. Mr Puttnam lived in hope of seeing positive proposals in the DNH's forthcoming policy paper. The problem was the size of the industry and the nature of the opportunity in the UK, partially because of its shared language with the USA. One method of funding he would like to see would be an internal mechanism, agreed within the industry, whereby, at each point of the distribution chain, a certain amount of revenue was recycled back into the industry as working capital. At the moment there was no European distributor who could distribute outside its own country, so distribution through a single distributor had to be carried out by a US company. The present practice was inefficient and time-consuming. One of the recommendations made by the EC Commission's Think Tank on Audio-Visual Policy had been the creation of a 'soft loan' facility which would assist the creation of some fully competitive pan-European distributors.

6.86. Mr Puttnam stressed the importance of training. Unless adequate training was provided, the UK industry would lose the skill base necessary to continue to make high-cost, high-value feature films and would, as a result, be unable to take advantage of the growth the audio-visual industry offered to the UK economy.

*Practices of the US majors*

6.87. We asked Mr Puttnam for his views on the leading US distribution companies. He said that he had found their UK distribution arms to be efficient and professional and prepared to distribute any independently-produced films that had serious revenue-earning potential. He made the following comments about the practices we had identified.

*Reserving screen space*

6.88. Reservation of screen space by distributors ensured a regular product supply. An exhibitor was influenced in its choice of whether to play a particular film, or to hold over an existing film, by the films that a particular distributor had lined up to offer in the future. Continuity of supply was very important and the US majors, rather than independents, were in a position to guarantee this.

*Alignment*

6.89. Alignment was a matter of convenience and did not have a particularly detrimental effect on the industry. Mr Puttnam said that present trends indicated that it was unlikely to exist at all in a few years' time.

*Exclusivity*

6.90. The practice of exclusivity was rapidly decreasing. Exclusive West End runs had now virtually been dropped because of the high cost of launch advertising. Mr Puttnam emphasized the importance of the cost of prints, advertising and distribution in the decision-making process. Changes in the distribution of films were increasingly driven by ever more sophisticated and cost-effective marketing techniques.

*Refusal to supply*

6.91. Mr Puttnam was a minority shareholder in the Richmond Filmhouse and said that he had first-hand experience of refusal to supply. He attributed this to the protectionist instincts of powerful exhibitors requesting exclusivity, sometimes even in very marginal situations. Mr Puttnam believed this practice to be very shortsighted, and not in the best interests of the industry overall.

# Others

## British Film Institute

6.92. The BFI's aims include encouraging the development of the art of film in the UK and promoting its use as a record of contemporary life. The BFI's concerns range across all aspects of film, television and video, including production, distribution and exhibition, both by active participation and by funding and supporting others. About half its funding comes from the DNH. The rest is raised by subscriptions, provision of services, sponsorship and donations. The BFI gave written evidence and attended a hearing.

### *Current state of the British film industry*

6.93. The BFI said that the main feature of the British film industry in the last ten years had been the growth in the market. Audience figures at cinemas had increased and new markets had arisen in the form of video rental and sale and satellite television channels. British cinema film production, in contrast, had slumped and there had been a reduction in the number of US and other foreign companies funding the production of films in the UK.

6.94. The decline in British film production was not due to a deficiency of UK talent. Moreover, the British television production sector was second only to the USA in terms of volume and value of output. This did not, however, provide a strong base for feature film production. The Eady Levy on box office revenues (see paragraphs 3.18 and 3.19) and tax incentives for film production were elements of the structure of assistance to British film production which had been removed in the mid-1980s. Since then, the UK distribution and exhibition markets had been increasingly dominated by US-produced films and there were fewer opportunities for UK films in the international market.

## *Vertical integration*

6.95. The BFI said that access to cinematic distribution for independent producers was limited. Of the 51 films produced in the UK in 1992, only 40 had received any form of distribution, and of those a significant number had only limited runs in a small number of cinemas. The BFI cited *Riff Raff*, *The Crying Game* and *Enchanted April* as examples of good British films which had not received appropriate distribution in the UK. Films from other European countries were now rarely distributed in the UK, in contrast to the situation a few years ago.

6.96. The major distribution companies operating in the UK, through their vertically integrated structure, were able to offset losses from box office failures with profits from successful films and receipts from secondary markets. UK film producers were generally not integrated with distributors or exhibitors and distribution of their films was uncertain. Often UK production companies were in existence for the production of only one film. In such a system, risk could not be spread and the companies were dependent on a 100 per cent success rate. The absence of vertical integration led to a lack of control over the marketing of the film, the spread of its distribution and the duration of its exhibition. These aspects were controlled by distributors and exhibitors whose interests might not coincide with those of the independent producer. The lack of control over distribution made the raising of production finance more difficult.

6.97. It was generally accepted within the industry that, in order to achieve the correct balance between successful and unsuccessful films, a 'critical mass' of films needed to be produced. The BFI told us that it had been estimated that the critical mass for the British film industry was 80 films a year, with a total budget of approximately £400 million. This was required to build up market share, support a viable infrastructure and establish a track record capable of attracting commercial investment and artistic success.

## *Control of the UK market*

6.98. The BFI said that much of the revenue from the exhibition market was repatriated overseas by the dominant players and, as a result, new British production was starved of capital from that potential source. In terms of shares of box office receipts, the UK was dominated by the US film industry to a far greater extent than other large Western European countries.

6.99. While cinema receipts had risen, their relative importance had declined with the introduction of video and satellite television markets. These had become the most important commercial markets, though success in the cinema was still vital as it generated demand in the other markets.

6.100. There were five major distribution companies which, together, dominated the exhibition market. Of the 50 highest-earning films in the period 1988 to 1990, 40 were produced in the USA. Of the 236 films released in UK cinemas in 1991, 56 per cent were produced in the USA, or with US finance, and these accounted for some 93 per cent of box office revenues. The video market exhibited parallel features.

*European film industries*

6.101. The BFI told us that European national film industries obtained assistance from their governments (as well as from the EC through the MEDIA 95 programme). These national schemes were intended to enable their film industries to compete in Europe, penetrate the US market and attract US production activity to Europe. The motivation in intervening to correct market distortions was usually cultural. The UK film industry did not obtain such benefits as it did not have such schemes. Without significant state subsidies, it was unable to compete on level terms with industries receiving governmental assistance.

*Restriction of choice and diversity*

6.102. Despite the growth in cinema audiences and the new markets opening up for feature films, the public had not enjoyed a greater variety of films. Nor had they been given access to the full range of films produced. Fewer films were being shown on more screens.

6.103. The exhibition of British films was being marginalized. They tended mainly to be shown at smaller independent cinemas and BFI RFTs. The bigger multiple-screen cinemas showed almost exclusively US films. The BFI said that conversations with audiences around the country indicated a widely-held view that there was insufficient variety in the films being exhibited and, in particular, that too few British films were shown.

*Cinema admission charges*

6.104. The BFI said that the UK was one of the most expensive places in the world to see cinema films and that London prices were alleged to be the most expensive in the world.

*Expression of British culture*

6.105. The BFI said that film was the most significant medium for expressing the cultural identity of a nation. The UK's ability to do so had been undermined and films relying on and exploring British culture were few and far between.

6.106. The BFI said that there was something fundamentally wrong with a country which had its most important cultural form dominated to such an extent that less than 10 per cent of the audience share went to indigenous material; where new talent had to go abroad to work; where the barriers to entry faced by independent producers were so enormous that they were practically insurmountable; where the financial returns on successful creativity were almost always expropriated out of the country and lost from the investment cycle; and where audiences could not express their preferences because their choice was restricted. The BFI found this situation, in public interest terms, unacceptable.

*The need for structural change*

6.107. In 1983 the MMC had concluded that scale monopolies existed in favour of the two major exhibition chains and two of their aligned distributors. The system of alignments was found to give rise to a complex monopoly situation. The BFI said that the MMC had concluded that the monopoly situation operated against the public interest but had not proposed any radical remedies. The very limited steps which had been taken had made little impact.

6.108. The BFI said that a great deal had changed in the industry since 1983. It believed nevertheless that one or more monopoly situations, within the meaning of the Act, continued to exist. Changes to the British film market were necessary because of the need for greater choice and diversity, the economic benefits which would result, and the expression of British culture in the film medium.

## Channel 4

6.109. Channel 4 gave written evidence and attended a hearing. It said that the channel had been set up in 1981 to cater for tastes and interests not catered for on ITV. Since the 1990 Broadcasting Act it had been a statutory corporation operating under licence from the Independent Television Commission. Channel 4 now sold its own advertising and was dependent on its own efforts to raise revenue. Its remit remained the same.

### *Channel 4 and films*

6.110. Channel 4 said that investment in original British films had always been a central part of its drama programming. It made the films available for theatrical release before broadcasting them on television. Between 1982 and 1992, 6.2 per cent of Channel 4's total programme budget had been spent on original feature films. In total £91 million had been invested in 264 different works.

6.111. Channel 4 supported films in various ways. Sometimes its interest was by way of a pre-purchase of the UK and other television rights, but more frequently it was a major investor. For many films the channel financed the development and script-writing process; others it financed fully, for example *Raining Stones*. However, most films had to seek a range of financiers such as British Screen, the European Co-production Fund and other more commercial sources. Channel 4 said that its policy had been very successful, not because the investments had produced real financial returns (in ten years only a handful of films had actually made a profit for the channel) but because it had gained access to original drama. A theatrical release prior to the television showing gave a film significant advance publicity and might lead to a larger television audience.

### *Film Four International*

6.112. Channel 4 sold the films in which it had rights through its sales agency, Film Four International, which was part of Channel 4 International Ltd. The channel also undertook other commercial activities, including the sale of programmes, publishing and video distribution, through Channel 4 International Ltd. Film Four International negotiated arm's length deals with outside distribution companies, in which Channel 4 did not have an interest. The channel did not own any cinemas.

### *Channel 4's concerns*

6.113. Channel 4 was concerned mainly with the access which British film producers had to a proper distribution system and a range of exhibitors. It said that, although cinema attendances in the UK had nearly doubled since 1984, over almost the same period the expenditure on films produced in the UK had halved. There were a number of reasons for this decline. In the mid-1980s the abolition of tax incentives for film production and the abandonment of the Eady Levy, coupled with an increasingly strong pound, had led to progressively fewer large-scale films being made in the UK.

6.114. In the past, Channel 4 had had difficulties in obtaining distribution in the UK for the films which it helped fund. An example of this was *Riff-Raff*, which was fully funded by Channel 4 and nominated as European Film of the Year, but had been seen in cinemas by more people in France than in the UK. However, the situation had now appeared to have improved. Channel 4's most recent releases, *Raining Stones* and *Naked*, had had widespread exhibition, both geographically and in terms of numbers of different exhibitors. Channel 4's view was, therefore, that despite the vertical integration of the US majors and their domination of all stages of the film chain, there was no longer a widespread problem about exhibition for UK independently-produced films. It said that 'barring' still persisted in some limited forms. For example, *Howards End* had effectively been prevented from being shown in any West End cinema other than the Curzon Mayfair.

6.115. US films still dominated the UK market to an extraordinary extent. US film production appeared to have stabilized at around 500 films a year, about 60 per cent of which had theatrical releases. Much of the lack of success of UK films was often attributed to their low marketing budgets. Film expenditure in the USA had increased dramatically recently, even though numbers of productions had stabilized. Although much of this extra expenditure went into increased production budgets, a substantial part had gone on increased marketing budgets. The average US film advertising budget was 32 per cent of total costs. No similar data were available for Europe, but Channel 4's marketing budget on average would currently be £50,000 on a total budget of £1.5 million.

6.116. In Channel 4's view, there were no simple explanations for the success of US films in the UK. It recently had the experience of relatively disappointing box office returns for *Raining Stones* and *Naked*, despite the widespread exhibition referred to in paragraph 6.114 and enhanced marketing budgets (at around £300,000). The two films would again be seen by more people in France than in the UK. The combination of high marketing spend, big production budgets and strong presence in all sectors of the industry helped to support the US film industry's dominant position in the UK. The problem did not seem to stem from abuse of their market power but nonetheless the extent of their power exacerbated the difficulties.

6.117. Cinema was a crucial part of the audio-visual culture. For those films which were shown theatrically the release was an important marketing tool. 27 per cent of global revenue for a US film would be raised through the cinema box office, compared with 49 per cent from home video, but the latter was heavily dependent on the former. This reflected Channel 4's experience that theatrical release helped the size of television audiences. Cinema's relationship with television channels and home video meant that, if anything, its role would be even more vital in the future. Other countries had introduced measures to control the market, coupled with subsidies and/or tax concessions for domestic production. Channel 4 would not support any sort of quota system in the UK (such as operated in Spain) but thought it perverse that the British tax system worked against film production and that the funds available from the National Lottery for film would be channelled through the Arts Council rather than into commercial film investment through an organization like British Screen.

## Mr Michael Henry

6.118. We received written submissions from Mr Henry of Nicholson Graham & Jones, solicitors. He stressed that the submissions were made in his personal capacity and not on behalf of his firm, and did not necessarily reflect the views of his firm.

### *Distributor commissions*

6.119. Mr Henry told us that the Motion Picture Association of America, Inc (MPAA) corporations (ie members of the MPAA) distributed their films in the UK via subsidiary companies. The MPAA corporations directly fixed the commission levels retained by their distribution subsidiaries at levels which were substantially less than the subsidiaries would have retained if they operated on an arm's length basis. They were also substantially less than the terms the UK subsidiaries offered when distributing films of third parties.

6.120. The UK subsidiaries retained a comparatively small percentage of the income they received from distributing the films of their parent companies. By contrast, the terms and conditions offered to independent producers allowed the subsidiaries to retain a commission of between 30 and 50 per cent of receipts (depending on the media exploited) and permitted them to deduct and recover all advertising, publicity and physical distribution expenses. These conditions put independent producers (in the USA, the UK and elsewhere in the EC) at a competitive disadvantage. Mr Henry argued that such activities contravened the provisions of Article 85 of the Treaty of Rome and also raised certain taxation issues—notably that of transfer pricing.

## Collusion among distributors in fixing prices and trading conditions

6.121. Mr Henry also argued that the MPAA corporations indirectly affected the prices at which films were made available to exhibitors. UIP's dominant position enabled terms it negotiated on behalf of one of its three shareholders to be applied for the benefit of the other two. Three of the MPAA corporations therefore shared market-pricing information in the UK.

6.122. By virtue of their common membership of the MPAA, the other MPAA corporations also had access to sensitive pricing information in the UK. This enabled them directly or indirectly to fix purchase and selling prices in the UK market. One MPAA corporation—MGM-Cannon—was able directly to fix purchase and selling prices at both the distribution and the exhibition level.

6.123. Mr Henry alleged that all other trading conditions in the distribution and exhibition sectors in the UK were either directly or indirectly fixed by the MPAA corporations as a result of UIP's dominant position; information sharing between UIP shareholders; information sharing between MPAA members; and the imposition on the exhibition sector of the *Standard Conditions*.

## Remittance of royalties

6.124. Mr Henry argued that the MPAA corporations made use of the UK/US double taxation treaty to remit the majority of their UK income to the USA, thereby avoiding the payment of UK corporation tax or the deduction of withholding taxes. The income extracted was used to fund film production in the USA.

6.125. UK tax legislation was, he said, more widely drawn than the requirements of the UK/US double taxation treaty necessitated. Under the treaty, the exemption removing the obligation to deduct withholding tax on royalties for films was not available for any company which had a permanent establishment in the UK. Since the UK subsidiaries acted as the agents of the MPAA corporations, the MPAA corporations should be treated as having a permanent place of business in the UK. This would disentitle them from the benefits of the exemption. Such disentitlement would result either in the MPAA corporations paying corporation tax or rearranging their affairs so as to carry on film production activity in the UK.

6.126. The remittance of royalty income to the USA was, according to Mr Henry, a concerted practice carried out by the MPAA corporations which had as its object or effect the prevention of competition in the UK in the financing and production of films. If the amounts of royalties remitted to the MPAA corporations by way of licence fees were greater than those which would be payable on an arm's length basis, a transfer pricing issue would arise, and UK corporation tax would be payable on the excess.

## Location of control

6.127. Mr Henry said that the sole or main priority of the UK subsidiaries of the MPAA corporations was to administer the business affairs of their parents in as profitable a manner as possible. They carried out very little business activity in their own name and appeared to be no more than the agents of the MPAA corporations.

6.128. The location of decision-making authority in the USA had a number of effects. Creative decisions were generally made in relation to US criteria and decisions to acquire or produce films in the UK were based on the criteria of the US market-place. The location in the USA of control of the UK subsidiaries was, he argued, a concerted practice carried out by the MPAA corporations which had as its object or effect the prevention of competition in the production of films in the UK.

*Acquisition of rights to distribute independent films*

6.129. Mr Henry stated that the films exploited by the UK subsidiaries might broadly be divided into two categories, namely:

*(a)* films produced by the MPAA corporations; and

*(b)* films acquired by the MPAA corporations for distribution.

6.130. Mr Henry alleged that a concerted practice existed between the MPAA corporations in relation to the acquisition of films from US independent producers. Where they acquired US distribution rights from an independent producer, the practice had evolved for the MPAA corporations to require such producers to sell distribution rights in the UK. The acquisition of UK distribution rights in the context of the acquisition of rights in a film for the US market had no connection, either by its nature or according to commercial usage, with the sale of distribution rights in the USA. This practice eliminated the possibility of independent UK distributors acquiring the greater part of US independently-produced cinemas films, and further restricted or distorted competition in the UK distribution sector.

*Withdrawal of financing from British film production*

6.131. Mr Henry asserted that the withdrawal of finance from British film production in order to favour US film production affected trade between the UK and the USA and constituted an abuse by the MPAA corporations and their UK subsidiaries of their dominant position. It was, therefore, a matter which affected the public interest. In previous years the two dominant cinema chains—Rank and Thorn EMI—could be relied on to provide finance for British film production. Thorn EMI was now part of MGM-Cannon, an MPAA corporation.

6.132. A number of industry sources would confirm that there had been no shortage over the last ten years of British and European film projects with strong commercial potential. The majority of these projects had been unable to secure investment support from Odeon and MGM Cinemas. Whilst the Rank organization continued (through its ownership of Odeon cinemas) to make substantial profits from the UK, it committed almost all its production financing activity to US projects.

6.133. The use by Rank of its dominant position in the exhibition and supply of films in cinemas to promote the production of US films to the detriment of UK films resulted in a restriction or distortion of competition in the UK market. The use by Rank of its profits derived from the patronage of its cinemas by UK cinema-goers in order to finance the production of non-UK cinema films was a matter which affected the public interest.

*BSkyB*

6.134. Mr Henry said that the acquisition by Fox Inc/News International of the two main pay-television cinema film channels in the UK had given the merged BSkyB channels exclusive access to films produced or acquired by Fox. BSkyB also had access to material acquired by the Fox Group's US television interests. In addition to having guaranteed access to Fox product, it had access to the output of other MPAA corporations. Because the UK film production sector was largely dependent on UK broadcasters for providing finance, the BSkyB-Fox-MPAA links had a direct effect on the UK market for films, and on their production and financing.

6.135. The interrelationship between the production sector and the television industries was complex. A number of factors merited examination. First, there was no competition in the UK market in the provision of cable or satellite movie channels. The price paid by BSkyB to acquire films was currently lower than the prices paid by Sky when it was in competition with BSB. Secondly, the vertical integration of BSkyB with Fox distorted competition for cinema films between the MPAA corporations in the pay-television area. Thirdly, the absence of external sources of finance in the UK film production sector had resulted in the sector relying on television companies as a source of finance. Prices paid by UK television channels for British films were reportedly lower than those paid by French or German television companies for their national cinema films.

## *UIP's exemption under Article 85*

6.136. Mr Henry sent us a copy of his submission to the EC Commission objecting to the extension of the exemption granted to UIP BV from the provisions of Article 85 of the Treaty of Rome. He argued that a number of significant commercial and technical developments had changed the market for the supply and distribution of films since the original notification of the UIP BV arrangements in 1982 and since the exemption was granted in 1989. Arguments justifying exemption for cinema exhibitors and distributors needed to be re-evaluated.

6.137. Mr Henry said that the UIP Group was in a dominant position in the UK and that its activities restricted, distorted and/or eliminated competition in the production, distribution and financing of films in the UK and the EC.

6.138. According to Recital 18 of the 1989 decision, UIP BV was required to distribute any films designated by the UIP corporations (the shareholders of UIP BV) for distribution outside North America. This restricted UIP BV's activities by requiring it to guarantee distribution access for US films to cinema screens and consequently to deny European films access to European screens.

6.139. Mr Henry submitted that, while the UIP corporations retained autonomy over their own product marketing, this did not guarantee free competition between them. Indeed Recital 39 acknowledged that by joining forces in the EC, UIP BV's parent companies had ceased distributing films independently from and in competition with each other. It was likely that they would eliminate competition by harmonizing the release dates of their films. Each of the partners could be individually appraised of the other partners' intentions for release dates. This afforded them the opportunity to share the market in terms of the type of films distributed and the timing of distribution and marketing strategies. This was likely to result in a distortion or restriction of competition. The increased efficiency in the distribution of films produced or acquired by the UIP Group enabled these entities to 'crowd out' cinema screens in the UK.

6.140. To describe the EC subsidiaries of the UIP corporations as local distributors was, in Mr Henry's view, misleading. While they might operate locally in the EC, control was exercised in the USA. UIP BV was obliged to consult with the UIP corporations on the distribution plan for each film before its release. The corporations reserved control over the number of prints and amount of advertising expenditure and they were also responsible for making payments for prints and advertising costs. It was generally acknowledged in the industry that there was a correlation between advertising expenditure and box office revenues. By retaining control of the amount spent on advertising, the UIP corporations were able to distort competition in the UK and the EC.

6.141. Recital 19 gave UIP the right to make or acquire non-English language films. By contrast there were no such express provisions in relation to English language films since, presumably, this would compete with the product of the UIP corporations. Thus the UIP corporations retained control over the production and financing of English language cinema films. This restricted or distorted competition in the production and financing of English language films in the EC and, in particular, in the UK. Such distortion resulted in the exclusion or denial of finance for English language films and had resulted in the substantial diminution in the production of English language films in the UK. The fact that all decisions relating to production, financing and distribution were taken in the USA could only be damaging to UK production and to the marketing of such films.

6.142. Mr Henry argued that the undertakings given by the UIP Group to the EC Commission did not create benefit for the EC and had permitted UIP UK to increase its market share and further distort competition.

6.143. As regards production and distribution, Recital 27 recorded that UIP undertook to make itself available, based upon its commercial judgment, to produce, finance, acquire distribution rights to or distribute feature films of third parties in the EC. Each UIP corporation also undertook to be available individually, based upon its commercial judgment, to produce, finance or acquire distribution rights to local products in the EC which were offered to UIP. It was reasonable to expect that this undertaking would have resulted in a significant number of EC films financed and produced and distributed by UIP in the EC. This would have created sufficient countervailing benefits to outweigh the anti-competitive effects previously noted by the EC Commission. The fact that no such countervailing benefits had resulted meant that the EC Commission could no longer continue the exemption on the grounds specified in Article 85(3). Far from UIP's efficiency having stimulated production in the EC, there had been a marked diminution in film production in the EC financed by the UIP Group.

6.144. Mr Henry said that exhibitors suffered detriment through the concentration of product in the hands of one distributor. This resulted in the elimination of competition between the UIP corporations. If they were truly independent, they might compete on the terms on which they offered films to exhibitors in order to spoil or compete with their competitors' release patterns. Consumers did not appear to benefit from the cost savings achieved by the UIP Group. The savings had not been passed on to exhibitors, who had not been able to lower cinema admission prices. Furthermore, there was no evidence that the range of choice of cinema films had been widened.

6.145. The UIP arrangements imposed restrictions in relation to the marketing of films which restricted competition. In view of the scale of the operations of the UIP corporations, no concession was required to these entities for them to achieve economy of scale. Moreover, the UIP arrangements contained numerous restrictions which were not indispensable to the attainment of their objectives. It appeared that the economic benefits received by the UIP Group had permitted its members to increase their market share in the EC, and in particular the UK, to the current dominant level.

## Department of National Heritage

6.146. The DNH gave written evidence and attended a hearing. It said that although there had been a general rise in cinema audiences in the UK over the last decade, British films had made a very limited impact on cinema-going. As the Department responsible for cultural interests, the DNH had, as one of its medium-term objectives, to expand opportunities for access to high-quality films from the UK and elsewhere. Another of the DNH's objectives was to increase the production of British films. It believed investment in British films might be inhibited by the difficulty they had in achieving UK-wide cinema release. The DNH had had consultations with the industry during a round of meetings held by the Secretary of State for National Heritage.

### *Lack of British films*

6.147. The DNH told us that, since its creation in April 1992, it had received 92 letters from the public and a petition of 2,500 signatures. These representations sought support for increased production of British films, implying that consumers wished to see more British films than were currently available.

# 7 Views of the leading exhibitors

## Contents

|  | Paragraph |
|---|---|
| Introduction | 7.1 |
| Observations on the market | 7.2 |
| Views on complex monopoly situation | 7.11 |
| Alignment | 7.16 |
| Exclusivity and refusal to supply | 7.46 |
| Minimum exhibition periods and restrictions on screen use | 7.69 |
| Influence or control over admission prices | 7.83 |
| SFD *Standard Conditions* | 7.90 |
| Vertical links to US production companies | 7.98 |
| Overseas decision-making | 7.110 |
| Domination of the UK markets by US films | 7.116 |
| Co-ordination of release dates | 7.124 |
| Exercise of market power by leading distributors | 7.133 |
| Exercise of market power by leading exhibitors | 7.136 |
| Code of practice and associated machinery | 7.141 |
| Prohibiting contracts based on box office receipts | 7.146 |
| Distributors to commit revenues to independently-produced films | 7.155 |
| Distribution/exhibition of films with a predominantly European theme or cultural content | 7.162 |
| Divestment or reduction of interests in exhibition | 7.174 |
| Termination of the UIP joint venture | 7.183 |
| Prohibition on distribution joint ventures | 7.188 |
| Termination of the UCI joint venture | 7.193 |
| Third party complaints | 7.200 |

## Introduction

7.1. In this chapter we summarize the views of MGM Cinemas, Natl Amusements, Rank,[1] UCI and Warner Theatres (the leading exhibitors). We first give their observations on the market and then their views on the matters raised in our issues letter of 14 February 1994. At the start of each of the sections dealing with these matters in turn, we summarize those views which are common to all, or the majority, of the leading exhibitors (though expressed by them individually). This is followed by a summary of the other views they put to us. All the leading exhibitors submitted written evidence; MGM Cinemas, Rank and UCI also attended hearings. We held a video conference with Mr Sumner Redstone, who with members of his family owns Natl Amusements.

---

[1] Rank submitted evidence on behalf of both Odeon and RFD. This evidence was partly common to both subsidiaries and partly covered one or the other respectively. We summarize in this chapter all of Rank's evidence other than that relating to RFD exclusively; the latter is summarized in Chapter 9.

## Observations on the market

7.2. The leading exhibitors recalled that at the time of the MMC's 1983 report the future of the UK film distribution and exhibition industry seemed bleak. The long-term and continuing decline in cinema admissions, together with the rapid growth in sales of video recorders, raised serious questions about the future viability of cinemas. This situation had been turned around since 1984, mainly as a result of major investment in the exhibition sector which had as a result become much more competitive. Since 1985 over £600 million had been invested in cinemas. New multiplex cinemas had been built, in particular by the leading exhibitors (MGM Cinemas, Natl Amusements, Odeon, UCI and Warner Theatres), and many existing cinemas had been upgraded and converted to multi-screen sites by new entrants and incumbents alike. Almost half the screens in the UK were now owned by exhibitors who had entered the market since 1983. Audience numbers had increased from 54 million in 1984 to approximately 114 million in 1993. Despite this, the UK remained, by international standards, under-screened relative to the number of admissions. With the exception of Rank, the leading exhibitors all saw considerable scope for additional multiplex cinemas to be built in the UK. While exhibitors sought to avoid building multiplex cinemas close to each other, there was keen competition for sites in areas of high population density.

### *Nature of the market*

7.3. Rank argued that it would be a mistake to consider the market for cinematic exhibition in isolation from the markets for pay television and video rental and sell through. Neither distributors nor exhibitors could operate without regard to the other media for viewing films. In particular, if cinema prices were to rise relative to the price of pay television or video cassettes, Odeon expected that more consumers would watch films in their homes. This conclusion was, it said, based on empirical evidence that consumers considered other media for watching films as substitutes for going to the cinema. Substitution into other leisure activities should also be expected if cinema prices rose.

7.4. UCI said that the exhibition of films in cinemas was not a separate market from video and television. Video and television were not perfect substitutes for the cinema but they did compete. A film which had a wide cinematic release and did well would go on to do well on video, satellite and other forms of television. The cinema was, it said, the launch pad for the life of a film.

### *Market power*

7.5. MGM Cinemas told us that when buying a distinctive, creative product such as a film, there was no alternative to that product. In the final analysis, therefore, the balance of market power must favour the distributor of the film rather than the exhibitor. The exhibitor had the freedom to refuse to show a major film if it was unhappy with the terms required by the distributor. In reality, however, it would agree to show the film. Smaller, independent exhibitors had no market power at all.

7.6. MGM Cinemas recognized that the fact that distributors wanted to show their films gave some bargaining power to the exhibitor. It cited *Jurassic Park* as a recent example of a situation in which the exhibitors were able to moderate the distributor's demands for special terms. If, however, MGM Cinemas was not able to negotiate adequate terms with a major distributor, that distributor could afford to refuse to supply it with any films. This was because the revenue generated by MGM Cinemas in the UK was insignificant to the distributor in terms of the overall world-wide revenue generated by each film.

7.7. MGM Cinemas did not accept that rental terms were largely determined by the exhibitors. It referred to the difficulty it experienced in obtaining increases in nut figures. It attributed the growth over recent years in the exhibitors' share of box office returns to the increase in the number of multiplex cinemas. These cinemas operated higher nut figures than did the more traditional type of cinemas. Also the ability to move a film between screens as audience numbers diminished tended to reduce the distributor's average share of the box office, while increasing the absolute level of rentals by prolonging the period of exhibition.

7.8. Rank told us that, from Odeon's perspective, the balance of market power was fairly even between exhibitors and distributors. It said that the exhibitors' share of box office returns in the UK was roughly equivalent to the average level in other European countries. It also said that rental terms were subject to negotiation and it was only rarely that an exhibitor would get the terms that it wished; indeed on an increasing number of films the distributors were able to negotiate special terms.

7.9. UCI described the relationship between distributors and exhibitors as symbiotic. UCI traded on equal terms with all distributors and realized the importance of maintaining good relationships. The balance of power between distributors and exhibitors varied from week to week depending upon the number of films on offer and the success of the films on release. On occasions the distributors would have the advantage; at other times it lay with the exhibitors.

7.10. UCI said that its share of box office receipts (ie the percentage of box office UCI retained after payment of film rental) had remained fairly flat over the last five years. It believed that multiplex cinemas paid a lower average rental percentage than had other cinemas. As more multiplex cinemas were built, therefore, it expected the overall average to decrease.

## Views on complex monopoly situation

7.11. We asked the leading exhibitors for their views on our provisional finding that a complex monopoly situation existed in respect of the supply of films for exhibition in cinemas in the UK in that they engaged in one or more of the following practices:

  (a) distributors systematically offering their films to the cinemas of either MGM Cinemas or Odeon in places where they are in competition one with the other, but not to both (alignment by distributors);

  (b) MGM Cinemas and Odeon accepting films from distributors in accordance with the practice of alignment (alignment by exhibitors);

  (c) distributors supplying, and exhibitors accepting, individual films on the basis that a particular cinema will have the exclusive right to show a film within a specified area and for a specified period (exclusivity);

  (d) distributors refusing to supply individual films to exhibitors who request them, either at all or at the time requested, for reasons other than creditworthiness and the need to cover the costs of supply (refusal to supply);

  (e) distributors requiring exhibitors to show a film at particular cinemas for a minimum period exceeding seven days (minimum exhibition periods);

  (f) distributors requiring exhibitors to show a film at all times during the licence period at which films are normally shown at the cinema in question, except for children's matinées and late night shows (restrictions on screen use);

  (g) distributors supplying, and exhibitors accepting, films on terms which require exhibitors to charge such admission prices during licence periods as shall be agreed by the distributors (distributors' influence over exhibitors' admission prices);

  (h) distributors and exhibitors observing the *Standard Conditions* for the licensing of the exhibition of films issued by the SFD (observance of SFD *Standard Conditions*); and

  (i) distributors and exhibitors with related companies based overseas reserving important decision-making functions (for example, as regards which films should be released or shown in the UK and as regards release strategies) to such companies (overseas-based decision-taking).

7.12. MGM Cinemas and Natl Amusements made no comment on our provisional finding. UCI said that it did not believe the practices listed were complex monopoly practices which were restrictive and/or affected the public interest but it did not challenge the complex monopoly finding as such or UCI's inclusion in it.

7.13. Warner Theatres argued that most of the practices listed related to the activity of distributors rather than exhibitors. Of the others, Warner Theatres did not engage in alignment or, with the exception of a single film at one of its cinemas, in negotiating exclusivity; nor did its overseas parent company influence its decisions on which films to show and for how long, or the rental terms. Warner Theatres argued that the two remaining practices—concerning distributors' influence over exhibitors' admission prices and the observance of the *Standard Conditions*—should not be classified as conduct engaged in by exhibitors as well as distributors. It therefore submitted that there was no justification for including Warner Theatres in the complex monopoly.

7.14. Rank submitted that Odeon was not a party to a complex monopoly. In its view, the reference market was highly competitive and the practices identified by the MMC did not prevent, restrict or distort competition. Rank commented on each of the practices in turn:

*(a)* and *(b)* To the extent that distributors systematically made the first offer of their films to Odeon rather than to other exhibitors, they did so from choice in order to secure the efficiencies available through establishing an ongoing working relationship with a national chain which could provide a basis for planning the release of their product nation-wide. Such distributors were not in any way restricted from choosing other routes for distributing their product and they did indeed regularly choose other routes. The existence of these working relationships could not of itself be regarded as preventing, restricting or distorting competition. Exhibitors had to be competitive with each other to retain the business of their respective aligned distributors.

*(c)* The grant of exclusive rights was a fundamental means of exploiting intellectual property. Supplying films on a basis that gave contractual or *de facto* exclusivity did not, in Rank's view, prevent, restrict or distort competition; rather it represented an efficient and pro-competitive means of distribution. For many films, simultaneous exhibition in neighbouring cinemas was likely to be inefficient, increasing the overall costs of exhibition without a corresponding increase in the revenue generated; as a result, the returns for exhibitor and distributor alike would be reduced to the ultimate detriment of the cinema-going public. In addition, simultaneous exhibition in neighbouring cinemas would reduce the choice of film available to consumers.

*(d)* For similar reasons, the ability of distributors to choose the mix of outlets through which they distributed their products was important to the efficient operation of the market. That necessarily involved the possibility of refusal to supply in certain circumstances. Such refusals were as likely to occur with the smallest distributor as with the largest. In such circumstances, refusals that were intended to achieve the most efficient release of the film, in competition with other films being released, should not be regarded as conduct that prevented, restricted or distorted competition.

*(e)* The duration for which a film was to be exhibited was a necessary part of any licensing contract between a distributor and an exhibitor, defining an essential element of the rights and duty of the parties. In circumstances where a film was sufficiently attractive for the distributor to believe that it could be offered for periods of more than seven days, then in conditions of effective competition it was to be expected that the distributor would indeed seek to obtain periods of more than seven days, thereby optimizing the use of the print. The offer of films on such terms did not prevent, restrict or distort competition; it was again a manifestation of competition.

*(f)* Another necessary part of the contract between distributor and exhibitor was that the frequency with which the film was to be shown should be agreed: the distributor needed to maximize the extent to which the print would be put to work. Agreeing that the film would be shown with the normal frequency of the cinema in question did not prevent, restrict or distort competition; it merely defined a part of the contract between the parties. The parties

could agree upon a different frequency where that was appropriate or suited their respective requirements.

(g) A distributor had a legitimate interest in the admission prices charged by the exhibitors in respect of the distributor's films where those films were supplied on a risk-sharing basis under which the rental was calculated by reference to the box office take. Rank believed supply of films on such a risk-sharing basis was entirely consistent with conditions of effective competition and represented the most effective means of financing and charging for films. In the absence of some provision giving the distributor a say over admission prices, the exhibitor would be free to reduce the rental payable, and undermine the basis of the contract, by reducing admission prices with a corresponding rise in charges for ancillary items in which the distributor did not participate (eg refreshments). The existence of a contractual provision guarding against such conduct could not be regarded as preventing, restricting or distorting competition.

(h) The *Standard Conditions* were agreed between representatives of both distributors and exhibitors as a reasonable basis for the conduct of business. Use of those conditions was in no sense obligatory and parties could and did agree different terms. The existence of standard conditions did, however, permit business to be contracted without the need on each occasion to negotiate new terms; it was common in many industries and did not prevent, restrict or distort competition.

(i) There were many companies in the UK that were owned by overseas parents. It was inevitable that for such subsidiaries some important decisions would be taken by the overseas parent. In Rank's view it would be a novel proposition to conclude that the taking of decisions by the parent of itself prevented, restricted or distorted competition. In any event, Rank said that whether or not a distributor had overseas related companies, decisions about such matters on the film to be released to the UK would inevitably be taken overseas to the extent that the rights in such films were owned overseas.

7.15. We also asked the leading exhibitors for their views as to whether it might be preferable to identify two complex monopoly groups, one comprising exhibitors and the other distributors, rather than one group comprising both exhibitors and distributors. None of the leading exhibitors objected to the identification of one group. Three of the leading exhibitors (Odeon, UCI and Warner Theatres) argued that their ultimate holding companies had no involvement in their business and no other interest beyond that of controlling shareholders and should, therefore, not be regarded as persons in whose favour the monopoly situation existed.

## Alignment

7.16. We asked the leading exhibitors whether the practice of alignment, by restricting the competition between MGM Cinemas and Odeon in negotiating for exhibition rights, made the market less responsive to consumer preferences. We also asked them to comment on the possibility that distributors and exhibitors might be prohibited from entering into any agreement or arrangement with each other relating to the showing of a film at a cinema, other than an agreement or arrangement which covered one cinema only, was made solely on the merits of that cinema and contained no condition as to the showing of that or any other film in any other cinema; and that distributors might be required to submit information to the OFT at six-monthly intervals showing, for each film distributed in the preceding period, all the cinemas of MGM Cinemas and Odeon to which prints had been supplied *(a)* on first release and *(b)* on subsequent dates. As an alternative, we asked them to comment on the possibility that the practice of alignment might simply be prohibited.

7.17. Most of the leading exhibitors told us that the practice of alignment was less widespread than at the time of the MMC's 1983 report, affecting MGM Cinemas and Odeon in approximately 20 locations. They said that the number of locations would continue to decline as more multiplex cinemas were built and as more of the older MGM Cinemas and Odeon sites closed. They did not accept that the practice had adverse effects. MGM Cinemas and Odeon argued that they had to be competitive to retain the business of their aligned distributors. Moreover, they also faced competition from other cinemas, particularly multiplex cinemas, in several of the aligned locations.

7.18. MGM Cinemas was strongly of the view that there was no detriment to customers through the operation of alignment. Its principal effect was to simplify negotiation with distributors, avoiding arguments on a day-to-day basis over particular films. It also provided a greater choice of product for customers. MGM Cinemas agreed that it had, to a degree, a preferential relationship with its aligned distributors which extended to its whole circuit. It also accepted that alignment gave it a say in the setting of release dates but denied that this gave it an unfair advantage over other exhibitors. MGM Cinemas also told us that differentials in rental terms applied to leading and independent distributors, which had favoured UIP and Warner Distributors, had been largely eliminated as a result of a recent review of its nut figures (see paragraph 4.142).

7.19. MGM Cinemas was concerned about the effects of alignment in two London locations. Its Fulham Road cinema did not receive films from Odeon's aligned distributors because it was considered to be in competition with Odeon's High Street Kensington cinema. MGM Cinemas did not accept this. It stated that its King's Road cinema was the same distance from Odeon's High Street Kensington cinema but was able to show films released by Odeon's aligned distributors. MGM Cinemas told us that its Trocadero cinema was a purpose-built multiplex cinema and by normal industry practice should be given free access to all films. It did not, however, receive films from Odeon's aligned distributors because it was considered to be in competition with Odeon's Leicester Square cinema.

7.20. Regarding the first proposed remedy, MGM Cinemas wondered whether the criteria for choosing a cinema on its merits would be customer-based (choice, size and comfort) or supply-side based (which screens paid the highest percentage rental). The additional difficulty with a merit criterion would be that it was self-fulfilling, with all of the top films going to the 'best' cinema and competitors making do with everything else. The effect would be that the 'best' would become better, with the weaker cinemas finding it increasingly difficult to compete. MGM Cinemas said that its principal concern was that if agreements were to be made on a cinema-by-cinema basis, with no individual booking being contingent on another, this should apply equally to the owners of the Leicester Square 'premiere' cinemas and outlaw their ability to insist on their cinemas being used in a general release in return for use of their prestige locations.

7.21. It seemed to MGM Cinemas that the overall effect of outlawing alignment would be a short-term hiatus while the dust settled. This would, it suggested, be followed by a new steady state in which the 'best' cinema in each location, whichever circuit it came from, would attract the most popular films.

7.22. The proposal would, according to MGM Cinemas, not only add to administrative overheads, but would greatly distort the balance of bargaining power in favour of the distributors. Currently, MGM Cinemas' aligned distributors would supply prints to all of its cinemas directly affected by alignment. Operating under the proposed remedy, they would decide on a film-by-film basis which of those cinemas to supply, thereby making it more difficult for MGM Cinemas to project which of them would be supplied. This would make entry to the exhibition market considerably less attractive to independent (ie not vertically integrated) exhibitors such as MGM Cinemas. It made no additional comments on the alternative remedy.

7.23. While not sufficiently familiar with the alignments of MGM Cinemas and Odeon to comment specifically, Natl Amusements said that, under certain circumstances, alignment could increase the number of films available to the consumer. This arose because whenever a film was licensed to an aligned exhibitor, the non-aligned exhibitor would have a screen available for showing a different film.

7.24. Rank argued that alignment was little more than a description of the working relationship between supplier and customer. In the film industry, as in all other industries, the customer was free to choose its supplier and the supplier free to choose its customers. Rather than restricting competition between exhibitors, the working relationships were the product of that competition. They did not make the market less responsive to consumer preferences. Rank cited the growth in cinema audiences as proof that Odeon and other exhibitors were succeeding in meeting consumer preferences. There was no evidence that the market was unresponsive to consumer preferences.

7.25. Rank denied that Odeon had a preferential relationship with its aligned distributors. It accepted that alignment gave it a say in the setting of release dates but denied that this gave it an unfair advantage over other exhibitors. Even if in those locations directly affected by alignment, the aligned distributors did not choose between circuit cinemas on the basis of their relative attractiveness, nevertheless that factor was of crucial importance in competing for customers and for the business of distributors across the circuits as a whole. Rank said that in those locations, the number of which had not changed since 1990, Odeon was particularly concerned to maintain a competitive edge over MGM Cinemas.

7.26. Rank went on to say that even if alignment in some way restricted competition between Odeon and MGM Cinemas, the market was not less responsive to consumer preferences as a result. To compete with other exhibitors, other methods of watching films and other leisure activities, Odeon had to be responsive to consumer preferences. Odeon decided on the extent to which it would show each film offered to it by reference to the commercial potential of the film in each of its locations. This assessment was based on its interpretation of consumer preferences and applied equally to films offered by aligned and non-aligned distributors.

7.27. Rank argued that alignments benefited the public in that they helped to minimize costs arising from negotiation and from the consequences of parties being unfamiliar with each other's working practices. They facilitated forward planning and permitted more effective marketing. Thus, alignments increased the efficiency of distribution and held down costs to the benefit of consumers.

7.28. Rank believed the first suggested remedy would be highly detrimental and should not be adopted. In particular:

— it would seriously undermine the efficiency of film distribution;
— it would be unworkable and pose major problems of compliance;
— it would be likely to distort competition; and
— it would be disproportionate and misdirected.

7.29. The suggested remedy would, Rank said, preclude distributors from operating efficiently by dealing with exhibitors on a multi-cinema basis and impose additional cost burdens on both distributors and exhibitors. To the extent that it proved impossible to negotiate the desired release pattern, the effective marketing and distribution of films would be undermined.

7.30. Rank argued that dealing on a multi-cinema basis was not a function of alignments but of efficiency in negotiation and booking. Thus, distributors dealt with the multiplex chains as chains, although they were outside any alignments. Equally, distributors who were aligned to MGM Cinemas, when they dealt with Odeon, did so on a multi-cinema basis, as did Odeon-aligned distributors when dealing with MGM Cinemas. It believed substantial additional costs would be incurred if each Odeon cinema had to negotiate separately. The costs would be even higher if it was necessary for each cinema to view films before booking. Moreover, without co-ordinated releases through the chain, the costs of Odeon's advertising would be increased and its effectiveness reduced.

7.31. In Rank's view, the suggested remedy would be unworkable and it would be impossible for the parties to demonstrate compliance. For example, when Odeon, with 73 cinema sites, was negotiating with a distributor for the exhibition of a popular film at one cinema only in accordance with the suggested remedy, it would necessarily expect that, having regard to the spread and location of its sites, the film in question would be booked into a least some of its other locations. But when that happened, how could it show that there was no agreement or arrangement to that effect? Equally, how could the distributor show that the film was booked into the cinema 'solely on the merits' of the cinema in question?

7.32. Rank suggested that the requirement that bookings be made solely on the merits of the cinema in question was unworkable. First, there were likely to be circumstances where a booking was made not on the merits of the cinema concerned but because no other screen in the relevant locality was available on the dates required. Secondly, the merits of a cinema, in terms of, for example, its location, appearance and efficiency of management (including reliability, integrity and adherence to contracts), were likely to be difficult to assess and compare in a way that could be relied upon to demonstrate compliance, particularly since different people might attach different weightings to the various elements and also since the merits of an individual cinema might vary according to the type of film concerned. Thirdly, such 'merits' could not be separated from the terms negotiated for a booking; apparent disadvantages in the 'merits' might be outweighed by advantages in the terms offered, or *vice versa*, making it still more difficult to demonstrate compliance in any particular case.

7.33. Rank said that because of the problems of compliance, it was likely that the imposition of the suggested remedy would force the participants in the industry to make choices that were determined not by the merits of the film or cinema in question but by the desire to be able to show compliance. For example, Odeon believed that each of its cinemas ought to be selected over neighbouring cinemas on its merits; but Odeon could foresee that, if the suggested remedy were implemented, distributors currently aligned to it might feel the need, at least on occasions, to select an alternative cinema not on the merits of that cinema but to satisfy the regulator. Thus, the suggested remedy would itself distort the working of the market.

7.34. Further, the suggested remedy would remove a significant aspect of competition. At present the exhibitor chains, including Odeon, competed with each other in offering distributors attractive networks of cinemas. The suggested remedy would remove the ability of distributors to respond to that competition by booking on a multi-cinema basis and would thus further distort competition. In addition, selection of cinemas solely on their respective merits would be likely to make it more difficult for the smaller independent cinemas to compete.

7.35. Rank submitted that, although raised in the context of alignments, the suggested remedy would bite irrespective of alignments and, as indicated in paragraph 7.30, would bite on agreements between parties who were not aligned. However, to limit the proposed remedy only to the two national circuits and their aligned distributors would produce a major distortion of competition. Further, alignments essentially constituted a practice of distributors in the choice they respectively made as to the exhibitors to whom they would first offer their films: as such, alignments were not dependent upon any agreement or arrangements between distributor and exhibitor. Thus, the suggested remedy, which focused on such agreements or arrangements, was in any event misdirected.

7.36. Moreover, as formulated, the suggested remedy would preclude an agreement between distributor and exhibitor which granted contractual exclusivity in any film (since the remedy would prohibit any condition 'as to the showing of that ... film in any other cinema'). Rank believed it would be against the public interest to remove the freedom to contract on that basis, which in any event was unconnected to the issue of alignment.

7.37. Rank submitted that, for these additional reasons, a remedy that would impose major adverse consequences on the industry would be wholly disproportionate to any perceived adverse effects of the practice of alignment, which was already of much reduced significance. Rank also argued that the suggested requirement for distributors to supply six-monthly data to the OFT would be administratively burdensome. In any event, such monitoring would be of no necessary assistance in seeing whether 'the pattern of supply was ... determined by the alignments that currently exist', as the MMC envisaged.

7.38. As to the alternative remedy, Rank said that this appeared to permit distributors to reach agreements with exhibitors on a multi-site basis, but envisaged that distributors would approach all chains and would select the appropriate mix of cinemas from amongst those on offer; this, it was apparently suggested, would lead to greater competition as between chains in order to ensure that as many of those cinemas as possible were selected. In fact, it was already the case that distributors approached the various chains and selected a mix of cinemas from amongst them. And it was already the case that there was highly effective competition as between exhibitors and with other forms of entertainment to provide cinema facilities of the highest standard. Rank said that the difference between the existing position and the suggested alternative was that distributors approached one or other of the two national chains first. By doing so they were able to secure the basic framework of a release pattern on which subsequently to build, without the logistical problems that would be involved in negotiating with more than one exhibitor in tandem to arrive at an acceptable release date and basic release framework. That each distributor habitually first approached one of the national chains rather than the other reflected their respective perceptions of the advantages to them of dealing with one rather than the other, whether that arose from the quality of the cinemas concerned, the number and location of the sites or the basis on which rentals were calculated (ie preferring MGM Cinemas for its use of the house nut or Odeon for its use of the sliding scale).

7.39. In Rank's view, the alternative remedy and the apparent rationale for it presented the following paradox: if the prohibition of alignments led to more intensive competition between the national chains with the result that one was perceived as clearly preferable to the other, it was to be expected that distributors, or at least those who perceived such a preference, would habitually approach the preferred chain rather than the other for their desired release patterns. Yet such habitual dealing was apparently the very conduct that the proposed remedy would be intended to prohibit. The problem was that the current arrangements were entirely consistent with being the product of fully effective competition and in fact were the product of such competition.

7.40. Rank submitted that in such circumstances it was impossible to identify the conduct to be prohibited. If a remedy was to be recommended, it must be capable of being implemented by some workable means. It could not be suggested that distributors should be prohibited from making the first offer of successive films to the same chain in preference to another, even if they were satisfied that the one was more competitive than the other. If nevertheless such pro-competitive conduct were to be prohibited, so that distributors were obliged to offer to both chains simultaneously, Rank believed that would not meet the perceived problem since it would leave distributors free to continue to contact their preferred chain. If distributors were prohibited from contacting a chain unless they were satisfied that it was the most competitive for their requirements, there was no reason to suppose that that would alter the status quo. If, on the other hand, distributors were prohibited from contacting the same chain for successive films in any circumstances, that would patently distort competition and remove the incentive for the exhibition chains to compete with each other. The difficulty of formulating a workable remedy itself called into question the desirability of introducing any such remedy and the need to do so. In Rank's view, there was no need to do so and it would be detrimental to seek to do so.

7.41. UCI said that it was not aligned to any distributor, nor was it affected by alignments. To the limited extent that alignments still existed, they reduced competition between MGM Cinemas and Odeon. Further investment in cinemas would continue to erode the practice which, it believed, would cease within five years.

7.42. UCI did not believe it would be affected by the first proposed remedy. Nevertheless, it doubted that regulatory intervention was necessary to hasten the demise of alignment. UCI would be concerned if the proposed remedy prevented central booking departments from holding discussions with distributors in relation to each of their cinemas; and if all exclusivity arrangements were prohibited. UCI made no further substantive comments on the alternative remedy other than to question the practicability of enforcement.

7.43. Warner Theatres believed that consumer preferences were currently well served by the market. Alignments did not, in its opinion, operate to make distributors or exhibitors less responsive to changes in consumer tastes. This was particularly the case as the multiplex cinemas were not affected by the practice. Alignments did not diminish the need for films to compete against each other or against the many other leisure pursuits available to the public. It was this competition which ensured that the market remained in touch with what the public wished to see.

7.44. Although Warner Theatres foresaw that alignment would wither away over the next few years, this did not mean that the MMC should try to speed up that process. If alignment were abolished without an adequate number of screens being available across the country, there was a risk that all exhibitors, including those operating multiplex cinemas, would be required to bid for films. It told us that this had happened when alignments were broken up in the USA. Film distributors sought 'best bids' from exhibitors stating the minimum number of weeks they would undertake to screen the film, the advance on rentals they were prepared to guarantee and the percentage rental they would offer. This proved very damaging for the smaller independent exhibitors who would stake a great deal of money on their bid for a major film; their business could not survive if their bid was successful and the film did not live up to expectations. A number of small exhibitors lost their businesses this way and the bidding system had to be replaced by a system of regional alignments. Warner Theatres feared that it would suffer if, like other chains, it was forced to bid for films even though at present it was not affected by alignment.

7.45. Warner Theatres said that the first remedy as worded would prevent it from negotiating centrally for the release of films in all its multiplex cinemas since to do so would not fulfil the requirement that it cover one cinema only. It assumed that it was not the intention to prevent the multiplex chains from negotiating centrally for the licensing of screens in all their cinemas.

## Exclusivity and refusal to supply

7.46. The leading exhibitors were asked whether exclusivity and refusal to supply unduly restricted consumers' choice of cinemas to see a given film on first release; were harmful to certain independent exhibitors, to the extent in some cases of causing their withdrawal from the market; and deterred new entry and investment in the exhibition sector. We also asked them to comment on the possibilities that the granting by distributors of exclusive rights to show a film might be prohibited, and that distributors might be required to supply prints to all competing cinemas in a given area which requested one, subject only to considerations of creditworthiness and the exhibitor guaranteeing as a minimum to cover the distributor's costs and a profit margin.

7.47. With the exception of Rank, the leading exhibitors said that they did not seek exclusivity. The three specialist multiplex operators nevertheless did not believe exclusivity had anti-competitive effects. Nor did they favour the suggestion that the practice should be prohibited. They believed that the market should decide.

7.48. Regarding refusal to supply, the leading exhibitors accepted that the distributors needed to have the ability to determine, on commercial grounds, the optimal number of prints for each release and the allocation of those prints. This fostered competition among exhibitors to attract audiences by the quality of their cinemas and hence persuade distributors to supply first-run prints. They said that refusal to supply cinemas which did not meet the commercial criterion had no anti-competitive effects. The leading exhibitors generally had no difficulty in obtaining prints of most films, especially for their multiplex cinemas (but see paragraph 7.51).

7.49. The leading exhibitors opposed the suggested remedy referred to in paragraph 7.46. They believed such a remedy would require them to bear more risk than they did at present, leading them to be more cautious about booking films of uncertain appeal. Because substantially the same total box office receipts would be spread over more cinemas, individual exhibitors' returns would suffer. This would harm the prospects for further investment in exhibition. Returns to distributors and producers would also decrease, leading to reduced investment in production. Their general view was that the existing methods of calculating rentals were necessary to reduce exhibitors' risks that a film would not attract audiences. The idea of switching to a flat percentage rental, a method which was used in a small minority of cases, did not commend itself to them.

7.50. Alone among the leading exhibitors, MGM Cinemas argued that exclusivity was anti-competitive and should be banned. It told us that it did not request exclusivity and considered the negotiation of exclusivity arrangements to be against the spirit of the 1989 Order on barring.[1] The practice was a means by which a large exhibitor could misuse its power to damage smaller competitors by pressurising distributors into refusing to supply them. It wanted decisions as to which cinemas received prints to be in the hands of distributors. MGM Cinemas said that it suffered from Odeon's demands for exclusivity only in London, however (see paragraph 7.19).

---

[1]MGM Cinemas said that, from time to time, it had agreed to exhibit marginal films in the West End on the understanding that they were not played concurrently in competing cinemas. It did not regard these as exclusivity arrangements because it would be happy to pass on the films to another exhibitor rather than show them itself.

7.51. MGM Cinemas told us that it regularly experienced difficulty in acquiring prints for some of its smaller cinemas because the distributors were not happy about the level of film rental generated by those cinemas. It made no complaint about this, which it regarded as the normal operation of a commercial market. It also found it difficult to exhibit certain British or European films for which only a limited number of prints were available. These were usually allocated to the BFI cinemas. Responding to Warner Distributors' comments on *The Witches of Eastwick* (see paragraph 8.103), MGM Cinemas described the behaviour of Cannon and Odeon on that occasion as Canute-like and as pointless.

7.52. Natl Amusements told us that the grant of exclusivity by a distributor might increase the diversity of films being exhibited in any particular market. While Natl Amusements did not seek to play films on an exclusive basis, it could conceive of situations where exclusivity might be justified as being pro-competitive. There was, it said, no way to determine whether either practice restricted consumer choice of cinemas without undertaking a close examination of the circumstances in each case. It recognized that the practices could impact on exhibitors. However, although certain exhibitors might not be able to obtain some films on first run, they were generally not prevented from showing such films later at a significantly lower charge to the public. Nor were they prevented from showing films on a first-run basis which were not being shown elsewhere by competing cinemas. It said that this resulted in a greater diversity of films, allowing smaller distributors access to screen time. It also argued that it allowed consumers to view films at a significantly reduced charge by waiting for a short time.

7.53. According to Natl Amusements, the distributors' ability to refuse to supply exhibitors and to supply on an exclusive basis encouraged new entry, investment and quality in the exhibition sector. By and large, however, distributors preferred to license films to multiplex cinemas, though Natl Amusements had been refused first-run prints from certain smaller distributors. This had encouraged a significant amount of new construction. Requiring distributors to supply prints would, it argued, virtually eliminate the second-run market which provided consumers with the ability to view films at significantly lower prices; reduce the ability of smaller distributors to have their films exhibited, since exhibitors would prefer to show more commercially viable and widely distributed films; and virtually eliminate any incentive to improve the quality of existing cinemas. It would also have the effect of discriminating against those exhibitors who had invested in new cinemas for the purpose of attracting larger numbers of patrons and better-quality films.

7.54. Mr Sumner Redstone told us of difficulties which Natl Amusements had experienced in obtaining films in the early stages when there were very few multiplex cinemas in the UK. The two circuit exhibitors had said to the distributors that, if they gave prints to new multiplex cinemas, their films would not be shown in other parts of the country where there were no multiplexes. Natl Amusements had made strong representations to the distributors about these problems, stressing that it was in the distributors' interests to encourage the development of multiplexes in order to reinvigorate the market and hence generate greater revenues.

7.55. Rank said that the grant of exclusive rights was a fundamental and widely recognized means of exploiting intellectual property. It argued that the possibility of granting exclusivity and refusing to supply were of fundamental importance in securing the efficient distribution and exhibition of films. They constituted a vital part of the machinery by which a distributor could tailor the release pattern for a film with a view to generating the necessary returns. They also maximized the audience reached by each print, minimized the costs of exhibition and maximized the variety of films exhibited in any locality at any given time. Showing the same film in neighbouring cinemas reduced the choice for customers; it would also be likely to reduce efficiency and increase costs. Rank cited the unprecedented level of new entry and the high level of investment in the exhibition sector over the last decade as proof that no significant deterrents to entry had operated.

7.56. Rank claimed that other exhibitors, including MGM Cinemas, also requested exclusivity. It also told us that, in Odeon's experience, all distributors granted contractual exclusivity in some circumstances; it was not aware of any differences between them in their attitude to exclusivity. Odeon sought exclusivity for many of the films it exhibited and usually succeeded in negotiating some exclusivity against neighbouring cinemas, although rarely against multiplex cinemas. It listed 30 cinemas, out of its total of 76, where it sought exclusivity and named the competing cinemas against which it did so. Odeon agreed that its negotiation of contractual exclusivity was to some extent a matter of 'belt and braces' since, in most cases, the distributor would in any event be likely to give *de facto* exclusivity as it would dilute its returns to show the film concurrently elsewhere in the locality. But it added that the practice also provided greater certainty, particularly in border-line cases where the distributor, left to itself, might choose to book a film into a competing cinema concurrently.

7.57. Rank described as wholly unworkable the suggestion that exhibitors should agree to cover a distributor's costs and a profit margin. The costs would include not only the acquisition of rights in the film but also prints and advertising, distribution, central administration and accounting and credit control. If these were to be passed on to exhibitors, guaranteeing distributors a profit on all films, the financial burdens on exhibitors would be substantially increased and many would rapidly go out of business. The whole basis of risk-sharing would be altered. Even if it were intended that exhibitors cover only the costs of the print and associated distribution costs, which would be inequitable for the distributors, it was likely that exhibitors would have to pay significantly more than under existing arrangements.

7.58. Providing prints on first release to all cinemas that requested one would, in Rank's view, reduce the choice of films available in a given area. It would require more prints to be produced, thereby increasing distribution costs, and it would be likely to fragment the audience for each film, dividing it between more cinemas and thereby increasing exhibition costs. Rank believed that the ability to exhibit a newly-released film concurrently with a neighbouring cinema would be unlikely to benefit many independent cinemas. Almost certainly each would achieve lower box office receipts.

7.59. It would, in Rank's opinion, be highly detrimental to the future of cinematic exhibition to introduce changes of the kind suggested. There was no more reason for giving exhibitors the right to obtain any film they wanted, regardless of the effects on the distributors' ability to maximize their returns, than there would be for giving distributors the right of access to any exhibitor's screens, regardless of the effect on the exhibitor's ability to maximize its profitability. It would be particularly inequitable to impose obligations in one direction only. Rank told us that Odeon had no knowledge of the incident concerning *The Witches of Eastwick* referred to by Warner Distributors (see paragraphs 7.51 and 8.103).

7.60. UCI told us that exclusivity should be a matter for negotiation between distributor and exhibitor on a case-by-case basis. A distributor had the discretion to agree supply on exclusive or non-exclusive terms. An exhibitor's ability to persuade a distributor to grant exclusivity would depend on its ability to offer more by way of return than the distributor would lose by forgoing revenue from competing cinemas. Provided that it was negotiated bilaterally, there should not be adverse effects. UCI believed the ability to grant exclusivity could encourage competition among exhibitors for the supply of films.

7.61. UCI saw no reason why distributors and exhibitors should be restrained by regulatory intervention from negotiating and agreeing exclusivity as part of the competitive process of supplying and acquiring prints. It should be left to the distributor, not the regulator, to choose whether to supply on an exclusive basis. Likewise, the exhibitor should remain free to seek exclusivity.

7.62. UCI said that refusal to supply meant inevitably that a film might not be played by all exhibitors who wished to do so. It did not, however, unduly restrict consumers' choice of cinemas in which to see a film on first release. This was because the distributor's discretion to refuse supply of a print where it believed a cinema's attendances would not generate adequate returns reflected the aim of matching the supply of prints with consumer demand. The onus on the exhibitor, when competing for prints, was to ensure that the ability of its cinema to attract audiences and thereby achieve high box office revenues justified the supply of a print. The failure of some exhibitors to compete for prints and audiences and their subsequent withdrawal from the market did not mean that refusal to supply operated against the public interest. In UCI's view, the failure of these exhibitors arose because they did not take sufficient steps to meet consumer demands, for example by upgrading their cinemas.

7.63. UCI told us that it had experienced some difficulties in obtaining prints in the late 1980s but that those had been overcome, partly thanks to the 1989 Order. Since 1983, the growth in the number of prints produced for release and in the number of screens meant that consumers had greater access to films. It believed refusal to supply could not be said to deter new entry and investment.

7.64. UCI said that the MMC's report on *Refusal to Supply* (see paragraph 4.179) identified three situations in which refusal to supply was likely to damage the public interest: refusals made for the purpose of influencing resale prices, those which were the result of a threatened boycott of existing outlets, and those made in conditions which were not reasonably competitive. UCI said that neither the first nor the second situations applied in this case. As to the third, UCI said that the industry was now competitive, partly as a result of the significant changes that had taken place since the previous MMC inquiry. Most importantly, refusal to supply in the film industry was concerned with the legitimate commercial objective of maximizing revenues or profits. UCI concluded that refusal to supply did not, therefore, operate against the public interest.

7.65. UCI believed that requiring distributors to supply prints to all exhibitors, subject only to covering costs and a profit margin and considerations of creditworthiness, would eliminate the competition for prints which had been a major incentive for exhibitors to invest in improved quality and service.

7.66. Warner Theatres said that the practices of exclusivity and refusal to supply did not have the effects suggested. Its cinemas had been refused a print on first release only when the distributor had decided to release the film in question initially to a very small number of cinemas.

7.67. Warner Theatres believed the prohibition of exclusivity would amount to an unnecessary interference with the flexibility of release strategies. Some films which were aimed at an up-market audience benefited from a slow release pattern in which screening was limited to a few cinemas, allowing audiences to develop over a number of weeks. This did not operate as a restriction on competition. Nor was it detrimental to the public interest.

7.68. Warner Theatres said that the enforced distribution of prints would be likely to reduce the aggregate level of rentals received by the distributor because it would result in the same audience being spread more thinly among the competing cinemas. As a result, fewer cinemas would reach the break points of box office receipts at which rental became payable at the higher level and more exhibitors would pay the minimum rental terms. This would hit the distributors particularly badly if the obligation were extended to the Leicester Square cinemas. A reduction in rentals would cause the distributors to seek improved terms. The wider availability of prints would also reduce the chances for independently-produced films, or films of less certain appeal, to be screened. All cinemas would prefer to take the safer option of showing the latest blockbuster rather than taking a risk with a less mainstream film.

## Minimum exhibition periods and restrictions on screen use

7.69. We asked the leading exhibitors to comment on whether the imposition by distributors of minimum exhibition periods and restrictions on screen use harmed smaller distributors by restricting their access to screens; harmed exhibitors by reducing their revenue; and unduly restricted consumer choice. We also asked them for views on the possibilities that minimum exhibition periods might be abolished or restricted to a maximum of two weeks on first release and one week subsequently, and that exhibitors might be given the right, as a minimum, to show other films on three occasions a week during licence periods, in addition to children's matinées and late night shows.

7.70. With the exception of MGM Cinemas, the leading exhibitors accepted the distributors' reasons for insisting on minimum exhibition periods and regarded them as part of a normal commercial relationship. They told us that while some distributors accepted that different locations had different potential for a film and would, accordingly, vary the length of the minimum playing time, others did not. Where a film's box office takings fell significantly below expectations, however, most distributors would reduce the minimum length of playing time.

7.71. Regarding restrictions on screen use, the leading exhibitors would prefer to have more flexibility to decide which films to show at any time but again they recognized why distributors insisted on such restrictions. They noted that most distributors were prepared to negotiate variations in screen use which allowed other films to be shown. With the exception of MGM Cinemas, they did not favour the suggestion that exhibitors should be free to show other films on three occasions a week during licence periods.

7.72. For its part, MGM Cinemas strongly opposed, and favoured the abolition of, minimum exhibition periods. At the very least it believed such periods should be restricted to a maximum of one week. It told us that, on major films which incurred heavy print and advertising costs, it was common practice for distributors to specify a minimum playing time before agreeing to supply a print. Two weeks was the norm. The practice was, in the opinion of MGM Cinemas, totally unsatisfactory. The distributor had made a commercial judgment regarding the amount of money to be spent on advertising a film and should let the market decide whether that judgment was correct. The policy of specifying minimum playing times could be interpreted as an attempt by distributors to prevent the competitive release of films as screens would not be available during that period for competing product. This was, however, less of a problem with the construction of multi-screen cinemas.

7.73. MGM Cinemas said that it was common practice, during the first four weeks of a film's run, for a distributor to refuse to allow an exhibitor to exhibit another film on the same screen during the cinema's normal working hours. This was specified in the *Standard Conditions*. It recognized that sharing playing time had become much more common, particularly where a cinema had a limited number of screens, but still more flexibility was required on the part of the distributors. For example, films appealing principally to children often performed very badly on the main evening show. Only rarely, however, did distributors permit the film to be moved to a smaller screen or the screen to be shared with another film, despite the fact that this was demonstrably more efficient to both the distributor and exhibitor.

7.74. Natl Amusements implied that the distributors could be more flexible in exercising their contractual rights, but said to the extent that smaller distributors had problems in gaining access to screens, this was not attributable to minimum exhibition periods. The problem arose from factors relating to the quality and audience appeal of the films, the release strategy and the level of promotional support. As an alternative to the proposed remedy, Natl Amusements suggested that the SFD establish a procedure, applicable on a film-by-film basis, whereby exhibitor and distributor could negotiate an agreement based upon the performance of the film in question. As an alternative to the proposed remedy on screen use restrictions, it suggested a similar procedure for dealing with disagreements on screen usage.

7.75. Rank did not believe these practices were likely to harm exhibitors by reducing their revenue. In Odeon's experience, films for which distributors sought extended exhibition periods tended to be those which could sustain such periods. Where they did not, it was generally possible to agree a variation with the distributor. Given the number of films released, there was extensive choice available to exhibitors who were not prepared to agree an extended exhibition period.

7.76. Rank said that the proposed remedy for restrictions on screen use would be impracticable. Given that box office revenue was not the same for each performance, it was possible that the three best attended performances could represent over 50 per cent of the total revenue for the week. The scheme would significantly increase the administrative burden for exhibitor and distributor and greatly complicate the marketing of films and the task of bringing exhibition dates and times to the public's attention. Even if given the right to share screens in the way proposed, therefore, Odeon would not necessarily choose to exercise it.

7.77. UCI said that the inevitable effect of minimum exhibition periods and restrictions on screen use was to restrict access to screens. Whether the minimum exhibition period harmed exhibitors and restricted consumer choice depended upon whether it exceeded the period in which the exhibitor would have played the film in the absence of such a requirement. Whether the restriction on screen use had such effects depended upon whether it resulted in the number of screenings at which an exhibitor played the film exceeding the number of times it would have played in the absence of such a restriction. UCI said that distributors were, in general, prepared to allow a film to be taken off if it was not meeting box office expectations.

7.78. UCI told us that minimum exhibition periods and restrictions on screen use were negotiated on a film-by-film basis and were reviewed weekly when it considered programming changes for the following week. It had to use its commercial judgment as to whether to concede or to resist the distributor's requirements. Sometimes UCI lost out by making a concession that it would have preferred not to have made. On other occasions it gained by, for example, obtaining a shorter minimum exhibition period or fewer restrictions on screen use than the distributor originally required. Where the distributor and exhibitor shared the same view on the appropriate conditions, the practices had neutral effects. Thus, the position was the same as in any commercial customer/supplier relationship and did not operate against the public interest.

7.79. UCI stated that, whilst it would prefer not to have any minimum exhibition periods and restrictions on screen use, it recognized that distributors would be likely to require a price for allowing increased flexibility, for example by way of a revised basis for calculating the rental fee. Distributors and exhibitors should be free to negotiate their own contractual terms and should not be circumscribed by minimum or maximum limitations imposed by regulation.

7.80. Warner Theatres did not feel that minimum exhibition periods or restrictions on screen use unduly limited its control over how it exhibited films. It showed films from smaller distributors, provided that they had commercial appeal. As an operator of multiplex cinemas, it had the capacity to show a variety of films, even if certain distributors imposed minimum exhibition periods for some films. It also had the flexibility to move films into smaller auditoria when admissions declined. If a film was not attracting audiences, Warner Theatres would not be held to the minimum agreed period, since the distributor recognized that to do so was not in its interest. Warner Theatres' revenue was not, therefore, materially reduced by the practices, nor did they affect its ability or willingness to screen films from smaller distributors. Consumer choice was not unduly restricted; an unsuccessful film would be withdrawn and replaced by another film.

7.81. Warner Theatres did not believe a remedy was necessary. If minimum exhibition periods were abolished, there would be greater pressure on exhibitors to take a film off during the early part of its run, even though experience suggested that some films took time to build up an audience. This might unfairly deprive the distributor and producer of revenue. There was a strong possibility that distributors would require a higher rental in the first two weeks of release if they thought this would be their only opportunity to recoup their expenditure. They would also be more likely to insist on the provision of minimum rental guarantees from exhibitors. Warner Theatres also believed that the existing ability to put on additional performances above those included in the nut calculations provided sufficient flexibility for exhibitors.

7.82. Two of the leading exhibitors told us that Buena Vista adopted an inflexible approach to requests to allow the showing of other distributors' films at certain times during the period that they were committed to a Buena Vista film, normally a children's film. One leading exhibitor, for example, told us that Buena Vista had refused to allow it to show a film of another distributor even though it had suggested an alteration in rental terms which would have been advantageous to Buena Vista.

## Influence or control over admission prices

7.83. Asked whether the influence or control exercised by distributors over exhibitors' admission prices caused those charges to be higher than they otherwise would have been, the leading exhibitors told us that admission charges were set by the exhibitors and regular increases were not discussed with the distributors. However, they recognized that the distributors had a legitimate right to approve variations in the notified admission prices, by way of free or discounted tickets, because film rentals were based upon a percentage of box office returns and a change in admission prices could affect the distributors' revenue expectations based upon the deals negotiated with the exhibitors. The right to approve variations did not cause admission prices to be higher than they otherwise would have been.

7.84. MGM Cinemas told us that distributors had, on occasions, refused to supply certain of its cinemas whose admission prices they regarded as too low to warrant the supply of top-quality films. It described as invalid the argument—sometimes advanced by distributors—that exhibitors might cut admission prices in order to boost concession revenue, all of which was retained by the exhibitor. According to MGM Cinemas, the bigger the audience, the less was taken per head in concession sales.

7.85. It was not obvious to MGM Cinemas that more freedom on pricing matters would necessarily lead to lower average prices overall. It would, however, be desirable to provide for greater flexibility in the price variation procedures set out in the *Standard Conditions*. In other words, exhibitors should be able to lower prices without seeking prior permission, so long as the admission price remained above a minimum level agreed between distributors and exhibitors.

7.86. Rank told us that, in Odeon's experience, distributors exercised little influence over admission charges at its cinemas and there was nothing to suggest that prices were higher than they otherwise would be. In fact, average ticket prices in the UK were lower than elsewhere in Europe. If rental payments were not based on risk sharing, calculated by reference to box office takings, and instead the exhibitor bore the risk of box office success or failure, admission charges might rise to reflect the increased risk.

7.87. Rank believed there was price competition between cinemas and that admission charges reflected the competitive position of each cinema. It cited examples of situations in which Odeon had reduced admission prices at cinemas in order to counter competition from another exhibitor.

7.88. UCI told us that distributors usually responded favourably to proposals for price cuts if an exhibitor could show that they were part of a well-thought-out commercial strategy. It recognized that it would be unacceptable for an exhibitor to have complete flexibility to alter admission prices without the distributor's consent. The distributor needed to protect its returns from box office revenues where those revenues were shared with the exhibitor. UCI believed this issue should be a matter for individual negotiation between distributors and exhibitors.

7.89. Warner Theatres said that, ideally, it would like to have complete flexibility to determine its own admission charges. However, it recognized that the distributors' ability to influence prices was the corollary of the nut system of determining film rentals. In practice, distributors were not able to dictate the level of ticket prices. In general, the nut system worked well and Warner Theatres would be reluctant to change to another method which might, for example, include fixed fees on a sliding scale. To do so might lead to an increase in the overall level of rental and in turn put pressure on admission prices.

## SFD *Standard Conditions*

7.90. We asked the leading exhibitors whether the widespread observance of the *Standard Conditions* strengthened the market power of distributors and exacerbated the anti-competitive effects of certain practices which were covered by the *Standard Conditions*. We also asked them to comment on the possibility that the SFD might be required to withdraw the *Standard Conditions* and that the future issue of such conditions might be prohibited.

7.91. While most of the leading exhibitors generally favoured the retention of some form of standard conditions, they also felt that the existing conditions were drafted in favour of the distributors. They did not agree that the *Standard Conditions* should be withdrawn and that the future issue of such conditions should be prohibited.

7.92. MGM Cinemas said that the observance of the *Standard Conditions* strengthened the power of the distributors. It was, however, necessary to operate within a mutually agreed framework. Some basis for negotiation needed to exist in an industry where both the supplier and the retailer participated in the retail takings.

7.93. Natl Amusements believed distributors should exercise greater flexibility, particularly in varying the terms of the *Standard Conditions* to reflect the actual performance of the film being exhibited. It said that the use of a standard form quickly and efficiently set out the legal relationship between parties. This was particularly beneficial in the film industry where numerous films were licensed on a day-by-day basis. The use of a standard form did not, however, mean that the terms could not be negotiated. Indeed, many of the critical terms were negotiated film by film. In view of the ability to negotiate particular terms with each distributor, Natl Amusements believed the use of the *Standard Conditions* did not strengthen the market power of the distributors.

7.94. Rank believed the existence of standard terms was important for the running of its business. Widespread use of some form of standard terms in an industry characterized by a high volume of similar contracts was, it argued, a symptom of business efficiency rather than of anti-competitive practices. Because the *Standard Conditions* were negotiated and used industry-wide, small exhibitors and distributors contracted on substantially the same terms as did their larger competitors. To this extent they facilitated the ability of such exhibitors and distributors to compete efficiently. Rank said that restrictions on screen use and influence or control over admission prices would be likely to arise irrespective of the use of the *Standard Conditions* and were not exacerbated by their use.

7.95. UCI described the *Standard Conditions* as a kind of 'highway code' which assisted distributors and exhibitors to resolve serious disputes. As UCI had never resisted a distributor's incorporation of the *Standard Conditions* into licence agreements, nor challenged a distributor's reliance upon them, it could not say whether they strengthened the distributors' market power. To the extent that the *Standard Conditions* had the effect of standardizing the terms upon which distributors dealt with exhibitors, they might discourage the kind of bilateral negotiation and contracts which were characteristic of many industries. UCI would prefer the background terms to licence agreements to be a matter for negotiation between exhibitors and distributors on an individual basis.

7.96. UCI told us that it was considering whether to adopt its own terms and conditions. But it believed that those distributors and exhibitors who wanted the convenience of using terms which they did not have to draft and update should be free, but not forced, to use any standard terms which could be agreed between the SFD and the CEA. The option for individual terms should concentrate the minds of the two trade bodies on finalizing terms agreeable to both sides of the industry which did not unduly restrict either side.

7.97. Warner Theatres said that the *Standard Conditions* did not operate in an anti-competitive way, nor could they be said to exacerbate the anti-competitive effects of any practices. If they were withdrawn, each distributor would be likely to develop its own standard terms which would cover the same aspects. The overall competitive position would not change materially. Warner Theatres would, however, welcome a review of the *Standard Conditions* which, it believed, were expressed in antiquated language.

## Vertical links to US production companies

7.98. The leading exhibitors were asked whether distributors and exhibitors with vertical links to US production companies used their position in the interrelated markets for distribution and exhibition to keep out competition from independent producers operating outside North America. They were also asked to comment on the allegation (see paragraph 9.11) that exhibitors reserved dates, many months in advance, for specified titles to be released by the distribution subsidiaries of the major studios, often before the film had been released in the USA or even completed. We also put to them the assertion (see also paragraph 9.11) that independent distributors were unable to get dates for independent films without first being able to show the completed films to the exhibitors, by which time they found that much screen space had been reserved for the majors' films.

7.99. MGM Cinemas said that the major distributors had a known timetable of films coming out of their parents' studios. They were, therefore, able to schedule their films with the exhibitors in advance, typically by 8 to 12 months before release. An independent producer or distributor might find it hard to break into this process at short notice, unless it had films with obvious commercial appeal.

7.100. MGM Cinemas told us that it reserved dates for films on the same basis for independent distributors as for the major distributors. All reservations were made on basis of available information about the commercial potential of a film (eg the involvement of leading actors, identity of the director) and were provisional until it could view the film. It insisted on prior viewing of any film whose commercial prospects were unclear before it would reserve a date. Few independent releases had clear commercial potential.

7.101. Natl Amusements told us that it attempted to book as many films as it could in order to maximize its revenue and satisfy the varied tastes of consumers. It said that it was in constant contact with all distributors regarding the availability of films, regardless of whether such films had been previously released in the USA. Its evaluation of a film was based on variety of factors and it generally requested prior screening of a film about which it had little information. It was not unusual for minor distributors to give little or no information about their films until just prior to release.

7.102. As regards the acquisition of Paramount by Viacom Inc, Mr Redstone told us that he did not expect the relationships between UIP, Natl Amusements and UCI to be changed by the merger.

7.103. Rank thought it unlikely that the US vertically integrated companies used their position in the interrelated markets for distribution and exhibition to keep out competition from independent producers operating outside North America. It did not consider that Odeon's screens were foreclosed to independent producers; on the contrary, it was always looking for good films. It was a lack of suitable films with strong commercial potential, rather than a refusal to distribute, that explained why such films did not play such a prominent part in the exhibition sector.

7.104. Rank told us that Odeon treated all distributors alike. Its only criterion was the commercial potential of a film. It was quite usual to discuss films many months before they were available for release; this was not limited to the major distributors. All provisional reservations were subject to viewing the film in question; Odeon would not make a booking without having first having seen a film. Rank gave examples of independent films which Odeon had reserved up to a year ahead of release.

7.105. UCI told us that when negotiating for exhibition rights, it dealt with a film's distributor, not the producer. The decision to exhibit a film was made purely on an assessment of its merits and commercial prospects, irrespective of the identity of the distributor or the producer. Indeed, UCI might not know the identity of the producer at the time it decided whether to exhibit a film. UCI dealt with all films, other than certain blockbusters, on the same terms. Thus it would give a US-owned distributor the same terms, irrespective of whether it was distributing its owner's film or the film of an independent producer.

7.106. UCI said that, in general, the leading distributors made exhibitors aware of product sooner than did the independent distributors. Their films were, therefore, included in provisional booking schedules. The actual booking of films was done on a week-by-week basis. The fact that a film was provisionally scheduled would not hinder another film being booked closer to its release date. UCI gave examples of forward booking of films from independent distributors ranging from two to four months ahead.

7.107. As regards the acquisition of Paramount by Viacom Inc, UCI told us that it had received no direction from its partners that it should change its stance towards Natl Amusements, which it regarded as a competitor. MCA Inc pointed out that while it had a half share in UCI, it had no financial relationship with Viacom; it would therefore be very concerned to ensure that the relationship between UCI and Natl Amusements did not change.

7.108. Warner Theatres said that it treated its affiliated distributor no differently from other distributors. It gave Warner Distributors no preference in the allocation of screens, in the negotiation of minimum exhibition periods, or in decisions to take films off. Warner Distributors did not receive more favourable rental terms than other distributors, save that it had been given guarantees of minimum rentals higher than the normal 25 per cent on three major films (out of the four films for which Warner Theatres had agreed such terms in recent years).

7.109. Warner Theatres told us that it was committed to showing a broad range of films which appealed to all sectors of the cinema-going public. As an operator of multiplex cinemas, it had the necessary spread of screens and the flexibility to put this into practice. The Warner West End cinema was used as a showcase for Warner Bros films. Warner Theatres was keen that it should also be used as a showcase for the films of other distributors, but to date they had been reluctant to use it for this purpose. Warner Theatres had, for a number of years, and in all its cinemas, offered Thursday programmes with special screenings, generally of EC-produced films. It told us that it had exhibited increasing numbers of films distributed by independent distributors. In recent years, the number of films taken, for example, from Guild and Entertainment had been almost as high as the number taken from Columbia and Fox. It was usually able to exhibit a film on the release date announced by the distributor.

## Overseas decision-making

7.110. We asked the leading exhibitors whether overseas-based decision-making made the market less responsive to consumer preferences than if decisions were made in the UK.

7.111. MGM Cinemas said that by definition, overseas decision-making must be less responsive to local customer needs. Generally, distributors used the performance of a film in the USA as a guideline to its likely success in the UK. In the majority of cases this expectation was borne out. MGM Cinemas recognized, however, that a local distributor, such as RFD with *Reservoir Dogs*, could often see local potential more readily.

7.112. Natl Amusements told us that, in view of the fact that it generally attempted to exhibit all available films, there was no impact on consumer preferences arising from overseas-based decision-making. Consumer preference formed the basis of its decision-making since it was clearly reflected in box office receipts, which in turn guided decisions.

7.113. Rank said that it would expect to be at an advantage *vis-à-vis* its US-based competitors if there was any substance to this issue. In practice it did not find itself at such an advantage.

7.114. UCI noted that it was decisions by overseas companies to invest in the UK exhibition sector which had halted the decline in admissions and led to the revival of the industry. Decisions as to which films would be exhibited were taken by UK-based personnel and had regard to the demands and preferences of local cinema audiences.

7.115. Warner Theatres said that all day-to-day decisions were taken in the UK. In particular, all decisions concerning the choice of films to be shown were taken here.

## Domination of the UK markets by US films

7.116. The leading exhibitors were asked whether the influence exercised by US companies in the UK markets for distribution and exhibition of films caused the markets to be dominated by US films, and whether the economic and cultural effects of this dominance were harmful. Those that commented on economic and cultural effects denied that the success of US films in the UK had adverse effects.

7.117. MGM Cinemas said that US films were the most commercially attractive products for the UK market and were rightfully popular. It made no comment on the economic and cultural effects.

7.118. Natl Amusements said that because it attempted to exhibit all available films, it did not have any particular influence on the exhibition of films. Its decisions were guided first and foremost by the consumer.

7.119. Rank said that it was no longer possible, other than for reasons of domestic legislation and regulation, to confine the market within purely national boundaries. There was a large international market for blockbuster films. The homogeneity of the market was particularly marked in English-speaking parts of the world. Thus, to focus on the influence exercised within the UK by US companies was to ignore the reality of the market. Rank argued that market homogeneity had been reinforced by the fact that the UK and US cultures were steadily becoming more alike. It was unclear whether the ever-increasing popularity of US films was the cause or effect of this. It was excessively paternalistic to argue that, by responding to demand in the UK market and supplying US films, distributors and exhibitors caused cultural damage. In any event, there was a large UK output of television product which reached a far greater audience in this country than did the cinema. This must limit any perceived cultural damage.

7.120. Rank said that RFD and Odeon supplied the films they believed the market wanted to see. The success of US films could not be attributed to the influence of US companies but to much wider cultural factors. Rank noted that, just as films of US origin were popular in the cinemas, so music of US origin had gained in popularity.

7.121. UCI argued that US films did not dominate the UK exhibition sector in a competition sense. A number of US studios had succeeded in ensuring that US films had achieved consistently high levels of box office revenue and admissions in recent years. There was no reason why this fact alone should operate against the public interest. Nor was the success of some US films surprising when US producers invested so much more and produced so many more films than producers in other countries. UCI did not accept that it was influenced by its US partners in such a way as to cause exhibition to be dominated by US films. It responded on a national and local level to consumers' wishes and selected films on commercial grounds. It selected those films, including non-US films, which it believed the consumer wished to see and could not force audiences into its cinemas.

7.122. UCI said that certain US films generated high returns. Earnings on these films enabled it to take the risk of exhibiting films of more uncertain appeal. UCI willingly exhibited films which catered for popular taste and which were not US-produced, such as *Much Ado About Nothing*, and it offered films of a 'cultural' nature in its Director's Chair programme. There was no evidence that US studios had attempted, through their interests in exhibition, to secure preference for their own films. UCI reiterated that it gave no preference to UIP's films, nor did it give preference to films handled by US distributors in general. For those British films where it received sufficient prints, the share of box office receipts reflected UCI's market share of exhibition in general. This demonstrated that it did not discriminate against such films.

7.123. Warner Theatres did not believe that any US company was able to influence its business so as to favour US films or exclude UK and European films. It was able to screen any British films which it considered were commercially viable and would willingly show more commercially viable British films if they were available. The substantial increases in admissions demonstrated that exhibitors were showing films which the public wished to see. It did not accept that US films had any harmful effect on the economic or cultural health of the public.

## Co-ordination of release dates

7.124. We asked the leading exhibitors whether leading distributors, by co-ordinating the release dates of their films, reduced consumers' choice of first-release films at any given time and crowded out other distributors. The leading exhibitors recognized that information about likely release dates was widely known within the industry but did not believe this had adverse effects.

7.125. MGM Cinemas said that a distributor might choose to alter the release date of a film in order to ensure that it did not clash with the release of another film. It did not accept that this involved any collusion between the distributors. In any event, the effects were generally beneficial to cinema-goers in that if two films which appealed to precisely the same market were released at the same time, patrons would be unlikely to see both. MGM Cinemas believed that a smaller distributor with an obviously commercial film would be able to have it exhibited. The leading distributors would probably reschedule their films to avoid clashing with such a film.

7.126. Natl Amusements said that to the extent the distributors were aware of the release dates of each other's films and scheduled dates to ensure minimal overlap, this was a logical and efficient business practice. It allowed for the maximization of revenues, with associated benefits to consumers. If distributors overlapped releases, exhibitors would have to make room to accommodate them. This would mean reducing the exhibition period of, or ceasing to exhibit, films that might, at that time, be of marginal appeal. Crowding out other distributors would be much more likely to result if larger distributors released films simultaneously; there would be an even greater impact if that were to occur during the peak periods.

7.127. Rank said that, as part of the service provided to distributors in assisting them to plan the release of a film, Odeon advised distributors of other films that would be on release on any proposed release date. In doing so, it gave no preference to any particular distributor. It believed a steady stream of releases would be more in the public interest than the simultaneous release of a large number of films.

7.128. Rank argued that, even if there were co-ordination of release dates, it could not affect the number of films released; it could only result in the release of those films being spread throughout the year rather than happening concurrently. Given the finite number of available screens and a finite number of films, the concentration of releases into one part of the year would not increase the overall choice of films available to consumers. On the contrary, it would be likely to reduce the frequency of cinema attendance and hence total admissions, thus increasing risks for investors and, in the long run, reducing the number of potential new films.

7.129. UCI told us that, whilst there was widely-held knowledge about release dates, distributors competed intensely for access to screens at particularly popular times of the year. There were, it said, times when it had to take off films that were doing reasonably well in order to make way for new releases. It believed a more even pattern of releases over the year might be desirable in order to avoid having to remove from its screens films which were performing well in order to make way for new releases at peak periods. The effect of the present system could be to deprive the public of the opportunity to see a film in a UCI cinema which UCI would otherwise have continued to show.

7.130. UCI said that the availability of information as to release strategies enabled all distributors, whether leading or otherwise, to decide whether to compete in the most crowded periods or to look for periods where there was less competition. This allowed each distributor to take its own competitive decision based on its individual strategy and assessment of the appeal of the film in question. The leading distributors received no particular benefit from this.

7.131. Warner Theatres said that, as a multiplex operator, it had no involvement in the setting of release dates. It was informed by the distributor of the date on which a film would be released. Warner Theatres said that, if several major films were released at once, most exhibitors, including those which operated multiplex cinemas, would not be able to show all the films. It was, therefore, in the exhibitors' interests that the leading distributors co-ordinated release dates. The leading distributors never opened more than two major films on the same day and even then the films would usually be of different genres, designed to appeal to different audiences. Over the long term, consumer choice would be enhanced because the public would have a greater opportunity to see films than if they were all released on the same date.

7.132. Warner Theatres said that it was able to show both blockbuster films and films of narrower commercial appeal. This did not adversely affect smaller distributors. There had been a number of recent examples of independently-released, up-market films where the distributor had been able to use the release dates it wanted and obtain the duration of playing time it wanted because of the strength of the film. The setting of the optimal release date was, Warner Theatres said, an important part of the competitive process. It would distort the market to place any restrictions on the ability of distributors to release films on the dates they thought most advantageous.

## Exercise of market power by leading distributors

7.133. The leading exhibitors were asked whether leading distributors, by exercising market power over independent exhibitors to persuade them to screen films which they would not otherwise choose, made the exhibition market less responsive to consumer preference; harmed the exhibitors concerned by reducing their revenue; and harmed independent producers, whose films were handled by other distributors, by reducing their films' access to screens. The leading exhibitors told us that they were not aware of any improper exercise of market power by leading distributors in the manner suggested.

MGM Cinemas, UCI and Warner Theatres said that they were unable to comment on a matter on which they had no information.

7.134. Natl Amusements was unaware of any instances of improper coercion. To the extent that distributors used their market power to coerce independent exhibitors into exhibiting any film against their wish, such a practice would be an improper use of market power. It would distort the market and should be restricted. Such a situation would, however, be significantly different from one involving attempted persuasion by the distributor. The latter case should not be restricted.

7.135. Rank said that Odeon did not see itself as being persuaded to take films which it otherwise would not have chosen.

## Exercise of market power by leading exhibitors

7.136. We asked the leading exhibitors whether, by exercising market power over distributors in order to secure preference over other exhibitors, they harmed those exhibitors by reducing their access to popular films, particularly on first release. The leading exhibitors did not accept that they acted in this manner.

7.137. MGM Cinemas agreed that other exhibitors would be harmed where this occurred. However, it did not negotiate exclusivity or conduct any other practice which might have this effect. To do so would not, in its opinion, be in the spirit of the 1989 Order. Natl Amusements said that on those occasions in which it had been unable to obtain a film, the distributor concerned had been able to give valid reasons for its decision.

7.138. Rank said that Odeon faced such a degree of competition that it could not be said to have any significant market power. To the extent that it was preferred over other exhibitors, this was due to the quality of service offered and its competitiveness. Rank denied that Odeon exercised market power when seeking exclusivity. It sought to define the terms on which a film would be licensed and to assess the audience potential and risks associated with the film. The circumstances in which Odeon secured contractual exclusivity would generally be those in which *de facto* exclusivity would likely be given in any event. Given that the grant of exclusivity was generally in the interests of both distributor and exhibitor, it was unlikely to be the product of the exercise of market power, even if Odeon had such power.

7.139. UCI said that it did not obtain preference because of any market power it might have over distributors. While it generally expected to receive prints of all films it wished to exhibit, the decision by a distributor to allocate prints to UCI in preference to, for example, an independent exhibitor reflected the demonstrated revenue-earning potential of the UCI cinemas. It was the quality of its cinemas, not market power, which distinguished UCI from exhibitors who were not given prints as frequently. Any harm suffered by other exhibitors was merely a result of competition between exhibitors for prints. UCI noted that in some cases, for example *The Remains of the Day*, it did not receive all the prints it wanted.

7.140. Warner Theatres said that it did not seek to obtain exclusive rights to exhibit any film. Nor did it attempt in any other way to deprive other exhibitors of access to films.

## Code of practice and associated machinery

7.141. The leading exhibitors were asked to comment on the possibility that a code of practice, dealing with the supply of prints, minimum exhibition periods and restrictions on screen use, might be drawn up by agreement between the SFD and the CEA; and that machinery, for example a committee with an independent chairman, might be set up to resolve disputes between distributors and exhibitors concerning the application of the code to particular circumstances.

7.142. MGM Cinemas supported the idea, provided that guidelines were put forward as to the basis for a code to be agreed by the industry. Natl Amusements said that if any type of remedy was to be imposed, this type of mechanism would be preferable since it would be responsive to the unique circumstances of each film.

7.143. Rank believed that a code of practice, though unnecessary and burdensome, would be preferable to the alternative remedies which the MMC had been canvassing. Any such code should be flexible and informal. It should seek to decrease the administration and resources needed to distribute films and leave distributors and exhibitors free to reach agreements which reflected market conditions and respond to changing consumer demands and preferences. A system with a formal structure and independent chairman would be unlikely to meet these criteria.

7.144. UCI doubted whether a code of practice and arbitration scheme could effectively cater for disputes on refusal to supply, minimum exhibition periods and restrictions on screen use which tended to arise on Monday mornings and had to be resolved at short notice. It believed it was in the best interests of distributors and exhibitors to resolve disputes on an individual basis within the scope of their contractual terms. The distributor would wish to ensure that disputes on such matters did not lead to an irretrievable breakdown of its relationship with the exhibitor concerned; likewise the exhibitor would not wish to jeopardize the potential source of supply of future product. These were powerful commercial incentives in a competitive market which ensured that disputes were resolved quickly and to the mutual satisfaction of distributors and exhibitors. Excessive regulatory intervention was unnecessary.

7.145. Warner Theatres did not object to a code of practice or a committee provided that it included representatives of the independent exhibitors and distributors as well as members of the CEA and the SFD. The usefulness of such a committee would necessarily be limited to major issues of principle. Most disputes related to the screening of particular films in particular weeks and had to be resolved very quickly.

## Prohibiting contracts based on box office receipts

7.146. We asked the leading exhibitors to comment on the possibility that distributors and exhibitors might be prohibited from entering into contracts under which the consideration received by the distributor was linked directly or indirectly to the exhibitor's box office receipts.

7.147. The leading exhibitors saw no reason to change the basis upon which rental payments were calculated. It was, they said, important that distributors and exhibitors shared the risks and rewards associated with showing films. Exhibitors, if forced to pay a predetermined price for each film, would have no incentive to pay for films of uncertain appeal. They would instead concentrate on popular films, declining to play high-risk product. The leading exhibitors had trouble envisaging a system of rental payments that was not linked to box office returns.

7.148. MGM Cinemas described the suggested remedy as superficially attractive. It warned, however, that an auction of films would ensue, ensuring the survival of only the most powerful exhibitors.

7.149. Natl Amusements said that, if distributors could not share the box office, there would be little incentive for producers to make films that were commercially desirable, or for distributors to promote films. A licensing system linked to box office receipts also made sense since, in essence, the distributor was selling a unique product, the value of which was directly linked to its success.

7.150. Rank told us that such a prohibition would be massively against the public interest. The present system spread the risks between distributors and exhibitors. If the risk was not shared, either the smaller distributors or the smaller exhibitors would be forced to withdraw from the market. If the rental could not be linked to the success of the film, either the rental for unsuccessful films would be uneconomically high, or the rental for successful films would be uneconomically low. In either event, the ability of distributors to obtain films, and of producers to finance them, would be undermined. If sharing box office receipts was prohibited, Rank expected that companies would seek alternative ways of sharing risk. The obvious solution would be to integrate vertically. Thus, an artificial advantage would be created for those companies that were already vertically integrated. This would act as an incentive to other companies to become vertically integrated.

7.151. UCI said that the different methods of determining rental payments reflected the desire in the industry to manage and share the risk involved in the production, distribution and exhibition of feature films. It believed that the ability of an exhibitor to share with the distributor the risk and reward of showing a new film was crucial to new investment in the UK exhibition sector. It doubted whether its partners would have been prepared to undertake the level of investment they had made since 1985, or would continue with such investment, under a system which did not allow for the risk and reward to be shared.

7.152. UCI argued that if an exhibitor had to pay a predetermined price for each film, it would have no incentive to pay for films of uncertain appeal. There would be a reduction in consumer choice as exhibitors concentrated on popular films and as distributors were deprived of box office revenue which would otherwise be invested in production.

7.153. Warner Theatres strongly opposed the proposed change in the method of calculating rental payments. Experience in the USA had shown that a fixed fee rental payment was likely to lead to the demise of many independent cinemas. In the USA, the exhibitor provided a guaranteed advance payment based on a certain level of expected box office receipts. Negotiations subsequently took place to settle on the final sum payable, taking account of the film's success. Many exhibitors had been unable to afford the initial guarantees and went out of business.

7.154. Warner Theatres argued that the current system benefited exhibitors in that payments were made in arrears and were limited to a proportion of the actual receipts. The cash flow benefits were very important to many marginal independent exhibitors.

## Distributors to commit revenues to independently-produced films

7.155. The leading exhibitors were asked to comment on the possibility that distributors might be required to commit a specified proportion of their revenues from film rentals in the UK to the production of films by independent producers in the EC.

7.156. All the leading exhibitors opposed this idea. It would, they argued, have adverse effects on the exhibition sector, such as increased admission prices resulting from distributors passing on the costs arising from the remedy or a reduction in choice as production was cut back in response to reduced returns to distributors and producers.

7.157. MGM Cinemas said that consumer preference and, therefore, commercial potential should be the only determinant for investment in film production. Natl Amusements said that the proposal would lead the distributors to increase the licence fee. Exhibitors would then be under pressure to increase ticket prices.

7.158. Rank said that it would be unlikely to be in the interests of UK consumers if the costs of distribution were to be increased by a levy designed to fund, at least in part, foreign language productions which, by their very nature, would have limited appeal in the UK. The availability of funds from such a levy would not guarantee that the films produced would be ones that the public wished to see. Indeed, such funds were likely to be used for uncommercial films, since those with commercial potential were likely to find funding in any event. The general public would, it argued, be little served by increased production of films of limited appeal.

7.159. UCI said that the suggested measures could have significant effects for exhibitors, since distributors would seek to pass at least part of the costs involved to exhibitors and, ultimately, the consumer. Admission prices could increase, thereby discouraging cinema-going. If there was no scope for increases in admission prices, the exhibitors and/or the distributors would have to bear the cost. This would inevitably threaten continued investment in the exhibition sector.

7.160. UCI argued that it should not be the responsibility of those currently participating in the industry on a commercial basis to finance the production of independent films for cultural purposes. Reallocating revenues to independent European production would not by itself encourage the promotion of commercially successful films. Whilst it would assist producers to make more European cultural films, it would not necessarily, and was unlikely to, encourage the production of commercially successful films as it would reduce by subsidy the incentive on a producer to have regard to consumer preferences. The remedy was, UCI argued, unjustified and inequitable.

7.161. Warner Theatres did not believe the imposition of a levy was likely to improve the position of the British film industry. A levy could be counter-productive, since it was likely to lead to an increase in rental payments and thereby ticket prices. This would threaten the continued expansion of the exhibition sector. It would also influence the expansion plans of exhibitors, such as Warner Theatres, who were considering the scope for further investment in the UK's cinema infrastructure.

## Distribution/exhibition of films with a predominantly European theme or cultural content

7.162. We asked the leading exhibitors to comment on the possibility that distributors might be required to distribute, and exhibitors to exhibit, a specified proportion of films with a predominantly European theme or other cultural content. The leading exhibitors responded that such a requirement would damage the exhibition sector by reducing revenues and discouraging cinema-going. This would result in reduced investment in exhibition.

7.163. MGM Cinemas told us that a previous quota system, abolished in the early 1980s, had achieved very little and led to what it described as 'nonsense screenings in order to make quota'. It said that the way to get a higher percentage of European films on to its schedules was to encourage the production of more films with commercial appeal to UK audiences. Whoever such films were distributed by, UK exhibitors would be very keen to obtain prints if they were likely to improve admission levels.

7.164. Natl Amusements said that the distribution and exhibition of such films should be responsive to consumer desires. Numerous avenues existed and were utilized for the exhibition of such films. In addition, they could also be made available on video and by way of pay and cable television. Consumers had the opportunity to see even those films which had an extremely narrow appeal and did not warrant cinematic exhibition.

7.165. Rank said that any such film which was likely to appeal to audiences would be exhibited without recourse to the suggested remedy. If a film had no audience appeal, a requirement that it be shown would serve only to increase costs unnecessarily and reduce the number of screens available for exhibiting films that consumers did want to see. Such a requirement would, in Rank's view, be against the public interest.

7.166. Rank told us that many of the films currently distributed by the major US producers could be said to be of predominantly European theme, for example *Robin Hood: Prince of Thieves* and *The Three Musketeers*. It warned that any attempt to discriminate against US films could have potentially damaging repercussions for continued US financing of 'British' productions such as *Shadowlands*, *The Remains of the Day* and *The Secret Garden*.

7.167. UCI argued that simply because US films had achieved consistently high levels of box office revenue and admissions in recent years, reflecting their attractiveness to consumers, it did not follow that the public interest was adversely affected. The suggested remedy assumed that consumers had, or ought to have, a greater cultural affinity with European than with US films. This ignored European-theme films, for example *The Remains of the Day, Dangerous Liaisons, In the Name of the Father* and *Schindler's List*, which were available without artificial stimulus. It also ignored the appeal of certain US films, the common language shared between the UK and the USA, and the extent to which British talent was employed in US productions. There was, UCI said, no evidence to suggest that UCI or other exhibitors favoured US films to the detriment of consumer preferences. Certain

US films simply generated high returns for the exhibitors. Such films enabled exhibitors to take the risk of accepting films of more uncertain appeal, which might include non-US films.

7.168. UCI argued that quotas would damage UK exhibition. Films which were commercially successful were generally US-produced. There was no guarantee that European films would generate the same level of admissions or revenue. Indeed the comparative lack of audience support for European films suggested the opposite. The imposition of quotas would be bound to reduce exhibitors' revenues unless, and UCI thought this inconceivable, they could charge higher admission prices on successful commercial films to generate sufficient additional revenues to compensate for the sacrifice imposed by the quota system. Any increase in prices would, in the longer term, tend to discourage cinema-going and would not be in the interests of consumers.

7.169. UCI said that the loss of revenue would mean less investment in building and upgrading cinemas. In some cases this could lead to cinema closures, which would have the effect of reducing consumers' access to films. Less revenue available to exhibitors would lead to lower rentals available to distributors and, ultimately, producers. This would reduce investment in the very films which, on the basis of box office records, consumers preferred.

7.170. UCI submitted that the price of promoting cultural objectives in this manner would be high, causing substantial damage to the industry and to the public interest. There was no reason why a quota system should be applied to the film industry to pursue cultural objectives, when other commercial activities having a cultural dimension, such as book publishing, the music industry and the theatre, were free from the distortions that a quota system would bring.

7.171. Warner Theatres believed that any form of screen quota system designed to favour British or EC films was likely to reverse the steady increase in cinemas attendances which had occurred since the MMC's last inquiry. It was aware of no evidence that potentially successful EC films were denied access to screens, either by shortage of screens or by any conduct on the part of distributors or exhibitors. The remedy would require distributors and exhibitors to substitute unpopular films for popular ones, with the loss of revenue which that would entail for both. A film which benefited from the quota system would be *ex hypothesi* a film which neither distributor nor exhibitor believed had the potential to bring in an audience. The public would not benefit from having screens occupied by films in which they were not interested, with the consequent reduction in the number of screenings of films which they wished to see.

7.172. Warner Theatres said that the only possible beneficiaries would be producers and financiers of films which had little or no commercial value and which would not be distributed or exhibited but for the quota. But since producers would still earn only a proportion of box office receipts, they were unlikely to recoup their investments if the film failed to attract an audience.

7.173. Warner Theatres believed, if the British film industry was to flourish, it must be because it made films which were able to compete internationally, not because it had protected status in its home territory. There was clearly a market for successful British films. But consumers would not go to see a film simply because it was being shown, as there were many other forms of entertainment available. Warner Theatres could not see any legitimate goal which was likely to be achieved by the suggested system. The imposition of a quota system would also be likely to dissuade existing exhibitors from expanding their cinema networks or investing in refurbishment since income would become more uncertain if they were not allowed to maximize revenues by showing the films that they believed would attract audiences.

## Divestment or reduction of interests in exhibition

7.174. The leading exhibitors were asked to comment on the possibility that companies with interests in film production and/or distribution might be required to divest any interests in exhibition, or to reduce such interests below a specified level, for example 10 per cent of the total number of screens in the UK.

7.175. MGM Cinemas believed competition between exhibitors would be best maintained by ensuring that exhibitors made all investment decisions on the basis of exhibition alone. If stand-alone exhibition was unprofitable or showed an inadequate return on shareholders' funds, the market would ensure that distributors' rentals and restrictions were adjusted to permit a healthy exhibition sector to continue to develop in the UK.

7.176. Natl Amusements said that it had not been harmed by the existence of vertically integrated companies. It did not favour the suggested remedy.

7.177. Rank told us that RFD and Odeon operated independently of each other and without giving rise to any cause for public interest concern. [

*Details omitted. See note on page iv.*

]

7.178. Rank suggested that any large-scale divestment of cinemas would lead to closure of at least some, reducing the number of screens available to the public.

7.179. UCI said that vertical integration, in the loose sense that it applied in the film industry, did not operate against the public interest. UCI did not favour the films of Paramount and MCA/Universal, the producers who were partners in UCI, nor the films of Paramount, MCA/Universal and MGM Inc, the partners in UIP, over those of other distributors. It argued that there was no evidence to demonstrate that such a remedy should be considered, let alone recommended.

7.180. UCI said that, in their 1983 report, the MMC concluded that vertical integration between producer and distributor was not something that should be condemned. No evidence had been presented to alter this conclusion. It said that the suggested remedy would have the serious adverse effects of halting the companies' significant investment programmes in the exhibition sector and depriving them of the opportunity to earn future revenues from their existing investment. Not only was the remedy unjustified, it would halt the industry's revival and risk a return to stagnation and decline.

7.181. UCI stated that Paramount and MCA/Universal had believed exhibition was a viable investment which would revive theatrical exhibition in the UK by attracting customers back to the cinemas; it was an investment which would thereby produce a direct return as well as stimulate interest and return on their studios' films. This investment had benefited both their films and the films of other studios. UCI rejected the charge that the investment was not commercial. UCI told us that it sought to achieve a minimum rate of return of 20 per cent on its cinema investments and a pay-back period of five years. Most of its cinemas were on target to meet this return. In assessing the suitability of a site it gave no consideration to the likely impact on its partners' films.

7.182. Warner Theatres did not believe vertical integration had any effect on its business, though it too agreed that its investments had been designed to help revitalize UK exhibition with a view to benefiting its parent studios' films, among others. It rejected the charge that its investments were not commercial. It assessed its investments purely on a stand-alone commercial basis and looked for at least 20 per cent return on investment on a cash flow basis. Again, most of its cinemas were on target to meet this return. There was no justification for imposing such a remedy.

## Termination of the UIP joint venture

7.183. We asked the leading exhibitors to comment on the possibility that the UIP joint venture in the distribution of films to cinemas in the UK might be terminated. Without exception they did not object to the continuation of the UIP joint venture.

7.184. MGM Cinemas told us that, if UIP were replaced by three distribution companies, the result would be increased costs and no advantage to exhibitors. It said that UIP already faced significant competition from other distributors. Natl Amusements said that it had not been harmed by UIP, nor did it believe UIP had harmed competition or the consumer. Rank told us that the removal of UIP would not increase the availability of suitable films from UK or other EC production sources.

7.185. UCI perceived no benefit that would accrue to exhibitors if the remedy were to be recommended. It told us that its pattern of trading with UIP was no different from its pattern and terms of trading with other studios which distributed only their own films. If the three studios whose product was distributed through UIP were to appoint separate distributors, UCI's task of booking films would be administratively more cumbersome. UCI could see little point in holding three sets of different discussions each week when the terms it received from UIP were consistent with those it received from the rest of the industry and when the service provided by UIP was efficient.

7.186. UCI was concerned that terminating the UIP arrangements could damage UK exhibitors and the public interest if UIP's three partners were obliged to cut film production or distribution in the UK as a result of increased costs of operating separate distribution organizations.

7.187. Warner Theatres said that the existence of UIP did not affect its business. There was no reason to propose its termination.

## Prohibition on distribution joint ventures

7.188. The leading exhibitors were asked to comment on the possibility that the formation of joint ventures in distribution between parties which together had more than 20 per cent of the market, measured by share of rental receipts over a rolling four-year period, might be prohibited. All the leading exhibitors believed joint venture distributors operated in the same way as other distributors and should not be prohibited.

7.189. MGM Cinemas opposed this suggestion on the grounds that it would increase distribution costs with no advantage to exhibitors. Natl Amusements said that approval of such joint ventures should be on a case-by-case basis, after a full examination of the relevant facts and the circumstances surrounding its operation.

7.190. Rank argued that, to meet the challenges of competing in the industry, all participants needed to be as free as possible to enter into commercial transactions as they sought fit. Given that existing legislation allowed the Secretary of State considerable powers over any merger which created or enhanced a market share of more than 25 per cent, there would be no evident benefits from the suggested prohibition. In fact, the inability to assess each case on its merits would be likely to be damaging in a rapidly changing market.

7.191. UCI could not see that any exhibitor would benefit from such a recommendation. Since it dealt with distributors on a film-by-film basis, the terms negotiated were unaffected by whether the distributor was a joint venture. It said that competition law was fully capable of dealing with joint ventures and unacceptable concentrations of market power which were shown to have detrimental effects on competition and/or consumers. To add a further layer of regulatory control was unnecessary and burdensome.

7.192. Warner Theatres did not object to joint ventures between distributors. They contributed to reducing costs and, therefore, ensured that rental payments were kept at a reasonable level.

## Termination of the UCI joint venture

7.193. We asked the leading exhibitors to comment on the possibility that the UCI joint venture in cinema exhibition in the UK might be terminated. The leading exhibitors either did not support the remedy or had no view.

7.194. MGM Cinemas said that it was happy with any competition which operated within reasonable norms within the exhibition market. Natl Amusements told us that it had not been harmed by UCI, nor did it believe UCI had harmed competition or the consumer. Rank expressed no view.

7.195. UCI argued that there was nothing to indicate that it operated or might be expected to operate against the public interest by virtue of the fact that it was a joint venture or that its ultimate parent companies were foreign companies. There was also nothing to indicate that it operated differently from any other UK exhibitor. It would be wholly unjustified to reach an adverse public interest finding in the absence of any facts which distinguished UCI from other exhibitors.

7.196. UCI said that the effect of the joint venture was neutral in competition terms. There was nothing to suggest that its market share was of such size as to create unacceptable distortions of competition which operated against the public interest. Moreover, the remedy ignored the public interest benefits that the joint venture had brought to UK exhibition, for example by promoting the development of new multiplex cinemas, facilitating new entry, and to employment and other business activities such as construction and retailing.

7.197. UCI reminded us that the EC Commission was considering the UCI partners' request for exemption under Article 85(3) of the Treaty of Rome. UCI said that our ability to apply national competition law should not prejudice the full and uniform application of EC law or the effects of measures taken, or to be taken, to implement it.

7.198. The MMC had, UCI argued, failed to show how the UCI joint venture might operate against the public interest and why break-up would be an appropriate remedy. Termination of the joint venture would be detrimental to the public interest. The remedy had no foundation in fact or in law, was unjustified and should not be recommended.

7.199. Warner Theatres said that the existence of UCI did not affect its business. There was no reason to propose its termination.

## Third party complaints

7.200. We asked the leading exhibitors to respond to the various complaints raised by third parties and summarized in Chapter 6. Their comments on the supply of prints, minimum exhibition periods, restrictions on screen use and the *Standard Conditions* are summarized earlier in this chapter. Their responses on other matters are summarized below. Warner Theatres had no additional comments to make in response to the complaints.

### *Independent exhibitors*

7.201. Responding to complaints about the availability of prints (see paragraphs 6.20 to 6.27), MGM Cinemas described as totally without foundation the claim (see paragraph 6.27) that it had a stranglehold over smaller distributors which acted to the detriment of independent cinemas. It said that its only cinema in Belfast was not accorded favourable treatment by distributors. The cinema did not compete with arthouse cinemas save to the extent that it had attempted to increase the range of films on offer.

7.202. With reference to the complaint from Richmond Filmhouse (see paragraph 6.23), Rank told us that the Odeon cinemas complemented the Richmond Filmhouse cinema; they did not compete with each other. Rank said that Odeon was surprised that Richmond Filmhouse, which had described itself as an arthouse cinema, chose to show more popular films. It denied that Odeon had sought to take films away from Richmond Filmhouse and suggested that distributors would be cautious about using Richmond Filmhouse for two reasons. First, Richmond Filmhouse charged higher admission prices than Odeon, which might reduce the level of admissions sufficiently to reduce box office revenues. Secondly, it had only one screen, which would inevitably limit its ability to hold over successful films.

7.203. Rank suggested that Richmond Filmhouse's experience as an operator of a single-screen, 150-seat town centre cinema was unlikely to be relevant to those contemplating the building of multiplex cinemas. Given the investment in new multiplex cinemas in recent years and the fact that such cinemas had access to all films, Rank believed the suggested deterrent was without foundation.

7.204. UCI said that it too had difficulties in obtaining prints where only limited numbers were released. UCI believed that an independent exhibitor willing to invest in building a multiplex cinema should obtain films from the distributors if it could demonstrate that the cinema was of sufficient quality and standard to appeal to local audiences. This belief was, it said, borne out by the experience of AMC and Natl Amusements, each of which had started out as an independent multiplex operator and was successful in obtaining films.

7.205. Responding to complaints about the calculation of rental payments (see paragraphs 6.32 and 6.33), Rank told us that Odeon did not believe there had been an increase in recent years in distributors demanding special terms for the most popular films. In any event it would always attempt to negotiate more favourable terms than those demanded by the distributors. However, these were always subject to negotiation and it was open to exhibitors to reject such terms.

7.206. Regarding the availability of British films (see paragraph 6.34), Rank told us that Odeon faced strong competition and made every effort to face that competition by exhibiting those films for which there was the greatest public demand. It did not give priority to films distributed by RFD and had every reason to exhibit as wide a diversity of films as it believed to be commercially sustainable.

7.207. UCI did not agree with the suggestion that independent multi-screen exhibitors were more likely to show a wider range of films than multiplex owners by reason of the latter's interest in distribution 'or other vested interests'. It pointed out that it had no distribution activities. Its only link with distribution was through its partly common ownership with UIP; relations between the two were carried out on an arm's length basis.

7.208. Responding to Mr Henshaw's comments on the supply of prints to multiplex cinemas (see paragraph 6.35), UCI told us that it was seldom supplied with two copies of popular films. In 1993 only seven films exhibited by UCI were supplied on the basis of two prints per cinema. Even then, less than half of UCI cinemas received two prints. UCI said that it used the practice of interlocking prints, whereby one print was shown in more than one screen simultaneously, significantly more often than it received two prints. UCI said that it retained prints for the period of time which offered good revenue-earning potential in comparison with other films. It never retained a print once it had decided to take off a film.

7.209. Responding to Mr Henshaw's complaint that distributors gave priority to their in-house interests without any concern for the traditional British-owned cinemas (see paragraph 6.37), Rank told us that Odeon had been a chain of traditional British-owned cinemas for many years and had consistently received high-quality films from all distributors. Odeon attributed this to the fact that it competed vigorously for films by offering a high quality of service and auditoria. UCI described as unfounded Mr Henshaw's comments on vertical integration securing preference for multiplex cinemas.

## *PACT*

7.210. Responding to PACT's comments on bias against independently-produced UK and European films (see paragraphs 6.53 to 6.55), MGM Cinemas said that the only bias that existed was in favour of the most popular films, wherever they came from. US market exposure was not the reason for UK films receiving a narrow release. To the extent that the implied assumption that UK and US films had the same commercial appeal was true: exposure in the USA and consequent 'weeding out' of the unsuccessful films reduced risk from showing US films in the UK. The extent of the theatrical release of a film was determined by the distributor's and exhibitors' commercial expectation of a film; this expectation was determined solely by the appeal of the film and not because of previous exposure in the USA.

7.211. Rank denied that Odeon preferred US-made films over any other film. Each film was regarded on its own merits. It considered any allegation that it was less willing to book a non-US film as false. Whilst it was clear that films which had already been market tested in the USA were likely to perform well in the UK, considerable expenditure was incurred in advertising a film in the UK. Increased expenditure on advertising and publicity reflected the strength of competition between exhibitors and between distributors. A film could only realize its potential if supported by a vigorous marketing campaign. It was not in the interests of Odeon to give little support to any of the films which it showed.

7.212. UCI acknowledged that it used publicly-available market information from the USA to assess the commercial potential of a film in the UK. The success of a film in the USA would often, although not always, be a measure of its likely success in the UK. UCI denied that it was biased against, or in favour of, particular films. It judged each film on its perceived commercial potential.

7.213. Responding to PACT's comments on reduction in choice (see paragraphs 6.56 and 6.57), MGM Cinemas attributed the difference in the number of films produced in the UK and other European countries to the common language and culture shared by the UK and the USA. Rank said that Odeon would book films into its multiplex cinemas if it considered that they had commercial potential. It believed that, within multiplex cinemas, it was possible to show films with minority appeal; the development of such cinemas had increased opportunities for these films.

7.214. UCI told us that the investment in UK exhibition by the UCI partners was made with a view to stimulating cinema-going in this country, which in turn would benefit their films. The investment did not, however, improve access for, or extend the life of, their films in preference to others. To the extent that investment increased audiences and screens, thereby creating improved opportunities for viewing films, it did so for all films.

7.215. Responding to PACT's comments on concentration of exhibition in the UK (see paragraphs 6.58 to 6.60), MGM Cinemas said that it had trouble seeing how the conclusion reached in respect of the number of cinema screens would of itself indicate that significant barriers to entry existed or that there was any detriment to the public. The fact that the proportion of screens to head of population in the UK was relatively low when compared with other western European countries implied, in its opinion, that the UK industry operated at a more efficient level of capacity. The UK tended to have an exceptionally low number of all kinds of retail outlet per million population, compared with other countries, because of the density of its population. It had never been suggested to MGM Cinemas that there was a shortage of exhibition capacity. There were, MGM Cinemas said, no significant barriers to entry arising from technology, goodwill or track record. Anybody could enter the exhibition market by investing in or constructing premises. Distributors would always want to supply an exhibitor who could show a reasonable commercial return on the prints supplied.

7.216. In relation to PACT's assertion that exhibitors in the UK retained an unusually large share of box office revenues (see paragraph 6.59), MGM Cinemas said that the cost of a new cinema in this country was typically 50 per cent higher than in the USA. In addition, operating costs were inflated by strict licensing requirements which were not to be found elsewhere in Europe or the USA. As a result, the fixed and operating cost of UK exhibitors were higher than elsewhere, dictating the need for a correspondingly larger share of box office receipts.

7.217. Regarding PACT's comments on transfer pricing (see paragraph 6.59), MGM Cinemas pointed out that not all the major US distributors owned cinemas. MGM Cinemas would have thought it commercially more beneficial for producers owning cinemas to transfer price the other way around. Revenues earned on the distribution of a film were subject to participation by, for example, actors and producers; it was likely to make better commercial sense to keep 100 per cent of the revenue within such of the cinemas as were vertically owned.

7.218. Rank agreed that the UK contained fewer screens per capita than many other countries; it doubted whether that justified a conclusion that the UK was under-screened. The number of screens was steadily rising as demand recovered and as the result of the high level of new investment that had taken place over recent years. In the light of the substantial level of new entry, it believed there were no substantial barriers to entry.

7.219. Rank did not accept PACT's claim that exhibitors in the UK charged relatively high prices for cinema tickets (see paragraph 6.59); it also believed that the assertions about the division of box office revenues between distributor and exhibitor were mistaken. RFD and Odeon operated at arm's length and the level of rental paid by Odeon reflected the market, both for films supplied by RFD and for all other films. Neither company believed their links in any way reduced competition, nor that opportunities for other exhibitors to take films from RFD were limited.

7.220. UCI queried PACT's comments on the barriers to entry which existed to prevent growth in the number of screens (see paragraph 6.58). It also queried what was meant by a natural level of growth in screens. UCI said that the investment which had taken place since 1983 showed that there had been, and continued to be, opportunities to invest. It questioned the usefulness of comparing the UK with other markets on the basis of screens per capita only. For example, in Italy about one-third of all cinemas were open fewer than 60 days a year; only just over one-third were open more than 240 days a year. It argued that this demonstrated that screen capacity did not necessarily reflect accessibility by consumers.

7.221. UCI disputed PACT's statement that, in the UK, the exhibitor's share of the total ticket price was 70 per cent. The actual figure was closer to 60 per cent, which was the norm suggested by PACT. UCI denied that it participated with its associated companies in internal transfer pricing and was aware of no evidence to support the PACT assertion.

7.222. UCI noted that PACT had failed to specify what restraints were exercised by distributors over exhibitors. It said that, as a result of the investment by new entrants, the exhibition sector was less concentrated than in 1983.

## *Producers*

7.223. Responding to the comments on the distribution of *Orlando* (see paragraph 6.71), Rank told us that Odeon did exhibit the film. Despite the shortage of prints, the film was shown in cinemas outside London. Rank said the complaint exaggerated the shortage of cinemas outside London which exhibited arthouse films, though there was no doubt only limited demand for such films.

## *BFI*

7.224. Responding to the BFI's comments on the current state of the British film industry (see paragraphs 6.93 and 6.94), MGM Cinemas attributed the dominance of US films in the UK to a lack of investment in UK films. This lack of investment had come about not because of the abolition of the Eady Levy but rather because of the poor returns achieved by investors in film production. It referred to the losses made in the mid-1980s by Thorn EMI Screen Entertainment which had attempted to compete directly with the US major studios in terms of its production and distribution budgets. It also noted that all the Hollywood studios had at some time been effectively bankrupt and suggested that the growth in earnings from videos and other ancillary markets sustained most of the studios.

7.225. MGM Cinemas did not understand the BFI's contention that there were fewer opportunities for UK films in the international market. The international market existed only for films that had universal appeal. Films of purely UK cultural significance would not necessarily appeal to this market. This situation was not unique to the UK. Small-town US films similarly did not do well on the international market.

7.226. Rank argued that the market for English language films was, at all levels of production and distribution, an international one. It was no longer possible readily to define a British film, except by the use of arbitrary criteria. For its part, Odeon would exhibit any film which it considered would make a worthwhile return, regardless of nationality.

7.227. Rank told us that Odeon did not favour the return of the Eady Levy or of any similar subsidy, even if it were used for the production of British films (as defined in the Films Act). It calculated that if such a levy were reintroduced at 2.5 per cent of net box office, the total sum available (£7.5 million) would not be sufficient to finance major film production. It should also be borne in mind that, since the termination of the Eady Levy, VAT had increased from 8 to 17.5 per cent. Therefore the tax on the box office had substantially increased and been passed on to the customer. Any reimposition of a levy would likely be passed on to customers through admission prices, with a consequent effect on admission levels, particularly given the competition from other media.

7.228. It seemed to Rank that the BFI's real complaint was about the taste of the cinema-going public in the UK rather than about any defect in the operation of the industry. Odeon was always willing to negotiate in respect of any film offered to it and, almost without exception, reached agreement as to the dates and terms on which the film would be shown.

7.229. UCI told us that US films accounted for approximately 80 per cent of admissions in the UK throughout the 1980s, with the exception of 1987. Thus it was not necessarily correct to say, as was suggested by the BFI, that removal of the Eady Levy and other elements of industry support had led the market to be increasingly dominated by US-produced films.

7.230. Regarding the BFI's comments on vertical integration (see paragraphs 6.95 to 6.97), MGM Cinemas said that the BFI seemed to assume that the 51 locally-produced films had the same commercial appeal as the US films that were shown. This was not the case. If British producers moved away from esoteric films to films with general appeal they would have more success. As for the BFI's claims about good films which did not receive appropriate distribution, with the exception of *Riff Raff*, MGM Cinemas had been unable to get as many prints as it wanted of the films cited.

7.231. Rank did not know on what basis the BFI stated that films from other European countries were rarely distributed in the UK (see paragraph 6.95). In 1991 the market share for national films (including co-productions) was 13.8 per cent; the market share for European films (not including national films) was 15.7 per cent.

7.232. UCI said that the BFI had offered no explanation or evidence as to how, by virtue of common ownership links between exhibitors, distributors and/or producers, independent producers' access to distribution was limited. Independent distributors did not always offer their films to UCI, particularly where only a few prints had been released. In the case of *Enchanted April* and *Riff Raff*, only one or two prints were available at any time. UCI was offered neither film on first release but played both at later dates at a limited number of its cinemas.

7.233. Responding to the BFI's comments on control of the UK market (see paragraphs 6.98 to 6.100), MGM Cinemas did not accept that, in terms of shares of box office receipts, the UK was dominated by the US film industry to a far greater extent than other large Western European countries. In Germany, for example, US films accounted for a similar percentage of box office receipts as in the UK. To the extent that there were differences, this might largely be the result of the lack of a common language which made the UK closer culturally to the USA than other European countries.

7.234. Rank acknowledged that revenue from UK cinemas would, in part, have gone back to those who invested in the films shown. But it did not accept the BFI's argument that this had starved British production of capital. Indeed, productions such as *Shadowlands* and *The Remains of the Day* were financed by US capital. Rank did not accept that the evidence supported the BFI's assertion that the UK was dominated by the US film industry to a far greater extent than other large Western European countries.

7.235. UCI said that its investment of £100 million in cinemas reflected the extent of investment into, rather than a drain on revenues away from, the UK. It did not remit its profits overseas via any kind of fee or commission arrangement and to date it had not made any dividend payments to its immediate parent company.

7.236. Responding to the BFI's comments on restriction of choice and diversity (see paragraphs 6.102 and 6.103), MGM Cinemas said that the industry had been concentrating into fewer cinemas each with more screens. This had resulted in more commercial films receiving a wider airing; consumers therefore had more opportunity to see them. More films were readily available to its customers. MGM Cinemas also rejected what it described as the assumption that the arthouse audience wished to see films in the same cinemas as the mainstream cinema-goer. Arthouse cinemas were generally inferior in quality to the multiplex cinemas but were still preferred by arthouse audiences. MGM Cinemas had concluded that mainstream and arthouse audiences were not compatible. The exhibition of British films was being marginalized because the bulk of British films fell into the arthouse category.

7.237. Rank did not accept the BFI's assertion that fewer films were being shown on more screens. It said that the number of films released in the UK rose from 278 in 1981 to 390 in 1990; the 1992 figure was in the region of 320. It appeared that the public had access in 1990 to 113 more new films than it did in 1981 and in 1992 to 42 more new films than in 1981. There were both more screens and more films.

7.238. Nor did Rank accept the BFI's claim that the exhibition of British films was being marginalized. It told us that Odeon monitored carefully the demand for films from each of its audiences and there had been no feedback requesting a greater number of UK- or European-produced films. Rank suggested that because the BFI specialized in exhibiting arthouse and UK-produced films, it was unlikely that its audiences were representative of mainstream commercial cinemas, or reflected the demands or tastes of such audiences. Furthermore, the BFI's funding structure was such that it was isolated from the financial pressures under which commercial exhibitors operated.

7.239. UCI queried how accurately the BFI reflected cinema-goers' views given that its comments were based on conversations with audiences around the country rather than a proper audience survey. It said that it did show British films which catered for popular tastes and responded further to consumer tastes via its Director's Chair programme.

7.240. Responding to the BFI's comments on admission charges (see paragraph 6.104), MGM Cinemas contested the BFI's assertion that UK cinema tickets were among the most expensive in the world. When the VAT element of the ticket price was excluded, the UK was not one of the most expensive places. The average seat price in the UK was slightly lower than the EC average.

7.241. Rank said that UK cinema admission prices compared favourably with those in other Western European countries. Exhibitors charged premium prices in a small number of auditoria in the West End which exhibited newly-released films and provided audiences with a high degree of comfort. Such cinemas were all within a short distance by public transport of much cheaper cinemas and most of their audiences had made a special journey to visit them. The admission prices reflected the high quality of service and amenity and the high level of demand; they were not anti-competitive.

7.242. UCI said that average admission charges in the UK in 1992 were just below the EC average and well below the average in Western European countries. It was wrong to suggest that UK admission prices were disproportionately high.

7.243. Regarding the BFI's comments on the expression of British culture (see paragraphs 6.105 and 6.106), MGM Cinemas said that film was no doubt a significant medium for the expression of British culture. But this included film for exhibition in other media, particularly television. It believed the importance of cinema exhibition should be placed in context. A made-for-television film, *One Foot in the Algarve*, was viewed by 22 million people in the UK in 1993. By contrast, the most popular feature film in recent times, *Jurassic Park*, was seen by approximately 14 million. The average person in the UK spent 26 hours a week watching television and only four hours a year watching films in cinemas. The cultural impact of television was, therefore, of far greater importance. According to MGM Cinemas, the only barriers to entry derived from commercial and investment decisions. There were no other barriers to commercial product.

7.244. Rank argued that there was extensive opportunity to express the cultural identity of the nation through television as well as through cinema films. But if the public were not willing to pay to see such expressions in the cinema, they could not be coerced into doing so.

*Mr Michael Henry*

7.245. Responding to Mr Henry's comments on collusion among distributors (see paragraphs 6.121 to 6.123), MGM Cinemas disputed the claim that members of the MPAA directly or indirectly fixed prices for exhibitors and distributors. Claims of price fixing were not, it argued, borne out by the facts; MGM Cinemas was constantly being challenged by distributors over the fact that it paid virtually the lowest film hire in the world. Nor was Mr Henry's assertion that MGM/Cannon was able to fix prices borne out by the facts. The average seat price of MGM Cinemas had been the same as the other circuits, notwithstanding its preponderance of cinemas in London where rentals and prices were higher. It also ignored the fact that MGM Inc had not produced a really commercially successful film for almost ten years. It further ignored the fact that, for some time, there had been no direct link between MGM Cinemas and the MGM studio.

7.246. Rank told us that Odeon did not regard its trading conditions as being directly or indirectly fixed by the MPAA corporations.

7.247. Responding to Mr Henry's comments on location of control (see paragraphs 6.127 and 6.128), MGM Cinemas argued that because the MPAA corporations made creative decisions in the USA, UK-based producers and distributors should have an advantage in this country, being closer to the market and local tastes.

7.248. Responding to Mr Henry's comments on the withdrawal of financing from British film production (see paragraphs 6.131 to 6.133), MGM Cinemas described as farcical the argument that the withdrawal of US financing for British films was an abuse of dominant position; US financing of production activity in the UK was of US rather than British films. The unfavourable exchange rate and the emergence of cheaper alternatives in other countries were the main reasons for the transfer of such financing. As the exchange rate had become more favourable, there was increased activity in the UK industry. Rank said that Mr Henry ignored the US financing of films such as *The Remains of the Day* and *Shadowlands*. Several films, including *Frankenstein* and *War of the Buttons*, which were financed from the USA were currently being made in this country.

# 8 Views of the leading distributors

## Contents

| | Paragraph |
|---|---|
| Introduction | 8.1 |
| Observations on the market | 8.2 |
| Views on complex monopoly situation | 8.21 |
| Alignment | 8.26 |
| Exclusivity and refusal to supply | 8.70 |
| Minimum exhibition periods and restrictions on screen use | 8.111 |
| Influence or control over admission prices | 8.148 |
| SFD *Standard Conditions* | 8.159 |
| Vertical links to US production companies | 8.172 |
| Overseas decision-making | 8.203 |
| Domination of the UK markets by US films | 8.211 |
| Co-ordination of release dates | 8.224 |
| Exercise of market power by leading distributors | 8.232 |
| Exercise of market power by leading exhibitors | 8.244 |
| Code of practice and associated machinery | 8.250 |
| Prohibiting contracts based on box office receipts | 8.257 |
| Distributors to commit revenues to independently-produced films | 8.265 |
| Distribution/exhibition of films with a predominantly European theme or cultural content | 8.277 |
| Divestment or reduction of interests in exhibition | 8.287 |
| Termination of the UIP joint venture | 8.293 |
| Prohibition on distribution joint ventures | 8.296 |
| Termination of the UCI joint venture | 8.302 |
| Third party complaints | 8.303 |

## Introduction

8.1. In this chapter we summarize the views of Buena Vista, Columbia, Fox, UIP and Warner Distributors (the leading distributors[1]). We first give their observations on the market and then their comments on the various matters raised in our issues letter of 14 February 1994. At the start of each of the sections dealing with these matters in turn, we summarize those views which are common to all, or the majority, of the leading distributors (though expressed by them individually). This is followed by a summary of the other views they put to us. All the leading distributors submitted written evidence; Columbia, Fox, UIP and Warner Distributors also attended hearings.

## Observations on the market

8.2. The leading distributors made the same general observations on the market as did the leading exhibitors (see paragraph 7.2), though UIP did not argue that the UK was under-screened.

---

[1] The views of the other distributors who are members of the complex monopoly group are summarized in Chapter 9.

*Nature of the market*

8.3. Buena Vista emphasized the uniqueness of every film. It said that the creation, production, marketing and distribution of each film required its own distinctive and separate judgments and decisions as to its potential audience appeal.

8.4. Buena Vista stressed that its main business was the distribution of films of mass appeal. Print and advertising costs in relation to these films were substantial and the release strategy adopted in respect of each was dictated by the degree to which selected cinemas would secure the best return on investment for Buena Vista and for Walt Disney. Buena Vista would seek those cinemas which attracted the largest audiences commensurate with the expected drawing power of the particular film (eg Buena Vista would not seek a high-capacity cinema for a film if it believed a significant percentage of the seats in that cinema would not be filled). It was not part of its strategy deliberately to exclude cinemas by discriminating unfairly against them. The notion of supply on demand ignored the legitimate business interests of distributors to maximize their returns and to ensure that their marketing strategy was properly exploited. Buena Vista submitted that, while no market was perfect or perfectly fair to each participant, the present system was highly responsive and functional.

8.5. Buena Vista argued that the current UK distribution climate increasingly met the public interest criteria. The interest of the consumer was, it claimed, exceptionally well catered for, while exhibitors were also well supplied with a wide diversity and number of films. In both cases, the prices charged represented value for money for high-quality goods. The comparative lack of success of British independent productions, with certain exceptions, was a reflection of consumer preferences. Buena Vista noted that the cost to the UK consumer of cinema-going was lower than in most other parts of Western Europe and substantially lower than in other developed countries. It also referred to the new distributors and exhibitors who had entered the market in the last ten years. New entrants had made, and were anticipated to make, significant investment in exhibition.

8.6. Columbia agreed that, for the purposes of economic analysis, it was sensible to regard the supply of films for exhibition in cinemas in the UK as a separate market. It told us that, unlike other consumer products, films had no brand-name identification or loyalty. No exhibitor would book, and no consumer would come to see, a new Columbia film because they had enjoyed the last one. Because of the lack of brand identification each film had to be distributed and promoted separately, in order to maximize revenues. Columbia's release strategies were designed to exploit the investment represented by each film to the maximum.

8.7. Columbia said that the release strategy was vital because the success of a film, both at the cinema and in subsequent media forms, was generally determined within the first four weeks of its theatrical release. Moreover, there was a high risk of failure; many films failed to recoup pre-release advertising and publicity expenses. Each film called for its own release strategy. For those with mass appeal, Columbia sought to have a large number of prints on screens on the opening day. Other films needed to be released slowly to build up an audience through word-of-mouth recommendation. The strategies used were based upon distribution expertise and knowledge of the market built up over many decades.

8.8. Columbia described film distribution in the UK as a hybrid of an alignment system, and a system based on negotiation between distributors and exhibitors. Columbia described itself as loosely aligned to Odeon, although this relationship was far less significant than it had been. Apart from Odeon, Columbia selected among competing cinemas by exercising judgment as to which would maximize its profits. The main factor taken into consideration was the economic potential of each cinema. Strategies varied from film to film; there was no preconception that one type of exhibitor would be favoured over another.

8.9. Columbia told us that it did not discriminate in its dealings as between MGM Cinemas, operators of multiplex cinemas or independent exhibitors. Indeed it did not recognize or use the category 'independent' in its commercial dealings. Successful independent exhibitors regularly received first-run releases. These included both established and new independents and also included city-centre independents which competed with nearby Odeon cinemas. Inevitably, some independent exhibitors performed less well due to poor location, small catchment area or, in some cases, under-investment or poor management. However, specific complaints of discrimination or unfair behaviour almost invariably turned out to be misconceived.

8.10. Columbia believed there was effective competition at both the distribution and exhibition levels and between the cinema and other entertainment media. There had been a rapid and beneficial development in the exhibition sector, notwithstanding earlier predictions of further decline in the face of video and other competitive media. It argued that most complaints made to the MMC concerned small individual components of a market mechanism which had worked as a whole effectively and to the public benefit.

8.11. Fox told us that the distribution market was competitive, being characterized by numerous independent competitors, intense film-by-film competition, ease of entry and exit, and rapid growth. It was also a very risky market being dependent upon audience taste which was often unpredictable and fickle. Only 2 per cent of films recovered their production costs.

8.12. UIP also told us that each film was a unique product, the success of which it was difficult to predict accurately prior to its release. It said that films were a perishable product; unless they were released expertly and widely on first release they would swiftly lose their appeal to consumers. Popular films were also extremely expensive to produce and market. Participation in the industry carried a high level of risk at all levels. It was, therefore, not surprising that relationships between producer, distributor and exhibitor involved an element of risk-sharing and revenue-sharing. In the absence of revenue-sharing, producers would find it very difficult to arrange for the distribution and exhibition of all but the evidently most commercial films.

8.13. UIP said that the US majors did not operate as a cartel to impose their films on the UK market. Nor, it said, had vertically integrated exhibitors discriminated in favour of their owners or against third party films. Distribution arrangements in the UK were not, it argued, biased in favour of US films and against UK films. It was wrong to treat the US majors as a cohesive group with common commercial interests. They competed for good film projects, for 'talent' and for quality cinemas. Nor did they act together on distribution. Each sought out what it regarded as the optimal strategy for each of its films.

8.14. UIP submitted that charges that distribution arrangements were biased in favour of US films and against independent films failed to take into account the existence of strong independent distributors (Guild, First Independent, RFD, PolyGram and Entertainment) which were large enough to pick up attractive films. It also ignored the fact that distributors could not force films on to exhibitors and that for much of the year and in much of the UK, there was no shortage of screens. The fact was that UK producers, with notable exceptions, had not been making films that attracted large UK audiences.

8.15. Warner Distributors referred to the conflicting aspirations which distributors were expected to meet. On the supply side, the British independent producers wanted greater exposure for their films, greater support for their production activities so that more British films were made and released, greater interest and commitment from the distributors to their films and more access to cinema screens across the country. In contrast, the independent exhibitors were largely concerned with obtaining easier access to mainstream films. They wanted to be supplied with more prints of the blockbusters and to receive them as soon as the films were released. They wanted to be free from any pressure, express or implied, to accept films of less certain commercial value and they wanted to be free to take a moderately successful film off their screens and replace it with a new major release as best suited their business. The independent exhibitors were not clamouring to show more arthouse, cultural, British or EC films—they wanted easier and faster access to the US films licensed by the leading distributors.

8.16. Warner Distributors said that the instinctive reaction of any observer of the industry was that the public interest favoured the revitalization and expansion of the British film industry but that it also favoured the growth and development of a strong independent exhibition sector. The difficulty lay in reconciling the wishes of the independent producers to find an outlet for their films with those of the independent exhibitors to maximize their revenue by concentrating on popular mainstream product. The distributor stood between these conflicting interests in attempting to serve the public interest by having a wide choice of films available that cinema-goers wanted to see and ensuring the best possible exposure for the films of which it held the distribution rights. The distributor's continued success depended both on a flourishing film production industry and the existence of sufficient high-quality venues where the public could see the films.

8.17. Warner Distributors told us that exhibitors made only a very limited contribution to the promotion of a film. It was almost entirely the efforts of the distributor which enabled the exhibitor to earn the revenue generated by the film's popularity. The methods used to calculate rental payments emphasized that the risk of the success or failure of the film was, to a great extent, placed on the distributor. The house nut was set to reflect the costs incurred by the cinema owner in operating the venue and only a minimum rental was charged if the box office receipts did not exceed those costs. The system ensured that the exhibitor had the greatest opportunity to recover its costs, even if this meant that the distributor did not recoup the investments made in promoting the film or supplying the print to that venue. The advantage for the distributor was that when the film was very successful, it could take a higher proportion of the revenue above the nut or other break threshold. Warner Distributors submitted that the practices which the MMC's inquiry had focused on were entirely reasonable and the minimum needed to provide an acceptable balance between the risks and rewards of distributors and exhibitors.

## *Ancillary markets*

8.18. Columbia told us that, in certain cases, it would take ancillary markets into consideration when considering how best to release a film into the theatrical market. If it had any doubts about the ability of a film to recoup the costs in the theatrical market, it might take into account the likely success in the video market (see also paragraph 8.183).

8.19. UIP agreed that expenditure on publicizing the theatrical release of a film was an investment which was likely to yield returns in the ancillary markets. It estimated that no more than two or three of the 20 or more films it released each year would recoup their costs from the theatrical market alone. Before any film was made, the relevant UIP partner estimated how well it was likely to do in all markets. Expenditure on promotion and advertising was determined on the expected performance of the film in all markets (see also paragraph 8.194).

8.20. Warner Distributors said that theatrical release would enhance the perceived value of a film to other markets. However, it would never release a film with 200 prints and a major media campaign unless it thought there was a chance of recouping the costs in the theatrical market. In questionable cases it might go ahead with a release, albeit with fewer prints and a smaller media campaign (see also paragraph 8.202).

## Views on complex monopoly situation

8.21. We asked the leading distributors for their views on our provisional finding that a complex monopoly situation existed in respect of the supply of films for exhibition in cinemas in the UK in that they engaged in one or more of the practices listed in paragraph 7.11.

8.22. Buena Vista made no comment on our provisional finding. Columbia questioned whether the practice of exclusivity existed in substance as opposed to form. It also stated that distributors did not supply films on terms which required exhibitors to charge admission prices agreed by the distributors. Exhibitors were free to charge whatever prices they wished. The only restriction was that exhibitors required consent before reducing admission prices in respect of films where booking commitments had already been made. It further expressed the view that overseas decision-making did not amount to a practice within the meaning of section 6(2) of the Act. UIP said that it did not believe the practices listed were complex monopoly practices which were restrictive and/or affected the public interest.

8.23. Warner Distributors said that it did not engage in many of the practices which had given rise to complaints and allegations of anti-competitive behaviour. It did not accept that it should be included in the complex monopoly when its involvement in the practices said to form the basis of the monopoly was so limited. It also believed it was not appropriate for the MMC to include, in the complex monopoly finding, such a varied range of practices which had very different effects on competition.

8.24. Fox submitted that there was no complex monopoly or that, if there was, Fox was not a beneficiary of it. This was because the conduct identified by the MMC as giving rise to a complex monopoly was neither conduct in which Fox engaged at all, nor, even if engaged in by others, was it conduct which prevented, restricted or distorted competition in connection with the production or supply of films. Fox commented on each of the practices in turn:

*(a)* and *(b)* Fox did not engage in alignment in any consequential sense. This was demonstrated by the fact that there was no difference in favour of Odeon in the proportion of Odeon cinemas and the proportion of independent cinemas exhibiting Fox films, in comparable circumstances. Fox normally approached Odeon to discuss the release strategy for its films and would either offer Odeon booking priority or explain why it was not doing so. There was no obligation or understanding that it would give precedence to Odeon. Alignment, even if engaged in by others, did not appear to affect the availability of films to independent exhibitors. Having regard to the structure of the film exhibition market, Fox did not accept that the practice of alignment prevented, restricted or distorted competition.

*(c)* Such exclusive rights as were granted by film exhibitors were of limited duration and related to a small geographic area. Fox believed the grant of such exclusive rights was a legitimate way of exploiting property rights and did not prevent, restrict or distort competition.

*(d)* Refusals to supply prints to exhibitors were a legitimate step taken by distributors to enable them to maximize profits from distribution of their films. This was particularly true where, as was generally the case in the UK, those films were distributed under licensing agreements insisted upon by exhibitor chains and the independents alike which required that each cinema cover its nut before revenue-sharing took effect.

*(e)* and *(f)* Distributors generally, and Fox in particular, did not engage in the practices of requiring minimum exhibition periods and imposing restrictions on screen use to any significant degree. When Fox did so, it was in order to maximize its profits and recover its costs. These provisions were part of the overall contract and compensated Fox for advertising and promoting a film. Given the limited extent to which these practices took place, Fox did not accept they were such as to prevent, restrict or distort competition to an extent capable of founding the existence of a complex monopoly.

*(g)* Fox said that distributors did not, in practice, exercise control over exhibitors' admission prices—for example, Fox had not prohibited its exhibitors from lowering their prices when they had wished to do so. In these circumstances, Fox maintained that this practice did not have any effect capable of founding the existence of complex monopoly.

*(h)* The use of the *Standard Conditions* arose because they reflected the industry norm, embodying a balance between risk and reward which was acceptable to both the distributor and the exhibitor. In these circumstances, the distributors' conduct was not such as to give rise to a complex monopoly and certainly did not prevent, restrict or distort competition.

*(i)* To the extent that Fox's related companies in the USA were involved in making decisions as to how to exploit films in the UK, such conduct derived from their legitimate interests in the proper exploitation of the property rights in their films. Their motive was to maximize revenues from exploitation of their films in the UK. Fox did not believe the overseas companies would have different motives or act differently if they were based in the UK. Therefore, it submitted that the practice of overseas companies being involved in certain decision-making functions did not have any consequences which would not otherwise occur, so that the practice did not prevent, restrict or distort competition.

8.25. We also asked the leading distributors for their views as to whether it might be preferable to identify two complex monopoly groups, one comprising exhibitors and the other distributors, rather than one group comprising both exhibitors and distributors. Of the leading distributors, only Fox objected to the identification of one group. Its solicitors submitted that, having regard to the wording of section 6 of the Act, it would be more appropriate for us to conclude (if the conditions described in that section were fulfilled) that separate complex monopoly situations prevailed in favour of exhibitors and in favour of distributors. Three of the leading distributors (Columbia, Fox and UIP) argued that their ultimate holding companies had no involvement in their business and no other interest beyond that of controlling shareholders and should not, therefore, be regarded as persons in whose favour the monopoly situations existed.

## Alignment

8.26. We asked the leading distributors whether the practice of alignment, by restricting the competition between MGM Cinemas and Odeon in negotiating for exhibition rights, made the market less responsive to consumer preferences. We also asked them to comment on the possible remedies detailed in paragraph 7.16.

8.27. The leading distributors generally argued that alignment was a sensible way of conducting business, reducing the uncertainty and costs which would be entailed in having to negotiate each release with the two main circuit exhibitors from scratch. Alignment was thus one of the industry's techniques for reducing risk. The benefits were enjoyed by independent distributors as well as the leading distributors. Most argued that alignment did not make the market less responsive to consumer preferences, pointing out that the number of cinemas affected by the practice had been substantially reduced since the MMC's 1983 report. Only 17 city centres outside London were now affected. Alignment did not affect the supply of films to multiplex cinemas or to independent exhibitors, nor did it enable the leading distributors to find screen space for non-commercial films.

8.28. Buena Vista said that, in its experience, the number of cinemas where alignment was meaningful was restricted. It suggested that the absence of price competition between distributors was significant in that alignment was unlikely to affect prices charged to consumers. In addition, at the time of the 1983 report, the manufacture of more than 200 prints was regarded as a mass release. Now films were released with substantially more prints. Thus, it would be reasonable to infer that popular films were more readily available to consumers. Buena Vista submitted that there had been a substantial change since the 1983 report in the proportion of receipts distributors received from their aligned circuit. The 1983 report tended to show how disproportionate the receipts of the aligned circuit were when compared with receipts from the non-aligned circuit, with the former being particularly dominant. That would appear no longer to be the case. In Buena Vista's experience, its receipts from the two circuits were almost equal.

8.29. Buena Vista said that the first proposed remedy was wholly unnecessary and the MMC seemed to have gone beyond the question of alignment into the area of exclusivity. The suggestion that contracts between exhibitors and distributors for each cinema, for each film, should contain 'no condition as to the showing of that or any other film in any other cinema' would prevent exhibitors and distributors from agreeing to exclusive engagements where that was commercially viable and justified. Buena Vista's particular objection was that the effects of the remedy would be far more extensive than were necessary to cure the ill that some believed existed. Buena Vista could see no reason for the second part of the proposed remedy. The premise for it depended upon the acceptance of the need for the first part of the remedy, which Buena Vista emphatically rejected. It would place an administrative burden upon the company which would involve unacceptable additional expense of time and money.

8.30. Columbia told us that alignment had no bearing on its dealings with multiplex operators or independent exhibitors. It said that alignment had a very much less exclusionary effect than in the past because of the smaller number of locations affected; the larger number of screens available to show competing films at aligned cinemas; and, most importantly, because of the arm's length relationship between Columbia and Odeon which precluded Columbia films receiving unfair preference over the films of competing distributors. Odeon was not obliged to screen Columbia films. Notwithstanding alignment, Odeon's decision as to whether, how widely and how long to screen Columbia films was ultimately driven by its view of their commercial potential.

8.31. Columbia accepted that the alignment system operated in a fairly rigid fashion in a number of provincial cities. The alignment system had also operated at certain 'platform' West End cinemas, though it believed alignment operated more flexibly in the West End than it had in the past. To give one recent example, *Shadowlands*, a UIP film, received its first release at the Odeon West End. Columbia considered that, subject to the constraints imposed by the alignment system in the 17 locations where alignment bit, films were distributed upon their merits. At any rate, Columbia considered that this was the case with its arrangements with Odeon, MGM Cinemas and other exhibitors.

8.32. Outside these locations, Columbia considered that the use of the term alignment had become increasingly misleading. For each release, Columbia discussed its plans not only with Odeon, but also with the multiplex operators, with MGM Cinemas, and with the operators of smaller cinema chains. Discussions with Odeon did not preclude simultaneous first-run screening of Columbia releases at any other location. Moreover, there was an understanding between Columbia and Odeon that discussion of release strategies was underpinned by the films offered by Columbia and the outlets offered by Odeon—as opposed to any legal or moral rights.

8.33. Columbia considered it important that the MMC accepted the practical necessity and utility of having advance discussions between distributors and exhibitors in order to plan release strategies and to obtain the maximum benefit from investment in advertising and publicity. Columbia stressed that, for each of its releases, advance discussions took place with all the cinema chain operators, and not merely with Odeon, though early discussions with Odeon helped to provide a release anchor and assisted in determining the release strategy. The advance planning of releases with other exhibitors was, it said, an essential prerequisite for a successful release and the recovery of advertising and publicity costs.

8.34. Columbia stressed that discussions between distributors and exhibitors necessarily dealt with the release of each film across the whole of the exhibitors' outlets. It was the essence of the distributor's task to plan its release strategies on a film-by-film basis, taking account of the assessment of the film's likely potential and the track record of the cinemas willing to exhibit it. Columbia said that it did not have the resources to carry out an exhaustive 'screen-by-screen' merit analysis; instead it aimed to grant first-run screening rights to the exhibitors which it considered would provide the best outlets for each film. This inevitably involved a degree of judgment on its part.

8.35. Columbia told us that exclusivity played no part in determining its release strategies. An independent cinema which merited a first-run release would be granted rights to screen a film, notwithstanding the fact that the film was being simultaneously screened nearby on the aligned Odeon circuit. Successful independent exhibitors regularly received first-run screenings, even in cities where they were competing with a nearby Odeon cinema.

8.36. Responding to the first possible remedy, Columbia said that there were always special factors determining the marketing of each film. For example, an independent exhibitor might argue that it would achieve a particularly good return on an arthouse film in a student area. Columbia already factored in such matters in deciding how to release films—a point that was illustrated by the fact that, for *The Remains of the Day*, it elected to date the film in rival screens rather than Odeon cinemas in some locations. Columbia did not have the resources to carry out an analysis on a film-by-film basis with such scientific rigour that it could be guaranteed to withstand complaints from any third party exhibitors.

8.37. Columbia pointed out that release strategies had to be planned upon the basis of its best estimate as to how a film would be received, and not with the benefit of hindsight. It was well known that distributors sometimes misjudged the public reception for particular films.

8.38. Columbia argued that the MMC must either accept the strategies which were now employed in the distribution of films, or come up with workable alternatives. If the MMC wished to prevent the continuance of present release strategies, there might be no alternative but to introduce a complex system of regulation imposing fixed and predetermined ground rules for the release of films and dealings between distributors and exhibitors. While Columbia was not out of sympathy with the spirit of the proposed hypothetical remedy, it considered that its arrangements with exhibitors (including Odeon) were driven by the merits of the cinemas selected. The remedy should not, in principle, require any alteration of its existing practice.

8.39. Columbia had a number of serious practical objections to the first proposed remedy. It was impossible to give any precisely ascertainable meaning to the term 'agreement or arrangement which covers one cinema only'. Columbia believed it essential that exhibitors and distributors were free to discuss release strategies. This necessarily involved the discussion in general terms of the exhibitors' cinemas where a film was to be screened. It was neither practicable nor desirable to prevent these discussions taking place. The proposed remedy could lead to formalistic compliance in which distributors and exhibitors exchanged large numbers of pieces of paper to demonstrate, in case of enquiry, that they were dealing with cinemas individually.

8.40. Columbia believed there would always be room for debate as to whether or not a cinema was selected on its merits. This went against the requirement that a remedy should be clear-cut and certain. Columbia selected, on their merits, all the Odeon cinemas to exhibit its films. If any Odeon cinemas were unsatisfactory, or Columbia took the view that there were other preferable cinemas within the same catchment area, it would resist pressure from Odeon to grant first-release screening rights.

8.41. Columbia believed it was essential that distributors were clear as to which actions were legal and which were not. Orders or undertakings given under the Act gave rise to the possibility of third party action and legal proceedings instigated by the DGFT. It submitted that distributors should not be subject to the jeopardy of such action or proceedings unless the nature of what was prohibited was unambiguously clear.

8.42. Columbia considered that the remedy would be an invitation for speculative complaints by aggrieved exhibitors. This would lead to a heavy burden of compliance for distributors and a heavy burden of regulation for the OFT. Columbia said that the MMC inquiry had provided an opportunity for complaints to be put by independent exhibitors. Where complainants had been identified, Columbia believed it had provided persuasive rebuttals of the complaints against it. If the proposed hypothetical remedy were instituted, it would be open to any exhibitor at any time to complain to the OFT that it had been denied a film because of 'arrangements' which contravened the order (or undertakings) made in implementation of the MMC's recommendations. The OFT would appear to have a continuing duty to investigate such complaints. Columbia had no doubt that many complaints would prove to be without foundation but foresaw that it would be in the repeated position of having to prove an extremely imprecise negative.

8.43. It was further unclear to Columbia how exactly the onus of proof would operate, or how the OFT would be expected to act in a 'balance of probabilities' case. Columbia hoped that the MMC would keep firmly in mind the need for a workable system of regulation, which would take account of the disproportionate expense which could be incurred by distributors in answering complaints against them, not all of which would prove to be justified in practice following detailed examination.

8.44. Columbia added that it had no strong opinion about the tight alignment system which operated in the provincial cities which contained cinemas of both Odeon and MGM Cinemas. In these locations, as a question of custom and arrangement, it was effectively precluded from offering its films to MGM Cinemas on a first-run basis. It said that this arose, not because Columbia was forbidden from offering films to MGM Cinemas, but because MGM Cinemas did not request Columbia films for screening at these locations. Columbia doubted very much whether any substantial public detriment arose from the operation of this system. However, if the MMC were minded to frame a remedy which was sufficiently clear-cut and precise to bring this situation to an end, Columbia would be indifferent to such a remedy.

8.45. Columbia had no objection to the second part of the remedy. It was reasonable that the OFT should be kept informed of distribution patterns. Furthermore, this part of the remedy had the advantage of certainty and absence of ambiguity.

8.46. Responding to the alternative remedy (see paragraph 7.16), Columbia said that it could not comment on a hypothetical remedy involving prohibition of the practice of alignment unless it was made specifically clear what practices now carried on by Columbia would cease to be permissible in the future and what alternative methods of dealing between distributors and exhibitors would be introduced in substitution for the practices which became illegal. If Columbia were to be prohibited from carrying out prior discussions with Odeon in order to establish its release strategies, presumably it would be prohibited from carrying out prior discussions with any other exhibitor either. In principle, that would amount to a mandatory requirement that all exhibitors would be simultaneously notified of each forthcoming release; and there would be some formal system of ensuring that each exhibitor's expressions of interest were dealt with in some kind of transparent fashion, so that no allegations of unfairness could arise. Logically, this amounted in effect to some kind of sealed bidding system.

8.47. As noted in paragraph 8.24, Fox argued that it was not aligned to any exhibitor, although it questioned the definition of the term 'alignment' proposed by the MMC. Fox did not believe alignment (in any sense) restricted competition between MGM Cinemas and Odeon. It was only in those locations which contained cinemas of both MGM Cinemas and Odeon that the two exhibitors could compete for exhibition rights and alignment could have any effect in restricting competition. Fox calculated that only 5 per cent of all localities in the UK fell within this category. In other areas, distributors licensed films without reference to alignment. Fox submitted that the significance of alignment was further reduced by the fact that it did not operate in the West End, nor did it apply to multiplex cinemas. In some cases, distributors would license films to competing cinemas owned by MGM Cinemas and Odeon.

8.48. Fox told us that it would have no objection to adoption of the first proposed remedy which, it said, could address possible concerns as to the anti-competitive exercise of market power by exhibitors who controlled a chain of cinemas. Fox would not regard the administrative burden of collating and providing the relevant information to the OFT as being excessive. It made no additional comments on the alternative remedy.

8.49. UIP said that alignment did not restrict the supply of films to operators of multiplex cinemas or to independent exhibitors. While UIP had no objections in principle to the termination of the remaining alignments, it would consider it to be against its own interests, and those of consumers, were it to be required to offer new films to both MGM Cinemas and Odeon in the 17 cities where both had cinemas. Such a requirement would prevent it from selecting customers so as to maximize returns. It would also reduce choice, contrary to the interests of consumers. UIP was willing to make its selection in the cities where alignment still had an effect on the same basis as elsewhere—selecting and contracting with those cinemas which, because of their quality and availability, it believed would best promote a film to realize its full value.

8.50. If the MMC were minded to recommend the first possible remedy, UIP said that it would need to ensure with the OFT that there were suitable transitional arrangements to take account of negotiations with exhibitors.

8.51. UIP was concerned that the possible remedy addressed not only alignments but also exclusivity, in that it proposed that distributors and exhibitors should be prohibited from entering into any agreement or arrangement for the showing of a film at a cinema which contained a condition as to the showing of that film in any other cinema. UIP said that the 1989 Order made it unlawful for 'an exhibitor or a distributor to make or carry out any agreement relating to the supply of any film for exhibition at a cinema if the agreement contains or provides for terms about exclusivity applied or to be applied to more than one film'. It was, therefore, already illegal to include a condition in any licence agreement for a particular film as to the showing of any other film in any other cinema. To this extent, the possible remedy simply duplicated existing legislation.

8.52. UIP said that the second part of the possible remedy would involve a very large amount of information. It believed that the huge effort of such reporting was not justified when the OFT could, for example, hold annual discussions on alignments with relevant parties and, at that stage, solicit more information if it felt the need. UIP made no additional comments on the alternative remedy.

8.53. Warner Distributors did not believe that alignment, in the manner in which it was currently practised, operated to make the market less responsive to consumer preferences or had any other adverse effect on the public interest. It said that the practice had relaxed considerably since the time of the last MMC inquiry as a result of the entry of multiplex cinemas into the exhibition market.

8.54. Although Warner Distributors was, broadly speaking, aligned with MGM Cinemas, it said that this policy was subject to a number of important exceptions. First, in areas where there were cinemas belonging to Odeon, MGM Cinemas and an independent exhibitor, alignment affected only the Odeon cinema. Warner Distributors would supply a first-run print to both MGM Cinemas and to the independent exhibitor, subject to the overall criteria of economic viability. Secondly, Warner Distributors supplied all multiplex cinemas with films at the date of first release. Thirdly, it supplied a print to all cinemas in the vicinity of the multiplex which were traditionally supplied with a print on the date of first release, even if the level of business now generated by those cinemas would not otherwise justify the provision of prints. It submitted that alignment did not affect the ability of the independent cinemas to obtain prints from Warner Distributors.

8.55. Warner Distributors submitted that, when considering the effect on the market of alignment, it was important to bear in mind that alignment did not oblige the aligned cinema chain to accept non-commercial films, nor did it mean that the distributor could force an exhibitor to continue to screen an unsuccessful film. To do so would be against the interests of both the exhibitor and the distributor. An independent cinema in a location where alignment 'bit', but which, nevertheless, received a print on first release, was not obliged to accept or continue to screen any film which did not prove to be commercially viable.

8.56. Warner Distributors argued that alignment provided the distributor with a greater degree of certainty that there would be a proper outlet for its films than would exist if it had to negotiate with each exhibitor over the release of each film. The planning of the publicity and advertising campaign for each film was carried out many months in advance of release and involved a substantial investment in terms of money and creative resource. That investment carried a large measure of risk because it was impossible to determine in advance whether the film would generate the audience needed to recoup the investment. Alignment to some extent also removed a further risk, namely that even those films which would be a great hit with the public would not be able to gain the wide release they deserved because insufficient cinema screens were available. It was important to appreciate that the security offered by alignment was enjoyed not only by the leading distributors but also by those independent distributors who were also aligned.

8.57. Warner Distributors suggested that, in the absence of alignment, the distributor would have to negotiate release arrangements every time a new film was released. As Warner Distributors released about 20 new films a year, the cost and complexity of organizing releases would be greatly increased if the abandonment of alignment meant that MGM Cinemas and Odeon no longer engaged in central booking and each film had to be released through a mixture of MGM Cinemas, Odeon and independent exhibitors across the country. At present, Warner Distributors negotiated release dates with the central booking manager of MGM Cinemas, who was responsible for the screening plans of each of its cinemas nation-wide. Once the date was settled, and taking into account the fact that the multiplex cinemas always had a screen available, Warner Distributors knew that there would be a significant coverage for the film in every region. This guaranteed coverage, with a reasonable geographical mix of cinemas, enabled Warner Distributors to formulate a coherent advertising and publicity campaign for the film.

8.58. Warner Distributors suggested that the abandonment of alignment could lead to three results. First, distributors might limit the release of a film to some only of the available cinemas at a given location. Exhibitors would have to bid for the film, which would lead to an increase in the rentals paid to the distributor without increasing the number of venues at which the film could be shown. This would have an adverse effect on independent exhibitors, who did not have the resources to match those offered by the cinema chains. Independent exhibitors would be less likely to have access to the most successful films. Whereas at the moment the independent exhibitors tended to play a film alongside the aligned cinemas, a bidding process would encourage more extensive exclusivity agreements as the winning bidder would need to be sure that it captured all possible audience for the film in order to support the additional payments made to the distributor. Warner Distributors suggested that bidding might well involve not only offers of higher rental payments but also offers to enter into longer minimum exhibition periods. This would leave less screen time available for other films and reduce the current flexibility with regard to minimum playing times. A bidding procedure would also be likely to lead to increases in admission prices.

8.59. The second possible result would be that every film would be shown at every cinema in a location. Warner Distributors said that this would serve to reduce consumer choice and increase the risky nature of the business for the distributor and the producer of the film concerned. If the abandonment of alignment led to every cinema in a particular town showing the same film, the cinema-going audience would have a smaller choice of films to see on a given evening than they had at the moment. Currently alignment meant that two or more 'blockbusters' could be released simultaneously, so that different tastes could be catered for at the same time.

8.60. The third possible effect would be the development of booking 'combines', which existed in certain other European territories where alignment was not practised. Warner Distributors said that this system interposed an intermediary between the exhibitors and the distributor. The combines did not own the cinemas but arranged bookings for many cinemas under different ownership in various parts of the country. In some cases, the combines had amassed greater market power than the aligned chains in the UK. Warner Distributors did not see any benefits from allowing such a system to become established here.

8.61. Commenting on the first proposed remedy, Warner Distributors submitted that it would impose constraints which went far beyond solving the perceived problems of alignment and was unworkable. The requirement that an agreement should cover only one cinema ignored the fact that the exhibitors' decisions as to which films to show in which cinemas were taken centrally by a head office or regional executive and not by the individual cinema managers. Even if the distributors and exhibitors were to attempt to negotiate over each cinema in a chain in turn, the centralized decision-making on both sides of the industry meant that it was inevitable that the final agreement reached with the exhibitor's central buyer would cover more than one cinema in the group, even if the inclusion of the individual cinemas in the deal was determined on a case-by-case basis. Warner Distributors submitted that, given the structure of the industry and the way in which business was done, it would be impossible for distributors to enter into agreements which covered one cinema only, regardless of the presence or absence of alignment. To do so would require a complete reorganization of the system for allotting screens, which was impracticable given the frequency and volume of new films being released over the year.

8.62. Warner Distributors described the requirement that decisions be based on the merits of the cinema as very vague and overly restrictive. It said that there were many factors which were taken into account in deciding whether to show a particular film at a particular cinema and many of these criteria went beyond the quality of the premises and the facilities on offer. First, there were the financial arrangements which the cinema was prepared to offer in terms of house nuts, break points and percentages. Secondly, the availability of screens at the cinema inevitably influenced whether the cinema would play the film on its initial release. Thirdly, the nature and quality of the film would influence the distributor's choice; an up-market film would not be shown at poor-quality screens which might be adequate for a more mainstream film which appealed to the lower end of the market. Warner Distributors said that it was difficult to see which of these criteria were included in the merits of the cinema. They were, it said, all entirely legitimate commercial factors which had nothing to do with alignment.

8.63. Warner Distributors believed that the prohibition on any condition as to the showing of that or any other film in any other cinema was unrealistic because of the way that the industry was structured. When dealing with a centralized buying structure, it was inevitable that the buyer would take into account, whether explicitly or implicitly, the advantages gained in one area of its responsibility when deciding whether to compromise on other points relating to other cinemas. This might not find its way into a formal condition in the agreement but it was not clear whether the MMC would regard this kind of balancing of advantages and disadvantages as contrary to the wording of the remedy.

8.64. Warner Distributors objected to the second part of the remedy on the ground that it covered much more material than was relevant to the question of alignment. It also suggested that the information would not permit the DGFT to draw any proper conclusions on the matter under investigation, since any conclusion concerning the continuation of alignment derived from that information was likely to be unreliable.

8.65. Alignments operated in a limited number of locations where there were competing MGM Cinemas and Odeon cinemas. Warner Distributors believed that the information sought by the OFT should be limited to those locations, as the distribution of prints in locations where alignment did not operate was irrelevant. Further, the practice of alignment related only to prints on their first release. Warner Distributors did not believe any significant complaint had been made, either by the MMC or by those making submissions to them, about the distribution of prints later on in the release period. Warner Distributors did not, therefore, believe that the information regarding the distribution of prints after first release had any relevance to the issue of alignment.

8.66. Warner Distributors said the remedy assumed that, if alignment were abolished, the DGFT would automatically see a change in the pattern of distribution so that, in relation to the initial release of films in the 20 locations, there would be a mixture of Odeon and MGM Cinemas sites supplied by a particular distributor. It argued that this would not be the case, as there were many other factors which influenced the choice of cinemas and which might lead to the maintenance of the same pattern of release as currently existed, even though alignment was no longer playing a role. For example, even if a distributor believed that the Odeon premises in the 20 alignment locations were generally of better quality than the MGM Cinemas facilities, it might, nevertheless, release its product through MGM Cinemas, partly because of the more favourable rental terms that MGM Cinemas was prepared to offer, or because the Odeon screens were already fully booked for the period when the distributor wished to release the film.

8.67. Warner Distributors suggested that the very fact that the distribution of prints would come under the scrutiny of the DGFT would distort the commercial decision-making of the distributors in an attempt to generate the kind of pattern of supply that they believed would satisfy the DGFT.

8.68. Responding to the alternative remedy, Warner Distributors said that a simple prohibition of the practice would raise problems because of the difficulty in identifying precisely what was meant by alignment. It wondered whether, if alignment were prohibited, distributors would be required to offer their films to, and discuss the timing and release strategy for those films with, both MGM Cinemas and Odeon. It also wondered whether distributors would be required to supply prints to both MGM Cinemas and Odeon in locations where they competed.

8.69. In conclusion, Warner Distributors submitted that, whatever the MMC's conclusions as to the virtues and vices of alignment, it should recognize that the market was in a process of growth and change. Any remedy would be unnecessary, ineffective and potentially damaging.

## Exclusivity and refusal to supply

8.70. The leading distributors were asked whether exclusivity and refusal to supply unduly restricted consumers' choice of cinemas to see a given film on first release; were harmful to certain independent exhibitors, to the extent in some cases of causing their withdrawal from the market; and deterred new entry and investment in the exhibition sector. They were also asked for their views on the possible remedies detailed in paragraph 7.46.

8.71. Certain of the leading distributors said that, outside the West End, contractual exclusivity was requested only by Odeon. Some of them said that they did not grant exclusivity, while others were prepared to do so, in certain circumstances. In most cases, the distributors would grant exclusivity only if it coincided with their own selected distribution patterns.

8.72. The leading distributors told us that the selection of exhibitors occurred on a film-by-film basis and was intended to ensure the optimal print run and maximum box office return from each film. The box office returns from some cinemas would not justify the cost of a print and associated costs. To supply all cinemas which could be expected to cover the cost of a print and associated costs was not the way to maximize profits, since it might raise total costs more than it raised total revenues. More generally, it was essential for distributors to retain control of supply decisions so that release strategies could be planned and carried out in the way best calculated to maximize the return on each film. Cinemas not supplied on first release were usually supplied on second run if they wished. Cases of absolute refusal to supply exhibitors were rare and were made solely on commercial grounds related to creditworthiness and other factors affecting the specific exhibitor. Some of the leading distributors argued that it was because some exhibitors had not invested in their cinemas that they did not receive first-run prints. The leading distributors argued that the substantial new entry and investment in the exhibition sector since 1983, particularly the construction of multiplex cinemas, demonstrated that exclusivity and refusal to supply had not deterred new entry and investment in cinemas. It was unlikely that either practice would result in undue restrictions on consumers' choice of cinemas.

8.73. Most of the leading distributors opposed the suggestion that the granting of exclusive rights should be prohibited. They argued that exclusivity was granted on rare occasions, being mainly confined to the West End. Some thought it was a valuable marketing tool in certain forms of release. They all opposed the suggestion that distributors should be required to supply prints to all competing cinemas in a given area which requested one, subject only to considerations of creditworthiness and the exhibitor guaranteeing as a minimum to cover the distributor's costs and a profit margin. They argued that it was crucial to their commercial interests that they retain the right to determine the most appropriate release patterns for each film, thereby ensuring that they were able to maximize their returns. They claimed that, in order to achieve this goal, they exercised their commercial judgment as to the number of prints of a particular film that would satisfy public demand.

8.74. The leading distributors argued that, if they were required to supply a print to any exhibitor that requested one, too many prints would be available in any given area. As a result, the available audience would be spread thinly across too many cinemas, thereby diminishing the box office return of each cinema. One result of reduced box office returns might be the closure of more cinemas. From the distributors' viewpoint, the rental available from certain cinemas would not cover the cost of producing a print and the advertising costs, let alone produce a profit. They argued that for them to be obliged to supply exhibitors on request would deprive them of the ability to exploit the distribution rights which they had acquired, as a result of their own or their parent companies' investments, according to their own commercial judgment. This would be contrary to the fundamental principles of the protection of intellectual property rights which were enshrined in UK and EC law and in international conventions.

8.75. Buena Vista did not accept that either practice prevented, distorted or restricted competition; if they did so, it was not contrary to the public interest. In its experience, exclusivity was as often requested by an exhibitor as by the distributor; refusal to supply was an infrequent occurrence, for which there was always a sound commercial reason.

8.76. Other than its alignment with specified Odeon cinemas, the only exclusivity relevant to Buena Vista was in relation to the West End, affecting films regarded as having outstanding commercial potential. Almost invariably in these circumstances, an exhibitor would seek exclusivity within the West End. Where this was consistent with Buena Vista's marketing strategy, it would normally be granted. It suggested that such exclusivity had no relevant adverse effect on competition. The very limited scale on which exclusivity existed could not unduly restrict consumers' choice of cinemas, since the period was short and the film in question was thereafter released without exclusivity.

8.77. Buena Vista argued that, because both practices were infrequent, and reflected the business judgment of those who catered to cinema patrons, it was highly unlikely that there were any undue restrictions on a consumer's choice of cinemas. Supplying prints in a particular order of priority was justified by the need to secure the best return, given the considerable investment in prints, advertising and in the cost of the films *per se*. It was the right of the distributor to develop and conduct its own marketing campaign and strategy designed to give it the best return. It would be an unsound business practice to make a print on demand or first run for a smaller, outlying cinema whose weekly audience would not cover the cost of a print and associated costs.

8.78. Buena Vista also suggested it was unlikely that the practices, in themselves, would cause independent exhibitors to withdraw from the market. It was much more likely that there were other sound sociological, demographic or economic reasons why the more marginal exhibitors were forced, from time to time, to close their cinemas. Indeed the notion that certain independent exhibitors were going out of business might be evidence of a healthy market. Assertions that independent exhibitors had been forced out by malign practices must, it suggested, be subjected to rigorous scrutiny. It also suggested that it was unlikely that the occasional and commercially warranted practice of exclusivity or refusal to supply would deter new entry or investment.

8.79. Buena Vista opposed any prohibition of exclusivity. It argued that to deny distributors the opportunity to create an exclusive platform release might well result in the type of film that secured such a release either not being made or not securing distribution. This would operate against the public interest. The compulsory supply of prints would, it submitted, disrupt an essentially orderly market and could lead to cinema closures as audiences were spread too thinly among cinemas. That would not be in the consumer's best interest.

8.80. Buena Vista submitted that supply on demand would amount to the granting of a compulsory copyright licence. It would not only be an unnecessary interference with a distributor's proprietorial rights but was not warranted by considerations of public interest as opposed to the narrow sectional interests of a handful of seemingly disgruntled exhibitors. The remedy would deprive the distributor of its fundamental freedom to select its own customers. Buena Vista also queried by whom and by what mechanism the guaranteed profit margin would be determined.

8.81. Columbia told us that it noted Odeon's requests for contractual exclusivity but complied with them only if they were consistent with its own release strategy. Since it did not have to change its decisions on which distributors to supply, it felt unable to demand any improvement in rental terms for meeting Odeon's request. There was, it said, no restriction of consumer choice, no impact upon independent exhibitors and no impact upon new entry and investment in the exhibition sector.

8.82. Columbia said that it refused to supply exhibitors only in a small number of cases of uncreditworthiness or suspected box office fraud. It believed that, if the issue of refusal to supply was considered in the round, the MMC would conclude that there was no restriction of consumer choice, even though individual exhibitors were not always allocated prints when they wished to have them. Films were allocated on an economic basis and there was no discrimination against independent exhibitors. Although independent exhibitors sometimes claimed losses through delay in receiving a print, Columbia did not believe these allegations always stood up and considered that they could not be assumed without proof. Some independent exhibitors, and indeed circuit cinemas, were detrimentally affected by the opening nearby of a multiplex cinema. But it was facile to say that whenever an independent exhibitor suffered in competition with a multiplex cinema this was due to refusal to supply as opposed to the normal and proper operation of market forces.

8.83. Columbia maintained its right to establish a release strategy, and to choose among cinemas for initial release, based on its judgment as to the best way to maximize revenues for a particular film. It also strongly contested the proposition that refusal to supply restricted new entry and investment in exhibition. Allocation of prints by reference to economic return was a market-driven system which rewarded successful exhibitors and provided an incentive both to investment and better management. In addition to the large-scale investment in multiplex cinemas over the past ten years, new independent exhibitors had successfully opened in favourable locations such as Greenwich, Clapham and Woking. Columbia argued that no policy or practice on its part deterred such investment.

8.84. While Columbia had no position on the suggestion that exclusivity be prohibited, it would strongly object to any interference with its ability to decide which cinemas should receive prints and when. It said that the compulsory supply of prints would have detrimental effects. These included restriction of consumer choice, because all exhibitors would seek to show blockbusters as soon as they were released, and shorter but more intensive periods of exhibition, which would require changed and more expensive practices in the advertising of films. Slow releases, such as it had chosen for *The Remains of the Day*, would become more difficult, to the detriment of exhibitors and distributors.

8.85. The proposed remedy would, Columbia argued, eliminate any incentive an exhibitor might have to compete for the first release of films, since it would grant equal access to exhibitors who had not invested in their cinemas nor established a successful track record in terms of box office returns. It would, therefore, reduce the competitive disciplines of a market-based system. There would also be severe difficulties in pricing film rental agreements, particularly in reaching a fair and acceptable basis for assessing distributors' costs.

8.86. Columbia submitted that, under both UK and European competition law, there was no general duty to supply on the part of a company which, like Columbia, possessed no market power. The EC Commission had recognized the right of a non-dominant supplier to withhold supplies for valid business considerations.

8.87. Fox said that, for consumers to have a choice of cinemas in which to see a given film on first release, it was necessary that two or more cinemas in a given locality should show the film concurrently. While this might stimulate competition in the exhibition of a single film, it would also diminish the choice of different films available at any one time. It was not clear to Fox that consumer welfare was enhanced by increased intra-film competition at the expense of inter-film competition.

8.88. Fox told us that, in practice, distributors rarely granted, and exhibitors rarely requested, exclusivity. Therefore any effects, were they to occur at all, would be inconsequential. Fox submitted that, nevertheless, it was important that a distributor be entitled to grant exclusive rights. The owner of copyright in a film entrusted the distributor with the task of maximizing rental income from the exploitation of the film. There was, it believed, a public interest in ensuring that the copyright owner, and those entrusted with the exploitation of the copyright, were able to grant exclusive rights to selected licensees when doing so increased rental income and thus provided an appropriate incentive to production of a greater number of new films than would otherwise be made. The public interest would be compromised if the grant of exclusive rights was prohibited or improperly controlled.

8.89. Fox said that, in many localities, there was only one exhibitor or a few exhibitors. In such cases, any restriction on consumer choice was not caused by the grant of exclusive rights to a local exhibitor, but by the limited screen capacity in the locality. Where an exhibitor did face local competition, there was no real risk that it would wrongfully exploit its exclusive right to show a film. It would be constrained from doing so by the knowledge that a competing exhibitor might be able to show the film at a later point, by the availability of other films in competing cinemas and by the prospect of the film becoming available on video and television.

8.90. Fox recognized that there would be occasions when it refused to supply a print to an exhibitor on the date requested, because to do so would be unprofitable. There was, however, no intrinsic reason to delay the supply of prints to exhibitors simply because they were independents. The exhibitors affected were those with single-screen cinemas and those located in less populous markets, where there were often inadequate audiences to support the cost of providing a new print at an earlier stage of the distribution process. Single-screen exhibitors might not receive a print on first release because they did not offer the flexibility and profit potential of multiplex cinemas, not because they were independently-owned. This reflected market realities and was not a distortion of competition. Fox submitted the results of an analysis of its supply decisions as between the two leading circuits on the one hand and independent exhibitors on the other. It said this showed that, although on average the first screening of a Fox film generally occurred at independent cinemas a week or so later than at circuit cinemas, this was due to their location and the fact that most of them had only one screen, not to the fact of their being independents.

8.91. Fox submitted that there was no reason why exclusivity or refusal to supply, as currently practised, should deter entry into or investment in exhibition. Nor was there evidence that they had. There had been substantial new entry in recent years and scope remained for further entry. An exhibitor who invested in good-quality exhibition facilities could be confident of obtaining good-quality films.

8.92. Fox told us that, if a distributor was obliged to make prints available as suggested, it could not be expected to accept the pricing terms currently demanded by exhibitors. If the suggested remedy were adopted, new pricing methods would need to be used which would transfer a greater share of the risk to the exhibitors. This would be likely to affect the prospects for continued investment in cinemas. It would also crowd out the films of smaller distributors as exhibitors would choose to opt for better-known US films. Fox also argued that the proposed remedy would also interfere with the economically efficient funding of film production. Some cinemas made a greater contribution than others to recovery of the production costs of a film. If distributors were confined to a formula of print cost plus a fixed return, the funds available to support film production would wither.

8.93. UIP said that it would grant exclusivity only if it were convinced by an exhibitor that it could so promote a particular film as to increase audiences either in a geographical area or nation-wide. In practice, it had not granted contractual exclusivity to Odeon or to any other exhibitor. In so far as a particular cinema exhibited a UIP-released film whereas competing cinemas did not, this was a factor of UIP's predetermined release pattern. It had nothing to do with requests for exclusivity. To date, the only convincing case UIP had heard for exclusivity was for a West End cinema which wished to show, on an exclusive basis, a film of unusual appeal for a relatively short time before general release. The grant of exclusivity in these limited circumstances should, it said, enhance consumer choice and encourage cinemas to compete through more intensive promotional activities. Save in these limited circumstances, the practice was becoming increasingly rare as distributors responded willingly to competition by exhibitors for prints on grounds of quality and ability to attract audiences.

8.94. UIP believed it would be inappropriate to introduce regulation prohibiting exclusive arrangements. Exclusivity should be left as a matter of negotiation between individual distributors and exhibitors. The public interest was safeguarded by the fact that distributors would grant exclusivity only on those rare occasions when the promotional value of doing so outweighed any possible detriment.

8.95. Regarding the selection of exhibitors, UIP also told us that it determined its release strategy on a film-by-film and a cinema-by-cinema basis. It required the freedom to contract with those exhibitors who would best promote a film and help realize its full value. UIP said that a distributor needed to choose high-quality cinemas which would show a film in optimal conditions. A distributor had to try to choose for each film the right number of prints to service the cinemas of sufficient quality; if too many were supplied, the costs of distribution would increase by more than the increase in total box office revenue; if too few were supplied, the reduction in print costs would quickly be more than offset by the reduction in revenue. UIP argued that the distributor's goals coincided with the public interest. If there were too many prints in the market, more screen space would be occupied than was necessary to satisfy public demand, to the possible exclusion in some cinemas of films the public would rather see. If there were too few prints, some members of the public would be denied the chance to see a film as soon as it was released. In either case, choice would be reduced, to the detriment of the public. A distributor could never precisely predict the public reaction to a particular film. If a film was more successful than expected, there would not be sufficient prints to meet demand and some exhibitors would complain that they had been denied first-run access. If a film did not live up to expectations, exhibitors would complain that they were forced to show a film they did not want.

8.96. UIP told us that selection of exhibitors promoted competition for prints on the basis of the quality of an exhibitor's facilities. All distributors knew that there was a clear correlation between high-quality cinemas and higher box office returns. Exhibitors knew that the surest way to obtain a print was to run the highest-quality cinema. This encouraged exhibitors to invest. UIP argued that, were prints to be made available to all cinemas, regardless of quality or other differentiating factors, the incentive to invest in improvements would be reduced. It also submitted that selection of exhibitors had benefited the public, increasing choice and quality in exhibition. It doubted whether, in the absence of selection based on quality, the UK would have seen the level of investment in cinemas over the last eight years. Without that investment, the decline in admissions which so threatened the industry in 1983 could have been permanent.

8.97. There was, UIP said, no justification for interfering with the principle of selection of exhibitors. The introduction of the suggested remedy would have very damaging effects on UIP's business and on the public interest. The promotional value of choosing appropriate outlets would be lost, with possible detrimental effects on the prospects of films. Exhibitors, faced with minimum guarantees, would be likely to concentrate on those films which seemed certain to produce a return, avoiding films perceived as risky or of uncertain appeal. This would lead to the over-supply of the most popular films and to an under-supply of other films. Public choice would be severely prejudiced. Distributors' returns would drop, since they would receive much less revenue from apparently less popular films and little if any additional return from the popular films. This would be likely to reduce the number of films released in the UK and harm producers.

8.98. UIP said that because more exhibitors would share the box office takings of successful films, their average earnings on such films would be lower. Apart from an increased unwillingness to take risks with less promising films, the fall in earnings would reduce their incentive to invest in cinema improvement and discourage new entry. There was no doubt, it said, that the remedy would end competition for prints on grounds of quality. UIP suggested that, in any event, it was highly unlikely that exhibitors would be willing to take the level of risk contemplated. Historically, exhibitors had been reluctant to increase their share of the risk. Instead they sought to minimize their exposure by break figure and nut arrangements which limited the prospect of failing to cover overheads. The remedy, if implemented, would increase their exposure to risk, with the adverse effects noted and without any offsetting public interest benefits.

8.99. UIP did not believe the possible remedy could be introduced, except on the basis that all exhibitors were required to trade on the basis of giving minimum guarantees. To expect some to give guarantees, but not others, would be inequitable and would be unlikely to reduce the number of complaints by exhibitors who did not receive prints for a particular film. UIP was unclear as to what minimum guarantee a distributor would be allowed to prescribe. If all exhibitors had to pay the same price for a print, the burden (per seat or admission) would fall most heavily on the smaller exhibitors and be especially burdensome for many independent exhibitors. A price that was reasonable in relation to costs might make many films inaccessible to many exhibitors.

8.100. Warner Distributors told us that, in recent years, the only film for which it had agreed an exclusive exhibition period was *The Fugitive* (for the West End only and for a limited period) for the purpose of launching the newly-refurbished Warner West End cinema. For ordinary film releases, it neither requested nor agreed to the grant of exclusivity when this was requested by exhibitors. Warner Distributors was aware that Odeon requested exclusivity for some of its cinemas against independent exhibitors when dealing with other distributors but said that the subject was never mentioned by Odeon in its dealings with Warner Distributors, because Odeon knew that exclusivity would not be granted. In those cases where a Warner Distributors film was exhibited at an Odeon cinema and not at any competing cinema, this was solely a function of the release strategy set by Warner Distributors before it spoke to Odeon about booking cinemas.

8.101. In Warner Distributors' experience, the grant of exclusivity was not sufficiently widespread or frequent to risk any of the adverse effects identified. It certainly did not appear to have deterred new entry or investment in the exhibition sector, since such new entry and investment had been the most important change in the industry since the last MMC inquiry. There had also been significant refurbishment in the infrastructure of the aligned chains, increasing the number of screens and generally improving the standard of facilities available in order to maintain their competitiveness. Warner Distributors said that its policy was to supply first-release prints to any cinema which had undertaken substantial investment, in order to encourage the increase in the number and quality of screens throughout the country, since this was in the best interests of Warner Distributors and the film exhibition market generally.

8.102. With regard to refusal to supply, Warner Distributors said that it did not refuse to supply cinemas, other than on the grounds of creditworthiness or the need to cover the costs of supplying the print, unless it had formed the view that a selective release strategy was the optimum way for the film to be released. It was very rare that Warner Distributors refused further supply on the grounds of creditworthiness and, as long as there appeared to be continuing cash flow from the exhibitor, a great deal of leeway was allowed. It believed that its policy regarding the provision of prints was considerably more liberal than that of many of its competitors.

8.103. Warner Distributors attributed the success of multiplex cinemas in obtaining prints on first release, regardless of whether they were near to, and competed with, cinemas of the two leading circuits, to an episode in 1988 when, for the first time, a multiplex had been opened within the catchment area of cinemas of both of the main circuits (Cannon—now MGM Cinemas—and Odeon).

Warner Distributors wanted to supply a print of *The Witches of Eastwick* to the new multiplex on first release but Cannon threatened to cancel all its bookings for the film if Warner Distributors did not observe the normal bars. When, despite this, Warner Distributors decided to stick to its intentions, not only Cannon but also the other leading circuit (Odeon) cancelled bookings for the film. The film therefore opened at a much reduced number of sites. It nevertheless proved an immediate success and the two circuits soon requested prints (see also paragraphs 7.51 and 7.59).

8.104. Warner Distributors submitted that the imposition of a requirement to supply prints would be a wholly unwarranted interference with the business of distributors and would risk severely damaging the film business in the long term. It would amount, in effect, to the introduction of compulsory licensing of every film distributor's copyright, regardless of the distributor's individual position in the market and before the distributor, as copyright holder, had an opportunity to exploit the copyright itself. Such a requirement might also conflict with the provisions of the EC Council's Rental Directive, due to come into force in July 1994.

8.105. Warner Distributors said that this form of compulsory licensing would also deprive the distributor of any discretion in the marketing of its product. The process of determining the release strategy for each film, in order to maximize its audience potential, would become redundant, since the decisions about the breadth of coverage would be entirely in the discretion of exhibitors, not distributors. There were some film releases in which an initial period of exclusivity, for example in one of the Leicester Square premiere cinemas, was an important part of the overall release strategy adopted by the distributor. In these cases, exclusivity was part of the plan adopted by the distributor to maximize the eventual impact of the film and, although it might result in some exhibitors not being able to screen the film as soon as they wished, it was entirely appropriate in an industry where distributors undertook the promotion of the film and incurred the considerable expense and creative effort in designing and implementing the advertising and promotional campaign for its launch. Exhibitors contributed virtually nothing to the overall appeal of the film. Yet the remedy would place all decisions on the breadth of the initial release and the timing of any increase in the number of prints in their hands.

8.106. Warner Distributors said that the reference to a guaranteed minimum 'to cover the distributor's costs and a profit margin' ignored the fact that the costs which had to be recouped in the longer term were those of the production of the film, not just the cost of advertising and distributing the prints in the UK. By depriving the distributor of the ability to adopt the best strategy, the remedy would reduce the willingness of film-makers to release their films in the UK.

8.107. Warner Distributors believed there were substantial practical difficulties with implementing such a remedy. For example, it was not clear whether the distributor would be required to supply a print to any cinema likely to generate enough income to cover the costs of the print, or whether the distributor's costs included the costs of promoting and advertising the film on television and in the national press, costs which could not be allocated to particular cinemas and which were far in excess of the cost of the individual print. It must be borne in mind too that the overhead costs of the distributors would increase with the increased number of cinemas which each had to serve. The burden of deciding, within a very short time frame each Monday morning, which cinemas would retain the print to show the film the following week and on which screens it would be shown, would be greatly increased. This point was crucial, since compulsory supply, in conjunction with the existing methods of rental calculation, was likely to lead to a reduction in the overall income of the distributor. There was no reason to suppose that a wider release would increase the total number of people who were interested in seeing the film. Consumer choice would be reduced by the non-availability of other films being screened at the same time and the same audience would simply be spread more thinly over a larger number of cinemas. This in turn meant that fewer of those cinemas would achieve income in excess of their house nut or of the minimum thresholds set for their royalty payments. The distributors' income was, therefore, likely to be restricted to the minimum percentages payable in a greater number of instances than at present, when the audience was concentrated in a smaller number of cinemas which, therefore, benefited from higher-capacity use. The remedy was, therefore, likely to result in a reduction in overall revenue for distributors, in conjunction with the increased costs of supplying a larger number of prints.

8.108. Warner Distributors also saw problems in deciding when the exhibitor would be obliged to make its decision about whether to call for a print of the film. At present, the release strategy for a film was decided many months in advance of its release in the UK, although the actual making of the prints took place only a few weeks before release. If exhibitors were required to ask for the print many months prior to the release strategy being determined in advance of release, this would greatly reduce their flexibility as to which films they screened. But it would be grossly unfair to expect distributors to make their decisions on advertising and promotional spend without having a clear idea of how many exhibitors were likely to want to screen the film until a few weeks before the release. If there were no time limit imposed on exhibitors, they would all be tempted to wait until the release of the film before requesting a print in the knowledge that, if the film was successful, the distributor would be bound to supply. This would undermine the whole basis on which the release of the film was planned.

8.109. Warner Distributors argued that, if the remedy were limited to the leading distributors, this would bring about a serious distortion in the market for distribution services to independent film-makers by placing the leading distributors at a great disadvantage to the smaller distributors, who would still, presumably, be free to select the exhibitors to whom they provided a print. Even if an independent film-maker admired the expertise of Warner Distributors in promoting films and wished to make use of its international links for the best exploitation of the film, the total loss of control over the distribution of the film through this compulsory licensing would be a major disincentive to that film-maker engaging Warner Distributors to distribute the film.

8.110. In conclusion, Warner Distributors believed such a remedy would bring about a fundamental change in the nature of the film distribution industry in the UK, and would necessitate a review of all aspects of the relationship between film-makers, distributors and exhibitors. There was nothing to suggest that there was currently any serious defect in the operation of the market to merit a change which would create a risk that the UK market would be significantly less attractive to film-makers both in the UK and overseas.

## Minimum exhibition periods and restrictions on screen use

8.111. We asked the leading distributors whether the imposition of minimum exhibition periods and restrictions on screen use harmed smaller distributors by restricting their access to screens; harmed exhibitors by reducing their revenue; and unduly restricted consumer choice. We also asked them for their views on the possible remedies detailed in paragraph 7.69.

8.112. The leading distributors argued that the question of minimum exhibition periods was one of the key elements in their negotiations with exhibitors concerning the supply of prints and could not be seen in isolation from the other elements, in particular the decision whether to supply a print on first run and the rental terms. It was necessary for distributors to have some assurance as to how long a film would be shown, so that they could plan their distribution strategies and decide how much to spend on publicity and advertising. Most said that it was not their standard practice to look for minimum periods longer than seven days. For those films where they did so, they did not insist that an exhibitor should continue to show a film whose box office performance was below expectations. But they would hold the exhibitor to the contractual period if the distributor considered that its film was doing reasonable business and the exhibitor wished to replace it with another which it thought would do better.

8.113. The leading distributors said that they incurred considerable costs (mainly on prints and advertising) when distributing a film, which were over and above the cost of producing the film in the first place. They required the freedom to negotiate minimum exhibition periods in order to have a reasonable opportunity to generate an adequate return on the investment. If this possibility were denied them, they would have to look for other ways of reducing their risks, for example through better rental terms.

8.114. The leading distributors argued that the substantial new entry and investment in the exhibition sector since 1983, particularly the construction of multiplex cinemas, demonstrated that the practices had not deterred entry and investment. Nor was either practice likely to result in undue restrictions on consumer choice.

8.115. The leading distributors argued that, in booking films, it was essential for them to know the extent of the exhibitor's commitment, since that helped to determine the potential benefits for the distributor. The restriction on screen use was part of the mechanism by which rental payments were assessed, since the house nut or break figures were set on the assumption that all performances were of the same film. It was essential that the distributor was able to renegotiate the rental when the film shared a screen. The question of sharing screens arose particularly with films aimed mainly at children. The distributor might want to see if such films attracted an adult audience as well, as *Aladdin* had done. If they did not, distributors were flexible, for example in agreeing that the film could be shown in a smaller screen in the evening, or allowing a reduced number of screenings (subject to an amendment to the rental terms).

8.116. They opposed the suggestion that exhibitors should have the right, as a minimum, to show other films on three occasions a week during licence periods, which they said would deprive them of the opportunity to earn the best possible return on their investment.

8.117. Buena Vista told us that it was not its standard practice to require a minimum period in excess of seven days, except for those films which it believed would have the widest public interest and support. Even in those circumstances, it would not insist that an exhibitor retain a film whose box office performance was below expectations. Occasionally there were differences of opinion at the margin about box office performance, but, in the vast majority of cases, the decision to continue to run a film, or to end it prematurely, was taken mutually. It was crucial for Buena Vista to be able to stipulate minimum exhibition periods for its children's films, the exploitation of which was concentrated in the holiday periods.

8.118. Buena Vista drew our attention to what it described as the contrary practice where, in the case of a successful film, exhibitors demanded the right to retain the film beyond the agreed minimum period and either refused to return the print or did so only with great reluctance. The reality of the exhibitors' position was that they wanted to be able to obtain films when they wanted without any particular obligation to distributors to exploit the film, even though the distributors would be obliged to supply the films which they requested. It argued that, in the absence of reasonable minimum exhibition periods, consumers would be disadvantaged because there would be a real disincentive to investment in film production.

8.119. As to restrictions on screen use, Buena Vista said that, partly because of the family nature of some of its films, it was prepared to be flexible with regard to the showing of other films on the same screen at different times. It told us that, for four of the five classic Disney animated films which it had released since it commenced trading, it had agreed from the outset that a different film could be shown in the evening. Responding to complaints about its practice in this area (see paragraph 7.82), Buena Vista told us that it typically received a request from an exhibitor who found that it unexpectedly had an 'over-performing' film on its hands but insufficient screen space (due to prior commitments to other films) to continue to show it. Buena Vista was asked to allow the 'over-performing' film to replace its film at the evening session, even though its film was performing to expectations. It was such situations which gave rise to most complaints from exhibitors, complaints which Buena Vista said were expected and understandable but wholly unjustified and unfair.

8.120. Buena Vista told us that more than half of its films were classified as 'U' and 'PG', meaning that they were particularly suitable for family viewing. It distributed more films with these classifications than all the other leading distributors together. While Buena Vista believed many of these films were also suitable for a purely adult audience, there was a tendency among exhibitors, mistakenly, to think that they were suitable only for family audiences. As a result, it inevitably received more requests to allow another film to show in the evening session than did the other leading distributors. Buena Vista said that because of this difference of opinion about its films, it tended to have more arguments with exhibitors than did the other leading distributors.

8.121. Buena Vista said that its primary task was to maximize revenues and to do so it was vital that it eliminated confusion. It argued that if an exhibitor, particularly with a single-screen site, was showing two or three films in the space of the same week, there was scope for confusion among potential customers. It was likely that the main film would be supported by an advertising campaign paid for by its distributor. It was equally unlikely that other films shown during that period would be promoted either by the exhibitor or the distributors concerned. Some members of the public would be unaware that different films were being shown and this could lead to disappointment if they found that the film which they were expecting to see was not being shown. This would harm the distributors' reputations and operations and would not benefit the consumer.

8.122. Buena Vista said that the proposed remedy implied that minimum exhibition periods were imposed by the distributor. As far as it was concerned, this was not the case. A minimum exhibition period was, it said, a joint decision made by distributor and exhibitor.

8.123. Regarding the right to show other films, Buena Vista said that a further, compulsory interference into established distribution practice would not benefit the customer. It would lead to confusion in the market and, in all probability, to consumer dissatisfaction. Distributors would be deprived of rentals upon which they were relying to generate a fair and adequate return since, presumably, it would be open to the exhibitor to nominate the showing of other films at times which might be most attractive to the distributor's own films (where there was common ownership between the exhibitor and the distributor).

8.124. Columbia described minimum exhibition periods as one of the three main economic variables, together with rentals and restrictions on screen use, which determined the economic relationship between distributors and exhibitors. They could not be regarded in isolation from each other; any compulsory change in the system could affect other variables, in particular rental terms. Exhibitors wished to decide which films to screen on a week-by-week basis, without prior commitment. Distributors, on the other hand, had heavy commitments to pre-release advertising and publicity and looked for a release 'anchor' to help ensure a return on their investment. Minimum exhibition periods were required strictly on a film-by-film basis and rarely for more than two weeks. It believed they represented a fair balance of interests between exhibitors and distributors.

8.125. Columbia argued that minimum exhibition periods were used equally by all distributors and did not operate against the smaller distributors. Nor was there evidence that they had reduced the revenue of exhibitors. Where they caused particular difficulties in specific cases, the matter was dealt with flexibly. Looking at the development of the market as a whole, they did not restrict consumer choice. Against the fact that a consumer might sometimes have to wait a short period to see a particular film at a particular screen, had to be set the growth of the market as a whole, which had led to more screens, with the result that consumers now had more choices in most areas. Minimum exhibition periods were also part of the release strategy which helped to support the costs of pre-release publicity and the distribution of large numbers of prints. Both factors increased awareness of and access to films.

8.126. Columbia believed restriction or abolition of minimum exhibition periods would be detrimental to the public interest. It would represent interference with a successful system based on free negotiation in light of market conditions. It would also give rise to particular difficulty for the release of films at school holidays. Abolition of minimum exhibition periods would also remove an important plank of Columbia's release strategy. It would lead to greater freedom of action for exhibitors but to countervailing reduction of certainty for distributors. This would lead to reconsideration of release strategies and decisions on numbers of prints, possibly to the ultimate detriment of consumers. It said that the films most affected would be those in the middle category, ie neither blockbusters nor minority films. They might receive less exposure than at present. Columbia did not believe any distinction should be made between first and subsequent releases.

8.127. Under the *Standard Conditions*, Columbia required full-time screening of its films, unless otherwise agreed, subject to standard exceptions, ie children's matinées and late night shows. It said that it dealt sympathetically with requests for variations from this standard practice. It did not receive many such requests and believed this was not widely seen as a problem.

8.128. Restrictions on screen use were operated equally by all distributors and Columbia did not believe the system operated to the detriment of smaller distributors. Given the small number of requests for release of restrictions and the flexible treatment given to them, Columbia contested that there was any material effect on exhibitors' revenues. It said that the issue of consumer choice had to be seen in the context of the fact that standard restrictions on screen use had been pervasive in a system which had delivered a large increase in the number of screens over the past ten years.

8.129. Columbia told us that rental negotiations were conducted from the starting point of an assumption that there would be full-time screening of films. If part-time screening were permitted at the whim of the exhibitor, this would be a fundamental change of the economic bargain. Rental agreements would need to be reconsidered and the consequences would be varied and complex. A right on the part of exhibitors to part-time screening would also affect the integrity of the present system of box office returns and could lead to increased fraud.

8.130. Fox submitted that the public interest did not demand either the abolition or control of minimum exhibition periods, or restrictions on screen use in the manner contemplated. Fox said that, if a film did less well than expected and a promising alternative was available, it was quite understandable that an exhibitor would wish to cut short the run. But to allow exhibitors to keep popular films for a protracted period, while replacing immediately those that were less popular, would shift all the risk on to distributors and make it impossible to plan the distribution of films. Thus, the inclusion in exhibition contracts of negotiated minimum exhibition periods and restrictions on screen use served to allocate risk between distributor and exhibitor.

8.131. Fox told us that it would press for a minimum exhibition period in excess of seven days only in special circumstances where, for example, it had committed itself to make a large investment in advertising a film. If it agreed with an exhibitor that a film would play for a longer minimum period and the film did not perform to expectations, Fox typically would agree to curtail the period to one week. It would, however, generally be unwilling to curtail the minimum period for a film which had performed well in its first week. To do so, normally to allow an exhibitor to show another film which it hoped would perform even better than the Fox film would fundamentally change the balance of commercial advantage. If both parties had agreed that the film merited a two-week run, both should bear the risks inherent in their agreement.

8.132. Fox said that similar considerations led distributors to reserve the right to impose restrictions on screen use. The distributor's objective was to ensure optimal use of the print and to maximize the benefit of its promotional activity. If the print was not used to the maximum extent, the distributor lost revenue and a return on its investment. Fox was, however, flexible in its dealings with exhibitors and was willing for its films to play alongside those of other distributors.

8.133. Fox believed that, if smaller distributors had less access to screens, this was attributable to the fact that their films generally lacked the mass appeal of the films of the leading distributors. It did not result from the imposition by the leading distributors of minimum exhibition periods and restrictions on screen use which were excessive in scope or duration, or disproportionate to the distributors' outlay to promote their films. It also doubted whether any difficulties experienced by some distributors were attributable to a shortage of screens, rather than to misallocation of existing screens. It believed that, as screen capacity continued to improve, this problem would resolve itself.

8.134. Fox did not accept that minimum exhibition periods and restrictions on screen use, if reasonable in duration and scope, harmed exhibitors. Indeed, they enabled exhibitors to promote and advertise films more vigorously than would otherwise be the case. Minimum exhibition periods of seven days were entirely reasonable and, in specific circumstances, longer periods might be appropriate. This was particularly so when, as occurred in practice, they were administered flexibly.

8.135. UIP described minimum exhibition periods and restrictions on screen use as necessary mechanisms which allowed a distributor to ensure that its return was as close as was achievable to that which a particular exhibitor in effect promised when acquiring its licence to show the film. The distributor needed to know the proposed period of exhibition, or intensity of exploitation, prior to selecting exhibitors, so that it might plan its distribution strategy and decide the amount of release costs and the level of promotional expenditure which were appropriate in light of the likely box office and rentals from the film.

8.136. UIP told us that distributors did not have the market power to impose terms on the exhibitors. Terms were a matter for negotiation on a film-by-film basis. They were negotiated up front as part of a package but were frequently renegotiated, after the fact, invariably in favour of the exhibitor. Ultimately, the decision on terms rested with the exhibitor who could, for example, refuse to take a film on terms which involved a minimum exhibition period of more than one week.

8.137. Each Monday morning, UIP spoke to exhibitors about the performance of its films over the weekend. If a film had under-performed, the exhibitors would refuse to hold it over, despite any previously agreed minimum exhibition period. If UIP felt that the film could still do reasonable business, it would try to persuade the exhibitor to continue to play the film. Sometimes it succeeded, more often it failed. In the latter case, there was nothing that a distributor could do to force an exhibitor to continue to show the film. UIP said that it would be highly damaging to the long-term relationship between distributor and exhibitor to force an exhibitor to take a film from which it felt unable to profit.

8.138. UIP believed both possible remedies would be against the public interest. In the absence of the ability to seek minimum exhibition periods and to place restrictions on screen use, the distributor would have no way to select between two exhibitors requesting a print. It would be virtually impossible to plan an effective sequential distribution strategy. Transactions costs would increase and flexibility would be removed. Distributors would be forced to demand some form of minimum financial guarantee. UIP could not see how a move away from the present flexible system would benefit exhibitors or be in the public interest.

8.139. Warner Distributors said that it was important to appreciate that the purpose of a minimum exhibition period and minimum screen use for a film was not to oblige the exhibitor to continue to show a film which was unsuccessful but to ensure that, where a film was successful, the distributor (and ultimately the producer) was able to reap the rewards of that success and that the public had an adequate opportunity to see the film before it was replaced by the next major release.

8.140. Warner Distributors said that its normal practice was to negotiate extended minimum periods only from cinemas with fewer than four screens, on the grounds that it was only in such cinemas that there was a real risk of its films being taken off prematurely. It also said that it would only seek an extended minimum exhibition period for films for which it had made a substantial promotional investment. It was essential that the film should be able to reach its maximum potential audience so that the investment of all those involved in the production and distribution of the film could be recouped and that revenues were available for further investment in films. If the audience, unfortunately, did not materialize when the film was released, it was better for all concerned for the film to stop playing and to be replaced. But if the film continued to attract a large audience, it should stay on screen: since the distributor, under the present method of rental calculation, took the risk of a film's failure, it should be entitled to enjoy a fair return from a film's success.

8.141. Warner Distributors submitted that the abandonment of minimum exhibition periods would operate against the public interest because it would make the ability of the film-maker and distributor to recoup their investment more uncertain and risky and hence reduce, in the long term, their willingness to make that investment. The importance of ensuring that the distributor had a fair opportunity to benefit from the potential audience for a film should override, in Warner Distributors' view, the short-term interest the exhibitor might have in rapidly replacing successful films with newer releases. The abandonment of minimum exhibition periods would particularly disadvantage the smaller independent film distributors who released fewer films over the year and, therefore, had less opportunity to recoup their costs across a range of films.

8.142. Warner Distributors suggested that a similar situation could arise in respect of films which were mainly aimed at children, but where the distributor required the exhibitor to show the film at all screenings, rather than show an adult film for the evening performance. The distributor would be concerned to ensure that, if the film did attract an adult audience, the distributor and production company would obtain the benefit of that appeal. Some films which were originally aimed at a young audience sometimes proved to be successful with adults, a striking recent example being *Aladdin*.

8.143. Warner Distributors said that the practice of screen restriction was not applied if it became clear that the film did not have a wider attraction. It must also be borne in mind that the restriction on screen use was part of the mechanism by which rental payments were assessed. The house nut was set in accordance with the expected number of performances during each week and was applied on the assumption that all the performances were of the same film. If a cinema reported its income and the house nut was applied, when in fact other films had been shown on the screen during the course of the week, the system would result in too low a rental payment being made to the distributor. It was essential, therefore, that the distributor be able to renegotiate the rental when the film shared a screen.

8.144. Warner Distributors submitted that the practices identified by the MMC did not have any adverse effect on competition. With regard to the position of smaller distributors, they also benefited from the ability to set a minimum period when they had a release which was very successful but which coincided with a release by one of the leading distributors. Again, it was important to bear in mind that any restriction of access to screens did not arise from the enforced showing of films which were not generating any business but from films which were still successful, though perhaps not making as much money as a new release on the same screen would.

8.145. The abandonment of the practices would, Warner Distributors suggested, lead to an adjustment of the rental calculation, which might leave the exhibitor no better off in the longer term. At present, an exhibitor might be tempted to break the minimum commitment and earn more money by showing a new blockbuster. But such a development would soon lead to the renegotiation of the rental terms for that cinema or to a general reduction in the break levels in the rental payments provisions. If there were no minimum exhibition period and the distributor, therefore, knew that it had only one or two weeks in which to benefit from the success of the film before it was taken off the screens, it would necessarily seek a greater proportion of the revenue from the shorter period to try to make the most of the audience that did have the chance to see the film. This would offset the extra revenue earned by the exhibitor from replacing one major release with another more rapidly than at present.

8.146. Warner Distributors argued that minimum exhibition periods for popular films also benefited the consumer in making the films available to as wide an audience as possible. A more rapid turnover of films in cinemas would reduce the period during which the public had the opportunity to see a particular film and would deprive some people of the chance to see the film if, for some reason, it was not convenient for them to visit the cinema during that time. Further, if the life of the successful films was artificially shortened in this way, it would greatly increase the uncertainty and risk surrounding the release of the films for which the largest promotional budgets were allocated. The potential for recoupment would then not depend only on whether the film was a hit with the public: even a popular film could be at risk of being taken off screen to make way for a competing film whilst it was still capable of generating substantial business. By concentrating the business in the first, say, two weeks after release, it would also make the film more vulnerable to extraneous influences such as the weather. Such an increase in the level of risk was likely to lead to a more conservative production policy and a greater dependence on films which were likely to withstand any opposition. The abandonment of these practices was likely, in the long term, to lead to a reduction in the range of films available and, therefore, would reduce rather than improve consumer choice.

8.147. Warner Distributors believed there was sufficient flexibility at present in the operation of screen use restrictions to make a remedy unnecessary. The current position struck the proper balance between the interest of the distributor in ensuring that the maximum potential audience had an opportunity to see the film and the interests of all parties, including the consumer, in a broad range of films being shown at appropriate times. It must also be recognized that such a remedy would increase the costs of distributors and exhibitors because of the need to renegotiate the house nut each time the number of performances of the main film fell below the number that was assumed when setting the nut.

## Influence or control over admission prices

8.148. Asked whether the influence or control they exercised over exhibitors' admission prices caused those charges to be higher than they otherwise would have been, the leading distributors told us that, in practice, they did not exercise influence or control over admission prices. They also said that because rental payments were based on box office returns, and given the distributor's investment in the film, it was only reasonable that the distributor should be consulted before an exhibitor reduced its admission prices, thereby affecting the distributor's share of the box office.

8.149. The leading distributors said that exhibitors' interests were not necessarily identical to those of distributors. A price reduction could, they said, reduce box office receipts, leading to reduced returns for both exhibitor and distributor, but give the exhibitor a more than compensating increase in profits from sales of ancillary, high-margin products such as popcorn, the profits from which were not shared with the distributors. They argued that it would be inequitable if exhibitors could unilaterally change prices, and alter the economic bargain, in a way which might benefit themselves but not the distributors. If exhibitors had such freedom, distributors might have to protect their economic position in some other way, such as requiring guaranteed minimum rentals.

8.150. Buena Vista said that it was a misconception to state that distributors exercised influence or control over exhibitors' admission charges. It had never sought a price increase for any particular film, nor had it refused a request made in advance for a decrease in prices for special groups or at slack times. It argued that it was not unreasonable that it should require some consultative mechanism *vis-à-vis* admission prices, in the light of the investment risk that had been taken. It said that this was even more understandable in the UK where the distributor took a smaller share of box office revenue than in other European countries where admission prices were higher. Because the method of calculating rental payments was decided essentially by the exhibitor, it was even more essential that the distributor should have some consultative mechanism over admission prices.

8.151. Buena Vista submitted that it was in nobody's interest for admission prices to be too high. It seemed reasonable, given the significant investments by both exhibitors and distributors and the substantial rise in admissions, to assume that the risk/reward balance between exhibitors and distributors for their respective investments had worked to the advantage of cinema-goers.

8.152. Columbia told us that it did not seek to influence, still less control, admission prices charged by exhibitors. It merely sought to protect its economic position and to obtain the benefit of its bargain with exhibitors. In practice, it usually consented to exhibitors' price promotions when asked in advance, even though, in many cases, the increase in admissions would be unlikely to compensate it for the price reductions. Because rentals were tied to box office receipts, any reduction in the admission price would reduce Columbia's revenues. It seemed only fair that it be consulted before such a change was made. Columbia was not aware of any other product or service where a retailer would be entitled to pass back retail level discounts to the supplier without obtaining prior consent. Columbia emphasized that nothing in the *Standard Conditions* prevented an exhibitor from announcing that it would generally reduce its prices for the future. The distributor then knew the position and could negotiate rental terms accordingly.

8.153. Fox denied that it influenced the setting of prices by exhibitors which showed its films: it had not prohibited exhibitors from lowering their prices when they wished to do so. The inclusion in contracts of the right to do so arose as a direct consequence of the manner in which the exhibitors required rental payments to be calculated. In order to ensure that its fee was not reduced unduly, the distributor needed to be able to prevent the exhibitor from trying to increase income from advertising and concessions, the benefit of which accrued solely to the exhibitor, by reducing admission prices and hence box office receipts. Fox suggested that, if exhibitors were willing to assume a greater proportion of the risk, it might not be necessary for a distributor to retain some control over admission prices. By way of example, it said that such control would not be necessary if the distributor were to receive a per capita fee of £x per ticket sold.

8.154. UIP argued that distributors had a direct and real interest in the level of admission prices. Reserving the right to approve any change in admission prices safeguarded the distributor's return. Without this control, an exhibitor could reduce the return to the distributor, while increasing its own return, by reducing admission prices so as to enhance admissions and concession sales. UIP told us that, in practice, it had rarely intervened in the pricing decisions of its exhibitors. It had never resisted bona fide reductions which were not designed to sacrifice box office revenue simply to increase concession income.

8.155. UIP said that an alternative system could exist, whereby the distributor was entitled to a share of notional box office calculated on a per capita basis. It would be prepared to discuss operating such a system with individual exhibitors. UIP's impression was that such a system would make it harder for exhibitors to charge lower admission prices, since they would bear all of the cost of reducing prices. The system might, therefore, offer exhibitors less real scope for price experimentation that existed currently.

8.156. Warner Distributors submitted that the ability to exercise some control over ticket prices was essential given that distributors' rental was calculated as a percentage of box office receipts. The distributor had an interest in ensuring that the full value of the film which was licensed to the exhibitor was realized by appropriate admission charges.

8.157. Warner Distributors said that the exhibitor's interest and the distributor's interest did not entirely coincide, because the distributors did not currently share in the income generated for the exhibitor by the highly profitable sale of refreshments. For the exhibitor there was a strong incentive to reduce the ticket price in order to attract a larger audience and increase sales of refreshments and hence the profits generated from these. Such a move might be to the disadvantage of the distributors, who would suffer the loss of revenue from ticket prices without being compensated by a share in the proceeds from refreshments or by an overall increase in the number of admissions. The shift in source of income would benefit the exhibitor, whilst the overall 'price' of the cinema visit to the consumer would remain static or increase. There was a further incentive to exhibitors to attract audiences by lower ticket prices since this might enable them to charge more for advertising on screen. The advertising revenue in a particular cinema depended on its audience figures. Again, the distributor did not share in this income, which for the five leading exhibitors was more than £12 million in 1992.

8.158. In Warner Distributors' experience, disputes over the level of admission prices were very rare. The distributors' power had not inhibited the ability of exhibitors to offer price reductions and innovative price packages where appropriate. Thus, many exhibitors offered cheaper tickets for pensioners or students and offered lower prices overall for some matinée performances when attendances were generally low. In fact, on certain occasions, particularly in relation to West End cinemas, Warner Distributors had succeeded in persuading exhibitors not to increase seat prices.

## SFD *Standard Conditions*

8.159. We asked the leading distributors whether the widespread observance of the *Standard Conditions* strengthened the market power of distributors and exacerbated the anti-competitive effects of certain practices which were covered by the *Standard Conditions*. We also asked them to comment on the possible remedies detailed in paragraph 7.90.

8.160. The leading distributors acknowledged the widespread use of the *Standard Conditions* in exhibition licences but did not accept that this was anti-competitive. The *Standard Conditions* were convenient both for distributors and exhibitors and had been negotiated between the SFD and the CEA, not imposed by the distributors. Some argued that, in the absence of the *Standard Conditions*, distributors would still require substantially the same conditions and these would appear in the individually negotiated contracts. In any event, the most important provisions were the subject of separate negotiation between distributor and exhibitor. The leading distributors tended to favour the continuing use of the *Standard Conditions* which, they believed, offered administrative convenience and cost savings. Some, however, said that they would not object to negotiating individual conditions with exhibitors. The leading distributors indicated that the SFD would be willing to consider any amendments to the *Standard Conditions* which the CEA might wish to suggest on behalf of the exhibitors.

8.161. Buena Vista accepted that there was widespread use of, and reference to, the *Standard Conditions*, but noted that the most important commercial provisions were frequently the subject of separate negotiation giving rise to express variations on the face of the licence document. Observance therefore was not slavish. It did not accept that certain practices covered by the *Standard Conditions* were anti-competitive. Buena Vista submitted that, in the absence of either the SFD or the *Standard Conditions*, each distributor would still require conditions in substantially the same form, albeit promulgated individually, for the economically efficient and effective organization of its distribution system.

8.162. Buena Vista said that the distributors' share of the UK box office had decreased over the last five years and was a lower percentage than in any other European or industrialized country, other than Australia. The amount obtained from the smaller independent exhibitors was lower, in percentage terms, than the average share from other exhibitors. It was, therefore, difficult to accept that the widespread use of the *Standard Conditions* had any effect on distributors' market power.

8.163. Buena Vista noted that the MMC's 1983 report did not find the concept of the promulgation of the *Standard Conditions* objectionable. No recommendations were made in that respect. Buena Vista argued that, because the market was considerably more competitive than was the case in 1983, it was unnecessary to recommend the withdrawal and/or prohibition of the *Standard Conditions*. Some form of standard conditions would, in any event, be reinvented by distributors and exhibitors.

8.164. Columbia said that the *Standard Conditions* were not imposed upon unwilling exhibitors. The development of industry standard terms, negotiated between the CEA and the SFD (parties of equal bargaining power), benefited both distributors and exhibitors. There was, it said, no evidence that the *Standard Conditions* strengthened the market power of the distributors. The principal purpose of the *Standard Conditions* was to establish the 'small print' terms for film rental. They allowed the distributors and exhibitors to devote their limited negotiating time to the key issues such as price and length of booking. Columbia had received no complaints about the conditions.

8.165. Because the main economic terms of film rental were negotiated individually, Columbia did not believe the *Standard Conditions* represented a material co-ordination of behaviour nor a restriction of competition. It was sensible and necessary to provide in the *Standard Conditions* that certain matters were fixed unless otherwise agreed; in particular, that there were no arbitrary changes of screening schedules or admission prices without consent. An agreed and stable system provided the framework within which rental agreements could be agreed with the maximum of certainty and the minimum of difficulty.

8.166. There was, Columbia argued, no evidence of anti-competitive or unfair practices which could justify the proposed remedy. If the *Standard Conditions* were prohibited, it seemed likely that the larger distributors and exhibitors would produce their own standard contracts with many 'small print' terms. The larger companies would be likely to impose their own standard terms on the smaller. Columbia said that it was hard to see how such a situation would be preferable to the present one, in which the terms were negotiated by parties of equal bargaining power. The present use of the *Standard Conditions*, if anything, redressed the imbalance of market power between individual contracting parties and saved unnecessary legal costs in contract negotiations and litigation.

8.167. For the reasons set out in paragraph 8.24*(h)*, Fox did not accept that the use of the *Standard Conditions* had the effects described, nor did it believe a remedy to be necessary. While it had no objection to abandoning the *Standard Conditions*, Fox believed contracts negotiated individually between distributor and exhibitor would include certain of the terms presently included in the *Standard Conditions*, as these were commercially sensible and would be acceptable to both parties.

8.168. UIP believed the *Standard Conditions* offered the industry savings in terms both of time and money. It would, however, be possible, albeit with greater transaction costs, for UIP to devise and negotiate its own standard terms with exhibitors. A switch to a series of individually negotiated standard terms could be a heavy burden for smaller distributors and exhibitors who might resist the move towards a different set of terms for each trading relationship. Such resistance would be understandable when the present terms had only a very limited number of provisions which affected competition.

8.169. Warner Distributors said that, although it was true that the *Standard Conditions* were routinely incorporated into the licence agreement with the exhibitors, those conditions which were usually the most controversial were still the subject of negotiation between the parties. It was only in exceptional circumstances that Warner Distributors would insist on observance of the letter of the *Standard Conditions*. This was particularly the case with regard to the provisions concerning minimum exhibition periods, where it was often not possible or desirable to seek to enforce the contractual terms if the public reaction to a film was disappointing. Similarly, with regard to the provisions on cinema ticket prices, disputes which arose were resolved by negotiation and there was usually compromise on both sides.

8.170. Warner Distributors did not believe that the fact that these matters were included in the *Standard Conditions* had any effect on their implementation in practice or could be said to exacerbate the practices. Members of the SFD were not bound to use the *Standard Conditions* but might vary or not apply them as they thought fit. The fact that they were widely incorporated by distributors into their licences simply indicated that they formed a convenient legal framework within which the negotiations over the more important terms of each individual licence could take place.

8.171. Warner Distributors said that, if the *Standard Conditions* were abandoned, distributors would have to draw up their own terms and conditions covering the same areas as those covered by the SFD terms. It was difficult to see why such terms would necessarily lead to greater flexibility or an improvement to the exhibitors' current position. A requirement that the SFD withdraw its *Standard Conditions* and a prohibition on any further such terms would not, in Warner Distributors' view, have any material impact on the operation of the market.

## Vertical links to US production companies

8.172. The leading distributors were asked whether distributors and exhibitors with vertical links to US production companies used their position in the interrelated markets for distribution and exhibition to keep out competition from independent producers operating outside North America. They were also asked to comment on the allegation (see paragraph 9.11) that they reserved dates with the two main circuit exhibitors (MGM Cinemas and Odeon) many months in advance, simply by putting forward a title which might relate to a film in the planning stage; and that if the film did not materialize the date was kept for another film from the same distributor. We also put to them the assertion that independent distributors were unable to reserve screen space in this way and that the practice prejudiced their efforts to get films screened.

8.173. We also asked the leading distributors to comment on the suggestion that the output deals under which Hollywood studios agreed to sell their films to BSkyB sometimes included provisions which linked the deal to the budget for the UK theatrical release of the films (see paragraph 9.3). Thus the deal might be triggered, or the payment by BSkyB increased, if spending on prints and advertising for the UK theatrical release exceeded certain figures. Such provisions, it was argued, gave distributors an artificial incentive to increase release budgets above what they would otherwise be.

8.174. All the vertically integrated leading distributors denied that they used their position in the interrelated markets for distribution and exhibition to keep out competition from independent producers operating outside North America. To differing degrees, they argued that they were prepared to encourage the making of such films and to distribute them.

8.175. Buena Vista was unable to comment upon the activities of those distributors with links to US production companies which also had exhibition interests in the UK, particularly as it had no such interests itself. Based on its experience, it said that while it was not aware of any duty to facilitate the making of films by any producers, whether inside or outside of North America, Walt Disney did in fact do so, offering the same terms to producers from outside North America as it offered to North American producers. Having entered into arrangements with non-US-based producers, it did not stultify those arrangements by failing to distribute their films.

8.176. Buena Vista denied that it reserved space with exhibitors. It drew an analogy between a major retail outlet and an exhibitor. Both required a reliable and consistent source of high-quality product. A major retailer achieved this by long-term arrangements with selected manufacturers. Likewise, an exhibitor might well examine the market-place and find that the most consistent suppliers of films were certain major distributors. It was of no use to an exhibitor to have an expensive facility if there was no product for it.

8.177. Buena Vista said that the lead time for mounting the proper campaign for the release of any film was a minimum of three months and, ideally, six months. It constantly updated exhibitors as to the likely product that it would have available in the coming year. At first, it could provide only a synopsis of the story, but as time went on it would furnish artwork or photographic materials and, finally, a screening print. There was no contractual commitment between an exhibitor and Buena Vista in relation to any film, until the exhibitor had had an opportunity to view the film in question. Only after such a viewing would firm contractual arrangements be negotiated and, possibly, entered into. Discussions with exhibitors were not confined to any one group of cinemas. It was thus wholly erroneous to describe this regular updating of information and of product availability as a feature of alignment. Instead, it was merely a normal function of a competitive market-place.

8.178. Responding to the suggestion about BSkyB (see paragraph 8.173), Buena Vista told us that it was only on very rare occasions that conditions relating to the UK theatrical release of a film were relevant to the arrangement between Disney and BSkyB. Buena Vista emphasized that it did not artificially inflate release budgets based on contractual arrangements between an affiliated company and BSkyB.

8.179. Columbia contested the distinction drawn between those distributors with links to US production companies and those with no such links. For its own part, it had neither the ability nor the desire to discourage the production of non-Hollywood films. It cited *The Remains of the Day*, *Mary Shelley's Frankenstein* and *Mary Reilly* as examples of films produced in the UK by its affiliated production companies. Columbia said that its primary business purpose was to distribute in the UK the output of its Hollywood affiliates. There was, it said, nothing unfair or anti-competitive about such a purpose. Columbia, and other US-linked distributors, had distributed many non-Hollywood films, such as *Gandhi*, *Hope and Glory*, *The Last Emperor*, *White Mischief*, *The Remains of the Day* and *Bitter Moon*. Columbia also acted as distribution arm for Sony Pictures Classics whose business was to pick up rights to distribute non-North American films. It denied that it had the market power which would allow it to impose its films upon exhibitors. Nor did it believe the overall failure of British films was attributable to distorting practices on the part of US-linked distributors. British audiences had, it said, indicated a preference for US rather than British films.

8.180. Columbia told us that it informed Odeon of films in production and sometimes put forward a proposed release date before the film was completed. This was, it said, a necessary part of the planning process, especially for those titles where specific dating periods were crucial to marketing success. This practice was not, however, invariably followed, since, in many instances, the time lag between US and UK release meant that the film was available for viewing by Odeon before the question of scheduling arose. An example could be a film which was being shot with the intention of being screened the following Christmas. In such cases, Columbia would put Odeon on notice, at an early date, that it was proposing a Christmas release and would ask Odeon to 'pencil in' dates for screening. The request would almost invariably be made when the film was committed or under way. Columbia could not think of any recent examples where Odeon had been asked to pencil in a date for a film which might not materialize. Columbia emphasized that Odeon was literally asked to 'pencil in' a diary date. It was fully understood by both parties that Odeon was not committed to a specific date and that a diary entry which was pencilled in by Odeon might be erased by it in the future. Odeon would have similarly 'pencilled in' requests for the Christmas date from other distributors, leading distributors as well as independents. At some point, still early on, Odeon might have half a dozen films 'pencilled in' for the two or three release slots available over the period. In this situation, to the extent that Odeon was in a position to view one of the 'pencilled in' films before the others, that film would, in many cases, be confirmed in priority over the others, whatever its provenance. There were any number of cases where Columbia had requested that a certain film be 'pencilled in' for a specific date, but had lost the date because a competitor's film (independent or major) was available for viewing earlier.

8.181. Columbia's experience was that Odeon virtually never committed to a release schedule until its chief booking officer or a senior member of his team had seen the film. There were extremely rare cases where the point at which Odeon could view a film was so close to the release date as to make a change in plan improbable. Typically, this could arise when the UK release was set to coincide with the US release, and the film in question was only completed a few days before the US release. But even in these cases, the decision to book the film in this fashion would have been made by Odeon based on its assessment, from the production details, that the film would be a very commercial proposition. In certain cases, distributors and exhibitors shared an expectation that a particular forthcoming film would be a commercial success. Such expectation would be based upon the stars, the subject, and the track record of the director. Expectations were often also set high for sequels of major hit films (although the commercial success of sequels could never be guaranteed). Where a film was pencilled in for a specific date and there was a high expectation of success, there was clearly a strong likelihood that Odeon would go firm upon the date first proposed, having seen the film. However, the decision was always made by Odeon after viewing, and not before.

8.182. Columbia believed independent distributors were in no different a position. To give a strictly hypothetical example, if Guild (which distributed *Basic Instinct*) picked up the rights to a hypothetical *Basic Instinct 2*, with the same female lead, Columbia believed Odeon would pencil in and, in due course, confirm a release date for Guild, as it would do for Columbia or Buena Vista. Columbia stated categorically that there was no system whereby 'slots' were reserved for an unspecified Columbia film. If Odeon pencilled in a Columbia film but then decided (after viewing) not to agree the proposed release date, then that release date would be available for competing distributors. Columbia would have no right to nominate another film in its place.

8.183. [

*Details omitted. See note on page iv.*

]

8.184. Fox believed that, because the market was competitive, each distributor and exhibitor was motivated to acquire the most attractive films available, from whatever source. A distributor would wish to cover its fixed overheads by maintaining a constant supply of new films. This was particularly important where the number of new films available from its associated production company was relatively low, as was the case for Fox. If a distributor were to decline to handle a commercially promising independently-produced film, it would be picked up by another distributor. Competition between distributors for such films protected their access to the market. In 1992 the majority of films distributed by Fox were independently-produced.

8.185. Fox submitted that there was no evidence that vertically integrated US companies discouraged the making of independent films. It noted that vertical integration was not limited to US-owned companies. Nor did it believe exhibitors refused to show independently-produced films, save for reasons related to their commercial viability. Any difficulty experienced by independent producers in gaining access to screens was, it argued, attributable to the shortage of screens and the frequent lack of widespread appeal of their films. It was not attributable to vertical integration among US-owned producers, distributors and exhibitors.

8.186. Fox told us that it did not 'cover' dates in the way described in paragraph 9.11. When Fox booked films on a provisional basis, the provisional booking would relate to a specific film and a specific intended release date. Any such booking was, however, subject to viewing by the relevant exhibitor and the exhibitor would be entitled, if it did not wish to take the film, to withdraw from any provisional arrangement which had been made. Fox would not then be entitled to require the exhibitor to take another film which Fox was then seeking to distribute.

8.187. Responding to the assertion about BSkyB (see paragraph 8.173), Fox said that, when deciding on how to release a film for the theatrical market, it would not take into account its parent studio's agreement to supply films to BSkyB. At no point did it take into account any incremental income when deciding on the amount of money to be put into promoting a theatrical release: the potential loss was too great for such an approach to be justified. It would not release a film theatrically which it thought would not recoup its costs simply in order to trigger a deal with BSkyB. Nor would it overspend on publicity to achieve the same end.

8.188. UIP said that other producers had equal access to the so-called vertically integrated exhibitors. If they offered films which were attractive to exhibitors and consumers, they would be shown. Vertical links did not keep out competition from independent producers operating outside North America.

8.189. Distributors in the UK were, UIP said, able to facilitate independent production by picking up the films of independent producers. UIP and its sister company had done so and their ultimate parent companies had financed independent productions. It believed that the terms on which it distributed films for independent producers were fair and competitive; if it did not offer such terms, the film would inevitably be picked up by a competitor. It noted that Lord Attenborough had recently expressed the view that UIP offered fair terms.

8.190. UIP said that, beyond picking up independent films, a distributor could facilitate independent production only if it were to give financial assistance to the producer. While UIP and other distributors occasionally did so, this was not the role for which they were principally qualified, nor was it one that could reasonably be expected of them. UIP was unclear how an exhibitor could seek to facilitate independent production, other than by dealing with films of independent producers on a non-discriminatory basis. Its experience was that exhibitors did trade in this manner. They would readily drop the film of a US studio if a more attractive film was offered, whether or not that film was an independent production. Indeed, if any bias had been observed, it was in favour of UK films.

8.191. UIP said that it did not discourage European production. It did not block UK screens by forcing films on exhibitors or by imposing unreasonable minimum exhibition periods and restrictions on screen use. It told us that in most areas, and for many periods of the year, there was ample screen space to accommodate the films of the US studios and of independent producers. Moreover, new screens continued to offer new viewing opportunities. Where, at a particular time, or in a particular area, there might be a temporary shortage of screens, exhibitors had enhanced negotiating power and would always choose the films which they believed were the most commercially promising. They regularly rejected UIP films and accepted films from other US studios and from independent producers.

8.192. UIP told us that it had discussions with MGM Cinemas and Odeon (as it did with other exhibitors) in respect of the 'positioning' of films which were not yet available for release and which probably no one in the UK would have seen at that stage. However, such discussions were always provisional in nature, subject to viewing of the film by the exhibitor and to satisfactory negotiations: either the exhibitor or UIP might decide that the film should not be exhibited at a particular MGM Cinemas or Odeon theatre at the date discussed. There was no agreement or understanding, between UIP on the one hand and MGM Cinemas or Odeon on the other, that if a particular film was not exhibited on the date discussed, the exhibitor must exhibit another UIP film on that date. Sometimes a UIP film which MGM Cinemas or Odeon did not take at the date originally envisaged would be replaced with another UIP film: sometimes with third party product—MGM Cinemas or Odeon had no obligation to UIP.

8.193. There was, UIP said, no reservation of screen space—just tentative planning. UIP would expect MGM Cinemas and Odeon to plan all releases on a tentative basis with all distributors but had no direct knowledge on this. UIP believed this tentative 'positioning' of films to be a sensible and flexible practice for both distributors and exhibitors. The practice could have an anti-competitive effect only if MGM Cinemas and Odeon applied it to tentative bookings in a discriminatory manner.

8.194. Regarding arrangements with BSkyB (see paragraph 8.173), UIP submitted information about its affiliated company's contractual arrangements with BSkyB which, it said, demonstrated that there was no artificial incentive for it to increase its theatrical release budgets.

8.195. Warner Distributors told us that its role was to gain the maximum exposure and hence revenue, for the films which it was licensed to distribute in the UK, and to compete effectively with all other films, whether they were made and distributed by the other major studios, by independents based in the USA or by independents based outside the USA. There was no policy of competing more strongly against non-US films or against independent films.

8.196. With regard to the encouragement of the making and distribution of independently-produced films, Warner Distributors said that it played an important part in facilitating the involvement of the Warner Bros group in such films through advising on their likely success in the UK. The group had an ongoing relationship with European-based independent producers. David Puttnam, for example, had a production deal whereby Warner Bros financed the development and production of various projects. Similar relationships had existed in the past with other producers. Warner Distributors also suggested films to Warner Bros International if it saw a film which it believed had potential.

8.197. Warner Distributors told us that the Warner Bros group financed films which had a strong European theme and involved independent producers, for example *Round Midnight*, *Vingt Ans Déjà* and *Frantic*. It also noted that a number of its major films had been made in Europe, for example *The Shining*, *Batman*, *Greystoke*, *Little Shop of Horrors*, *Gorillas in the Mist*, *The Secret Garden*, *Black Beauty*, *Memphis Belle*, *Ladyhawke* and most recently, David Puttnam's latest film, *The War of the Buttons*. Warner Bros had, it said, financed the production of some of the most influential European films over a long period, including *O Lucky Man*, *A Clockwork Orange*, *La Nuit Americaine*, *Barry Lyndon* and *Amarcord*.

8.198. In the light of this, Warner Distributors submitted that there was no substance in the complaints that it failed to facilitate, or discouraged, the production of independently-produced non-US films, or that it failed to distribute such films or did so on unfavourable terms. More generally, it had to be recognized that the factors which determined the scale of independent film production, particularly outside the USA, were varied and included the willingness of financiers to invest in film production and government policies on subsidies and taxation. Warner Distributors was not aware of a significant body of opinion, among those expressing concern at the state of the British film industry, which regarded the conduct in the market of distributors and exhibitors as a material factor in influencing the volume of film production here. On the contrary, many of those currently putting forward various proposals to encourage investment in British film-making recognized the importance of vertical integration in the success of a film industry.

8.199. With regard to the suggestion that exhibitors refused to show independent non-US films despite their commercial prospects, Warner Distributors was not aware of such conduct ever having taken place. On the occasions where it had distributed an independently-produced film, there had not been particular reluctance from exhibitors to show the film, provided they were satisfied that it was commercially viable. Warner Distributors rejected any suggestion that it obliged exhibitors to take all or most of its films. The organization of the industry, as it presently operated, benefited exhibitors in ensuring for them a steady stream of product which had been effectively promoted and advertised by distributors. There were no 'tying' provisions, either formal or informal, and Warner Distributors did not believe independent films of value were being excluded from the market by any conduct on the part of distributors or exhibitors.

8.200. Warner Distributors confirmed that it set provisional release dates for its films with its aligned circuit (MGM Cinemas), often many months in advance. It was typically the case that Warner Distributors would set a date furthest in advance for those films which it considered were likely to be the biggest box office successes. It was very rare for a film, which it considered to be a likely blockbuster, to be 'dated' and then never be released. Where a film which had been provisionally dated did not materialize, Warner Distributors would try and keep the date for another of its films. However, all release dates were only set provisionally and exhibitors would not hesitate to substitute another distributor's film if they thought it was stronger.

8.201. Warner Distributors said it was true that the leading distributors would tend to discuss release dates earlier than independents. This was largely because the independents tended not to know which films they would be handling until much nearer the release date. Clearly, the leading distributors would know what films were in production and could estimate further in advance when a film would be made available to them. Nevertheless, the exhibitor's choice of which film to show on any given date would primarily be determined by its assessment of that film's merits as against competing films. If the independent distributor was handling a strong enough film it would have no difficulty finding screen space.

8.202. Regarding arrangements with BSkyB (see paragraph 8.173), Warner Distributors told us of the various criteria which determined whether a film qualified for inclusion under its affiliated company's output agreement. In the few cases where qualification depended on the nature and extent of a film's theatrical release in the UK, only one film had been released by Warner Distributors which satisfied the relevant criteria and, in that case, Warner Bros did not control the television rights. Warner Distributors assumed that the BSkyB agreement had not influenced Warner Bros International's decision on films' release strategies.

## Overseas decision-making

8.203. Asked whether overseas-based decision-making made the market less responsive to consumer preferences than if decisions were made in the UK, the leading distributors argued that there was no evidence that overseas decision-making, to the extent that it took place, forced on to the UK market films that might otherwise not have been exhibited. Although overseas parent companies decided which films should be distributed and how much should be spent on prints and advertising, they relied on the local expertise of their UK subsidiaries and rarely overruled their recommendations.

8.204. Buena Vista told us that the advice tendered by the UK distribution executives was almost always accepted. This meant that a film would typically not be distributed in the UK where the local management felt it was unlikely to attract a sufficient audience. This freed up screens for other films.

8.205. Columbia said that decisions as to which films to distribute were made jointly by local executives with great expertise in the UK market and by US-based executives. Although ultimate decisions were made in the USA, release strategies were effectively determined by its UK-based employees.

8.206. Columbia argued that the current practice was not in any way anti-competitive. A practice either did or did not 'prevent, restrict or distort competition'; it was irrelevant in which country the decision to implement the practice was made. It queried whether overseas-based decision-taking was 'conduct' capable of restricting competition within the test of section 6(2) of the Act. Columbia said that, in any event, the suggestion that overseas decision-making made the market less responsive to consumer preferences was unfounded. In 1993 films released by the five US-linked distributors together earned 80 per cent of all box office receipts. Columbia argued that it was obvious that these companies were extremely aware of and responsive to UK consumer preferences.

8.207. In Fox's experience, overseas-based decision-makers were influenced by the same motives as local decision-makers. Accordingly, the sharing of decisions with persons based overseas, to the extent that it occurred, did not make the market less responsive to consumer preferences. Those decision-makers were advised by Fox's UK management as to which films were likely to prove popular. It would be illogical to require the distribution of a film which the UK management believed would be unpopular, or to deny access to films which they felt would be successful.

8.208. UIP told us that it prepared recommendations for its sister company and the relevant studio as to how a film would perform in the UK. Each of the UIP partners reserved the ultimate decision on the release of its films but, in the vast majority of cases, each accepted the expert advice given by UIP. It was then up to UIP, subject to overview by the partner, to devise the most appropriate distribution strategy, responding to local preferences.

8.209. Warner Distributors said that it had a significant input into the decision whether a particular film would be released in the UK. The ultimate decision as to which films to exhibit rested with the owners of the cinema chains. Warner Distributors undertook considerable market research in terms of test screenings and audience surveys to ascertain changing trends in UK audience preferences and these influenced the decisions on how to market the film as well as, to some extent, decisions as to whether the film should be released in the UK. The results of the market research were sent, *inter alia*, to Warner Bros International. The corporate link with Warner Theatres had no influence on the terms and conditions on which films were supplied.

8.210. Warner Distributors suggested that the extent to which decisions of US film production companies influenced or determined what was shown on UK cinema screens reflected the fact that it was they who were able and willing to make the investment necessary to make films. Overseas decision-making did not, in Warner Distributors' view, make the market less responsive to UK consumer preferences. The global audience potential of a film was an increasingly important consideration for US production companies. Tastes among UK audiences were not markedly different from those of US audiences, save with regard, for example, to films centred on baseball, with which UK audiences were unfamiliar.

## Domination of the UK markets by US films

8.211. The leading distributors were asked whether the influence exercised by US companies in the UK markets for distribution and exhibition of films caused the markets to be dominated by US films, and whether the economic and cultural effects of this dominance were harmful. All the US-owned distributors strongly disagreed that there were any harmful economic and cultural effects arising from the success of US films. Most queried how such effects could be measured.

8.212. Buena Vista argued that it was a gross over-simplification to suggest that US films unfairly dominated the UK market and thereby excluded UK films or films produced by independent producers. Walt Disney, in common with all the Hollywood studios, engaged the services of independent producers from any country (including British production companies), provided they were judged to have a project that would appeal to a mass audience. Buena Vista believed that the 'disproportionate' success of films distributed by the US majors was attributable to consumer preference. The increase in admissions and the significant increase in the proportion of the box office attributable to US films since 1983 (whilst the proportion of such films available for distribution had fallen slightly) indicated that the consumer was showing greater interest in the cinema and, particularly, a preference for US films. The success of US films, it argued, was the best evidence of their quality and it believed such films possessed substantial variety. Buena Vista said that it sought to distribute some films with limited or specialist appeal and it argued that such films were distributed in totally different circumstances from, and were not affected adversely by the influence of, US films which were of general appeal. Buena Vista queried the alleged harmful effects to British culture and argued that it would not seem to be an appropriate part of the function of the MMC to consider matters of taste and culture. Buena Vista also noted that the vast proportion of box office receipts remained in the UK.

8.213. It was unclear to Columbia how to define or quantify cultural harm, or indeed what standpoint was to be used to judge this issue. It also wondered how a film's country of origin, as opposed to its content, was related to the issue of cultural harm. Columbia said that many of its recent films had won critical acclaim, including *Groundhog Day*, *The Remains of the Day*, *The Age of Innocence* and *Philadelphia*. These films all concerned universal human values and could not be said to be culturally harmful.

8.214. Columbia said that the effects of intervention in the market for the greater cultural good were hard to foresee. British film makers had not made many films recently with mass appeal. If the system were distorted to favour British films, it might foster the production of low quality British films for a subsidised market. There might also be a transfer of the viewing public to video and satellite television where they might be viewing films of lower cultural quality.

8.215. Fox believed US films would remain as popular in the UK if they were distributed and exhibited by UK-owned and -based companies. The influence exerted by the US companies did not, therefore, give rise to harmful economic effects; on the contrary, it reflected the outcome of competitive market forces. It submitted that there were no harmful effects to consumers if the dominance of US films resulted from consumers' preference for those films. It was often difficult to classify a film as being culturally British or American. Often a film reflected themes common to more than one culture, for example *Mrs Doubtfire*, *Star Wars*, *Crocodile Dundee* and *The Piano*. Fox suggested that in order to assess whether US films dominated British culture, it would be necessary to examine not only the prevalence of US films in UK cinemas, but also the prevalence of British product in other media and the effects on culture of other phenomena. It was impossible to quantify and evaluate the effects of US films in UK cinemas by viewing them in isolation from other important factors.

8.216. UIP pointed out that only one of its three owners was in fact a US company. It also told us that no producer could force films on to an unwilling market. If a film did not appeal to the public they would not go to see it. So-called US films attracted a significant share of box office receipts in this country because:

*(a)* they were produced by highly-skilled companies which competed internationally for film projects and for the 'talent' who would enhance a film's appeal;

*(b)* US film-makers more accurately read popular tastes than did film-makers in other countries;

*(c)* US film-makers invested far more in producing their films than did film-makers in other countries; and

*(d)* US films were made in the English language and the UK and the USA shared common cultural frames of reference.

8.217. UIP submitted that the success of a commercially attractive US film could prejudice the prospects of a more attractive UK film only if there were insufficient screen space for both films and US producers had the power to tie up that screen space, which was not the case. For most of the year and for most of the country, there was sufficient screen space to show all commercially attractive films and no producer had the power to tie up screen space for any significant period.

8.218. UIP said that there might be those who would like the UK public to be more susceptible to a different type of film. But the fact was that the public chose the films that they wished to see. It would be unthinkable to try, by official intervention, to divert readers from 'lowbrow' to 'highbrow' newspapers, nor could quotas be imposed on non-UK or non-European books. Yet some producers felt that it was fair to request regulation which would seek to divert viewers from US to UK films. Not only was this protectionism, and contrary to the principles of a free market and free competition, it was also misconceived. A film-goer was as unlikely to give up an evening watching *The Terminator* to watch *Much Ado About Nothing*, as a reader of *The Sun* was to switch to *The Independent*.

8.219. Warner Distributors did not believe that the influence of the US companies over the distribution and exhibition of films was the cause of the prevalence of US films in UK cinemas. Rather, this reflected two other factors: the strength of the US film production industry and the popularity of US films amongst the cinema-going audience. There was no doubt that US films appealed to the mass UK audience in a way that films made in Europe and popular with audiences there did not.

8.220. Warner Distributors noted that some UK and European films, made to a smaller budget and for a more sophisticated audience, achieved success both in the UK and abroad. Recent films, such as *The Crying Game* and *Enchanted April*, were considerably more successful in the USA than they were in the UK. French films, such as *Cyrano de Bergerac* or *Jean de Florette/Manon des Sources*, also reached a limited but appreciative audience here. But it was not possible to force the public to view films which some might regard as more worthy by removing from cinema screens the kind of films which the majority of the public chose to see, however regrettable British film producers and critics might find that choice. It would, therefore, be wrong to suggest that, in the absence of US product, British cinemas would be filled with high-quality European films appealing to a mass audience. Such films were not being produced for reasons which had nothing to do with the availability of distribution networks or cinema screens. The absence of US films would simply mean a drastic reduction in the number of films being released, since there was no European product available to fill such a vacuum.

8.221. Warner Distributors believed that to suggest the cultural effects of US films might be harmful was to make elitist assumptions about the comparative merits of US and European films which were not borne out by the facts. It would be wrong to regard all British films as 'highbrow' or 'improving' for the cultural health of the public. Most people with an interest in the cinema as an art form would agree that the cultural life of British people would be the poorer without the films of Woody Allen, Martin Scorsese, Robert Altman and Francis Coppola. Many of the most popular US films had the highest standards of creative invention, acting and technical achievement and would be regarded as classics of the cinema long after many European films had faded from the public's memory.

8.222. Warner Distributors said that British television provided a popular and widely accessible means for the expression of British culture and the exploration of domestic issues and concerns in programmes of the same length and with the same high production values as film. Many of these television programmes found a ready market overseas.

8.223. Warner Distributors argued that, although a proportion of the cinema box office receipts flowed through to US producers, there were positive economic benefits to the UK from the successful marketing of popular US films here. A huge amount was spent, effectively by the US production studios, on advertising and on print production in the UK. The US studios also provided important opportunities for British actors to gain a wider audience. It noted that the US film industry was present in the UK before the domestic industry began. In 1925 an estimated 95 per cent of films shown in Britain were of US origin.

## Co-ordination of release dates

8.224. Asked whether, by co-ordinating the release dates of their films, distributors reduced consumers' choice of first-release films at any given time and crowded out other distributors, the leading distributors acknowledged that information about likely release dates was widely available but denied that there was active collaboration between them. Decisions as to release dates were taken by each distributor in consultation with each exhibitor. A decision by one distributor to shift a release date to avoid head-to-head competition with another distributor's film would benefit consumers in that they would be able to see both films on different dates rather than having to choose one or the other. Smaller distributors remained free to set their own release dates.

8.225. Buena Vista argued that there was no evidence that leading distributors co-ordinated release dates. It denied that it did so. There was, it said, no active collaboration or participation between distributors as a whole in the co-ordination of release dates. Indeed, that was the area of greatest competition; the essence of successful distribution was to position product to achieve maximum audiences by outwitting competing distributors by, among other things, carefully planned release schedules. Buena Vista said that if a distributor shifted a release date to avoid significant head-to-head competition with another film, this would act in the consumer's favour. The consumer would be able to see both films on different dates rather than having to choose one or the other. Given that US films accounted for only 56 per cent of all films released in the UK in 1992, there seemed to be no evidence that other distributors were crowded out.

8.226. Columbia said that it was entirely open about its release dates, as were all distributors, but did not in any sense co-ordinate release dates with its competitors. Release dates were sometimes deferred when the market was congested; this ensured an even flow of releases. Columbia failed to see how the present system reduced consumer choice. As smaller distributors were free to select their release dates, there was no question of their being crowded out.

8.227. Fox denied that it co-ordinated release dates with other distributors. It fixed dates having regard to public information as to the dates on which competing films were to be released. Selection of release dates, far from being co-ordinated, was one aspect of the competitive strategy developed by distributors to maximize revenues from each film. Fox believed that, to the extent a distributor determined its release strategy in the light of public information regarding the release dates of its competitors, the resulting pattern of releases maximized consumers' opportunity see new films on first run.

8.228. UIP said that it did not participate in any discussions with other distributors about release dates. It did not, however, seek to keep its release dates secret and would respond to enquiries about release plans. Each distributor planned its release dates for the time when it thought its film would earn maximum revenue. Among other factors, it took into account how well its film was likely to perform against other films which it knew were scheduled for release. This information was available from, for example, advance publicity and from exhibitors who had already booked other films and who might counsel that release be set for another date. UIP submitted that a decision by a distributor, acting independently, to delay or advance a release date because of likely competition did not mean that there was co-ordination among distributors. It meant that the distributor believed a delay or advance would increase the film's box office. In any event, exhibitors had very considerable control over release dates. By way of example, UIP told us that, as a result of pressure from exhibitors, the release of *Beethoven's 2nd* was delayed. UIP said that it was a common plea from exhibitors that distributors should co-ordinate release dates, with a view to ensuring a regular flow of films. They complained that distributors regularly competed without any sensible co-ordination, frequently allowing films to open head-to-head. During the period 1990 to 1993, films with print runs exceeding 100 prints opened head-to-head on 52 occasions (ie on one in four occasions). UIP told us that it would not determine a release date so as to crowd out another distributor's film if it believed it could make a better return by delaying its release date.

8.229. UIP denied that it was able, under the UIP arrangements, to co-ordinate the release dates for its partners' films. It devised what it believed to be the optimal release plan for each film. This was discussed only with the partner who produced the film. Part of that discussion would focus on the release date. It was the partner who finally decided whether to go head-to-head with a competing film—no committee or individual in UIP could decide. In any event, the number of films with large print runs made by each partner was too small for the question of co-ordination to arise with any frequency. By the same token, UIP could not flood UK screens in order to keep out its competitors.

8.230. Warner Distributors said that the release dates set by distributors for their major features rapidly become widely known in the industry. There was some co-ordination of these dates, in the sense that other distributors would avoid releasing their own directly competing films on those dates. There was no co-ordination in the sense of distributors agreeing or sharing out dates amongst themselves. The reason why distributors attempted to co-ordinate release dates to some degree was to achieve precisely the opposite effect from that cited, namely to increase the range of films available to the consumer and to ensure that each distributor's film had the best chance of success. It must also be borne in mind that this activity was not limited to the leading distributors: the independent distributors were also concerned that their films should not be released at the same time as a film designed to appeal to the same audience.

8.231. Warner Distributors submitted that such co-ordination had no influence over the number of films made or released. It could not, therefore, reduce customer choice or affect other distributors as suggested. Nor did it allow only one major release on to the market at the same time. For example, at the time that *The Fugitive* was released by Warner Distributors, the highly successful *Sleepless in Seattle* was also released. Although these could both be described as mass appeal films, they were different in nature and appealed to different though overlapping audiences. The consumer therefore had a choice of what type of film to see, though they might not have a choice of two romantic comedies at the same time. Warner Distributors believed release co-ordination benefited the consumer as it meant that the release patterns of films better reflected the patterns of cinema-going. Most people preferred to go on one cinema outing every few weeks, rather than concentrate their viewing in one week followed by a period in which there were no films which they were interested in seeing. By spreading the release of similar films across the year, distributors helped to ensure that there was always a range of films available appealing to many different tastes.

## Exercise of market power by leading distributors

8.232. The leading distributors were asked whether, by exercising market power over independent exhibitors to persuade them to screen films which they would not otherwise choose, they made the exhibition market less responsive to consumer preference, harmed the exhibitors concerned by reducing their revenue, and harmed independent producers, whose films were handled by other distributors, by reducing their films' access to screens.

8.233. The leading distributors denied that they were involved in conditional booking. Each film was, they said, a unique product and the success of one could not be used to sell another. Exhibitors would only show those films which they considered would attract customers.

8.234. Buena Vista said that there did not seem to be any convincing evidence of the exercise of market power by leading distributors in a way that would lead to these consequences. The evidence suggested that independent exhibitors did not regard themselves as showing films they would not otherwise have shown. Consumer preferences were, it suggested, demonstrated by the fact that consumers went to the cinema twice as often as was the case a decade ago. Buena Vista had no knowledge of any harm done to independent distributors by way of a reduction in their revenue.

8.235. Columbia asserted that it had no market power on its own account; nor did it exercise market power jointly with any other distributors. It said that its lack of market power was evidenced by its frequent inability to 'sell' films to a large number of exhibitors. Columbia firmly denied that it engaged in the practice of conditional booking, either in the sense of imposing a requirement or expressing an expectation that exhibitors would book one film as a condition of receiving another. This had been Columbia's policy for many years. Columbia explained that its small team of salesmen had to conduct sales discussions by telephone with large numbers of exhibitors in a very short space of time. Inevitably the conversations would cover the availability of prints for more than one film. Columbia inferred from our survey results (see Appendix 4.4) that a minority of exhibitors had taken discussions of this kind as suggesting subtle or implied pressure on the exhibitor to agree to conditional bookings. No such pressure was in fact exerted. Columbia did not know why more exhibitors had identified Columbia as engaging in informal conditional booking than had identified other distributors but thought it might be due to the fact that the survey had been conducted at a time when it was selling two films—*The Remains of the Day* and *The Age of Innocence*—which were of great interest but which Columbia had decided, for marketing reasons, to issue in limited print numbers. Any complaint about conditional booking was refuted by the fact that many exhibitors who screened the popular *Sleepless in Seattle* declined other, less sought-after films which it was marketing during the same period.

8.236. Columbia denied any suggestion that the practices of the distributors had distorted or restricted competition within the exhibition sector. There had been very significant recent market entry into exhibition, with three major new operators of multiplex cinemas. Market entry through investment in multiplex cinemas remained open to a wide variety of leisure companies. In the independent sector there had been successes among entrepreneurial operators. Columbia was convinced that, with rising attendances, there remained the potential for further market entry and investment by independent operators in well-chosen locations.

8.237. Fox told us that, in practice, a distributor had little market power by virtue of its enjoyment of exclusive rights to license a film to exhibitors. At any time, a distributor had to compete with films of similar creative merit and films which offered exhibitors comparable opportunities for profitable exhibition. Accordingly, the uniqueness of a film conferred little market power on the producer or distributor. Fox said that independent exhibitors were, generally, in a particularly strong bargaining position since they were concentrated in monopoly markets where they controlled the only cinema. If a distributor attempted to force an exhibitor to show a film, the exhibitor would turn to any of the other distributors to obtain a suitable alternative.

8.238. UIP told us that it was structured so as to ensure that it did not restrict or distort competition. It had succeeded in delivering cost savings to its partners while leaving each with complete autonomy with respect to the sale and marketing of its films. The relationship between each partner and UIP was much the same as that between any producer and its distributor. The only difference of note was that UIP had a right of first refusal over the films of its partners. This was the basis of the joint venture and achievement of cost savings. It did not gain preferential terms or preferred access at UCI (with which it had two common owners) or MGM Cinemas (which was owned by UIP's third partner) by virtue of the common ownership links. UIP said that if it were to trade with UCI on a preferential basis, MGM Inc would object, and if it were to trade with MGM Cinemas on a preferential basis, Paramount and MCA Inc would object.

8.239. UIP described as misplaced the idea that the leading distributors, acting collectively or individually, forced independent exhibitors to screen films against their will. It was not aware of, and did not take part in, any collaboration between distributors. UIP said that it did not book films as part of a package; each was booked separately. UIP denied that any distributors suggested to independent exhibitors that they must take less appealing films if they wanted the blockbusters.

8.240. UIP submitted that no distributor had market power in relation to its films. Each film was a unique selling proposition. If a film seemed likely to be able to attract substantial box office revenue it would be easy to sell. A small independent distributor would be able to sell such a film even if it had no previous experience with a blockbuster. Equally, a leading distributor would be unable to sell a film if exhibitors believed it had no potential or less potential than an available competing film. Neither distributors nor producers earned goodwill from one film which could be transferred to the next. While a distributor like UIP might increase its market share in a particular year because it had a major success, it did not thereby achieve market power which would enable it to make greater demands for its next film or force it on unwilling exhibitors. UIP said that its success with *Jurassic Park* did not help it sell any of its partners' other films.

8.241. Warner Distributors also denied that it tied the provision of prints for successful films to that of a less successful film. The ability to persuade an exhibitor of the commercial value of the film was, it said, an important part of the distributor's function. Exhibitors and distributors had to maintain good working relationships since they had to negotiate and deal on a daily basis and from year to year. As part of maintaining this relationship, exhibitors might be prepared to accept films even where they had doubts about their commercial potential rather than simply 'cherry-picking' the safest, most popular films. This was a feature of any industry where suppliers and buyers had to conduct business together and was not related in any way to the alleged existence of the complex monopoly. Such a relationship also operated in the public interest in encouraging exhibitors to show films of uncertain appeal. Warner Distributors' salesforce were under instruction not to engage in conditional booking. They were paid a basic salary plus an annual bonus but the latter was not based on any quantifiable measure of their performance in booking films. There were many instances of independent exhibitors refusing to screen films offered to them by Warner Distributors, which nevertheless continued to offer them films on first release.

8.242. Warner Distributors did not accept that exhibitors had any realistic concerns that they would be refused supply of a successful film because they had refused to show an unsuccessful one. A distributor would be acting against its own interests if it did so. Competition between distributors was very fierce and ruled out such conduct.

8.243. Warner Distributors did not accept that the leading distributors had market power over independent exhibitors. The number of films released over the year was very large compared with the capacity of an independent exhibitor with a small number of screens to exhibit new releases.

## Exercise of market power by leading exhibitors

8.244. We asked the leading distributors whether the leading exhibitors, by exercising market power over distributors in order to secure preference over other exhibitors, harmed those exhibitors by reducing their access to popular films, particularly on first release. None of the leading distributors accepted that the leading exhibitors improperly exerted market power over distributors. If an exhibitor was favoured by a distributor, that was attributable to the quality of the exhibitor's cinema, location and the demographics of its audience.

8.245. Columbia claimed that, in contrast to distributors, exhibitors did have market power. This was due in large part to the historic market position of the two leading circuits and to the fact that the UK was significantly under-screened. This market power was further evidenced by the comparatively low percentage of box office receipts paid to the distributors. In the UK, average rentals were 38 per cent of box office compared with, for example, 48 per cent in France. If the share of rentals rose to the French levels, this would have a dramatic impact upon the profitability of distributors' UK operations. The only explanation of this dramatic loss of potential revenue was, it said, the exhibitors' market power.

8.246. Fox argued that an exhibitor might enjoy bargaining power by virtue of its control over the use of its screens. Such market power would result where, for example, an exhibitor had a monopoly in a particular locality or, with respect to an exhibitor with a large chain of cinemas, where a number of those cinemas enjoyed local monopolies. Fox noted that, despite the recent growth in numbers, the UK still had one of the lowest number of screens in Europe in relation to its population. Fox told us that independent exhibitors faced no effective competition from other exhibitors in 75 per cent of the markets in which they operated. These local monopolies accounted for over 70 per cent of all independent exhibitors. Moreover, in comparable situations, there was a greater probability that a typical Fox film would be exhibited by an independent exhibitor than by one of the two main circuits.

8.247. Fox said that the considerable market power of the leading exhibitors in certain local markets explained why it acceded to demands to bear the exhibitor's risk by covering its nut or break figure. Exhibitors did not provide independent verification for the calculations on which the nut and break figures were based and this illustrated the way in which exhibitors utilized their market power. The exhibitors' power also explained why Fox earned lower returns than did distributors of Fox films in other countries. Fox said that the exhibitors' insistence that rental payments be calculated by reference to nut and break figures discouraged distributors from granting concurrent exhibition rights to two or more exhibitors in the same geographic market. This was because the distributor would derive greater revenues if all box office takings covered the nut or break figure of one exhibitor rather than two or more. Fox emphasized that the adherence to nut and break figures was not confined to leading exhibitors. It was the preferred pricing method of all exhibitors because it transferred more of the risk of low attendance on to the distributor. The exhibitor recovered its claimed costs and, possibly, a profit margin before the distributor was free to share the revenues. Moreover, the exhibitor retained a higher share of the first increment of rent after its nut had been recovered than of subsequent increments. This further shifted risk to the distributor.

8.248. UIP said that to grant exclusivity in the vast majority of cases would be inconsistent with its objective of maximizing returns. Accordingly, it was not its practice to license on exclusive terms, but it would consider doing so where an exhibitor could demonstrate that the grant of exclusivity enabled an exhibitor to make a promotional effort which would ultimately enhance the value of the film to the benefit of the distributor and the public. Distributors and exhibitors should, however, be free to negotiate exclusivity on the few occasions when to do so would be likely to stimulate competition. UIP submitted that, in any event, a distributor with a popular film could not be forced to license it on exclusive terms. The strength of the film would enhance the distributor's negotiating position. UIP said that it did not grant preferentially favoured terms to leading exhibitors. Terms were broadly standard across the industry; deviations were highly unusual.

8.249. Warner Distributors referred to its attitude to exclusivity (see paragraphs 8.100 and 8.101). This practice was now rarely found in the industry and was not severe enough to have any appreciable effect on other exhibitors.

## Code of practice and associated machinery

8.250. The leading distributors were asked for their views on the suggestion that a code of practice, dealing with the supply of prints, minimum exhibition periods and restrictions on screen use, might be drawn up by agreement between the SFD and the CEA; and that machinery, for example a committee with an independent chairman, might be set up to resolve disputes between distributors and exhibitors concerning the application of the code to particular circumstances.

8.251. Most argued that such interference in the operation of the market was not required or justified and doubted whether such a scheme could work effectively. Disputes between exhibitors and distributors tended to arise on Monday morning, when programmes for the week commencing on the following Friday were discussed. The disputes had to be quickly resolved between the parties involved. An external party could not resolve disputes with sufficient speed.

8.252. Buena Vista said that the operation of the market did not warrant either direct prescriptive interference or a voluntary mechanism. There were, it suggested, so many variables currently dealt with by direct negotiation that it would be virtually impossible to draw up a code that would cover them in a practicable way.

8.253. Columbia contested the need for a disputes committee. It believed that the nature of the exhibitors' complaints could not practically be dealt with through such a committee. Such a committee would, it argued, increase the cost and time incurred in dealing with vexatious complaints. There was, it believed, a genuine mutual interest between exhibitors and distributors in dealing with specific complaints informally.

8.254. Fox contended that the remedy was unnecessary and could provide a forum for collusion among distributors and exhibitors. This would be contrary to the public interest. It was not, however, averse to the establishment of an independent body which could address issues which arose between distributors and exhibitors, provided that the interests of both were properly represented and that the costs were proportionate to the benefit.

8.255. UIP told us that it would be very difficult for a committee to convene quickly enough to contribute in any useful way to disputes over allocation terms. It was inappropriate for an additional committee or code of conduct to be established to deal with issues of minimum exhibition periods or restrictions on screen use. These issues were freely negotiated between distributor and exhibitor and were part of a package of financial terms. A code of conduct dealing with these terms would inevitably introduce a degree of rigidity to terms which had to be determined flexibly and had to be adjusted at very short notice when a film performed below expectations.

8.256. Warner Distributors did not believe such a system would work in practice. The fact that the previous TDC had fallen into disuse suggested that such a procedure had no practical value. It referred to the need for quick decisions to be made when distributors and exhibitors disagreed. There was no room for reference to a committee which might issue a decision many weeks after a film had ended its run. Nor would a code of practice be of any value. Guidelines would have to be qualified by many exceptions drafted so broadly as to be meaningless.

## Prohibiting contracts based on box office receipts

8.257. The leading distributors strongly opposed the suggestion that distributors and exhibitors might be prohibited from entering into contracts under which the consideration received by the distributor was linked directly or indirectly to the exhibitor's box office receipts. They pointed out that the sharing of box office receipts with exhibitors was the norm in most countries and enabled both parties to share the risks in what was a high-risk business. The proposed remedy would inevitably upset the risk-sharing that currently existed, to the disadvantage of both parties. Distributors had trouble envisaging a system of rental payments that was not linked to box office returns.

8.258. Buena Vista said that the existing system allowed for the sharing of risk and reward; it was totally in keeping with the philosophy of distributors and exhibitors and should not be disturbed. Even in those areas of UK copyright law where compulsory licences could be imposed by the Copyright Tribunal, or licensing schemes of collective copyright licensing bodies could be reviewed by that Tribunal, the Tribunal consistently recognized that payment to the copyright licensor measured by the licensee's receipts or turnover was fair and proper.

8.259. Columbia said that the remedy would dramatically change the nature of the industry, yet did not appear to arise from any complaints of anti-competitive behaviour. There was, it said, no basis for abolishing the present system. If the present system were abolished, exhibitors and distributors would need to negotiate a firm rental price or guarantee for each film. Faced with such a system, exhibitors might decline to book films without assured mass appeal or insist upon a much lower rental to cover themselves against the economic risk of screening such films. This could have a detrimental effect upon the production of films without mass appeal. The effect of such a remedy would, Columbia believed, be very uncertain given the lack of known precedent anywhere in the world. It would be liable to lead to new pricing structures based on opaque bilateral deals, which might operate to the benefit of the most powerful distribution and exhibition companies.

8.260. Fox believed it would be very difficult to devise a formula for sharing risk that would be as efficient as the current system. If relevant sharing arrangements were prohibited, distributors could resort to less efficient means of sharing risk or they could adopt more complex pricing arrangements to achieve substantially the same effect. Greater risk and costs could be imposed without any countervailing benefit.

8.261. UIP argued that distributors' and exhibitors' earnings must, in the long run, be related in some way to box office receipts, since these were the principal revenues derived from distribution and exhibition. The current formula was simply a feature of the desire in the industry to manage and share the risk involved. The proposed remedy would inevitably increase the risk to one or both parties and increase transaction costs. A system which divorced payments for products of uncertain appeal from the revenues from those products could be highly damaging. It could damage the prospects for releases of all but the potentially most successful films; and it could hinder future investment in the UK exhibition infrastructure.

8.262. Warner Distributors told us that it would be impossible to devise a payment system which was not linked directly or indirectly to box office receipts and which would not create severe difficulties for the future of film production as well as the distributors and exhibitors concerned. It suggested that it would be absurd for the current system to be replaced by a flat fee payment system which was the same regardless of how successful a film was expected to be or the size of the audience. Either the fee would be set at a very low level, so that the exhibitor could afford to screen risky films, or it would be set at a high level, so that the distributors and the producers could at least have a chance to recoup their investments. Either approach would have a disastrous effect on the range of films distributed in the UK. A low flat fee would mean that it was not worth releasing big budget films since there would be no chance of recouping the investment. While it might be worthwhile for US studios to release their films in the UK if they were prepared to regard it as a marginal activity, this would affect British-made films in a particularly adverse manner since their main market was the UK and their revenues would be greatly reduced. It would, therefore, greatly increase the difficulties already faced by British producers in obtaining finance for all but the most limited budget films.

8.263. Warner Distributors said that if the flat fee were set high, this would discourage exhibitors from showing films with limited audience appeal, since they would risk not being able to cover the cost of the rental payment. This would reduce the range of films available and make the market more reliant on blockbusters, which tended to originate in the USA. It would, therefore, increase the dependence on US films. It would also put many films beyond the budget of the smaller exhibitors. If the flat fee were not fixed for all films but was negotiated for each, it would substitute an imperfect risk-sharing arrangement for the one currently in operation. The level of the fee would represent the parties' assessment of the likely success of the film rather than the actual level as at present. This would throw the risk of the unexpected failure on the exhibitor. Most distributors and exhibitors would agree that it would be unfair to shift the risk in this manner, since it was the distributor who was responsible for the promotion of the film and the exhibitor had little influence over the audience size. It would also remove the incentive on producers and distributors to make the right decisions when deciding which films to make and release in the UK.

8.264. Warner Distributors submitted that the present system was typical of agreements for the licensing of intellectual property rights, where the licensee paid a royalty in accordance with the actual use made or revenue generated by the use of the licensed patent or copyright. It could not be suggested, therefore, that there was anything anti-competitive about the current system or that it operated in any way against the public interest.

## Distributors to commit revenues to independently-produced films

8.265. The leading distributors were asked to comment on the suggestion that they might be required to commit a specified proportion of their revenues from film rentals in the UK to the production of films by independent producers in the EC.

8.266. All the leading distributors opposed this suggestion, arguing that they did not operate discriminatory policies against independent producers located outside North America. They welcomed viable projects from whatever source but objected to what they saw as an obligation to subsidize independent European producers.

8.267. Buena Vista was not aware of any leading distributor which operated a discriminatory policy against independent producers from outside North America. There was, it said, no closed door policy so far as independent producers in the EC were concerned. It pointed out that the average share of box office takings paid by exhibitors in the UK was substantially lower than in other European countries. There was, it said, no justification for confiscating any of the rentals received for the purposes suggested in the remedy. Buena Vista also submitted that it was outside the scope of the terms of reference of the inquiry to consider the funding of production in the EC. In these circumstances, it had difficulty in understanding the relevance of a remedy of this nature and rejected the possible inference that films were supplied to exhibitors in a manner which had the object or effect of distorting or restricting competition in the production of films in the UK.

8.268. Columbia rejected the suggested remedy as unnecessary, unfair and wholly impractical. It would require Columbia to provide a portion of its already low film rentals to a fund of some kind, which would be disbursed on some unknown basis to independent EC producers. This would foster a subsidized film-making culture but it could not be guaranteed that the beneficiaries would be films of high artistic quality. A 'Film Council' appointed to disburse compulsory levies would be involved in making impossible decisions between the claims of competing film-makers and would be likely to encounter difficulties under the state aid rules of the Treaty of Rome.

8.269. Columbia noted that British film production was showing a recovery from its 1992 low point. It shared the overwhelming consensus within the industry that further revival required, above all, a more favourable tax regime. If there was a case for public subsidy this should be spent in training and other facilities for the benefit of the industry as a whole.

8.270. Fox said that the issue was not the volume of European films but their commercial viability. There was, it suggested, no shortage of European films. But although, in 1992, they accounted for 60 per cent of the films released in the UK, they accounted for only 20 per cent of box office receipts. This suggested either that the films were not popular or that they did not receive the promotional support which they needed. Fox said that it was not clear that the proposed remedy would solve these problems. It would, however, drive up admission prices and reduce the availability of popular films.

8.271. UIP suggested that the remedy would require producers and distributors, who had invested significant sums and taken significant risks in producing and distributing films, to pay a part of their legitimate reward to others, who either would not have made the same investment or taken the same risk. If they had done so, they would have succeeded and would not, therefore, need to be subsidized. UIP believed that the reallocation of revenue from film rentals in the UK in this way was unjustified. The incentive for producers to seek UK distribution of their films would be reduced if part of their revenue was to be paid as a tax to other producers. For some films, the potential tax on earnings might even be a disincentive to production. This would be against the interests of exhibitors and consumers.

8.272. UIP submitted that a subsidy to finance EC films, if thought desirable, should come from central Government funds as did, for example, subsidies for Covent Garden and the National Theatre. It should not be taken from the rewards of those who had invested in film production at their own risk. For these reasons, it was not thought appropriate for the popular to subsidize the less popular or cultural in any other industry. It could not be right to treat films differently.

8.273. Warner Distributors objected to the remedy, both as a matter of principle and because of its impracticality. The imposition of such a levy would, it said, result either in an increase in the level of film rental sought by the distributor or in a reduction in the level of royalty remitted to the producer. It did not believe there could be any justification for diverting the revenues available for investment in new production away from the companies which had demonstrated their ability to make such investment decisions successfully to those which had been substantially less successful in producing films that the public wished to see. The proposed levy would inevitably generate antagonism between US and European film-makers and might jeopardize the fruitful co-operation that currently existed.

8.274. Warner Distributors submitted that the diversion of funds to independent producers would make that investment less responsive to consumer tastes because those producers were not subject to the disciplines imposed by vertical integration. By divorcing the production function from the distribution function, and by dulling the need to take into account the commercial viability of a film, there would be a greater risk that producers would ignore audience tastes and that the film would fail. Subsidizing European film production would be likely to reduce further its competitiveness. The disadvantages of film production subsidy could be seen from the experience of other countries where such subsidies were widespread. In Germany, where all film production was subsidized, 72 films were produced in 1991 (compared with 51 in the UK), yet they accounted for 11 per cent of box office returns. In France, 156 films were produced in 1991, nearly all of which benefited from subsidies or favourable loans. Whilst they accounted for 43 per cent of all releases in France, they captured only 35 per cent of local box office revenues.

8.275. Warner Distributors argued that there could be no justification for a system under which revenues generated in the UK from the sale of seats for US films were used to finance films made outside the UK, and which might not appeal to UK audiences. This was especially true as there were no reciprocal arrangements under which British film-makers could benefit from income generated in other EC member states.

8.276. Warner Distributors submitted that previous experience with levies demonstrated that they performed no useful function. The Eady Levy was paid to British films in accordance with their box office receipts. When it became clear that the commercial viability of cinemas was under grave threat, the levy was phased out to relieve the pressure on admission prices and to encourage exhibitors to stay in business.

## Distribution/exhibition of films with a predominantly European theme or cultural content

8.277. We asked the leading distributors to comment on the suggestion that they might be required to distribute, and exhibitors to exhibit, a specified proportion of films with a predominantly European theme or other cultural content.

8.278. They opposed any suggestion that a quota system be introduced. Such a system would, it was argued, require them to distribute some films which would not be commercially viable. The ability of the public to see the films of their choice would be reduced and lower box office returns would be to the detriment of both distributors and exhibitors.

8.279. Buena Vista was utterly opposed to being unable to select the films which it distributed and to having imposed upon it a requirement to distribute films. It submitted that there was no evidence of consumer dissatisfaction with the range of films available. On the contrary, the evidence of increasing admissions suggested that the opposite was true. To require distributors to distribute films with European themes or other cultural content would be an unwarranted interference with freedom of expression. It would amount, directly, to a form of positive discrimination and, indirectly, to a form of censorship.

8.280. Columbia said that the proposed remedy would deprive it of the right to determine for itself which films it wished to sell. It already distributed a good number of films with European themes or content, such as *The Remains of the Day*. It did so in pursuit of its best business judgment and in pursuit of profit. The remedy would transform Columbia into a kind of cultural public utility, obliged to distribute films it might not deem profitable.

8.281. Columbia said that it was unable to understand the concept of films with a European theme or other cultural content. Not all European film production had high cultural content. Sub-titled and dubbed films commanded a very small audience in the UK. Columbia questioned whose benefit the remedy was designed to serve. It also believed that any form of compulsory European quota would be a gross distortion of the market which could ultimately work to the detriment of high-quality film-making. In any event, it lacked the business infrastructure to carry out the proposed remedy.

8.282. Fox said that the proposed remedy was unnecessary and would, in any event, infringe the European Convention on Human Rights. It would be inappropriate for the MMC to make any recommendation as to how European film production should be stimulated, particularly as the cultural and economic issues relevant to the promotion of a European film production industry were under active consideration by a variety of public bodies in the UK and in the EC. Fox suggested that concerns as to dominance by US culture needed to be considered in the context of other cultural industries, such as television. These industries fell outside the scope of the MMC's inquiry. As these wider issues could not be addressed, this issue was not an appropriate subject for recommendations.

8.283. In UIP's view, such a quota system would interfere unjustifiably with competition and would adversely affect the public interest. It would force exhibitors to choose a certain proportion of films on the basis of culture rather than commercial appeal; distributors would be forced to distribute films which they felt unable to distribute effectively. It would reduce the ability of the public to see the films they wanted to see at the venue and time of their choice. It would reduce box office returns to the detriment of exhibitors and to the detriment of those distributors and producers who had convinced exhibitors that their film was, on a competitive comparison, more attractive than any other available.

8.284. UIP suggested that, ultimately, certain exhibitors might have to close if forced to show films which the public would not pay to see. This could mean that screen capacity became scarce, to the detriment of distributors and consumers. It would restrict the number and variety of US films distributed in the UK and reduce the incentive to release films in the UK. It would also be extremely detrimental to the continued revival of the UK film market.

8.285. Warner Distributors described as elitist and unwarranted the assumption that European films were more artistic, more worthy or more culturally improving than US films. Any test of cultural content would be unworkable and there was a danger that such a criterion would simply become synonymous with commercially unviable. The remedy assumed that people would visit the cinema to see whatever film happened to be showing and that, by imposing quotas, it would be possible to force them to go to see films which someone else had determined they should want to see or which would be good for them. Warner Distributors suggested that, in fact, a quota system was more likely to reduce the number of people visiting cinemas. The existence of alternative ways in which films could be viewed and, more generally, the number of different leisure alternatives meant that there was no captive cinema audience. If exhibitors could not show the films that people wanted to see, they could not hope to remain viable. It was also likely to discourage further investment in cinema construction.

8.286. Because of the damage that quotas caused to exhibitors' revenues, there was a temptation to comply with the letter rather than the spirit. When quotas were applied in the 1950s and 1960s, this gave rise to the production of 'quota quickies', short films of poor quality which were shown before the main feature film simply to meet the quota requirement. This did nothing to improve the fortunes of British film-makers or to increase the public's appreciation of British films. Warner Distributors suggested that experience in the Spanish industry confirmed that such a policy caused widespread damage to distribution and exhibition and, paradoxically, to the production industry which it was designed to help.

## Divestment or reduction of interests in exhibition

8.287. The leading distributors were asked to comment on the suggestion that companies with interests in film production and/or distribution might be required to divest any interests in exhibition, or to reduce such interests below a specified level, for example 10 per cent of the total number of screens in the UK. This was opposed by the distributors concerned, on the grounds that it would serve no purpose since they did not favour their associated exhibitors. They also argued that it would act as a disincentive to further investment in the UK exhibition sector.

8.288. Buena Vista did not believe there was any justification for the remedy, particularly as the investment in multiplex cinemas had demonstrably benefited the UK cinema-goer.

8.289. Fox submitted that, if the objective was to reduce vertical integration in order to prevent foreclosure or to stimulate investment in exhibition, the remedy was unnecessary. There was, it suggested, no evidence that vertically integrated exhibitors enjoyed favourable treatment from their associated distributors/producers such as to damage other exhibitors. Indeed, the growth in the number of screens had resulted from investment by, *inter alia*, such vertically integrated groups.

8.290. UIP submitted that this remedy was neither appropriate nor justified. The investment in exhibition carried out, primarily, by vertically integrated companies should not be susceptible to competition law attack and proposed remedial action, unless it created a preference in favour of the films of those who owned the exhibition outlets, and not necessarily even then. There was, UIP said, no such preference. To deny those who had invested the opportunity to earn a return on their investment was grossly inequitable. It would act as a severe deterrent to any future investment and, ultimately, might halt the revival of the exhibition sector, to the detriment of the public interest.

8.291. Warner Distributors submitted that the MMC would have to find that a very serious public interest detriment existed in the industry before they could justify imposing such a draconian remedy as divestment. There was no evidence to suggest that vertical integration had any effect on the ability of distributors to gain access to the market. Warner Distributors did not believe that MGM Cinemas' links with the US production studio had affected Warner Distributors' ability to book screens for its films, or that its business had been adversely affected by any preferential treatment by MGM Cinemas of its affiliated distribution or production companies. Similarly, Warner Distributors did not gain any competitive advantage with regard to the Warner Theatres multiplex chain (save to a limited extent with regard to the special circumstances of the Warner West End complex). Since all negotiations took place at arm's length, there was no need for divestment.

8.292. Warner Distributors argued that it was important to note that the majority of the investment in exhibition infrastructure in the UK had been undertaken by companies which had interests in film production as well as in distribution and exhibition. It was primarily the vertically integrated groups that had taken the lead in bringing about the marked improvement in the standard of cinemas and the range and quality of the facilities offered to the consumer. This had been largely responsible for the revitalization of cinema attendances in recent years. Such a turnaround from the position at the time of the last MMC inquiry would not have been achieved if such vertical integration had been prohibited, since those groups had, perhaps, particularly strong incentives to invest.

## Termination of the UIP joint venture

8.293. We asked the leading distributors for their views on the suggestion that the UIP joint venture in the distribution of films to cinemas in the UK might be terminated. They either did not object to the continuation of the UIP joint venture or had no comment to make on the proposed remedy.

8.294. UIP noted that, in their 1983 report, the MMC found that it was not pursuing a course of conduct which operated or might be expected to operate against the public interest. The purpose, structure and operation of UIP had not changed since 1983. UIP said that it was not a cartel and did not have the market power which would enable it to restrict competition, and its structure did not affect the terms on which the films of its partners were distributed. The only effect of terminating the joint venture would, it claimed, be to raise significantly the distribution costs for its partners, to reduce the return to the partners and to reduce the revenue available for reinvestment in productions of its partners or independent producers.

8.295. UIP also noted that the EC Commission was currently considering whether to renew UIP's exemption under Article 85(3) of the Treaty of Rome. The MMC should take into account the legal requirement that no action must be taken nationally which would prejudice the full and uniform application of EC law. The MMC must take appropriate measures to avoid any conflict between its recommendation and any decision of the EC Commission.

## Prohibition on distribution joint ventures

8.296. The leading distributors were asked for their views on the suggestion that formation of joint ventures in distribution between parties which together had more than 20 per cent of the market, measured by share of rental receipts over a rolling four-year period, might be prohibited. They opposed the remedy, arguing that joint ventures were already subject to control under existing UK and EC competition law.

8.297. Buena Vista saw no justification for the remedy. It argued that it was the consumer, by electing which films to see, who determined the success of any distribution company. This was not affected by the existence of joint ventures.

8.298. Columbia had no opinion on any currently existing joint venture. It did, however, believe the proposed remedy was excessive. Though not currently party to such a venture, it had been so in the past. It believed that the high level of distribution expenses relative to box office returns in the UK might make joint sales operations desirable in the future to save overheads. A further factor was the fragmented nature of the European market, which meant that distribution operations had to be replicated in many European territories, leading to higher costs. Any joint sales ventures should be dealt with on the basis of their specific characteristics, and in the light of prevailing competition law.

8.299. Fox did not believe such a general remedy was appropriate. If a specific circumstance which distorted competition were to be identified, the appropriate course would be to address that circumstance.

8.300. UIP suggested that the introduction of a new level of regulation for joint ventures having a market share of 20 per cent was unnecessary. It said that a 20 per cent market share test was arbitrary and meaningless; it would be highly inflexible and would ignore normal competition law considerations. It could outlaw ventures, such as UIP, which were designed to be competitively benign or neutral but fail to catch ventures which might, for example, engage in revenue or profit pooling but whose market share fell just below 20 per cent. UIP submitted that a strict market share test was particularly ill suited to an industry in which market share was a poor indication of economic or market power.

8.301. Warner Distributors said that, although it had no plans to enter into a joint venture, it did not believe there was any reason for prohibiting such ventures, particularly those where the marketing and sales functions were kept separate. The aggregation of market share for the purpose of determining which joint ventures to permit and which to prohibit was misconceived, since market share even on a rolling four-year basis was no indication of true market power. Consequently, the merging of two distribution activities did not create any increment in the separate market position of the two participants.

## Termination of UCI joint venture

8.302. Most of the leading distributors opposed the possibility that the UCI joint venture in cinema exhibition in the UK might be terminated. Some pointed out that UCI had been a major investor in the UK exhibition sector and were concerned that to terminate the joint venture would jeopardize future investment. Others had no comment to make on the proposed remedy.

## Third party complaints

8.303. We asked the leading distributors to respond to the various complaints raised by third parties and summarized in Chapter 6. Their responses on supply of prints, minimum exhibition periods, restrictions on screen use, influence over admission prices and the *Standard Conditions* are summarized earlier in this chapter. Their comments on other matters are summarized below.

## The CEA

8.304. Responding to the CEA's comments on exchanges of information (see paragraph 6.16), Fox told us that, in its experience, exhibitors wished to fix a standard house nut and break figures with each distributor with whom they dealt. An exhibitor might, on occasion, invite Fox to verify with other distributors the nut which they had agreed for the cinema(s) in question. UIP said that it was not its policy to share confidential information with third parties concerning its arrangements with customers. Warner Distributors refuted the suggestion that distributors exchanged commercially sensitive information with each other, whether under the auspices of the SFD or in any other way. On the contrary, often it was the exhibitors themselves who revealed to the distributor the house nut or break figures they claimed to have agreed with other distributors, as part of their negotiating tactics to persuade a distributor to agree to the same figure.

## Independent exhibitors

8.305. Responding to the comments on availability of prints (see paragraphs 6.20 to 6.27) and conditional booking (see paragraph 6.28), Fox said that there was no reason why an independent exhibitor should not be willing to invest in a multiplex cinema. Generally, a high-quality multiplex cinema was a more attractive outlet to a distributor than was a single-screen cinema. A distributor would wish to license its films for exhibition in such a cinema, regardless of whether it was independently owned or formed part of a circuit. Fox said that it did not engage in conditional booking. There was a wide choice of films available to exhibitors. They were, therefore, not obliged to accept films which they did not want to exhibit.

8.306. UIP said that it was because multiplex cinemas were particularly attractive to customers that it sought to play most of its films there. Inevitably this would often mean that they received prints before competing non-multiplex cinemas which were not of the same quality and were not able to attract significant audiences. It might, for a film of exceptional appeal, for example *Jurassic Park*, offer a multiplex cinema two prints. In such cases it would also supply prints to many more independent exhibitors than it would for the general run of films. UIP denied that it operated a key town priority system. Such a system would, it said, cut across the basis on which it selected customers and across its principle of determining release strategy on a film-by-film basis. It also denied that it engaged in conditional booking.

8.307. Warner Distributors recognized that the huge overall investment made by a number of parties in improving the exhibition infrastructure in the UK would not have been possible if the multiplex cinemas had not been sure of receiving first-run prints. Overall, there was no doubt that the growth of multiplex cinemas had been a very positive development for distributors, exhibitors and the cinema-going public, although it had inevitably made life harder for those exhibitors who were unable to compete with the better quality of facilities offered by the multiplex cinemas. Warner Distributors said that it had not given preferential treatment to multiplex cinemas but, on the contrary, had assisted some of those cinemas which had suffered a drop in their audiences by continuing to provide them with first-release prints. Beyond this, it did not believe it would be possible or even desirable to protect the position of the independents from competition from the multiplex cinemas.

8.308. Warner Distributors rejected the suggestion that cinema operators had been deterred from investing in new cinemas, or in refurbishing existing cinemas, by uncertainty about the provision of prints. On the contrary, whenever it had been approached by a potential investor, Warner Distributors had been prepared to offer an assurance that the cinema would receive prints on first release. It denied that it operated a key town priority system.

8.309. Responding to complaints about restrictions on screen use (see paragraphs 6.30 and 6.31), Buena Vista described the 8.30 pm ruling as simply a yardstick, since obviously there were occasions when the agreed evening film was of a length to cause a licensing problem. It was a negotiable point which many exhibitors were happy to debate.

8.310. Responding to complaints about the calculation of rental payments (see paragraphs 6.32 and 6.33), Fox recognized that some exhibitors might pay a larger proportion than others of their box office revenue by way of rental payments. It said that this was to be expected. It did not believe independent exhibitors generally paid a higher percentage of revenues by way of rental fees than did circuit cinemas. UIP told us that it frequently received requests from exhibitors to increase their break points or nut figures. Such requests were considered carefully, having regard to the overheads of the exhibitor as well as the need for rentals to cover the cost of providing prints and handling the account. Warner Distributors said it was noteworthy that only seven exhibitors had complained about the level of rental payments, indicating that the overwhelming majority regarded the current split of income between the licensor and the licensee as fairly reflecting their respective costs and risks.

8.311. Warner Distributors submitted that Mr Henshaw's complaints (see paragraphs 6.35 to 6.37) were based on misconceptions, at least as far as its distribution policy was concerned. There was certainly no preferential treatment given to multiplex cinemas operated by Warner Theatres.

## *PACT*

8.312. Responding to PACT's comments on bias against independently-produced UK and European films (see paragraphs 6.53 to 6.55), Buena Vista said that the difficulty facing the independent production sector in the UK did not arise from any dominance of exhibition by US films. US films dominated because there were insufficient British films with wide popular appeal. This was, in part, attributable to the fact that there was no leading global distributor owned or backed by British investors. Independent British producers were not owed a living by US distributors. If there had been a failure by British capital investors to appreciate the global opportunity that existed for the exploitation of English language audio-visual works, that was scarcely the fault of the US distributors.

8.313. Fox said that it was only to be expected that US-produced films were highly popular in the UK. This was because, *inter alia*, US films were made for the world market and their costs were amortized over many territories. This enabled production companies to invest more in sets, stars, location and promotion. In the case of the UK, this trend was reinforced by the existence of a common language. Fox submitted that many of the problems encountered by independent producers in distributing their films in the UK did not stem from the fact that the major producers owned and controlled their own distributors. PACT had identified that many independently-produced films did not appeal to a US audience and were likely to be offered for distribution in the UK without a record of successful distribution in the USA. This had two effects. Because exhibitors had no evidence of how such a film was likely to perform, it carried greater risks than a film which was known to have succeeded in the USA or in other English-speaking markets. A film which had succeeded in the USA was likely already to be known and to have built up audience anticipation and curiosity in the UK. The marketing of such a film in the UK could proceed to build on the image created in the USA. Fox said that there was no reason why only US-produced films should acquire a successful track record in the USA before their release in the UK. It was simply that European producers tended to produce films which appealed less to US and to European audiences than did US-produced films. In addition, in some cases European producers and their distributors failed to promote their films successfully.

8.314. UIP told us that distributors and exhibitors judged each film on its perceived appeal to the UK consumer. Clearly they took into account the success or otherwise of a film in the USA but the determining factors were the preferences of UK consumers. US films were not advantaged by the vertically integrated structure of certain US companies, nor were UK films disadvantaged. UIP did not believe there were significant barriers to entry in exhibition in the UK. Nor did it believe that, in most areas and for most of the year, there was a shortage of screens.

8.315. Warner Distributors regarded it as most unfair, though perhaps not surprising, for UK film producers to place the blame for the lack of success of their films on the arrangements for distribution and exhibition rather than on the quality of their own work. It was noteworthy that PACT appeared to be calling for an increase in the level of cinema rentals whereas the independent exhibitors complained that rentals were already too high and threatened their continued viability.

8.316. Responding to PACT's comments on the concentration of exhibition in the UK (see paragraphs 6.58 to 6.60), Fox agreed that there was a shortage of screens in the UK. But since the removal of the Eady Levy and other features which rendered investment in exhibition unattractive, the number of screens had increased and the problem was correcting itself.

8.317. UIP understood that all the vertically integrated cinemas traded with all distributors on an arm's length basis. It traded with UCI and MGM Cinemas on that basis; there was no adjustment to prices which distinguished the terms on which it traded with those exhibitors.

## *The BFI*

8.318. Responding to the BFI's comments on the current state of the British film industry (see paragraphs 6.93 and 6.94), Fox submitted that the Eady Levy was one factor which contributed to the slump in cinema attendances in the 1970s and early 1980s, by inducing exhibitors to play films for which there was little public demand and by raising admission prices. Fox said that it would be harmful to reintroduce such a scheme. Fox agreed that investment was increasingly being made in the production of television programmes. If this was drawing finance away from the production of films for cinema exhibition, it was by no means clear that the production of such films should be supported by regulatory intervention or state subsidy.

8.319. UIP submitted that the effect of the abolition of the Eady Levy had not been to increase the number of US-produced films in the UK market. The removal of the subsidy might, however, have made it more difficult for projects from British producers, which were not seen to be commercially promising, to obtain financing. This might have led to a decline in the making of such films.

8.320. Warner Distributors said that it shared the BFI's concern about the fragile state of the British film industry but did not believe this was due to the conduct of distributors or exhibitors. It was rather due to a combination of factors, including lack of incentives for proper investment and, in some cases, a failure by the film-maker to read correctly what kind of films the British public wished to see. If British film-makers chose to concentrate on making arthouse films they could not expect to attract the audiences which went to see the latest Arnold Schwarzenegger film. Many US producers, whether or not linked to the major studios, also concentrated their efforts on producing smaller budget films which had no mass appeal but which would nevertheless appeal to the more discerning sector of the market. These films competed with television productions, as well as with other films, and they too had to be content with lower audience figures. There were many failures among the US releases and a number of films made by the Warner group were never released in the UK.

8.321. Responding to the BFI's comments on vertical integration (see paragraphs 6.95 to 6.97), Fox submitted that independent producers enjoyed good access to distribution channels. The examples cited by the BFI were, it said, misleading. For example, *The Crying Game* was often cited as a British film which was prevented from fulfilling its potential in the UK exhibition market. It was the view of the film's producer that its relative failure was not attributable to its being denied access to UK distributors but, more probably, to mistakes in the distribution strategy. An additional reason was that the film had been released at the time of an IRA bombing campaign on mainland UK. Fox cited examples of non-US films which were successful in the UK.

8.322. UIP said that it distributed third party films and was always looking for commercially viable films to distribute. Where it picked up a film, it would try to bring it effectively to a wide audience.

8.323. Warner Distributors disagreed with the BFI in seeking to blame vertical integration for the absence of British films on cinema screens here. In fact, many of those putting forward ideas for the regeneration of the British film industry regarded vertical integration as one of the great strengths of the industry and believed British film producers should emulate the US corporate structure. Vertical integration meant that the film production business was kept in touch directly with the ultimate market for the film, so that it could be more responsive to exhibitor and audience trends and tastes.

8.324. The BFI had cited three films as examples of good British films which were poorly distributed (see paragraph 6.95). Warner Distributors said that *Riff Raff* and *Enchanted April* were both financed in part by television companies and had only a limited exhibition window before being shown on television. *The Crying Game* did suffer from poor distribution. The success of the film was also unexpected, since the story of an IRA terrorist's relationship with a transsexual was hardly a theme one would expect to attract a large audience. This might well be an example of a misjudgment of the scope of a film's appeal and the inability of the distributor to cope with the sudden demand for prints on the film's release.

8.325. Responding to the BFI's comments on control of the UK market (see paragraphs 6.98 to 6.100), Buena Vista said that it was not surprising that US films claimed a larger share of audience in the UK than in other Western European countries, since the UK and the USA shared a common language and shared the same pool of talent. The BFI's own figures showed that the percentage of box office receipts derived by US films in Germany and Italy was very close to that in the UK.

8.326. Fox said that it was true that it paid over a proportion of its revenues to its US licensor. This was not, however, a means of repatriating the revenues to avoid UK taxation. The payments were compensation for, and helped to recover, the vast investments made by the copyright holder in producing a film. The UK exhibition of a film contributed to the recovery of production costs. It was, therefore, entirely logical that a proportion of the UK distributor's revenues should be paid to the US licensor. The fact that there was an arm's length relationship between Fox and its licensor was borne out by the fact that the Inland Revenue was satisfied that the sums paid by Fox represented a fair price for the films supplied.

8.327. UIP told us that it remitted a proportion of its turnover to its US partners by way of licence fees for their respective films. This remittance represented the return on investments made by its partners. It suggested that there was nothing strange in this arrangement. UIP submitted that the success of a film at the box office did not depend on whether it was a US film or a UK film but rather whether it was commercially appealing to the consumer. It was not surprising, given the common language, that US films were more appealing to UK consumers than, for example, were foreign language films.

8.328. Responding to the BFI's comments on restriction of choice and diversity (see paragraphs 6.102 and 6.103), Buena Vista said that it did not believe BFI audiences were representative of the bulk of the UK cinema-going public. It would be interesting to know the manner in which the audiences were consulted. Buena Vista also wondered by what criteria a film was adjudged to be British.

8.329. UIP understood that, on average, year on year, the public had been able to see a similar number of films but recently had much greater and more immediate access to those films. Whether there had been a change in the variety of films on offer was a highly subjective matter. UIP's perception was that the films on release today were not significantly less varied than ten years ago. UIP did not accept that British films were being marginalized. British films with commercial appeal would be shown by all exhibitors; those which appealed to a niche audience would be shown by exhibitors who catered to such audiences. The multi-screen cinemas wished to exhibit films which maximized audiences, regardless of whether they were US or UK films. Moreover, a significant number of so-called major Hollywood films were British- or European-inspired films made with British or European talent and crew.

8.330. Buena Vista did not agree with the BFI's comments on admission charges (see paragraph 6.104). Admission charges in the UK were, it said, in line with those in other EC countries and lower than in most comparable countries, eg Germany, Italy and France. UIP also disputed the BFI's comments on admission charges. Its perception was that the large increase in cinema-going indicated that prices were set at a level which consumers believed offered good value for money. Warner Distributors did not accept that cinema prices were high in the UK.

8.331. Responding to the BFI's comments on the expression of British culture (see paragraphs 6.105 and 6.106), Buena Vista submitted that what was fundamentally wrong with the British film industry was the relative failure of investors to recognize the global opportunity that investment in feature film production and distribution represented. In order to compete effectively in the global market with the existing leading distributors, it was necessary to take a long view and to commit very substantial sums of money.

## Mr Michael Henry

8.332. Responding to Mr Henry's comments on distributor commissions (see paragraphs 6.119 and 6.120), UIP told us that the fee it received for distributing its partners' films had been agreed with the Inland Revenue as representing proper arm's length profits. Terms offered to third parties were, it believed, comparable with terms offered by its competitors. The difference in terms offered to third parties and terms agreed with the UIP partners reflected the fact that the partners were responsible for the UIP overhead and offered sufficient product to benefit from economies of scale in distribution.

8.333. Warner Distributors was unable to comment on Mr Henry's criticism relating to differential commission terms applied to independent producers as compared with the major studio producers. Warner Distributors said that it generally did not enter into direct contracts for the distribution of independently-produced films in the UK and when such films were licensed to it by Warner Bros International, it was not informed of the terms covering the remuneration of the producer of the film. The origin of the film did not affect the level of royalty paid by Warner Distributors to Warner Bros International under its Franchise Agreement.

8.334. Responding to Mr Henry's assertion that the percentage distribution commission retained by the UK subsidiaries of the MPAA corporations was substantially less than it would be if they were engaged on an arm's length basis, Warner Distributors said that UK tax legislation contained transfer pricing provisions (section 770 of the Income and Corporation Taxes Act 1988) which enabled the Inland Revenue to substitute an arm's length price if it believed that transactions between associated persons were at an under or over value. This legislation was specifically designed to ensure that an appropriate level of profits was taxed in the UK. The arrangements between the Warner group companies had been agreed with the Inland Revenue as being arm's length after considerable scrutiny and discussion. These arm's length rates had, as was usually the case, been adopted in the relevant UK and US companies' accounts. It was wholly wrong to suggest that MPAA corporations did not pay their fair share of tax in the UK.

8.335. Responding to Mr Henry's comments on collusion among distributors (see paragraphs 6.121 to 6.123), UIP denied that it had market power or that it was dominant. It did not accept that trading conditions in distribution and exhibition in the UK were directly or indirectly fixed by the MPAA corporations; such conditions had been agreed by the trade associations for all distributors and exhibitors.

8.336. Warner Distributors regarded most of Mr Henry's claims as unfounded and irresponsible. There was, it said, no grand conspiracy amongst the leading distributors with regard to their activities in the UK or elsewhere; on the contrary, they competed strongly at every stage of production and distribution to gain the widest audience on the best terms for their films.

8.337. Warner Distributors described the allegations made about collusion in fixing prices and trading terms as extravagant and without any substance. It strongly denied that any such collusion took place. The MPAA was a legitimate trade association dealing with matters of common interest to the industry, such as anti-piracy activities and political lobbying over copyright and other matters. Any information, for example on average ticket prices in a territory, was published in an aggregate and non-commercially sensitive basis. There was no 'fixing' of prices or other terms at MPAA meetings. The participants were well aware of their legal obligations under US and European competition law and the meetings were conducted in accordance with those obligations.

8.338. Responding to Mr Henry's comments on remittance of royalties (see paragraphs 6.124 to 6.126), Fox denied that it acted as the agent of its US licensor in consideration of a commission payment.

8.339. UIP also denied that it was the agent for its partners, nor did the Inland Revenue suggest that it should be taxed as such. UIP said that it traded as a distributor of films in the UK and paid taxes on the profits of that trade. Remittance of royalty income from the UK to another jurisdiction was a normal feature of a commercial relationship where a UK entity was granted the right to exploit in the UK property belonging to a non-UK entity. Double taxation treaties between the UK and most major countries provided that royalties in respect of copyright might be paid without withholding tax.

There was no suggestion that, in such cases, this had a detrimental effect on competition or the public interest in the UK.

8.340. Warner Distributors said that section 536 of the Taxes Act 1988 provided that basic rate UK tax was to be withheld from copyright royalties where the owner of the copyright was abroad. However, this section specifically did not apply to the copyright in a cinematograph film or video recording and, therefore, no withholding of tax was required from film royalties. Mr Henry's inference that the MPAA corporations were in some way improperly making use of this section to avoid deducting UK tax from royalties was misleading as it was Parliament that had specifically legislated that withholding tax did not apply to film royalties.

8.341. Warner Distributors described Mr Henry's reference to the UK/US double taxation treaty, and his comments in relation to exemptions from the need to deduct withholding tax from royalties, as misconceived. There was no such obligation under UK domestic legislation and so the exemption was not relevant. Under the UK/US Treaty, cinematograph royalties were classed as business profits and not royalties. Under the treaty, business profits were only to be taxed in the country of the licensor unless the licensor had a permanent place of business in the country of source. The relevant article in the UK/US tax treaty which dealt with permanent establishment acknowledged the fact that the existence of a subsidiary in the UK did not of itself constitute the subsidiary as a permanent establishment of the US company, since it was a separate legal entity. Mr Henry's argument that the subsidiary should be treated as agent for the parent, and thus as constituting a permanent establishment, was therefore misleading, since neither Warner Distributors nor Warner Home Video (UK) Limited carried out any agency activity. The suggestion that the UK subsidiaries of the MPAA corporations be required to withhold tax on royalties would involve primary legislation to bring cinematograph royalties within the provisions of section 536 of the Taxes Act. Furthermore, if the companies rearranged their affairs so as to carry on film production in the UK, this would only affect the level of corporation tax and not withholding tax.

8.342. Warner Distributors submitted that the proposals put forward by Mr Henry to increase the level of tax on cinema royalties would greatly increase the disincentives for US companies to make films in the UK and invest in film production, distribution and exhibition here. His comments ran directly counter to the proposals put forward by British producers and others involved in the industry, who saw the further relaxation of the current tax deterrents as essential if the British film industry was to survive. Any moves to penalize US companies for choosing British locations or showing their films in the UK was likely to be entirely self-defeating. The suggestion that the remittance of royalty income, to the studio which undertook the risk and investment in making the film, amounted to a concerted practice was clearly nonsense.

8.343. Responding to Mr Henry's comments on location of control (see paragraphs 6.127 and 6.128), UIP denied that the location of its partners in the USA had any of the effects suggested. Warner Distributors said that there was nothing surprising or anti-competitive in the fact that the major studios retained the main decision-making powers concerning how their films were distributed throughout the world, since they had the key interest in the success of the film.

8.344. Responding to Mr Henry's comments on the acquisition of rights to distribute independent films (see paragraphs 6.129 and 6.130), Fox said that it acquired independent films on the same terms as films produced by its associated companies. UIP denied that its partners required independent producers who sold them US distribution rights also to sell them the UK rights. Warner Distributors said that there was no standard practice with regard to the scope of the rights acquired in independent films. There was certainly no policy within the Warner group or among MPAA corporations whereby they insisted on acquiring the UK rights for the film. On the contrary, in the majority of cases where Warner Bros International obtained distribution rights, these did not include rights for the UK. The suggestion of a concerted practice was nonsense.

8.345. Responding to Mr Henry's comments on the withdrawal of financing from British film production (see paragraphs 6.131 to 6.133), UIP said that its partners had not withdrawn financing from British film projects; UIP and the partners all acquired independent production for distribution in the UK. Warner Distributors said that the scale of US investment in British film production was influenced to a considerable extent by the tax incentives available for such investment and the convenience or inconvenience of making arrangements to film here. It had nothing to do with the supposed strength of MPAA corporations. In fact there had been no 'withdrawal' of finance. On the contrary, the Warner group had been involved with a number of projects to make films in the UK.

8.346. Responding to Mr Henry's comments on BSkyB (see paragraphs 6.134 and 6.135), Fox told us that News International plc had a 50 per cent shareholding in, but did not control, BSkyB. BSkyB did not have exclusive access to cinema films produced or acquired by 20th Century Fox. While BSkyB enjoyed certain exclusive rights, of short duration, to exhibit some 20th Century Fox films on pay television in the UK, other broadcasters were entitled to exhibit certain 20th Century Fox films on free terrestrial television or on pay television outside the period of BSkyB's licence period. BSkyB's contract with 20th Century Fox was an arm's length agreement and its terms were not affected by vertical integration.

8.347. Responding to Mr Henry's comments on its exemption under Article 85 of the Treaty of Rome (see paragraphs 6.136 to 6.145), UIP submitted that issues as to Article 85 were solely for consideration by the EC Commission and not, therefore, for the present inquiry. To the extent that the UIP joint venture was relevant to the UK public interest, UIP's views were expressed in its response to the issues and possible remedies. It described Mr Henry's allegations as incorrect both in fact and substance. It told us that it had commissioned research from consulting economists which substantiated this statement.

# 9 Views of the other distributors in the complex monopoly group

## Contents

| | Paragraph |
|---|---|
| Introduction | 9.1 |
| Observations on the market | 9.2 |
| Views on complex monopoly situation | 9.6 |
| Alignment | 9.9 |
| Exclusivity and refusal to supply | 9.13 |
| Minimum exhibition periods and restrictions on screen use | 9.24 |
| Influence or control over admission prices | 9.36 |
| SFD *Standard Conditions* | 9.39 |
| Vertical links to US production companies | 9.43 |
| Overseas decision-making | 9.47 |
| Domination of the UK markets by US films | 9.49 |
| Co-ordination of release dates | 9.52 |
| Exercise of market power by leading distributors | 9.55 |
| Exercise of market power by leading exhibitors | 9.59 |
| Code of practice and associated machinery | 9.62 |
| Prohibiting contracts based on box office receipts | 9.65 |
| Distributors to commit revenues to independently produced films | 9.68 |
| Distribution/exhibition of films with a predominantly European theme or cultural content | 9.71 |
| Divestment or reduction of interests in exhibition | 9.73 |
| Termination of the UIP joint venture | 9.75 |
| Prohibition on distribution joint ventures | 9.77 |
| Termination of the UCI joint venture | 9.79 |
| Complaints | 9.81 |

## Introduction

9.1. In the previous chapter we summarized the views of the leading distributors. In this chapter we summarize the views of the other distributors who are members of the complex monopoly group: Entertainment, First Independent, Guild and Rank.[1] We first summarize their observations on the market and then their comments on the various matters raised in our issues letter of 14 February 1994.

## Observations on the market

9.2. Entertainment told us that the major development in the market over the last ten years had been the introduction of multiplex cinemas. It said that access to those cinemas was still dominated by the US studios.

---

[1] Rank submitted evidence on behalf of both Odeon and RFD. This evidence was partly common to both subsidiaries and partly covered one or the other respectively. In this chapter we summarize Rank's evidence relating to RFD exclusively. All the remainder of Rank's evidence was summarized in Chapter 7, to which cross-reference is made where appropriate.

9.3. Entertainment told us that the output deals of the Hollywood studios under which they agreed to sell their films to BSkyB often included provisions which linked the deal to the budget for the UK theatrical release of the films. Thus the deal might be triggered, or the payment by BSkyB increased, if spending on prints and advertising for the UK theatrical release exceeded certain figures. Such provisions, Entertainment argued, gave distributors an artificial incentive to increase release budgets and encouraged the Hollywood studios to take up screen time in cinemas with films for which there might not be any consumer demand.

9.4. First Independent said that film distribution in the UK was still dominated by the major US studios, with US films taking an average of 80 per cent of box office receipts over recent years. Referring to the increase in cinema admissions since 1984, it said that approximately half of all admissions were now accounted for by multiplex cinemas. It considered that the advent of the multiplex cinemas had helped the smaller independent exhibitors. Any film released with over 200 prints would, in an area served by a multiplex cinema, a circuit cinema (belonging to MGM Cinemas or Odeon) and an independent, be given to all three simultaneously. The video boom of the 1980s had helped to fund the distribution of films, with profits being ploughed back into the production of films. Now, however, the dynamics of the video rental industry had changed substantially and it could not support theatrical losses. Each medium now had to stand on its own.

9.5. Guild referred to the substantial investment made by the operators of multiplex cinemas. It said that these greatly improved venues were in the public interest. Rank's views on the nature of the market are summarized in paragraph 7.3.

## Views on complex monopoly situation

9.6. We asked these distributors for their views on our provisional finding that a complex monopoly situation existed in respect of the supply of films for exhibition in cinemas in the UK in that they, along with the leading distributors and exhibitors, engaged in one or more of the practices listed in paragraph 7.11.

9.7. Entertainment disputed its inclusion in the complex monopoly group saying that it was the only truly independent company in the list, it was privately owned and it did not own cinemas, nor did it have control over exhibitors. First Independent made no comment on our provisional finding. Guild said it did not agree that a complex monopoly existed but presented no arguments in support of this view.

9.8. Rank submitted that RFD was not a party to a complex monopoly. In its view, the reference market was highly competitive and the practices identified by the MMC did not prevent, restrict or distort competition. Rank's detailed comments on each of the practices are summarized in paragraph 7.14.

## Alignment

9.9. We asked the distributors whether the practice of alignment, by restricting the competition between MGM Cinemas and Odeon in negotiating for exhibition rights, made the market less responsive to consumer preferences. We also asked them to comment on the possible remedies detailed in paragraph 7.16.

9.10. Entertainment did not consider that it was aligned to either of the two main circuits. More of its films were released through Odeon than through MGM Cinemas because Odeon had a greater number of available release dates. Entertainment distinguished between release and non-release films. With the former, it sought exhibition dates, in the first instance, from Odeon. If enough prints were available, it offered to supply the whole Odeon circuit. In the case of a non-release film, it sought exhibition dates from Odeon, MGM Cinemas and other exhibitors more or less at the same time. The decision as to whether a film would be a release or non-release film was largely a marketing decision which took into account the form of advertising to be used. If Entertainment intended to arrange television advertising, it would release the film as widely as possible. If the film required careful nurturing, it would be released on a very selective basis. On occasions it might wish to release a film in key cities only, supporting it with national press or a national poster campaign targeted at those cities. Since the beginning of 1992, it had had one full MGM Cinemas release.

9.11. Entertainment said that the practice of alignment was originally instigated by the US studios and enabled them to reserve release dates for the entire year. Independent distributors were denied access to screens on certain dates and the market was made less responsive to consumer preferences. Alignment enabled the leading distributors to reserve dates with the two main circuit exhibitors (MGM Cinemas and Odeon), many months in advance, simply by putting forward a title which might relate to a film in the planning stage; if the film did not materialize the date was kept for another film from the same distributor. Entertainment said that the independent distributors were unable to reserve screen space in this way and that the practice prejudiced their efforts to get films screened.
[

*Details omitted. See note on page iv.*

]

9.12. First Independent told us that it was not aligned to either of the two main circuits. It did not believe alignment had any adverse effects. It pointed out that neither MGM Cinemas nor Odeon had a cinema in every location. A successful film would, it said, play in almost every town that had a cinema. Guild did not accept that alignment operated against the public interest. It said that it had a flexible policy and offered films to both MGM Cinemas and to Odeon. Rank's views on alignment and the possible remedies are summarized in paragraphs 7.24 to 7.40.

## Exclusivity and refusal to supply

9.13. The distributors were asked whether exclusivity and refusal to supply unduly restricted consumers' choice of cinemas to see a given film on first release; were harmful to certain independent exhibitors, to the extent in some cases of causing their withdrawal from the market; and deterred new entry and investment in the exhibition sector. We also asked them to comment on the possible remedies detailed in paragraph 7.46.

9.14. Entertainment agreed that exclusivity and refusal to supply restricted consumer choice, though not unduly. It said that there were numerous reasons which might warrant a refusal to supply. For example, unreliable booking by an exhibitor and concerns regarding the security of the print could be relevant. New entry and investment in the exhibition sector were not being deterred, as was evidenced by the fact that cinemas were being built and admissions had increased.

9.15. Entertainment said that a distributor had to make a commercial decision whether to supply a print to an exhibitor and whether exclusivity should be granted. Several factors played a part in making such a decision. For example, certain films required a slow build-up and could be damaged if released too quickly or too widely. It was counter-productive to play too many cinemas in the same area. To do so would split the audience between the cinemas and thereby reduce the distributor's share of the box office returns. This would, it suggested, be an argument for not supplying every exhibitor even if they were to guarantee a minimum return to the distributor.

9.16. Entertainment said that creditworthiness was the most important factor to be taken into consideration when deciding whether to supply a print. Timely payment to the distributor was also important. Entertainment said that it often took a very long time to collect its share of box office receipts from independent exhibitors. Indeed, they might choose not to pay until they knew whether Entertainment was offering another film which they wanted to book. Entertainment argued that it would be harmful if independent exhibitors were to be supplied with films when it was clear that this would be unprofitable for the distributor. If it had to book films on an uneconomic basis, Entertainment would be forced to withdraw from the market.

9.17. First Independent said that distributors were in business to make a profit. The costs of prints and advertising were an extremely important factor which had to be taken into account when developing the release pattern for a film. It attempted to recoup these costs from the cinemas which had booked the film. First Independent did not accept that these practices were harmful to independent exhibitors; nor did it accept that they deterred new entry and investment in the exhibition sector.

9.18. First Independent opposed the suggestion that exclusivity might be prohibited. If every cinema in a given area was able to play the same film at the same time, the public's choice of films would be reduced. Regarding the suggestion that distributors might be required to supply prints, it said that distributors and exhibitors would never agree over profit margins. It said that creditworthiness was the most important consideration when deciding which exhibitors to supply with prints.

9.19. Guild did not believe occasional exclusivity acted against the public interest. On the contrary, it could enhance the profile of a film that might otherwise disappear quickly if exhibited widely. Exclusivity did not deter new entry and investment in the exhibition sector. Many independent exhibitors were expanding their businesses by acquiring additional cinemas and adding new screens.

9.20. Guild said that it could provide evidence of numerous exhibitors who declined offers of prints on release. It wondered whether this practice had adverse effects. It said that it was not a public service industry. All its activities were directed towards achieving profit within the limits of good business conduct.

9.21. Rank said that, given the high level of risk inherent in film distribution and the low level of return achieved by distributors in respect of many films, it was vital that distributors were free to seek to maximize the returns by means of granting exclusivity and selecting outlets, as appropriate. Without such freedom, the risks involved in production and distribution would be disproportionate and the level of investment would be likely to be reduced, limiting further the range of films available to the public. The ability to control the distribution of prints in order to maximize returns was fundamental to efficient distribution. The right to refuse to supply a print was essential.

9.22. Rank argued that the grant of exclusive rights constituted a recognized and acceptable means of exploiting intellectual property rights in many fields. There was no justification for restricting this right in respect of cinematic exhibition. Such a restriction would limit the efficiency and competitiveness of the means of distribution and would be against the public interest. Prohibition of contractual exclusivity would deprive exhibitors of the ability to reduce the risks associated with showing films and could be expected to reduce the rental that they were able or willing to pay.

9.23. Rank also argued that requiring distributors to supply prints to all exhibitors, subject only to covering costs and a profit margin and considerations of creditworthiness, would involve compulsory licences of doubtful legality under EC law, in the light of Council Directive 92/100, and under the Berne Convention. Rank's other views on these issues are summarized in paragraphs 7.55 to 7.59.

## Minimum exhibition periods and restrictions on screen use

9.24. We asked the distributors whether the imposition of minimum exhibition periods and restrictions on screen use harmed smaller distributors by restricting their access to screens; harmed exhibitors by reducing their revenue; and unduly restricted consumer choice. We also asked them to comment on the possible remedies detailed in paragraph 7.69.

9.25. Guild, First Independent and RFD did not feel that they were denied access to screens as a result of the minimum exhibition periods negotiated by the leading distributors.

9.26. Entertainment was concerned that the leading distributors were able to obtain longer minimum exhibition periods than were the independent distributors. Whereas the leading distributors usually negotiated a two-week booking plus holdover, the independents could only negotiate one week plus holdover. It believed that, apart from special cases where a distributor only had a limited opportunity to recoup its advertising and print costs, there should be a level playing field between the leading distributors and the independents. It also argued that the leading distributors were able to impose unreasonable minimum exhibition times on the exhibition circuits, thereby exacerbating the problems faced by independent distributors and restricting consumer choice.

9.27. Entertainment said that because the exhibitors did not contribute towards the cost of prints and advertising, distributors felt that it would be financial suicide to agree to reduce the playing time of a major film. Agreeing that one exhibitor could reduce the playing time on a film would weaken the distributor's ability to reject similar requests from other exhibitors.

9.28. First Independent told us that the extended minimum exhibition periods required by the leading distributors had never affected its ability to place its films with MGM Cinemas, Odeon or the multiplex operators. The effect on exhibitors would depend entirely on which films were being shown at any particular time. It did not believe these practices would restrict consumer choice.

9.29. First Independent said that the public always complained that films came and went too quickly. Films should, it said, continue to be shown for as long as the box office takings warranted. It agreed with the suggestion that exhibitors should have the right to show other films, as long as adequate compensation was paid to the distributor who lost a showing on its contracted booking.

9.30. Guild said that it was not denied access to screens either by minimum exhibition periods or by restrictions on screen use. Nor did it accept that these practices harmed exhibitors by reducing their revenues. For its own part, Guild always sought a minimum exhibition period of seven days; for some films it sought a longer period. Where agreement on the minimum exhibition period had been reached and box office returns were disappointing, consideration would be given to revising the minimum period.

9.31. Guild said that no evidence was available about the effects on consumer choice. It did not agree that minimum exhibition periods should be abolished or restricted. Each film should be allowed to maximize its potential for both exhibitor and distributor. Allowing exhibitors to show other films was, it said, a matter for negotiation. Guild said that if exhibitors were not profitable, distributors would also suffer. Distributors would not engage in practices which were harmful to their profitability.

9.32. Rank said that it was the strength of the film which determined a distributor's ability to negotiate an extended exhibition period. It described the usual exhibition period as seven days plus holdover. It told us that agreement on the duration of the exhibition period and the frequency of exhibition was a necessary part of the contract between distributor and exhibitor. The distributor needed to know what obligations the exhibitor was prepared to accept in return for receiving a print. Given the cost of prints and the limitations on their availability, the distributor needed to ensure that each print was used as effectively as possible. If an exhibitor was prepared to show a film only part time, the distributor would prefer to place the print with another exhibitor who was willing to make better use of it. It would be against the public interest if exhibitors were free to take prints and not use them fully, or if distributors were precluded from seeking to place prints where they would be used most effectively.

9.33. Rank told us that, where a film was not of exceptional potential, distributors would wish to maximize the use made of the available prints by transferring them between cinemas. Given the risks involved in distribution and the relative infrequency of exceptional films, it was of the greatest importance that distributors were able to exploit such films to the full. This was particularly important for independent distributors who would have acquired such films at a high price and would inevitably incur significant release costs. Thus, in Rank's view, the ability to seek minimum exhibition periods, and to specify frequency of screen use, was valuable to the smaller distributors. It was unlikely to restrict their access to screens since there were few films capable of supporting an extended exhibition period.

9.34. Rank did not accept that consumer choice was restricted by these practices. The ability of a distributor to seek an extended exhibition period on the basis of the quality of the film reflected the strength of consumer demand and preference. There was, it said, no justification for restricting minimum exhibition periods. Any restriction would prevent distributors from achieving the optimum distribution pattern for their films and securing the most efficient use of prints. If distributors were unable to direct prints to those exhibitors who were prepared to commit to minimum periods, distribution costs would be likely to increase, to the ultimate detriment of consumers.

9.35. Rank also argued that any reduction in the number of times that a film was shown in a week would be likely to lead to a reduction in the distributor's income and would increase risks. It would also reduce the efficiency with which prints were used and render less effective the distributor's national marketing campaign, thus increasing overall costs. Those prints that were used by exhibitors for reduced frequency showings would be unlikely to be available elsewhere during the week in question. Thus, public access to prints would be reduced. Rank's other comments on these issues are summarized in paragraphs 7.75 and 7.76.

## Influence or control over admission prices

9.36. We asked the distributors whether the influence or control exercised over exhibitors' admission prices by distributors caused those charges to be higher than they otherwise would have been.

9.37. Entertainment said that income generated from concession sales, games machines and screen advertising could enable an exhibitor to lower its admission prices. This would adversely affect the distributor whose revenue was solely derived from its share of the box office takings. First Independent did not accept that the influence or control exercised over exhibitors' admission prices by distributors caused those charges to be higher than they otherwise would have been. Guild said that it had never been involved in price fixing, nor did it exercise controls which had that effect.

9.38. In Rank's view, a distributor had a legitimate interest in the admission prices charged by exhibitors and it was entirely reasonable that the distributor should have some influence over them. However, the extent of that influence was limited, extending only to giving or withholding consent to a reduction in prices during the licence period for a film supplied by the distributor in question. The distributor could not require an exhibitor to increase admission prices. Rank's other views on this issue are summarized in paragraphs 7.86 and 7.87.

## SFD *Standard Conditions*

9.39. We asked the distributors whether the widespread observance of the *Standard Conditions* strengthened the market power of distributors and exacerbated the anti-competitive effects of certain practices which were covered by the *Standard Conditions*. We also asked them to comment on the possible remedies detailed in paragraph 7.90.

9.40. Entertainment said that, without the *Standard Conditions*, distributors would have to negotiate a fresh contract for each film to be exhibited. This would create an impossible and chaotic situation in which to conduct business. It believed independent distributors could be put out of business as the leading distributors attempted to obtain more favourable trading conditions from the exhibitors.

9.41. First Independent did not accept that the widespread observance of the *Standard Conditions* strengthened the market power of distributors and exacerbated the anti-competitive effects of certain practices which were covered by the *Standard Conditions*. It said that there had to be some logic to buying and selling films. The *Standard Conditions* were a matter of common sense.

9.42. Guild said that the observance of the *Standard Conditions* did not have anti-competitive effects. Terms and conditions were negotiated on a film-by-film basis. Withdrawal of the *Standard Conditions* would, it suggested, create total confusion with thousands of separate negotiations each year. It would be ludicrous to depart from the *Standard Conditions*. Rank's views on the *Standard Conditions* are summarized in paragraph 7.94.

## Vertical links to US production companies

9.43. The distributors were asked whether distributors and exhibitors with vertical links to US production companies used their position in the interrelated markets for distribution and exhibition to keep out competition from independent producers operating outside North America.

9.44. Entertainment said that US-linked distributors and exhibitors tended to be more reliant upon films from US producers and rarely supported independent producers from outside North America. They generally only acquired such films for distribution when completed. The exhibitors would give dates for commercial British films only if they did not clash with dates sought by an aligned studio.

9.45. First Independent said that the majority of the films handled by the leading distributors had been produced by independent producers. It believed exhibitors would negotiate on a film-by-film basis at arm's length from their parent companies. It did not accept that the films of independent producers outside North America were unable to obtain screen space. It had released *City Slickers* through Odeon, not MGM Cinemas, and had had no difficulty making bookings (see paragraph 9.11).

9.46. Guild had no comments to make. Rank told us that RFD was not unreasonably excluded from screens at cinemas outside Odeon. Its other views on vertical links are summarized in paragraphs 7.103 and 7.104.

## Overseas decision-making

9.47. We asked the distributors whether overseas-based decision-making made the market less responsive to consumer preferences than if decisions were taken in the UK.

9.48. Entertainment and Guild had no comments to make. First Independent said that the public decided which films it wanted to see. Many films that succeeded in the UK failed elsewhere and vice versa. Rank's views are summarized in paragraph 7.113.

## Domination of the UK markets by US films

9.49. The distributors were asked whether the influence exercised by US companies in the UK markets for the distribution and exhibition of films caused the markets to be dominated by US films, and whether the economic and cultural effects of this dominance were harmful.

9.50. Entertainment was concerned about the output deals between the major US studios and BSkyB. It claimed that they subsidized the wide release of inferior US product which the studios were able to force on the exhibition circuits due to the strength of the alignment system. The deals were, it said, used by most distributors to underwrite the size of their theatrical releases, both in terms of print numbers and advertising budgets. They had, therefore, a distorting effect on the exhibition of films in the UK. Entertainment also believed that the economic and cultural effects of US dominance were extremely harmful both in terms of employment and the impact on cultural identity.

9.51. First Independent said that the UK public had been brought up on a diet of US films. In its opinion, this was not harmful. It suggested that UK producers had to stop complaining about lack of finance and Government assistance and get on with producing commercially attractive films that the public wanted to see. Guild did not believe that the influence exercised by US companies caused the UK markets to be dominated by US films. Nor did it believe that the economic and cultural effects were harmful. Rank's views on the domination of the markets are summarized in paragraphs 7.119 and 7.120.

## Co-ordination of release dates

9.52. We asked the distributors whether, by co-ordinating the release dates of their films, the leading distributors reduced consumers' choice of first-release films at any given time and crowded out other distributors.

9.53. Entertainment told us that it did not co-ordinate release dates with other distributors. It chose what it felt to be the most effective dates for its films. It reiterated the point that the leading distributors reserved dates throughout the year, thereby denying release dates to the independents (see paragraph 9.11). First Independent denied that the leading distributors, by co-ordinating the release dates of their films, reduced consumers' choice of first-release films at any given time. It said that when too many films were released in the same week, there could be an adverse effect on the availability of press coverage for its films. Guild told us that the co-ordination of release dates did not reduce consumers' choice of first-release films. It had not experienced any problems in arranging release patterns in competition with other distributors.

9.54. Rank denied that distributors co-ordinated release dates. Rather, individual distributors used publicly available information about release dates when deciding upon their own dates. It was sensible commercial conduct for any producer or distributor, when considering the launch of a new product, to consider all the factors that might influence demand at any time. A distributor who failed to do so would be ignoring commercial prudence. The need to book screens and develop a lengthy pre-release marketing campaign meant that release dates were announced well in advance. In addition, the fact that most films were first released in the USA meant that generally they were heralded in the UK well before release. Even before US release, details of films in production were likely to be known. Rank's other views on co-ordination of release dates are summarized in paragraphs 7.127 and 7.128.

## Exercise of market power by leading distributors

9.55. The distributors were asked whether, by exercising market power over independent exhibitors to persuade them to screen films which they would not otherwise choose, the leading distributors made the exhibition market less responsive to consumer preference, harmed the exhibitors concerned by reducing their revenue, and harmed independent producers, whose films were handled by other distributors, by reducing their films' access to screens.

9.56. Entertainment did not believe, as an independent distributor, it was able to exercise market power over independent exhibitors. It said that the excessive power of the US studios might cause exhibitors to book films which it might not be in their economic interests to take. The effect on independent producers depended on how commercial their films were. When an independently-produced film proved to be more successful than a film released by a leading distributor, exhibitors would make more screen space available.

9.57. First Independent said that it had yet to find an independent exhibitor who would play a film that it did not want. A few would only play the films of the leading distributors. It did not accept that the revenue of independent exhibitors was reduced. If an independently-produced film was commercially attractive and opened well at the box office, screen space would be available. Guild did not believe distributors exercised market power over independent exhibitors to persuade them to screen films which they would not otherwise choose.

9.58. Rank said that RFD had no material market power, nor did it seek to persuade exhibitors to screen films which they would not otherwise choose, save in the sense that it tried to persuade them to choose its film rather than one of the many others that would be available. RFD was generally, though not always, able to secure a showing for its films. Any difficulty experienced in persuading independent exhibitors to take its films was attributable to the fact that the exhibitors had access to other films which they believed had greater commercial potential, rather than to pressure from leading distributors to take films which the exhibitors would not otherwise have wanted. Rank's other views on the exercise of market power by the leading distributors are summarized in paragraph 7.135.

## Exercise of market power by leading exhibitors

9.59. We asked the distributors whether the leading exhibitors, by exercising market power over distributors to secure preferences over other exhibitors, harmed those exhibitors by reducing their access to popular films, particularly on first release.

9.60. Entertainment told us that the distributor's decision was based solely on a commercial assessment of the release plan most suited to the film in question. First Independent said that independent exhibitors always wanted to know which of the circuits would be showing a film. With the exception of the BFI cinemas, they would never book a film that had not first been booked either by MGM Cinemas or Odeon. This allowed them to assess the potential of a film based on the opening figures at either MGM Cinemas or Odeon.

9.61. Guild said that it actively sought exhibitors in order to maximize the market for its films. In so doing, it did not reduce other exhibitors' access to the market. Certain exhibitors would not take a film unless it was showing nearby in a leading exhibitor's cinema. Rank's views on the exercise of market power by leading exhibitors are summarized in paragraph 7.138.

## Code of practice and associated machinery

9.62. The distributors were asked for their views on the possibility that a code of practice, dealing with the supply of prints, minimum exhibition periods and restrictions on screen use, might be drawn up by agreement between the SFD and the CEA; and that machinery, for example a committee with an independent chairman, might be set up to resolve disputes between distributors and exhibitors concerning the application of the code to particular circumstances.

9.63. Entertainment believed the SFD had adequate procedures for handling disputes between exhibitors and distributors. It also said that direct discussions between distributor and exhibitor worked well. First Independent said that the suggested code of practice and associated machinery might work for the leading distributors. It would, however, cause problems for independent distributors as prints and advertising costs often had to be agreed between distributor and producer before release.

9.64. Guild said that the suggestion might have the appearance of an efficient means of resolving disputes but would be impracticable to put into operation. It opposed the establishment of any 'quangos' when the means of resolving disputes already existed. Rank's views on the code of practice and associated machinery are summarized in paragraph 7.143.

## Prohibiting contracts based on box office receipts

9.65. We asked the distributors to comment on the possibility that distributors and exhibitors might be prohibited from entering into contracts under which the consideration received by the distributor was linked directly or indirectly to the exhibitor's box office receipts.

9.66. Entertainment said that distributors received a smaller share of box office receipts in the UK than they did in other territories. Given that distribution was such a risky business, it believed it would be fairer if the terms were more in line with those achieved elsewhere. It was right, however, that distributors should receive a share of the box office receipts. It was the distributor who supplied the film and who had to account to the producer. First Independent said that there was no alternative to the existing system. Producers would never agree to a flat rate system. Guild made no comment on this suggestion.

9.67. Rank said that it was the prospect of participating in a box office success that justified the risk incurred by the producer and distributor. If the distributor was unable to charge the exhibitor by reference to box office receipts, it could neither participate in the success of the film nor pass on the benefits of such success to the producer. The distributor would have to charge the exhibitor on some other, presumably flat rate, basis unrelated to box office receipts, determined before the success of the film was known. The impracticality of negotiating a fee in such circumstances was, in Rank's view, self-evident. Rank's other views on this subject are summarized in paragraph 7.150.

## Distributors to commit revenues to independently-produced films

9.68. The distributors were asked to comment on the possibility that they might be required to commit a specified proportion of their revenues from film rentals in the UK to the production of films by independent producers in the EC.

9.69. Entertainment did not believe this would be a good idea. While it was very supportive of British films, it did not think that any company should be forced to invest in a film that might not be commercial. First Independent opposed this suggestion. It would be another burden which independent distributors would have to bear. Furthermore, producers and sales agents would probably not accept the suggestion. Guild also opposed this suggestion.

9.70. Rank said that the business of an independent distributor, such as RFD, was not particularly profitable. An obligation of the sort suggested could have significant implications for its continuing viability. RFD invested in films from independent producers. Its decision in each case was based on commercial, rather than chauvinistic, criteria. Rank's other views are summarized in paragraph 7.158.

## Distribution/exhibition of films with a predominantly European theme or cultural content

9.71. We asked the distributors to comment on the possibility that they might be required to distribute, and exhibitors to exhibit, a specified proportion of films with a predominantly European theme or other cultural content.

9.72. Entertainment believed exhibitors should be encouraged to book British films but believed it would be very difficult to legislate for such a proposal. First Independent said that this would be a retrograde step. When previously tried, the net result was poor-quality films which were produced to meet the requirements of the quota. Guild said that it was already involved in distributing films with a European theme. It cited *Germinal* as an example. Rank's views are summarized in paragraphs 7.165 and 7.166.

## Divestment or reduction of interests in exhibition

9.73. The distributors were asked to comment on the possibility that companies with interests in film production and/or distribution might be required to divest any interests in exhibition, or to reduce such interests below a specified level, for example 10 per cent of the total number of screens in the UK.

9.74. Entertainment felt that, given the investment being put into exhibition and production, it would be unwise to restrict vertically integrated companies, so long as they did not use that integration to give them an unfair advantage in placing films. First Independent could not see that the proposal would be advantageous. Guild was not sure that the proposal was in the public interest. Rank's views are summarized in paragraphs 7.177 and 7.178.

## Termination of the UIP joint venture

9.75. We asked the distributors to comment on the possibility that the UIP joint venture in the distribution of films to cinemas in the UK might be terminated.

9.76. Entertainment told us that the fact that UIP was a joint venture gave it muscle in the market. First Independent said that the effect would be that the UIP partners would distribute their own films, thereby creating more jobs. Given that the partners required a return on their investments, it might be best to leave UIP alone. Guild said that it was not qualified to comment. Rank's views are summarized in paragraph 7.184.

## Prohibition on distribution joint ventures

9.77. The distributors were asked to comment on the possibility that the formation of joint ventures in distribution between parties which together had more than 20 per cent of the market, measured by share of rental receipts over a rolling four-year period, might be prohibited.

9.78. Entertainment believed this should be examined on a case-by-case basis. First Independent had no comment to make. Guild's reaction was that it might help to increase competition. Rank's views are summarized in paragraph 7.190.

## Termination of the UCI joint venture

9.79. We asked the distributors to comment on the possibility that the UCI joint venture in cinema exhibition in the UK might be terminated.

9.80. Entertainment said that UCI had done a lot for the exhibition business by investing a large amount in new cinemas. It would be foolish to terminate a growing venture. First Independent did not agree that the UCI joint venture should be terminated. It said that UCI was the only company with the courage to invest in UK exhibition when the industry was in decline. The UK exhibitors had stood on the sidelines. Neither Guild nor Rank expressed a view.

## Complaints

9.81. We asked the distributors to respond to the various complaints raised by third parties and summarized in Chapter 6. Their comments on the supply of prints, minimum exhibition periods, restrictions on screen use and the *Standard Conditions* are summarized earlier in this chapter. Their responses on other matters are summarized below. Other responses by Rank to complaints are summarized in paragraphs 7.202, 7.203, 7.205 and 7.206, 7.209, 7.211, 7.213, 7.218 and 7.219, 7.223, 7.226 to 7.228, 7.231, 7.234, 7.237 and 7.238, 7.241, 7.244, 7.246 and 7.248.

### *The CEA*

9.82. Responding to the CEA's complaint about the sharing of information (see paragraph 6.16), Rank told us that RFD did not share commercially sensitive information about members of the CEA with other members of the SFD. It did, from time to time, check break figures with other distributors.

### *Exhibitors*

9.83. Responding to the complaint by Richmond Filmhouse (see paragraph 6.23), Entertainment denied that Odeon had put any pressure on it with regard to the booking of *Much Ado About Nothing*. The Odeon cinema in Richmond was better situated than the Richmond Filmhouse and was frequented by a mainstream audience. Entertainment believed that for some films, particularly *Much Ado About Nothing*, the Odeon would attract a far wider audience than would the Richmond Filmhouse, which it described as an arthouse cinema.

9.84. Regarding the complaint about the unfair treatment of exhibitors and its effect on investment (see paragraph 6.24), Rank said that RFD could not reasonably be accused of treating independent exhibitors unfairly. All multiplex owners, whoever they were, received access to a wide variety of films from most distributors. This lent no support to the suggestion that investment in multiplex cinemas had been deterred.

9.85. Rank denied that RFD operated a key town priority system (see paragraph 6.26). While RFD would usually seek to arrange the exhibition of its films in the major cities as soon after release as possible, this did not mean that it would not consider requests from cinemas in towns nearby.

9.86. Rank did not know on what basis, or by what measure, Richmond Filmhouse claimed that the diversity of choice for films in the UK was not as wide as it could be (see paragraph 6.34). 44 per cent of the films released in the UK in 1992 were of non-US origin. Although US films accounted for about 86 per cent of total box office revenue, this was well within the range typical of other European countries, notwithstanding that the UK might, as an English language country, have been expected to have a greater US penetration. Although RFD distributed US films along with films from other countries, and Odeon was a major cinema operator, Rank said that it had no vested interest when deciding which films to show. Odeon did not give priority to films distributed by RFD.

9.87. Rank rejected Mr Henshaw's claim that prints were allocated to independent exhibitors on a random basis (see paragraph 6.35), saying that there was no random element in planning the release of a film. It was uncertain what was meant by the consideration given to multiplex cinemas (see paragraph 6.37). RFD treated multiplex cinemas in essentially the same way that it treated other cinemas to which it regularly supplied films on first release. It treated Odeon multiplex cinemas in the same way as it treated other multiplex cinemas.

## PACT

9.88. Responding to PACT's comments on bias against independently-produced UK and European films (see paragraphs 6.53 to 6.55), Rank said RFD did not consider that a narrow release led to restricted marketing and advertising budgets. Rather, it was the restricted budgets or the limited appeal of a film which usually limited the number of prints.

9.89. RFD did not accept that non-US films which were distributed by companies not vertically integrated with the major US studios were, by virtue of that fact, less attractive to UK audiences (see paragraph 6.54). If that were so, RFD would operate under a permanent handicap.

9.90. Regarding PACT's comment that distributors contributed very little finance to the making of films in the UK (see paragraph 6.55), Rank told us that RFD had contributed to the financing of 12 UK-made films in the last ten years.

9.91. Responding to PACT's comments on reduction in choice (see paragraphs 6.56 and 6.57), Rank agreed that many films generated most of their revenue in the first four weeks after release. It did not, however, agree that a film's potential revenue was exhausted after that time. RFD had, on a number of occasions, opened a film in a limited number of cinemas around the country, after which it was released in stages over a period of time. *Reservoir Dogs* was still being shown successfully after 14 months.

9.92. Regarding PACT's comments on internal transfer pricing (see paragraph 6.59), Rank said the suggestion that, for vertically integrated companies, the exhibitor's share of box office returns was simply a matter of internal transfer pricing was mistaken. RFD and Odeon operated at arm's length and the level of rental paid by Odeon reflected the market, both for films supplied by RFD and for all other films. The links between the two did not reduce competition, nor were opportunities for other exhibitors to take RFD's films in any way limited.

## The BFI

9.93. Responding to the BFI's statements on the current state of the British film industry (see paragraphs 6.93 and 6.94), Rank said that RFD would participate in the financing and distribution of any film which it regarded as commercially viable. The criteria that it applied in deciding the commercial potential of a film might not, however, be the same as the criteria used by the BFI in deciding what was a good film. Rank also told us that barriers to entry were low (see paragraph 6.106) as was evidenced by the level of output and critical acclaim of a number of low-budget British producers.

## Michael Henry

9.94. Responding to Mr Henry's comments, Rank said that, so far as RFD and Odeon were concerned, they did not regard their trading conditions as being directly or indirectly fixed by the MPAA corporations (see paragraph 6.123). In referring to the withdrawal of US financing from British cinema film production (see paragraph 6.131), Mr Henry ignored films such as *The Remains of the Day* and *Shadowlands*.

# APPENDIX 1.1

*(referred to in paragraphs 1.1, 2.5, 2.41 and 3.1)*

## The reference and conduct of the inquiry

1. On 29 September 1993 the Director General of Fair Trading sent to the MMC the following reference:

> The Director General of Fair Trading in exercise of his powers under sections 47(1), 49(1) and 50(1) of the Fair Trading Act 1973 hereby refers to the Monopolies and Mergers Commission the matter of the existence or the possible existence of a monopoly situation in relation to the supply of films for exhibition in cinemas in the United Kingdom.
>
> The Commission shall investigate and report on the questions whether a monopoly situation exists and if so:
>
> *(a)* by virtue of which provisions of sections 6 to 8 of the said Act that monopoly situation is taken to exist;
>
> *(b)* in favour of what person or persons that monopoly situation exists;
>
> *(c)* whether any steps (by way of uncompetitive practices or otherwise) are being taken by that person or those persons for the purpose of exploiting or maintaining the monopoly situation and if so by what uncompetitive practices or in what other way;
>
> *(d)* whether any action or omission on the part of that person or those persons is attributable to the existence of that monopoly situation and, if so, what action or omission and in what way it is so attributable; and
>
> *(e)* whether any facts found by the Commission in pursuance of their investigations under the preceding provisions of this paragraph operate or may be expected to operate against the public interest.
>
> In this reference:
>
> 'cinema' means any premises used for the exhibition of films;
>
> 'exhibition' means exhibition to the public;
>
> 'film' means any record, however made, capable of being used as a means of showing a sequence of visual images as a moving picture.
>
> The Commission shall report upon this reference within a period of ten months from the date hereof.
>
> 29 September 1993
>
> *(signed)* BRYAN CARSBERG
> *Director General of Fair Trading*

2. The questions in the reference are answered in the following paragraphs of the report:

   whether a monopoly situation exists: paragraphs 2.10 and 2.35;

   *(a)* paragraphs 2.10 and 2.35;

   *(b)* paragraph 2.40;

   *(c)* paragraphs 2.128, 2.164, 2.173 and 2.180;

*(d)* paragraphs 2.141 and 2.151; and

*(e)* paragraphs 2.129, 2.141, 2.154, 2.164, 2.173 and 2.180.

3. The composition of the group of members responsible for the present investigation and report is indicated in the list of members which prefaces this report.

4. Notices inviting interested parties to submit evidence to the MMC were placed in the *Financial Times* and *Screen International*. In addition we sought information and views from film producers, distributors and exhibitors and their representative organizations, film studios, television companies and consumer bodies, the DNH, the BFI and the EC Commission. Evidence received from these parties is summarized in Chapters 6, 7, 8 and 9. We held 23 hearings and one video conference.

5. Having regard particularly to the number of parties involved in the inquiry, we decided that the most efficient and helpful method of conducting the inquiry would be to look to each party's written submission for a comprehensive statement of its position and to ask only such parties as we considered necessary to attend hearings. This approach was drawn to the attention of the parties; their comments were invited; and it was made clear that, if a party which had not been invited to a hearing nevertheless wished to make oral representations, an opportunity would be given. The approach was somewhat different from the procedure followed in the majority of monopoly inquiries. Having considered the circumstances of the inquiry in the light of our statutory duties (in particular, section 81 of the Act) and our duty to act fairly, we are satisfied that the procedure adopted was both sensible and correct.

6. Members and staff of the MMC visited a five-screen cinema, a multiplex cinema and an independent exhibitor in Coventry and a multiplex cinema in Warrington. Visits were also made to Warner Distributors' head office in London and UCI's in Manchester, to the Centre National de la Cinématographie (CNC) in Paris and to the EC Commission.

7. Some of the evidence received during the course of our inquiry was of a commercially confidential nature and our report contains only such information as we consider necessary for a proper understanding of our conclusions.

8. We thank all those who helped with our inquiry, particularly the companies principally involved.

APPENDIX 2.1
*(referred to in paragraphs 2.17, 2.31, 2.35 2.128, 2.151, 2.164 and 2.238)*

## Schedule of practices engaged in by the members of the complex monopoly group

| | Alignment | Exclusivity | Refusal to supply | Minimum exhibition periods | Restrictions on screen use | Distributor influence on admission prices | SFD conditions |
|---|---|---|---|---|---|---|---|
| *Distributors* | | | | | | | |
| Buena Vista | Yes | Yes | Yes | Yes | Yes | Yes | Yes |
| Columbia | Yes | Yes | Yes | Yes | Yes | Yes | Yes |
| Entertainment | Yes* | Yes | Yes | Yes | Yes | Yes | Yes |
| First Independent | No† | Yes | Yes | Yes | Yes | Yes | Yes |
| Guild | Yes | Yes | Yes | Yes | Yes | Yes | Yes |
| RFD | Yes | Yes | Yes | Yes | Yes | Yes | Yes |
| Fox | Yes‡ | Yes | Yes | Yes‡ | Yes‡ | Yes‡ | Yes |
| UIP | Yes | No | Yes | Yes | Yes | Yes | Yes |
| Warner Distributors | Yes | No | Yes | Yes | Yes | Yes | Yes |
| *Exhibitors* | | | | | | | |
| MGM | Yes | No | N/A | N/A | N/A | Yes | Yes |
| Natl Amusements | No | No | N/A | N/A | N/A | Yes | Yes |
| Odeon | Yes | Yes | N/A | N/A | N/A | Yes | Yes |
| UCI | No | No | N/A | N/A | N/A | Yes | Yes |
| Warner Theatres | No | No | N/A | N/A | N/A | Yes | Yes |

*Source:* MMC, based on the companies' evidence.

*Entertainment does not consider that it is aligned to either of the two main circuits (see paragraph 9.10). Our conclusion that it is aligned to Odeon is explained in paragraph 2.22.

†First Independent provided information on the release of its films which substantiated its statement (see paragraph 9.12) that it is not aligned to either of the two main circuits.

‡Fox submitted that it did not engage in alignment, minimum exhibition periods, restrictions on screen use or distributor influence on admission prices (see paragraph 8.24). Our conclusion that it does engage in these practices is explained in paragraphs 2.19 to 2.21.

*Note:* N/A = not applicable.

APPENDIX 2.2

*(referred to in paragraph 2.36)*

## Original list of persons in whose favour the complex monopoly situation was provisionally considered to exist

The MMC's issues letter of 14 February 1994 said that the Commission had provisionally found that the complex monopoly situation existed in favour of the members of the complex monopoly group (listed in paragraph 2.12) and the following other persons:

Chargeurs SA
Crédit Lyonnais SA
Fox Inc
Matsushita Electric Industrial Co Limited
The News Corporation Limited
Paramount Communications Inc
The Rank Organisation Plc
Sony Corporation
Sony Pictures Entertainment Inc
Mr Sumner M Redstone
Time Warner Inc
United Cinemas International Multiplex BV
United International Pictures BV
The Walt Disney Company

APPENDIX 3.1

(referred to in paragraphs 2.2 and 3.3)

## Summary of the Monopolies Commission's 1966 report on *Films*

1. The following is a summary of the Monopolies Commission's report *Films: A Report on the Supply of Films for Exhibition in Cinemas* (HC 206, October 1966) made under the Monopolies and Restrictive Practices (Inquiry and Control) Act 1948 (the 1948 Act); and of action taken in response. References below in parentheses are to paragraph numbers in that report.

### Conclusions as to the conditions defined in the 1948 Act

2. More than one-third by value (as measured by the licence fees paid by exhibitors to distributors) of the films supplied to exhibitors in Great Britain were supplied to The Rank Organisation Ltd (Rank) companies. (178)

3. More than one-third by value (as measured by the licence fees paid by exhibitors to distributors) of the films supplied to exhibitors in Great Britain were supplied for exhibition in cinemas controlled by Associated British Picture Corporation Ltd (ABPC) and by Rank. ABPC and Rank so conducted their respective affairs as to restrict competition in connection with the supply of films in that for circuit deals each made a practice of booking films mainly from certain distributors, and in general did not deal with distributors who supplied the other. (180)

4. More than one-third by value (as measured by the licence fees paid by exhibitors to distributors) of the films supplied to exhibitors in Great Britain were supplied to exhibitors who so conducted their respective affairs as to restrict competition in connection with the supply of films in that by the operation of time and distance bars they restricted the freedom of distributors to offer films to other exhibitors. (182)

5. More than one-third by value (as measured by the licence fees paid by exhibitors to distributors) of the films supplied to exhibitors in Great Britain were supplied by persons who so conducted their respective affairs as to restrict competition in connection with the supply of films in that each sometimes made the supply of a particular film conditional upon the acceptance of other films. (187)

6. More than one-third by value (as measured by the licence fees paid by exhibitors to distributors) of the films supplied to exhibitors in Great Britain were supplied by members of the Kinematograph Renters' Society (the Society) who so conducted their respective affairs as to restrict competition in that, by agreement, they:

   *(a)* prevented exhibitors booking films on behalf of other exhibitors; and

   *(b)* limited the extent to which exhibitors used their premises for purposes other than the exhibition of films. (194)

### Conclusions on the public interest

7. Restrictions were operated by a large number of those engaged in the industry. In assessing the effect on the public interest, it was necessary to take into account not only the consequences which could be identified as resulting from each separate limitation of competition, but also the total effect of all the limitations. Thus the Monopolies Commission were not solely concerned with a straightforward monopoly situation, notwithstanding that Rank had a sufficient share of the supply of films to exhibitors to qualify as a monopoly under the 1948 Act. Nevertheless, although the anti-competitive practices of other parties could not be overlooked, the outstanding feature of the film industry's structure was the fact that it was effectively dominated by two companies, ABPC and Rank, and this fact inevitably played a large part in the consideration of the public interest. (195)

8. ABPC and Rank conducted their affairs so as to restrict competition, both because they did not compete with each other in obtaining films from distributors, and because by the exercise of bars they limited the freedom of other exhibitors to compete with them. Their dominance was reflected in the pattern of film distribution with only two regular channels of release, the ABPC release and the Rank release. Substantially all feature films which achieved public exhibition were distributed in the pattern set by one or other of these releases. This meant that they were shown not only in most of the cinemas of the circuit in question, but also in an even larger number of independently-owned cinemas which habitually followed the major circuits. In this situation, which was peculiar to Great Britain, a booking on one or other of the main circuits was essential to the financial success of any feature film produced in Great Britain. Without such a booking a film had little chance of reaching the public at large. The importance of a circuit booking thus put ABPC and Rank in a position to determine very largely which films should be given public exhibition, and hence what films should be made, since those who put up money for film production took account of what they believed to be the circuits' booking policies in their assessment of a proposed film's chances of success. (196)

## Summary of conclusions and recommendations and action taken in response

9. The introduction of a larger measure of competition into film exhibition would be advantageous both to the industry and the public. Competition was deficient partly because of the various practices customary in the industry, but mainly because of the structure of the industry which resulted from the dominant position of the two main exhibition circuits. To give the industry a new and competitive structure would mean breaking up the circuits, but that would be a drastic step the results of which would be uncertain. Instead the Commission recommended a series of less drastic remedies which were intended to eliminate practices which restricted competition. Although each remedy individually could not be expected to have far-reaching consequences, provided they were all carried out, their combined effect should be to permit the development of greater and more effective competition. (261)

10. The conditions to which the 1948 Act applied prevailed as respects the supply in Great Britain of films to exhibitors for exhibition in cinemas by virtue of Rank's share of the supply of films (178); the lack of competition between ABPC and Rank for films (180); the practice of barring (182); the practice of making the hire of one film conditional upon the hire of another (187); and two practices of the Society (194). All the conditions operated and might be expected to operate against the public interest. (230, 232, 234 and 238)

11. The preference which Rank gave to its own documentary films in cinemas which took more than one-third by value of the total supply of films was a thing done as a result of its monopoly position which operated and might be expected to operate against the public interest. (215)

12. By way of remedies the Commission made a number of recommendations which the Board of Trade discussed with the relevant sectors of the industry. The discussions resulted, in May 1967, in a joint agreement for the implementation of the recommendations, known as the Statement of Intent. The Commission's recommendations, and the action taken in response to them, may be summarized as follows:

(a) ABPC and Rank should undertake to extend the practice of giving trial runs to films whose appeal to the public was in doubt and giving limited or partial circuit bookings to films of limited appeal. *The undertakings were given.*

(b) Machinery should be set up to deal with disputes over the allocation of product; and exhibitors should have the right to bid for films in competition. *A Trade Disputes Committee was established to deal with complaints about the allocation of product, and an Appeals Tribunal with an independent chairman was also set up. The industry did not consider the introduction of competitive bidding was necessary and wished for consideration of its introduction to be deferred until after a review of the new disputes machinery in 1969. No further action was taken by the Board of Trade.*

(c) Rank should discontinue its practice of giving preferential bookings to its own documentaries and short films. *An undertaking on these lines was given.*

*(d)* The Board of Trade should keep under review the arrangements for settling disputes over time and distance bars. ***The recommendation was accepted.***

*(e)* No cinema (other than a West End cinema) should operate a bar on a film for longer than a four-week run. It should be left to the distributor to decide whether or not to let another cinema in the same town have a film while a long extended run was in progress. ***This recommendation was accepted with the reservation that it would not affect the right of a distributor to decide upon the availability of films in the light of its assessment of the commercial advantages.***

*(f)* Distributors should not make the hire of any film conditional upon the acceptance of others. ***All interested parties accepted the recommendation on the understanding that it would not prohibit transactions between willing purchasers and sellers.***

*(g)* The Society should cease its actions restricting co-operative bookings and limiting the use to which exhibitors put their premises. ***These recommendations were accepted.***

APPENDIX 3.2

*(referred to in paragraphs 2.2 and 3.8)*

## Summary of the MMC's 1983 report on *Films*

1. The following is a summary of the conclusions and recommendations of the MMC's report *Films: A Report on the Supply of Films for Exhibition in Cinemas* (Cmnd 8858, May 1983) made under the Act; and of action taken in response. References below in parentheses are to paragraph numbers in that report.

## The monopoly situation

2. In the four years 1978 to 1981, the average market shares of Columbia-EMI-Warner Distributors Ltd (CEW) and Cinema International Corporation Ltd (UK) (CIC (UK)) amounted to 30.7 and 21.8 per cent respectively. Since November 1981 United International Pictures (UK) (UIP (UK)) had distributed not only on behalf of those distributors previously served by CIC (UK) but also on behalf of United Artists, whose market share in recent years had been of the order of 10 per cent, so that UIP (UK)'s market share might be expected to be substantially larger than that of CIC (UK) and greater than 25 per cent. Over the same period of four years the average market shares of EMI Cinemas Ltd (EMI) and Rank Leisure Ltd (Rank) amounted to 32.2 and 26.2 per cent respectively. Because all these market shares, as expressed, exceeded 25 per cent, a monopoly situation existed by virtue of section 6(1)*(a)* in favour of the distributors CEW and (if allowance was made for the market share of United Artists) UIP (UK) and in favour of the exhibitors EMI and Rank. (8.3)

3. Many distributors, including CEW and UIP (UK), adopted a practice (referred to as the practice or system of alignments) of normally offering their films in the first instance either to EMI or to Rank in preference to all other exhibitors, but never to both.[1] EMI and Rank adopted the practice of accepting films on that basis. This practice restricted competition between distributors who did not obtain competing offers for licences to exhibit from EMI and Rank or from any other exhibitors. It also restricted competition between EMI and Rank who did not make such offers. A complex monopoly situation existed by virtue of section 6(1)*(c)* in favour of those distributors, including CEW and UIP (UK), who adopted the practice, and in favour of EMI and Rank who accepted films on the basis on which they were offered by those distributors. (8.4)

4. The bars which applied between cinemas were the results of long-standing settlements between exhibitors as to the order in which cinemas would show a film. Distributors accepted the bars, and implemented them by inclusion in their film hire agreements. Competition between distributors was restricted because they did not generally offer to license films to exhibitors except in the sequences determined by the bars. Competition between exhibitors was restricted because they did not generally attempt to obtain licences except in accordance with the bars. A complex monopoly situation existed by virtue of section 6(1)*(c)* in favour of those exhibitors, including EMI and Rank, and those distributors, including CEW and UIP (UK), who adopted the practice of barring. (8.5)

## The alignments between distributors and EMI and Rank

5. The system of alignments was no doubt a convenient way of doing business between the major distributors and the two major exhibition circuits, but it restricted competition, because EMI and Rank did not compete to obtain films at first run, nor were the major distributors taking any steps to encourage them to do so. Within a single system of decision-making operated by EMI and its aligned distributors on the one hand, and by Rank and its aligned distributors on the other, there was

---

[1]The only exception which occurred regularly was that seven cinemas which had an allocation of product received some films on a first-run basis instead of the relevant EMI or Rank cinemas.

effective control of some 60 per cent of the film exhibition market and a still greater share of the film distribution market in Great Britain. (8.17)

6. Alignments provided some certainty of outcome, as compared with the risks of a more competitive system. However, the dominant market share of EMI and Rank as exhibitors prevented others from becoming effective competitors in circumstances of very limited price competition. The alignments both helped to create the situation and to maintain it. They enabled EMI and Rank to exploit the scale monopoly situations which existed in their favour. The alignments operated and might be expected to operate against the public interest. (8.21)

7. An effective remedy would necessitate substantial reductions in the market shares of both EMI and Rank as exhibitors, in ways which would not lead to the re-creation of the existing degree of concentration in exhibition. Such a remedy would be likely to require the divestment of substantial numbers of EMI's and Rank's cinemas. Taking into account the decline in cinema audiences, the continuing need to close cinemas, and the fact that some surviving cinemas were making losses, such a remedy was not practicable and could not be recommended. (8.22)

## The system of barring

8. There might be somewhat less cost involved in operating the present system of barring instead of taking all exclusivity decisions on a case-by-case basis. But distributors had in any event to deal with many cinemas, and with most if not all exhibitors, in respect of films released on a substantial scale. It was not thought that their costs would increase to any substantial extent were they to operate differently (8.29). The present system of barring gave predetermined answers to questions of exclusivity, except on infrequent occasions. But the industry needed to choose between a number of release strategies and apply them to suit different films, in greatly varying numbers of cinemas. This required rapid responses to the public's reception of a film, and if necessary changes to the strategy of release. It had, for example, already become necessary to have a substantial—but itself predetermined—variation on the present set of 'general' bars to provide for television area releases. (8.30)

9. An exhibitor, when entering into a hire agreement to show a film at a particular cinema, would need to know whether other cinemas which were in effective competition with its own cinema were intending to show the film at the same time or immediately before, because in its judgment that would be likely to reduce the audience it could hope to obtain. The exhibitor would then need to decide whether to enter into an agreement on that basis, or on a different basis as regards those other cinemas if the distributor was prepared to agree to one, or whether instead to show a different film if it thought that would give a better result. When the exhibitor entered into the agreement, it would need to see that it reflected the terms for exclusivity agreed with the distributor. In the above sense, the need to define exclusivity was accepted. There was no great practical difficulty in terms for exclusivity being reached on a case-by-case, film-by-film basis, in the way outlined. Such a process might produce broadly similar results to the present system at least for some time. However, the present system of deciding exclusivity produced results which were determined, largely, by EMI and Rank. It did not achieve sufficient competition during the full period in which films were released. Although much of the industry was in favour of keeping some barring, many operators wanted to see changes made, towards less restriction and greater freedom of action and decision. Taking all those things into account, together with the restriction of competition caused by the alignments, on which the places of EMI and Rank in the system of barring partly depended, the present system of barring operated and might be expected to operate against the public interest, and other arrangements should be made to determine exclusivity. (8.31)

10. Appropriate steps should be taken to ensure that both distributors and exhibitors brought to an end the system whereby bars were decided and implemented, that they did not replace it with a like system, and that they conducted their respective businesses thereafter in such a way that provisions for exclusivity could be negotiated for each film hire agreement on a case-by-case basis (8.32). If such steps were implemented, it would follow that some of the *Standard Conditions* of the SFD, which dealt with barring and related matters, would either no longer apply (in which case the

SFD would doubtless wish to withdraw them) or would need to be amended to reflect the new circumstances in which exclusivity provisions would appear in film hire agreements. (8.33)

## Delays in the release of popular films to exhibitors other than EMI and Rank

11. Exhibitors who competed with EMI and Rank were disadvantaged when EMI and Rank obtained exclusive runs of unknown duration during which the film was unavailable to other exhibitors (8.34). Given the dominant market positions of EMI and Rank, reinforced by the effects of their alignments with CEW, UIP and most other distributors, a situation existed which worked generally to the disadvantage of exhibitors other than EMI and Rank, with the result that those other exhibitors obtained films later that they would have obtained them in the absence of the dominant positions of EMI and Rank, and of the alignments. The public had an interest in being able to see popular films early in their release, in places and at prices which suited their choice. Some people preferred to go to the city centre cinemas; others preferred to see the films locally, often at lower admission prices and perhaps lower costs of travel. The public did not have such a choice if the city centre cinema alone showed the film for a prolonged period. (8.43)

12. Delays in the release of popular films, particularly where this had happened in the large cities, were a distortion of competition between exhibitors. They affected the choice available to the public. In almost all cases they constituted an advantage gained by EMI and Rank by reason of their market power as scale monopolists in exhibition, which power was reinforced by the system of the alignments between them and most distributors. Such delays operated and might be expected to operate against the public interest. (8.44)

13. Arrangements should be made to provide that, at any stage in the release of a popular film, that film would not be exhibited for more than four weeks—nor thereafter re-exhibited—in any cinema unless or until the film had been made available to all other cinemas in effective competition which had sought to exhibit the film. For the distributor to meet this requirement, cinemas in effective competition with the first cinema to show the film, or with any subsequent cinema to show the film, must be able to obtain the right to exhibit the film when they sought to do so (within the terms of the preceding sentence), and to conclude a film hire agreement on terms consistent with those applying generally to film hire in the industry. When a film was first released to EMI and for as long as the distributors remain aligned either to EMI or Rank, Rank cinemas would not be regarded as being in effective competition with any EMI cinema showing the film. Likewise, in the case of first release to Rank, an EMI cinema would not be regarded as being in effective competition with any Rank cinema. (8.45)

14. The definition of a popular film should exclude films which did not obtain a first-run release in the EMI and Rank circuits and those which were not expected to achieve any substantial film hire rentals. A popular film could be currently defined as one for which 60 or more prints were or had become available in Great Britain. This definition should be reviewed after it had been in operation for a suitable period of time (8.47). The arrangements should not apply to the well-known cinemas in the West End of London in which film premières were staged (8.46). The primary criterion for deciding whether two cinemas were in effective competition with each other was whether, in the relevant circumstances, one would take significant audience from the other. Distributors and exhibitors would be able to decide on this matter, and would have information to support their judgments. Any dispute as to whether one cinema was competing with another should be capable of being referred to the Trade Disputes Committee (TDC). (8.49)

15. Film hire agreements should be negotiated on terms consistent with those applying generally in the industry. Cases might arise, nevertheless, in which a distributor or an exhibitor might feel that it was being subjected to undue pressure, in a subsequent-run situation, to depart from such terms. If that happened sufficiently often as to be considered a course of conduct, as distinct from an occasional and mutually acceptable departure from generally accepted terms, the matter should be capable of being referred to the TDC. If the Committee felt able to decide whether the situation was or was not in accordance with the recommended arrangements, its decision should then be taken into account in future negotiations by the exhibitor and distributor concerned. (8.50)

## Other possible effects of the scale monopoly situations

16. Concentration in the distribution sector had developed to the point that CEW and UIP were scale monopolists, and were likely to remain so (8.53). The degree of concentration in the distribution sector had recently increased as a result of the creation of UK Film Distributors Ltd, a joint venture between Twentieth Century Fox and Walt Disney. Concern was expressed at the possibility of still further concentration, because the way in which films were released, and the way in which the existing groups operated, could change; and because nearly all distributors were involved in the complex monopoly arising from the system of alignments, which had been found to operate against the public interest, but against which it had not been possible to recommend any remedy. Any further moves which would increase the degree of concentration in film distribution in Great Britain, and especially if it involved any of the three existing groups, should be looked at carefully under the arrangements for dealing with mergers under the Act. (8.56)

17. It appeared unlikely that EMI or Rank would seek to acquire cinemas, with the result that they increased their market shares in exhibition. But in the eventuality that they did, it would be detrimental to the public interest. (8.57)

## The Trade Disputes Committee and the Appeals Tribunal

18. Representatives of the industry should continue to have a voice in decisions made by its TDC. Independent persons could with advantage play a major role. Two of the four members should become persons who did not have active involvement in the industry, while the other two should be persons who had such involvement. An independent person should be appointed as Chairman of the TDC thus bringing its membership to five. A single stage procedure should replace the present two-tier arrangement of the TDC and the Appeals Tribunal, by dispensing with the Appeals Tribunal. (8.60)

19. The removal of the present system of barring, as recommended, would mean that no further disputes about that system or its operation would arise for the TDC to consider. However, if the recommendations to limit exclusive runs were implemented, there would be a need to decide whether one cinema was in effective competition with another or not. If the operation of the new arrangements were to give rise to complaints or disputes, these could be made to the TDC, which should be empowered to deal with those matters (8.61). The TDC should also be empowered to deal with disputes or complaints about the terms on which film hire agreements were negotiated, in connection with the arrangements recommended to limit the delays in popular films being released to exhibitors other than EMI and Rank (8.62). The recommendations were not intended to restrict the TDC from considering any other problems in the distribution or exhibition of films which the industry might see fit to refer to the committee (8.63). The TDC should continue to consider applications for allocation of product. (8.64)

## The SFD's *Standard Conditions*

20. The SFD argued that there was no basis for a finding that a recommendation by the SFD to its members that they should use standard terms and conditions in transactions with exhibitors could be said to form the basis of a complex monopoly situation comprising the members of the SFD. The SFD said that it had so ordered its affairs that its *Standard Conditions* related exclusively to an agreement under which its members did no more than grant a licence to exhibit a film. This was not an agreement which related to the supply of goods or services and accordingly, the SFD argued, could not be dealt with under the reference to the MMC. (8.69 and 8.70)

21. In law a distinction might at times be drawn between the right to exhibit and the right to acquire the means to exhibit. But in practice no cinema exhibitor would enter into a transaction under which it would pay for the right to exhibit a film to the public in its cinema without, at the same time and in the course of the same transaction, securing the right to the film itself (8.71). It was clear that for the cinema exhibitor, dealing with a distributor who was the only source of supply to which it could turn, the purchase of exhibition rights alone without the supply of the film itself would be

pointless. The same could be said of the distributor, since its right to payment in respect of exhibition to the public was dependent upon the attendance of the public at a cinema which had been supplied with the film in question. For both parties to the transaction, the right to exhibit was inextricably bound up with the agreement to supply, and the transaction would be meaningless in the absence of one or the other. Attempts to distort this position, and thus to avoid the consequences of competition law in the UK, by purporting to distinguish between what would otherwise be regarded as the inseparable elements of a straightforward (albeit particular) commercial transaction between distributor and exhibitor were inappropriate and unconvincing. (8.72)

22. Three of the standard conditions dealt with barring, advertising in relation to the operation of bars, and with runs. If the recommendations were adopted, it would be necessary for those standard conditions, and any others that might be affected by those recommendations, to be amended or withdrawn (8.73). As regards the other standard conditions and recommendations, some appeared to restrict the freedom of individual distributors and exhibitors to negotiate agreements, particularly as regards terms of credit. Some conditions dealing, for example, with the programming of films and with equipment in cinemas also appeared to be outdated or unnecessary. (8.74)

## Summary of conclusions and recommendations and action taken in response

23. Scale monopoly situations existed in favour of CEW and UIP (UK), and EMI and Rank. The system of alignments gave rise to a complex monopoly situation which operated and might be expected to operate against the public interest. Divestment was considered but not recommended.

24. The present system of barring gave rise to a complex monopoly situation which operated and might be expected to operate against the public interest. The system should cease to operate, and be replaced by arrangements under which exclusivity would be negotiated for each film hire agreement on a case-by-case basis. *Following consultation with the industry, the 1989 Order prohibiting barring came into effect in April 1989* (see Appendix 3.3).

25. Delays in the release of popular films to exhibitors other than EMI and Rank were a consequence of the market power which those companies possessed as scale monopolists, which power was reinforced by the system of alignments as a complex monopoly. Arrangements should be made to place limits on the length of time for which cinemas might exhibit popular films in certain circumstances. *Consultation with the industry revealed strong opposition to the imposition of a four-week limit. The recommendation was not proceeded with.*

26. The procedures and membership of the TDC and the Appeals Tribunal should be changed. The TDC should be empowered to deal with disputes relating to the extent of competition between individual cinemas. It should also be empowered to deal with disputes or complaints in connection with film hire agreements in certain circumstances. The arrangements for awarding allocations of product to independent exhibitors should continue. *Developments in the industry between 1983 and 1989 led the DTI and the OFT to agree that the remit envisaged for the TDC had disappeared. The recommendations relating to the TDC were considered to be no longer relevant, particularly as the question of the allocation of product was addressed by the 1989 Order. The recommendations were not proceeded with.*

APPENDIX 3.3

*(referred to in paragraphs 2.3 and 3.15)*

## The Films (Exclusivity Agreements) Order 1989

*Made*                                          *28th February 1989*
*Laid before Parliament*             *7th March 1989*
*Coming into force*                     *4th April 1989*

Whereas the Secretary of State, in accordance with section 91(2) of the Fair Trading Act 1973(a), published on 19 August 1988 a notice stating his intention to make this Order, indicating the nature of the provisions to be embodied in it and stating that any person whose interests were likely to be affected by it and who was desirous of making representations in respect of it should do so in writing before 30 September 1988;

And whereas the Secretary of State has considered the representations made to him in accordance with that notice;

Now, therefore, the Secretary of State, being the appropriate Minister within the meaning of section 56 of the said Act, in exercise of the powers conferred by sections 56(2) and 90(2) and (4) of, and paragraphs 1, 2 and 4 of Schedule 8 to, the said Act and for the purpose of remedying or preventing adverse effects specified in a report of the Monopolies and Mergers Commission entitled 'A Report on the Supply of Films for Exhibition in Cinemas'(b), hereby makes the following Order:—

**Citation and commencement**

1. This Order may be cited as the Films (Exclusivity Agreements) Order 1989 and shall come into force on 4th April 1989.

**Definitions**

2. In this Order—

'cinema' means any premises in Great Britain which are used for the exhibition of films and which require a licence or consent for that purpose under section 1 or 2 of the Cinemas Act 1985(c);

'distributor' means a person carrying on the business of supplying films to exhibitors for exhibition;

'exhibition' means exhibition to the public;

'exhibitors' means a person carrying on the business of exhibiting films;

'film' means any record, however made, capable of being used as a means of showing a sequence of visual images as a moving picture;

'terms about exclusivity means terms restricting a distributor from authorising the exhibition of a film at a cinema.

3.—(1) Subject to paragraphs (3) and (4) of this article, it shall be unlawful for an exhibitor or a distributor to make or carry out any agreement relating to the supply of any film for exhibition at a

---

(a) 1973 c.41.

(b) Cmnd. 8858.

(c) 1985 c.13.

cinema if the agreement contains or provides for terms about exclusivity applied or to be applied to more than one film.

(2) Paragraph (1) above shall apply to prohibit the carrying out of an agreement already in existence on 4th April 1989 (including any agreement already in existence on 28th February 1989) and any distributor or exhibitor who is a party to such an agreement shall terminate it before 2nd May 1989.

(3) This article shall not apply to an agreement in so far as it is or, if made, would be an agreement to which the Restrictive Trade Practices Act 1976(a) applies or, as the case may be, would apply.

(4) This article shall not apply to an agreement if it relates to not more than three films in respect of their exhibition at the cinema in question as a single programme.

**4.** It shall be unlawful for an exhibitor to withhold or to threaten to withhold any order for exhibition of a film at a cinema on the ground that terms about exclusivity in respect of any other film have not been agreed or are not being complied with.

28th February 1989

*Francis Maude*
Parliamentary Under Secretary of State
for Corporate Affairs,
Department of Trade and Industry

### EXPLANATORY NOTE
*(This note is not part of the Order)*

This Order makes it unlawful for any distributor or exhibitor to make or carry out an agreement (whether existing or future) for exhibition of a film at a cinema if that agreement contains exclusivity terms (terms restricting distribution) relating to more than one film. The Order also makes it unlawful for an exhibitor to refuse to deal with a distributor on the ground that exclusivity terms for more than one film have not been agreed or complied with.

The Order does not apply to agreements in so far as they are agreements to which the Restrictive Trade Practices Act 1976 (c.34) applies. Nor does it apply to two or three films being shown as a single programme.

Copies of the report of the Monopolies and Mergers Commission on which the Order is based (Cmnd. 8858) may be obtained from Her Majesty's Stationery Office.

---

(a) 1976 c.34.

APPENDIX 4.1

*(referred to in paragraphs 4.30, 4.32, 4.63 and 4.83)*

# Distributors and exhibitors in the UK

## Distributors

*Note:* An asterisk against the title of a film mentioned in this appendix indicates that the film was British-made.

### *UIP*

1. UIP BV was formed in 1981 in the Netherlands, a joint venture by MCA/Universal, MGM Inc and Paramount (the UIP partners). Its purpose was to distribute feature films and short films produced and acquired by the three partners and their affiliates for theatrical and non-theatrical exhibition outside the USA and Canada. UIP BV licenses the films of its three partners to United International Pictures, a UK-based unlimited company which is responsible for the distribution of the partners' films in all countries outside North America. This company sub-licenses the film rights which it receives from UIP BV to the various national distribution companies. In the UK the distribution company is United International Pictures (UK), referred to in this report as UIP. UIP has a right of first refusal to distribute films produced or distributed by each of the three joint partners in its parent company. It has distributed on average about 29 films in the UK each year since 1988. The great majority (80 per cent) of these films emanated from two of the three partners, Paramount and MCA/Universal, with very few from MGM Inc (except in 1988). Paramount has been the source of many of UIP's most successful films since 1988, including *Fatal Attraction* (first released in 1988), *Crocodile Dundee II* (1988), *Indiana Jones and the Last Crusade\** (1989) and *Ghost* (1990). *Jurassic Park*, first released in the UK in July 1993, was produced by Universal, as was *Schindler's List* (1994). UIP also distributed *Shadowlands\** (1994) produced in the UK by Shadowlands Productions.

### *Warner Distributors*

2. Warner Distributors began operating in the UK in 1931 and is now a subsidiary of Time Warner Entertainment Company LP (a Limited Partnership registered in the US state of Delaware) which in turn is majority owned by Time Warner. Time Warner's Entertainment Group comprises companies engaged in film entertainment and related businesses. Between 1988 and 1992 Warner Distributors distributed Walt Disney films in addition to those films produced or acquired by Warner Bros International (a division of Time Warner) or any other company within the Time Warner Entertainment Group. Since the end of 1992 Disney films have been distributed in the UK by Buena Vista, a Walt Disney subsidiary company. Warner Distributors distributed on average about 16 Warner Bros International films in the UK each year since 1988. Among the more successful in recent years were *Batman\** (1989), *Robin Hood: Prince of Thieves\** (1991), *Lethal Weapon* (1992), *Batman Returns* (1992), *The Bodyguard* (1993), *The Fugitive* (1993) and *The Secret Garden\** (1993). *Pretty Woman* (1990) and *Three Men and a Little Lady* (1991) were two of the Walt Disney films distributed by Warner Distributors.

### *Columbia*

3. Columbia is the division of Columbia Pictures Corporation Limited (CPCL) which has been responsible since at least 1983 for theatrical and private screen distribution of films in the UK. It distributes the film output of its affiliated US companies, Columbia Pictures Industries Inc and Tristar Pictures Inc. CPCL is a UK registered company and is now ultimately owned by the Japanese company Sony Corporation. Columbia has distributed, on average, 20 films each year since 1989. Its most successful recent films in the UK include *Look Who's Talking* (1990), *The Addams Family*

(1991), *Hook* (1992), *Bram Stoker's Dracula* (1993), *Sleepless in Seattle* (1993), *The Remains of the Day\** (1993) and *Philadelphia* (1994).

## *Buena Vista*

4. Buena Vista, a wholly-owned subsidiary of The Walt Disney Company, started distributing films in November 1992. Between 1988 and 1992 Disney films had been distributed in the UK by Warner Distributors. Buena Vista distributes films from three main film production companies, namely Walt Disney Pictures, Touchstone Pictures and Hollywood Pictures (all of which are owned by Walt Disney). In its first full year of trading in the UK Buena Vista distributed 18 films. Its first release was *Sister Act* (1992), and among its other releases some of the most popular were *Honey, I Blew Up The Kids*, *The Jungle Book*, *What's Love Got To Do With It* and *Aladdin*, all released in 1993, and *Cool Runnings*, *Sister Act II*, *The Three Musketeers\** and *My Father the Hero*, all released in 1994.

## *Fox*

5. Fox is a subsidiary of Fox Inc, which since 1985 has been a wholly-owned subsidiary of The News Corporation Limited based in South Australia. Fox distributes mainly those films covered by a franchise agreement with Twentieth Century Fox International Corporation, but it also acquires rights from third parties to license other titles for cinema exhibition. In the period 1988 to 1992 Fox distributed on average about seven films each year in the UK. *Sleeping with the Enemy* and *The Commitments\** (both released in 1991), *Alien III* (1992), *Home Alone 2: Lost in New York* (1992) and *Mrs Doubtfire* (1994) have been among the more successful of recent Fox titles.

## *Independent distributors*

6. There are about 24 independent distributors who trade on their own account, and the majority of them distribute fewer than ten films each year (see paragraph 4.31). The main independent distributors include Guild, Entertainment, First Independent, RFD, Electric Pictures, Artificial Eye and Metro Tartan. The last four named distributors also have some interest in cinema exhibition. In May 1994 Mayfair and Artificial Eye announced their intention to merge their distribution interests. Independents have distributed a number of successful films. Examples include: Artificial Eye's *Farewell my Concubine* (1994) and *Short Cuts* (1994); Entertainment's *Highlander II* (1991), *Peter's Friends\** (1992), *Super Mario Brothers* (1993), *Much Ado About Nothing\** (1993), *The Piano* (1993), *Mr Nanny* (1993), *The Man Without a Face* (1993), *Tombstone* (1994) and *The Crow* (1994); Guild's *Total Recall* (1990), *Dances with Wolves* (1991), *Terminator 2* (1991), *Basic Instinct* (1992) and *Cliffhanger* (1993); First Independent's *The Lawnmower Man\** (1991); Mayfair's *Howards End\** and *The Crying Game\**, both distributed in 1991; and RFD's *The Krays\** (1990), *Silence of the Lambs* (1991), *Reservoir Dogs* (1993), *Malice* (1994) and *Four Weddings and a Funeral\** (1994).

## Exhibitors

### *MGM Cinemas*

7. MGM Cinemas is the largest operator of cinemas in the UK. It currently (July 1994) operates 119 cinemas with a total of 394 screens. It originated in a series of structural changes affecting EMI Cinemas Ltd, which had the largest cinema chain at the time of the MMC's last report. EMI Cinemas was acquired by Cannon Group (Cannon) in 1986 and four years later Cannon acquired MGM Inc, the Hollywood studio. The studio is now owned by Crédit Lyonnais, the third largest bank in France, as a result of loan default. MGM Cinemas told us that since September 1993 it had operated separately from, and was no longer controlled by, MGM Inc, but reported to Crédit Lyonnais through a separate reporting chain.

8. Many of MGM Cinemas' cinemas are quite small. It has 9 single-screen cinemas, 29 with two screens and 56 with three screens. Thus 94 of its 119 cinemas have fewer than four screens. MGM Cinemas trades as Cannon except in the West End of London and at its 17 multiplex cinemas. The locations of all MGM Cinemas' cinemas in the UK are shown in Figure 1.

## *Odeon*

9. Odeon, owned by Rank, is the second largest operator of cinemas in the UK, with 73 cinemas containing 319 screens in total. Forty-seven of its 73 cinemas have three, four or five screens, and it has so far invested in eight new multiplex cinemas. Figure 1 also shows the location of all the Odeon cinemas in the UK.

## *UCI*

10. UCI is the UK subsidiary of UCI BV, a joint venture between Paramount BV and MCA BV. These two partners are also the joint owners of Cinema International Corporation NV, whose UK subsidiary, CIC UK (CIC), owns two London West End cinemas (the Empire and Plaza) which are managed on its behalf by UCI. UCI, now the leading multiplex operator in the UK, is a new entrant to the industry since the MMC's 1983 report. In December 1988 UCI's partners acquired, from American Multiplex Cinemas Inc, a chain of 19 multiplex cinemas (built or under development), including the UK's first multiplex cinema (The Point in Milton Keynes) which had opened in November 1985. UCI has since built new multiplexes, mostly on out-of-town sites, and it now operates 24 multiplex cinemas containing 225 screens. Figure 2 shows the location of all multiplex cinemas in the UK, including those of UCI.

## *Natl Amusements*

11. Natl Amusements operates ten multiplex cinemas containing 127 screens, mainly in the Midlands and North of England, having entered the UK exhibition market in 1988. Natl Amusements operates these cinemas under lease from National Amusements Ltd, which owns the land and the buildings. Mr S M Redstone (a US citizen) and certain members of his family own Natl Amusements, and the companies' day-to-day operations are actively managed from the company headquarters in Dedham, Massachusetts. National Amusements Inc, which is in the same ownership as Natl Amusements, is one of the eight largest cinema circuits in the USA and one of the earliest to build multiplexes there; it also owns National Amusements Ltd. Mr Redstone is also Chairman and, together with members of his family through National Amusements Inc, the majority shareholder of Viacom Inc (Viacom), one of the world's largest communications and entertainment companies. Viacom owns cable television networks and produces television programmes, as well as operating radio and television stations in the USA. In early 1994 Viacom acquired Paramount, the acquisition being completed in July 1994.

## *Warner Theatres*

12. Warner Bros Theatres Limited was incorporated in 1931 solely to own and operate the Warner cinema in Leicester Square in the West End of London (known as the Warner West End). A second company, Warner Bros Theatres (UK) Limited, was incorporated in 1987 to develop a national chain of multiplex cinemas. The two companies, which are both part of the Time Warner Entertainment Group, are managed together. The Warner West End cinema served for many years as a showcase cinema for Warner films. It was closed in September 1991 for conversion into a nine-screen cinema and reopened in September 1993. Warner Theatres opened its first multiplex in Bury in 1989, and has since opened seven other multiplexes, mainly in the Midlands and the North of England. Together with its Warner West End cinema, it now operates nine cinemas containing 84 screens.

# FIGURE 1

# Locations of cinemas operated by MGM Cinemas and Odeon, July 1994

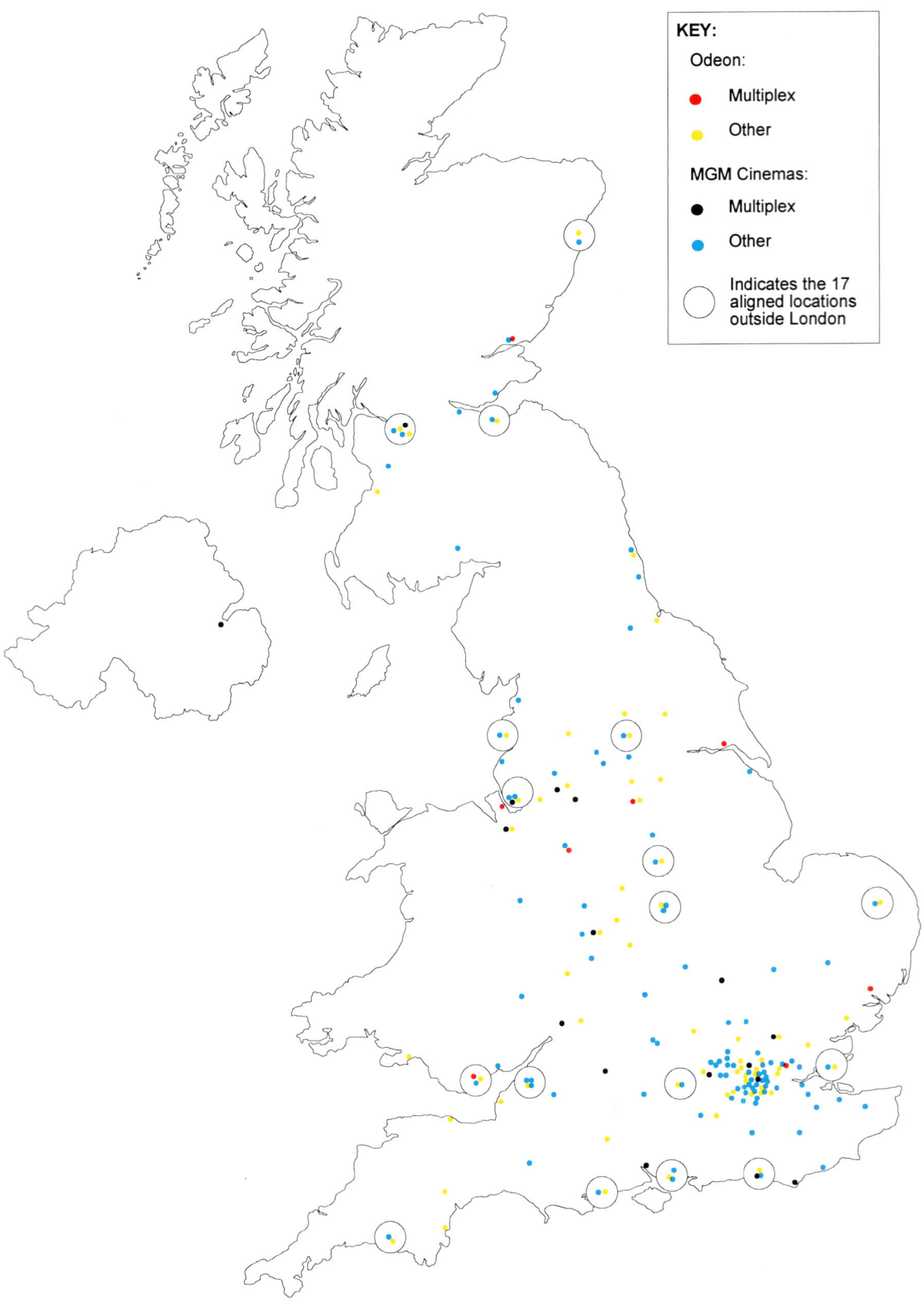

Source: MMC.

FIGURE 2

**Location of multiplex cinemas in the UK, July 1994**

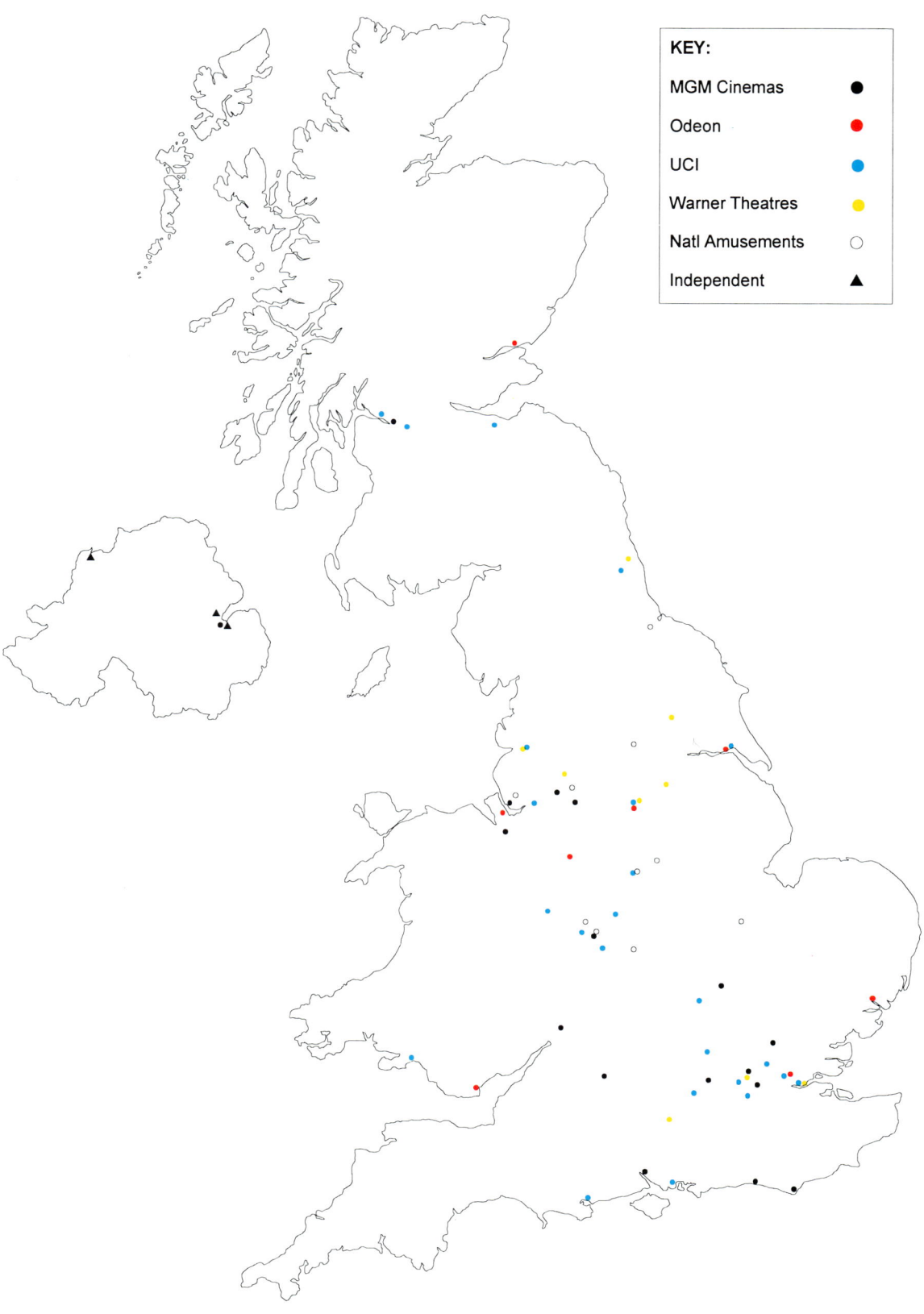

*Source:* MMC.

## *Independent exhibitors*

13. Most of the independent exhibitors operate either single-screen cinemas or a small number of multi-screen cinemas. These are mostly in small towns, but a few are in cities. Figure 3, which shows the locations of all the cinemas in the South-West region of England, illustrates the extent to which the less densely populated areas of the UK are served by independent cinemas. The seven counties in this region (Avon, Cornwall, Devon, Dorset, Gloucestershire, Somerset and Wiltshire) currently have just three multiplex cinemas: MGM Cinemas' multiplex cinemas in Gloucester (six screens, which opened in December 1990) and Swindon (seven screens, which opened in March 1991); and UCI's ten-screen cinema in Poole, which opened in December 1989). Two more are to open in August 1994: a Natl Amusements 12-screen multiplex cinema in Bristol, and Odeon's five-screen multiplex cinema in Taunton. There are also a further seven cinemas operated by MGM Cinemas and nine by Odeon, with 58 independent cinemas (including ten part-time cinemas and three RFTs).

FIGURE 3

**Locations of cinemas in the South-West Region of England, July 1994**

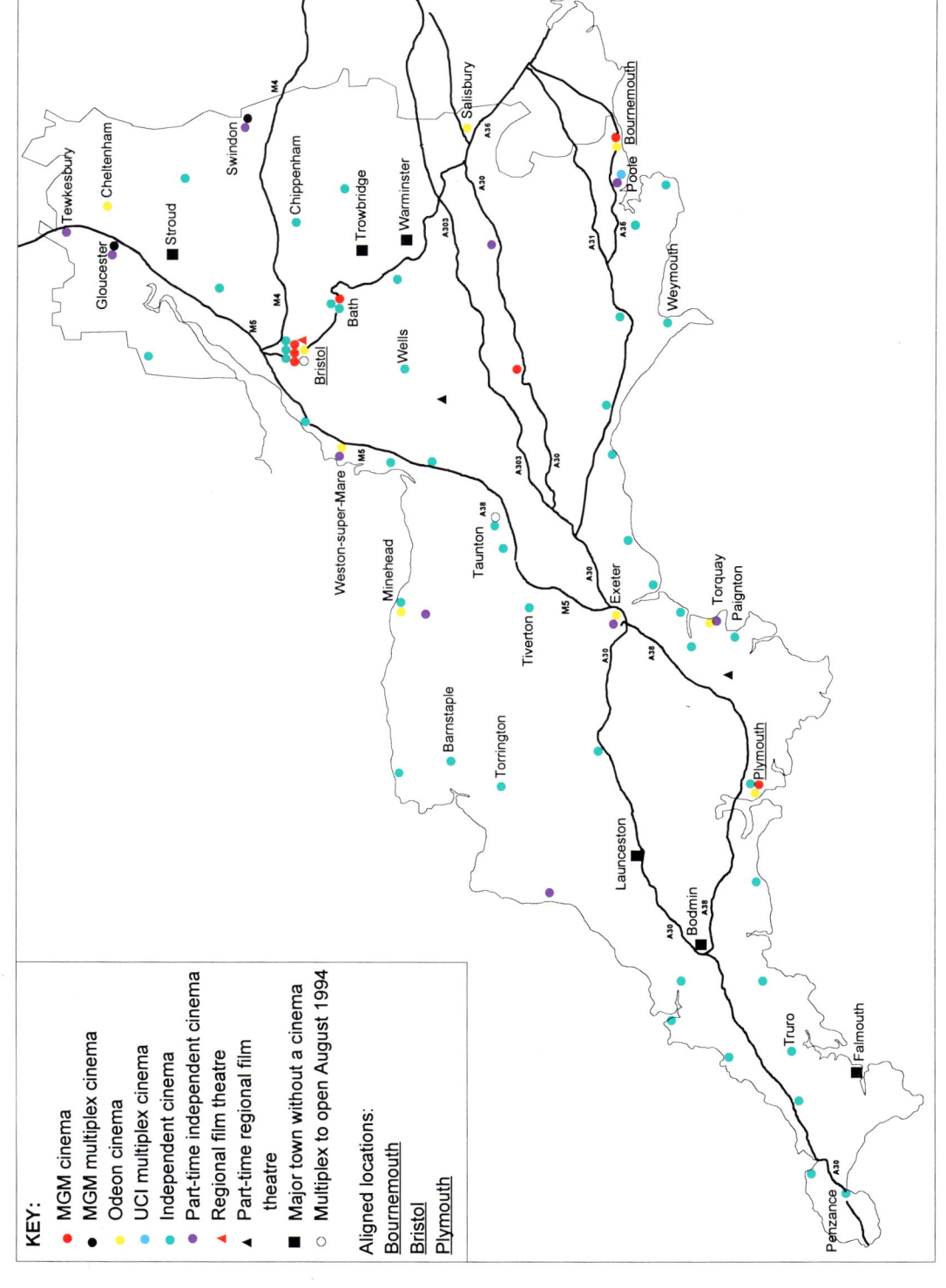

*Source:* MMC, based on cinema information published in the BFI's *Film & Television Handbook*, 1994.

APPENDIX 4.2

*(referred to in paragraph 4.49)*

# Taxation: a summary of the main issues affecting film production in the UK

## Introduction

1. We were told by several parties of the concern expressed by some in the industry that film production in the UK had been hindered by what was regarded as an unfavourable tax regime here compared with the tax regimes in other countries. A number of research papers, pamphlets and articles have been written on this subject during recent years, some in preparation for, or following up from, the Downing Street seminar in June 1990 (see paragraph 3.20). The effects of many of these taxation and other issues on film production in the UK are set out and considered in a series of booklets published by the BFI under the series title *UK Film Initiatives* (the first was published in 1991, and the sixth and most recent in 1993).

2. Two aspects of the UK tax regime have been highlighted as causing difficulties for the film industry here. The first concerns tax relief for expenditure on film production and for new investment in film production facilities, and the second concerns the treatment of income tax (and in particular, the effect of bilateral and other taxation agreements between different countries).

3. No two countries' tax regimes and tax rates are the same, and great care must be taken in comparing and assessing the particular effects of individual aspects of each regime in isolation from the whole of which they are part. In presenting the summary information in this appendix, we do not wish to imply that we have come to any conclusion about any detrimental effects the present UK tax regime may have on the making of films in the UK. Such an assessment would have to be based on a thorough understanding not only of the taxation issues, but also of the many other factors which may influence a production company's film-by-film decisions on where to make their films.

## Tax relief on expenditure and investment

4. Until 1979 expenditure on the production of a film had been treated as a revenue expense for tax purposes, but an Inland Revenue statement that year confirmed that such expenditure could be treated as expenditure on plant. This statement created incentives for companies to invest in films and achieve tax savings or deferrals by means of a variety of transactions, some involving the sale and leaseback of films, others involving the 'gearing' of investments by way of non-recourse loans. It is thought that the availability of capital allowances attracted into the film production industry a substantial amount of investment from the industrial sector and provided a great stimulus to film production in the UK.

5. Significant changes in Corporation Tax were announced in 1983, particularly that the rate payable was to be reduced in stages from 50 to 35 per cent. It was also announced that Capital Allowances were to be reduced in stages from 100 per cent of expenditure in the first year to 25 per cent a year of the reducing balance. These changes, the implementation of which was completed by 1988, applied to all companies and were not specific to the film industry. The overall effect for nearly all companies, however, was to reduce the amount of tax payable. The effect on the film industry was a marked decrease in outside investment, which had principally been tax-driven.

6. In 1992 additional rules for the treatment of expenditure on British-made films were introduced. In outline, these allowed 100 per cent of pre-production costs (to a maximum of 20 per cent of a film's production costs) to be written off as incurred, and for the remainder of the production costs to be written off in three equal instalments once a film had been delivered. Commenting at the time, the Director of the BFI said that the new measures were a first step towards relieving the cash-flow problem for producers, but they did not solve the investment shortage problem. The Director felt that

the industry wanted to get back to its position in 1979, and that while these new measures were helpful, the solution was to repeal section 68 of the Capital Allowances Act 1990 in its entirety.

7. In considering the impact of various taxation measures on film production in the UK, it should be borne in mind that the production of individual films is generally carried out by companies specially established for that purpose. Receipts will usually only cover the production budget, so that the production company will not record a profit; for an unsuccessful film it will show a loss. Royalties in the resulting films will be owned in companies separate from those which distributed and exhibited them, and their profits will be taxable. Thus, while increased Capital Allowances would be of no benefit to newly-established production companies, since they have no immediate tax liabilities against which allowances could be offset, they might be of some benefit to established companies which financed several productions and which could use the allowances to defer payments of Corporation Tax.

## Withholding of income tax

8. The second taxation issue concerns the application of a base rate withholding tax assessment by the UK Government of foreign film stars. Since April 1987, payments to non-resident entertainers (broadly defined) have been subject to deductions of income tax at the basic rate (this provision excludes the directors of films, and others employed behind the scenes). All non-resident workers are subject to UK income tax on their UK earnings, and the withholding tax amounts essentially to a payment on account. This tax provision is a widely used anti-avoidance measure aimed at taxpayers who are unlikely to be resident in a country for more than a few weeks. It applies to a wide range of entertainers, including musicians, and sports people, and not just to film actors.

9. In most cases non-resident entertainers should be able to claim tax relief in their own countries for any UK taxes paid. But it may take them a year or more to do this, and in the meantime they are out of pocket. The effect is often that the film producer has to agree to indemnify the film stars against their UK tax liability, causing an increased production budget, and a nuisance which may be sufficient to switch the film's production to (say) the Irish Republic or to another European country.

APPENDIX 4.3
*(referred to in paragraphs 2.20, 4.76, 4.131, 4.188, 6.8 and 6.39)*

## SFD: Standard Conditions
## for licensing the commercial exhibition of a film or films

(adopted by the Council on 14th January 1960, revised 12th January 1961, May 1973, 10th February 1977, 8th February 1990, 20th June 1991 and 15th April 1993).

THE CONDITIONS set out below are the Standard Conditions which will be deemed to be incorporated in all Agreements for the licensing of the exhibition of cinematograph films entered into between members of the Society of Film Distributors Limited and Exhibitors unless and except to the extent to which any particular Agreement specifically provides to the contrary:—

1. **DEFINITIONS**

    In these Standard Conditions the following expressions have the following meanings:—

    'SFD' means the Society of Film Distributors Limited.

    'The Agreement' means any particular Agreement for the grant by a member of SFD to an Exhibitor of a licence to exhibit a single cinematograph film or a licensed programme.

    'The Distributor' in the case of any particular Agreement means that member of SFD who is a party to that Agreement and its successors and assigns as owner or licensee of the copyright in the film or films the exhibition of which is licensed by that Agreement.

    'Distributor' or 'Distributors' means a member or members of SFD.

    'The Exhibitor' means the exhibitor party to the Agreement and his permitted assigns.

    'The Film' means the cinematograph film or each cinematograph film comprised in a licensed programme the exhibition of which is licensed by the Agreement and "film" includes any record, however made, of a sequence of visual images, which is a record capable of being used as a means of showing that sequence as a moving picture.

    'Licensed Programme' means any two or more films the exhibition of which is licensed by the Agreement and which are indicated in the Schedule to the Agreement as comprising a single programme.

    'The licence period' means the licence period mentioned in the Agreement.

    'The cinema' means the cinema cinemas or other place or places at which the rights of exhibition granted to the Exhibitor under the Agreement are to be exercisable and includes for the purposes of Condition 2 all premises used by the Exhibitor in connection with his business at the cinema.

    'Receipts' means all moneys received by the Exhibitor in connection with the exhibition of the film at the cinema including all fees commissions and premiums on bookings or reservations and on the sale of seats by whomsoever received less Value Added Tax on such money.

    'Fixed licence fee' means the fee payable to the Distributor by the Exhibitor in respect of the licence to exhibit the film if the Agreement provides for the payment of a fixed sum in that connection which fee for all the purposes of the Agreement and these Standard Conditions shall be deemed to accrue from day to day.

'Distributors share' means the share of the receipts payable to the Distributor by the Exhibitor if the Agreement so provides.

'Month' means calendar month.

'The Schedule' means the Schedule to the Agreement.

Any reference to a statute shall be deemed to include any statutory modification or re-enactment thereof.

2. **PAYMENT, SHARING TERMS AND DISTRIBUTOR'S RIGHTS OF INSPECTION AND COLLECTION**

   (a) The Distributor's share shall be deemed to belong to the Distributor as and from the time of payment by customers at the pay boxes at the cinema and the Distributor may if it thinks fit appoint any person or persons to collect at the cinema during the licence period the Distributor's share and any other moneys due to the Distributor from the Exhibitor under the Agreement. If the commencement of any such collection does not coincide with the commencement of the licence period the person or persons so appointed may collect and retain for the Distributor all moneys paid at the pay boxes during the licence period until there has been collected the Distributor's share in respect of receipts during the part of the licence period prior to the moment of collection and any other moneys due as aforesaid. The Distributor may if it thinks fit similarly appoint any person or persons to collect the fixed licence fee from moneys received at the pay boxes.

   (b) If the Distributor shall not exercise its right of collection under sub-clause (a) of this Condition the Exhibitor shall pay to the Distributor the Distributor's share or the fixed licence fee if the licence period does not exceed seven days within seven days after the last day of the licence period and if the licence period does exceed seven days within seven days after every seventh day and after the last day thereof, subject to any provision to the contrary in the Agreement and to the provisions of Condition 3 where applicable.

   (c) At the conclusion of business on every day during the licence period the Exhibitor shall prepare a detailed return (if so required in the form for the time being prescribed by the Distributor) of all tickets (including complimentary tickets) issued (whether by the Exhibitor direct or through any agent) and moneys taken during the day in question such return to state the serial and machine numbers of all such tickets and to indicate separately tickets issued and moneys taken in respect of every class of seat and in respect of transfers and any charge made by the Exhibitor for the reservation of seats or for advance bookings and (if more than one) at every pay box and also to indicate separately complimentary tickets issued. Every such daily return shall be signed by the Exhibitor or on his behalf by his responsible representative and the returns shall be posted to the Distributor on the day following the last day of the licence period or if the licence period exceeds seven days on the day following every seventh day and the last day thereof (except where the day concerned is a Sunday, when returns should be posted on the following Monday). If required by the Distributor the Exhibitor shall send to the Distributor by post within two days after the last day of the licence period a detailed return as aforesaid certified by the person in charge of the theatre or (if the Distributor shall so require) by an Accountant (who shall be a member of a body of accountants recognised for the purposes of Section 161(1)(a) of the Companies Act 1948) and if the licence period shall exceed seven days then if required by the Distributor such a certified return shall be sent to the Distributor by the Exhibitor within two days after every seventh day and after the last day of the licence period.

   (d) The Exhibitor shall keep all records and operate such a system of checks and exercise such supervision and control (including the supervision and control of his staff) in connection with admissions to the cinema the issuing of tickets the receipt of moneys and the separation of moneys from the sale of tickets from other receipts at the cinema as may be necessary to ensure that such matters are properly regulated conducted and recorded to the Distributor's reasonable requirements. The Exhibitor shall give to SFD as agent for the Distributor as hereinafter mentioned notice of any proposed change or alteration in the ticket issuing system or the ticket issuing machines at the theatre which is to be introduced prior to the commencement of the licence period and obtain the prior approval of SFD thereto (which approval shall not be unreasonably withheld). Where advance bookings are included in a return without details of the ticket numbers, the Exhibitor shall preserve the daily booking plans and ticket counterfoils (as required under sub-clause (e) of this Condition) for a period (unless otherwise agreed with SFD) of not less than two calendar months from the date of performance to which each ticket relates and produce the same to the Distributor or its agents or representatives on demand.

(e) No person shall be admitted to the cinema without a ticket. Each person on admission shall produce a ticket for the class of seat which he is to occupy and shall not be permitted to transfer to a higher-priced seat without a proper transfer ticket. Each ticket issued shall state its price and shall be numbered at each end and shall be torn in half before admitting the holder. The retained halves of tickets issued at each performance (or where performances are continuous each day) shall be filed on a separate string immediately after tearing and such strings of half tickets shall be retained in safe custody by the Exhibitor for twenty-four hours and destroyed by burning or by such methods as approved by the SFD by the Exhibitor as soon as conveniently possible thereafter. Provided that if any query has in the meantime been raised by the Distributor or its agents the half tickets for the period in question shall be retained by the Exhibitor until the query is satisfied. No half tickets once filed shall be removed except at the request of HM Customs and Excise or after retention as aforesaid for immediate destruction as aforesaid. Tickets shall be issued for each price of seat consecutively and in series of not less than 10,000 and in the case of transfer, complimentary and emergency tickets in series of not less than 1,000. Emergency tickets shall only be used in the event of a failure of a ticket issuing machine or in the absence of tickets in the ordinary series. If two or more series of tickets of the same price are in use concurrently they must be clearly distinguishable from each other by a difference in colour or printing. The foregoing requirements of this sub-clause shall also apply to tickets for advance bookings. Unless separately printed for specific dates and performances tickets for advance bookings shall be numbered and issued for each price of seat consecutively in series of not less than 10,000. All such tickets shall be issued from a book with counterfoils to be retained by the Exhibitor and each counterfoil shall show the same particulars as appear on the corresponding ticket. A separate ticket shall be issued for each seat reservation. Series of tickets in use for admission to cinematograph performances shall not be used for admission to any other type of entertainment. Provided however that SFD may approve in writing on behalf of its members any other method of checking and recording admissions which the Exhibitor may seek to introduce in which event the method so approved shall be strictly observed by the Exhibitor.

(f) No person shall be admitted free of charge to a performance at the cinema except within the normal issue of complimentary tickets at the cinema or as shall be agreed between the Distributor and the Exhibitor. The Exhibitor shall issue to each person admitted free a complimentary ticket. Complimentary tickets and tickets issued for admissions to children's matinees shall be drawn from separate stocks, each appropriately marked to avoid the possibility of tickets being incorrectly issued.

(g) The Exhibitor shall charge such admission prices at the cinema during the licence period as shall be agreed by the Distributor. In the absence of agreement the Exhibitor shall charge admission prices not less than those in force at the cinema at the time of signing the agreement for a similar type of film and shall not in any case, without the prior consent of the Distributor, make any reduction in prices.

(h) The Exhibitor shall on the ticket or on the machine or clearly display at the pay box the current admission prices including reserved seat prices (if any). Ticket issuing machines (if any) at the cinema shall be locked when not in use and the keys held by the Manager or the person responsible for signing returns on the Exhibitor's behalf. In the event of a breakdown of any ticket issuing machine involving its adjustment or the realignment of tickets with the machine register, the Exhibitor shall obtain a certificate from the manufacturer or the servicing agent and produce it to the Distributor or its agents or representatives whenever required.

(i) The Distributor shall be entitled to take any reasonable steps for the purpose of satisfying itself that all matters relating to admission to the cinema are and have been regularly conducted, that returns and payments are have been and will be duly made and that the film is and has been only exhibited and used in accordance with the Agreement and these Standard Conditions.

(j) The Exhibitor shall permit the agents or representatives of the Distributor at all reasonable times to have access to all parts of the cinema to which the public by purchase of tickets have access and the Exhibitor shall produce or make available to the Distributor or its agents or representatives at all reasonable times on demand the tickets returns records ticket-issuing machines filed half-tickets retained by the Exhibitor in accordance with subclause (d) of this Condition and any other things relating to admission to the cinema and the receipts therefrom for inspection and shall permit (where appropriate) the making of copies or extracts therefrom.

(k) The Exhibitor shall supply information and answer questions asked for or put to him by the Distributor or its agents or representatives on any of the matters mentioned in sub-clauses (a) to (h) of this Condition and shall provide all facilities required to satisfy the Distributor or its agents or representatives on any such matters, and to enable the Distributor to carry out his rights under sub-clause (a) of this Condition shall request his employees to supply information and answer questions as aforesaid if so requested by the Distributor or its agents or representatives.

(l) The Distributor has appointed SFD as its agent for all the acts and things to be done on behalf of the Distributor as aforesaid and the Exhibitor shall accept as the Distributor's agent any person producing evidence that he is authorised for this purpose by SFD. The appointment of SFD in no way limits or excludes the right of the Distributor to act through other representatives.

(m) The Exhibitor shall forthwith give to SFD as agent of the Distributor notice of any irregularity in regard to tickets, moneys or returns which could directly or indirectly affect the interests of any Distributor as soon as the same becomes known to him and whether such irregularity occurs during or prior to the licence period.

(n) If the Irregularities Committee of SFD shall appoint any accountant or other person to investigate the conduct of the business of the cinema such accountant or other person shall be entitled to the same facilities and rights as are provided for under subclauses (j) and (k) of this condition as if he were the Distributor.

(o) Where due to the operation by the Exhibitor of computerised system(s) the Exhibitor is unable to meet any of the obligations set down in Condition 2(a) to (n) then the Exhibitor shall advise the SFD accordingly whereupon the Exhibitor and the SFD shall discuss and agree alternative arrangements to ensure the security and information requirements of the SFD are met.

3. **CREDIT**

   (a) If the words:—

       (i)    'credit five days' or
       (ii)   'credit seven days' or
       (iii)  'credit tenth and twenty-fourth monthly' or
       (iv)  'credit tenth monthly'

or words to the like effect shall appear in the Agreement then, notwithstanding anything to the contrary contained in these Conditions, the Exhibitor shall pay the fixed licence fee plus Value Added Tax (if any) or the Distributor's share (as the case may be) and any other moneys then due to the Distributor whether under this Agreement or otherwise:—

in case (i) not later than five days after the last day of the licence period

in case (ii) not later than seven days after the last day of the licence period

in case (iii) not later than the tenth day of the month next following if the end of the licence period is on or between the fifteenth day and last days of a month or not later than the twenty-fourth day of the same month if the end of the licence period is on or between the first and fourteenth days of that month

in case (iv) not later than the tenth day in the month next following the end of the licence period.

(b) If this Condition applies to the Agreement then in the event that:—

(i) at the end of the third day (Saturday and Sunday being excluded from the calculation) before the first day of the licence period any moneys which became due from the Exhibitor to the Distributor otherwise than under the Agreement shall be still owing or

(ii) at end of such third day any moneys which became due from the Exhibitor to any other Distributor before such third day shall be still owing or

(iii) any cheque given in payment or any moneys referred to in (a) or (b) shall be dishonoured on or before the first day of the licence period

The Agreement may be determined by notice by letter or telemessage given by the Distributor or by SFD on the Distributor's behalf notwithstanding that the Exhibitor shall in the meantime have paid such moneys.

4. **CASH IN ADVANCE**

In the event that:—

(a) At the end of the fifth day before the commencement of the licence period (Saturday and Sunday being excluded from the calculation) any sum which shall have become due from and payable by the Exhibitor to the Distributor on or before such fifth day otherwise than under the Agreement shall still remain unpaid or

(b) at the end of such fifth day any moneys which became due from the Exhibitor to any other Distributor within six months before such fifth day shall still be owing or

(c) any cheque given in payment of any moneys referred to in (a) or (b) shall be dishonoured on or before the third day of the licence period or

(d) the Irregularities Committee of SFD shall recommend that owing to irregularities in the conduct of the theatre or of any other theatre in the same ownership or control as the theatre it is in the best interests of Distributors to require payment of cash in advance.

The Distributor or the SFD on the Distributor's behalf by letter or telemessage may require the Exhibitor to pay to the Distributor not less than two days before the first day of the licence period:—

(i) the sum referred to in (a) and

(ii) the fixed licence fee plus Value Added Tax (if any) or (if the Agreement provides for the payment of a Distributor's share) such sum as the Distributor shall reasonably require on account and in advance of the Distributors share (such sum to be subject to adjustment at the end of the licence period) and in such case if the Exhibitor shall fail to make such payment the Agreement shall be automatically determined but without prejudice to the Exhibitor's liability to the Distributor whether under the Agreement or otherwise.

5. **METHOD OF EXHIBITION**

    (a) The Exhibitor shall not exhibit the film or permit the same to be exhibited except to the public at the cinema and shall exhibit the film in the usual manner on every day of the licence period permitted by law and in particular the Exhibitor shall exhibit the film in its entirety including credit titles trade marks and classification certificate (if any) and without any breaks or intermissions save such as are provided for by the producer of the film or the Distributor and not otherwise. The Distributor will use his best endeavours when so requested by the Exhibitor to obtain from the producer agreement to the inclusion of an intermission in the screening of the film, where it is licensed to play in a single feature programme.

    (b) The Exhibitor shall exhibit the film at such times as shall be agreed with the Distributor. The agreement of the Distributor to a variation in such times may be sought after the signing of the Agreement and shall not be unreasonably withheld. In the absence of agreement, the Exhibitor shall exhibit the film at all times during the licence period at which films would normally be exhibited at the cinemas at the time of the signing of the Agreement (excluding children's matinees and late night shows) and at such additional times as shall be agreed with the Distributor.

    (c) Any form of reproduction or copying of the film, and exhibition by means of any such reproduction or copy, is also strictly forbidden. The Exhibitor shall take reasonable security precautions to ensure that this Condition is complied with. Legal proceedings will be taken at once in respect of any breach of this Condition without prejudice to any other remedies arising therefrom.

    (d) If the cinema has two or more auditoria (screens) the Exhibitor and the Distributor shall agree in which auditorium (screen) the film shall be exhibited. The Exhibitor shall not exhibit the film in any other auditorium (screen) in the cinema without the prior agreement of the Distributor. If the Distributor agrees that the film may be moved to an auditorium (screen) other than the one originally licensed, the Exhibitor must ensure that each daily return indicates the correct auditorium (screen) number for each performance.

6. **PROGRAMME**

    The Exhibitor shall not exhibit the film in a programme which includes more than one feature film and a supporting programme without the consent of the Distributor.

7. **ADVERTISING**

    (a) The Distributor reserves the right to require that the Exhibitor shall not use any advertising matter in connection with the exhibition of the film except that which is approved by the Distributor. The Exhibitor shall observe such conditions as to advertising matter as are binding on the Distributor and communicated in writing or by means of the advertising campaign book to the Exhibitor. Unless the Distributor shall otherwise direct all programmes lobby displays advertising and publicity issued by the Exhibitor in connection with the exhibition of the film shall contain such reference to the Distributor and the film as the Distributor shall require.

    (b) The Exhibitor shall advertise the exhibition of the film at the cinema in such a manner and during such period as may be agreed with the Distributor and in the absence of agreement in the manner customary with the cinema. Unless otherwise agreed the Exhibitor shall himself bear all advertising expenses.

(c) Unless the Schedule otherwise stipulates the Exhibitor shall not advertise or make any amendment concerning the film or Licensed Programme until such date as is specified in or to be ascertained in accordance with the Schedule (as to which applicable date the Exhibitor shall enquire of the Distributor who shall inform the Exhibitor as soon as the said date is known shall also inform the Exhibitor of any subsequent alterations of the said date) except by means of (i) announcement on the screen (ii) programmes leaflets and other publicity distributed within the auditorium or by post to regular patrons (iii) announcements photographs posters and notice boards placed in the vestibule of the cinema in such a position that the advertisement shall not be legible from the exterior of the cinema. Inasmuch as the principal object of this Condition is the protection of the exhibition rights *inter se* of the Exhibitor and other exhibitors having under contracts similar to the Agreement successive runs of the film the following provisions shall have effect:—

(1) If the Exhibitor shall make any breach of this condition to the detriment of any other exhibitor who may have a contract with the Distributor for a prior run of the film the Exhibitor shall be liable to pay the amount of the damage suffered by such other exhibitor notwithstanding that there is no privity of contract between the Exhibitor and such other exhibitor.

(2) If any other exhibitor with whom the Distributor may have a contract for a run of the film subsequent to that of the Exhibitor shall make any breach of the condition therein corresponding to this condition to the detriment of the Exhibitor the Exhibitor shall be entitled to damages against such other exhibitor notwithstanding that there is no privity of contract between the Exhibitor and such other exhibitor.

For the purpose of effectuating (by arbitration as hereinafter provided) the provisions of sub-clause (1) and (2) of this condition:—

(a) In case (1) the Distributor may and at the request of such other exhibitor will proceed against the Exhibitor and, as the Exhibitor hereby agrees, join in such proceedings such other exhibitors.

(b) In case (2) the Distributor will at the request of the Exhibitor proceed against such other exhibitor and may as the Exhibitor hereby agrees join in such proceedings the Exhibitor.

In all such proceedings the Distributor and the Exhibitor and such other exhibitor shall each be entitled to appoint an arbitrator but otherwise all such proceedings shall so far as practicable be taken in accordance with the provisions of Condition 25 and all parties affected shall submit to the jurisdiction and be bound by the award of the arbitrators which may be that the offending exhibitor shall pay to the complaining exhibitor the amount of damages suffered by the latter.

The Exhibitor shall pay to the Distributor any legal costs incurred by the Distributor in consequence of any breach by the Exhibitor of the provisions of this clause.

## 8. TRAILERS

The Distributor or his agent will use their best endeavours to ensure that any material supplied promoting a film or films conforms with the law and that if a complaint arises will assist the licensee if such a complaint proves subsequently to be actionable.

## 9. EQUIPMENT AND SOUND EFFECTS

(a) The Exhibitor shall maintain the equipment for picture presentation and sound reproduction installed at the theatre in good and efficient working order and condition and suitable for the picture presentation and sound reproduction of the film. The Distributor shall have the right at any time to inspect the said equipment.

(b) If the Distributor has reasonable cause to consider that the said equipment is not in such order and condition as aforesaid, he shall be entitled to call upon the Exhibitor to carry out any necessary adjustments, repairs or renewals to the said equipment prior to the exhibition or further exhibition of the film.

(c) The Exhibitor shall not permit any musical or any other sound accompaniment of any kind to be used during the exhibition of the film other than that which forms part of the film.

(d) In the event of any breach by the Exhibitor of (a) or (c) or if the Exhibitor shall fail to carry out any necessary adjustments, repairs or renewals to the said equipment so as to restore it to good and efficient working order and condition immediately upon being called upon by the Distributor so to do the Agreement shall be automatically determined but without prejudice to the Exhibitor's liability to the Distributor whether under the Agreement or otherwise.

10. **LIQUIDATED DAMAGES**

If the Agreement is determined under Condition 3 Condition 4 or Condition 11 the Exhibitor shall nevertheless remain liable to pay forthwith to the Distributor the fixed licence fee or a sum ascertained as below mentioned in respect of the Distributor's share as the case may be. In the case of a Distributor's share the sum to be so paid by the Exhibitor shall be the sum which would represent the Distributor's share if the film had been exhibited at the cinema during the licence period and the daily receipts at the cinema had equalled the average daily receipts thereat during the licence periods covered by the six last preceding performed agreements between the Exhibitor and the Distributor under which a Distributor's share and not a fixed licence fee (or rental) was payable to the Distributor and which comprise the same days of the week as the licence period or if less than six such agreements shall have been performed then all such performed agreements.

11. **AGREEMENT AS TO LIQUIDATED DAMAGES**

Any sum which may become payable by the Exhibitor under Condition 9 Condition 15 or Condition 18 is agreed to constitute a genuine pre-estimate and limitation of the damage to be suffered by the Distributor through the non-exhibition of the film at the cinema the precise amount of which damage it would not be possible accurately to ascertain and accordingly such sum is agreed to consist solely of liquidated damages and to contain no element of penalty.

12. **CANCELLATION FOR DEFAULTS OR IRREGULARITIES**

(a) If the Exhibitor shall:—

(i) make default for seven days in complying with a notice in writing from the Distributor requiring him to remedy any breach of his obligations under Condition 2 (c) or

(ii) make default for seven days in payment of any moneys owing by him to the Distributor under the Agreement or

(iii) commit any breach of his obligations under Condition 5

the Distributor by giving notice in writing to the Exhibitor may determine the Agreement and also any other agreement with the Exhibitor for the licensing by the Distributor of the exhibition of any cinematograph film subsisting at the date of such notice.

(b) If the Irregularities Committee of SFD shall recommend that owing to the unsatisfactory conduct of the Exhibitor's business or of the business of any other cinema in the same ownership or control as the theatre it is no longer in the best interests of Distributors to remain in business relations with the Exhibitor the Distributor or SFD on the Distributor's behalf by giving notice in writing to the Exhibitor may determine the Agreement and also any other agreement with the Exhibitor for the licensing by the Distributor of the exhibition of any cinematograph film subsisting at the date of such notice.

13. **EXCLUSIVITY**

    The Distributor

    (i) Shall not authorize the exhibition of the film or the licensed programme at any cinema mentioned in the relative column of the Schedule until after the end of the licence period and of any further period mentioned in the relative column of the Schedule.

    (ii) Shall not authorize any advertising of the film or the licensed programme (save advertising of the nature excepted in Condition 7 (c) in respect of a subsequent run at any such theatre until after the commencement of the licence period or such other date as may be mentioned (in a special condition) in the Schedule.

14. **RESTRAINT ON PERFORMANCE**

    (a) If any legal proceedings shall be commenced or threatened against the Distributor and the Exhibitor or either of them for the purpose of restraining the exhibition of the film at the cinema or of establishing any claim in respect of such exhibition the Exhibitor if so required by notice in writing from the Distributor shall refrain from exhibiting or if exhibition has already commenced shall cease from exhibiting the film and the Distributor shall use its best endeavours to license the exhibition of a substitute film but shall be under no other liability.

    (b) If any legal proceedings shall be commenced or threatened against the Distributor and the Exhibitor or either of them for the purpose of establishing that the film infringes any right (other than the right to perform musical works within the repertoire of the Performing Right Society Limited) or is defamatory of any person the Distributor on behalf of the Exhibitor shall conduct defend settle or otherwise dispose of such proceedings and (provided that the Exhibitor duly complies with all the Exhibitor's obligations under this Condition) shall indemnify the Exhibitor from all damages and costs in connection therewith.

    (c) The Exhibitor shall not communicate in any way with any party by whom any such proceedings as aforesaid shall be commenced or threatened or his agents but shall promptly transmit to the Distributor any communication received by the Exhibitor from such party or his agent and shall give to the Distributor all such information and assistance in his power as the Distributor may require in relation to such proceedings.

15. **MUSIC LICENCE**

    The Exhibitor shall be responsible for acquiring from the Performing Right Society Limited or its successors an effective licence covering the public performance at the cinema of such musical works as may be within the repertoire of that Society and which form part of the film.

16. **BANKRUPTCY OR LIQUIDATION**

    (a) If the Exhibitor shall be adjudicated bankrupt or (being a company) shall enter into liquidation whether compulsory or voluntary (save for the purpose of reconstruction or amalgamation) or if a receiver of the property of the Exhibitor or any part thereof shall be appointed or if the Exhibitor shall make any arrangement or composition with or for the benefit of his or its creditors the Distributor by giving notice in writing to the

Exhibitor may determine the Agreement without prejudice to the rights and remedies of the Distributor thereunder and in such case the Exhibitor shall nevertheless continue liable to pay the fixed licence fee or sum representing the Distributor's share (as the case may be) the sum to be so paid being ascertained (if need be) in accordance with Condition 18.

(b) Provided nevertheless that the Distributor may permit the trustee in bankruptcy or liquidator or receiver of the Exhibitor to carry out the Agreement in place of the Exhibitor upon giving such security or making such arrangements as the Distributor may require for the purpose of ensuring payment to the Distributor of all moneys to become payable to the Distributor under the Agreement in respect of the exhibition of the film thereunder.

## 17. FORCE MAJEURE

(a) If the Exhibitor shall be prevented from exhibiting the film in accordance with the provisions of the Agreement and these Standard Conditions owing to any cause of whatsoever nature outside the control of the Distributor or the Exhibitor as the case may be or the film shall not pass the British Board of Film Classification or the Official Censor in the Republic of Ireland or be licensed for exhibition by the local authority as the case may be the Agreement shall cease to have effect in respect only of the period during which the exhibition is so prevented or in respect of the licence period if exhibition is so prevented at the commencement of the licence period in either of which cases neither party shall be under any liability to the other party in respect of the appropriate period. Where the Agreement licenses the exhibition of the film at more than one cinema or place the prevention of the Exhibitor from exhibiting the film at one cinema or place shall not affect the Agreement so far as it relates to the exhibiting of the film at any other cinema or place.

(b) No censorship cut shall invalidate the Agreement or give rise to any claim by the Exhibitor.

## 18. DEFAULT BY DISTRIBUTOR

If through any default of the Distributor the film cannot be exhibited during the licence period or some part thereof such of the following provisions as shall be applicable shall have effect:—

(a) If the film shall not be exhibited at all the Distributor shall pay the Exhibitor (i) a sum equal to the deficiency (if any) in the receipts (as defined in Condition 1) from the exhibition of films at the cinema during the licence period (the Exhibitor having used his best endeavours to provide a replacement) as compared with the average daily receipts thereat from the exhibition of films under the six last preceding performed agreements (whether incorporating these Standard Conditions or otherwise) between the Distributor and the Exhibitor which licensed the exhibition of a film on the same days of the week as those comprised in the licence period or if less than six such agreements shall have been performed then all such performed agreements and (ii) the cost incurred by the Exhibitor in advertising the film pursuant to Condition 7.

(b) If the film shall be exhibited on any day during the licence period the Distributor shall pay or allow to the Exhibitor a sum equal to the deficiency in the receipts mentioned in (a) above on the day or days during the licence period on which the film is not exhibited as compared with the average receipts for the corresponding day or days of the week under the six last preceding performed agreements (or if less than six all such performed agreements) as aforesaid.

Less in either case (a) or case (b) above a sum representing (i) the fixed licence fee or a proportionate part if the Agreement provided for the payment of such fee or (ii) the Distributor's share in respect of the period in question if the Agreement provides for the payment of a Distributor's share. Provided always that the Distributor's liability in case of default in respect of supporting programme or any part thereof shall not exceed the amount usually paid by the Exhibitor for supporting programme or an equivalent part thereof (as the case may be).

19. **DEFAULT BY EXHIBITOR**

   If the Exhibitor shall fail to exhibit the film on any day during the licence period in accordance with the terms of the Agreement and if the Agreement provides for the payment of a Distributor's share the Exhibitor shall be deemed to have received on such day a sum equal to the average daily receipts on the days on which exhibition of the film shall have taken place and shall pay to the Distributor in respect of the Distributor's share for such day on which default shall have occurred a sum equal to the Distributor's share of the sum so deemed to have been received and if such default shall extend to the whole of the licence period the Exhibitor shall pay to the Distributor the sum which would have been payable to the Distributor under Condition 9.

20. **POSTPONEMENT**

   If at the request of the Exhibitor the Distributor agrees that the licence period be postponed the Exhibitor shall accept the circumstances existing at the date of commencement of the postponed licence period and shall have no claim whatever against the Distributor in respect of any prior or concurrent runs resulting from the postponement which have been disclosed by the Distributor prior to the Agreement to postpone by reason of the fact that owing to such postponement the Exhibitor may have the film for a run subsequent to that originally contracted for.

21. **ASSIGNMENT BY DISTRIBUTOR**

   The Distributor shall be entitled to assign the benefit and burden of the Agreement to any other Distributor of repute who shall be capable of carrying out the terms of the Agreement without the consent of the Exhibitor but shall promptly give to the Exhibitor notice in writing of any such assignment.

22. **ASSIGNMENT BY EXHIBITOR**

   The Exhibitor shall not be entitled to assign the benefit and burden of the Agreement except with the previous consent in writing of the Distributor which consent shall not be unreasonably withheld.

23. **TELEVISION**

   (a) Subject as below-mentioned the Distributor warrants that he will not authorise the televising of the film during the licence period or within three months thereafter.

   (b) The warranty contained in (a) above shall not apply to

   (i) the televising of the film after the expiration of two years from the date of the first cinema trade showing of the film or the date of certification of the film by the British Board of Film Classification, whichever date is the earlier or

   (ii) the televising of an excerpt or excerpts aggregating not more than five minutes playing time in any one programme or

   (iii) the televising of the film if it has a playing time of forty five minutes or less.

(iv) the televising of the film if the film's audited production costs did not exceed £4,000,000 at 15th September 1988 or such higher audited production cost as results from the addition of the increase in the British Retail Price Index since 15th September 1988 plus 3.5% (three and one half percent) to £4,000,000, or the addition to £4,000,000 of £300,000 for each year since 15th September 1988 or

(v) the film if the film has received exemption from the warranty by the British Screen Advisory Council Films on Television Committee.

(c) If between the date of the Exhibitor's offer for the film and the first day of the licence period the film shall be televised in its entirety or the date on which the film is to be televised shall be publicly advertised the Exhibitor shall have the right by notice in writing given not later than twenty-one days after such televising and prior to the first day of the licence period to determine the Agreement and if the Exhibitor so desires to require the Distributor to license the exhibition of a replacement film which the Distributor shall use his best endeavours to do.

(d) In this Condition 'televising' means the televising of the film so that it shall be visible and audible over a television service transmitted from any part of Great Britain and Northern Ireland or the Republic of Ireland by the general public (without separate payment for the particular programme or period of viewing) and 'televised' has a corresponding meaning.

## 24. IRELAND

These Standard Conditions shall apply to Agreements for the licensing of the exhibition of a film or films in a cinema situate in Northern Ireland or the Republic of Ireland subject to the following modifications:—

(a) The Distributor may at any time not less than six months before the first day of the licence period by notice in writing to the Exhibitor cancel the Agreement.

(b) In relation to Agreements for the licensing of the exhibition of a film or films in the Republic of Ireland the words 'HM Customs and Excise' in Condition 2 (e) shall be understood to mean the Authority in the Republic of Ireland responsible for the collection of tax on admission to theatres.

## 25. INTERPRETATION ETC

(a) The Agreement shall be governed by the laws of England and shall be deemed to have been entered into at the Head Office in England of the Distributor.

(b) No granting of time or indulgence by the Distributor to the Exhibitor shall prejudice the Distributor's rights.

(c) The Agreement shall be deemed to be a separate contract in respect of each licensed programme if more than one programme is mentioned in the Schedule or in respect of each film forming part of a programme if the exhibition of a complete programme is not licensed by the Agreement.

(d) Nothing in the Agreement shall operate or be construed so as to infringe The Films (Exclusivity Agreements) Order 1989 and to the extent that any provision of the Agreement purports to do so, it will be null and void.

26. **ARBITRATION**

   Subject as below provided any dispute or question which may arise concerning the construction meaning or effect of the Agreement or concerning the rights and obligations under the Agreement of the parties or either of them or otherwise howsoever arising out of or in connection with the Agreement shall be referred to a single arbitrator if the parties can agree upon one and otherwise to two arbitrators one to be appointed by the Distributor and the other by the Exhibitor and in the event of such arbitrators failing to agree to an independent umpire appointed by those arbitrators and pursuant to any legislation relating to arbitration for the time being in force in the territory in which the theatre is situate. Provided that notwithstanding the foregoing provision for arbitration the Distributor shall be entitled to recover by legal proceedings any moneys which are due to the Distributor from the Exhibitor under the Agreement and either party shall be entitled to take such steps as are necessary to obtain an injunction to restrain any breach or threatened breach of the Agreement by the other.

27. Nothing in the Agreement shall entitle the Exhibitor to be supplied with or in any way concern a print of the film or to be supplied with advertising material or any other goods required for the exhibition of the film.

A copy of these Standard Conditions will be kept at the Head Office and at every Branch Office of the Distributor and also at the office of SFD and will be available for inspection by the Exhibitor during normal business hours.

APPENDIX 4.4

*(referred to in paragraphs 2.27, 2.28, 2.80, 2.106, 2.146, 2.161, 2.170, 2.192, 4.85, 4.117, 4.187, 6.19 and 8.235)*

## Survey of operators of independent cinemas in the UK

### Background

1. The MMC received a number of letters from operators of independent cinemas and their comments are summarized in Chapter 6. We felt it necessary, however, to obtain more systematically the views of such operators and information on particular aspects of their cinema activities. The MMC therefore sent a short postal questionnaire to all the small independent cinemas in the UK which could be identified, ie all exhibitors apart from the five majors and the main independents referred to in Chapter 4.

2. The main objective of the survey was to obtain some basic quantitative data on independent cinemas in the UK, and to obtain the views of their operators on a range of matters relevant to the present inquiry. In particular, we sought information about:

— their box office takings, and average rental payments to distributors;

— recent and planned investment;

— the local competition they faced and the competitiveness of different types of cinemas;

— the effects of the 1989 Order; and

— specified features of the relationship between the exhibitors and the distributors which supplied films to them.

### *Method and sample structure*

3. Addresses were obtained from, and cross-checked between, three sources: the BFI's *Film and Television Marketing Handbook, 1994*; the addresses of members of the CEA; and addresses shown in *Yellow Pages* directories.

4. A total of 428 questionnaires were sent out (411 to cinemas in Great Britain and 17 to cinemas in Northern Ireland), the main mailing being on 21 December 1993, and responses were requested by 14 January 1994. A reminder letter was sent out on 28 January 1994 to those which had not responded by that date.

5. One hundred and seventy-eight replies were received. We found that the questionnaire was not applicable to a further 75 cinema operators which were sent copies (eg because the cinema had closed, or more than one questionnaire had been sent to the same cinema because, for example, one was sent to the operator's home or office address as well as to the cinema's address, or the cinema showed films only during very limited periods each year). The effective response rate to the questionnaire was therefore 50 per cent.

### Main findings

### *Nature of respondents*

6. The great majority of respondents were operators of one cinema with a single screen. Eight respondents owned two cinemas, and in most of these cases the two cinemas were situated within

about 30 miles of each other. Six others owned small chains of between four and seven cinemas. Some of the independent cinemas in rural areas and those on university campus sites receive financial and programming assistance from the BFI.

## *Ticket prices*

7. Admission charges for adults for evening performances quoted by the 167 respondents which answered this question varied from £1.50 to £4.50. Taking as a bench-mark other information which suggests that admission charges at multiplex cinemas tend to be around £3.50 or more, 24 of the respondents said that they charged more than £3.50, 30 charged £3.50 and 113 charged less than £3.50. On this basis, admission charges at independent cinemas are typically lower than at multiplex cinemas.

## *Box office receipts*

8. Total box office receipts (including VAT) in 1993 were reported to be £27.5 million (£26.4 million in Great Britain and £1.1 million in Northern Ireland), an average of about £180,000 per cinema (see Table 1). On the assumption that the respondents are representative of independent exhibitors in general, this suggests that total box office receipts for all independent cinemas in 1993 were about £65 million (or about £55 million excluding VAT, which is a little lower than the equivalent figure of £60 million we estimated on the basis of distributors' 1993 data as shown in Table 4.7). The increase in box office receipts from 1992 to 1993 was about 11 per cent.

TABLE 1  **Box office receipts (including VAT), average rental payments and other revenue**

|  | Box office receipts | | Average film rental payments | | Revenue other than from ticket sales* | |
| --- | --- | --- | --- | --- | --- | --- |
|  | 1992 £m | 1993 £m | 1992 % | 1993 % | 1992 % | 1993 % |
| Base† | (156) | (154) | (154) | (163) | (137) | (139) |
| Total | 24.8 | 27.5 | - | - | - | - |
| Average | 0.16 | 0.18 | 34.5 | 36.1 | 18.5 | 19.4 |

*All revenue other than ticket sales as a proportion of total revenue.
†The total number of questionnaire responses which included an answer to this question.

## *Average film rental payments*

9. The average film rental payment reported for 1993 was 36.1 per cent, which is an increase on the 1992 figure of 34.5 per cent (see Table 1). The average percentage rental reported for 1993 suggests that rental payments by respondents amounted to about £9.9 million in that year, and that the total rental payments by all independent cinemas in 1993 were about £23.7 million (which is a little higher than the equivalent figure of £21.4 million we estimated on the basis of distributors' 1993 data as shown in Table 4.8).

10. Although, as mentioned, the average rental payment in 1993 was about 36 per cent, there was a quite wide range when comparing the individual figures for particular cinemas. While 60 per cent of the cinemas reported that their average annual rental payments were in the range 30 to 39 per cent, 13 per cent said that they paid less than 30 per cent and 27 per cent said that they paid 40 per cent or more (see Figure 1).

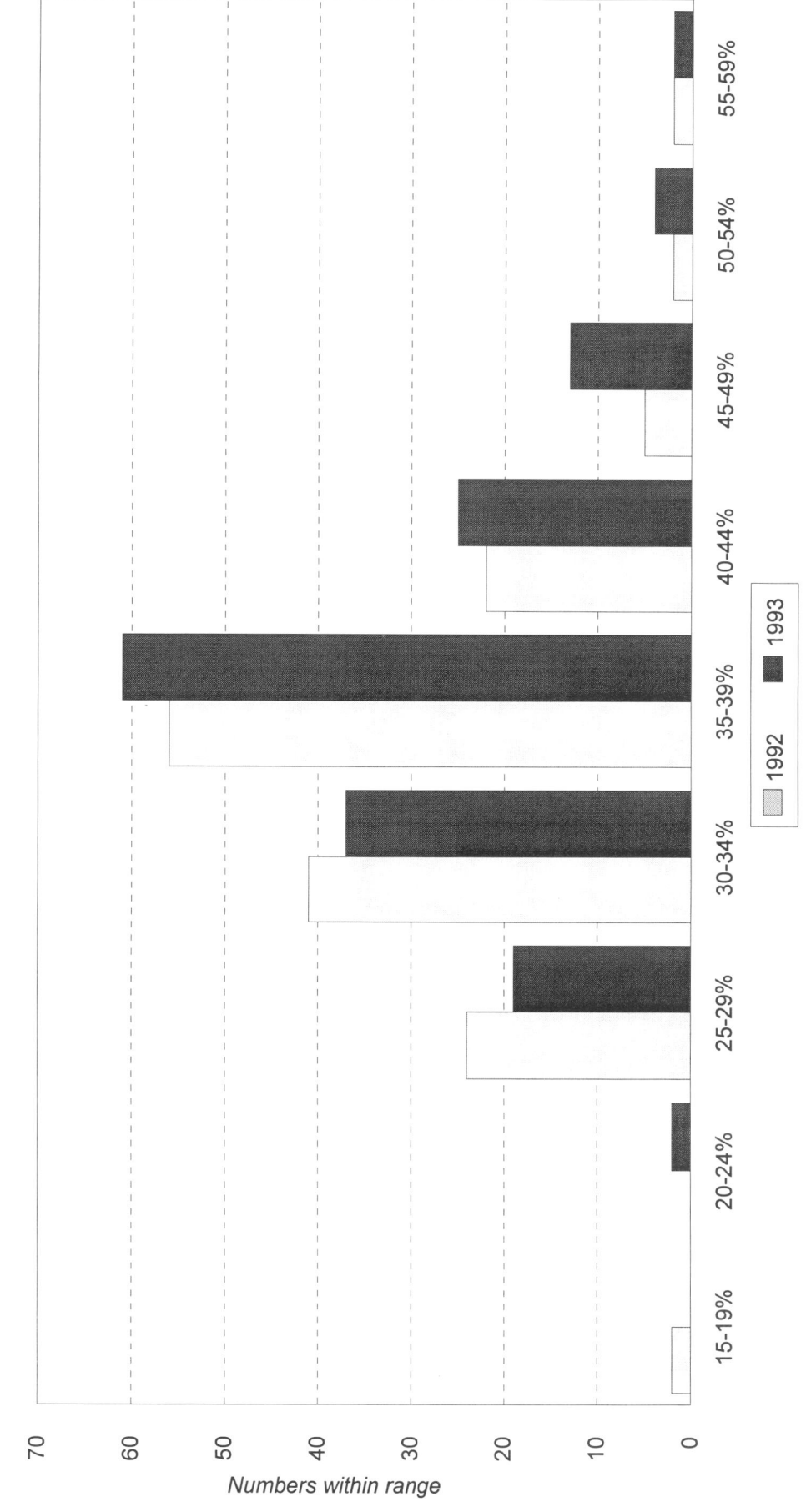

FIGURE 1

**Average percentage film rental**

Source: MMC.

## Other revenues

11. Respondents reported that in 1993 revenue other than from admission tickets (eg from sales of confectionery, drinks, screen advertising, car parking, souvenirs, etc) accounted for about 20 per cent of their total revenues from the operation of cinemas (see Table 1).

## Recent and planned investment

12. About three-quarters of respondents said that they had undertaken some investment in their cinemas in the last three years (see Table 2). The total investment by respondents over this period amounted to almost £8 million, with an overall mean figure per cinema (averaged over only those cinemas on which some investment was incurred) of about £69,000. However, these figures include some quite large investment expenditures by a few of the respondents: ten cinemas each reported spending over £200,000 over the last three years. Excluding these ten cinemas has the effect of reducing the total figure by about £4 million, and the average per cinema to about £27,000. If respondents are typical of independent exhibitors in general, these data suggest that total investment by all independent cinemas over the three-year period 1991 to 1993 was about £14 million, or roughly £5 million a year.

TABLE 2  **Recent investment expenditure**

| *Base: (178)* | % |
|---|---|
| Answered NO | 24.7 |
| Answered YES | 75.3 |
| *Types of investment* | |
| Refurbishment, redecorating and rebuilding | 70.8 |
| Projection equipment | 35.1 |
| Sound equipment | 29.8 |
| New or replacement seats | 22.4 |
| Electrical fittings and security systems | 18.6 |
| New or replacement screens | 14.1 |
| Heating systems | 12.7 |
| *Years in which expenditure was incurred* | |
| 1991 | 19.0 |
| 1992 | 35.5 |
| 1993 | 45.5 |

13. Slightly over half of the respondents reported that they planned some expenditure in their cinemas over the next two years (see Table 3). The total planned expenditure over the next two years was stated to be about £4.8 million, with a mean figure of about £52,000 per cinema (the figure is about £23,000 if investments at individual cinemas of more than £200,000 are excluded).

TABLE 3  **Planned investment over the next two years**

| *Base: (178)* | % |
|---|---|
| Answered NO | 47.2 |
| Answered YES | 52.8 |
| *Types of investment* | |
| Refurbishment, redecorating and rebuilding | 64.9 |
| New or replacement seats | 24.5 |
| New or replacement screens | 19.1 |
| Sound equipment | 19.1 |
| Projection equipment | 11.7 |
| Heating systems | 5.3 |
| Electrical fittings and security systems | 3.2 |
| *Years for which the investment is planned* | |
| 1994 | 80.0 |
| 1995 | 20.0 |

## Nearest competing cinemas

14. Respondents were asked to identify the nearest competing cinemas to their own, and to indicate which one of those identified they considered to be their strongest competitor. Respondents identified a total of 474 competing cinemas (the majority being within ten miles). This suggests that, on average, each independent cinema regards three nearby cinemas as competing directly with it. Almost 25 per cent of respondents were of the view that their strongest competitor was not the nearest cinema to the respondent's own cinema.

15. Of the 474 cinemas, 371 were identified in response to the question which asked about competing cinemas getting first-run releases of films before the respondent. Of these 371, 113 (34 per cent) were cinemas operated by the five major exhibitors and which always took first-run releases before the respondent independent cinema could show them (see Table 4).

TABLE 4 **Competing cinemas taking first-run releases before the respondent's cinema has shown them**

| Competing exhibitors | Always | Always from certain distributors | Often | Sometimes | Never |
| --- | --- | --- | --- | --- | --- |
| MGM Cinemas | 41 | 7 | 15 | 16 | 4 |
| Odeon | 46 | 10 | 8 | 13 | 6 |
| UCI | 26 | 2 | 2 | 5 | 1 |
| Natl Amusements | 7 | 4 | 0 | 6 | 1 |
| Warner Theatres | 6 | 0 | 2 | 2 | 0 |
| Other independents | 40 | 12 | 45 | 23 | 20 |

## Effects of the Films (Exclusivity Agreements) Order 1989

16. Of the 178 respondents which answered this question, 64 per cent thought that the Order had no effect on their film exhibition activities and 45 per cent were also of the view that the Order had no effect on the pattern of film distribution and exhibition in the UK more generally. Some respondents said that they were unaware of the Order, some felt unable to comment on its impact because they had recently entered the industry and had no knowledge of the situation before 1989, while others said that because their programming needs were satisfied by the BFI they had no direct knowledge on which to base a response.

17. A number of respondents made substantive comments, the main points of which were:

— standard barring had been replaced with the frequent use of the claim that prints were unavailable because of extended playing time at first-run cinemas;

— the Order had led to greater competition for a limited supply of prints; and

— respondents still could not obtain new prints on a film's release date.

Thus, a concern of many respondents was the shortage of prints, and the unduly long playing times of first-run cinemas which delayed the availability of prints. In this situation several independent cinema operators felt that barring of another sort had replaced the system of standard barring made unlawful by the 1989 Order.

## Relations with distributors

18. We asked respondents to read ten different statements, as listed below, and to tick a box in a table showing which individual distributors, if any, they thought the statements applied to. The 154 responses are summarized in Table 5, and in the text following it.

TABLE 5  Percentages of respondents placing a tick in the relevant box

| Distributors | 1 Minimum period for first run | 2 Minimum period for subsequent run | 3 Must also accept other films | 4 Expected to accept other films | 5 Restrictions on other films | 6 Charges/ terms comparisons | 7 Delayed releases | 8 Will not supply | 9 Problems in obtaining some films | 10 Other conditions which may affect competition | Conditions mentioned* |
|---|---|---|---|---|---|---|---|---|---|---|---|
| Warner Distributors | 80.5 | 46.1 | 2.6 | 17.5 | 50.0 | 14.9 | 46.8 | 0.6 | 11.7 | 9.1 | ABDEF |
| UIP | 81.8 | 48.7 | 1.9 | 13.0 | 49.4 | 26.6 | 51.9 | 1.9 | 15.6 | 11.7 | ADEF |
| Columbia | 79.2 | 44.2 | 1.9 | 24.7 | 49.4 | 20.8 | 55.2 | 3.2 | 18.2 | 12.3 | ABDEF |
| Buena Vista | 79.2 | 48.1 | 1.3 | 9.7 | 55.2 | 13.0 | 42.2 | 3.9 | 13.6 | 11.0 | CDE |
| Fox | 77.3 | 45.5 | 1.3 | 13.0 | 45.5 | 10.4 | 42.9 | 1.9 | 9.7 | 9.1 | ADE |
| Guild | 71.4 | 43.5 | 1.3 | 18.2 | 44.2 | 14.3 | 44.8 | 1.9 | 11.7 | 7.1 | DE |
| RFD | 66.2 | 39.0 | 1.3 | 5.2 | 39.6 | 7.1 | 42.2 | 1.9 | 8.4 | 7.1 | DE |
| Entertainment | 62.3 | 31.2 | 0.0 | 2.6 | 41.6 | 5.2 | 51.9 | 3.2 | 19.5 | 4.5 | DE |
| Mayfair | 51.3 | 26.6 | 0.0 | 1.3 | 33.8 | 5.2 | 39.6 | 2.6 | 14.9 | 4.5 | DE |
| Other distributors | 6.5 | 3.2 | 0.6 | 0.6 | 1.3 | 0.6 | 3.2 | 0.0 | 3.2 | 0.6 | ADE |

*The conditions mentioned by respondents who ticked column 10 were:

A.  Refusal to allow matinée products to be screened during a '15' or '18' certificate film.
B.  Certain films must be screened on the largest screen in the cinema, even though this may not be economic to the cinema.
C.  Buena Vista only allowed 'over' films to be shown after 8.30 pm.
D.  Distributors were now making increasing use of 'overage' terms.
E.  Could not obtain the guarantee of a film until other cinemas had turned it down.
F.  Minimum exhibition period of (say) four weeks was too long to sustain for this cinema.

— *Statement 1: The distributor always or mostly specifies a minimum period for which a first-run film is expected to be kept running at your cinema.*

77 per cent or more of respondents were of the view that this statement was true for each of the five major distributors, and between 50 and 70 per cent considered it to be true of the four independent distributors mentioned in the questionnaire. Several respondents said that a minimum run of three to four weeks (and occasionally more) did not make commercial sense, particularly for one-screen cinemas in small towns or country areas.

— *Statement 2: The distributor always or mostly specifies a minimum period for which a subsequent-run film is expected to be kept running at your cinema.*

Between 44 and 50 per cent of the respondents were of the view that this statement was true for the five major distributors, and between 26 and 44 per cent considered it to be true of the four independent distributors mentioned in the questionnaire. In relation to both statements 1 and 2, about 47 per cent of those who responded said that the distributor always or usually refused permission for the film to be taken off before the end of the minimum period, while 36 per cent said that such permission was given (the other 17 per cent said that the question did not apply, which suggests that they did not ask).

— *Statement 3: The distributor insists, when agreeing the rental of a particular film(s) you want to show, that if you were to be allocated that film you must also accept another film(s) which you might not otherwise have chosen.*

Only a very small minority of the cinemas said that Statement 3 applied to them.

— *Statement 4: You understand or recognize that, though the distributor may not have indicated this formally to you, if you were to be allocated the film(s) you wanted you would also be expected to accept another film(s) which you might not otherwise have chosen.*

The only distributors to have anything other than a very small response to this statement were the five majors and Guild. The figures for Columbia (25 per cent), Guild (18 per cent) and Warner Distributors (17 per cent) were noticeably higher than for the other distributors (but see paragraphs 4.181 and 4.182).

— *Statement 5: The distributor specifies that other films should not be shown on the same screen in the same week as the film which it rents to you.*

About one-half of the respondents were of the view that this statement was true of the five leading distributors (the range was from 46 to 55 per cent). A smaller percentage considered it to be true for the four independent distributors named in the questionnaire (the range was from 34 to 44 per cent). Several respondents stated that providing programmes for all sections of the community demanded a variety of films and timings through the week: this was inconsistent with the restriction on showing another film on the same screen as the one supplied by a given distributor. It was also pointed out that the requirement that the showing of another film should not commence before 8.30 pm caused difficulties for cinema-goers who relied on public transport for the journey home. About 22 per cent of respondents expressed the view that distributors always or usually refused them permission to show other films if asked, 65 per cent said that permission was not refused, and 13 per cent said that the question did not apply.

— *Statement 6: A broad comparison of the distributor's rental charges or terms for a particular film(s) shows that its charges are usually above or more stringent than those of most other distributors.*

The figures for UIP (27 per cent) and Columbia (21 per cent) were noticeably higher than for the other distributors. (*Note:* The point was made by Columbia, on seeing the figures, that independent exhibitors may have been influenced by specific popular films released in 1993, including UIP's *Jurassic Park* and Columbia's *Sleepless in Seattle*.)

— *Statement 7: The distributor, for whatever reason, provides your cinema with popular films (ie for which 150 or more prints are made) only after the films have been on release for more than a certain number of weeks.*

Between 42 and 55 per cent of respondents said that this was true of the five major distributors and between 40 and 52 per cent said that it was true of the four independents listed.

— *Statement 8: The distributor, for whatever reason, will not provide your cinema with any of the films it distributes.*
Most respondents did not find this to be the case.

— *Statement 9: The distributor has given your cinema problems in obtaining particular films or categories of films (eg films with a British or European theme or content, films for ethnic minorities).*
Up to 20 per cent of respondents expressed the view that there were difficulties in obtaining certain types or categories of film from certain distributors.

— *Statement 10: The distributor imposes rental contract conditions or other conditions of supply, not covered in the above statements, in respect of your cinema which are onerous or burdensome or otherwise decrease your cinema's ability to meet the competition it faces for patrons.*
Distributors appear to have presented additional problems for up to 12 per cent of independent exhibitors, with the most common observations listed at the bottom of Table 5.

## *Appeals procedure*

19. There were very few responses to the question seeking information on how exhibitors resolved disagreements with distributors concerning the availability of particular films and the terms on which they were offered. Of those which did reply, most stated that in cases where they felt aggrieved they were obliged to press their case as best they could on a personal basis. Some respondents referred to the possibility of seeking help from either the CEA or the SFD. No respondent referred to the Trade Disputes Committee and Appeals Tribunal established following the MMC's 1966 report.

## *General comments*

20. The last question in the questionnaire gave respondents an opportunity to comment on any aspect of their business they wished to. Nearly half of the respondents did offer comments. These predominantly concerned:

— the terms on which films were made available (including timing, minimum periods and restrictions on use of screens);

— the service given to independent cinemas compared with multiplexes; and

— the quality of prints.

21. On the terms on which films were made available to independent cinemas, a recurring issue was the 'catch-22' that independent cinema operators felt affected them with respect to major new releases. They had to wait sometimes up to four or six weeks before they received a film, by which time much of the publicity surrounding the release was likely to have prompted people to travel to a large town to see the film. Thus, when the print was eventually made available, much of the potential local market for the film had already been lost to the independent cinema. But such exhibitors were told by distributors that a print could not be made available any sooner on the grounds that their box office receipts would be too low.

22. A number of respondents said that planning their future schedules was made more difficult by late cancellations of bookings, or late confirmations of availability.

23. About a third of those commenting criticized what they saw as the inflexibility of current supply arrangements. Some respondents said that while, as a commercial reality, they could not expect their small rural cinema to obtain a print on release date, distributors were inflexible in not accepting shorter playing times, and the showing of films under or over the main film. Greater flexibility in these respects would allow the programming of the smaller cinemas to be made more commercial. Some also commented that when small cinemas received prints many weeks after first release, their attraction to cinema-goers was much less given the knowledge that such films would soon be available in video format.

24. About a quarter of those commenting felt that distributors were now preoccupied with satisfying the multi-screen cinemas, and had become almost oblivious to the needs of the single- or twin-screen independent exhibitors.

25. A few respondents also complained of the poor technical quality of the prints they received. As a result, these operators received complaints from their customers about the standard of their cinema sound and projection equipment, even though the faults were mostly in the prints themselves. The respondents said that they were usually unable to do anything about poor-quality prints as they were often delivered to them at the last moment (eg because of overbooking). They felt they needed to receive prints as good as those made available to the major cinema circuits.

APPENDIX 4.5
*(referred to in paragraphs 2.206, 4.136 and 4.142)*

# Cinema nuts: comparisons between different distributors

## Introduction

1. In principle the nut or break figures used in calculating film rentals for any given screen are based on the weekly operating costs (plus a profit margin) for the cinema concerned, and allocated to the various screens (if there are more than one) in relation to the number of seats in each. In practice, the base figure is arrived at through negotiations between the exhibitor and each distributor.

2. In general, it appears that exhibitors aim to agree the same nut or break figures with each distributor, since having different figures adds a further layer of complication to decision-making about which films to show. Nevertheless the element of negotiation means that certain distributors may succeed in agreeing nut figures more favourable to them (ie lower nut values) compared with those negotiated with other distributors.

3. One independent distributor told us that, in its view, independent distributors had received inferior terms from the two main circuit exhibitors, compared with those enjoyed by the leading distributors. It considered, therefore, that on a particular film it had received less rental income than any of the leading distributors would from similar box office figures. The operators of multiplex cinemas, on the other hand, had always offered similar terms across the board to all distributors.

## Data analysis

4. In the light of these and other comments, we analysed the nut figures for all the cinemas of MGM Cinemas, Natl Amusements, UCI and Warner Theatres (ie all four of the leading exhibitors which use the nut method), as given to us by five different distributors: UIP and Warner Distributors (aligned to MGM Cinemas), Columbia and Fox (aligned to Odeon), and an independent distributor (which only gave us figures in respect of MGM Cinemas). The figures related to the end of 1993 and in most cases the exhibitors told us that revised figures had since been negotiated.

5. Odeon uses the sliding scale method rather than the nut method for calculating rental payments. It told us that its break figures were applied equally to all distributors subject to two categories of exemption:

*(a)* Those popular films for which Odeon agreed to grant the distributor more favourable terms than usual. Of the 31 films in this category which Odeon exhibited in the period January 1992 to June 1994 all but one were released by the leading distributors.

*(b)* Those films which Odeon considered of above-average commercial risk and for which it increased its monetary break figures above the normal level. All the 65 films in this category in the period January 1992 to June 1994, being 6 per cent of all the films shown by Odeon in that period, were released by independent distributors. Odeon told us, however, that, as it had expected, these films did not draw large audiences, with the result that the rental was in all cases at the minimum percentage level of 25 per cent. The application of higher break figures had made no practical difference to the rentals paid.

## MGM Cinemas

6. The MGM Cinemas situation is complex. Out of the 119 cinemas for which we had comparable data, at ten of them the screen nuts were the same for all five distributors, all these being cinemas with six or more screens (though we found differentials at the other four cinemas with six or more screens). For the remaining cinemas, the pattern of nuts was roughly as follows:

— For MGM Cinemas' two aligned distributors there were small differences, with Warner Distributors' nut total being about 0.4 per cent below UIP's.

— Both Columbia and Fox (aligned with Odeon) had nuts which were on average about 1 or 1.5 per cent higher than UIP's.

— The independent distributor's nuts were on average about 4.5 per cent higher than UIP's. At some individual cinemas, however, the differences were much greater, ranging up to 16 per cent more than those for UIP.

7. MGM Cinemas told us that these differentials had disappeared when it renegotiated its nut figures early in 1994.

## Natl Amusements

8. Natl Amusements uses the same nut figures for all its screens in all its cinemas except one, Derby, which has a lower figure (but again applying to all the screens in the cinema). These nuts apply equally to all distributors.

## UCI

9. We found that seven UCI cinemas showed differences between the nuts applying to different distributors. In six cases UIP and Fox had between 4 and 6 per cent more favourable terms than Warner Distributors and Columbia, and in one case (Tamworth) it was the other way around. The net effect of all these differences, averaged over the whole UCI circuit, was that UCI's rental payments to Warner Distributors were based on nuts which were about 1 per cent higher than those for UIP and Fox, and that in the case of Columbia they were almost 2 per cent higher.

## Warner Theatres

10. Three of Warner Theatres' cinemas had different nuts for different distributors, and five did not (these figures exclude the Warner West End, for which the data were incomplete). While differences on individual screens were as much as 17 per cent, the overall average was less than 1 per cent, with Columbia and Fox having slightly less favourable terms than UIP and Warner Distributors.

## Significance of these nut figures

11. Using the nut system, the weekly rental payment for a film is the greater of:

*(a)* 90 per cent of box office receipts above the nut; and

*(b)* 25 per cent of total receipts.

So long as the box office receipts remain below the level at which the 90 per cent calculation comes into play, the size of the nut is irrelevant and rental payments are the same for all films (ie 25 per cent of receipts) regardless of which company distributes them. Differential nuts only bite, therefore, on films which attract relatively good audiences. The effect is best shown by the following example:

> *Example:* Take one screen which has two different nuts: for Distributor A the nut is £4,000; and for Distributor B the nut is 4.5% higher at £4,180.

*Therefore:*

(a) When box office per film is £4,000
    Rentals are: Dist A = £1,000
                 Dist B = £1,000

(b) When box office per film is £5,000
    Rentals are: Dist A = £1,250
                 Dist B = £1,250

(c) When box office per film is £5,600
    Rentals are: Dist A = £1,440
                 Dist B = £1,400   or 3% less

(d) When box office per film is £5,800
    Rentals are: Dist A = £1,620
                 Dist B = £1,458   or 10% less

(e) When box office per film is £6,000
    Rentals are: Dist A = £1,800
                 Dist B = £1,638   or 9% less

(f) When box office per film is £7,000
    Rentals are: Dist A = £2,700
                 Dist B = £2,538   or 6% less.

APPENDIX 4.6

*(referred to in paragraph 4.145)*

# The market in the USA

## The production, distribution and exhibition of films in the USA

1. More than half as many films again were released in the USA in 1993 as in the UK. Approximately a third of them were produced by the seven major studios, a somewhat lower proportion than in this country.

2. The structure of the US industry is similar to that of the UK in one respect: the major studios themselves distribute all the films they make (or make in conjunction with independent production companies). But market shares at the exhibition level are less concentrated than in the UK, with no company having more than a 10 per cent share. At the same time there are only three major producers/distributors (Columbia/Tristar, Paramount[1] and Warner Bros) that have exhibition interests, and none of these has a market share in exhibition greater than 5 per cent.

3. The fact that producers/distributors have few exhibition interests is largely the result of action taken by the US competition authorities. As a result of action by the US Department of Justice, the Supreme Court found in 1948 that the Sherman Act had been violated by the eight major Hollywood studios. There followed a series of decrees (known collectively as the 'Paramount decrees'—see below) which brought about a separation between producer/distributor interests and exhibition businesses, as well as laying down a number of rules aimed at open and transparent competition in the industry. In the years following the Paramount decrees the Department of Justice was active (in 1980) seeking to prevent exhibitors agreeing with each other on the patterns of film releases and (in 1988) in enforcing the rule against block-booking of films that formed part of the Paramount decrees.

4. In the 1980s, however, the Department of Justice began to take a more relaxed view of the need for regulation in the film industry and made clear that it could envisage that in some particular cases a relaxation of the Paramount decrees would be justified, if it were sought by the companies themselves (see below).

5. The system in the USA for allocating films to cinemas is similar but not identical to that in the UK. It is usually done through bilateral negotiations between exhibitors and distributors, but where competition among exhibitors is particularly strong such negotiations are sometimes replaced by a bidding process, whereby exhibitors respond to a bid request from distributors.

6. Arrangements for allocating shares of the box office between distributor and exhibitor are similar to those in the UK. Minimum length of run is also a common term in US agreements. A feature that does not exist in the UK is the provision of guarantees or advances by exhibitors to distributors. A guarantee is non-refundable irrespective of the eventual box office receipts and the normal exhibitor share, whereas an advance is refundable to the extent that it exceeds the film rental. With a figure of about 42 per cent for 1993, average rental payments in the USA are higher than in the UK.

## Action by the US competition authorities: the Paramount decrees

7. In 1938 the Department of Justice filed suit against eight major Hollywood studios alleging violation of the Sherman Act by way of price-fixing and attempts to monopolize trade in films through cinema ownership. It was not until 1948 that the suit was finally resolved by decision of the Supreme

---

[1]Paramount has also a link now with National Amusements Inc (which has a share of exhibition of around 3 per cent) as the result of its acquisition in 1994 by Viacom Inc. National Amusements Inc is the majority shareholder of Viacom Inc.

Court. A series of decrees (known collectively as 'the Paramount decrees') covering the eight studios followed over the next few years.

8. At the time when the suit was filed the eight studios owned cinema circuits accounting for around 45 per cent of total box office receipts, and in 92 cities with populations over 100,000 at least 70 per cent of all first-run cinemas were affiliated with one or more of the eight studios.

9. The decrees fell into two parts, the first setting down requirements and prohibitions in respect of the defendants, and the second laying down a number of general rules for the distribution and exhibition of films. The main purpose of the requirements and prohibitions was to bring about, and maintain, a structure of the industry in which distribution businesses were not owned by the same companies as exhibition businesses. In the second part there were three main rules which were aimed at ensuring that competition for the showing of films was as open and transparent as possible; they required that:

*(a)* there should be no agreement on pricing among exhibitors or among distributors;

*(b)* distributors should license films for exhibition on the merits of each individual cinema without regard to its affiliated cinemas; and

*(c)* the right to show a film should not be conditional on agreement to show one or more other films.

10. In 1981 the Department of Justice launched a review of the Paramount decrees. It concluded that there might be cases where a modification of the decrees was justified and made clear that it would support a company that sought modification or termination where it (the Department) saw a public interest case.

11. The first major test of the decrees came in 1987 when Warner Bros, having decided that it would like to re-enter the exhibition business, sought the appropriate permission from the District Court. The Court decided in favour of Warner Bros but on condition that it kept its interests in the exhibition business separate from its other film interests and that any dealing between the two was at arm's length. The company decided, however, to go to appeal, and the Appeals Court decided in favour of Warner Bros, ie that it could acquire the exhibition interests that it proposed (a 50 per cent holding in a company that would control around 2 per cent of the total number of screens in the USA) without any restrictions on ownership structure and mode of operation.

APPENDIX 4.7

*(referred to in paragraphs 2.201, 2.202, 2.203 and 4.152)*

# Shares of rental payments and box office receipts

1. Table 1 gives, for each of the years 1988 to 1993, data showing:

   *(a)* the percentages of UCI's rental payments and box office receipts accounted for by UIP films; and

   *(b)* UIP's percentage share of all box office receipts and exhibitors' rental payments in the UK.

Table 2 gives, for each of the years 1988 to 1993, data showing:

   *(a)* the percentages of UIP's rental income accounted for by receipts from UCI cinemas and the two CIC cinemas in the West End of London which are managed by UCI; and

   *(b)* the percentages of distributors' total rental income accounted for by payments made by UCI and CIC.

TABLE 1  **Data relating to the exhibition of UIP films in UCI cinemas**

| | UCI* Percentage of box office attributable to UIP films | UIP Percentage share of box office at all exhibitors | UCI* Percentage of rentals attributable to UIP films | UIP Percentage share of rentals from all exhibitors |
|---|---|---|---|---|
| 1988 | [ | | | |
| 1989 | | | | |
| 1990 | | *Figures omitted.* | | |
| 1991 | | *See note on page iv.* | | |
| 1992 | | | | |
| 1993 | | | | ] |

*Source:* MMC, based on data from the companies.

*Excludes CIC data.

TABLE 2  **Net rental payments by UCI and CIC**

| Year | Exhibitor | As a percentage of UIP's rental receipts | As a percentage of total rental payments by all exhibitors |
|---|---|---|---|
| 1988 | CIC | [ | |
| | AMC | | |
| 1989 | CIC | | |
| | UCI | | |
| 1990 | CIC | | |
| | UCI | *Figures omitted.* | |
| 1991 | CIC | *See note on* | |
| | UCI | *page iv.* | |
| 1992 | CIC | | |
| | UCI | | |
| 1993 | CIC | | |
| | UCI | | ] |

*Source:* MMC, based on data from the companies.

2. The data in Table 1 suggest that UCI gained a larger share of its box office receipts from UIP films, and paid a larger share of its rental payments to UIP, than might be expected given UIP's overall market share. Taking the figures for the four most recent years, the disparities appear only in 1991 and 1992 as far as box office receipts are concerned, and in those years together with 1990 as far as rentals are concerned. Similarly, the data in Table 2 suggest that in each of the years a higher percentage of UIP's rental receipts was accounted for by receipts from UCI/CIC than might have been expected given the market shares (in terms of rental payments) of these two exhibitors. Again, focusing on the more recent years, and leaving aside the figures for CIC whose cinemas are often used as the West End platform for UIP films, the disparities are more marked in 1991 and 1992. In both tables the disparities had virtually disappeared in 1993.

3. We put these two tables to both UCI and UIP for their comments. In UCI's view, UIP's share of UCI's rental payments was higher than its share of UCI's box office receipts because UIP's films performed particularly well in UCI's cinemas. In four of the five years covered by the data, UIP's films achieved the highest revenue per film of all the leading distributors.

4. The box office data in Table 1 show that in the four years when UIP's share of box office receipts was relatively high ([*] per cent [ * ]), its share of total rentals was significantly above its share of box office. In the other two years, when its share of box office receipts was under [*] per cent, its share of rentals was slightly below its share of box office. This is largely the result of the 'blockbuster effect', whereby the bigger the audience for a film, the greater the distributor's share of the box office receipts. The pattern of differences between shares of box office and shares of rentals is broadly similar as between UCI and all exhibitors. These data do not indicate that UCI is out of line in this respect.

5. On the specific point that the data in Table 1 suggest that UCI and UIP trade with each other more than one would expect, UCI listed a number of factors which may have influenced the figures (including the fact that different exhibitors use different methods for calculating the amounts of rental payments to be made, the effects of alignment, the effects of each exhibitor using different monetary values for the nut or break figures for different distributors, the relative success of the same film in different cinemas in the UCI circuit, the number of weeks over which the revenue was earned and the use of estimates in assessing rental and box office shares in respect of independent exhibitors).

6. In commenting on Table 2, UCI suggested that the figures in the two columns (excluding the CIC figures) were affected by a number of factors, and that no valid conclusions could be drawn from them.

7. UCI provided alternative data relating to the top 20 films each year. It pointed out that these figures showed that its market share figures in respect of UIP films did not differ significantly from the market share figures for exhibition generally. UCI pointed out that its policy and practice of matching films to audience demand were reflected in its achievements as the exhibitor with the highest level of attendance per screen and per seat.

8. UIP was unable to comment in detail on the figures in Tables 1 and 2 as it had no access to the confidential information on which those tables were based or on the comparative position of other distributors and exhibitors. It did consider, however, that on the basis of the information available to it, there was no evidence of preference in its trading with UCI. UIP provided EDI box office data for key cities in the UK during the years 1992 and 1993 (the only years for which the data are available). The figures were said to cover all multiplexes and to account for about two-thirds of the total UK market. In comparing the box office for the three multiplex operators (UCI, Natl Amusements and Warner Theatres), UIP showed that there was very little difference (in these two years) between its shares of UCI box office figures and those for all three multiplex operators together, ie that it traded with all multiplex operators on a similar basis. This confirmed, in UIP's view, the absence of any trading preference between it and UCI by virtue of the fact that Paramount and MCA/Universal were interested in both companies. Rather, it traded on similar terms with all operators of cinemas achieving equivalent standards and audience-winning potential.

9. As regards Table 2, UIP acknowledged that it had received slightly higher average rental payments (as a percentage of box office) from UCI than from other major exhibitors. This was due to

---

*Details omitted. See note on page iv.

UCI's success in utilizing its cinema capacity more fully than other exhibitors. As a result, UIP said that UCI's share of its rental receipts would tend to be higher than UCI's share of its box office revenue.

10. UIP drew attention to one other point, that UIP distributed very few specialist or arthouse films, and UCI exhibited very few films of this type. UIP estimated that such films accounted for around [†] per cent of total box office receipts in the UK.

11. We also made a comparison between UCI's and Natl Amusements' data; they have similar operations in the UK, though on a different scale, and their ownership in the period concerned was quite different. Table 3 shows the percentage of rental payments attributable to UIP films for each of the five leading exhibitors. The figures for UCI and Natl Amusements are similar except, again, for the years 1991 and 1992.

TABLE 3  **Share of rental payments: UIP**

| Year | Percentage of rental payments attributable to UIP films | | | | | UIP's percentage share of rentals paid by all exhibitors |
| --- | --- | --- | --- | --- | --- | --- |
| | MGM Cinemas | Odeon | UCI* | Natl Amusements | Warner Theatres | |
| 1988 | [ | | | | | |
| 1989 | | | | | | |
| 1990 | | | | Figures omitted. | | |
| 1991 | | | | See note on page iv. | | |
| 1992 | | | | | | |
| 1993 | | | | | | ] |

Source: MMC, based on data from the companies.

*Excludes CIC.

12. Similar comparisons were made for each of the other leading distributors and for Guild and RFD. These figures are shown in Tables 4 to 9.

TABLE 4  **Share of rental payments: Warner Distributors**

| Year | Percentage of rental payments attributable to Warner Distributors' films | | | | | Warner Distributors' percentage share of rentals paid by all exhibitors |
| --- | --- | --- | --- | --- | --- | --- |
| | MGM Cinemas | Odeon | UCI* | Natl Amusements | Warner Theatres | |
| 1988 | [ | | | | | |
| 1989 | | | | | | |
| 1990 | | | | Figures omitted. | | |
| 1991 | | | | See note on page iv. | | |
| 1992 | | | | | | |
| 1993 | | | | | | ] |

Source: MMC, based on data from the companies.

*Excludes CIC.

TABLE 5  **Share of rental payments: Columbia**

| Year | Percentage of rental payments attributable to Columbia's films | | | | | Columbia's percentage share of rentals paid by all exhibitors |
| --- | --- | --- | --- | --- | --- | --- |
| | MGM Cinemas | Odeon | UCI* | Natl Amusements | Warner Theatres | |
| 1988 | [ | | | | | |
| 1989 | | | | | | |
| 1990 | | | | Figures omitted. | | |
| 1991 | | | | See note on page iv. | | |
| 1992 | | | | | | |
| 1993 | | | | | | ] |

Source: MMC, based on data from the companies.

*Excludes CIC.

† Figure omitted. See note on page iv.

TABLE 6  **Share of rental payments: Fox**

| Year | MGM Cinemas | Odeon | UCI* | Natl Amusements | Warner Theatres | Fox's percentage share of rentals paid by all exhibitors |
|---|---|---|---|---|---|---|
| | *Percentage of rental payments attributable to Fox's films* | | | | | |
| 1988 | [ | | | | | |
| 1989 | | | | | | |
| 1990 | | | *Figures omitted.* | | | |
| 1991 | | | *See note on page iv.* | | | |
| 1992 | | | | | | |
| 1993 | | | | | | ] |

*Source:* MMC, based on data from the companies.

*Excludes CIC.

TABLE 7  **Share of rental payments: Buena Vista**

| Year | MGM Cinemas | Odeon | UCI* | Natl Amusements | Warner Theatres | Buena Vista's percentage share of rentals paid by all exhibitors |
|---|---|---|---|---|---|---|
| | *Percentage of rental payments attributable to Buena Vista's films* | | | | | |
| 1988 | [ | | | | | |
| 1989 | | | | | | |
| 1990 | | | *Figures omitted.* | | | |
| 1991 | | | *See note on page iv.* | | | |
| 1992 | | | | | | |
| 1993 | | | | | | ] |

*Source:* MMC, based on data from the companies.

*Excludes CIC.

TABLE 8  **Share of rental payments: Guild**

| Year | MGM Cinemas | Odeon | UCI* | Natl Amusements | Warner Theatres | Guild's percentage share of rentals paid by all exhibitors |
|---|---|---|---|---|---|---|
| | *Percentage of rental payments attributable to Guild's films* | | | | | |
| 1988 | [ | | | | | |
| 1989 | | | | | | |
| 1990 | | | *Figures omitted.* | | | |
| 1991 | | | *See note on page iv.* | | | |
| 1992 | | | | | | |
| 1993 | | | | | | ] |

*Source:* MMC, based on data from the companies.

*Excludes CIC.

TABLE 9  **Share of rental payments: RFD**

| Year | MGM Cinemas | Odeon | UCI* | Natl Amusements | Warner Theatres | RFD's percentage share of rentals paid by all exhibitors |
|---|---|---|---|---|---|---|
| | *Percentage of rental payments attributable to RFD's films* | | | | | |
| 1988 | [ | | | | | |
| 1989 | | | | | | |
| 1990 | | | *Figures omitted.* | | | |
| 1991 | | | *See note on page iv.* | | | |
| 1992 | | | | | | |
| 1993 | | | | | | ] |

*Source:* MMC, based on data from the companies.

*Excludes CIC.

APPENDIX 4.8
*(referred to in paragraph 4.160)*

# Locations affected directly by alignment

**The aligned locations**

| City or town | Total population in 1992 '000 | Other MGM cinemas | Other Odeon | Natl Amusements | UCI | Independent cinemas |
|---|---|---|---|---|---|---|
| Aberdeen | 217 | | | | | ✓ |
| Blackpool | 152 | | | | | |
| Bournemouth | 159 | | | | | |
| Brighton | 155 | ✓ | | | | ✓ |
| Bristol | 397 | | | | | ✓ |
| Cardiff | 296 | | ✓ | | | ✓ |
| Edinburgh | 440 | | | | ✓ | ✓ |
| Glasgow | 684 | ✓ | | | | (✓) |
| Leeds | 722 | | | ✓ | | ✓ |
| Leicester | 285 | | | | | (✓) |
| Liverpool | 479 | | | ✓ | | |
| Norwich | 128 | | | | | (✓) |
| Nottingham | 283 | | | ✓ | | ✓ |
| Plymouth | 258 | | | | | |
| Portsmouth | 190 | | | | ✓ | |
| Reading | 137 | | | | | (✓) |
| Southend | 165 | | | | | |

London:
  Fulham Road (MGM) & Kensington (Odeon)
  Hampstead (MGM) & Swiss Cottage (Odeon)
  Streatham (both)

**Other locations where alignment has direct effects**

| City or town | Total population in 1992 '000 | Other MGM cinemas | Other Odeon | Natl Amusements | UCI | Independent cinemas |
|---|---|---|---|---|---|---|
| Bath | 84 | | | | | (✓) |
| Coventry | 305 | | | ✓ | | (✓) |

# Summary

Of the 17 aligned locations outside London listed above, 13 have other cinemas (in addition to those of MGM Cinemas and Odeon which are subject to alignment) which are not aligned. This number falls to 10 if arthouse or part-time cinemas are excluded.

*Notes*:
1. There are no Warner Theatres cinemas in any of the locations listed.
2. MGM Cinemas has two conventional cinemas in Leicester and three in Bristol, and these all appear to be subject to alignment. As well as the cinemas which are subject to alignment, it also has multiplex cinemas in Brighton and Glasgow.
3. Odeon has a multiplex cinema in Cardiff, but it is only its conventional cinema there which is subject to alignment.
4. For locations where the only independent cinema is a BFI or other arthouse cinema, or is a part-time cinema, the tick is shown in brackets.
5. In Bath a form of alignment exists in that, while there is no Odeon cinema, distributors aligned to Odeon normally supply their films (as first choice) to a particular independent cinema and not to the cinema operated by MGM Cinemas. The position in Coventry is similar except that it is MGM Cinemas which has no cinema, its aligned distributors supplying (as first choice) a particular independent cinema and not Odeon. We have not included these two cities in our definition of aligned locations.
6. The locations listed exclude the Odeon Haymarket, Odeon Leicester Square, Odeon Marble Arch, Odeon West End and MGM Trocadero cinemas in London's West End which are also affected by a form of alignment.

# APPENDIX 4.9
*(referred to in paragraph 4.166)*

# Effects of alignment on MGM Cinemas' and Odeon's smaller cinemas

## Introduction

1. To test whether the effects of alignment on the supply of films in the UK extended beyond the aligned locations, we conducted a study of data from both MGM Cinemas and Odeon on the number of films, box office takings and (in the case of MGM Cinemas) rentals from their cinemas grouped into different categories according to the number of screens in each cinema. In terms of numbers of screens in each cinema, the majority (94 out of 119) of MGM Cinemas' cinemas are of small size (ie with three or fewer screens), and 18 of these small cinemas are in the aligned locations. Of Odeon's cinemas, 13 out of 73 are small cinemas on this definition.

## MGM Cinemas

2. Table 1 shows how each distributor's share of both box office takings and rentals in MGM Cinemas' smaller cinemas compares with its share in the larger cinemas (both groups exclude the cinemas in aligned locations), its share in MGM Cinemas' circuit as a whole, and its share in the total market.

3. The following points emerge from Table 1:

  *(a)* Aside from the aligned locations, MGM Cinemas' aligned distributors take a higher share of box office and rentals in its smaller cinemas than in its larger ones, and higher than in the total market.

  *(b)* Correspondingly, other distributors (with the exception of Buena Vista) have a lower share of box office and rentals in MGM Cinemas' smaller cinemas than in its larger ones, and lower than in the total market.

  *(c)* For the most part, distributors' shares of box office and rentals in MGM Cinemas' larger cinemas are similar to their shares in the total market.

4. These findings show that alignment also has effects outside the aligned locations. However, these effects are mostly on MGM Cinemas' smaller cinemas, where screen space is scarce, rather than in MGM Cinemas' larger cinemas which are able to show a wider range of films.

## Odeon

5. Table 2 shows distributors' shares of box office takings both in the 13 of Odeon's smaller cinemas which are outside the aligned locations and for the total market. (Odeon said that it could not readily provide cinema-by-cinema data on rentals.) However, for comparative purposes, Tables 2B and 2D show distributors' shares of Odeon's total rental payments in both 1992 and 1993 together with equivalent data for the total market.

6. The following points emerge from Table 2:

*Box office takings*

  *(a)* Both Fox and Columbia (which are aligned to Odeon) accounted for a higher share of the box office in the 13 smaller cinemas in both 1992 and 1993 than they did in the total market.

TABLE 1  **Distributors' shares of MGM Cinemas' box office and rental payments**

*TABLE 1A  Percentage shares of box office takings, 1992*

|  | MGM Cinemas' small cinemas (excluding aligned locations) | MGM Cinemas' large cinemas (excluding aligned locations) | MGM Cinemas' circuit as a whole | Total market |
|---|---|---|---|---|
| Buena Vista | [ | | | |
| Columbia | | | | |
| Entertainment | | | | |
| First Independent | | | | |
| Guild | | *Figures omitted.* | | |
| Mayfair | | *See note on* | | |
| RFD | | *page iv.* | | |
| Fox | | | | |
| UIP | | | | |
| Warner Distributors | | | | |
| Others | | | | ] |
| | 100.0 | 100.0 | 100.0 | 100.0 |

*TABLE 1B  Percentage shares of rental payments, 1992*

| Buena Vista | [ | | | |
|---|---|---|---|---|
| Columbia | | | | |
| Entertainment | | | | |
| First Independent | | | | |
| Guild | | *Figures omitted.* | | |
| Mayfair | | *See note on* | | |
| RFD | | *page iv.* | | |
| Fox | | | | |
| UIP | | | | |
| Warner Distributors | | | | |
| Others | | | | ] |
| | 100.0 | 100.0 | 100.0 | 100.0 |

*TABLE 1C  Percentage shares of box office takings, 1993*

| Buena Vista | [ | | | |
|---|---|---|---|---|
| Columbia | | | | |
| Entertainment | | | | |
| First Independent | | | | |
| Guild | | *Figures omitted.* | | |
| Mayfair | | *See note on* | | |
| RFD | | *page iv.* | | |
| Fox | | | | |
| UIP | | | | |
| Warner Distributors | | | | |
| Others | | | | ] |
| | 100.0 | 100.0 | 100.0 | 100.0 |

*TABLE 1D  Percentage shares of rental payments, 1993*

| Buena Vista | [ | | | |
|---|---|---|---|---|
| Columbia | | | | |
| Entertainment | | | | |
| First Independent | | | | |
| Guild | | *Figures omitted.* | | |
| Mayfair | | *See note on* | | |
| RFD | | *page iv.* | | |
| Fox | | | | |
| UIP | | | | |
| Warner Distributors | | | | |
| Others | | | | ] |
| | 100.0 | 100.0 | 100.0 | 100.0 |

*Source:* MMC, based on data from the companies.

TABLE 2  **Distributors' shares of Odeon's box office and rentals**

*TABLE 2A  Percentage shares of box office takings, 1992*

|  | Odeon's small cinemas (excluding aligned locations) | Odeon whole circuit | Total market |
|---|---|---|---|
| Buena Vista | [ |  | [ |
| Columbia |  |  |  |
| Entertainment |  |  |  |
| First Independent |  |  |  |
| Guild |  |  |  |
| Mayfair | * |  | * |
| RFD |  |  |  |
| Fox |  |  |  |
| UIP |  |  |  |
| Warner Distributors |  |  |  |
| Others | ___] |  | ___] |
|  | 100.0 |  | 100.0 |

*TABLE 2B  Percentage shares of rental payments, 1992*

| Buena Vista (included in Warner Distributors) | [ |  | [ |
|---|---|---|---|
| Columbia |  |  |  |
| Entertainment |  |  |  |
| First Independent |  |  |  |
| Guild |  |  |  |
| Mayfair |  | * | * |
| RFD |  |  |  |
| Fox |  |  |  |
| UIP |  |  |  |
| Warner Distributors (including Walt Disney films) |  |  |  |
| Others (including the four independents listed above as N/A) |  | ___] | ___] |
|  |  | 100.0 | 100.0 |

*TABLE 2C  Percentage shares of box office takings, 1993*

| Buena Vista | [ |  | [ |
|---|---|---|---|
| Columbia |  |  |  |
| Entertainment |  |  |  |
| First Independent |  |  |  |
| Guild |  |  |  |
| Mayfair | * |  | * |
| RFD |  |  |  |
| Fox |  |  |  |
| UIP |  |  |  |
| Warner Distributors |  |  |  |
| Others | ___] |  | ___] |
|  | 100.0 |  | 100.0 |

*TABLE 2D  Percentage shares of rental payments, 1993*

| Buena Vista |  | [ | [ |
|---|---|---|---|
| Columbia |  |  |  |
| Entertainment |  |  |  |
| First Independent |  |  |  |
| Guild |  |  |  |
| Mayfair |  | * | * |
| RFD |  |  |  |
| Fox |  |  |  |
| UIP |  |  |  |
| Warner Distributors |  |  |  |
| Others |  | ___] | ___] |
|  |  | 100.0 | 100.0 |

*Source:*  MMC, based on data from the companies.

*Figures omitted. See note on page iv.

*(b)* Buena Vista's share of the box office in the 13 cinemas was somewhat higher than its share of the total market in 1993 (this was the only year for which data are available as Buena Vista only began trading at the end of 1992).

*(c)* Of the two distributors aligned with MGM Cinemas, UIP had a markedly lower share of the box office in the 13 Odeon cinemas in 1992 and Warner Distributors a lower share in 1993. UIP's share of these cinemas' box office in 1993, and Warner Distributors' in 1992, were broadly in line with their overall market share.

*Rentals*

*(d)* Fox's and Columbia's shares of rentals in the Odeon circuit was higher in both 1992 and 1993 (and especially so in the case of Columbia).

*(e)* Buena Vista's share of rentals in 1993 was higher in the Odeon circuit than in the market as a whole.

*(f)* UIP and Warner had markedly lower shares of rentals in the Odeon circuit compared with the total market.

7. We considered whether these findings from the Odeon data supported those arising from the MGM Cinemas data, which suggested that alignment has an impact outside the 21 aligned locations. Rank said that the data from the 13 smaller Odeon cinemas could not be relied on for the following reasons: first, the data only related to 13 cinemas and this was so small a sample that the results were affected by the particular circumstances of each of the 13 cinemas; secondly, the total market data were provisional and incomplete and were for a calendar year whereas the Odeon data were for the 12 months November to October; and thirdly, there was no reason to suppose that the results shown in the MMC tables represented anything other than random variations around the averages that were to be expected, and were certainly not to be relied on as establishing any clear pattern (eg the behaviour of the annual figures for Fox and Columbia was different from that of RFD and Entertainment even though all four were aligned to Odeon, the differences for Columbia in the second year and for Buena Vista in the same year were only marginal, and the figures for UIP and Warner Distributors appeared to move randomly between the two years).

APPENDIX 4.10

*(referred to in paragraphs 4.176 and 5.9)*

# Case studies

## Background

1. In this appendix we summarize the findings from a number of case studies that we undertook of a variety of different films released in the UK over the last six years. We asked the leading distributors, Guild and RFD to provide data on 15 films which they had supplied to cinemas in the UK during the five-year period from 1988 to 1993. They were asked to choose these 15 films according to the following criteria:

*(a)* their top five releases as measured by gross box office receipts;

*(b)* five typical releases; and

*(c)* their five most disappointing releases (again as measured by gross box office receipts).

2. In addition to the basic statistical information requested for these 15 films, the same distributors were also asked to provide self-contained case studies on three of the 15 films. The case studies were to relate to films which they distributed in 1991 or 1992, and were to be one from each of three categories:

*(a)* wide distribution (in terms of numbers of prints);

*(b)* average distribution; and

*(c)* limited distribution.

Five distributors (Warner Distributors, Fox, UIP, Columbia and RFD) provided these case studies.

## Characteristics common to the top films

3. The case study data showed that the top releases received a minimum of 500 different screenings in their first six months of release. The highest numbers were for RFD's *Silence of the Lambs* (1,501) and Warner Distributors' *Robin Hood: Prince of Thieves* (1,111 different screenings). The highest number of prints reported for any one film was 412 for UIP's *Jurassic Park*. The normal print figure in recent years was in the range 250 to 300 prints, although RFD's *Reservoir Dogs* had only 124 prints (RFD had a notably higher print utilization figure, compared with the other distributors, with each of its prints receiving about three or four screenings). By a small margin, UIP made the largest number of prints (an average of 315 in their first six months) for its top films compared with Warner Distributors (302), Fox (282), and Guild (277).

4. The most successful of the top films in the case studies was UIP's *Jurassic Park*. Its UK gross contribution (to the end of 1993) was £[*] million. The smallest gross contribution (ie before the cost of the acquisition rights) by a top film was RFD's *The Krays* at £[*] million. The average was £[*] million. UIP's top five films (released during the period 1988 to 1993) achieved about £[*] million (ie £[*] million per film) in net rentals by the end of 1993, far more than the next highest (Warner Distributors at £[*] million, or £[*] million per film). Advertising and publicity expenditure for the top films was about £[ * ] on average. In almost all cases, however, advertising and publicity expenditure was a notably smaller percentage of rental income than it was for the typical or the most disappointing films.

---

*Figures omitted. See note on page iv.

## Characteristics common to the typical films

5. Typical films received at least 200 different screenings in their first six months. The highest numbers were for Warner Distributors' *Last of the Mohicans* (793) and Columbia's *My Girl* (725). The highest number of prints reported for any one film was 315 for Fox's *Alien III*. The normal figure appeared to be around the 200 mark, although four films had fewer than 60 prints.

6. The typical releases more often made negative rather than positive gross contributions (though Fox's *Alien III* made a £[*] million contribution). Both Buena Vista and UIP showed two typical releases each making a negative contribution of at least £[*] million. Net rental receipts for typical releases ranged between £[*] million and £[ * ]. Advertising and publicity costs were, on average, equivalent to about three-quarters of net rentals (for four films the advertising and publicity costs alone were greater than the net rental payments). UIP's typical five films achieved in total about £[*] million in rentals (or about £[*] million per film), about half that of Columbia (at £[*] million per film) and notably less than Warner Distributors (£[*] million). Revenue per print figures were much smaller in comparison with the top films, particularly for those of UIP and Warner Distributors.

## Characteristics common to the most disappointing films

7. Even the most disappointing films, with notable exceptions, each received at least 150 different screenings in their first six months. The highest numbers were for UIP's *An American Tail* (430 screenings) and Guild's *Chaplin* (409). All of Fox's films in this category received fewer than 70 screenings, and one of RFD's titles received only nine. The leading distributors (notably UIP, Warner Distributors and Columbia) achieved over 260 screenings per film, having made mostly over 100 prints for each title. The highest number of prints reported were 243 for RFD's *Christopher Columbus*, and 238 for UIP's *An American Tail*. The usual figure appeared to be around the 120 mark, although for UIP, Warner Distributors and Columbia it was about 160.

8. UIP's five most disappointing films achieved about £[*] million (or about £[ * ] per film) in net rentals. All the disappointing films on which we had the necessary information made a negative gross contribution. Net rentals ranged between £2,000 and £600,000, with an average of £150,000. In all cases the advertising and publicity costs alone exceeded, sometimes considerably, the net rental payments. Rental payments per print were surprisingly low, often less than £1,000.

---

*Figures omitted. See note on page iv.

APPENDIX 4.11
*(referred to in paragraph 4.176)*

# Pattern of release for UIP's film *Ghost*

1. Information on the release pattern for prints of UIP's film *Ghost* (its most successful film in the UK when it was released on 5 October 1990) is shown in Table 1.

TABLE 1  **UIP: distribution of prints for *Ghost*, October to November 1990**

| *List one:* | *First run* | | *Second run* | | *Total* | |
| --- | --- | --- | --- | --- | --- | --- |
| | No | % | No | % | No | % |
| Cannon | 102 | 45.5 | 10 | 12.3 | 112 | 36.7 |
| Odeon | 37 | 16.5 | 5 | 6.2 | 42 | 13.8 |
| UCI | 19 | 8.5 | - | - | 19 | 6.2 |
| Natl Amusements | 7 | 3.1 | - | - | 7 | 2.3 |
| Warner Theatres | 4 | 1.8 | - | - | 4 | 1.3 |
| Other | _55_ | _24.6_ | _66_ | _81.5_ | _121_ | _39.7_ |
| | 224 | 100.0 | 81 | 100.0 | 305 | 100.0 |
| *List two:* | | | *Second run* | | *Total: lists 1 & 2* | |
| | | | No | % | No | % |
| Cannon | | | 14 | 26.9 | 126 | 35.3 |
| Odeon | | | 3 | 5.8 | 45 | 12.6 |
| UCI | | | 1 | 1.9 | 20 | 5.6 |
| Natl Amusements | | | - | - | 7 | 2.0 |
| Warner Theatres | | | - | - | 4 | 1.1 |
| Other | | | _34_ | _65.4_ | _155_ | _43.4_ |
| | | | 52 | 100.0 | 357 | 100.0 |

*Source:* MMC, based on data from UIP.

2. About 75 per cent of the initial print run of 224 prints went to cinemas operated by the five leading exhibitors, and the remaining 25 per cent went to other exhibitors. On second run, 81 (36 per cent) of the 224 prints were released, and of these only about 19 per cent went to cinemas operated by the five majors (in fact only to Cannon, the predecessor of MGM Cinemas, and Odeon cinemas). As the film was unexpectedly popular, UIP made 52 additional prints from early November 1990, and of these about one-third went to cinemas operated by the five leading exhibitors (in fact all but one went to Cannon or Odeon cinemas).

3. Thus, during the period early October 1990 to early January 1991, out of the 357 screens at which *Ghost* was shown, 155 (or 43 per cent) were at independent cinemas, but only 55 (or 15 per cent) were available for first-run release at independent screens. The case study data (see paragraph 4.176) showed that *Ghost* eventually received 619 screenings in total.

APPENDIX 4.12
(referred to in paragraphs 2.147 and 4.178)

# Booking of films by distributors

1. We asked each of the five leading distributors, RFD and Entertainment to supply us with information on the film bookings they made in the four-month period November 1993 to February 1994. This information included details of all requests from exhibitors for prints which were not met, together with the reasons and information about any alternative dates or films offered. We also sent a short questionnaire to all the exhibitors whose requests were not met asking them to verify the details and provide further information as appropriate (82 of these short questionnaires were sent out, of which 56 (68 per cent) were completed and returned).

2. In the remainder of this appendix we summarize our main findings from this survey by distributor.

## Buena Vista

3. Buena Vista booked seven different films during the period of the study, but bookings were refused for only two of them. Most of Buena Vista's refusals concerned *Aladdin* (332 prints supplied with 14 refusals). A number of these were connected with the exceptionally long (five weeks) minimum exhibition period required by Buena Vista. Two exhibitors said that they were refused a print despite having made a preliminary reservation of the film well in advance. However, when it came to be confirmed these exhibitors were unwilling to meet Buena Vista's minimum exhibition requirement. In the case of the other film, *Another Stakeout*, there were only two refusals and neither exhibitor involved returned our questionnaire.

4. Buena Vista pointed out that for the other films which it released in the period there were no refusals. In fact, on 105 occasions exhibitors had refused bookings offered to them by Buena Vista (60 in the case of *The Three Musketeers* and 45 in the case of *Cool Runnings*).

## Columbia

5. Refusals arose on four of Columbia's films, but the only one for which the number of refusals exceeded three was *The Remains of the Day* (101 prints supplied with 12 refusals). It seems that the high incidence of refusals for this film was the result of Columbia's decision to release the film gradually and progressively in order to derive maximum benefit from 'word of mouth' and the publicity surrounding the Academy Awards. Four of the cinemas refused were part-time.

## Entertainment

6. The only film with more than two refusals was *The Piano* (80 prints supplied with eight refusals). The case appears similar to Columbia's *The Remains of the Day*, in that the film was not seen as a mainstream commercial product but as an arthouse film with cross-over potential. Entertainment's decision on the number of prints, which dictated that there would be a significant incidence of refusals, appears to have been based on a combination of financial and marketing factors. Three of the five exhibitors who returned our questionnaire regarded Entertainment's decision to refuse their requests as reasonable.

## Fox

7. The only film which Fox released in the period was *Mrs Doubtfire* (365 prints supplied with nine refusals). This was a big hit, second only to *Jurassic Park* in UK box office returns over the past year.

While there were a variety of reasons for the nine refusals, which Fox explained in detail, two general reasons emerged: first, Fox chose which of two competing cinemas to supply in four locations; and secondly, Fox chose not to supply four cinemas partly because of the limited length of run they were able to offer.

## RFD

8. RFD was accepting bookings for 14 new films during the period of the study, but it only refused one request (from Odeon) in respect of any of them.

## UIP

9. UIP supplied the most comprehensive information, including details of the length of run negotiated with each exhibitor and the length of time each film actually played. UIP gave information about bookings for 17 films but we looked in detail at only eight of them (because the other films were released some time before November 1993 but UIP was still accepting a trickle of late bookings). The basic results were as follows as follows:

|  | Total prints supplied | Bookings made or attempted in period | Refusals in the period |
|---|---|---|---|
| Addams Family Values | 290 | 449 | 6 |
| Beethoven 2 | 280 | 47 | 2 |
| Carlito's Way | 187 | 261 | 2 |
| In the Name of the Father | 88 | 70 | 3 |
| Schindler's List | 147 | 32 | 1 |
| Shadowlands | 145 | 63 | 1 |
| Undercover Blues | 231 | 118 | 2 |
| Wayne's World 2 | 231 | 312 | 5 |

10. UIP's main reason for refusing requests was that it considered that supplying a print would have an adverse effect on the net revenue it was expecting for the film concerned (ie that it expected its costs to increase by more than its revenues). In a few cases the exhibitor was unwilling to agree to the minimum period sought by UIP. The overall incidence of refusals was low and several of the exhibitors who returned our questionnaires said that they regarded UIP's decision as reasonable.

## Warner Distributors

11. For the three films released by Warner Distributors in the period there was a handful of refusals in two cases (*A Perfect World*, 314 prints supplied with four refusals, and *The Pelican Brief*, 269 prints with five refusals), and just one refusal in the other case. In each case Warner Distributors' reason was that it would have had to make additional prints, and considered that it would be unlikely to recover fully the costs of supplying the exhibitors concerned. Such comments as we received from exhibitors did not generally indicate a strong sense of grievance.

## Views of exhibitors

12. Table 1 shows the numbers of respondents who regarded the distributors' decisions on three particular matters as reasonable or not, together with the numbers commenting that the distributors' behaviour had changed recently (this was to test the view expressed by some exhibitors that the distributors were on their best behaviour during our inquiry).

TABLE 1 **Refusals to supply, November 1993 to February 1994: summary of answers to the exhibitors' mini-questionnaire**

|  | Was the distributor's decision to refuse supply reasonable? | | Was the distributor's offer of a print on a later date reasonable? | | Was the distributor's position on the minimum exhibition period reasonable? | | Has the distributor's behaviour regarding supply of prints changed in the last six months? | |
| --- | --- | --- | --- | --- | --- | --- | --- | --- |
|  | Yes | No | Yes | No | Yes | No | Yes | No |
| Buena Vista | 1 | 7 | 1 | 6 | 3 | 5 | 4 | 3 |
| Columbia | 7 | 6 | 7 | 5 | 9 | 0 | 1 | 13 |
| Entertainment | 3 | 4 | 3 | 2 | 3 | 0 | 1 | 6 |
| RFD | 1 | 0 | 0 | 0 | 0 | 0 | 0 | 1 |
| Fox | 0 | 2 | 1 | 1 | 1 | 1 | 0 | 3 |
| UIP | 6 | 5 | 5 | 4 | 7 | 1 | 2 | 9 |
| Warner Distributors | 4 | 1 | 3 | 2 | 2 | 1 | 2 | 3 |

*Source:* MMC.

*Notes:*
1. In some cases the exhibitor's view as to the reasonableness of the distributor's position regarding a minimum exhibition period refers to a shorter period specified for a second run, following a refusal to supply on first release.
2. In most cases a statement that the distributor's behaviour has changed in the last six months indicates an improvement.

13. In general, the results in Table 1 show a fairly even balance between respondents who found the distributors' decisions to refuse supply, and to offer a print on a later date, reasonable and those who did not. On minimum exhibition periods most exhibitors found the distributors' position reasonable. Relatively few exhibitors commented that the distributors' behaviour had changed recently.

14. Given the small numbers of cases involved in this survey, we have not placed much weight on these findings alone, but they did provide us with a further indicator to be weighed alongside other evidence we received.

APPENDIX 5.1
*(referred to in paragraphs 2.75, 4.62, 4.79, 5.11, 5.12, 5.14,
5.16, 5.17, 5.18, 5.21, 5.22, 5.24 and 5.25)*

# Financial performance and licensing arrangements of the distributors

1. We received financial information from the five leading distributors, each of which is owned by one or more Hollywood studios which are also their principal suppliers. They also supplied us with details of the arrangements under which they acquire films from their affiliated companies. In addition we received financial information from Guild and RFD. RFD gave us a detailed description of the various types of agreement into which it enters. Guild, the largest independent, also gave a brief description of its licensing arrangements.

## Buena Vista

2. Buena Vista's principal supplier is its affiliated company, Buena Vista International Inc (BVI). Receipts from a film licensed by BVI to Buena Vista are applied as to 90 per cent royalty to BVI and 10 per cent distribution fee to Buena Vista. Buena Vista pays BVI the royalty after deducting distribution expenses (advertising, publicity, prints, trailers etc) incurred from the 90 per cent. If the distribution expenses exceed the royalty, Buena Vista recovers the excess from amounts due to BVI on other films. BVI is owned by Walt Disney, and Buena Vista primarily distributes Disney films.

3. Buena Vista's results covered only the period from the commencement of trading on 20 November 1992 to its next financial year end on 30 September 1993 and are set out in Table 1.

TABLE 1  **Buena Vista: financial results from UK film distribution**

|  | Period to September 1993 £'000 |
|---|---|
| *Turnover* | |
| Gross rentals | 9,373 |
| Other revenue | 0 |
|  | 9,373 |
| *Direct costs* | |
| Prints, trailers etc | [ |
| Advertising and publicity | |
| Other direct costs | |
| Contribution | |
| *Indirect costs* | |
| Staff costs | * |
| Accommodation | |
| General administration | |
| Other | |
| Operating profit before cost of distribution rights | |
| Cost of distribution rights | |
| Operating profit after cost of distribution rights | ] |
|  | % |
| *Percentages of turnover* | |
| Prints, trailers etc | [ |
| Advertising and publicity | |
| Other direct costs | |
|   Direct costs | |
| Contribution | * |
|   Indirect costs | |
| Operating profit (ROT) before distribution rights | |
|   Cost of distribution rights | |
| Operating profit (ROT) after distribution rights | ] |

*Source:* Buena Vista.

---

*Figures omitted. See note on page iv.

## Columbia

4. Columbia's primary business is the distribution in the UK of films from its affiliated US companies, Columbia Pictures Industries Inc and TriStar Pictures Inc, both of which are subsidiaries of Sony Pictures Entertainment Inc. Columbia's rights to distribute films in the UK arise under a licence from its connected company, Columbia TriStar Film Distributors International Inc (CTFD). Columbia recovers from CTFD 100 per cent of distribution expenses, 1 per cent of monies received from certain overseas territories and a fee representing 110 per cent of its operating costs.

5. The period ending in February 1993 was Columbia's most successful with films such as *Hook* and *Bram Stoker's Dracula* contributing to rentals of £20.7 million and an operating profit before the cost of distribution rights of more than £[*] million. Columbia's results are set out in Table 2. In 1993 it moved its year end from January to February, so that its results to February 1993 cover a 13-month period.

TABLE 2  **Columbia: financial results from UK film distribution**

£'000

|  | Year to Jan 1990 | Year to Jan 1991 | Year to Jan 1992 | 13 months to Feb 1993 | Year to Feb 1994 | Total |
|---|---|---|---|---|---|---|
| *Turnover* | | | | | | |
| Gross rentals | 7,779 | 7,491 | 8,359 | 20,717 | 11,150 | 55,496 |
| Other revenue | 0 | 0 | 0 | 0 | 0 | 0 |
|  | 7,779 | 7,491 | 8,359 | 20,717 | 11,150 | 55,496 |
| *Direct costs* | | | | | | |
| Prints, trailers etc | [ | | | | | |
| Advertising and publicity | | | | | | |
| Other direct costs | | | | | | |
| Contribution | | | | | | |
| *Indirect costs* | | | | | | |
| Staff costs | | | Figures omitted. | | | |
| Accommodation | | | See note on page iv. | | | |
| General administration | | | | | | |
| Other | | | | | | |
| Operating profit before cost of distribution rights | | | | | | |
| Cost of distribution rights | | | | | | |
| Operating profit after cost of distribution rights | | | | | | ] |
|  | | | | | | per cent |
| *Percentages of turnover* | | | | | | |
| Prints, trailers etc | [ | | | | | |
| Advertising and publicity | | | | | | |
| Other direct costs | | | | | | |
| Direct costs | | | | | | |
| Contribution | | | Figures omitted. | | | |
| Indirect costs | | | See note on | | | |
| Operating profit (ROT) before distribution rights | | | page iv. | | | |
| Cost of distribution rights | | | | | | |
| Operating profit (ROT) after distribution rights | | | | | | ] |

*Source:* Columbia.

## Fox

6. The rights to most films distributed by Fox are obtained under a franchise agreement with its affiliated company, Twentieth Century Fox International Corporation (Fox International). Fox recovers its distribution costs on these films, plus an appropriate proportion of its operating costs (related to its receipts from these films as a proportion of its receipts from all films). It then retains 1 per cent

---

*Figure omitted. See note on page iv.

of gross receipts as its distribution fee and remits the balance to Fox International. The effect of these arrangements is to prevent Fox from covering losses on some films by profits on others, so that there were losses in all five years.

7. The results for Fox for the five years to 22 May 1993 are shown in Table 3. With a few exceptions, the company distributes only those film titles covered by its franchise agreement with Fox International.

TABLE 3  **Fox: financial results from UK film distribution**

£'000

| | Year to May | | | | | |
|---|---|---|---|---|---|---|
| | 1989 | 1990 | 1991 | 1992 | 1993 | Total |
| *Turnover* | | | | | | |
| Gross rentals | 4,145 | 3,247 | 8,929 | 7,520 | 8,776 | 32,617 |
| Other revenue | 0 | 0 | 0 | 0 | 0 | 0 |
| | 4,145 | 3,247 | 8,929 | 7,520 | 8,776 | 32,617 |
| *Direct costs* | | | | | | |
| Prints, trailers etc | [ | | | | | |
| Advertising and publicity | | | | | | |
| Other direct costs | | | | | | |
| Contribution | | | | | | |
| *Indirect costs* | | | | | | |
| Staff costs | | | *Figures omitted.* | | | |
| Accommodation | | | *See note on page iv.* | | | |
| General administration | | | | | | |
| Other | | | | | | |
| Operating profit before cost of distribution rights | | | | | | |
| Cost of distribution rights | | | | | | |
| Operating profit after cost of distribution rights | | | | | | ] |

per cent

| | | | | | | |
|---|---|---|---|---|---|---|
| *Percentages of turnover* | | | | | | |
| Prints, trailers etc | [ | | | | | |
| Advertising and publicity | | | | | | |
| Other direct costs | | | | | | |
| Direct costs | | | | | | |
| Contribution | | | *Figures omitted.* | | | |
| Indirect costs | | | *See note on* | | | |
| Operating profit (ROT) before distribution rights | | | *page iv.* | | | |
| Cost of distribution rights | | | | | | |
| Operating profit (ROT) after distribution rights | | | | | | ] |

*Source:* Fox.

8. The contribution of Fox's five most successful films is shown in Table 4. They account for more than 95 per cent of the total contribution from UK film distribution over the five years.

TABLE 4  **Fox: contribution of top five films, 1989 to 1993**

£'000

| | Rentals | Prints | Advertising and publicity | Other direct costs | Contribution |
|---|---|---|---|---|---|
| Home Alone | [ | | | | |
| Home Alone 2 | | | | | |
| Sleeping with the Enemy | | | | | |
| The Commitments | | | *Figures omitted.* | | |
| Alien 3 | | | *See note on page iv.* | | |
| All others | | | | | ] |

*Source:* Fox.

# UIP

9. UIP is the largest distributor on the basis of rentals received over the five years 1989 to 1993. It mostly distributes films produced by its joint venture parent companies, MGM Inc, Paramount and MCA/Universal. Although it is the main distributor for its parent companies, it is not the only distributor. UIP told us that it had a right of first refusal over its parents' films, which was not always exercised. When it was not exercised, the parent might well distribute the film through an independent distributor. UIP also told us that each partner paid for the direct costs of its films and received all the rentals less the distribution fee. There was therefore a negligible financial benefit to each of the joint venture partners from the films of the other partners; the advantage of the joint venture arose from sharing some of the fixed costs of a distribution company.

10. UIP obtains the distribution rights for most of the films it distributes in the UK under a licence agreement with its connected company, United International Pictures (International). Under this agreement UIP pays International the rentals it receives, less its distribution costs, administrative expenses and a fee of 2.4 per cent of rentals receivable less distribution costs. (Until 1 January 1993 this fee was 1.5 per cent of rentals before any deductions.)

11. UIP changed its accounting year end from June to December in 1990. Its most successful recent films include *Crocodile Dundee II* (1989), *Indiana Jones and the Last Crusade* (1990) and *Ghost* (1990). But UIP's best year was 1993 which was dominated by *Jurassic Park*, by far the most profitable film for any distributor in the five years 1989 to 1993. In spite of this spectacular success, its operating profit for that year after the cost of distribution rights was only £[ * ]. Its results are set out in Table 5.

---

*Figure omitted. See note on page iv.

TABLE 5  **UIP: financial results from UK film distribution**

£'000

|  | Year to June 1989 | 18 months to Dec 1990 | Year to Dec 1991 | Year to Dec 1992 | Year to Dec 1993 | Total |
|---|---|---|---|---|---|---|
| *Turnover* | | | | | | |
| Gross rentals | 26,096 | 41,807 | 15,217 | 16,205 | 32,014 | 131,339 |
| Other revenue | 876 | 1,560 | 924 | 747 | 1,171 | 5,278 |
|  | 26,972 | 43,367 | 16,141 | 16,952 | 33,185 | 136,617 |
| *Direct costs* | | | | | | |
| Prints, trailers etc | [ | | | | | |
| Advertising and publicity | | | | | | |
| Other direct costs | | | | | | |
| Contribution | | | | | | |
| *Indirect costs* | | | | | | |
| Staff costs | | | *Figures omitted.* | | | |
| Accommodation | | | *See note on page iv.* | | | |
| General administration | | | | | | |
| Other | | | | | | |
| Operating profit before cost of distribution rights | | | | | | |
| Cost of distribution rights | | | | | | |
| Operating profit after cost of distribution rights | | | | | | ] |

per cent

| | | | | | | |
|---|---|---|---|---|---|---|
| *Percentages of turnover* | | | | | | |
| Prints, trailers etc | [ | | | | | |
| Advertising and publicity | | | | | | |
| Other direct costs | | | | | | |
|   Direct costs | | | | | | |
| Contribution | | | *Figures omitted.* | | | |
|   Indirect costs | | | *See note on* | | | |
| Operating profit (ROT) before distribution rights | | | *page iv.* | | | |
|   Cost of distribution rights | | | | | | |
| Operating profit (ROT) after distribution rights | | | | | | ] |

*Source:* UIP.

## Warner Distributors

12. Warner Distributors' primary function is to market and distribute in the UK the films produced, co-produced or acquired by Warner Bros International (WBI). It is the second largest of the distributors after UIP. Virtually all the films distributed by Warner Distributors are licensed to it under its franchise agreement with WBI. It pays WBI a royalty of 80 per cent of rentals for those films and is reimbursed by WBI for 80 per cent of its advertising costs and all its print costs. The same agreement covered the Walt Disney films licensed to Warner Distributors by WBI until 1992. Warner Distributors also has agreements with other connected companies to distribute films that they co-finance.

13. Over the last five years Warner Distributors' rentals have varied little, with a low of £21.3 million in 1991 and a high of £24.9 million in 1992. In 1993 it maintained its rentals close to the levels achieved in previous years, in spite of the loss of UK distribution rights for Walt Disney films. Although less dependent on individual films than Fox, it would have made an operating loss in 1991 before the cost of distribution rights without the contribution from *Robin Hood: Prince of Thieves*. Its results are set out in Table 6.

TABLE 6  Warner Distributors: financial results from UK film distribution

£'000

Year to November

| | 1989 | 1990 | 1991 | 1992 | 1993 | Total |
|---|---|---|---|---|---|---|
| *Turnover* | | | | | | |
| Gross rentals | 23,549 | 24,202 | 21,275 | 24,883 | 23,891 | 117,800 |
| Other revenue | 0 | 0 | 0 | 0 | 918 | 918 |
| | 23,549 | 24,202 | 21,275 | 24,883 | 24,809 | 118,718 |
| *Direct costs* | | | | | | |
| Prints, trailers etc | [ | | | | | |
| Advertising and publicity | | | | | | |
| Other direct costs | | | | | | |
| Contribution | | | | | | |
| *Indirect costs* | | | | | | |
| Staff costs | | | *Figures omitted.* | | | |
| Accommodation | | | *See note on page iv.* | | | |
| General administration | | | | | | |
| Other | | | | | | |
| Operating profit before cost of distribution rights | | | | | | |
| Cost of distribution rights | | | | | | |
| Operating profit after cost of distribution rights | | | | | | ] |

per cent

| | | | | | | |
|---|---|---|---|---|---|---|
| *Percentages of turnover* | | | | | | |
| Prints, trailers etc | [ | | | | | |
| Advertising and publicity | | | | | | |
| Other direct costs | | | | | | |
| Direct costs | | | | | | |
| Contribution | | | *Figures omitted.* | | | |
| Indirect costs | | | *See note on* | | | |
| Operating profit (ROT) before distribution rights | | | *page iv.* | | | |
| Cost of distribution rights | | | | | | |
| Operating profit (ROT) after distribution rights | | | | | | ] |

*Source:* Warner Distributors.

# Financial results of the leading distributors

14. The turnover of the five leading distributors is summarized in Table 7.

TABLE 7  The five leading distributors: components of turnover

£'000

Periods*

| | 1989 | 1990 | 1991 | 1992 | 1993 | Total |
|---|---|---|---|---|---|---|
| *Gross rentals (excl VAT)* | | | | | | |
| Buena Vista | - | - | - | - | 9,373 | 9,373 |
| Columbia | 7,779 | 7,491 | 8,359 | 20,717 | 11,150 | 55,496 |
| Fox | 4,145 | 3,247 | 8,929 | 7,520 | 8,776 | 32,617 |
| UIP | 26,096 | 41,807 | 15,217 | 16,205 | 32,014 | 131,339 |
| Warner Distributors | 23,549 | 24,202 | 21,275 | 24,883 | 23,891 | 117,800 |
| | 61,569 | 76,747 | 53,780 | 69,325 | 85,204 | 346,625 |
| *Other revenues* | | | | | | |
| UIP | 876 | 1,560 | 924 | 747 | 1,171 | 5,278 |
| Warner Distributors | 0 | 0 | 0 | 0 | 918 | 918 |
| | 876 | 1,560 | 924 | 747 | 2,089 | 6,196 |
| *Turnover* | | | | | | |
| Buena Vista | | | | | 9,373 | 9,373 |
| Columbia | 7,779 | 7,491 | 8,359 | 20,717 | 11,150 | 55,496 |
| Fox | 4,145 | 3,247 | 8,929 | 7,520 | 8,776 | 32,617 |
| UIP | 26,972 | 43,367 | 16,141 | 16,952 | 33,185 | 136,617 |
| Warner Distributors | 23,549 | 24,202 | 21,275 | 24,883 | 24,809 | 118,718 |
| | 62,445 | 78,307 | 54,704 | 70,072 | 87,293 | 352,821 |

*Source:* MMC using the five leading distributors' data.

*Accounting periods ending in the year shown or early in the following year. Columbia's 1992 accounting period covered 13 months and UIP's 1990 accounting period covered 18 months.

15. The principal items of expense and profit have been calculated as a percentage of turnover for each of the five leading distributors and are set out in Table 8.

TABLE 8  **The five leading distributors: costs and profits as percentages of turnover**

per cent

| | \multicolumn{6}{c}{Periods*} | | | | | |
|---|---|---|---|---|---|---|
| | 1989 | 1990 | 1991 | 1992 | 1993 | Total |
| *Prints, trailers etc* | | | | | | |
| Buena Vista | [ | | | | | |
| Columbia | | | Figures omitted. | | | |
| Fox | | | See note on | | | |
| UIP | | | page iv. | | | |
| Warner Distributors | | | | | | ] |
| Average | 10.3 | 10.9 | 16.2 | 12.4 | 11.8 | 12.1 |
| *Advertising and publicity* | | | | | | |
| Buena Vista | [ | | | | | |
| Columbia | | | Figures omitted. | | | |
| Fox | | | See note on | | | |
| UIP | | | page iv. | | | |
| Warner Distributors | | | | | | ] |
| Average | 34.5 | 39.1 | 59.9 | 50.2 | 41.3 | 44.3 |
| *Indirect costs* | | | | | | |
| Buena Vista | [ | | | | | |
| Columbia | | | Figures omitted. | | | |
| Fox | | | See note on | | | |
| UIP | | | page iv. | | | |
| Warner Distributors | | | | | | ] |
| Average | 8.0 | 8.1 | 9.1 | 7.1 | 6.9 | 7.8 |
| *Operating profits before cost of distribution rights* | | | | | | |
| Buena Vista | [ | | | | | |
| Columbia | | | Figures omitted. | | | |
| Fox | | | See note on | | | |
| UIP | | | page iv. | | | |
| Warner Distributors | | | | | | ] |
| Average | 46.5 | 41.2 | 13.8 | 29.5 | 39.1 | 35.0 |
| *Cost of distribution rights* | | | | | | |
| Buena Vista | [ | | | | | |
| Columbia | | | Figures omitted. | | | |
| Fox | | | See note on | | | |
| UIP | | | page iv. | | | |
| Warner Distributors | | | | | | ] |
| Average | 44.6 | 40.5 | 12.9 | 29.5 | 36.3 | 33.7 |
| *Operating profits after cost of distribution rights (ROT)* | | | | | | |
| Buena Vista | [ | | | | | |
| Columbia | | | Figures omitted. | | | |
| Fox | | | See note on | | | |
| UIP | | | page iv. | | | |
| Warner Distributors | | | | | | ] |
| Average | 1.9 | 0.7 | 0.9 | 0.0 | 2.8 | 1.3 |

*Source:* MMC using the five leading distributors' data.

*Accounting periods ending in the year shown or early in the following year. Columbia's 1992 accounting period covered 13 months and UIP's 1990 accounting period covered 18 months.

# Guild

16. Guild is the largest of the independent distributors. Although it was acquired by Chargeurs SA in 1992, it receives few films from associated companies and its business has not so far been much affected by the change of ownership.

17. Guild told us that the price payable for the distribution rights for a film was usually negotiated in the light of the production budget, the script, the cast, the director and the forecast of its profitability in the UK market. Guild's normal agreement with a US producer provided for a minimum guarantee payment for the rights acquired (eg theatrical, television, video rental and video sell-through rights) payable as to 10 per cent on signature of the agreement, 40 per cent on delivery of the material and 50 per cent on the video release. In addition, royalties, generally of 50 per cent, were payable once Guild's minimum guarantee payment and distribution expenses had been covered by the rentals earned, so that profits in excess of the minimum guarantee and distribution costs were shared equally between Guild and its supplier.

18. Guild's results are set out in Table 9. It has made an operating profit after payments for distribution rights in only one year, 1991, when it had two successful films.

TABLE 9  **Guild: financial results from UK film distribution**

£'000

| | | | Year to December | | | |
|---|---|---|---|---|---|---|
| | 1989 | 1990 | 1991 | 1992 | 1993 | Total |
| *Turnover* | | | | | | |
| Gross rentals | 594 | 4,103 | 13,002 | 9,287 | 5,411 | 32,397 |
| Other revenue | 0 | 0 | 0 | 0 | 0 | 0 |
| | 594 | 4,103 | 13,002 | 9,287 | 5,411 | 32,397 |
| *Direct costs* | | | | | | |
| Prints, trailers etc | [ | | | | | |
| Advertising and publicity | | | | | | |
| Other direct costs | | | | | | |
| | | | | | | |
| Contribution | | | | | | |
| | | | | | | |
| *Indirect costs* | | | | | | |
| Staff costs | | | *Figures omitted.* | | | |
| Accommodation | | | *See note on page iv.* | | | |
| General administration | | | | | | |
| Other | | | | | | |
| | | | | | | |
| Operating profit before cost of distribution rights | | | | | | |
| Cost of distribution rights | | | | | | |
| Operating profit after cost of distribution rights | | | | | | ] |
| | | | | | | per cent |
| *Percentages of turnover* | | | | | | |
| Prints, trailers etc | [ | | | | | |
| Advertising and publicity | | | | | | |
| Other direct costs | | | | | | |
|   Direct costs | | | | | | |
| Contribution | | | *Figures omitted.* | | | |
|   Indirect costs | | | *See note on* | | | |
| Operating profit (ROT) before distribution rights | | | *page iv.* | | | |
|   Cost of distribution rights | | | | | | |
| Operating profit (ROT) after distribution rights | | | | | | ] |

*Source:* Guild.

## RFD

19. RFD, as an independent distributor, rarely has access to films made by or for the Hollywood studios, which usually supply them to their own vertically-integrated distribution companies. It acts independently in acquiring rights in films, distributing them for theatrical exhibition in the UK and, if it acquires other rights in those films, licensing them in other media in the UK and in all media world-wide, normally excluding North America. The basis on which it acquires these rights varies from film to film but usually takes one of the four forms described in the paragraphs below.

## Co-financing deals

20. RFD commonly part-finances film production to help secure its distribution supply. This may occasionally involve participating at an early stage in decisions to ensure that the completed product will achieve its distribution potential. Frequently, however, a decision to part-finance has to be made with little information about the finished product and with limited opportunity to be involved in creative decisions.

21. In a typical production, financing and distribution agreement RFD will agree to provide funds equal to the smallest of a specific sum, a percentage of the production budget or the same percentage of the actual cost of the film. This percentage is now usually around [*] per cent, which roughly represents the proportion of the total income of a film generated by foreign (ie world-wide outside North America) rights. In return, RFD is normally granted the right to distribute, and to license the distribution of, the film in all media throughout the world excluding North America. In a typical co-financing deal, RFD's distribution commission will be the following percentages of revenues received:

|                | %   |
|----------------|-----|
| UK theatrical  | [   |
| Television     |     |
| Video          | *   |
| Other          |     |
| Overseas       | ]   |

In addition, it would expect to recover its distribution costs and its investment.

22. RFD will pay for theatrical distribution in the UK, including prints and advertising, and will seek to recover these costs from the rentals it receives, after deducting its distribution fees. In North America, RFD would normally require the film to be theatrically distributed by a domestic distributor, often with an agreed minimum level of print and advertising expenditure to ensure a reasonably wide release.

23. There are generally two sets of fees: one for distribution in the UK and certain related territories, and the other for all other territories where RFD has bought the rights. The fee for UK distribution is higher because RFD undertakes more responsibility there.

24. In addition, in return for investing in the production, RFD will share in net profits, if any, arising from the distribution of the film in its territories. If its financing contribution is around [*] per cent of the cost of production, the net profit split between RFD and the producer will usually be [ * ]. Profits are calculated on net revenues received by RFD from the distribution of the film in all media throughout its territories, after the deduction of its fees and expenses, the recovery of its investment with interest and, in some cases, other costs and guarantees. Net revenues for this purpose include the exploitation of ancillary rights (merchandising etc) whether or not this exploitation is undertaken by RFD.

25. RFD does not usually obtain better terms on a film merely because it agrees to provide cash flow financing, nor does it receive a separate payment for that financing, except interest on the monies advanced. However, by providing such financing, RFD is in a better position to obtain film rights in competition with other distributors.

## Purchase deals

26. These deals involve the purchase of rights to distribute a film in specified media within a specified area. They can be made at any stage during the film's development or production. On a typical purchase deal, RFD's commission will be the following percentages of revenues received:

---

*Figures omitted. See note on page iv.

|  | % |
|---|---|
| All theatrical | [ |
| Video | * |
| Television | ] |

On many purchase deals RFD will also be expected to pay the supplier of the film an advance against its share of revenues. RFD would expect to recover its distribution costs and any such advance out of the balance of revenues after its commission has been deducted, although this is far from a foregone conclusion.

## Output deals

27. These are deals under which RFD agrees to distribute all films made or acquired by a supplier, either for a specified period or up to a specified number of films. When RFD makes an output deal it usually does so on the basis of the producer's record without any specific information about the quality and commercial potential of the films to be acquired. These deals are usually made either on a 'straight distribution' or a 'minimum guarantee' basis. On a straight distribution basis, RFD does not guarantee the supplier's share of receipts and generally does not bear the risk of marketing costs. Instead, it provides finance for the print and advertising costs associated with the release, on the basis that the supplier refunds any sums that remain unrecovered after a certain period has expired. If the deal involves only UK theatrical rights, RFD will retain a commission of [*] to [*] per cent of revenues. This lower level of commission reflects the fact that it does not bear the risk of marketing costs. Conversely, on a minimum guarantee basis, RFD takes the risk on promotion and marketing costs and gives a guarantee (frequently based on the production budget of the film) of the supplier's or producer's share of the revenue of exploitation of rights acquired by RFD.

## First-look deals

28. RFD also enters into 'first-look' deals under which it is entitled to first refusal of the chance to invest in and acquire film rights on a pre-arranged basis. The financial arrangements for these deals are usually similar to those described under co-financing deals.

## Other arrangements

29. If RFD has acquired the home video rights in a film it will seek to license a third party to distribute the film on video. A licence for video distribution is generally agreed prior to theatrical release. RFD will normally take a share of the revenues from distribution (sales or rentals) and may require a minimum advance payment on account of that share.

30. If RFD has also acquired the pay television rights, it will endeavour to license the film to BSkyB. However, since BSkyB became the only purchaser of films for satellite transmission in the UK, RFD told us that it had found it difficult to obtain commercial returns from pay television.

31. RFD will also endeavour to sell the free television rights in any film for which it has such rights. Despite the development of Channel 4 during the last ten years, the BBC and ITC (acting for the independent television companies jointly) remain the only significant purchasers of films for free television from RFD.

## Financial results

32. As noted in paragraph 5.18, RFD was unable to provide us with financial information in the form that we had requested. It provided us instead with analyses of its trading profits for the last five years, together with allocations of its indirect costs to UK theatrical distribution. Its results are set out in Table 10.

---

*Figures omitted. See note on page iv.

TABLE 10  **RFD: financial results, 1989 to 1993**

£'000

*Year to October*

|  | 1989 | 1990 | 1991 | 1992 | 1993 | Total |
|---|---|---|---|---|---|---|
| *Turnover* | | | | | | |
| UK theatrical | 2,808 | 3,949 | 9,736 | 2,162 | 2,502 | 21,157 |
| Other | 10,089 | 10,038 | 5,365 | 4,153 | 7,534 | 37,179 |
| Overseas | 12,068 | 12,071 | 12,516 | 16,794 | 9,407 | 62,856 |
|  | 24,965 | 26,058 | 27,617 | 23,109 | 19,443 | 121,192 |

*Commission*
UK theatrical  [
Other
Overseas

Production income

*Indirect costs*
Staff costs
Accommodation
General administration
Other indirect costs

Operating profit

*UK theatrical results*
Turnover

Commission

*Indirect costs*
Staff costs
Accommodation
Other costs

Operating profit

*Tangible capital employed*
Tangible fixed assets
Films and film rights
Other net current assets
  (excluding net borrowings)
Capital employed                                                                                                                             ]

*Percentages of UK*                                                                                                                  per cent
  *theatrical turnover*
UK theatrical commission  [
Indirect costs
Operating profit

*Percentages of total turnover*
UK theatrical commission
Total commission
Production income

Indirect costs
Operating profit

*Percentage of average*
  *capital employed*
Operating profit (ROCE)                                                                                                                        ]

*Figures omitted. See note on page iv.*

  Source: RFD.

APPENDIX 5.2

*(referred to in paragraphs 2.88, 2.89, 5.27, 5.28, 5.30–5.32, 5.34, 5.35, 5.38–5.41 and 5.43–5.45)*

## Financial performance of the five leading exhibitors

1. We received financial information from the leading exhibitors for their financial years ending in 1989 to 1993.

## MGM Cinemas

2. MGM Cinemas is one of the two national circuits. The financial information for MGM Cinemas includes its operations in the Republic of Ireland, which account for 1.9 per cent of turnover. Its results are set out in Table 1.

TABLE 1  **MGM Cinemas: financial results, 1989 to 1993**

£'000

| | | | | Year to December | | | |
|---|---|---|---|---|---|---|---|
| | 1988 | 1989 | 1990 | 1991 | 1992 | 1993 | Total |
| *Turnover* | | | | | | | |
| Box office takings | | [ | | | | | |
| Screen advertising | | | | *Figures omitted.* | | | |
| Concessions | | | | *See note on page iv.* | | | |
| Other revenue | | | | | | | |
| | | 84,645 | 82,050 | 90,311 | 98,279 | 106,678 | 461,963 |
| *Costs* | | | | | | | ] |
| Film rental payments | [ | | | | | | |
| Concession cost of sales | | | | | | | |
| Advertising and publicity | | | | | | | |
| Staff costs | | | | | | | |
| Depreciation | | | | | | | |
| Other operating costs | | | | | | | |
| | | | | | | | |
| Operating profit | | | | *Figures omitted.* | | | |
| | | | | *See note on* | | | |
| | | | | *page iv.* | | | |
| *Tangible capital employed* | | | | | | | |
| Tangible fixed assets | | | | | | | |
| Fixed asset investments | | | | | | | |
| Net current assets | | | | | | | |
| | | | | | | | |
| Average capital employed | | | | | | | ] |
| | | | | | | | per cent |
| ROCE | | [ | | *Figures omitted. See note on page iv.* | | | ] |

*Source:* MGM Cinemas.

## Natl Amusements

3. The financial results of Natl Amusements are made up of all the results of Natl Amusements (UK) Ltd, which operates the Showcase chain of multiplex cinemas, and the UK portion of the results of National Amusements, Ltd, a Delaware corporation, which owns all the cinema sites and rents them to its UK affiliate at a rental which is based on box office takings. The financial results of Natl Amusements are set out in Table 2.

4. The head office function of Natl Amusements is carried out from the offices of its parent company in Dedham, Massachussetts. No charge is made to the UK company for this service, and the cost of it is not included in Table 2, which consequently overstates the profitability of the Showcase operation in the UK.

TABLE 2  **Natl Amusements: financial results, 1989 to 1993**

£'000

| | 1988 | 1989 | 1990 | 1991 | 1992 | 1993 | Total |
|---|---|---|---|---|---|---|---|
| *Turnover* | | | | | | | |
| Box office takings | | [ | | | | | |
| Screen advertising | | | | *Figures omitted.* | | | |
| Concessions | | | | *See note on page iv.* | | | |
| Other revenue | | | | | | | ] |
| | | 7,538 | 18,367 | 20,812 | 23,763 | 31,248 | 101,728 |
| *Costs* | | | | | | | |
| Film rental payments | [ | | | | | | |
| Concession cost of sales | | | | | | | |
| Advertising and publicity | | | | | | | |
| Staff costs | | | | | | | |
| Depreciation | | | | | | | |
| Other operating costs | | | | | | | |
| Operating profit | | | | *Figures omitted.* | | | |
| *Tangible capital employed* | | | | *See note on* | | | |
| Tangible fixed assets | | | | *page iv.* | | | |
| Fixed asset investments | | | | | | | |
| Net current assets | | | | | | | |
| Average capital employed | | | | | | | ] |
| | | | | | | | *per cent* |
| ROCE | | [ | | *Figures omitted. See note on page iv.* | | | ] |

*Source:* Natl Amusements.

## Odeon

5. Odeon is the other national circuit. Odeon revalued its cinemas in 1990 which led to a large increase in the value at which they were stated in the statutory accounts. A later revaluation in 1993 reduced the revaluation surplus. In Table 3 the results of Odeon exclude these revaluations, and depreciation has been calculated on the historical cost of the cinemas.

TABLE 3  **Odeon: financial results, 1989 to 1993**

£'000

| | 1988 | 1989 | 1990 | 1991 | 1992 | 1993 | Total |
|---|---|---|---|---|---|---|---|
| *Turnover* | | | | | | | |
| Box office takings | | [ | | | | | |
| Screen advertising | | | | *Figures omitted.* | | | |
| Concessions | | | | *See note on page iv.* | | | |
| Other revenue | | | | | | | ] |
| | | 57,192 | 65,582 | 74,343 | 69,789 | 76,377 | 343,283 |
| *Costs* | | | | | | | |
| Film rental payments | [ | | | | | | |
| Concession cost of sales | | | | | | | |
| Advertising and publicity | | | | | | | |
| Staff costs | | | | | | | |
| Depreciation | | | | | | | |
| Other operating costs | | | | | | | |
| Operating profit | | | | *Figures omitted.* | | | |
| *Tangible capital employed* | | | | *See note on* | | | |
| Tangible fixed assets | | | | *page iv.* | | | |
| Fixed asset investments | | | | | | | |
| Net current assets | | | | | | | |
| Average capital employed | | | | | | | ] |
| | | | | | | | *per cent* |
| ROCE | | [ | | *Figures omitted. See note on page iv.* | | | ] |

*Source:* Odeon.

## UCI and CIC

6. CIC NV, a joint venture between Paramount and MCA/Universal, acquired cinemas in a number of countries through its subsidiaries, including two West End cinemas, the Empire and the Plaza, which are now owned by CIC and operated by UCI. CIC opened a multiplex cinema at High Wycombe in 1987, which was transferred to UCI in 1988. In the same year CIC NV and United Artists acquired from American Multiplex Cinemas Inc a chain of 19 multiplex cinemas (built or under development), the first of which had opened in Milton Keynes in 1985. Also in 1988 CIC NV transferred its multiplex operations to UCI BV, a joint venture between Paramount BV and MCA BV and immediate parent company of UCI. Some of UCI's freehold and leasehold cinemas are owned by UCI BV.

*UCI*

7. The results of UCI are shown in Table 4. In this table the cinema operations of Milton Keynes Entertainment Company Ltd (MKEC) have been consolidated as if it were a wholly-owned subsidiary of UCI.

TABLE 4  **UCI: financial results, 1989 to 1993**

£'000

| | 1988 | 1989 | 1990 | 1991 | 1992 | 1993 | Total |
|---|---|---|---|---|---|---|---|
| *Turnover* | | | | Year to December | | | |
| Box office takings | | [ | | | | | |
| Screen advertising | | | | *Figures omitted.* | | | |
| Concessions | | | | *See note on page iv.* | | | |
| Other revenue | | | | | | | ] |
| | | 30,150 | 50,393 | 63,967 | 69,774 | 80,490 | 294,774 |
| *Costs* | | | | | | | |
| Film rental payments | [ | | | | | | |
| Concession cost of sales | | | | | | | |
| Advertising and publicity | | | | | | | |
| Staff costs | | | | | | | |
| Depreciation | | | | | | | |
| Other operating costs | | | | | | | |
| Operating profit | | | | *Figures omitted. See note on page iv.* | | | |
| *Tangible capital employed* | | | | | | | |
| Tangible fixed assets | | | | | | | |
| Fixed asset investments | | | | | | | |
| Net current assets | | | | | | | |
| Average capital employed | | | | | | | ] |
| | | | | | | | per cent |
| ROCE | | [ | | *Figures omitted. See note on page iv.* | | | ] |

*Source:* UCI.

*CIC*

8. The results of CIC are shown in Table 5.

TABLE 5  CIC: financial results, 1989 to 1993

£'000

Year to December

|  | 1988 | 1989 | 1990 | 1991 | 1992 | 1993 | Total |
|---|---|---|---|---|---|---|---|
| *Turnover* | | | | | | | |
| Box office takings | | [ | | | | | |
| Screen advertising | | | | *Figures omitted.* | | | |
| Concessions | | | | *See note on page iv.* | | | |
| Other revenue | | | | | | | ] |
| | | 9,071 | 6,466 | 5,190 | 5,218 | 5,845 | 31,790 |
| *Costs* | | | | | | | |
| Film rental payments | [ | | | | | | |
| Concession cost of sales | | | | | | | |
| Advertising and publicity | | | | | | | |
| Staff costs | | | | | | | |
| Depreciation | | | | | | | |
| Other operating costs | | | | | | | |
| | | | | *Figures omitted.* | | | |
| Operating profit | | | | *See note on page iv.* | | | |
| *Tangible capital employed* | | | | | | | |
| Tangible fixed assets | | | | | | | |
| Fixed asset investments | | | | | | | |
| Net current assets | | | | | | | |
| Average capital employed* | | | | | | | ] |
| | | | | | | | per cent |
| ROCE | | [ | | *Figures omitted. See note on page iv.* | | | ] |

Source: UCI.

*CIC could not provide 1988 year-end capital employed. 1989 year-end capital employed has been used to calculate 1989 average.

9. In Tables 8 to 13 of this appendix and in Chapter 5, the information for UCI and CIC has been combined, and is shown as UCI.

## Warner Theatres

10. Warner Theatres consists of two separate companies: Warner Bros Theatres Limited, which operates the Warner West End cinema, and Warner Bros Theatres (UK) Limited, which has constructed and operates a chain of multiplexes.

### *Warner Bros Theatres Limited*

11. The results of Warner Bros Theatres Limited are set out in Table 6. The company's only cinema was closed for conversion into a multiplex between 12 September 1991 and 24 September 1993, and our calculation of average capital employed has been adjusted accordingly.

TABLE 6  **Warner Bros Theatres Limited: financial results, 1989 to 1993**

£'000

| | 1988 | 1989 | 1990 | 1991 | 1992 | 1993 | Total |
|---|---|---|---|---|---|---|---|
| | | | | Year to November | | | |
| *Turnover* | | | | | | | |
| Box office takings | | [ | | | | | |
| Screen advertising | | | | *Figures omitted.* | | | |
| Concessions | | | | *See note on page iv.* | | | |
| Other revenue | | | | | | | ] |
| | | 3,666 | 3,480 | 2,832 | 0 | 1,577 | 11,555 |
| *Costs* | | | | | | | |
| Film rental payments | [ | | | | | | |
| Concession cost of sales | | | | | | | |
| Advertising and publicity | | | | | | | |
| Staff costs | | | | | | | |
| Depreciation | | | | | | | |
| Other operating costs | | | | | | | |
| | | | | | | | |
| Operating profit | | | | *Figures omitted.* | | | |
| | | | | *See note on* | | | |
| *Tangible capital employed* | | | | *page iv.* | | | |
| Tangible fixed assets | | | | | | | |
| Fixed asset investments | | | | | | | |
| Net current assets | | | | | | | |
| | | | | | | | |
| Average capital employed* | | | | | | | ] |
| | | | | | | | per cent |
| ROCE | | [ | | *Figures omitted. See note on page iv.* | | | ] |

*Source:* Warner Theatres.

*The calculation of average capital employed has been adjusted for the closure of the company's only cinema, the Warner West End, between 12 September 1991 and 24 September 1993 for conversion into a nine-screen cinema.

## *Warner Bros Theatres (UK) Limited*

12. The results of Warner Bros Theatres (UK) Limited are shown in Table 7.

TABLE 7  **Warner Bros Theatres (UK) Limited: financial results, 1989 to 1993**

£'000

| | 1988 | 1989 | 1990 | 1991 | 1992 | 1993 | Total |
|---|---|---|---|---|---|---|---|
| | | | | Year to November | | | |
| *Turnover* | | | | | | | |
| Box office takings | | [ | | | | | |
| Screen advertising | | | | *Figures omitted.* | | | |
| Concessions | | | | *See note on page iv.* | | | |
| Other revenue | | | | | | | ] |
| | | 1,113 | 6,791 | 12,243 | 15,683 | 22,486 | 58,316 |
| *Costs* | | | | | | | |
| Film rental payments | [ | | | | | | |
| Concession cost of sales | | | | | | | |
| Advertising and publicity | | | | | | | |
| Staff costs | | | | | | | |
| Depreciation | | | | | | | |
| Other operating costs | | | | | | | |
| | | | | | | | |
| Operating profit | | | | *Figures omitted.* | | | |
| | | | | *See note on* | | | |
| *Tangible capital employed* | | | | *page iv.* | | | |
| Tangible fixed assets | | | | | | | |
| Fixed asset investments | | | | | | | |
| Net current assets | | | | | | | |
| | | | | | | | |
| Average capital employed | | | | | | | ] |
| | | | | | | | per cent |
| ROCE | | [ | | *Figures omitted. See note on page iv.* | | | ] |

*Source:* Warner Theatres

## Aggregated results

13. The financial results of the exhibitors are summarized in Tables 8 to 13. In addition to the financial information in Tables 1 to 7, we have obtained from the exhibitors details of admissions and facilities during the five-year period, and we have used this information to calculate a number of operating ratios. In all the following tables and those in Chapter 5, 'UCI' combines the results of UCI and CIC, and Warner Theatres combines the results of Warner Bros Theatres Limited and Warner Bros Theatres (UK) Limited.

TABLE 8  **The five leading exhibitors: composition of turnover, 1989 to 1993**

£'000

| | | | Financial years ending in | | | |
|---|---|---|---|---|---|---|
| | 1989 | 1990 | 1991 | 1992 | 1993 | Total |
| *Box office takings (excl VAT)* | | | | | | |
| MGM Cinemas | [ | | | | | |
| Natl Amusements | | | | | | |
| Odeon | | | | | | |
| UCI | | | | | | |
| Warner Theatres | | | | | | |
| *Screen advertising* | | | | | | |
| MGM Cinemas | | | | | | |
| Natl Amusements | | | | | | |
| Odeon | | | | | | |
| UCI | | | | | | |
| Warner Theatres | | | | | | |
| *Concessions* | | | | | | |
| MGM Cinemas | | | | | | |
| Natl Amusements | | | | | | |
| Odeon | | | *Figures omitted.* | | | |
| UCI | | | *See note on page iv.* | | | |
| Warner Theatres | | | | | | |
| *Other revenue* | | | | | | |
| MGM Cinemas | | | | | | |
| Natl Amusements | | | | | | |
| Odeon | | | | | | |
| UCI | | | | | | |
| Warner Theatres | | | | | | |
| *Total turnover* | | | | | | |
| MGM Cinemas | | | | | | |
| Natl Amusements | | | | | | |
| Odeon | | | | | | |
| UCI | | | | | | |
| Warner Theatres | | | | | | ] |

per cent

| | 1989 | 1990 | 1991 | 1992 | 1993 | Total |
|---|---|---|---|---|---|---|
| *Box office takings: turnover* | | | | | | |
| MGM Cinemas | [ | | | | | |
| Natl Amusements | | | *Figures omitted.* | | | |
| Odeon | | | *See note on* | | | |
| UCI | | | *page iv.* | | | |
| Warner Theatres | | | | | | ] |
| *Average* | 74.3 | 72.7 | 72.1 | 72.0 | 72.3 | 72.6 |
| *Concession sales: turnover* | | | | | | |
| MGM Cinemas | [ | | | | | |
| Natl Amusements | | | *Figures omitted.* | | | |
| Odeon | | | *See note on* | | | |
| UCI | | | *page iv.* | | | |
| Warner Theatres | | | | | | ] |
| *Average* | 19.1 | 21.1 | 21.9 | 22.2 | 22.6 | 21.6 |

*Source:* MMC using the five leading exhibitors' data.

14. In Table 9 we show some of the significant operating ratios for each of the leading exhibitors.

TABLE 9  **The five leading exhibitors: operating ratios, 1989 to 1993**

*per cent*

*Financial years ending in*

| | 1989 | 1990 | 1991 | 1992 | 1993 | Total |
|---|---|---|---|---|---|---|
| *Film rentals: box office takings* | | | | | | |
| MGM Cinemas | [ | | | | | |
| Natl Amusements | | | *Figures omitted.* | | | |
| Odeon | | | *See note on* | | | |
| UCI | | | *page iv.* | | | |
| Warner Theatres | | | | | | ] |
| Average | 40.9 | 36.8 | 34.5 | 33.9 | 36.0 | 36.1 |
| | | | | | | |
| *Concession gross profit* | | | | | | |
| MGM Cinemas | [ | | | | | |
| Natl Amusements | | | *Figures omitted.* | | | |
| Odeon | | | *See note on* | | | |
| UCI | | | *page iv.* | | | |
| Warner Theatres | | | | | | ] |
| Average | 53.7 | 59.5 | 63.2 | 64.7 | 67.3 | 62.7 |
| | | | | | | |
| *Operating profit: turnover (ROT)* | | | | | | |
| MGM Cinemas | [ | | | | | |
| Natl Amusements | | | *Figures omitted.* | | | |
| Odeon | | | *See note on* | | | |
| UCI | | | *page iv.* | | | |
| Warner Theatres | | | | | | ] |
| Average | 9.5 | 12.1 | 15.0 | 13.4 | 16.9 | 13.8 |
| | | | | | | |
| *Operating profit: average capital employed (ROCE)* | | | | | | |
| MGM Cinemas | [ | | | | | |
| Natl Amusements | | | *Figures omitted.* | | | |
| Odeon | | | *See note on* | | | |
| UCI | | | *page iv.* | | | |
| Warner Theatres | | | | | | ] |
| Average | 8.5 | 10.1 | 13.0 | 11.2 | 15.3 | 12.2 |

*Source:* MMC using the five leading exhibitors' data.

## *Profitability of the exhibitors*

15. Three ratios, operating profit (before interest and tax) per admission, admissions per seat and capital employed per seat, can be linked to give ROCE. In the section following we set out these ratios and their components for the leading exhibitors.

### *Profit per admission*

16. Table 10 sets out box office receipts, concession gross profit and the principal variable costs per admission for each of the leading exhibitors.

TABLE 10  **The five leading exhibitors: average revenues and costs per admission, 1989 to 1993**

£

*Financial years ending in*

|  | 1989 | 1990 | 1991 | 1992 | 1993 |
|---|---|---|---|---|---|
| *Box office receipts* | | | | | |
| MGM Cinemas | [ | | | | |
| Natl Amusements | | *Figures omitted.* | | | |
| Odeon | | *See note on* | | | |
| UCI | | *page iv.* | | | |
| Warner Theatres | | | | | ] |
| Average | 2.16 | 2.39 | 2.62 | 2.70 | 2.74 |
| *Concession gross profit* | | | | | |
| MGM Cinemas | [ | | | | |
| Natl Amusements | | *Figures omitted.* | | | |
| Odeon | | *See note on* | | | |
| UCI | | *page iv.* | | | |
| Warner Theatres | | | | | ] |
| Average | 0.30 | 0.41 | 0.50 | 0.54 | 0.58 |
| *Film rental* | | | | | |
| MGM Cinemas | [ | | | | |
| Natl Amusements | | *Figures omitted.* | | | |
| Odeon | | *See note on* | | | |
| UCI | | *page iv.* | | | |
| Warner Theatres | | | | | ] |
| Average | 0.88 | 0.88 | 0.90 | 0.92 | 0.98 |
| *Other costs less other revenues* | | | | | |
| MGM Cinemas | [ | | | | |
| Natl Amusements | | *Figures omitted.* | | | |
| Odeon | | *See note on* | | | |
| UCI | | *page iv.* | | | |
| Warner Theatres | | | | | ] |
| Average | 1.30 | 1.52 | 1.68 | 1.82 | 1.70 |
| *Profit before interest and tax* | | | | | |
| MGM Cinemas | [ | | | | |
| Natl Amusements | | *Figures omitted.* | | | |
| Odeon | | *See note on* | | | |
| UCI | | *page iv.* | | | |
| Warner Theatres | | | | | ] |
| Average | 0.28 | 0.40 | 0.54 | 0.50 | 0.64 |
| | | | | | '000 |
| *Admissions* | | | | | |
| MGM Cinemas | 32,416 | 27,325 | 26,005 | 27,496 | 29,600 |
| Natl Amusements | 2,583 | 5,663 | 6,103 | 6,699 | 8,467 |
| Odeon | 18,378 | 19,415 | 19,867 | 17,439 | 19,257 |
| UCI | 11,673 | 15,824 | 18,489 | 18,977 | 21,349 |
| Warner Theatres | 1,363 | 2,593 | 3,751 | 4,641 | 6,993 |
| Total | 66,413 | 70,820 | 74,215 | 75,252 | 85,666 |

*Source:* MMC using the five leading exhibitors' data.

17. In 1989 Warner Theatres only had a single West End cinema, with higher costs and revenues than the other exhibitors. With its growing chain of multiplex cinemas and the closure of Warner West End for refurbishment, its results have come to resemble more closely those of its competitors. Of the other exhibitors, Odeon has had the highest box office prices and until 1993 it also generated the highest rentals per admission. The new multiplex operators have higher concession gross profits than MGM Cinemas and Odeon, but all the exhibitors have increased their profits from this source. With low operating costs, Natl Amusements has emerged as the most profitable exhibitor in terms of profit before interest and tax per admission.

18. It is more useful to look at the fixed costs of the exhibitors in terms of seats rather than admissions. Table 11 sets out the principal fixed costs, staff costs, depreciation, advertising and other operating costs per seat.

TABLE 11 **The five leading exhibitors: average fixed costs per seat, 1989 to 1993**

£

*Financial years ending in*

| | 1989 | 1990 | 1991 | 1992 | 1993 |
|---|---|---|---|---|---|
| *Staff costs* | | | | | |
| MGM Cinemas | [ | | | | |
| Natl Amusements | | *Figures omitted.* | | | |
| Odeon | | *See note on* | | | |
| UCI | | *page iv.* | | | |
| Warner Theatres | | | | | ] |
| Average | 159.20 | 172.47 | 185.16 | 192.26 | 199.05 |
| *Advertising and publicity* | | | | | |
| MGM Cinemas | [ | | | | |
| Natl Amusements | | *Figures omitted.* | | | |
| Odeon | | *See note on* | | | |
| UCI | | *page iv.* | | | |
| Warner Theatres | | | | | ] |
| Average | 21.27 | 24.54 | 27.15 | 29.77 | 29.91 |
| *Depreciation* | | | | | |
| MGM Cinemas | [ | | | | |
| Natl Amusements | | *Figures omitted.* | | | |
| Odeon | | *See note on* | | | |
| UCI | | *page iv.* | | | |
| Warner Theatres | | | | | ] |
| Average | 42.54 | 66.38 | 72.31 | 74.45 | 76.18 |
| *Other operating costs* | | | | | |
| MGM Cinemas | [ | | | | |
| Natl Amusements | | *Figures omitted.* | | | |
| Odeon | | *See note on* | | | |
| UCI | | *page iv.* | | | |
| Warner Theatres | | | | | ] |
| Average | 161.87 | 157.83 | 173.76 | 181.97 | 186.03 |

Units

| | 1989 | 1990 | 1991 | 1992 | 1993 |
|---|---|---|---|---|---|
| *Average number of seats* | | | | | |
| MGM Cinemas | 130,413 | 131,955 | 133,767 | 134,651 | 130,664 |
| Natl Amusements | 10,981 | 22,353 | 22,632 | 27,203 | 31,011 |
| Odeon | 85.571 | 86,704 | 89,550 | 92,818 | 95,646 |
| UCI | 25,125 | 38,174 | 44,773 | 48,585 | 50,673 |
| Warner Theatres | 5,486 | 11,884 | 15,642 | 17,549 | 20,803 |
| | 257,576 | 291,070 | 306,364 | 320,806 | 328,797 |

*Source:* MMC using the five leading exhibitors' data.

## *Admissions*

19. All the leading exhibitors except MGM Cinemas have increased the number of seats. The number of admissions, the average (not year-end) number of seats and average admissions per seat for each of the exhibitors are set out in Table 12.

TABLE 12  **The five leading exhibitors: average admissions per seat, 1989 to 1993**

'000

*Financial years ending in*

|  | 1989 | 1990 | 1991 | 1992 | 1993 |
|---|---|---|---|---|---|
| *Admissions* | | | | | |
| MGM Cinemas | 32,416 | 27,325 | 26,005 | 27,496 | 29,600 |
| Natl Amusements | 2,583 | 5,663 | 6,103 | 6,699 | 8,467 |
| Odeon | 18,378 | 19,415 | 19,867 | 17,439 | 19,257 |
| UCI | 11,673 | 15,824 | 18,489 | 18,977 | 21,349 |
| Warner Theatres | 1,363 | 2,593 | 3,751 | 4,641 | 6,993 |
|  | 66,413 | 70,820 | 74,215 | 75,252 | 85,666 |
| | | | | | *Units* |
| *Average number of seats* | | | | | |
| MGM Cinemas | 130,413 | 131,955 | 133,767 | 134,651 | 130,664 |
| Natl Amusements | 10,981 | 22,353 | 22,632 | 27,203 | 31,011 |
| Odeon | 85,571 | 86,704 | 89,550 | 92,818 | 95,646 |
| UCI | 25,125 | 38,174 | 44,773 | 48,585 | 50,673 |
| Warner Theatres | 5,486 | 11,884 | 15,642 | 17,549 | 20,803 |
|  | 257,576 | 291,070 | 306,364 | 320,806 | 328,797 |
| *Admissions per seat* | | | | | |
| MGM Cinemas | 249 | 207 | 194 | 204 | 227 |
| Natl Amusements | 235 | 253 | 270 | 246 | 273 |
| Odeon | 215 | 224 | 222 | 188 | 201 |
| UCI | 465 | 415 | 413 | 391 | 421 |
| Warner Theatres | 248 | 218 | 240 | 264 | 336 |
| *Average* | *258* | *243* | *242* | *235* | *261* |

*Source:* MMC from the leading exhibitors' data.

## Capital employed

20. Tables 1 to 7 show that for all the leading exhibitors the bulk of capital employed is made up of fixed assets less a small amount of net current liabilities. Capital employed has increased because of the construction of new cinemas by all the leading exhibitors. Their capital expenditure is set out in Table 13.

TABLE 13  **The five leading exhibitors: capital expenditure, 1988 to 1993**

£'000

|  | 1988 | 1989 | 1990 | 1991 | 1992 | 1993 |
|---|---|---|---|---|---|---|
| MGM Cinemas | [ | | | | | |
| Natl Amusements | | | | | | |
| Odeon | | | *Figures omitted.* | | | |
| UCI | | | *See note on page iv.* | | | |
| Warner Theatres | | | | | | ] |

*Source:* The five leading exhibitors.

21. For each of the exhibitors we have calculated average capital employed as a simple average of opening and closing capital employed, except for Warner Theatres, where an adjustment was made for the closure of the Warner West End cinema from September 1991 to September 1993. Our calculation of average capital employed per seat is set out in Table 14.

TABLE 14  **The five leading exhibitors: average capital employed per seat, 1989 to 1993**

£'000

*Financial years ending in*

|  | 1989 | 1990 | 1991 | 1992 | 1993 |
|---|---|---|---|---|---|
| *Average capital employed* | | | | | |
| MGM Cinemas | [ | | | | |
| Natl Amusements | | | | | |
| Odeon | | | *Figures omitted.* | | |
| UCI | | | *See note on page iv.* | | |
| Warner Theatres | | | | | ] |

Units

| *Average number of seats* | | | | | |
|---|---|---|---|---|---|
| MGM Cinemas | 130,413 | 131,955 | 133,767 | 134,651 | 130,664 |
| Natl Amusements | 10,981 | 22,353 | 22,632 | 27,203 | 31,011 |
| Odeon | 85,571 | 86,704 | 89,550 | 92,818 | 95,646 |
| UCI | 25,125 | 38,174 | 44,773 | 48,585 | 50,673 |
| Warner Theatres | 5,486 | 11,884 | 15,642 | 17,549 | 20,803 |
|  | 257,576 | 291,070 | 306,364 | 320,806 | 328,797 |

£

| *Capital employed per seat* | | | | | |
|---|---|---|---|---|---|
| MGM Cinemas | [ | | | | |
| Natl Amusements | | | *Figures omitted.* | | |
| Odeon | | | *See note on* | | |
| UCI | | | *page iv.* | | |
| Warner Theatres | | | | | ] |
| *Average* | 838 | 963 | 1,017 | 1,053 | 1,091 |

Source: MMC using the five leading exhibitors' data.

# APPENDIX 6.1
*(referred to in paragraphs 6.19 and 6.48)*

# Independent exhibitors and distributors who gave evidence

## Exhibitors

The Aldeburgh Cinema Ltd, Aldeburgh, Suffolk (a single-screen cinema)

Apollo Leisure (UK) Ltd, Oxford (19 cinemas comprising 54 screens)

Border Entertainment Cinema, Kelso (a two-screened cinema in Fife, and single screens in Kelso and Galashiels)

Canolfan Adloniant Llanelli Entertainment Centre, Llanelli

Cheshire County Cinemas Ltd, Northwich (a two-screen cinema)

Circle Cinemas Ltd, Cardiff (four screens on three sites)

Contemporary Entertainments Ltd (for some years ran cinemas in Kensington, East Finchley and Oxford—now disposed of)

Cosmo Leisure Group (two cinemas in Ashton-under-Lyne and Stalybridge)

Edkey Cinema Co Ltd, Marple, Stockport (a single-screen cinema)

Empire Cinema, Kirkham, Lancs (a single-screen cinema)

Full Circle Film and Theatre Company, Wellington, Somerset (a single-screen cinema)

Hippodrome (Wrexham) Ltd, Wrexham, Clwyd (a two-screen cinema)

Little Theatre, Bath (a two-screen cinema)

The Macclesfield Majestic Picture House Ltd, Macclesfield, Cheshire (a single-screen cinema)

Mainline Pictures, London (five small cinemas, some one and some two screens, three of which are in central London)

North West Leisure (Manchester) Ltd, Withington, Manchester (a three-screen cinema)

Parkway Entertainment Company Limited, Scunthorpe (a five-screen cinema which competes with multiplexes in Doncaster and Hull)

Playhouse Cinema, Louth, Lincs (a single-screen cinema)

Plough Arts Centre, Torrington, Devon

Queens Film Theatre, Belfast (a cultural theatre owned and operated by Queen's University)

AJS Regal Cinema, Boston, Lincs (a single-screen cinema)

Rex Cinema, Wilmslow, Cheshire (a single-screen cinema)

Richmond Filmhouse, Richmond, Surrey (a single-screen cinema). This cinema was sold to new owners during our inquiry. The evidence given to us came from the original owners.

## Distributors

Artificial Eye Film Company Ltd[1]

Colstar International Limited

Mayfair Entertainment UK Ltd[1]

Metro Tartan Ltd

Oasis Film Distribution Ltd

---

[1] In May 1994 these two companies announced the merger of their distribution interests.

# Glossary

**20th Century Fox**  
**Twentieth Century Fox Film Corporation**, one of the **Hollywood studios**.

**Alignment**  
The practice whereby, in the first instance, a distributor normally offers its films to, and discusses the timing and release strategy for those films with, either **MGM Cinemas** or **Odeon**, but not both. In the 20 locations where **MGM Cinemas** and **Odeon** operate directly competing cinemas (other than **multiplex cinemas**), aligned distributors normally supply prints of their films to the cinemas of their aligned circuit but not to those of the other circuit.

**Ancillary markets**  
Film markets which are additional to the **theatrical** market, being mainly home video (both rental and sell-through), **free-television** and **pay television**. Also known as the secondary markets.

**Arthouse cinemas**  
Cinemas which exclusively or predominantly show **arthouse films**.

**Arthouse films**  
Specialized **feature films** (ie not **mainstream films**) usually (but not always) made by **independent producers** and designed to appeal to minority audiences. Some **arthouse films** may have **cross-over** potential.

**BBFC**  
The British Board of Film Classification.

**BFC**  
The British Film Commission. The Commission's aims are to promote the UK as a location for the production of, *inter alia*, **feature films**; to provide a comprehensive information service to producers; and to facilitate filming in the UK.

**BFI**  
The British Film Institute. The national body charged with fostering the development and understanding of the moving image as an element in British cultural life. Its duties range across all aspects of film, television and video including production, distribution and exhibition, both by active participation and by funding and supporting others.

**Blockbuster**  
A very successful film (ie **feature films** currently achieving UK box office totals of at least £10 million each).

**Break figures and sliding scale**  
A method of calculating the film rental payments to be made by exhibitors to distributors. Under this method, the percentage of weekly box office takings for each screen paid to the distributor rises (usually from a minimum of 25 per cent in steps of five percentage points to a maximum of 50 per cent) as those box office takings rise over the pre-set break figures for the screen.

**British film**  
Any **feature film** for which the UK was the prime source of the ideas or cultural values portrayed.

**British-made film**  
Any **feature film** which was produced or **co-produced** by a UK production company or which was made in the UK by an overseas producer.

**British Screen**  
British Screen Finance Limited. A private company which receives financial support from the British Government and whose purpose is to provide support for British film-makers seeking to develop and produce films for the cinema.

| | |
|---|---|
| **Buena Vista** | Buena Vista International (UK) Limited, a **leading distributor** of films in the UK. |
| **CEA** | The Cinema Exhibitors' Association. A trade association which represents approximately 90 per cent of UK cinema operators including all the **leading exhibitors**. |
| **CIC** | Cinema International Corporation UK, owner of two West End cinemas which are operated by **UCI**. |
| **CNC** | Centre National de la Cinématographie. The French National Film Centre. |
| **Columbia** | Columbia Pictures Corporation Limited, a **leading distributor** of films in the UK. |
| **Columbia/TriStar** | The name used in this report to refer to Columbia Picture Industries Inc and TriStar Pictures Inc (owned by Sony Pictures Entertainment Inc), jointly one of the **Hollywood studios.** |
| **Concession income/ gross profit** | A cinema's income/gross profit derived from sales of popcorn, ice cream and other refreshments. |
| **Co-production** | A film produced through the co-operation of, and with substantial contributions from, two or more production companies. Many countries, including most European countries, Canada and Australia, have formal co-production treaties with other countries relating to the financing and production of films. |
| **Cross-over film** | An **arthouse film** which is originally released to a specialized audience but which attracts a broader audience beyond **arthouse cinemas**. |
| **DNH** | Department of National Heritage. The department of the British Government responsible for policy towards the film industry. |
| **Eady Levy** | A levy on the price of cinema admissions introduced in 1957, principally to provide money from film exhibition and distribution to support film production in the UK. It was terminated in 1985. |
| **EDI** | Entertainment Data International Ltd. A private sector body which collects and disseminates data on box office takings. |
| **Entertainment** | Entertainment Film Distributors Limited, one of the main **independent distributors** of films in the UK. |
| **European film** | Any **feature film** for which a European country (including the UK) was the prime source of the ideas or cultural values portrayed. |
| **European-made film** | Any **feature film** which was produced by a European production company or which was made in Europe by a non-European producer. |
| **Feature film** | A film over 72 minutes in length made with the intention of obtaining **theatrical** release. |
| **First Independent** | First Independent Films Limited, one of the main **independent distributors** of films in the UK. |
| **First-run releases** | Films made available to exhibitors at the time of their first release to the UK **theatrical** market. |

| | |
|---|---|
| **Free television** | Television financed by either an annual fee or by the revenue from on-screen advertisements. Normally received direct from ground-based transmitters. |
| **Fox** | Twentieth Century Fox Film Company Limited, a **leading distributor** of films in the UK. |
| **Guild** | Guild Film Distribution Limited, one of the main **independent distributors** of films in the UK. |
| **Holdover** | The continued showing by an exhibitor of a **feature film** beyond the initial minimum period of exhibition time set out in the licence agreement, with the agreement of the distributor. The term is also used to mean an agreement that such continued showing will be considered in the light of box office receipts for the film. Thus a licence agreement may specify, for example, that the film is to be shown for a minimum of two weeks 'plus holdover', meaning that the exhibitor will consider keeping the film beyond the two-week minimum period, and the distributor will allow the exhibitor to keep the print for further weekly periods if the exhibitor so wishes. |
| **Hollywood studios** | Certain US-based companies which own the physical locations and other facilities for the development, **pre-production**, production and **post-production** of **feature films**. The studios may also have subsidiaries carrying on business as film production companies, film distributors, and (in some cases) film exhibitors. The most well known of these companies are now **Columbia/TriStar, MCA/Universal, MGM Inc, Paramount, 20th Century Fox, Walt Disney** and **Warner Bros**. |
| **Independent distributor** | A distributor which does not have corporate vertical links to one of the **Hollywood studios**. |
| **Independent exhibitor** | An exhibitor other than one of the **leading exhibitors**. |
| **Independent film** | A film made without the financial participation of a **Hollywood studio**. |
| **Independent producer** | Any production company not wholly- or majority-owned by a **Hollywood studio**. |
| **Leading distributor** | Any of the five distributors operating in the UK which are owned by one or more of the **Hollywood studios** (namely **Buena Vista, Columbia, Fox, UIP** and **Warner Distributors**). |
| **Leading exhibitor** | Any of the five largest exhibitors operating in the UK (namely **MGM Cinemas, Natl Amusements, Odeon, UCI** and **Warner Theatres**). |
| **Mainstream film** | A **feature film** which is designed to have broad commercial appeal and to attract large audiences in both the producer's home market and internationally. |
| **MCA/Universal** | The Universal film studio, one of the **Hollywood studios**, owned by MCA Inc. |
| **MGM Cinemas** | Metro-Goldwyn-Mayer Cinemas Ltd, a **leading exhibitor** of films in the UK. |
| **MGM Inc** | Metro-Goldwyn-Mayer Inc, one of the **Hollywood studios**. |

| | |
|---|---|
| MPAA | Motion Picture Association of America, Inc. A US trade association which represents and promotes the interests of its members within the USA. Its members are Buena Vista Pictures Distribution Inc, **MGM Inc**, **Paramount**, Sony Pictures Entertainment Inc, **20th Century Fox**, Universal Studios Inc and **Warner Bros**. |
| MPEAA | Motion Picture Export Association of America, Inc. A trade association which represents and promotes the interests of its members on industry matters outside the USA. Its members are Buena Vista International Inc, **MGM Inc**, **Paramount**, Sony Pictures Entertainment Inc, **20th Century Fox**, Universal International Films Inc and Warner Bros International. |
| Multiplex cinema | A purpose-built cinema with at least five screens and usually offering extensive free parking. The first multiplex cinema in the UK was opened in November 1985. |
| Natl Amusements | Natl Amusements (UK) Ltd, a **leading exhibitor** of films in the UK. |
| Nut | A monetary figure, negotiated between exhibitor and distributor, notionally representing the weekly cost (plus a 10 per cent profit margin) of operating each cinema screen. Used in calculating film rentals under the **nut method**. |
| Nut method | A method of calculating the film rental payments to be made by exhibitors to distributors. Under this method, the distributor normally receives the larger of 25 per cent of the box office and 90 per cent of the amount by which the film's box office exceeds the **nut**. |
| Odeon | Odeon Cinemas Limited, a **leading exhibitor** of films in the UK. |
| Output deal | An agreement between a film producer and a film distributor, or between a film producer and a television company, under which the distributor or the television company obtains in advance the distribution or television rights to a number of films to be made or distributed over a period of time. |
| PACT | Producers Alliance for Cinema and Television. An organization which represents, among others, independent television and film producers in the UK and operates a range of business services, which include running industrial relations agreements with the trade unions involved in **feature film** production. |
| Paramount | Paramount Pictures Corporation, one of the **Hollywood studios**. |
| Pay television | Television for which viewers pay a subscription. Normally received directly from satellites or via cable. |
| Pay-per-view | A television service under which viewers pay for each individual programme that they watch. |
| Pick-up | A film for which the distribution rights are acquired after it has been made. |
| Post-production | The late stages of film production after filming, including editing, adding music, special effects and titles. |
| Pre-production | The early stages of film production, preceding the principal photography. Pre-production activities include, for example, crew and cast preparation, finalizing the film's script and budget, and finding outdoor locations. |

| | |
|---|---|
| **Rank** | The Rank Organisation Plc, owner of **Odeon** and **RFD**. |
| **Regional film theatres** | A network of independently-owned cinemas throughout the UK. Some are supported financially by the **BFI** through grants, and most are supported by the **BFI** through film booking and publicity services. |
| **RFD** | Rank Film Distributors Ltd, one of the main **independent distributors** of films in the UK. |
| **ROT** | Return on turnover. |
| **ROCE** | Return on capital employed. |
| **SFD** | Society of Film Distributors Limited. The trade association representing film distributors in the UK. It has 11 members, including all the **leading distributors** and the larger **independent distributors**. |
| **Theatrical** | Related to film exhibition in cinemas as in, for example, theatrical release, theatrical distribution rights. |
| **Twentieth Century Fox** | See **20th Century Fox**. |
| **UCI** | United Cinemas International (UK) Limited, a **leading exhibitor** of films in the UK, jointly owned by MCA Inc and **Paramount**. |
| **UIP** | United International Pictures (UK), a **leading distributor** of films in the UK, jointly owned by MCA Inc, **MGM Inc** and **Paramount**. |
| **Under or over** | Describes the showing of films, on any given day or series of days, before or after the showing of the main film licensed for exhibition on the screen in question. |
| **US film** | Any **feature film** for which the USA was the prime source of the ideas or cultural values portrayed. |
| **US-made film** | Any **feature film** which was produced or largely produced in the USA. |
| **Video-on-demand** | A telephone line or fibre optic service by which consumers may view on their television sets in their homes, at any time they want to, films they have chosen from a large range of available titles. |
| **Walt Disney** | The Walt Disney Company, one of the **Hollywood studios**. |
| **Warner Bros** | One of the **Hollywood studios**. |
| **Warner Distributors** | Warner Bros Distributors Ltd, a **leading distributor** of films in the UK. |
| **Warner Theatres** | The name used in this report to refer to Warner Bros Theatres Limited and Warner Bros Theatres (UK) Limited, a **leading exhibitor** of films in the UK. |
| **Window** | The period for which a film is available for viewing in any particular medium, eg **theatrical** window and video rental window. |

# Index

Advertising 1.5, 2.65, 2.103, 4.66-4.68, 4.113
Alignment
    conclusions 1.10, 2.24, 2.113-2.129, 2.256
    conclusions of MMC 1983 report 1.10, 2.2, 3.4-3.5, App 3.2
    description 4.159-4.167
    locations affected 2.120, 4.160, App 4.8
    recommendations 2.231-2.238
    study of effects App 4.9
    views of Cinema Exhibitors' Association 6.17-6.18
    views of David Puttnam 6.89
    views of distributors 8.26-8.69, 9.9-9.12
    views of exhibitors 7.16-7.45
American Multiplex Cinemas Inc (AMC) 2.101, 4.103
Ancillary markets 1.6, 2.67, 2.94, 4.8-4.11
Apollo Leisure Group PLC 4.33
Appeals Tribunal
    conclusions of MMC 1983 report 3.6, App 3.2
    present status 3.16
Arthouse films, definition 2.58
Artificial Eye Film Co 4.31, 4.33, 4.55, App 4.1
Audio-visual EUREKA programme 3.28

Barring
    conclusions of MMC 1983 report 2.2, 3.4, App 3.2
    experimental prohibition by OFT 2.3, 3.9-3.13
    prohibition by Order 2.3, 2.103, 2.131, 2.133, 2.249, 2.252, 3.14-3.15, 4.130, 4.168, App 3.3
BFI—see British Film Institute
Bloom Theatres Limited 4.33
Brent Walker Distributors Ltd 4.52
British Board of Film Classification (BBFC) 4.3-4.7
British Film Commission 3.22
British film industry
    current size 1.5, 2.55, 4.41
    definitions 2.55, 4.40
    difficulties faced 2.107-2.110, 4.43-4.50, App 4.2
        conclusions 1.15-1.16, 2.218-2.226, 2.260
    film budgets 4.42
    Government initiatives 3.17-3.25, 4.48
    views of British Film Institute 6.93-6.94, 6.103, 6.105-6.106
    views of Channel 4 6.113-6.117
    views of David Puttnam 6.76-6.86
    views of distributors 6.50
    views of exhibitors 6.34
    views of Producers Alliance for Cinema and Television 6.52-6.70
British Film Institute (BFI)
    activities 4.2, 4.85-4.86
    information provided by 2.55, 4.5, 4.6, 4.11, 4.42, 4.46, 4.58, 4.61
    views 6.92-6.108
        response of distributors 8.318-8.331, 9.93
        response of exhibitors 7.224-7.244
British Screen Finance Limited (British Screen) 3.24-3.25, 4.42, 6.111
British Sky Broadcasting Ltd (BSkyB) 2.60, 4.47, 6.82, 6.134-6.135, 8.173, 8.178, 8.346
Buena Vista International (UK) Limited (Buena Vista)
    financial results 5.11-5.25, App 5.1

Buena Vista International (UK) Limited (Buena Vista—contd
    history 2.9, 4.53, App 4.1
    licensing arrangements App 5.1
    market share 2.61, 4.59-4.61
    membership of complex monopoly group 2.12, 2.35, App 2.1
    minimum exhibition periods 4.183
    refusal to supply App 4.12
    rental receipts 4.56
    views 2.171, 8.3-8.5, 8.28-8.29, 8.75-8.80, 8.117-8.123, 8.150-8.151, 8.161-8.163, 8.175-8.178, 8.204, 8.212, 8.225, 8.234, 8.252, 8.258, 8.267, 8.279, 8.288, 8.297, 8.309, 8.312, 8.325, 8.330-8.331

Cable broadcasting 4.8-4.11
CAC Leisure Limited 4.33
Carolco Pictures Inc 2.70
Centre National de la Cinématographie, discussions with Monopolies and Mergers Commission 3.38, App 1.1
Channel 4 2.54, 4.42, 4.47, 6.79
    views 6.109-6.117
Chargeurs SA 2.60, 5.17, App 2.2
Charles Scott Cinemas 4.33
Cinema Exhibitors' Association
    description 2.81, 4.114
    information provided by 2.101
    views 2.27-2.29, 2.106, 2.144, 2.150, 2.160, 2.169, 2.185, 2.232, 2.241, 6.2-6.18
        response of distributors 8.304, 9.82
        response of Society of Film Distributors 6.46-6.47
Cinema International Corporation UK (CIC) 2.76, 4.98, 5.28, 5.30, App 5.2
Cinema Ltd 4.33
Cinemas
    advertising 4.113
    booking of films 2.79, 4.108-4.112
    box office receipts 4.96-4.97
        shared between distributors and exhibitors 4.13, 5.4-5.10
    concession income 2.99, 4.100, 5.34
    exercise of market power
        views of distributors 8.244-8.249, 9.59-9.61
        views of exhibitors 7.136-7.140
    financial results 2.88, 2.99, 5.26-5.50
    independent exhibitors 4.33, 4.84-4.86, 4.117, 4.187, 8.235, App 4.4, App 6.1
        views 6.19-6.38
    leading exhibitors 2.76-2.78, 4.32-4.33, App 4.1
        views 7.1-7.248
    market entry 4.126-4.129
    market shares 2.77, 4.96-4.100
    market size and trends 1.3, 2.82-2.88, 4.82-4.95
    multiplexes 1.5, 2.78, 2.101, 4.101-4.107, 4.123-4.124, 4.127-4.129, App 4.1
    new investment 4.122-4.125, 5.44
    number of admissions 1.5, 2.100-2.103, 3.17, 4.87-4.89, App 5.2
    number of cinemas 2.103, 4.34, 4.90-4.91
    number of screens 4.90-4.91, 4.94

Cinemas—*contd*
    relationship with distributors 1.4, 2.97, 2.253, 4.131-
        4.198, 7.5-7.10
    rental payments for films 2.89-2.91, 2.93, 2.149-
        2.150, 4.98-4.99, 4.135-4.142, App 4.5
        views of distributors 8.257-8.264, 9.65-9.67
        views of exhibitors 6.32-6.33, 7.146-7.154
        views of Society of Film Distributors 6.45
    seat capacity 4.92-4.93
    ticket prices 1.5, 2.80, 2.87, 4.115-4.121
        conclusions 2.29, 2.174-2.180
        views of British Film Institute 6.104
        views of distributors 8.148-8.158, 9.36-9.38
        views of exhibitors 7.83-7.89
    views 6.19-6.38, 7.1-7.248
Code of practice
    views of distributors 8.250-8.256, 9.62-9.64
    views of exhibitors 7.141-7.145
Columbia Pictures Corporation Limited (Columbia)
    conditional booking 2.192-2.194, 2.195, 4.180-4.182
    financial results 2.75, 5.11-5.25, App 5.1
    history 4.53, App 4.1
    licensing arrangements App 5.1
    market share 2.61, 4.59-4.61
    membership of complex monopoly group 2.12,
        2.35, App 2.1
    minimum exhibition periods 2.162, 4.183
    refusal to supply App 4.12
    rental receipts 4.56
    views 2.14, 2.175, 2.183, 8.6-8.10, 8.18, 8.22, 8.25,
        8.30-8.46, 8.81-8.86, 8.124-8.129, 8.152, 8.164-
        8.166, 8.179-8.183, 8.205-8.206, 8.213-8.214, 8.226,
        8.235-8.236, 8.245, 8.253, 8.259, 8.268-8.269, 8.280-
        8.281, 8.298
Columbia-EMI-Warner Distributors Ltd 4.52-4.53
Columbia/TriStar 2.50, 2.198, 4.145-4.147
Competition 1.12-1.14, 1.17, 2.71-2.75, 2.84-2.87, 2.250-
    2.252, 2.261, 4.192-4.198
Complaints machinery 1.12, 2.245-2.246
    views of distributors 8.250-8.256, 9.62-9.64
    views of exhibitors 7.141-7.145
Complex monopoly situation
    conclusions 1.8, 2.11-2.41, 2.228-2.229
    issues arising 2.112-2.226
    parties involved 2.36-2.41
    practices engaged in by parties to the monopoly
        2.13-2.23, App 2.1
    views of British Film Institute 6.107-6.108
    views of distributors 8.21-8.25, 9.6-9.8
    views of exhibitors 7.11-7.15
Conditional booking 4.180-4.182
    conclusions 2.192-2.196, 2.245-2.246
    views of independent exhibitors 6.28
Council of Europe, audio-visual support schemes
    3.28-3.29
Crédit Lyonnais 2.36, 2.50, 2.198, App 2.2, App 4.1

Department of National Heritage (DNH)
    support for film industry 3.23-3.25, 4.2
    views 6.146-6.147
Distributors
    activities 2.62-2.64, 4.62-4.76
    description 2.59-2.60, 4.30-4.31, App 4.1
    exercise of market power
        views of distributors 8.232-8.243, 9.55-9.58

Distributors, exercise of market power—*contd*
    views of exhibitors 7.133-7.135
    financial results 2.75, 2.98, 5.11-5.25
    influence over admission prices—*see* Cinemas,
        ticket prices
    licensing agreements 5.12-5.13, App 5.1
    market entry 4.77-4.81
    market shares 2.61, 4.59-4.61
    market size and trends 1.2, 2.68-2.70, 4.52-4.58
    relationship with exhibitors 1.4, 2.63-2.64, 2.97,
        4.131-4.198, 7.5-7.10
    rental receipts 4.56-4.57, 5.19-5.21
    views 6.48-6.51, 8.1-8.347, 9.1-9.94
Divestment of interests in exhibition
    views of distributors 8.287-8.292, 9.73-9.74
    views of exhibitors 7.174-7.182
Downing Street seminar (1990) 3.20-3.21

Eady Levy
    purpose and history 3.18-3.19
    views of David Puttnam 6.73, 6.79
    views of Warner Distributors 8.276
Electric Pictures 4.31, App 4.1
Entertainment Film Distributors Limited
(Entertainment)
    activities 2.60, 4.31, 4.55, App 4.1
    market share 2.61, 4.59-4.61
    membership of complex monopoly group 2.12,
        2.35, App 2.1
    refusal to supply App 4.12
    rental receipts 4.56
    views 2.14, 2.22, 2.116, 2.157, 2.183, 9.2-9.3, 9.7,
        9.10-9.11, 9.14-9.16, 9.26-9.27, 9.37, 9.40, 9.44,
        9.48, 9.50, 9.53, 9.56, 9.60, 9.63, 9.66, 9.69, 9.72,
        9.74, 9.76, 9.78, 9.80, 9.83
Eurimages programme 3.29, 3.32
European audio-visual support schemes 3.25-3.29,
    6.101
European Co-Production Fund 3.25
European Commission
    Article 85 exemptions 2.4, 2.213, 3.33-3.36, 6.136-
        6.145, 8.295
    audio-visual support schemes 3.26-3.28
    discussions with Monopolies and Mergers
        Commission 3.38
    Green Paper on audio-visual sector 2.220, 3.37
    role in GATT negotiations 3.31-3.32
Exclusivity
    1989 Order—*see* Films (Exclusivity Agreements)
        Order 1989
    conclusions 2.25, 2.130-2.141
    description 4.169-4.172
    views of David Puttnam 6.90
    views of distributors 8.70-8.110, 9.13-9.23
    views of exhibitors 7.46-7.68
Exhibitors—*see* Cinemas

Feature films—*see* Films
Film Four International 6.112
Films
    case studies of specific films App 4.10
    categories 2.58
    definition 4.14-4.15
    financial risk involved 1.14, 2.49, 2.92-2.96, 4.12-
        4.13, 4.37

Films—*contd*
  financing 2.51-2.54, 4.38-4.39
  investment required 4.12, 4.37
  number certified and released in UK 2.56, 4.3-4.6
  production 2.49-2.58, 4.35-4.37
  release patterns 4.65, 4.176, App 4.11
  rental payments by cinemas 2.89-2.91, 2.149-2.150, 4.98-4.99, 4.135-4.142, App 4.5
    views of distributors 8.257-8.264, 9.65-9.67
    views of exhibitors 6.32-6.33, 7.146-7.154
  share of revenue between distributors and exhibitors 4.13, 5.4-5.10
Films (Exclusivity Agreements) Order 1989 2.3, 2.103, 2.131, 2.133, 2.249, 2.252, 3.14-3.15, 4.130, App 3.3, App 4.4
  conclusions 2.249
First Independent Films Limited (First Independent)
  market share 2.61, 4.59-4.61
  membership of complex monopoly group 2.12, 2.35, App 2.1
  ownership 2.60, 4.55
  rental receipts 4.56
  views 2.157, 9.4, 9.12, 9.17-9.18, 9.28-9.29, 9.41, 9.45, 9.51, 9.53, 9.57
Fox—*see* Twentieth Century Fox Film Company Limited
Fox Inc 2.40, App 2.2, App 4.1
French film industry, views of David Puttnam 6.84

GATT Uruguay Round, negotiations on audio-visual services 3.30-3.32
General Agreement on Trade in Services (GATS) 3.30-3.32
Guild Film Distribution Limited (Guild)
  activities 2.70, 2.72, 2.75, 4.31, 4.55, App 4.1
  financial results 2.75, 5.11-5.25, App 5.1
  licensing arrangements App 5.1
  market share 2.61, 2.69, 4.59-4.61
  membership of complex monopoly group 2.12, 2.35, App 2.1
  ownership 2.60
  rental receipts 4.56
  views 2.14, 2.157, 2.167, 9.5, 9.19-9.20, 9.25, 9.30-9.31, 9.42, 9.46, 9.61, 9.64

Henry, Michael
  views 6.118-6.145
    response of distributors 8.332-8.347, 9.94
    response of exhibitors 7.245-7.248
Henshaw, Geoffrey B, views 6.35-6.38
Hollywood studios
  competition 2.226, 2.250-2.251
  cost of films 2.49, 4.37
  domination of UK box office 1.14, 2.217-2.221, 2.255
  ownership 2.50
  sources of finance 4.38-4.39
  vertical links 1.2-1.3, 1.13, 2.104, 2.107, 2.198, 2.251, 2.253, 4.143-4.147
HTV Group plc 2.60, 4.55
Hutchinson Leisure Group of Companies Ltd 4.33

Independent distributors
  description 2.60, 2.255, 4.31, 4.63, App 6.1
  views 6.48-6.51
    response of exhibitors 7.201-7.209

Independent exhibitors
  description 2.76, 4.33, 4.84-4.86, App 6.1
  survey by Monopolies and Mergers Commission 4.85, 4.117, 4.187, 8.235, App 4.4
  views 6.19-6.38
    response of distributors 8.305-8.311, 9.83-9.87
  (*see also* Cinemas)
ITC Film Distributors Ltd 4.52

Joint ventures
  EC exemptions 1.1, 2.4, 3.33-3.36
  views of distributors 8.293-8.302, 9.75-9.80
  views of exhibitors 7.183-7.199

Levy for independently produced films
  views of distributors 8.265-8.276, 9.68-9.70
  views of exhibitors 7.155-7.161

Mainline Pictures 4.33
Mainstream films, definition 2.58
Market definition 2.42-2.48, 4.14-4.26
  views of distributors 8.6
  views of exhibitors 7.3-7.4
Market shares
  cinema operators 2.77, 4.96-4.100
  distributors 2.61, 4.59-4.61
Matsushita Electric Industrial Co Limited 2.50, App 2.2
Mayfair Entertainment UK Limited (Mayfair) 4.31, 4.55, App 4.1
MCA Inc 2.39-2.40, 2.50, 2.198, 2.216, 4.147
  (*see also* Universal Studios)
MEDIA programme 3.27
Metro Tartan Ltd 4.31, App 4.1
Metro-Goldwyn-Mayer Cinemas Ltd (MGM Cinemas)
  activities 2.84, 2.208
  alignment study App 4.9
  financial results 5.26-5.50, App 5.2
  history App 4.1
  market share 2.77, 4.96-4.100
  membership of complex monopoly group 2.12, 2.35, App 2.1
  number of cinemas 2.76, 4.90, App 4.1
  number of multiplexes 2.84, 4.104
  ownership 2.198, 4.147, App 4.1
  rental payments 2.206-2.207, 4.98, App 4.5
  scale monopoly situation 1.7, 2.10, 2.36, 2.40, 2.111
  ticket prices 2.87, 4.117-4.118
  views 2.97, 2.118, 2.123, 2.137, 2.159, 2.168, 2.176, 7.5-7.7, 7.12, 7.17-7.23, 7.50-7.51, 7.70-7.73, 7.84-7.85, 7.92, 7.99, 7.100, 7.111, 7.117, 7.125, 7.133, 7.137, 7.142, 7.148, 7.157, 7.163, 7.175, 7.184, 7.189, 7.194, 7.201, 7.225, 7.243, 7.245, 7.247-7.248
Metro-Goldwyn-Mayer Inc (MGM Inc) 2.39-2.40, 2.50, 2.198, 4.53, 4.147
MGM Cinemas—*see* Metro-Goldwyn-Mayer Cinemas Ltd
MGM Inc—*see* Metro-Goldwyn-Mayer Inc
Minimum exhibition periods 4.183-4.187
  conclusions 1.11, 2.27, 2.155-2.164, 2.259
  recommendations 2.239-2.244
  views of Cinema Exhibitors' Association 6.5-6.7
  views of distributors 8.111-8.147, 9.24-9.35
  views of exhibitors 6.29, 7.69-7.82

Monopolies and Mergers Commission (MMC)
   consultations with other bodies 3.38
   report *Films: a report on the supply of films for exhibition in cinemas* (Cmnd 8858, 1983) 2.2, 2.100, 3.2, 3.4-3.8, 4.27, 4.130, App 3.2
   report *Films: a report on the supply of films for exhibition in cinemas* (HC 206, 1966) 2.2, 3.2-3.3, 4.130, App 3.1
   report *Refusal to supply* (Cmnd 4372, 1970) 4.179
   survey of independent exhibitors 2.106, 4.85, 4.117, 4.187, 8.235, App 4.4
   terms of reference 1.1, 2.5, 2.36, 2.41, 3.1, App 1.1
Multiplex cinemas—*see* Cinemas, multiplexes

Natl Amusements (UK) Limited (Natl Amusements)
   financial results 5.26-5.50, App 5.2
   history App 4.1
   market share 2.77, 2.82, 4.96-4.100
   membership of complex monopoly group 2.12, 2.35, App 2.1
   number of cinemas 2.76, 4.90, App 4.1
   number of multiplexes 4.104
   ownership 2.198, 4.147, App 4.1
   rental payments 2.206, 4.98, App 4.5
   ticket prices 2.87, 4.117-4.118
   views 2.133, 2.158, 2.190, 2.241, 7.12, 7.52-7.54, 7.74, 7.93, 7.101, 7.112, 7.118, 7.126, 7.134, 7.142, 7.149, 7.164, 7.176, 7.184, 7.189, 7.194, 7.204
The News Corporation Limited 2.50, App 2.2, App 4.1
Nut figures—*see* Films, rental payments by cinemas

Oasis Cinemas Ltd 4.33
Odeon Cinemas Limited (Odeon)
   activities 2.84
   alignment study App 4.9
   exclusivity 2.135, 2.138-2.140
   financial results 2.88, 2.211, 5.27, 5.29-5.30, 5.34, 5.39, 5.41, 5.44-5.45, 5.50, App 5.2
   history App 4.1
   market share 2.77, 2.82, 4.96-4.100
   membership of complex monopoly group 2.12, 2.35, App 2.1
   number of cinemas 2.76, 4.90, App 4.1
   number of multiplexes 4.104
   ownership 2.198, 4.147, App 4.1
   rental payments 2.206, 4.98
   ticket prices 2.80, 2.87, 4.117-4.118
   views 2.118, 2.123, 2.127, 2.159, 7.8, 7.14, 7.16-7.17, 7.19, 7.23-7.25, 7.30-7.31, 7.33-7.34, 7.38, 7.41, 7.56, 7.59, 7.75-7.76, 7.86-7.87, 7.103-7.104, 7.127, 7.135, 7.138, 7.177, 7.202, 7.205-7.206, 7.209, 7.211, 7.213, 7.219, 7.223, 7.226-7.228, 7.238, 7.246
Office of Fair Trading
   experimental scheme to prohibit barring 2.3, 3.9-3.13
   role in implementing MMC recommendations and proposals 1.13, 2.217, 2.231-2.238, 2.245-2.248

Paramount decrees App 4.6
Paramount Pictures Corporation (Paramount) 2.39-2.40, 2.50, 2.198, 4.147
Pay television 4.8-4.11, 4.18-4.20, 6.82, 6.134-6.135, 8.173, 8.178
Pinewood Studios Limited 4.31, 4.45

Prices—*see* Cinemas, ticket prices
Producers Alliance for Cinema and Television (PACT)
   views 6.52-6.70
      response of distributors 8.312-8.317, 9.88-9.92
      response of exhibitors 7.210-7.222
Production—*see* Films, production
Production companies
   views 6.71
      response of exhibitors 7.223
Public interest issues 2.105-2.226
   conclusions 2.227-2.229
Puttnam, David, views 2.54, 6.72-6.91

Quota system for European films
   views of distributors 8.277-8.286, 9.71-9.72
   views of exhibitors 7.162-7.173

Rank—*see* Rank Organisation plc
Rank Film Distributors Limited (RFD)
   activities 2.72, 2.75, 4.31
   financial results 5.11-5.25, App 5.1
   licensing arrangements App 5.1
   market share 2.61, 2.69, 4.59-4.61
   membership of complex monopoly group 2.12, 2.35, App 2.1
   ownership 2.60, 2.198, 4.147, App 4.1
   refusal to supply App 4.12
   rental receipts 4.56
   views 2.120, 2.157, 2.167-2.168, 2.240, 9.5, 9.8, 9.21-9.23, 9.32-9.35, 9.38, 9.42, 9.46, 9.48, 9.51, 9.54, 9.58, 9.61, 9.64, 9.67, 9.70, 9.72, 9.76, 9.78, 9.81, 9.82, 9.84-9.88, 9.90, 9.93-9.94
The Rank Organisation Plc 2.15, 2.25, 2.60, App 2.2
   views—*see* Odeon; Rank Film Distributors Limited
Redstone, Sumner 2.133, 2.198, App 2.2, App 4.1
Refusal to supply 4.173-4.179, App 4.12
   case studies App 4.10
   complaints machinery proposed 2.154, 2.245-2.246
   conclusions 1.12, 2.26, 2.142-2.154, 2.245-2.246, 2.258
   views of Cinema Exhibitors' Association 6.3-6.4
   views of David Puttnam 6.91
   views of distributors 8.70-8.110, 9.13-9.23
   views of exhibitors 6.20-6.27, 7.46-7.68, App 4.12
   views of Society of Film Distributors 6.42
Regional film theatres (RFTs) 4.2, 4.86
Release dates
   co-ordination 4.64-4.65
      conclusions 2.188-2.191
      views of distributors 8.224-8.231, 9.52-9.54
      views of exhibitors 7.124-7.132
   competition 2.73
Release patterns 4.65, 4.176, App 4.11
Rental payments—*see* Cinemas, rental payments for films
Restrictions on screen use—*see* Screen use, restrictions
RFD—*see* Rank Film Distributors Limited
Robins Cinemas Ltd 4.33

Satellite broadcasting 4.8-4.11, 6.82, 6.134-6.135, 8.173, 8.178
Scale monopoly situation
   conclusions 1.7, 1.9, 2.7-2.10, 2.36-2.40, 2.227

Vertical integration—*contd*
   views of distributors 8.172-8.202, 9.43-9.46
   views of exhibitors 7.98-7.109, 7.174-7.182
Viacom Inc 2.198, 2.216, 4.147, App 4.1
Video cassettes
   effect on cinema attendance 2.67, 4.18-4.20
   growth in market 1.6, 2.94, 4.8-4.11, 6.51
   number released in UK 4.4

The Walt Disney Company (Walt Disney) 2.9, 2.39-2.40, 2.50, 2.198, 4.53, App 2.2, App 4.1
Ward Anderson group of cinemas 4.33
Warner Distributors
   conditional booking 2.192, 2.195-2.196, 4.180-4.182
   financial results 2.75, 5.11-5.25, App 5.1
   history 4.53, App 4.1
   licensing arrangements App 5.1
   market share 2.61, 2.68, 4.59-4.61
   membership of complex monopoly group 2.12, 2.18, 2.35, App 2.1
   minimum exhibition periods 2.162, 4.183
   refusal to supply App 4.12
   rental receipts 4.56

Warner Distributors—*contd*
   scale monopoly finding 2.9
   views 2.18, 2.32, 2.132, 2.135, 8.15-8.17, 8.20, 8.23, 8.53-8.69, 8.100-8.110, 8.139-8.147, 8.156-8.158, 8.169-8.171, 8.195-8.202, 8.209-8.210, 8.219-8.223, 8.230-8.231, 8.241-8.243, 8.249, 8.256, 8.262-8.264
Warner Theatres
   activities 2.210, 2.215
   financial results 5.26-5.50, App 5.2
   history App 4.1
   market share 2.77, 2.82, 4.96-4.100
   membership of complex monopoly group 2.12, 2.35, App 2.1
   number of cinemas 2.76, 4.90, App 4.1
   number of multiplexes 4.104
   ownership 2.198, 4.147, App 4.1
   rental payments 2.206-2.207, 4.98, App 4.5
   ticket prices 2.80, 4.117-4.118
   views 2.158, 2.210, 7.2, 7.13, 7.15, 7.43-7.45, 7.66-7.68, 7.80-7.81, 7.89, 7.97, 7.108-7.109, 7.115, 7.123, 7.131-7.133, 7.140, 7.145, 7.153-7.154, 7.161, 7.171-7.173, 7.182, 7.187, 7.192, 7.199
White Paper on Film Policy (1984) 3.17-3.19

Scale monopoly situation—*contd*
  issues arising 2.111
Screen use
  competition 2.74
  restrictions 4.188-4.191
    conclusions 2.28, 2.165-2.173, 2.245-2.246
    views of Cinema Exhibitors' Association 6.8-6.11
    views of distributors 8.111-8.147, 9.24-9.35
    views of exhibitors 6.30-6.31, 7.69-7.82
    views of Society of Film Distributors 6.43-6.44
Shepperton Studios 4.45
Society of Film Distributors Limited (SFD)
  description 2.66, 4.74-4.76
  interest in price promotions 2.177, 4.132
  *Standard Conditions* 2.66, 4.76, 4.131-4.134, App 4.3
    conclusions 2.13, 2.30, 2.181-2.187
    views of Cinema Exhibitors' Association 6.12-6.15
    views of distributors 8.159-8.171, 9.39-9.42
    views of exhibitors 7.90-7.97
  views 6.39-6.47
Sony Corporation 2.50, App 2.2, App 4.1
Sony Pictures Entertainment Inc 2.40, App 2.2

Taxation, effect on British film industry 4.49, App 4.2
Television
  effect on cinema attendance 2.67, 4.18-4.20
  as medium for showing films 1.6, 2.94, 4.8-4.11
  role in British film industry 2.54, 4.47
Time Warner Inc 2.40, App 2.2, App 4.1
Trade Disputes Committee
  conclusions of MMC 1983 report 3.6, App 3.2
  present status 3.16, 4.130
Twentieth Century Fox Film Company Limited (Fox)
  financial results 2.75, 5.11-5.25, App 5.1
  history 4.53, App 4.1
  licensing arrangements App 5.1
  market share 2.61, 2.68, 4.59-4.61
  membership of complex monopoly group 2.12, 2.19-2.21, 2.35, App 2.1
  minimum exhibition periods 2.20, 4.183
  refusal to supply App 4.12
  rental receipts 4.56
  views 2.19-2.21, 2.25, 2.34, 8.11, 8.24-8.25, 8.47-8.48, 8.89-8.92, 8.130-8.134, 8.153, 8.167, 8.184-8.187, 8.207, 8.215, 8.227, 8.237, 8.246-8.247, 8.254, 8.260, 8.270, 8.282, 8.289, 8.299, 8.313, 8.326
Twentieth Century Fox Film Corporation 2.50, 2.198, 4.145-4.147

UCI—*see* United Cinemas International (UK) Limited
UCI BV—*see* United Cinemas International Multiplex BV
UIP—*see* United International Pictures (UK)
UIP BV—*see* United International Pictures BV
UK Film Distributors Ltd 4.52-4.53
United Cinemas International Multiplex BV (UCI BV) App 2.2, App 4.1
  joint venture 2.4, 3.36
    views of distributors 8.302, 9.79-9.80
    views of exhibitors 7.193-7.199

United Cinemas International (UK) Limited (UCI)
  activities 2.208, 2.210, 2.215
  financial results 2.211, 5.26-5.50, App 5.2
  history 2.101, App 4.1
  market share 2.82, 4.96-4.100
  membership of complex monopoly group 2.11, 2.35, App 2.1
  number of cinemas 2.76, 4.90, App 4.1
  number of multiplexes 4.103
  ownership 2.198, 4.147, App 4.1
  pattern of trading with UIP 2.201-2.204, 2.214, 4.152-4.154
  rental payments 2.206-2.207, 4.98, App 4.5
  ticket prices 2.87, 4.117-4.118
  views 2.14, 2.74, 2.133, 2.158, 2.179, 2.184, 2.190, 2.210, 2.241, 7.4, 7.9-7.10, 7.41-7.42, 7.60-7.65, 7.77-7.79, 7.88, 7.95-7.96, 7.105-7.107, 7.114, 7.121-7.122, 7.129-7.130, 7.139, 7.144, 7.151-7.152, 7.159-7.160, 7.167-7.170, 7.179-7.181, 7.185-7.186, 7.191, 7.193-7.199, 7.204, 7.207-7.209, 7.212, 7.214, 7.220-7.222, 7.229, 7.232, 7.235, 7.239, 7.242
United International Pictures BV (UIP BV)
  history App 4.1
  joint venture 2.4, 2.213, 3.33-3.35
    views of distributors 8.293-8.295, 9.75-9.76
    views of exhibitors 7.183-7.187
    views of Michael Henry 6.136-6.145
United International Pictures (UK) (UIP)
  financial results 2.75, 5.11-5.25, App 5.1
  licensing arrangements App 5.1
  market share 2.61, 2.68, 4.59-4.61
  membership of complex monopoly group 2.12, 2.35, App 2.1
  minimum exhibition periods 2.162, 4.183
  ownership 2.198, App 4.1
  pattern of trading with UCI 2.201-2.204, 2.214, 4.152-4.154
  refusal to supply App 4.12
  release pattern of *Ghost* App 4.11
  rental receipts 4.56
  scale monopoly finding 2.8
  views 2.14, 2.135, 2.203, 8.12-8.14, 8.19, 8.49-8.52, 8.93-8.99, 8.135-8.138, 8.154-8.155, 8.168, 8.188-8.194, 8.208, 8.216-8.218, 8.228-8.229, 8.238-8.240, 8.248, 8.255, 8.261, 8.271-8.272, 8.283-8.284, 8.290, 8.294-8.295, 8.300, 8.304, 8.306, 8.310, 8.314, 8.317, 8.319, 8.322, 8.327, 8.329, 8.339, 8.343, 8.344-8.345, 8.347
Universal Studios 2.50, 4.31
  (*see also* MCA Inc)
US film industry
  description App 4.6
  dominance of UK market 2.57, 2.107-2.110, 4.6-4.7, 7.110-7.123
    conclusions 2.31, 7.110-7.123
    views of British Film Institute 6.98-6.100
    views of distributors 8.203-8.223, 9.47-9.51
    views of exhibitors 6.34, 7.110-7.123
    views of Producers Alliance for Cinema and Television 6.52-6.70

Vertical integration 1.1, 1.13, 2.1, 3.1, 4.143-4.158, App 4.7
  conclusions 2.197-2.217, 2.247
  views of British Film Institute 6.95-6.97